How to M
Commercial M

How to Master Commercial Mediation: An Essential Three-Part Manual for Business Mediators

David Richbell

with

Specialist Contributors

Bloomsbury Professional

Bloomsbury Professional Limited, Maxwelton House, 41–43 Boltro Road, Haywards Heath, West Sussex RH16 1BJ

© Bloomsbury Professional Limited 2015, unless otherwise indicated in the text

Reprinted 2015
Reprinted 2016

Bloomsbury Professional is an imprint of Bloomsbury Publishing plc

All rights reserved. No part of this publication may be reproduced in any material form (including photocopying or storing it in any medium by electronic means and whether or not transiently or incidentally to some other use of this publication) without the written permission of the copyright owner except in accordance with the provisions of the Copyright, Designs and Patents Act 1988 or under the terms of a licence issued by the Copyright Licensing Agency Ltd, Saffron House, 6–10 Kirby Street, London EC1N 8TS. Applications for the copyright owner's written permission to reproduce any part of this publication should be addressed to the publisher.

Warning: The doing of an unauthorised act in relation to a copyright work may result in both a civil claim for damages and criminal prosecution.

Crown copyright material is reproduced with the permission of the Controller of HMSO and the Queen's Printer for Scotland. Any European material in this work which has been reproduced from EUR-lex, the official European Communities legislation website, is European Communities copyright.

A CIP Catalogue record for this book is available from the British Library.

Every effort has been taken to ensure the accuracy of the contents of this book. However, neither the authors nor the publishers can accept any responsibility for any loss occasioned to any person acting or refraining from acting in reliance on any statement contained in the book.

ISBN: 978 1 78043 682 1

Typeset by Phoenix Photosetting, Chatham, Kent
Printed and bound in the United Kingdom by CPI Group (UK) Ltd, Croydon, CR0 4YY

Preface

There are several reasons for me writing this book. I have been mediating since 1992 and training mediators for most of that time. So there is a knowledge and experience that I hope will be of use to others. In that time the practice of mediation has become a serious activity and there is an undoubted move towards it becoming an established profession. My time with the Civil Mediation Council has been devoted to helping the emerging profession have credibility and realistic standards that may ensure the profession has practitioners that are both effective and worthy ambassadors, both in the United Kingdom and overseas, of a process that not only puts common sense back into resolving disputes but also offers a better form of justice.

When I was Director of Training at CEDR I partly wrote and also compiled the CEDR Handbook, of which there have been many revisions since. Not only was it a pleasure to bring it into being but it also has been a reference point for many mediators who were trained and accredited by CEDR. Many mediators have told me that it is the most used book on their shelves; however, that may mean that the other books are not used at all! The downside was that the Handbook was only available to those who went on the CEDR Mediator Training Course. Part of this book, which was written initially for the Chartered Institute of Arbitrators MTC on the understanding that it would one day be part of a larger book, makes that basic knowledge available to anyone who is interested in becoming a mediator, or who wants the skills they already have to be refreshed. The rest is for those who are already mediating, whether new, established or at the top of their profession.

Whilst MATA was operating, we ran for ten years an Advanced Mediator Retreat (only mediators can advance and retreat at the same time!), held most years in Italy. Twelve participants and four faculty shut themselves away for a week in a converted monastery in the hills of Umbria and just soaked up mediation. Most years the faculty was Lawrence Kershen, Heather Allen, Joanna Kalowski and me – all of whom have contributed to this book. I mention them later. This was a unique event and, without exception, everyone who went on that course said it was the best experience they had, some even said it was lifechanging. A few went on it more than once. Some of the material we used on that course has been further developed and included in this book.

In total, 86 people have contributed to the three parts of this book. They are all named in the acknowledgements and I am very grateful that almost without exception they responded to my request for a contribution with enthusiasm and pleasure. A few I had to nag and pester but they produced the goods in the end. I am humbled by the fact that most contributions were gifted, a few have been licensed, and I very much appreciate their generosity and willing support.

Because there are so many contributors I thought it only right that the royalties from the book – on the optimistic assumption that we do sell some copies – will go to TalkingWorks, a charity that teaches mediation skills to schoolchildren. Janine Edge, the founder of TalkingWorks writes:

Preface

> 'TalkingWorks brings the mediation profession into schools to teach young people how to handle conflict in a non-violent way. The mediation skills training provided by TalkingWorks can fit into one school day, and is delivered with the assistance of volunteer mediators who coach the students through role plays and tell stories about their mediation experience to give the training context and relevance.
>
> TalkingWorks was created not only to give students conflict resolution skills which they can immediately use in their lives, but also to educate the next generation of school leavers on the power of mediation to resolve disputes in many areas of life. If you wish to volunteer as a coach or support TalkingWorks in any other way, please contact us through www.twis.org.uk. TalkingWorks is a UK registered charity.'

It is my conviction that if we can teach children non-violent ways of dealing with conflict, the world will be a much better place. I am full of admiration for those that do this poorly funded work and it is a privilege to support them.

Finally, I must say thank you to a number of people. I mentioned the other three members of the Advanced Retreat. Lawrence is the nearest to a brother that I could ever have and has shared my ups and (few) downs in mediation. He is a gracious and generous man and my life has been greatly enriched by him. Heather is a talented and perceptive mediator and trainer, a deep thinker who has advanced the theory and practice of mediation. Joanna is a humorous, entertaining and vastly experienced mediator and trainer who is a joy to work with. I am so grateful for their support, loyalty and wisdom over so many years. Joanne Claypole deserves a mention. For many years she was my right hand (secretary, assistant, cheerleader and enabler). She took over the managing of In Place of Strife when her sister, Jane, died and I miss her still. And finally, Jane Gunn, my partner in MATA and co leader of many training courses. We undoubtedly modelled empathy, respect, humour and harmony to all that we taught and I look back on those many years together with real pleasure, even pride.

I am now of an age when retirement is expected, though resisted with energy on my part. When retirement does come, I hope this book will be seen as something useful that I left behind!

David Richbell

November 2014

Foreword

As a young trainee attorney I had occasion to pick up the telephone to Nelson Mandela asking me to act as his agent in an appeal to the Supreme Court in Pretoria. I was in admiration of him then for his ability to practise law in the teeth of apartheid tyranny. I am now in awe of him for his successfully negotiating a peaceful transition with President de Klerk despite his years of imprisonment on Robben Island. His approach to that negotiation has its resonance in any commercial mediation:

> 'To make peace with your enemy you must talk to your enemy. Then your enemy becomes your partner. As your partner you can strive to make arrangements in the best interests of the partnership and to the mutual advantage of the partners.'

Mediation is now the Black and Decker tool to be used to further civil justice. It is, as Lord Neuberger of Abbotsbury describes it, the twin of litigation and, as Lord Dyson MR says:

> 'ADR Is now a well established part of every lawyer's practice. If there was ever any doubt that the consensual settlement of disputes – facilitated through the use of ADR – served the public interest, it has been laid to rest. Consensual settlement ... is an essential aspect of any civil society. The effective promotion of ADR is unquestionably in the public interest'. (From his foreword to the Jackson ADR Handbook)

As the judgments of the Court of Appeal extol its virtues, its use will increase. Soon only the ostrich will refuse to mediate. Negotiated settlements, 'where an independent third party (the mediator) helps the parties reach their own solution, in private' – 'cooperative problem-solving', to cite David Richbell in Chapter 1 of this book – is increasingly accepted to be better than fighting to the death, leaving blood on the court room floor. The role of the mediator in achieving that mutually satisfying outcome is crucial and success depends on the skill of the mediator.

In this Handbook, David Richbell draws on his vast expertise to instruct us in the skills needed to get started as a mediator, to get better as a mediator and then to get to be the best mediator. David is himself one of the very best. Coming from a business background, he understands commercial negotiation. He has been in full-time practice as a mediator for nearly 20 years. He amply meets every qualification he prescribes for a mediator, who must be 'patient, tenacious, enthusiastic, positive, energetic, humorous, humble, wise, non-judgemental, accepting and encouraging. In other words, a saint, or an angel – probably both!' He can justly boast of a remarkable settlement record. Both the *Chambers* and *Legal 500* Directories acknowledge his pre-eminence in the field. He commands the respect of his peers across the world. Who better than David to write a definitive manual on mediation?

The triumph of this Handbook is that it distils the wisdom not only of David himself but also of an academy of accomplished and successful practitioners, who

Foreword

contribute to the sector specialisms ranging from agriculture to sport, from faith mediation to restorative justice, from mediation in Austria to mediation in Turkey. It is a masterly encyclopaedia. It is, moreover, written with clarity and with wit. Like a good novel it is hard to put down. It should be made compulsory reading for undergraduates in law schools and business schools, for in-house counsel as well as for lawyers in private practice and it would do no harm for Her Majesty's judges to read it to learn how mediation works. Whether you are an eager beginner or a hoary old hack, you will learn from every page of this book.

The Rt Hon Sir Alan Ward

Chairman of the Civil Mediation Council

November 2014

Dedication

This book is dedicated to two people.

Karl Mackie had the courage to invite me, a non-lawyer, newly trained mediator, onto the CEDR training faculty and then to make me CEDR Director of Training. He started me off on the road which was a coming home for me, a place where I was, and still am, made to be.

Chris, my wife, has still not realised that I got the best deal when we came together in 1977. She has been the enabler and supporter that has made possible my life as a mediator and now as an author. Thanks are not enough, but thank you anyway. I love you.

Contents

Preface	v
Foreword	vii
Contributor Profiles	xxix
PART 1 MOULDING	1
Chapter 1 Introduction	3
Overview	3
The reason to be	3
Why the only route to justice?	4
Commercial mediation in the dispute resolution landscape	5
Mediation models	6
Mediation overview	8
Summary of the mediator's role	8
A word of warning	9
Chapter 2 The Core Skills	11
Overview	11
The mediator is a 'friend' to all	11
Rapport building	12
Empathy	12
Hearing	13
Summarising	13
Reframing	14
Active listening	14
Silence	15
Reflecting	15
Managing Emotion	15
The mediator as negotiator	16
Strategic use of information	16
Problem solving	16
Hitting the zone	17
Saving face	17
The mediator as communicator	17
Questioning appropriately	17
Non-verbal communication	18
From history to future	19
Modelling other's behaviour	19
The mediator as manager	20
Overview	20
Patience and tenacity	20
Time management	21
Using visual aids	21
Finally	22

Contents

Chapter 3   Case Study   **23**
   General information   23
      Background   23

Chapter 4   Preparing Stage   **25**
   Getting appointed   25
   Profile   25
   Fees   26
   Dates   27
   Assistant/pupil   27
   Confirming the appointment   28
   Summaries and supporting documents   29
   Venue and facilities   30
   Equipment   31
   Pre-mediation contact   31
   Who attends?   34
   Role of lawyers, parties, experts and others   34
   Site visit   35
   On the day   35
   First private meetings   35
   Agreement to Mediate   35
   Preparing in a nutshell   37
   Case study   38
      First contact   38
      The calls   39
      On the day   41
   Mediator challenges   41
      Preparation stage   41

Chapter 5   Opening Stage   **43**
   Purpose of the first open session   43
   Seating and facilities   43
   Setting the scene   44
   Opening statements   46
   Telling their stories   46
   Stimulating dialogue   46
   Using the flipchart   46
   Managing emotion   47
   Breaking up   48
   Opening stage – in a nutshell   48
   Case study   48
      The first open session   48
   Mediator challenges   51
      Opening stage   51

Chapter 6   Exploring Stage   **53**
   Purpose of the exploring stage   53
   Private (caucus) sessions   53
   Saving face   54
   Topping and tailing   55
   Positions and interests   55
   Relationships v problem solving   56
   Moving on   56

Exploring stage – in a nutshell	56
Case study	57
Private meetings	57
Mediator challenges	62
Exploring stage	62

Chapter 7 Negotiating Stage 65

Shaping the deal	65
Negotiation styles, techniques and strategies	65
First and final offer	66
Salami slicing	66
Low offer	66
Mediator's advice	66
Coaching	67
Reality testing	67
Overcoming deadlock	69
Power imbalance	70
Cultural aspects	70
Negotiating stage – in a nutshell	71
Case study	71
More private meetings	71
Mediator challenges	77
Negotiating stage	77

Chapter 8 Concluding Stage 79

Getting the deal	79
Deals with dignity	79
Pain-pain	80
Mediator recommendation	80
Settlement Agreements	81
Settling, or not	83
Aftercare	83
Concluding stage – in a nutshell	84
Case study	84
Open meeting	84
Mediator challenges	86
Concluding stage	86

Chapter 9 Setting Up a Mediation Practice 89

Introduction	89
What have you got to offer?	89
Create experience	89
Personal network	90
Joining mediator groups/panels	90
Marketing	91
Conclusion	91

Chapter 10 An Overview of the English Legal System 93

The court system	93
The Court Rules	94
Redress through the court system	96
Limitation periods	97
Costs and funding	98

Employment tribunals 101
Contract 102
Negligence and personal injury 102
Confidentiality and without prejudice 103

Appendix 1 Responses to Mediator Challenges 105
Preparing stage 105
   1 Conflict of interest 105
   2 Papers 105
   3 Support documents 105
   4 Inflammatory summary 106
Opening stage 106
   1 Participants 106
   2 Joint session 106
   3 No honest intent 106
   4 Counsel 106
   5 Decision maker 107
   6 Room allocation 107
   7 Key document 107
   8 Brown envelope 107
   9 Demonised party 108
   10 Crowd control 108
   11 Urgent text 108
Exploring stage 109
   1 Assertive lawyer 109
   2 Needs 109
   3 Arithmetical error 109
   4 No money 109
   5 Unrepresented party 110
Negotiating stage 110
   1 Key information 110
   2 First and final 110
   3 Giving a steer 110
   4 Bug 111
   5 Mediator not wanted 111
   6 Relaying offer 111
   7 Walk-out 111
Concluding stage 112
   1 Authority 112
   2 Ratification 112
   3 Second thoughts 112
   4 Tears 113
   5 CFA 113
   6 Better deal 113
   7 Counsel 113
   8 Deals with dignity 114
   9 VAT 114
   10 Too late for the deal 114
   11 Full and final settlement 114
   12 Serial user 114

Appendix 2 Recommended Reading List 115

PART 2 MATURING   **117**

Chapter 1 Introduction   **119**

Chapter 2 Psychology in Mediation (Paul Randolph)   **121**
- Emotions   122
- Self-esteem   124
  - The need to be heard   125
- Values   126
- Perceptions   127
- Conclusion   127

Chapter 3 It's All About Relationships (David Richbell and Henry Brown)   **129**
- The non-evaluative mediator   130
  - A (good) example   130
  - A (not so good) example   131
  - Transformative mediation   131
  - Conclusion   131
- Having difficult conversations   131
  - Different stories   133
  - Conflict can be positive   133
  - Separate people from the problem   133
  - Step into each other's shoes   133
  - Face the demon   133
  - Turn assumptions into facts   134
  - Look to the future, not back at the past   134
  - Save face   134
  - Prepare and rehearse   134
  - End positively   135
  - Look out for ... and avoid ...   135
  - Finally   135
- High conflict disputes   136
  - The special meaning of 'high conflict'   136
  - Distinguishing high conflict from other factors   137
  - High conflict personalities   137
  - Attachment disorganisation   137
  - Personality disorders and maladaptive traits   138
  - Cautions and reservations   139
  - Strategies for working with high conflict   139
  - High conflict dispute endings   141
- Who is at the centre of mediation?   141
  - The party   142
  - The lawyer   142
  - The mediator   143
  - The providers   143
  - The Civil Mediation Council (CMC)   143
  - Conclusion   144

Chapter 4 Intercultural Mediation: The Fundamentals (Joanna Kalowski)   **145**
- Knowing what intercultural signifies – and what it does not   145
  - Case study   147

Contents

Which approach to take?	148
The broad cultural approach	148
The importance of understanding high and low context communication	150
Case study	151
The comfort of familiarity with one or more frameworks	152
Geert Hofstede's Five Dimensions of National Culture	152
Some insights for mediators based on Hofstede's model	153
How should intercultural mediators speak?	154
Beyond behaviour: assumptions, expectations and intentions	154
Case study	155

Chapter 5 Further Communications Skills (Jane Walmsley) — 157

The foundations: presence, self-awareness and self-confidence	158
Prepare and plan	158
Challenge your own assumptions and judgements	158
Self-confidence	159
Establishing and developing rapport	160
Openness: make mental space for everything	160
Show them that you are listening and are interested	160
Match their language	160
Match their body language	161
Fostering a conducive atmosphere	161
Tell people that that and what you have heard and understood	161
More about phrasing patterns	162
Match their language, continued …	163
Conclusion	164

Chapter 6 Sector Specialisms — 165

Mediating farming and rural disputes (Anthony Glaister)	165
Variety, volatility and volume	165
The mediator's perspective	166
Mediating disputes in the Armed Forces (Susan Morgan MBE)	167
Mediating banking and financial services disputes (Charles Flint QC)	170
Mediating charity sector disputes (David Richbell)	173
Volunteers and management	173
Management v trustees	174
Fundraising v fiduciary duties	174
Profit v principles	174
Service v trade	174
Conclusion	175
Mediating clinical negligence disputes (Tony Allen)	175
Mediating competition disputes (William Wood QC)	178
Mediating construction/engineering disputes (David Richbell)	180
Introduction	180
Construction and engineering mediations	181
Smaller cases	181
Larger cases	181
Bespoke process	181
Experts and expert mediators	182
Co-mediation	182

Papers and numbers	182
Summary	183
Mediating employment disputes (Liz Rivers)	183
Tips for handling the practicalities of employment mediations	184
Handling the emotional and relational aspects of the dispute	185
And finally ...	187
Mediating energy disputes (Jane Player)	187
Mediating entertainment and media sector disputes (Andrew Hildebrand)	190
The entertainment industry	191
The industry's attitude towards litigation	192
The industry's attitude towards mediation	192
Typical industry disputes	192
The suitability of mediation	193
What does the sector want from their mediator and what is unusual about the people at a mediation	194
Mediating franchise disputes (Michael Cover)	194
Mediating insolvency disputes (Chris Fitton)	196
Introduction and scope	196
Types of insolvency dispute	196
Some issues typically arising at insolvency mediations	197
Costs	199
Conclusions	199
Mediating insurance/reinsurance disputes (Jane Andrewartha)	200
An historic view	200
Direct insurance as opposed to reinsurance	201
Insurance	201
Brokers	202
Reinsurance and retrocession	203
The insurers	203
Summary	204
Mediating intellectual property and IT disputes (Jon Lang)	205
Intellectual property mediation	206
IT mediation	207
Mediating partnerships and family business disputes (David Richbell)	208
Separating people and problem	209
High emotion	209
Historic relationships	210
Justice	210
Attachment	210
Law	211
Mediating personal injury claims (Neil Goodrum)	211
Introduction	211
It's about the people	211
Early process management	212
Who should be there?	212
It's a negotiation isn't it?	213
The costs mediation	213
More personal injury mediations?	214
Conclusion	214
Mediating planning related disputes (John Pugh-Smith)	214
Mediating probate and trust disputes (Beverly-Ann Rogers)	218

Contents

Mediating professional indemnity disputes (Nicholas Pryor)	220
Mediating property disputes (Mark Jackson-Stops and Michael Wyldebore-Smith)	224
The domestic property dispute	224
Neighbour disputes in multi-occupied buildings	225
Landlord/tenant disputes – residential properties	226
Non-domestic property disputes	226
Choice of mediator for property cases	227
Boundary disputes	227
Mediating public sector disputes (Jon Lang)	229
Appreciation of statutory framework	229
Public accountability	230
Decision-making and authority	230
Post-mediation approval	231
Attendees	231
Mediating shareholder disputes and post-transaction warranty claims (Stephen Walker)	231
Shareholder disputes	231
Essential law	232
Remedies	232
Particular features of shareholder dispute mediations	232
Post-transaction warranty claims	235
Essential law	235
Particular features of warranty claims	235
Mediating shipping disputes (Silas Taylor)	237
Mediating sports disputes (Quentin Smith)	240
Chapter 7 Learning from Other Mediation Disciplines	**243**
Transformative mediation (Jane Gunn)	243
Scenario 1	243
Scenario 2	244
What exactly is transformative mediation and what has it got to teach commercial mediators?	244
The problem – destructive dialogue	245
The solution – constructive dialogue	245
Self determination	245
Client centred	246
Skills and tools	246
Lesson for commercial mediators	247
Evaluative mediation (Andrew Goodman)	247
Mediation and decision making	248
Using evaluation within facilitative mediation	250
Merits and reality testing	250
Dealing privately with lawyers or technical experts	250
Ovecoming deadlock	251
Appraising technical solutions	251
Commissioning evaluative mediation	252
Preparation	252
Form	253
Consequences	254
Community mediation (Eve Pienaar)	255
Overview of the community mediation process	256

Process outline	258
Tools for the mediators	258
Who are the parties?	259
Some particular features of community mediation	260
Conclusion	261
Family mediation (Mary Banham-Hall)	262
The history of family mediation	262
Compulsory referral to hear about mediation from a mediator – increases mediation take up	264
The Children and Families Act 2014	264
Family mediation models	265
Training, accreditation and legal aid agency recognition	265
The family mediation process	266
Types of mediation and direct consultation with children	266
Property and financial mediations	267
The couple	268
Managing the process of family mediation	269
Shuttle mediation	269
Mediation at court	270
The right time to mediate	270
Facilitative mediation v evaluative mediation	271
What civil and family mediation might learn from each other	271
Conclusion	272
Workplace mediation (Clive Lewis OBE DL)	272
The historical context	272
The organisational background	274
Why mediation in the workplace works?	276
Workplace or employment mediation?	276
The business case for workplace mediation	277
Return on investment	278
The future of mediation at work	281
Peer mediation in schools (Chris Seaton)	282
Storytelling (Geoffrey Corry)	285
Mediating in faith communities (David Richbell with Zaza Elsheikh)	288
Introduction	288
Issues commonly in dispute	289
Issues behind the dispute	290
Expectation and needs	290
Choice of mediator	290
The mediation process	291
What mediation in faith communities may offer commercial mediators	291
Conclusion	292
Environmental and public policy mediation (Andrew Floyer Acland)	292
Restorative Justice (Lawrence Kershen QC)	297
The limits of adjudication	297
From retribution to restoration	297
Restorative principles	298
Shared values	298
Restorative justice and commercial mediation compared	299
Distinctions	300
What can restorative justice offer commercial mediation?	300

Contents

Enhancing commercial mediation	303
Co-mediation (Eve Pienaar)	304
Introduction	304
Benefits of co-mediation	305
Challenges of co-mediation	306
Co-mediation in practice – process stages	307
Conclusion	309
Assistantships (David Richbell)	309
Why?	310
Appointment	310
What I do	310
Role of the assistant	311
Debriefing	312
Conclusion	312
Chapter 8 Analysing risk (Elizabeth Jones QC and John Clark)	**313**
Why analyse risk in mediation?	313
Barriers to rational risk analysis	314
Asymmetric attitudes to gains and loss	315
Anchoring	315
Overconfidence	315
Confirmation bias	316
Fundamental attribution error	316
Groupthink	316
Sunk cost fallacy	316
Approaches to risk analysis	317
Structure	318
Probabilities	318
Outcome values	319
Determine best decision	319
Pros and Cons of risk analysis	322
Summary	323
Chapter 9 Mediation ethics (with Michel Kallipetis QC)	**325**
Introduction	325
Why an ethical code?	325
Types of mediation	326
Regulation	327
The European Code of Conduct for Mediators	327
The United States Experience	328
Monitoring the settlement agreement	330
Mediator's obligations	331
Impartiality	334
Conflicts of interest	325
Competence	336
Confidentiality	337
Conclusion	339
Chapter 10 Achieving Excellence – a Delicate Balance (Heather Allen)	**341**
Chapter 11 Conclusion (David Richbell)	**347**
PART 3 MASTERING	**349**
Chapter 1 Introduction	**351**

Chapter 2 The Route to Mastery — 353
- What is mastery? — 353
- Building on the foundations — 354
- The internal mediator – being rather than doing — 355
- The external mediator – doing rather than being — 355
- Achieving mastery — 356
- Peer review — 356
  - Role of reviewer — 357
  - Debrief — 357
  - Giving the review — 357
  - Receiving feedback — 358
- Mentoring — 358

Chapter 3 From Mastery to Incompetence — 359
- Introduction — 359
- Horror stories — 360
- Mediator's role — 360
- What are the dangers? — 361
- What keeps masters masterly? — 362
  - Acknowledgement — 363

Chapter 4 Trust, Truth, Love and Forgiveness (or rather Greed, Lies, Hatred and Revenge) — 365
- Trust — 365
- Truth — 365
- Love — 366
- Forgiveness — 366

Chapter 5 Mediator Bias (Paul Gibson) — 369
- Introduction — 369
- What is bias? — 371
- The necessary purpose of bias — 371
- Conscious and unconscious bias — 372
- Common personal biases — 373
- Identification of biases — 375
- Rules and standards — 375
- NMAS Practice Standards — 376
- ICC Mediation Rules — 376
- Mediator neutrality — 377
- Dealing with biases — 379
  - Awareness — 380
  - Acceptance — 380
  - Mindfulness — 380
- Conclusion — 381

Chapter 6 Intercultural Mediation: A Digest of Theory and Practice (Joanna Kalowski) — 383

Chapter 7 One Continent, Many Methods (introduction by Bill Marsh) — 393
- Introduction — 393
  - The framework — 395
  - The values — 395
- Austria (with Thomas Kustor) — 395
  - Introduction — 395

Contents

EU Directive (2008)	395
The Austrian Mediation Act (2004)	396
Mediation and conciliation	396
Definition of mediation	396
Register of mediators	397
Voluntary/mandatory process	397
Enforceability of mediation clauses	397
Confidentiality	397
Mediation style and procedure	397
Enforceability of Mediated Settlement Agreements	398
Mediator training, accreditation and post-qualification standards	398
Mediator exemption	398
Conclusion	398
Belgium (Anna Doyle)	399
The Belgian experience – sharing perspective	399
The Future of Mediation in Belgium	399
The European Parliament perpective	400
International organisations' perspective	401
Bulgaria (Eliza Nikolova)	401
Regulation	401
Style	402
Who does mediation?	403
Training	403
Croatia (Mladen Vukmir)	404
Cyprus (Christos Theodoulou)	409
The legal framework	409
The bodies involved	410
The need for mediation in Cyprus	410
Czech Republic (Tatjana Šišková)	410
Cost	411
Community mediation	411
Act on the Probation and Mediation Service (PMS)	411
Consumers' mediation	412
Act on Civil and Commercial Matters	412
Important features	412
Trends in mediation	414
Denmark (Gerd Sinding)	414
The courts system	414
Mediation within the courts	415
Mediation outside the courts system	416
Conclusion	417
Estonia (with Triinu Hiob)	417
Introduction	417
EU Directive (2008)	417
The Estonian Conciliation Act	417
Definition of mediator	418
Voluntary/mandatory process	418
Sanctions if parties do not mediate	418
Confidentiality	418
Mediation style and procedure	418
Enforceability of Mediated Settlement Agreements	419
Mediator training, accreditation and post-qualification standards	419

Register of mediators	419
Mediator exemption	419
Conclusion	419
Finland (Petri Taivaloski)	419
Legal framework	420
Mediation under the Rules of the Finnish Bar Association	420
Court mediation	421
Conclusion	422
France (Thierry Garby)	422
The legal status of mediation in France in 2014	422
The development of mediation in France in 2014	423
The structure of the mediation market	425
Germany (Renate Herrmann)	425
Background	425
The German Mediation Act	426
Structure of the German Mediation Act	426
Enforceability of Settlement Agreements	428
Statute of limitation	428
Style of mediations	429
Certified mediators	430
Types of mediation	430
Legal aid/court fees	432
Conclusion	433
Greece	433
Introduction	433
EU Directive (2008)	433
Mediation Act	433
Definition of mediator/mediation	433
Voluntary/mandatory	434
Confidentiality	434
Mediation style and procedure	434
Enforceability of Mediated Settlement Agreements	434
Mediator training, accreditation and post-qualification standards	434
Register of mediators	435
Mediator exemption	435
Conclusion	435
Hungary (Tibor Tajti)	435
Introductory caveats	435
General overview	436
Private and commercial mediation	437
Conclusions	439
Ireland (including Northern Ireland) (Jim Halley)	440
Introduction	440
Training and accreditation	440
Overview of legal provision for mediation in Ireland	441
Commercial disputes	441
Employment disputes	442
Family disputes	442
Elder mediation	442
Other areas	442
EU Directive	443
Anticipated Mediation Bill	443
Northern Ireland	444

Conclusion	444
Italy (Carlo Mosca)	444
Introduction	444
The legal framework	445
Recourse to mediation	447
Mediators' style and approaches	448
Conclusions	449
Latvia (Rada Matjušina)	450
Lithuania (Natalija Kaminskiene)	452
Introduction	452
The Conciliatory Mediation in Civil Disputes Act of the Republic of Lithuania (2008) amended 2011	452
EU Directive (2008)	453
Definition of mediation and mediator	453
Voluntary/mandatory process	453
Sanctions if parties do not mediate	453
Confidentiality	453
Mediation style and procedure	453
Enforceability of Mediated Settlement Agreements	454
Register of mediators	454
Mediator exemption	454
Conclusion	454
Luxembourg (with Alain Grosjean)	454
Introduction	454
EU Directive (2008)	455
The Civil Procedure of Luxembourg (2012)	455
Definition of mediation and mediator	455
Voluntary/mandatory process	455
Confidentiality	455
Mediation style and procedure	455
Enforceability of Mediated Settlement Agreements	455
Mediator training, accreditation and post-qualification standards	455
Register of mediators	455
Mediator exemption	455
Malta (Austin Sammut)	456
Netherlands (with Manon Schonewille and Dr Fred Schonewille)	459
Introduction	459
EU Directive (2008)	459
The new Dutch Mediation Act (draft)	459
Definition of mediation	460
Voluntary/mandatory process	460
Sanctions if parties do not mediate	460
Enforceability of mediation clauses	461
Confidentiality	461
Mediation style and procedure	461
Enforceability of Mediated Settlement Agreements	461
Mediator training, accreditation and post-qualification standards	462
Register of mediators	462
Mediator exemption	462
Conclusion	462
Norway (Anna Nyland)	463
Introduction	463
Legal regulation on out-of-court mediation	463

Out-of-court mediation in the private sphere	465
Court-connected mediation	466
Poland (Sylwester Pieckowski)	466
Polish Mediation Law of 2005	466
General assessment of the Polish Mediation Law vis-à-vis the EU Directive 2008/52/EC	468
Definition of civil mediation	468
Referral to mediation	469
Quality assurance	469
Enforcement of settlement agreements	470
Confidentiality safeguards	470
Interruption of statues of limitation	470
Barriers to successful growth of mediation in civil and commercial matters in Poland	471
Cognitive barriers	471
Conclusion	471
Portugal (Ana Maria Maia Gonçalves, François Bogacz and Thomas Gaultier)	471
Overview of mediation in Portugal	471
The legal status of mediation in Portugal	472
Confidentiality	473
Settlement	474
Mediators	474
Use of mediation in Portugal	475
Romania (Constantin-Adi Gavrilă and Luminita-Jana Trifan)	476
Legal status of mediation in Romania	476
Extent of use of mediation in Romania (particularly commercial mediation)	477
Who is doing mediation in Romania?	478
The common styles of mediation in Romania	479
Slovakia (with Renata Dolanska and Slavka Karkoskova)	480
Introduction	480
EU Directive (2008)	480
The Slovak Mediation Act (420/2004)	480
Definition of mediation and mediator	480
Voluntary/mandatory	481
Confidentiality	481
Mediation style and procedure	481
Enforceability of Mediated Settlement Agreements	481
Mediator training, accreditation and post-qualification standards	482
Register of mediators	482
Mediator exemption	482
Conclusion	482
Slovenia (Simona Mlakar)	482
Place of mediation in Slovenian law	482
Alternative Dispute Resolution in Judicial Matters Act	483
Who are mediators?	484
Style of mediators	485
The regulations and training that apply	485
Spain (Mari Cruz Taboada)	486
Voluntary/mandatory mediation	486
Credible institutions	487
Confidence	487

Contents

The role of lawyers in mediation	488
Mediation fees	488
Endorsement	488
Sweden (Eric Runesson)	489
Switzerland (Jeremy Lack)	491
Outline of civil and commercial mediation in Switzerland	491
The current legal status of mediation in Switzerland	492
The extent and use of mediation in Switzerland	495
Common styles of mediation	496
United Kingdom with Scotland	497
England and Wales (David Miles)	497
In the beginning	497
The courts today	498
Who are the mediators	499
The lawyers	500
Non-lawyers	500
The participants	500
Insurers	500
Experts	501
Confidentiality	501
Mediator's confidentiality	501
Litigation funding	501
Mandatory mediation	502
The EU Directive 502	
Conclusion	502
Scotland (Pamela Lyall)	503
Russia (Dr Tsisana Chamlikashvili)	505
Turkey (Deniz Artan Ilter and Samil Demir)	510
Background overview	510
Legal status of mediation	511
Current practice of mediation	515
Chapter 8 Use of Interpreters in Mediation (Xiaohui Yuan)	**517**
Introduction	517
Interpretation versus translation	518
Interpretation in arbitration versus in mediation	519
Non-verbatim interpretation for rapport management	519
Example 1: bridging cultural differences in building rapport	520
Example 2: protecting a party's face needs and defusing potential conflicts	521
Working with interpreters on deciphering body language	523
Pitfalls of using party's relatives or lawyers as interpreters	524
Dos and don'ts for using interpreting in mediation	525
Chapter 9 Enhancing the Political Process (John Sturrock)	**527**
Chapter 10 Beyond Mediation (Tony Willis)	**533**
Introduction	533
Possible new fields to conquer	534
Sovereign state negotiations	534
Collective labour negotiations	535
Commercial deal making	536

Settlement counsel	537
Conclusions	537

Chapter 11 Standards and Regulation **539**
    High standards   539
    Aspirational standards   541
    Regulation   542

**Chapter 12 What We Do Changes the World
(with Stephen Ruttle QC)** **543**
    The potential of mediation   544

Index   **549**

Contributor Profiles

Andrew Acland

Andrew Acland has worked for 25 years as a mediator and facilitator in contexts ranging from the political, social and environmental to the legal, corporate and organisational. He specialises in designing and facilitating public and stakeholder dialogue processes in complex, multi-party, multi-issue contexts, often with environmental and social sustainability dimensions.

E: andrewacland@btinternet.com

Heather Allen

Heather mediates commercial contract, employment, inheritance, property, shareholder and other matters. She has commercial experience in the oil industry and book publishing, and is trained as a barrister. As Head of the CEDR Faculty since 2004, she contributes to the development of mediation in Africa, Asia, the Middle East and closer to home. Heather currently serves as an elected mediator member of the CMC Board.

E: heather@heatherallen.com

Tony Allen

Formerly a practising solicitor, then a Director of CEDR, Tony is now a mediator with particular experience in personal injury, clinical negligence and related professional indemnity disputes. He trains for CEDR worldwide and is the author of *Mediation Law and Civil Practice* and co-author of *The ADR Practice Guide*.

E: tony@allensmediate.com

Jane Andrewartha

An international Mediator for 20 years, Jane has been recognised as a leader in mediation by the professional directories since the 1990s, being named 2012 Cross Border Mediator of the Year. She is a senior litigation and arbitration partner with global law firm Clyde & Co, advising on major international disputes across (re)insurance, maritime, aviation, energy, banking and finance sectors. A former director of CEDR, she now holds various positions in the insurance industry including that of non-executive Chair of an insurance company.

E: Jane.Andrewartha@clydeco.com

Contributor Profiles

Mary Banham-Hall

Mary Banham-Hall has mediated since 1999, practised as a solicitor since 1979, and dispute resolution is her vocation. Mary set up Focus Mediation in 1999 and it has an established reputation for family and civil mediation. Mary has conducted thousands of mediations and specialises in family and probate disputes.

E: Mary@focus-mediation.co.uk

Francois Bogacz

François Bogacz has experience as a mediation trainer, international mediator and business executive. François is an Accredited Mediator of *International Mediation Institute, ADR group, Who's Who Legal 2014.* He is the co-founder of Convirgente and the CEO of Neuroawareness Consulting Services, a company specialised in the application of neuroscience to professional skills development.

E: Fb@neuroawareness.com

Henry Brown

PIM Senior Mediator Emeritus and family and commercial mediation trainer, Henry wrote the Law Society's *ADR Report* and co-wrote *ADR Principles and Practice* and *Managing Difficult Divorce Relationships.* Awarded the CMC's 2013 Lord Slynn Prize for developing mediation in the UK and the International Academy of Mediators' 2013 Lifetime Achievement Award.

E: henry@brownadr.com

Tsisana Chamlikashvili

Tsisana Chamlikashvili is an International expert in ADR, practicing international mediator, CEDR-accredited mediator, mediator of JAMS International (USA-UK), and a member of the Association for Integrated Mediation. She is President of the National Organization of Mediators (NOM), academic and scientific chair of the Federal Institute of Mediation, Chair of the Subcommittee on ADR and Mediation in the *Russian Association of Lawyers,* founder of the Scientific and Methodological Center for Mediation and Law, editor-in-chief of the magazine 'Mediation and Law', professor of the MSUPE

E: president@mediacia.com

John Clark

John Clark is a management consultant who advises on economics, strategy and negotiation. He has been mediating since 2001. He believes that understanding the science behind the dynamics of negotiation and mediation is critical to helping parties make good decisions. He has a PhD in Game Theory.

E: jc@mediation-negotiation.com

Contributor Profiles

Geoffrey Corry

Geoffrey Corry is a family and workplace mediator and runs his own mediation training courses. He has been involved with the Glencree Centre for Reconciliation since 1974 during the difficult years of the Troubles in Northern Ireland. His search for interactive approaches to conflict resolution led him to dialogue facilitation. Between 1994 and 2006, he facilitated over 50 Political Dialogue Workshops between politicians from Northern Ireland, Britain and the Republic of Ireland. He has trained peacemakers in Colombia, facilitated workshops between Israelis and Palestinians, and visited Haiti twice to train local gang leaders and the police in conflict resolution.

E: Geoffreycorry@eircom.net

Michael Cover

Michael Cover is a full time and independent specialist in dispute resolution. He is a barrister, accredited mediator and Chartered Arbitrator. He has been serving as an independent third-party neutral since 2002 and is on the panels of many well-known and respected UK and international groups and institutions. He is the current Chairman of the Mediation Sub-Committee of the Chartered Institute of Arbitrators.

E: mc@michaelcover.com

Samil Demir

Samil Demir was born in Ankara in 1976. He graduated from the Anatolian University, Faculty of Law (LLB) in the year 1997 and from Başkent University, Institute of Social Science (LL.M) in the year 2011. He still pursues his doctorate studies in the field of civil procedure law. Demir, who has published three books and written 10 articles published in peer-reviewed journals, has worked as a lawyer and a licensed mediator since 1998. Demir is the President of the Turkish Alternative Dispute Resolution Association.

E: samildemir@demirlaw.com

Renata Dolanska

Renata Dolanska, lawyer, mediator, founder and manager of the Mediation Centre for Out-of-Court Dispute Resolution in Kosice, which also operates the Specialist Mediator Preparation, which is a prerequisite for registered Mediators. She is Deputy Chair of the Slovak Association of Mediators and of the European Women Lawyers Association of Slovakia.

E: dolanska.advokat@gmail.com

Anna Doyle

Anna Doyle is Mediator & Ethics Officer at EUROCONTROL, European Organisation for Safety of Air Navigation, Brussels. She specialises in mediation, conflict resolution, international public service, HR, social dialogue and training and is a Practitioner Member of the Mediators' Institute of Ireland and a Certified Mediator with the International Mediation Institute.

E: Anna.Doyle@eurocontrol.int

Zaza Elsheikh

Dr Zaza Johnson Elsheikh, a mediator of 10 years and formerly a medical doctor and solicitor, has used her professional experience and mixed cultural (Afro-Arab-Caribbean) and religious (Baptist-Muslim) heritage to found the charity BIMA, a multi-faith group of mediators and arbitrators who resolve disputes within and between faith communities.

E: zaza@bimagroup.org

Chris Fitton

Chris was a partner at Pinsent Masons LLP for 15 years, resolving disputes for insurers and corporates. He started mediating in 1999 and is now a full time mediator with In Place of Strife. Chris specialises in financial services (including insolvency disputes), professional negligence and business-related disputes. Chris has been chairman of the Association of Midlands Mediators since 2012.

E: office@chrisfitton.com

Charles Flint QC

Charles Flint QC of Blackstone Chambers is a commercial barrister and an accredited mediator who mediates commercial disputes, primarily in the banking and financial services field. He is rated by *Chambers UK 2013* and *Legal 500 2012* as a leading barrister in financial services law.

E: charlesflint@blackstonechambers.com

Thierry Garby

Thierry Garby was originally an attorney. He has been one of the most renowned commercial and international mediators and trainers in France since 1998. He is the founder of the World Forum of Mediation Centres. Thierry is IMI certified. He teaches and mediates worldwide, particularly for the World Bank Group.

E: t.garby@me.com

Thomas Gaultier

Thomas Gaultier is a New York qualified attorney, and of Counsel at AAA Advogados. He graduated from the University of Paris X Nanterre Law School and has an LL M in ADR from the University of Texas in Austin, during the sitting of which he became a certified mediator. He is the co-founder of the Instituto de Certificação e formação de Mediadores Lusófonos, and teaches mediation and negotiation in several Portuguese universities.

E: gaultier@gmail.com

Constantin-Adi Gavrilă

Constantin-Adi Gavrilă is an IMI certified mediator and mediation trainer, general manager of the Craiova Mediation Center Association, the first president of the Romanian Mediation Centers Union and the first vice-president of the Romanian Mediation Council. He was honoured with the ACR's 2009 Outstanding Leadership Award for outstanding contributions to international conflict resolution.

E: mediator@adigavrila.com

Paul Gibson

Dr Paul Gibson has been a full-time professional mediator since 2006, prior to which he had 25 years of dispute resolution using facilitation, negotiation and conciliation techniques. He combines 40 years of management, consulting, training and dispute resolution experience, with current international knowledge of mediation practice and specialist training. He was the first Australian mediator to be qualified and registered to mediate cross-border disputes in the EU and works out of Sydney and Brussels. He is currently Executive Director of the Centre for Conflict Resolution, based in Sydney.

E: paul@gibsonadr.com.au

Anthony Glaister

Anthony Glaister FCIArb is a mediator conciliator and arbitrator. He has been chairman of the Association of Northern Mediators since 1996, based near York, and is a member of the CMC registration committee. Anthony is a mediation and ADR adviser to the agricultural and property sectors.

E: resolve@anthonyglaister.co.uk

Grant Goodlad

Grant was a solicitor, and is now a barrister at Farrar's Building, specialising in employment and personal injury. He trained as a commercial mediator in 1996 and since then has mediated disputes in a wide range of civil and commercial cases. He is also a member of the training faculty on the Chartered Institute of Arbitrators mediator training course.

E: ggoodlad@farrarsbuilding.co.uk

Contributor Profiles

Ana Maria Maia Gonçalves

Ana Maria Maia Gonçalves has experience as a lawyer, teacher, international mediator and executive for multinational organisations. Ana is an Accredited Mediator with the International Mediation Institute, ADR group, Who's Who Legal 2014 and Julgados de Paz. Ana is the co-founder of Convirgente and the President of ICFML, an NGO representing the IMI for the certification of Portuguese speaking mediators. She is also a lecturer and author on mediation.

E: ana@anagoncalves.com

Andrew Goodman

Professor Andrew Goodman PhD has been a civil/commercial mediator for 23 years. Director of SCMA and AMATI, member of the Independent Standards Commission of the IMI and UK regional representative of the WMO, Andrew is a leading exponent and international trainer of mediation advocacy and author of mediation titles, and lecturer in conflict management in the United Kingdom, the Gulf and the Far East.

E: agoodman@1chancerylane.com

Neil Goodrum

A CEDR-accredited mediator since 1997, Neil has mediated numerous personal injury and clinical negligence cases as well as a wide range of commercial and civil disputes. In addition to mediating, he is a mediation trainer, principally with the CEDR Faculty and a consultant solicitor with a prominent law firm.

E: neil@meilgoodrum.com

Alain Grosjean

Alain Grosjean is a certified Mediator at the Centre de Médiation Civile et Commerciale, and a partner in Bonn & Schmitt in charge of the dispute resolution department. He is a member of the Luxembourg Bar Council and has conducted numerous mediations. He has written several articles on mediation and speaks frequently at conferences.

E: agrosjean@bonnschmitt.net

Jane Gunn

Jane Gunn is an international mediator and speaker. She is President of the Professional Speaking Association and has been invited to speak at the United Nations, The European Commission and the White House. Jane travels and speaks all over the world. She is also the author of a popular book on conflict management *How to Beat Bedlam in the Boardroom and Boredom in the Bedroom*.

E: jane.gunn@corpeace.com

Contributor Profiles

Jim Halley

Jim Halley is Managing Director of 2-Collaborate Ltd and has been at the forefront of mediation in Ireland since 1994. He specialises in corporate and workplace mediation, investigation, facilitation, consultation and change management. He has also held lectureships in mediation and dispute resolution in Stanford University (United States), the Institute of Public Administration (Ireland) and the National University of Ireland, Maynooth.

E: jim@2-collaborate.ie

Renate Herrmann

Renate Herrmann's more than 25 years' experience of risks and liabilities in commodity financing, trading and shipping are particularly suited for solving and settling disputes arising under commercial contracts, dry bulk and containerised cargo shipping disputes, but also financial and banking disputes, including disputes in relation to finance agreements, letters of credit, structured loan agreements and guarantees. Renate is certified mediator and accredited arbitrator in England and Germany.

E: Renate_Herrmann@gmx.de

Andrew Hildebrand

Andrew is a commercial mediator, with a specialist entertainment/media/sport practice. He has spent his career working in industry, successfully managing negotiations and brokering settlements as a top-ranked in-house counsel, including at Channel 4 and FilmFour and as a partner at Mishcon de Reya. He has litigated and mediated as a client and knows what it feels like. Andrew mediates independently and through In Place of Strife. He is an IFTA arbitrator and a dispute resolution partner with Gunner Cooke.

E: Andrew@hildebrandmediation.com

Triinu Hiob

Triinu Hiob is senior associate at LAWIN Attorneys at Law. She has nearly 15 years of legal experience in dispute resolution matters, including litigation, domestic and international arbitration, and other forms of alternative dispute resolution.

E: triinu.hiob@lawin.ee

Mark Jackson-Stops

Mark Jackson-Stops has been mediating for 20 years following a successful first career in property. He founded the mediation provider, In Place of Strife The Mediation Chambers, in 1995. He is passionate about the power of negotiation

Contributor Profiles

as the basis for resolving disputes and that the role of the mediator is to help the parties to engage in that process.

E: mjs@mediate.co.uk

Elizabeth Jones QC

Elizabeth Jones QC is a chancery/commercial litigator who has also been mediating since 1999. She has mediated cases with 2–10 parties, alone and as co-mediator, across a wide number of sectors. Her aim is to assist parties in making decisions they can live with and so she attaches particular weight to thorough preparation and risk analysis.

E: Ejones@serlecourt.co.uk

Deniz Artan Ilter

Dr Deniz Artan Ilter is an Associate Professor in Construction Management at Istanbul Technical University, teaching and supervising research in contract administration, construction claims and disputes, sustainable construction and green buildings. She is an accredited BREEAM International Assessor, joint coordinator of CIB TG89 Construction Mediation Practice task group and a member of TG69 Green Buildings and the Law task group. She is author of many papers and book chapters.

E: artande@itu.edu.tr

Michel Kallipetis QC

Michel is a full time professional civil and commercial mediator with over 40 years' experience as a practising barrister in the field of general commercial, professional negligence and employment work. He is accredited with CEDR, ADR Chambers and the ADR Group, and an international panel member of HKIAC and SIMC. Michel is a Distinguished Fellow and a director of the International Academy of Mediators; a PIM Senior Mediator and a Chartered Arbitrator.

E: michel@kallipetis.com

Joanna Kalowski

Joanna Kalowski is a workshop leader, judicial educator and senior mediator with wide experience in facilitating public participation and decision-making processes. She has been working with groups for over 30 years in sensitive intercultural and political settings. She writes and presents on operating effectively across cultures in Australia, Asia and Europe.

E: jok@jok.com.au

Natalija Kaminskienė

Associate Professor Natalija Kaminskienė is the Director of the Institute of Communication and Mediation at Mykolas Romeris University (Lithuania), a practicing attorney at law, mediator and negotiator, and member of several institutional committees on mediation set up in Lithuania. She was one of the first to introduce ADR and mediation to Lithuania and work on its' implementation into the legal system of this country. Her dissertation 'Alternative civil dispute resolution' was the first in Lithuania to open scientific discussions on ADR and mediation in Lithuania.

E: natalijak@mruni.eu

Slavka Karkoskova

Slavka Karkoskova is a university lecturer and leader of specialist courses and further education for mediators. She is the founder of ASCEND, a non-governmental organisation which offers counselling and education on child sexual abuse. Trained in psychotherapy and psychotraumatology she is an expert in the area of abuse, its characteristics, long-term effects, therapeutic needs of victims and intervention strategies towards offenders.

E: slavka.karkoskova@gmail.com

Lawrence Kershen QC

Lawrence Kershen has facilitated commercial and other mediations since he was accredited as a mediator in 1994, and more recently as a restorative practitioner. With a background as a barrister, from 2003 to 2012 he was a board member and latterly Chair of the Restorative Justice Council.

E: kershen@europe.com

Thomas Kustor

Thomas Kustor is a dispute resolution lawyer in Vienna and specialises in the conduct of lawsuits in the field of business law, with a focus on proceedings for corporations and financial institutions. He holds a Doctor of Laws (Dr iur) degree from the University of Vienna and a Master of Laws (LLM) degree from Exeter University.

E: thomas.kustor@freshfields.com

Jeremy Lack

Jeremy Lack is an independent lawyer, mediator and arbitrator, based in Geneva, Switzerland. He is the Co-Chair of the Swiss Chamber of Commercial Mediation (Section Romande) and the Vice-Chair of the Independent Standards Commission of the International Mediation Institute (IMI), and a member of its taskforces on cross-cultural mediation, investor-state disputes, mediation advocacy, ADR Hybrids, and IMI's Qualified Assessment Programs and QAP Audit Committee. He is also a certified mediator and mediation advocate, is the advisor to the Geneva Chamber of Commerce and Industry on mediation, and sits on the Oversight Commission on Civil and Criminal Mediation created by the Republic and Canton of Geneva.

E: jlack@lawtech.ch

Contributor Profiles

Jon Lang

Listed in the first tier of mediator rankings of both the Chambers & Partners and Legal 500 directories, Jon Lang is recognised as one of the top mediators in the United Kingdom. CEDR accredited, Jon became a full-time mediator in May 2005, having spent almost 20 years as a solicitor in private practice, the last six as a partner in the disputes group of White & Case in London. Jon is a past Chair of the Mediation Committee of the International Bar Association and author of the book, *A Practical Guide to Mediation in Intellectual Property, Technology & Related Disputes*, published by Sweet & Maxwell in 2006.

E: jl@jonlang.com

Clive Lewis OBE DL

Clive Lewis is a HR professional specialising in employee and industrial relations. He is the founding director of the Globis Mediation Group. He has worked at government level, most recently representing the United Kingdom in Algeria and Jordan. He is a fellow of the Chartered Institute of Personnel and Development. Clive is the author of ten books including *Difficult Conversations: Ten Steps to Becoming a Tackler, not a Dodger* which featured in the *Sunday Times*. In addition, he is also a Non-Executive director at an NHS Foundation Trust, a Trustee and Board Member of the National Youth Jazz Orchestra, and Trustee of E-Act Academies. He was awarded the OBE for Public Service in the Queen's Birthday Honours List of 2011 and commissioned as a Deputy Lieutenant in 2012.

E: clive.lewis@globis.co.uk

Liina Linsi

Liina Linsi has nearly 30 years of legal experience, specialising in dispute resolution, construction and real estate, and she is a well-known litigator in the Estonian market. She has worked for the Law firm LAWIN since 1991, and has been a partner since 2006. Liina heads LAWIN's dispute resolution and real estate practice groups.

E: liina.naaber-kivisoo@lawin.ee

Pamel Lyall

Pamela is one of Scotland's most experienced mediators. A full-time mediator, coach and facilitator, she has mediated in disputes across commercial sectors. Pamela has extensive experience in leading training courses in mediation and negotiation. She was a partner in a large national law firm and was accredited as mediator by CEDR in 2000. She is a senior mediator associated with Core Solutions Group.

E: pamela.lyall@yahoo.com

Bill Marsh

Bill has been a professional mediator for the last 25 years, working on commercial, religious, ethnic and political disputes. He also acts as adviser to numerous governments and international organisations on issues of conflict and mediation, and trains mediators. He is the *Who's Who 2014-15* Global Mediator of the Year.

E: wm@billmarsh.co.uk

Rada Matjušina

Rada Matjušina, practising attorney-at-law in Latvia, was a member of the working group on the draft mediation law .She is chairman of the board of 'Mediation and ADR', chairman of the ethics committee of the Mediation Council, and author of several publications, including publications about mediation.

E: rada.matjusina@gmail.com

David Miles

David Miles is a solicitor and a consultant with Blake Morgan. An original founding Director of CEDR, David is accredited by CEDR. He has been a member of CEDR training faculty since its inception. He is a Fellow of the Chartered Institute of Arbitrators (Mediation and Arbitration). He has trained judges, lawyers and others around the world. He has mediated disputes in the United Kingdom and overseas. David is Chairman of PIM Senior Mediators.

E: David.Miles@blakemorgan.co.uk

Simona Mlakar Frumen

Simona Mlakar Frumen is lawyer, mediator and mediator trainer in Slovenia and abroad. She has written several articles on mediation and contributed a chapter to a white paper on mediation in 2008. She is one of the mediation professionals who are members of the Council for ADR at the Ministry of Justice.

Email: Simona.mlakar@dogovor.si

Susan Morgan MBE

Susan Morgan MBE received the highest acclaim for her pioneering work in the introduction of Workplace Mediation in the Armed Forces. Susan is the longest serving female in the history of the Royal Navy, having dedicated over 34 years to the service,. Her life experiences and transferable skills have enabled the success of Morgan Mediation Ltd.

E: info@morganmediation.co.uk

Carlo Mosca

Carlo Mosca studied law at Bologna University and become a specialist in overseas business operations. He has been practising as a lawyer in this sector for 30 years.

Contributor Profiles

He has an LLM from Queen Mary's College in international commercial law. Accredited by CEDR in the mid-90s, he set up and encouraged the creation of mediation centres, such as Curia Mercator, and Quadra. He is now a member of the board of the Institute for the Study of Conflict Transformation (ITSC), the transformative mediation think-tank based in Dayton, Ohio.

E: c.mosca@lexmill.com

Eliza Nikolova

Eliza Nikolova works as a business lawyer, partner at NKN Law firm (Sofia, Bulgaria). She is also a mediator and mediation trainer. Her professional focus is to support communication and dialogue on various levels. In her practice of business she is a solution finder, assisting and encouraging her clients to use different methods of alternative dispute resolutions and bringing together counter positions. Eliza Nikolova is a founder and chairperson of Professional Association of Mediators in Bulgaria. Eliza lives in Sofia, the capital of Bulgaria.

E: eliza.nikolova@nknlaw.com

Anna Nylund

Anna Nylund is professor of law at the University of Tromsø, the Arctic University of Norway. She earned her LL D at the University of Helsinki, and has studied mediation at the University of Texas and Hamline University. Her main research interests are civil litigation and mediation and Europeanisation of civil procedure.

E: anna.nylund@uit.no

Sylwester Piekowski

Sylwester Piekowski is an advocate, international arbitrator and mediator, and head of the dispute resolution department at Chadbourne & Parke LLP, Warsaw. He is President of the Polish Arbitration Association (2006–present), Deputy Director of the Business Mediation Centre in Warsaw, Co-Founder of the Court of Arbitration at the Polish Confederation of Private Employers Lewiatan (2005), and President of the Civic Council on ADR at the Ministry of Justice (2012–2013). Sylwester is a member of ICDR, VIAC, KIG Arbitration Court in Warsaw, Lewiatan Arbitration Court in Warsaw and the Czech Court of Arbitration in Prague, and is the author of *Mediation in Civil Matters* (Difin, 2006).

E: spieckowski@chadbourne.com

Eve Pienaar

Eve is a solicitor by training and currently heads up the legal, governance and procurement functions for the Royal Institution of Chartered Surveyors. She is also an independent mediator and Faculty member of CEDR. Eve became accredited in 2007 and regularly mediates a wide range of disputes, specialising in property and construction matters. Eve is a passionate advocate for mediation and delivers peer mediation training as well as community mediation services.

E: info@mediationwise.com

Jane Player

Jane Player is an accredited mediator and has mediated a number of disputes both domestic and international. She is a member of CEDR faculty and CEDR Solve panel, IPOS, IMI Users Council and Commercial Mediation Group. Jane is also a disputes partner at King & Spalding International LLP.

E: jplayer@kslaw.com

Nicholas Pryor

Nicholas Pryor is a former solicitor in the City of London and the London insurance market. He has been mediating since 1986 and was amongst the pioneers of mediation in Europe. He is recognised as one of the leading English mediators over the last 25 years, and writes and lectures frequently.

E: nicholas.pryor@sotheby-road.co.uk

John Pugh-Smith

John Pugh-Smith is a barrister, mediator and coach practising from Thirty-Nine Essex Street Chambers. He has not only mediated a diverse range of issues but also pioneered the use of mediation in his specialist practice field of planning and related areas, mostly recently as a DCLG 'broker' for 'stalled developments'.

E: john.pugh-smith@39essex.com

Paul Randolph

Paul Randolph, is a barrister, mediator and author, with special expertise in the psychology of conflict, lecturing on the subject in the UK, Europe, and Asia. He is the mediation course leader, training and accrediting mediators at Regent's University London; and is co-author of *Mediation – A Psychological Insight into Conflict Resolution* (Continuum, 2004).

E: paul@paulrandolph.net

Elizabeth Rivers

Liz Rivers is an expert in employment and workplace mediation, with over 25 years' experience. She supports individuals to create rewarding careers and organisations to have harmonious workplaces. Liz teaches mediation skills around the world and is also a highly experienced women's leadership coach and a psychotherapist.

E: liz@lizrivers.com

Contributor Profiles

Beverly Ann Rogers

Described by Chambers and Partners as 'a mediator of great renown', Beverly's core expertise lies in chancery work ranging from trust and probate matters through property to company and partnership disputes. She has a wealth of experience in multi-party and cross-cultural disputes and trains and mediates in the Far East and Middle East.

E: BARogers@serlecourt.co.uk

Eric Runesson

Eric M Runesson combines his practice as a lawyer with research and tutoring in the fields of contract law and dispute resolution. He is the author of several books and articles. He is often retained as mediator and arbitrator in Swedish and international disputes. He has for many years been chairman of the Mediation Institute of the Stockholm Chamber of Commerce and is considered one of the Swedish pioneers within that area. He is accredited with CEDR and appointed by the Swedish government as one of its three mediators at the International Centre for Settlement of Investment Disputes (ICSID).

E: eric.runesson@sandart.se

Stephen Ruttle QC

Stephen's background is a commercial practice at Brick Court Chambers. He trained with CEDR and was accredited in 1999. Since 2002 he has done no 'proper [legal] work' and has worked solely as a commercial mediator.

In addition to commercial mediation, Stephen is active in the community mediation field. He is the founder of Wandsworth Mediation Service, a registered charity. He is also involved in mediating disputes within and between faith-groups, and in the broader political peacemaking field.

E: stephen.ruttle@brickcourt.co.uk

Austin Sammut

Austin Sammut is an accredited mediator to CEDR and received intensive training at the Singapore Mediation Centre. Chair of Malta Public Broadcasting Services, Austin has been a contributor for many years to radio and television, newspapers and journals, both local and overseas, also as a political analyst including parliamentary correspondent, and to historical and law reviews.

E: asammut@fff-legal.com

Fred Schonewille

Dr Fred Schonewille is legal mediator, mediation advocate, consultant and trainer in the Legal Mediation Firm Schonewille & Schonewille in the Netherlands, He runs a family mediation practice, is co-initiator and director of a national family mediation-network business (Hoefnagels Family Mediation) and is also a part-time judge. He is a researcher on the fields of mediation, negotiation, divorce law, inheritance law and family property law and is an author of books and articles in scholarly journals.

E: fred@schonewille-schonewille.com

Manon Schonewille

Manon Schonewille is a partner in dispute resolution and deal-making training and resource centre, Toolkit Company, a partner in the Legal Mediation Firm Schonewille & Schonewille in The Netherlands and President of ACB Foundation, Corporate ADR & Mediation. She is an IMI certified mediator, legal business mediator, IMI certified mediation advocate, deal facilitator, trainer, lecturer and author.

E: manon@schonewille-schonewille.com

Chris Seaton

Chris began life as a lawyer, but after working in church and voluntary organisations he established Peaceworks in 1999. Through Peaceworks, hundreds of community mediators and tens of thousands of peer mediators in schools have been trained. Chris also leads Schoolsworks, a multi-academy trust based on healthy relationships.

E: chris@peaceworks.org.uk

Gerd Sinding

Gerd Sinding is judge at the District Court of Glostrup, Denmark, where she deals with both civil and criminal cases. She is trained as a mediator and was formerly Head of Human Resources and Head of Reform and Development at the Danish Court Administration.

E: GESI@domstol.dk

Tatjana Šišková

Tatjana Šišková is founder Chairwoman of the Association of the Mediators of the CR (AMČR), and founder of the Centrum Mediace Praha, s.r.o. In 2012 she was named by the Ministry of Justice as commissioner and examiner of the future registered mediators.

Her interest is concentrated into two spheres: family and interethnic mediation and facilitation.

E: amcr@amcr.cz

Quentin Smith

Quentin qualified as a lawyer in 1985 and an accredited Mediator in 1998. He was a partner with Addleshaw Goddard until 2007 when he moved to being a full time mediator. Renowned for his preparation, energy, creativity and persuasiveness combined with the ability to balance fine details, commercial pragmatism and the bigger picture. He is the Chairman of Premiership Rugby, a Director of England Rugby 2015 Limited (the company delivering the 2015 Rugby World Cup in England) and a Member of the Chartered Institute of Arbitrators.

E: quentin@quentinsmith.co.uk

John Sturrock QC

John Sturrock QC has pioneered mediation and conflict strategy in business and professions in Scotland and elsewhere. A Harvard-trained negotiator, with huge experience in commercial mediation, he is an internationally recognised coach in negotiation, mediation and collaboration, and works with leaders, senior executives, top athletes and politicians. He founded Collaborative Scotland, promoting respectful dialogue in the Scottish independence referendum.

E: John.Sturrock@core-solutions.com

Mari Cruz Taboada

Mari Cruz is a lawyer and trained mediator since 1998. She is currently the Managing Director at Iberian Legal Group, an international consultancy and publishing group based in Madrid. In 1997 she started her career at CEDR before being recruited to a pioneering position as BD manager to one of the largest mediation service in London. She then worked for 4 years as a sole mediator for Brighton & Hove City Council.

E: maricruz.taboada@iberianlegalgroup.com

Petri Taivaloski

Petri Taivalkoski heads Roschier's Dispute Resolution practice in Finland. His practice includes litigation, arbitration and alternative dispute resolution. He has extensive experience of a wide variety of business disputes. Petri has been extensively involved in the development of facilitative mediation schemes in Finland and internationally, and in the training of mediators.

E: petri.taivalkoski@roschier.com

Tibor Tajti

Tibor Tajti (Thaythy) is a professor of law at the Legal Studies of Central European University, Budapest (Hungary) since 2002, teaching bankruptcy and secured transactions law, corporate finance and governance, as well as capital markets and securities regulation. Each course is comparative law-based. His research interests include advanced contracts, law reforms and transplantation of law, the industry-law-growth nexus and the role of substantive law in alternative dispute resolution. Some of his publications are available at SSRN or Researchgate.

E: tajtit@ceu.hu

Contributor Profiles

Silas Taylor

Silas practised as a shipping solicitor in Hull for over 35 years, developing the largest shipping law firm outside of London. He was one of the first mediators to be accredited in 1991 and has an international reputation as a skilled and experienced mediator of complex, high value shipping disputes.

E: Silas.taylor@seamediation.com

Christos Theodoulou

Christos is a barrister-at-law from Lincoln's Inn, London and a Licencié and Docteur es sciences politiques from the prestigious Institut de hautes études internationales of Geneva, Switzerland. He was called to the Bar in 1961. He worked at the UN in New York as a Human Rights Officer (1971–73), in the Greek Government in Athens advising on special international matters (1974–76), and as an Assistant Professor of Political Science at the Panteion University, Athens (1974–1976). He is a Member of IMI and the WIPO Panel of Neutrals and is the Honorary Consul of Tunisia in Cyprus.

E: patent.theodoulou@cytanet.com.cy

Luminiţa Trifan

Luminiţa Trifan is a mediator, lawyer and mediation trainer in Romania, training manager of the Craiova Mediation Center Association. She has also been a speaker and a member of the organising team of various conferences and congresses on mediation in Romania. She has written studies and articles on conflict resolution in mediation magazines and journals.

E: luminitatrifan@yahoo.fr

Mladin Vukmir

Mladin Vukmir is a distinguished Neutral (mediator) at the International Institute for Conflict Prevention and Resolution (CPR) (2006–), working as a neutral on the CPR trademark, domain names, IP and IT lists. He is an arbitrator and mediator at the Permanent Arbitration Court and the Mediation Centre of the Croatian Chamber of Commerce, mediator at the Croatian Bar Association's Mediation Centre, certified mediator by the Croatian Ministry of Justice (2011), and UDRP panelist and mediator at the WIPO Arbitration and Mediation Centre.

E: mladen.vukmir@vukmir.net

Stephen Walker

Stephen was a civil and commercial litigation solicitor in London for 30 years. In 2013 he published a book written (with David Smith) for clients and their representatives: *Advising and Representing Clients At Mediation* (Wildy's). He did

Contributor Profiles

this to help people get the best out of the mediation process. It has been well received and was chosen by the ICC as a prize in the 2014 International Mediation Competition. Stephen is also dual accredited as a mediator in the United States through INADR and has undertaken specialist training in workplace mediation. He is a visiting lecturer in mediation at King's College London on the MSc in Construction Law.

E: Stephen@swalkermediation.com

Jane Walmsley

Jane practises as a commercial and workplace mediator, coach and trainer. She is completing her training as a psychotherapist at the School of Psychotherapy and Psychology, Regents University, London and is broadening her private practice to include psychotherapeutic and counselling support to her clients. Jane is a non-practising barrister.

E: jane@janewalmsley.demon.co.uk

Tony Willis

Tony Willis is an eminent full time commercial mediator. He was, for 27 years, a litigation partner in Clifford Chance including two years as a full time Managing Partner and transferred to the Bar in 2004. He has mediated in all parts of the United Kingdom and in many other jurisdictions. He has long ranked at the top of the lists of mediators in Directories such as *Chambers*, the *Legal 500* and *Who's Who Legal*.

E: tony.willis@brickcourt.co.uk

William Wood QC

Bill Wood QC is one of the UK's leading commercial mediators. His mediation practice now takes him to Dubai, Hong Kong, Paris and New York as well as to all parts of the United Kingdom. He sits as an ICC arbitrator, and mediates for the ICC. Former Vice-Chair of the Civil Mediation Council, Bill has been extremely influential in the development of mediation as a profession in the United Kingdom.

E: william.wood@brickcourt.co.uk

Michael Wyldbore-Smith

Michael Wyldbore-Smith is a fellow of the Royal Institution of Chartered Surveyors, Agent for the President of the RICS and Surveyor to the Town Trust in Stratford upon Avon – a charity formed over 500 years ago with a large property porfolio. Michael enjoys the challenge of mediating boundary disputes and finding a successful outcome.

E: michael@wyldbore-smith.co.uk

Xiaohui Yuan

Xiaohui Yuan is a qualified mediator with CEDR and the course director on the MA in Translation and Interpreting at the University of Bristol, and previously the University of Nottingham. She interpreted for the UN Geneva office between 2006 and 2010. She was the principal investigator on UK Research Council funded projects on intercultural competence and use of interpreters in mediation.

E: Xiaohui.yuan@bristol.ac.uk

Part 1
Moulding

Contents

	Page No.
Chapter 1 Introduction	3
Chapter 2 The Core Skills	11
Chapter 3 Case Study	23
Chapter 4 Preparing Stage	25
Chapter 5 Opening Stage	43
Chapter 6 Exploring Stage	53
Chapter 7 Negotiating Stage	65
Chapter 8 Concluding Stage	79
Chapter 9 Setting Up a Mediation Practice	89
Chapter 10 An Overview of the English Legal System	93
Appendix 1 Responses to Mediator Challenges	105
Appendix 2 Recommended Reading List	115

Chapter 1

Introduction

Overview

This is the first part of a three-part Handbook and its aim is to set the solid foundations for an effective commercial mediator (Part 2 is 'Maturing' – going into more detail on the skills and process – and Part 3 is 'Mastering' – being the BEST every time as a commercial mediator, no matter how experienced you may be).

Part 1 uses a case study, which is based upon an actual case with some extra detail added to illustrate particular points and to anchor the 'teaching' to real experience. Each of the five stages of mediation (preparing, opening, exploring, negotiating, concluding) has a few challenges (personal experiences of sticky moments), and Appendix 1 has the responses to those challenges from the actual case.

This chapter gives:

- the reason why mediation is the best dispute resolution process;
- the context of mediation in the dispute resolution landscape and its legal status in the UK;
- the models currently practised;
- an overview of the process and skills;
- a summary of the mediator's role;
- word of warning to end!

The reason to be

Mediation puts common sense back into dispute resolution. Outside face-to-face negotiation, I see it as the only real route to justice. It puts the power for a solution back into the hands of those most affected – the parties – and enables them to construct a solution that works for them. No one imposes a solution, no one tells them what the answer is, no one wins or loses. The deal is whatever the parties decide (so long as it is legal!) and the mediator's job is to give the parties the best opportunity to achieve that deal.

That last point is important. In non-evaluative commercial mediation (I used to call it 'facilitative' mediation until someone described me as being very 'laid back',

Introduction

suggesting that I sat back and let it all happen around me – which was outrageous as I always work my socks off in a mediation – so I changed it to 'non-evaluative' as it sounds more energetic!) the mediator's role is to give the parties the best chance of achieving a solution. There are two parts to that:

- it is managing a process; and
- it is enabling parties to achieve a solution, particularly by listening, questioning, challenging and building a relationship of trust.

If the parties don't make the best of the opportunity provided by the mediator, that is their problem. Most do make the best of the opportunity because most commercial mediations settle on the day, or very soon afterwards.

Why the only route to justice?

There is no doubt that the quickest, cheapest and most effective way of resolving disputes is face-to-face negotiation. If that fails then mediation, which is an assisted negotiation, is the next best. That is another important point – if face-to-face negotiation has failed, mediation won't be easy. If it was easy, they wouldn't need a mediator, so mediation can be tough, and usually is, both for the parties and for the mediator. That means patience and tenacity from the mediator, a belief that the process works (which it does), and a willingness to be non-judgemental and accepting, no matter how difficult a party (or their lawyer, expert or partner) may be.

I have to say that, in our western society, mediation can be seen as unnatural, especially to the male of the species. I say 'male of the species' and risk sounding as if I am pigeonholing. Later in this book we will look at culture and the danger of stereotyping, but my experience is that co-operation appeals to the feminine side of human nature, and women tend to be more feminine than men! Therefore, mediation at its best means co-operative problem-solving, not fighting; it means seeing the issues as joint problems, which can be difficult in a blame culture; it means finding solutions that meet all parties' needs, not winning. So, for mediation to become really established, it needs a culture change. That is gradually happening but one of the challenges is that, for the present at least, lawyers are the gatekeepers. They decide if, when and who, and the trouble is that litigation lawyers (and it is inevitably they who handle disputes) are trained to build the best case, to fight it and to win. It is therefore a real challenge to adapt to a more conciliatory approach and to encourage the parties to work together to find a solution. Not only that, mediation is a party-centred process, which means that lawyers, experts and others are supporters, rather than leaders or soldiers.

When a party has a dispute out of which they cannot negotiate, the automatic next step, in western culture at least, is to consult a lawyer. Necessarily, the lawyer puts a legal framework around the dispute and it becomes a legal argument, no longer a commercial problem. Thereafter the argument is about the legal rights, interpretation of facts in dispute and the strategic 'game' that is litigation, each lawyer finding legal precedent to prove their particular position. The longer it goes on, and the more the commercial dispute recedes, costs increase and more and more management time is wasted. What mediation does is to open the legal framework, for a day, and allow the commercial dispute to be in focus again. Of course, the legal framework is still in the background, but mediation provides the forum for a commercial negotiation once more. The legal arguments (should) largely fall away as the mediation progresses and the role of lawyers (and others) becomes one of support and advice as to risk, whilst the party negotiates a settlement that meets his/her needs. I say 'should' because not all lawyers can let go of the legal arguments and their client's rights. But the sad fact is that when I ask a party what they need to be able to achieve a settlement most say, 'I want to put an end to this misery.' Disputes take over people's lives, they can become like dark clouds hanging over them every day, they waste time in defending or pursuing a claim instead of creating wealth for their business (or leisure time with their family) and they affect relationships, both personal and business. Mediation allows the parties to bring that misery to an end. Of course, to get there will inevitably cause some, if not a lot of pain – mediation used to be called 'win-win' but I now call it 'pain-pain' – but it brings finality. Settle, and tomorrow is cloud-free and brings new opportunities.

That has got to be better than going to court, or arbitration, and having an anonymous stranger impose a decision that means one party wins and the other loses. Life is not like that, not black or white but all shades in between. People see the same facts and events through different eyes, for a whole range of different reasons (education, culture, religion, gender, age, ego, wealth (or not), political belief, residency, authority (or reaction to it), principles, needs, sexual orientation and many more); they interpret facts and events differently as a result, and it doesn't necessarily mean that their 'truth' is any more right or wrong than another's, just different. To put someone who does not know the parties, or the circumstances, into a position of deciding a winner cannot be fair. Worse, for that person to make that decision based upon legal, rather than commercial, argument cannot be, in my view, just. Mediation allows (or should allow) the parties to be in control of the outcome, to find a solution that is anywhere on the spectrum from outright win to outright lose; even better, that solution can take into account a whole number of matters that a judge or arbitrator cannot – personal and commercial circumstances, relationships, future business, ability to pay, settlements in kind and so on. The parties decide, and that has to be more just than a stranger imposing a judgment in favour of one or the other.

Commercial mediation in the dispute resolution landscape

Mediation sits next to negotiation at the far end of the dispute resolution spectrum. It is, after all, an assisted negotiation, and is only sensible if direct face-to-face negotiation fails. It is a consensual process and, unless other processes introduce a consensual stage (such as arbitration turning into a mediation to avoid an imposed decision), it is the only process that allows the parties to shape their own settlement. Beyond this there are recommended solutions such as experts opinions, neutral fact-finding, early neutral evaluation (usually a judge forecasting the likely outcome if the case goes to court) and dispute resolution boards (three neutrals giving a recommended solution); there are also imposed outcomes such as by the Ombudsman, expert determination, tribunals, adjudication, arbitration and the courts.

In the UK the term 'ADR' (alternative dispute resolution) usually means mediation; in other countries it can also mean arbitration as this is not a common process in

Introduction

some jurisdictions. Because mediation has become established in the UK, ADR has now come to mean 'appropriate dispute resolution' (although there are several other, some not so complimentary, explanations).

Although there is no mandatory mediation in the UK, most courts give a very strong nudge to parties to consider ADR, particularly mediation. They assume that the courts should be the last resort and so mediation, and other forms of ADR, should be 'first resort'. Indeed, the courts are able to sanction costs if a party does not consider mediation or enter into it in good faith. Quite how the judge would decide such an issue if the mediator cannot be called as a witness (because it is a confidential process) is difficult to imagine, but does happen.

Because it is still a (relatively) new process, there is little case law on mediation in the UK. Such as there is has reinforced its position in the accepted UK dispute resolution spectrum. The courts recognise the importance of mediation as a confidential process. However, as users get experienced in using that process, there will be more challenges and abuses.

For a regular update on mediation-related cases see the great website set up by David Cornes: www.mediatewithcornes.co.uk/caselawalpha.html.

Mediation models

As mentioned earlier, I practise non-evaluative commercial mediation. In other words, I don't give opinions on parties' rights, the relevant law, the likely chances if a case goes to court or relative merits. Unfortunately some mediators are undoubtedly evaluative and do all of those things. Not only do I consider that dangerously challenges the mediator's neutrality, but when it happens it is most likely to be because it is an easy way out of a deadlock situation, and therefore more to the mediator's comfort, not the party's benefit. Non-evaluative mediators have to find other (and better) ways.

Nor do I sit back and let the parties slug it out whilst I read a book (although I am told some mediators do just that!). Mediation is a tiring process, though fuelled by adrenalin, and it is not unusual for ties to be loosened and sleeves rolled up as the day goes on. The mediator should be the first to arrive, the last to leave and constantly engaged throughout.

Although I would prefer otherwise, evaluative commercial mediation is now being widely practised in the UK, following the trend in the United States. It would appear to be lawyer-driven and practised predominantly by barristers, and seems to achieve a reasonably high settlement rate. However, in my opinion it takes away so many of the benefits of mediation and is a trend to be regretted.

Transformative mediation concentrates on the parties' relationships and is much less structured than conventional problem-solving mediation. It often spans several days and does not seek solutions, its premise is that parties will find a path to resolve their conflict through each side narrating their story. Some would say there is no place for such a process in commercial disputes, but I fear many commercial mediators focus too much on the solution at the expense of the parties' relationships. Time spent on the emotional dimension of disputes can often yield a much richer solution.

There are several strands of mediation in the UK. Community, or neighbourhood, mediation, which deals primarily with local issues, sometimes overlaps with commercial mediation in boundary disputes and rights of way. Mostly it deals with tensions between neighbours with limited resources, mainly noise disputes which cause immense stress, but also cultural issues over the behaviour of children, vandalism, etc. Peer mediation teaches children in schools mediation skills in a safe model. This can be a powerful tool for children who do not feel heard, both at school or at home, and who tend to try and resolve conflict with violence. Arguably, it should be part of the curriculum because it teaches children ways of dealing with conflict in a non-violent way – what a legacy for the world! Unfortunately there is little to no funding for this in this country at present. To be effective, these schemes should also teach mediation skills to governors, teachers and parents as well as the children. Victim-offender mediation, or restorative justice schemes, enable, after lots of preparation, the perpetrator of a crime to meet face-to-face with their victim(s). It is a growing and effective strategy for reducing repeat offending and helping to bring closure for victims.

Family mediation is primarily about contact with children and the division of possessions, and very rarely with reconciliation. Having said that, anything that reduces the pain of separation and divorce has a vital place in society. Family mediation occasionally overlaps with commercial mediation in areas of contested wills and splitting family business.

Environmental mediation is as much about consensus building between a large number of stakeholders, as finding solutions. It deals with major issues such as routes of new railways or roads, pollution, conservation and so on. It can overlap with commercial mediation in planning issues, particularly large housing and commercial developments.

Faith disputes deal with conflict within and between faith communities. It can overlap with both commercial and community mediation and often draws on Mediators from all strands.

Although the mediation process varies with each strand, – for example, Community mediation is usually co-mediated, whereas family mediation rarely involves private meetings, although the principles are the same – all are based upon a confidential process where an independent third-party helps the parties reach their own solution.

It is worth noting that in some jurisdictions mediation is mandatory for certain cases. In the UK we have not gone that far and all the signs are that a 'firm nudge' is about as far as the courts, or the government, will go. However, there are many advocates for compulsory mediation, and not just from mediators who are under-employed! It would mean that ignorance – the main reason for many cases not going to mediation – would no longer be an issue. It would also mean that reluctant lawyers or parties would have to take their case to mediation at some time. It would probably mean that parties have more influence over when to mediate, and possibly who with. The down side is that more parties who are reluctant or against mediation would still have to participate – and that would probably mean that settlement rates would come down. Having said that, my experience is that

Introduction

reluctant parties often become quite positive once they realise that settlement is within their power. Mediation is a very seductive process!

Mediation overview

So mediation is an assisted negotiation where an independent third-party (the mediator) helps the parties reach their own solution, in private. It is non-binding until reduced to writing and signed by the parties and without prejudice (that is, what is said and produced for the mediation cannot be used if the case does not settle and goes to court). It is therefore party-focused; the lawyers and others are there in support, and the mediator manages the process. The best way to use the process is for the parties, and their advisers, to see the dispute as a joint problem and to co-operate to find a joint solution. So, principled (needs-based, ie what the parties need to agree a settlement) negotiation is more effective than positional (rights-based, ie their legal rights under the law) negotiation. Better deals come from co-operating than from fighting.

Most mediations take a full day although some (particularly low-value claims) may be time-limited. There is a main room and a private room for each party. The day usually starts with separate private meetings between the mediator and each party and then everyone gathers in the main room for an open session where all the issues are tabled and a strategy for the day is agreed. At some stage the parties will then return to their room and the mediator will shuttle between them, exploring the issues and helping to shape an eventual deal. There may well be further open, or joint, sessions or working meetings between experts or lawyers. Often the key decision makers will meet to finalise the settlement and then the lawyers will write up the settlement agreement for signature by the parties.

Summary of the mediator's role

As mentioned earlier, the mediator's role is to:

- manage the process in the most efficient way;
- reopen often fractured lines of communication between the parties;
- actively listen and allow parties to tell their story;
- build a relationship of trust with all parties and their advisers so that they will be prepared to disclose sensitive information and know that it will not be used to their disadvantage;
- be seen to be unbiased and even-handed;
- manage emotions so that they do not become destructive;
- use information strategically (what to hold, what to give, what to reframe);
- help parties achieve the best settlement; and
- oversee a deal that sticks.

The mediator must be patient, tenacious, enthusiastic, positive, energetic, humorous, humble, wise, non-judgemental, accepting and encouraging. In other words, a saint, or an angel – probably both! The headline is the mediator is there to help the parties get a deal – managing and enabling, not directing or advising. What follows is intended to get you, as an effective mediator, there in one, accomplished piece.

A word of warning

Most of Part 1 of this book is based on my personal experience over more than 20 years of mediating commercial (and some workplace and faith) disputes. Mediation is a solitary profession. At best, some of us co-mediate occasionally and some of us take assistants who have been newly trained, but most commercial mediators work alone. So I don't know what my peers get up to, other than what we share at mediator gatherings, and maybe the occasional peer review. I only know what I have taught and what I practice (they are not necessarily the same!), so some experienced mediators may well say this is not what they do. All I know is that what I do works, most of the time, and, whilst I recognise that I am still learning as I go, I believe it is the best way to resolve disputes.

Chapter 2

The Core Skills

Overview

This chapter deals with the essential skills needed to be an effective commercial (or any) mediator. Some skills are natural, instinctive and can be highlighted and polished. Others can be learnt. The result will be people who a potent force for settling disputes and even for reconciliation – and the world needs lots of such people!

An effective mediator must be a good:

- manager – orchestrating the day in the most efficient and effective way, helping the parties to make the best of the opportunity and getting the best deal as a result;
- communicator – bringing clarity to an often confused and deadlocked situation and helping parties to speak with each other in a safe and unthreatening environment;
- negotiator – using the information provided in the best and most positive way and helping parties to shape and settle the best deal possible that is realistic and that will stick;
- 'friend' – building relationships of trust with the parties and their advisers through giving time, carefully listening to their story and understanding their emotions, so that they will share sensitive information and know that it will not be used to their disadvantage.

We will now take a look at these in reverse order.

The mediator is a 'friend' to all

The success of the mediation process depends upon the mediator's ability to build a relationship of trust with the parties and their advisers, quickly and effectively. All in a day! Without that trust the parties will not share sensitive information and the mediator will not know the key issues and real needs of the parties, and so will have little or nothing to work with. So building a relationship of trust is crucial – I would say the ability to do that should be mandatory in any assessment of a potential mediator. In technical jargon this comprises the following competencies.

The Core Skills

Rapport building

Rapport can be built in different ways, but the purpose must always be to create a relationship of trust and respect. Typical ways of creating rapport are:

- including everyone in the discussions;
- listening attentively to what is being said and demonstrating that you have heard;
- demonstrating understanding by responding or summarising;
- being neutral and non-judgemental;
- being approachable, open, honest and friendly;
- being harmonious in verbal and non-verbal language;
- maintaining eye contact (and taking few notes);
- being even-handed and treating everyone equally;
- observing and demonstrating confidentiality at all times.

This is much more than being 'nice' to people. It is effectively communicating with them at their level both verbally and non-verbally.

Rapport has a physical dimension. The personal space between the speaker and listener (and obstacles such as the desk or computer screen between them), the body posture, the tone and pace of voice and the words that are used are all key to being in harmony (or not) with a person. For harmony to be created there needs to be a respect of a person's own space, and being too close, or too distant, can inhibit rapport. Sitting behind a desk or table, sitting on chairs of different heights, or, worst of all, being distracted by a computer screen, keyboard or wristwatch while a person is speaking, are all challenges to creating and maintaining rapport. Good rapport is created by matching the speaker's body position (standing, sitting, walking) and posture (relaxed, energetic), and by using the voice pitch, tone and even words (jargon, metaphor) that are similar, without mimicking the speaker. The effective mediator will create an atmosphere that is comfortable and unthreatening to the parties, will demonstrate interest and will 'honour' the individual by ensuring that his or her actions and words (those of the mediator) are in harmony.

Fundamentally good rapport means that other people feel comfortable and relaxed in your presence and because of that they are prepared to speak freely and openly. It arises as much from the mediator being comfortable in their own skin and projecting an atmosphere of openness and acceptance. If you don't have it, it is not easily learnt. This is probably the key difference between an ordinary mediator and a masterly one. To a master it is natural and intuitive. However, natural or not, there are some key skills that can be learnt/polished that will enable rapport to be built.

Empathy

It is important to distinguish between empathy and sympathy. Empathy is demonstrating understanding of a person's experience, behaviour and feelings without judging, evaluating or confronting the speaker. It means conveying that understanding without sharing the person's feelings and emotions. Empathy means not joining the speaker in the issue. Sympathy is getting in there with the speaker, identifying with the issue and sharing the speaker's feelings and emotions. A statement from the mediator such as, 'Oh, I know how you feel...,' is definitely showing sympathy, whereas, 'I appreciate how upsetting this must be for you...,' demonstrates empathy. A good mediator shows empathy but not sympathy. They see the situation through the speaker's eyes.

Hearing

People need to feel heard. Hearing is subtly different to listening. So many people listen in part but are more focused on how they are going to reply or are more concerned with their own thoughts and story than the one being told. When someone feels heard, they feel valued and that makes a huge difference to the frustration that arises from knowing that the listener is distracted or not giving proper attention to what is being said. However, hearing is only part of the process. The hearer must show that what has been said has been received and understood. And the best way of doing that is to summarise what has been said, which has the dual advantage of showing that the speaker has been heard, and that the key points have been understood, and also allows the speaker to correct or reframe what is being fed back, if they do not agree (or wish to change what has been said).

Summarising

Summarising is a valuable method of:

- checking understanding;
- demonstrating that the listener has heard;
- focussing on key issues;
- allowing parties to change what they have said;
- putting order into an otherwise disordered statement;
- changing the direction of a conversation; and
- buying time, both for the party to reflect and also for the mediator (who may be wondering what to do next!)

It is particularly important not to move on from summarising until the party has said 'Yes'. This ensures that there is a common understanding and that the mediator and party are in agreement. Waiting for confirmation allows the party to review what has been said and then to adjust the emphasis or interpretation.

It is good practice for the mediator to be in the habit of summarising what has been said in a private meeting and checking what is confidential before they leave the room. It gives value to what has been said and allows the parties to be in control of the information flow to the other side. There are other times, even with a party's opening statement in the first open meeting, when the mediator can summarise, to bring some order to an otherwise fragmented statement, show that what has been said has been understood, and to give the party an opportunity to amend or agree and give confidence to the mediator that they have heard correctly. However, it can be overdone and therefore its true value diminished. No one wants to have what they have said summarised back to them after every few sentences.

Summarising can also be a valuable way to reframe a negative statement.

Reframing

Reframing is adjusting, reordering or changing the words of a statement to give it a more positive meaning. It is a (hopefully) subtle way of making a negative or provocative statement more acceptable or palatable. It can take the sting out of the statement and help parties avoid losing face. A small example is how a demand for an apology can be reframed into an expression of regret. Or a statement that the other side are liars and cheats could be reframed as a need to be able to trust what is being said and to have confidence that they are being treated fairly. Admittedly not a positive reframe, but a lawyer stating that his client has a 70 per cent chance of winning if the case goes to Court, can be reframed as a 30 per cent chance of losing!

Another example would be if a party makes a statement early in the mediation such as 'My bottom line is £100,000'. Such a definite statement may cause deadlock later and risk the party losing face. A reframe could be something like, 'So money is important to you in any settlement'. This gives the party space to manoeuvre should that become necessary later in the mediation.

Active listening

Being a good listener implies not talking (very much)! It means being prepared to listen to what the other person has to say without interrupting or taking over the conversation. As mentioned earlier, it means hearing what is being said and demonstrating that you have heard. It means leaving silence, and not filling the space, and encouraging the other person to carry on by giving a few gentle prompts. There are ways of demonstrating that what is being said is being heard without actually saying anything. Minimal prompts such as 'Mmm...,' and 'Uh-ha...,' will encourage the speaker to continue. When the flow falters then 'Tell me more...,' and 'Then.....?' will encourage the flow. A raising of the eyebrows or gesture of the hands can invite more. Or just silence.

It also means not bettering their story with one of your own. It is not easy being a good listener!

A mediator needs to gather information and encourage people to talk. The measure of how effective they are being is the balance of 'air time'. If the mediator is occupying more than, say, 20 per cent of the speaking time in the early stages of a mediation, then they are probably talking too much. It is worth stepping back and checking why this might be. It could be that the mediator is not asking encouraging (open) questions, or that the speaker is uncomfortable, or that there is a particularly sensitive issue lurking below the surface that has yet to be liberated. The mediator needs to be 'in tune' with the speaker in order to recognise, and respond to, these possibilities.

Silence

Silence is a very powerful tool for the mediator. It is, perhaps, difficult to use because it can make people, including the mediator, feel uncomfortable, but real gems can result if the mediator has the confidence to wait. People feel the need to fill the silence and will often say something that is quite revealing because it has not been rehearsed. Not least when they have just been very emotional.

Reflecting

Reflecting is a form of summarising but focuses on the feelings. So by recognising and acknowledging a person's emotional response to a situation it helps that person to consider and clarify their feelings and the reasons behind them. Not only does it give the mediator the opportunity to recognise and value those feelings (even if they appear to be unreasonable, they are still real to the person), it also provides an opportunity for the mediator to check their understanding of what has been heard or sensed. Reflecting non-verbal communication is also important and that is dealt with later. I believe that it is important to confront emotion (I don't mean be confrontational but recognise and acknowledge) and spend time with it.

Managing emotion

There are few rules in mediation but one is that if the parties (or anyone in the mediation for that matter) are becoming emotional, DON'T sit on it and DON'T avoid it. If the mediator stops it there will be a head of steam that will affect the mediation and eventually burst. If the mediator avoids it because it is uncomfortable (who for?) the same will happen, with the party also feeling ignored and undervalued.

There is no better way to build rapport with a party than to let them freely vent their emotion, and then to acknowledge and value what has been said. Best done in the open session so that the cause of their emotion, usually the other party, can see the strength of feeling. It can be scary. The last thing the mediator wants is for the parties to feel that he or she is not in control, and, because it can be uncomfortable for everyone, there is a tendency for people to want it to end. Resist it! Let the demonstration of emotion continue until it fades, or if it becomes abusive or destructive. Why shouldn't an injured party show how strongly they feel? Come to that, why shouldn't the listener respond strongly as well? After all, it is their dispute. If it does become abusive or destructive then the mediator needs to intervene to break the flow. That could be to pick up a particular point the party has made, to suggest focusing on another area or even taking a break – so long as it is done without demeaning the speaker and with an acknowledgement of their strong feeling.

The parties are not the only ones who come to the mediation with an emotional investment. The lawyers have an investment. They have advised their client to come to mediation, have chosen a mediator, have developed their mediation strategy and, usually by the day itself, they want it to settle – after all, a satisfied client will bring more business. The experts, if they attend, also have an investment. Their credibility is being scrutinised, their expertise may be questioned, their

The Core Skills

'performance' noted. Other supporters/advisers come with their own emotional investment, – and don't forget the mediator! Mediation can be a very emotional activity for the mediator – there is a huge personal investment involved. After all, the mediator is the 'conductor of the orchestra' and they need to get the best from all the various 'instruments' involved (hopefully all eventually playing the same tune). I advise new mediators to have an easy day after a mediation, to recover and reflect, and ideally, crystallise key learning points in a mediation journal. Every mediation brings about something unexpected from which to learn.

The mediator as negotiator

Strategic use of information

The mediator is in an incredibly powerful position in a mediation. They are likely to know more about each party's true position – their underlying interests and needs – than either party and so have insights into how to influence the process to obtain the best deal for everyone. A subtle, but vital, part of that is knowing what to do with the information provided. After all, the 'exploring' stage (Chapter 6) is about gathering information, whilst the 'negotiating' stage (Chapter 7) is filtering and using that information to help the parties achieve the best deal. So throughout the mediation the mediator must decide how best to use the information – what to pass on, what to hold (whether to give later or never), what to reframe and what to edit. All this is to give the parties the best opportunity of achieving a settlement. It is a crucial role and worth thinking about how best to use the information before acting. That is another benefit of having a room to go to and an assistant with whom to talk options though.

Problem solving

Although a vital part of mediation is that it is the parties' problem, and THEIR solution, it is also an important part of the mediator's role to help with the problem solving. There is absolutely no reason for the mediator to hold back from throwing in suggestions of possible solutions – indeed the mediator comes to this as an independent, virtually ignorant of the past, and is a fresh mind to the problem. However, the key is that, having lobbed in a few suggestions, the mediator allows the parties to pick them up or ignore them.

The trouble is that most mediators see a solution quite early on in the mediation; indeed many mediators are trained problem solvers – it is part of their job. It is so tempting, if not to actually tell the parties the obvious answer, then to make it clear to them how sensible a particular solution might be. But it is a no-go area. It is the parties' problem and THEIR solution. If they choose to ignore yours and even settle on an inferior one, that is their right and responsibility. After all, the mediator only knows what the parties choose to tell him/her and the real reason for doing a particular deal may never be known.

The mediator is in a position to help bring logic and clarity to the issues by:

- exploring the original cause of the problem (and asking what lessons have been learnt);

- discussing ideas, especially non-financial possibilities in a settlement;
- reality-testing a proposed deal to ensure it will work; and
- checking the various actions that are necessary for the settlement to be fulfilled.

Never forget that the role of the mediator in mediation is to give the parties the best chance of achieving settlement, but that it is their settlement.

Hitting the zone

I think that one of the most valuable roles for the mediator in mediation is to understand, manage and, if necessary, coach the parties into effective business negotiation. It is one reason why I believe that non-lawyer mediators have an edge on their lawyer mediator colleagues – if the mediator has lived in the business world then negotiation (that is proper negotiation as opposed to doing deals for someone else) is second nature and so they should add significant value to the process. Part of that is understanding the difference between positional and principled negotiation and the certainty that co-operation invariably leads to the best deals. If the mediator handles the early phases of the mediation well, establishing the parties' needs and shaping a deal that meets those needs, then the first offers and counteroffers are likely to be in the zone of probable agreement (ZOPA in Pepperdine University jargon). Hitting that zone leads to the best settlement because parties see a deal that meets their needs and don't want to lose it. There is more about this in Chapter 7.

Saving face

Saving face is a universal need. Everyone wants to leave a negotiation with head held high and a feeling that they have obtained a deal with dignity. This is not a cultural matter; it is a human matter. And the effective mediator will do their very best to ensure this happens by anticipating issues where a party might be cornered or make a statement from which they will have difficulty escaping (eg, '£x is my bottom line and not a penny more') or even make a statement of 'principle' which becomes a solid barrier against settlement. Reframing, softening language, challenging statements, even refusing to accept a statement are all ways in which an effective mediator may help a party to avoid a face-saving issue later in the mediation.

The mediator as communicator

Questioning appropriately

There are other skills used by an effective mediator that have a considerable effect on the course of the mediation. The style and method of questioning, the ability to challenge without appearing to be partial, of being deeply interested without being inquisitorial, and of reframing negative or adversarial statements into positive, more conciliatory words, can be a key to helping the parties to move on. The wrong questions can risk blocking communication and even destroying rapport.

The Core Skills

Of course, different types of questions can be effective at different times, but some types of questions are rarely appropriate in a mediation. These include *leading* questions where the questioner indicates the expected answer, and *multiple* questions where the questioner asks the same question in several different ways and confuses the listener en route. The best questions are simple and short (my mantra is 'Short, Simple, Shut up!')

When the mediator is gathering information, particularly in the 'exploring' phase, *open* questions are the most appropriate. Questions that start 'How....?' or 'What.....?' or 'Why...?' or 'Tell me about....' invite the listener to speak at length, whereas *closed* questions invite a 'Yes' or 'No' answer that provide little or no information. We tend to ask closed questions more instinctively but often it is just a matter of reordering the words to change a closed question into an open one. For example: 'Do you feel OK about that?' (= 'Yes' or 'No') could be 'Tell me how you feel about that'. Or 'Do you want payment terms?' (= 'Yes' or 'No') could be 'What payment terms do you need?'.

Of course, there are times when closed questions are appropriate, particularly to obtain confirmation of understanding or acceptance of an offer, but they are not appropriate for encouraging people to speak. The use of *hypothetical* ('What if....?') questions is a powerful technique when exploring possible solutions. It depersonalises the suggestion and allows it to be examined dispassionately, for example, 'What if they agreed to stage payments....?' or 'What if they were to provide alternative accommodation...?'

Challenging questions can be used to great effect, particularly when reality-testing. 'Why...?' is one of the best. The challenge to the mediator, however, is to be sure that the questions are worded so as not to imply criticism or judgement of the party's position.

Non-verbal communication

Non-verbal is what it says – we communicate with much more than words. Unfortunately in our age of emails and texting, we rely on the written word much more than verbal and it is fraught with the danger of being misunderstood. The written word has the meaning that is received rather than the meaning that was sent, and they may not be the same – without explanation the meaning is entirely how the receiver interprets the words. How much more meaningful then are words that have expression, tone, volume and pace to accompany them – telephone conversations are much better able to convey the true meaning of the words and also enable the speaker to explain further if the listener has misunderstood.

Even then, communication is incomplete. Face-to-face communication is so much more effective and that is one of the benefits of the initial open session in mediation, where parties face each other and, hopefully speak, and listen, to each other. Face-to-face, people can see expression, have eye contact (or not), read the body language, interpret inconsistencies between posture and words, cease to demonise the other person and recognise that they are also human with feelings and needs.

Part of building rapport mentioned earlier is being in harmony with a person. The mediator can enhance that by *matching* a party's body language. That does not mean mimicking or appearing to parody – harmony is the key word. When a group of friends are sitting round a table or in a pub, relaxed and at ease with each other, their body posture is often the same. Legs crossed, sitting back, arms moving when they talk. Unconsciously they are matching, being in harmony with each other. When one reaches for their drink, the others often do so. So it is with rapport-building – having a body posture that is consistent with the other person, subtly matching their pace and tone of voice, using key words that they have used, all helps the person to relax and feel valued. But 'subtle' is the word; more than that and it can seem artificial or insulting. The main message here is that a mediator whose body language is almost horizontal is not going to be in rapport with someone who is pacing the room in agitation. Keep that picture in mind and matching will come more easily – and if the person is pacing the room, it is not a bad move for the mediator to stand and maybe pace with them.

There is potentially a place for *mismatching* in mediation although there needs to be a strong health warning. Bringing a ranting monologue, or a meeting, to a close by standing up, or looking at your watch (although that can easily be interpreted as indicating boredom), or turning up the energy, or the volume, all send a very positive message. The danger is that all the careful rapport-building that has gone before may be undone in an instant – and if there has not been careful rapport-building before it might lead to bloodshed!!

From history to future

Parties in mediation tend to be anchored in the past. After all, that is when the problem started. Linked with that, however, is their almost desperate wish to end the misery of their dispute and to get on with life again. That is the prize – or one of the prizes at least. So one of the mediator's tasks is to get parties to look forward, not back. I often say to them: 'You can't change history but you can control the future'. Used at the right time, this can be a powerful and compelling message and will often be the point where a party lets go of their negative behaviour and start to consider the shape of a deal. The vision of a future without the cloud of a dispute overshadowing their business and personal lives can be immensely attractive.

Modelling other's behaviour

A valuable technique for the mediator is to get each party to 'step into the other's shoes' and view the issues from that perspective. Parties see the same facts and events differently, hence the dispute, and this is compounded by their legal advisers interpreting the facts in the way best suited to their case. Getting parties to understand why the other is interpreting the same situation differently can enable them to see the dispute in a new light, and even help them to accept that the other's position may not be as unreasonable as first assumed. It will also help them to construct a settlement that takes account of these insights.

Getting parties to 'step into the other's shoes' is a useful technique for the mediator when being asked to take settlement offers to the other side. Asking 'How do you think they will react?' is a useful challenge in reality-testing an offer.

Unconsciously or not, the mediator's very demeanour can model other's behaviour. Being open, accepting, light-hearted and believing has an affect on others and tends to offer a more co-operative approach. Often, when asked 'Do you believe them (the other side)?' I respond 'I believe everything that I am told – but I know that some people do not tell me the truth'. Dare they tell me an untruth after that?

The mediator as manager

Overview

Many of the qualities of the mediator as an effective manager of the mediation process are covered elsewhere in this book. In summary the mediator needs to be:

- seen to be 'in control', a firm manager of the process;
- accepted as a safe pair of hands who will deal with sensitive issues (and people) carefully;
- seen to be efficient and purposeful;
- seen to be even-handed and independent;
- constantly optimistic, knowing that the process works and that settlement occurs in the vast majority of mediations; and
- energetic, particularly when others are flagging.

Part of this is routine:

- the confirmatory email needs to be clear in its directions about information required, timetable and practical issues such as timing, venue, fees, etc;
- preparation needs to be thorough and sufficient for the mediator to be confident about the issues and claims, particularly the financial details;
- the initial telephone contact needs to be structured and with purpose;
- the mediator needs to arrive early on the day, checking the rooms, the seating, access, smoking area, toilets, pens, pads, water, the food, fire alarms and so on;
- they need to be reassuring and clear about what is expected of the parties and advisers in the first private meeting before the initial open session;
- they must lay clear ground rules for the day (confidentiality, courtesy, responsibility, format and so on);
- timekeeping including keeping everyone informed of progress and timing;
- having a settlement agreement template available; and
- being aware of the need for refreshments, particularly if the mediation goes into the evening.

In addition, there are specific skills and techniques required of the effective mediator that are not specifically covered elsewhere

Patience and tenacity

If I had a label as a mediator I guess it would be that I am patient and won't let go. I believe the mediator should be the last to leave and should always be optimistic about the mediation settling, no matter how difficult it, and/or the parties, has become. Belief that the process works and that we only get the difficult ones to sort out (the easy ones are sorted by the lawyers before they ever reach the mediator!), is sufficient for the mediator to be confident that patience, perseverance and hanging on in there despite reaching the point of despair will prevail. Most settle, so that confidence is not misplaced. What is more, it is often the mediator's optimism and confidence that keeps the parties going as well – another way of the mediator modelling parties' behaviour.

Time management

One of the potential weaknesses of mediation is the idle time (and the potential boredom that goes with it). It is crucial that the mediator keeps everyone informed about what is happening through out the day, not least:

- 'The initial open session could last until (lunchtime), but we will see how it goes.'
- 'Let's assume we finish in normal working hours. That means signing a settlement agreement at 6pm, shaking hands on a deal at 4pm (the lawyers usually need a couple of hours to get the wording right) which means being in serious negotiation at 2pm, so all the detail (facts and issues) needs to be dealt with in the next (two) hours.'
- 'I shall be with them for about half an hour, so should be with you by xx.'
- 'I am just going to xy's room to talk about yz, so should be with you by xx.'
- 'I have suggested that the decision makers/lawyers/experts meet in the main room to finalise this issue. How long do you need to prepare?'

The assistant should be used as timekeeper and runner if the time allowed is exceeded.

Using visual aids

Some parties may use computerised presentations in mediations and some mediators may have risk analysis programmes in reserve. The use of electronic aids in mediation is bound to increase. However, the visual aid or technique that some experienced mediators, including me, most often use is writing on the flipchart. The effect can be dramatic. Not only can it present the reality of a situation, or clarify where the real issues are, it can also be a tool for changing the dynamic of a meeting. Getting people to focus on what is being written takes them away from focussing on each other and can therefore change an otherwise confrontational situation.

I use the flipchart (but no other visual aid) in every mediation (see in Chapter 5 – 'Using the Flipchart'). It can be to record the key issues to be tackled on the day; it may be to draw a plan of a site/right of way/boundary; it could be to summarise (or reframe) financial claims; it often is to relay offers, and counteroffers on the same sheet; it could be to brainstorm solutions (either all together or, more likely, in separate rooms); it could even be to run several solutions in parallel until one emerges as the final deal. I often use it to keep a record of the various parts of a settlement as they are agreed – often that is the basis for the lawyers to write up the agreement. On one occasion the parties signed the flipchart, considering it to be a sufficient record of the deal, and we recorded the settlement taking a picture on everyone's smartphone (the lawyers drew it up formally the next day)!

Of course when the flipchart is being used, it doesn't have to be the mediator who does the writing up. It can be anyone present, but the person who holds the pen is in a very powerful position (which may be a reason for the mediator to hold on to it!) so it can be a challenge for the mediator to hand over the pen, but very empowering for the person who takes it.

There are, of course, techniques for using the flipchart that make its use most effective. Mixing colours (but not using yellow), writing in capital letters and using graphics all help to make the use of a flipchart interesting and powerful. Also putting up a heading first is a good reference point as to the purpose of the exercise and a reminder for later.

Finally, be careful where the flipchart is sited. It is sensible to have it where everyone can see it but most conference rooms have glass vision or side panels and a lot of modern offices have glazed atriums. So make sure the flipchart is sited in a position where it cannot be seen by a third party (and potentially give away a confidence).

Finally

This may all seem to be expecting the effective mediator to be superhuman. Not so. Most of us have all of this within us, although consciously bringing together these skills requires patience and real effort. Much of it is a matter of being more aware of, and polishing, what we know. This is a human activity and it is putting common-sense back into the dispute resolution process. It is also a seductive process – once you are doing it you never want to stop. For some, like me, it is a coming home, a working of the soul. At its best it is almost a spiritual activity.

Chapter 3

Case Study

General Information

Background

The Claybeam family has been farming for at least five generations on around 1,000 acres of agricultural land, some of which is rented from neighbouring smallholdings. The farm (land and property) is currently owned by Harry and his two younger siblings, Chris and Jo, Harry having 40 per cent, Chris and Jo each owning 30 per cent. Harry owns and manages the farm business, Chris runs the farm shop and Jo is a teacher at the local upper school (although contributes to the farm at the weekends and school holidays).

The farm has several barns and grainstores, some of which are stone-built but somewhat derelict, and two pairs of farm cottages, one pair of which is occupied by long-serving farm workers, the other pair being empty but in need of renovation.

The farm borders Over Leys, a village to the north that has developed in ribbon fashion along the main road. Elsewhere the boundaries are shared with other farms. Harry has recently set up a development company with the intention of developing the redundant farm buildings. It is currently a shell company because ownership of the buildings is joint with his siblings and both Chris and Jo are not in favour of diversifying into development of property, as they believe Harry's energy should be in making the farm a success, which has been a real struggle for them all in recent years. Harry's position is that he has quite a lot of experience in building because the various farm buildings are always in need of repair and maintenance. He has become quite cross with his siblings about all this. Matters have come to a head with Harry insisting that:

- Chris and Jo sign a mortgage deed allowing him to obtain a £500,000 loan against the land (the mortgage provider requires all three owners to sign the deed) to fund the property development.
- Chris and Jo sign over the group of stone barns and adjoining paddock (about two acres) to the north boundary (adjoining Over Leys) on the basis that they are currently worthless due to them being derelict.

Up to now both Chris and Jo have resisted Harry's demands but then finally decided to agree, to stop the bad feeling this dispute is causing within the family. Harry has produced various forms for them to sign but, at the last moment, a friend (Stephen Atkins) urged them to go to mediation, feeling that Jo and Chris were about to sign

Case Study

away their rights to valuable property. Harry was furious, but eventually relented, as it seems to be the only route to getting this sorted.

The following attended the mediation:

- Harry Claybeam
- Angela Pearce (Harry's solicitor)
- Quentin Phillips (Harry's barrister)
- Charles Pugh-Smith (Harry's valuation expert)
- Chris and Jo Claybeam
- Stephen Atkins, Chris and Jo's friend (a general practice surveyor)
- David Richbell (mediator)
- Mags Bishop (assistant)

Plan of farm (part)

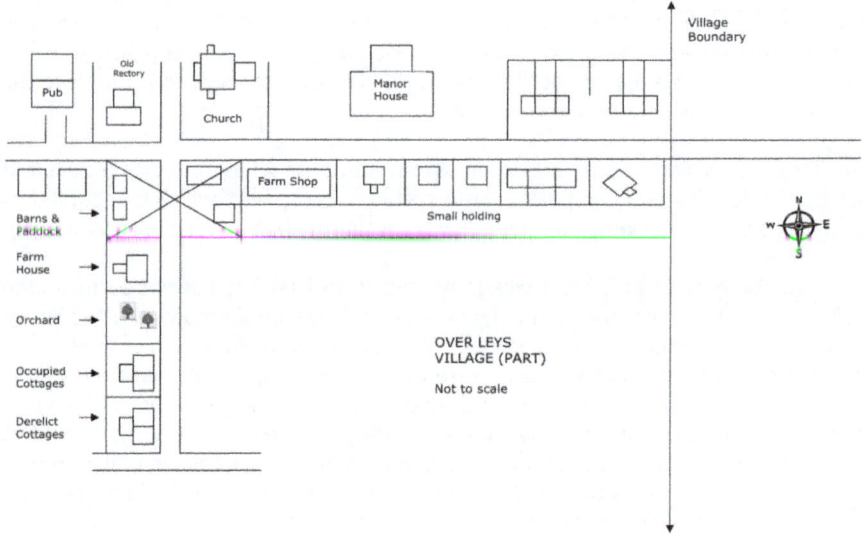

Chapter 4

Preparing Stage

This chapter deals with what happens in setting up a mediation, from the first contact to the parties' arrival and first meeting with the mediator. It covers the practicalities of venue, who attends and their roles, documents, checklists and the Agreement to Mediate. It ends with the preparing stage of the case study.

Getting appointed

There are three main ways of being appointed:

- directly;
- through a provider; or
- by a court or other scheme.

It is also possible that a mediator is named in a contract, and so has been agreed by the parties at the time of the contract being formed, but this is rare, although it would be a welcome step in any contract (especially for the named mediator).

Most mediators are on at least one panel, although the criteria for joining are getting increasingly onerous. For a provider to be accredited with the Civil Mediation Council (CMC), its panel members must meet minimum training, CPD, experience and insurance requirements. That already sets a challenging level for newly accredited mediators without the provider setting their own, higher criteria. However, most mediators manage to get on a panel, even if they have to form it themselves, and get appointments from it.

Whether from a panel or from a direct enquiry, the first contact may well be an enquiry for a CV and the likely cost. If the mediator is known, the contact is usually about dates. When is the mediator available? Or, is the mediator available on a certain date?

Profile

CVs (which should really be 'profiles') are very important. They may make the difference between you being chosen and some other keen and competent mediator being booked instead. Some panels have standardised formats but every mediator should have their own bespoke profile. When putting a profile together, ask yourself the following questions:

Preparing Stage

'What do I offer that others don't?'

'Why should someone book me in preference to 1,000 others?'

What is going to grab the reader's attention? A photograph is good, whereas it is unlikely that a mediator's school and university record are going to be the reason for appointment. Nor is your historic employment record. Which is why I prefer to call it a 'profile'. It needs to highlight personality, experience (both mediation and professional) and feedback – anything that puts colour on the facts. Unfortunately the modern trend is for parties to seek a specialist mediator, so noting the sectors mediated (or experienced – so observations/pupillages are relevant) and any professional expertise is important. If possible, the text needs to be contained on a single A4 sheet so that anyone reading it will persevere and not bin it because they are bored. The profile can also refer the reader to further details on your website, but it is unlikely that anyone will take the trouble to look. The first page is the critical one. The profile is the mediator's public face and so it is worth spending time on refining it and then up-dating it regularly.

The other early question may be the matter of fees.

Fees

It shouldn't be the case but fees may be significant in choosing a mediator. It is a sad fact that the mediator's fee is likely to be less that any lawyer present (let alone the likely team of lawyers) but it can still be an area of concern and negotiation. I put my 'Guide to Fees' on my website, so most enquiries are not for my profile or my fees but usually for availability. I prefer to charge a lump sum for the day and preparation and travel time, so that parties know in advance the level of their commitment. The charges are scaled according to the amount in dispute, with one scale up to £1 million and another above that figure, the logic being that over £1 million the level of my fee becomes incidental. However, there is an important rider – I say in the Guide to Fees 'according to need' and so it gives the opportunity for a party to plead a case for lower or no fees. I have only once turned down a case because the fee was too low and that was because I felt the lawyer was game-playing and not genuine.

When a mediator is new and developing a practice, fee levels can be sensitive. You want the work but you need to be paid for it. So do you pitch a low fee (and perhaps set an unfortunate precedent for the future) or stick to a set scale? That is why I say the fee is set 'according to need', so the door is open if negotiation is necessary – it rarely is.

One other important issue – I always invoice for payment before the mediation date. Except with insurance companies, this has never been a problem and it avoids the potential difficulty of chasing for payment after the event, a difficulty that may be increased if the mediation didn't settle! My Guide to Fees also covers cancellation charges. That is a difficult one because, whilst the fees are normally shared equally, most would consider that the cancelling party should bear the cost in total. This is another reason to be paid in advance – if the fees have already been paid then the argument is between the parties!

Preparing Stage

I suppose that I should mention 'success' fees – the mediator being paid a fee or an enhanced fee if the mediation settles. A number of years ago, there was a mediator provider organisation that tried such a scheme but it failed. At the time it raised a lot of questions in the mediator community because it potentially caused the mediator to have a vested interest in the outcome – a stronger and more personal interest than every mediator wanting every case to settle. The provider's scheme paid the mediator a fee whether the mediation settled or not, and the provider took a much larger fee if it did settle. In theory that kept the mediator in a neutral position but in practice there was still a real pressure for the mediator to get a settlement.

The 'brown envelope' should be mentioned. I don't know if it is true or not, but there is a story of a mediator being offered a brown envelope containing significant cash with the message: 'If you get us a deal this is yours'. I understand the mediator refused (and presumably told the other party) – which I believe, otherwise the story would not have been told. I am still waiting for it to happen to me.

Finally, if you are appointed by a mediator provider, it sets the fee. Sometimes its fee is considerably higher and it can be a real irritation to the mediator to know that they do the work and the provider gets the spoils. My reaction, having experienced such a feeling myself, is you don't have to take the case. If you do, then don't moan.

Dates

As I mentioned earlier, the first contact is often about dates. It is not unusual for more than one mediator to be asked the same question because getting all the parties and their respective teams in the same place on the same date can be a nightmare. So it would not be unusual for the date to be settled before the enquiry.

My only comments are to be realistic about allowing sufficient time to prepare, to avoid back-to-back mediations if at all possible, and to be kind to yourself the next day. My belief is that all mediators should give their best every time and there is a danger that busy mediators may default to being on auto-pilot rather than being 'on their toes'.

If a provider is involved, sharing an electronic calendar is a very efficient way of establishing availability – dependent of course upon it being updated on a daily basis.

Assistant/pupil

I always say that when a mediator mediates alone it is a missed opportunity for newly-accredited mediators to gain experience of the real thing. So I always have an assistant – this is often someone I have trained, but it may be someone who has made cold contact. The system is simple: as soon as the mediation is confirmed I send a group email to all the people on my 'Assistants' list. The first response will normally get the booking, although I do give priority to people based outside the UK as their opportunities are fewer. I either attach their details with my confirmatory emails or forward them as soon as the assistant is known. I don't ask permission

Preparing Stage

from the parties – it is a given – although if there was an objection I would certainly withdraw the assistant. This has only happened once when a proposed assistant was a lawyer who practised in the town in which the dispute was centred. One lawyer objected, presumably because he did not want a competitor (my assistant) to witness his negotiation skills and tactics. Of course, I agreed and someone else was appointed as my assistant. The downside for any assistant is that there is no pay (although I do try to pay something towards expenses). The upside is that the assistant has the rare privilege of being able to see several different mediators at work, which will not be possible once you become established.

The Civil Mediation Council (CMC) requires all providers to give opportunities for their mediators to have assistants. I believe most do although there are still more assistants looking for bookings than there are opportunities.

Confirming the appointment

If the appointment comes through a provider, they will usually confirm the details and provide the paperwork. So what follows assumes that this is a direct appointment.

I have a standard confirmatory email which is altered to suit each case:

> Greetings all!
>
> Following our exchange of e-mails, I have now booked (date) for your mediation and assume that the mediation will start at 09.30. Please try to arrive in plenty of time for a prompt start.
>
> I attach a copy of my standard Agreement to Mediate that I propose using. I will bring the hard copy with me for signature on the day. Meanwhile, any contact that we have will be deemed to be covered by the confidentiality provisions of the Agreement.
>
> Please let me have a note of the value of the dispute so that we can confirm a fee. I attach my fee guide for your information. It is usual for my fee to be shared equally between the parties and I will email an invoice to each of you for payment seven days before the first mediation date (ie by [xxx]). I presume that the invoice should be made out to you as the parties' legal representatives.
>
> I will be preparing for the mediation on [date] and I would appreciate a summary BEFORE then from each of you of 5–10 A4 sheets covering:
>
> - brief history of the dispute
> - key issues in dispute (legal/commercial)
> - details of claims/counterclaims and your respective positions on them
> - matters that are not in dispute
> - settlement discussions and offers
> - suggestions that might help settlement
> - confirmation of who is attending the mediation (and their roles)
> - costs to date and through trial.

Preparing Stage

You may also wish to provide a 'mediator's eyes only' paper. These can all be emailed to me if you wish, without hard copy backup. Support documents should be brief and, if possible, agreed between you.

I understand that the venue will be at [address] and that [person] will be making the arrangements. Please ensure that the main room will be large enough to take everyone attending plus my assistant and me and that each party has a comfortable room as their base. I would also like a flipchart in the main room (and the others if possible) please.

Finally, I will have an assistant with me at the mediation. (Her/his) name is [xxx] and (s/he) is attending mainly to gain experience. Of course, [name] attends without cost and will be bound by the confidentiality provisions. I attach (her/his) profile for your information.

Feel free to contact me whenever you wish.

All the best

David

You will see that in mentioning the date on which I will be preparing, I emphasise receiving the documents BEFORE that date. It rarely happens. Either the lawyers don't bother to read the email or they consider it to be unimportant – they are often up late at night reading papers, often at the last minute, so why shouldn't the mediator? It is a problem, and usually one caused by inefficiency or maybe the lawyer just being inconsiderate, but I don't want to state a preparation date which is untrue, so I have to plan to prepare several days ahead and have a cushion of a day or two to compensate.

One reason why I need time between preparing and the mediation date is so that I may speak with the lawyers and my assistant before the day.

Summaries and supporting documents

The confirmatory e-mail gives guidance on the case summaries and assumes an agreed bundle of supporting documents. The mediator does not need much – or at least I don't. The mediator's role is to give the parties the best opportunity of achieving a settlement to their dispute. It is therefore about managing the process, creating a safe and flexible environment, asking the right questions, reality-testing and challenging in a safe way, listening and encouraging and supporting. None of that is about substantive knowledge of the case. Of course, the mediator needs to know what the dispute is about, but much of the mediator's work is to help parties get out of the detail and to see the bigger picture. Detailed knowledge will not help that. It is really a matter of balance and confidence. Some mediators need to read every piece of paper to give them confidence, others do not.

But what happens when 15 lever-arch files of papers arrive by courier on your doorstep and you are being paid for three or five hours' preparation? It is a matter of the mediator's judgement, but intimate knowledge of 300 time sheets and 1,000 copies of invoices is rarely needed for the mediator to help parties to get to a deal. In fact, if there is a need (for a document that hasn't been read) then it is quite acceptable to ask to be directed to an individual document if it becomes important. In the alternative (to use a legal phrase), it is quite sensible to ring the responsible lawyer and ask for the documents to be prioritised. A third alternative is to estimate the time required and ask permission to clock those hours above those included in the agreed fee. If this happens then all parties need to give permission as the cost is likely to be shared equally between them.

Included in my confirmatory email is the suggestion of papers that are for 'mediator's eyes only'. It is quite rare for this to happen, but if it does it is rarely useful. Most times it is just a bit of mischief-making by one party, and so of no use to the mediator. Sometimes it may give useful insight into relationships and characters of the parties, and sometimes it may reveal the parties' true needs and negotiation strategy. If such a paper does arrive, it must be handled with care. It is a confidential document and so must not be included with the document exchange. It may also create assumptions, which is bad for the mediator, and it may provide sensitive knowledge that must be stored away, rather than used. An example of this was a party who revealed that they would drop their counterclaim in the mediation, and so the mediator (me) took this for granted and spent no time in discussing their claims. The counterclaiming party felt that this weakened their negotiating position. I do wonder why they gave me the information in the first place.

Venue and facilities

Rarely, in my experience, is the mediator asked to arrange the venue. Ideally it should have a separate room of sufficient size for each party's team plus the mediator and assistant/pupil and a main room to take everyone comfortably. I use the word 'comfortably' deliberately. A party is likely to spend most of the day in their room and it is not in anyone's interest for them to be stuffed into an overheated, airless room with no natural light where temperatures and tempers are likely to rise as discomfort grows. Much better to have plenty of space with natural light and air, and ideally with external areas in which to walk.

Food is also important. Constant coffee/tea and water should be available – and biscuits to keep the blood sugar up. Most mediators would suggest lunchtime sandwiches served to the rooms but there is a strong case for communal dining – there is something humanising in a shared table. I had one case in Jersey where, because I and my colleague were flying out the night before and knowing that several lawyers were doing the same, we issued a general invitation to everyone involved to join us in the restaurant for dinner, on condition that no one talked about the case. Fourteen people turned up and we had a very convivial evening. The next day the atmosphere in the main room when everyone gathered was so different to normal – light-hearted and friendly and not at all confrontational. The mediation settled mid-afternoon, and it underlined the advantages of taking food together. Unfortunately I had not mentioned that each person should pay their own bill, so the mediator paid for 16 dinners!

Another point is that energy levels tend to dip in the late afternoon, and when that happens, people often become irritable, just when the deal is emerging and the mediator needs parties to be co-operating and agreeing the details of their deal. So biscuits, chocolate and other energy-raising food can be very useful. If the mediation goes into the evening, get the pizzas ordered! Even when the deal seems very close, it usually is not, so my advice (not always heeded by myself I should admit) is to order the food once 6.30pm arrives.

Equipment

As mentioned in the previous chapter, I am a flipchart fan. I don't necessarily use it in the open session, or in private meetings, but I almost always use it at some time. It may be to record the bits of a deal, or as a checklist of the issues that need to be included in the deal, or it might be to group or summarise figures. Almost always it will be to record one party's offer, if there is a logic to it or if there are several parts. I can then get their agreement and take it to the other party (and leave it with them if appropriate). So my confirmatory email requests flipcharts to be provided. I take my own pens because the selection provided is usually small and most probably won't work anyway.

Occasionally a party will want PowerPoint or other facility. It may be useful but it is certainly worth asking why. The benefits may be questionable if the reason is to convince the mediator of their case. Whatever the reason and benefits, the other party should be made aware of their intention so that they are given a similar opportunity or, at the very least, are not taken by surprise.

Sometimes parties bring their own equipment – or rather, props. I had one where a prototype car was brought to the mediation, and I was offered a ride (I didn't accept). A colleague tells of a case she mediated where one party brought her husband's ashes and put them on the table at the first open meeting. It rather set the tone for a quiet session!

Having read the documents (or most of them), the next stage is to speak with the lawyers (rarely the parties).

Pre-mediation contact

Although by far the most pre-mediation contact is by telephone with the lawyers, occasionally there is a pre-mediation meeting. This may well be an added cost but when it does happen the actual day of the mediation tends to start in a much more positive and co-operative way, compared with the normal separate contact. The meeting would usually be with just the lawyers and it would cover the strategy for the day, who is attending and similar practical matters. It may take place before documents are exchanged so discussion may include what should be in the agreed support bundle.

Rarely, mainly in medical negligence or personal injury cases, or employment/workplace disputes, pre-mediation contact will also be with the parties. The purpose of the call is to have a confidential chat, partly to 'touch base' but also to settle any queries and reinforce the fact that mediation is a party-centred process and provides an opportunity for the parties to speak as well as the lawyers. This can be a challenge for the lawyers because it allows their client to speak uncontrolled, but most lawyers now have the confidence to allow their client to make the best of the opportunity to look the other party in the eyes and tell their story. I have a mental checklist that I try to follow in these calls, but, as with the mediation itself, this is a flexible process and the list is only there if appropriate. It goes something like this:

Preparing Stage

REASON FOR CALL
- Touching base before the day
- Confidentiality rules in operation (during call)
- Need to outline the process? Especially about opening statements *(depends upon their experience)*
- Role of mediator
- Agreement to Mediate approved? *(sent out with the confirmatory email)*

WHO ATTENDS?
- Lawyer? If not, line of contact? If so, then their role as supporter
- If no lawyer then partner/companion if party is alone
- Keep team small (lean and keen)

WHAT HAS HAPPENED SO FAR?
- Settlement discussions/offers?
- Current state of court case/arbitration (if any). Future timetable
- Costs to date/through trial/arbitration?
- Publicly funded?
- CFA, ATE Insurance?

HOW MIGHT IT SETTLE?
- Barriers preventing settlement to date?
- Any limits of authority? Need for out-of-hours contact?
- How might it settle?
- Risk analysis done? What type?

ON THE DAY
- Be on time/ arrive early
- Any special needs? Diet? Access? Smoking?
- Confirm mediator contact details
- Strategy for idle time

ANYTHING ELSE?
- Documents/breakdown of quantum
- Settlement agreement pro-forma
- Assistant

There are a few headings worth explaining.

CFA (*Contingency Fee Agreement*) is when a lawyer is on a success fee. If a deal is done, or they win in court, the lawyer is paid base rate plus an uplift of up to 100 per cent (although this may be restricted in certain claims). This arrangement has to be declared to the other party and it can complicate the mediation negotiations for two reasons:

- the lawyer has an interest in the settlement and so is not a detached adviser to the client; and
- other parties' lawyers consider such an arrangement to be fair game for negotiation, if not outright dismissal.

Some limitation on the extent of recoverability of CFA fees, in court, was introduced in April 2013 following the Jackson report. These limitations mainly affect personal injury cases.

CFAs are often backed by ATE (after the event) Insurance. The premiums are huge and again this can have a significant effect on the negotiations because:

- the cost is significant; and
- it takes much of the pressure off the party to settle as the insurance (although often capped) covers legal costs through trial. The party is not as influenced by the cost of going to trial, which is often one of the significant reasons for a party reaching agreement during a mediation.

Limits of authority – the parties sign an Agreement to Mediate that states that they come in good faith to negotiate a settlement. The reality is that most come with limits of authority (usually maximum/minimum settlement sums) and this may be breached during the mediation. This raises the importance of having someone contactable, particularly out-of-hours, who can agree to change the authority. In my experience, even a sole proprietor wants to speak with someone (usually the spouse) before signing the Settlement Agreement.

Strategy for idle time – the main disadvantage with mediation is the idle time. When the mediator is with one party in private session, the other is idle. Ideally the mediator has left them with a task so that they are actively engaged whilst alone, but that is not always possible. So it must be the responsibility of the lawyer (who has put the team together) to have a strategy for idle time so that everyone is still engaged with the mediation process even when the mediator is elsewhere for significant times. This also highlights the need for the mediator to keep a party aware of time – I always state a time when I will return and ask my assistant to keep time for me.

Settlement Agreement pro forma – it almost always takes two hours for the lawyers to write up a Settlement Agreement. Every word becomes significant. In theory, one way of reducing the time is to come with a pro forma, containing all the stock phrases and with a checklist for guidance. The trouble is that these pro formas grow with age and so the time is spent discussing why a particular clause is in or is deleted, so it still takes as long, but for a different reason. There is more on Settlement Agreements in Chapter 8.

Preparing Stage

Who attends?

It is usual in commercial mediations for lawyers to be present with their client. It is rare for me to have an influence on who attends because the pre-mediation contact is close to the mediation date and the teams are already in place. My advice would always be to keep the teams lean and keen – the highest level of decision maker and the lawyer; after that be very sure of the reason for a person attending. Often big teams come just for the comfort of the decision maker. The problem with that is they could become bored and disengaged and eventually be a barrier to settlement.

Role of lawyers, parties, experts and others

The party should come with the highest level of authority possible, be properly prepared and understand the mediation process, and be prepared to tell their story, to listen (especially to the other party), to take the mediator into their confidence and to adjust position according to what is said and done in the mediation.

The lawyer should help to assemble the best team, brief everyone on the mediation process and on their individual roles, prepare the summary and support documentation before the mediator's preparation date, carry out a risk analysis of the case (and do a regular reappraisal throughout the mediation), be a supporter and adviser but allow the party to take a prominent part in the process, and draft, or assist in the drafting of, the Settlement Agreement.

Counsel, ie a barrister, may also be present, and in fact often is. Unfortunately, no matter how skilled and co-operative counsel may be, it is inevitable that they assume leadership, and be the spokesperson, negotiator and settler. In such circumstances it ceases to be a party-centred process and the whole dynamic changes. Quite apart from the significant financial cost, parties should seriously consider the other costs to the therapeutic process of mediation where the party can tell their story and take control of the outcome. If one party insists on bringing counsel, the mediator should ensure the other side also has this option in advance as it can lead to very imbalanced meetings if only one party has their barrister present.

Experts often attend mediations but there is a danger in this. Ideally, parties' experts should have met before the mediation and identified areas of commonality, so that only the items of disagreement are left. It is unlikely that an expert will change their opinion during the mediation – indeed it is more likely that each will become more entrenched. This can become a real barrier to settlement so it would be better, and cheaper, for them to be available by telephone if needed in the mediation, or to attend the initial open session, make their statements, and then leave.

Assistant mediators should do just that – assist the mediator. This could be as just an additional pair of eyes and ears, another brain at work, a runner, timekeeper, friend and supporter. In turn, the mediator should remember that this is meant to be a learning opportunity for a less experienced mediator, and so be prepared to discuss what has happened, the techniques used and the thinking behind them, ideally over a glass of wine at the end of the mediation.

Preparing Stage

Site visit

Sometimes parties request a site visit either on the day of the mediation or beforehand. In boundary and right-of-way disputes this can be invaluable. In other cases it can be of limited use. The important thing is that the mediator must be seen to be even-handed and transparent in all things. So if a site visit is arranged, all parties should be invited to attend but on condition that the main debate is left for the mediation table. Site visits are information-gathering in support of the mediation day, and should not be clouded by excessive arguments. The rule is to set the ground rules before the start and to remind people if they get broken.

On the day

I always say that the mediator is the first to arrive and the last to leave. It is important to arrive well before the parties so that you can check the rooms and other facilities, wifi codes, photocopying and printing facilities, find the toilets, check the fire alarm test and confirm refreshments. It is pretty certain that the room seating will have to be altered – so often you are faced with a huge boardroom table when there will be only six or eight people. I no longer dictate where people should sit, although sometimes, where a lot of people are involved, I consult with the lawyer(s) as to how they prefer to arrange their team.

As people arrive I, and my assistant, will welcome them, show them to their room and settle them down. When everyone has arrived, I have a private meeting in each room.

First private meetings

The purpose of the first private meetings is to get the Agreement to Mediate signed – and I like everyone present to sign – and to answer any questions. This is usually the first mediation that a party has attended, and may well be their last, so they are often rather nervous about what lies ahead. So the underlying purpose of the first private meeting is to reassure, show that they are in safe hands, encourage them to speak in the open session and to give an outline of the day. I also check for any time constraints and authority issues – it is best to do so in private rather than risk it being an issue in the open session. If it is an issue (eg needing to get committee or Board ratification of any deal) then a strategy can be agreed on how best to inform the other party.

The process is repeated with each party and may well mean that the first open session starts as much as an hour after the official start time.

Agreement to Mediate

Most mediators now get the Agreement to Mediate signed on the day. Occasionally they are sent out early for signature but that means multiple documents and no one document with all the signatures. If one document is sent out to each of the

Preparing Stage

parties in turn, it is usually lost by the time it reaches the final party, and it also means that not everyone will have signed. Getting it signed on the day is therefore the most efficient and symbolic way.

Many Agreements to Mediate are lengthy, enlarged by unfortunate experience and fear of being sued. I prefer a simple agreement which sets out the principles, not least because, despite having seen a copy which was attached to the confirmatory email, many lawyers feel the need to read it and go through it with their client. So, as with so many things in mediation, keep it short and simple.

AGREEMENT TO MEDIATE

Date: Time: 09:30

Venue:

Parties:

(1)

(2)

Mediator: David Richbell   Assistant mediator:

The Dispute:

[*short description of the case and claim value*]

The Agreement:

The undersigned parties hereby agree to participate in mediation in accordance with the following terms:

1. Whilst it is recognised that mediation is a voluntary process and that the mediator will not and cannot compel the parties to settle, nor even to continue negotiating, the parties agree to participate in negotiations in good faith with the aim of achieving a settlement.
2. The parties agree to have present at the mediation such persons as are authorised to agree settlement terms.
3. The parties agree to keep confidential:
   - all information, whether oral, written or otherwise, produced for or at the mediation, and
   - the terms of any Settlement Agreement arising from it;

   provided that nothing in this clause prevents the parties (including the Mediator) discussing the mediation with the parties' professional advisers and/or insurers and those necessary to implement or enforce the Settlement Agreement and/or making disclosure to any relevant authority or person, whether under the Proceeds of Crime Act 2002 and/or under any Regulations relating thereto, if obliged to do so by law.

   Note: Evidence that is otherwise admissible or discoverable shall not be rendered inadmissible or non-discoverable simply as a result of its use in the mediation.

Preparing Stage

4. The parties agree that:
    - all offers, promises, conduct and statements made in the course of the mediation proceedings are inadmissible in evidence in any subsequent litigation or arbitration;
    - any agreement reached at or following the mediation shall not be binding on the parties unless it is recorded in writing and signed by the parties and/or their authorised representatives;
    - they will not call the mediator nor any co-mediator nor any assistant mediator as a witness, nor require the production of records or notes relating to the mediation;
    - no recording or transcript will be made at the time of the mediation.
5. The mediation will terminate when:
    - a settlement has been reached
    - a Party withdraws
    - the Mediator retires for any reason provided by the Chartered Institute of Arbitrators' Code of Conduct.
6. Neither the Mediator nor any Co-Mediator nor Assistant Mediator shall be liable to the parties for any act or omission in connection with the services provided.
7. This agreement will be governed by English Law.

Note: The referral of the dispute to mediation does not affect any rights that may exist under Article 6 of the European Convention on Human Rights. If the dispute is not settled by mediation, the parties' rights to a fair trial are unaffected.

Signed: Date:

Declaration of Attendees

I, the undersigned, agree with each of the attendees at the mediation, including the Mediator, that in consideration of my being present at this mediation, I will not disclose to any person not expressly authorised by the parties to receive such information, anything which I have heard or read or seen in the course of this mediation unless obliged by law to do so.

Note: The wording of this agreement is based upon that used by In Place of Strife.

Signed: Date:

Preparing – in a nutshell

- Spend time on compiling a compelling profile with a good photograph
- Be pro-active in managing the documents and pre-mediation contact
- Ensure the venue helps rather than hinders anxious people
- Be attentive to food and special needs (including smoking)

Preparing Stage

- Prepare well, if only to be confident and positive. Your mood is infectious
- Be clear about what you want from the pre-mediation contact
- Ensure the lawyer takes responsibility for the size of their team and keeping them committed throughout, especially in idle time
- Use the first private meeting to reassure the party and build their trust
- Highlight that mediation is a party-centred process – they are in charge of the problem and the outcome; the mediator's role is to manage the process

CASE STUDY

First contact

David, the mediator, had confirmed his appointment by email to the parties' lawyers. (Chris and Jo had consulted a lawyer but he was not attending the mediation to keep their costs down. He was available by telephone if they felt the need.) The email had also confirmed the date, time, fee (shared equally by the two parties), document exchange, venue requirements and the fact that Mags Bishop was attending as his assistant (without cost to the parties). Mags had recently trained as a commercial mediator and this was her first experience of the real thing.

The email had also indicated the sort of information that should be included in the case summary, and had included confirmation as to who was attending and a statement of each side's legal costs to date and through trial. David attached a copy of his standard Agreement to Mediate, mentioning that it would be signed on the day but that the confidentiality provision applied to any contact in the meantime.

A few days before the date he had set for receipt of documents, David emailed a reminder to the lawyers and, whilst Jo and Chris' lawyer confirmed they were on time, Angela Pearce (Harry's lawyer) responded that their summary was being prepared by counsel and, as he was currently in court on another case, he would not be able to complete it and get Harry's confirmation until the day after the deadline. Resisting a bad-tempered response, David reorganised his diary so that he could prepare a day later than planned.

A bundle arrived by courier the next day. It contained three lever-arch files of papers, including two experts' reports and drawings of the proposed development of the redundant farm buildings, together with planning permission and conservation area approval. The bundle also contained plans for a second scheme, which included three new houses in the paddock, but this scheme did not appear to have planning or other approvals. There were also some budget costings but nothing of much detail. Finally, there was a stack of mortgage papers offering the loan against the entire farmland, together with a file of correspondence.

Eventually the case summaries arrived, that from Jo and Chris first thing in the morning, and from Harry's solicitor (after another chasing email from David) in the early afternoon. The solicitors exchanged summaries that afternoon. The main points arising from the paperwork were as follow.

Preparing Stage

From Harry (the claimant, although formal proceedings had not commenced):

- There is a clear and compelling case for the development.
- The planning authority supports it.
- Most of the buildings are derelict and worthless in their present state.
- Chris and Jo seemed happy with the deal until Stephen Atkins interfered.
- Chris and Jo have missed the opportunity to be part of the development company but Harry will consider paying them a small share of the profits on completion if they sign the mortgage deed and so allow it to happen.

From Jo and Chris:

- Harry is not a developer and should stick to farming.
- They are worried that the mortgage will not be repaid and they will lose the farm.
- They do not want to lose the cottages.
- They are upset at the worry and fighting this has caused within the family, particularly the stress it has caused to their widowed and elderly mother.

The calls

For no particular reason, David chose to ring Jo and Chris' solicitor first. He had a grasp of the key issues from the papers and now wanted to get some 'off the record' comments. This is how part of the conversation went:

David: *I just wanted to touch base with you before the mediation to have a chat and answer any queries that you have about the day. This is all in confidence of course.*

Solicitor: *Thanks. As you know, I won't be coming but I have told the girls what to expect and I'm on the end of the phone if they need me.*

David: *That is something that I wanted to raise with you – the other side have both a solicitor and a barrister with them, but Chris and Jo are not represented at all. Are you concerned about that?*

Solicitor: *Of course, but the girls have no money and they are aware of the danger of me not being there. They have Stephen Atkins with them who will look after them. He is quite a strong character. The girls know they will be bullied – that is Harry's style and his legal team have all the signs of being in the same mode.*

David: *Well, it is Chris and Jo's decision not to be represented and I will do my best to see they are not too disadvantaged by it.*

Solicitor: *Thanks. I've explained the mediation process and your role. I don't think I have any questions for you.*

David: *Please explain to them that I want them to tell their story in the first open session. It is very important that they have their say in front of Harry and his team – they will only have themselves to talk to when they are back in their room.*

Preparing Stage

Solicitor: *OK. I'm not sure that they will as they feel quite threatened by Harry and his lawyers, but I will pass on what you say.*

David: *Thanks. Anything else?*

Solicitor: *I don't think so.*

David: *How do you think this will settle?*

Solicitor: *The girls just want to put an end to the misery. There is a danger that they will agree to anything but Stephen will help them and I am here if they need me, but, as I have said to them more than once, they have the whip hand. Bottom line is, Harry needs them to sign, and they don't have to.*

The second call was to Angela Pearce, Harry's solicitor. This is how part of that conversation went:

David: *I just wanted to touch base with you before the mediation to have a chat and answer any queries that you have about the day. This is all in confidence of course.*

Angela: *Thanks. I don't think I have any queries. I am experienced in mediation and know what to expect. Will you be having a general session at the beginning? My experience is that they can be a waste of time.*

David: *Definitely. Obviously I don't want anybody to be disadvantaged by it and will end it when I feel it has served its purpose, but it is so important that each side tells their story, and listens to the other's story as well. I want Harry to speak.*

Angela: *Oh, I don't know about that. We have counsel to do the speaking.*

David: *And he will have his chance, and so will you. But this is a party-centred process and Harry will be given the opportunity to talk about what is important to him and why.*

Angela: *I hear what you say but need to speak to counsel about it.*

David: *Tell me why you are bringing counsel – the other side will not even be represented.*

Angela: *He is the expert and he has prepared the statements.*

David: *OK, but I urge you to prepare Harry to say something.*

The conversation continued, lasting around half an hour. Towards the end, David asked:

David: *How do you think this might settle?*

Angela: *Harry won't give in. The future of the farm depends on it.*

David regretted not following up that comment.

David's third call was to Mags, his assistant on the day. Mags had trained as a commercial mediator but had no experience of the real thing. David summarised

Preparing Stage

what had been said in his calls to the two solicitors and then explained what he expected of his assistant:

- be early;
- be part of the team, not an observer;
- make it the best learning experience for her;
- take notes of learning points and any conflicts with the teaching; and
- be supportive, a listening ear, an extra pair of eyes.

David ended by suggesting that they have a debrief after the mediation, assuming that it finished at a reasonable hour.

On the day

David arrived an hour before the scheduled start and checked the rooms, toilets, fire alarm test, flipchart pens and arrangements for refreshments. The main room had seating for 20 and he arranged for the table to be reduced in size with seating for 10 plus water, glasses, paper and pens in each position and coffee/tea and biscuits in each room. He checked that reception had a list of all those attending and to which room they should be sent and asked that he should be informed of all arrivals.

Mags arrived soon after and David briefed her and showed her the rooms.

As people arrived he and Mags met them, introduced themselves and showed them to their room. Chris, Jo and Stephen arrived together and, after leaving them for a little while to settle in, David visited them and went through the Agreement to Mediate, asking all three to sign.

Harry's team arrived individually, Quentin Phillips (his counsel) arriving last, a few minutes after the agreed start time. David delivered the Agreement to Mediate and was told that Quentin required half-an-hour with his clients before starting. Concealing his annoyance, David agreed so long as half-an-hour was realistic and stated that he would be using the time usefully with the other party.

Mediator challenges

Preparation Stage

1 **Conflict of Interest**

   Conflicts of interest seem to have been taken to ridiculous extremes. One well-known lawyer mediator does a conflicts check throughout all offices of her international firm and withdraws if anyone has acted for one of the mediation parties at any time. What are the real conflicts that should cause a mediator to withdraw?

2 **Papers**

   It is the day before the mediation. No papers have arrived. Does the mediation go ahead?

Preparing Stage

Mediators are experiencing papers arriving later and later. What can be done about it?

3 **Supporting documents**

A banker's box of eight lever-arch files arrives with the parties' summaries. Your fee agreement assumes three hours' preparation. What do you do?

4 **Inflammatory summary**

Counsel delivers (late) an extremely inflammatory, if not insulting, position statement. Aside from such comments as 'you will lose this one (five times)', 'ridiculously trivial', 'ill-considered', 'self-serving evidence' and 'grossly exaggerated', it personally attacked the claimants' expert – '…typifies the quality of expert chosen by the defendants, being a nationally recognised expert to whom Mr F (claimant's expert) can barely light a candle' – and the claimants' 'bad animal husbandry', 'appalling hygiene record ', 'extremely poor standards' and 'distinctly inept'. The mediator receives a call from the claimant's solicitor saying that his clients are so upset with the summary that they are withdrawing from the mediation. What do you do?

Chapter 5

Opening Stage

This chapter deals with the start of the mediation day, the first open session, and the mediator's and parties' opening statements up to the break into private meetings. In particular it covers the mediator setting the scene and the ground rules (such as they are).

Purpose of the first open session

The main purpose of the first open session is for information exchange – 'first' because there are likely to be other times when it is sensible to bring all the parties together again, and 'main purpose' because there are many other potential benefits of this meeting:

- the mediator setting the scene and showing that s/he is a safe pair of hands;
- reopening lines of communication (cases usually come to mediation because communication has broken down and parties have reached deadlock);
- each party hearing the other side's version of the legal case, experts' opinion, etc;
- the opportunity for the parties to tell their truth, their story (and listen to the other side's version of that same truth/story);
- observing how parties, experts and others are likely to perform in the witness box; and
- creating an opportunity to start co-operating to find a solution (although most open sessions start in an adversarial way and co-operation comes later).

It can be difficult. If the opening is very adversarial it can dishearten people and set the settlement process back. That is why some mediators either abandon the first open session or terminate it after each side has outlined their case. To me that is a terrible waste of an opportunity for dialogue and understanding and so it is worth holding your nerve and having some strategies to keep the meeting going.

Seating and facilities

I mentioned in the previous chapter about rearranging the room to get the best effect. Early wisdom used to be that a circular table is best because it is less confrontational. That may be so where the mediator is just facilitating dialogue but, in normal mediations, I want the parties to talk to each other. So sitting opposite at

Opening Stage

a rectangular table is best. Where everyone actually sits is less important. In the early days I would put the decision makers next to me, then their lawyers. Now, because teams are generally no more than five or six people, I let the lawyers decide who sits where. With more than five or six people, I would dictate where the decision makers sit and let the lawyer decide the rest (although this may be difficult in some international disputes where some cultures dictate that the real decision maker is the most silent and lowest profile). Multi-party cases pose a different problem and I would generally get the lawyers into the main room with me and discuss where each team sits. Consulting the lawyers on even such a small issue creates an atmosphere of co-operation (with the mediator at least). I would normally sit at the end of the table with my assistant beside me. Other than managing the process effectively, the mediator is the least important in this scenario. This is a party-centred process and so the focus should be on them. It is also a very unique gathering because it is very unlikely that all these people have sat around a table before to discuss this problem, and certainly not with a neutral third-party (the mediator), so that in itself creates a new dynamic that can lead to settlement.

Setting the scene

The first open session would normally start with the mediator setting a few ground rules. In fact, I would start with a welcome and then get everyone to introduce themselves and state what their role is in the mediation. I do a table plan as they speak so that I get the right name to the right face. It can devalue the mediator's role and authority if you get the names wrong. Most people will sit at the same seat again if they return to the main room – it is their territory.

I want to create a feeling of safety and flexibility so I will follow with an overview of the opportunity they have:

- **C**onfidentiality – two levels:
  - as a group, that what is said in the open session will not be repeated to others; and
  - in private meetings, where what is said to me as the mediator (and to my assistant) will not be repeated to the other side unless I have been given permission. This is to encourage the parties to speak frankly to me without fearing that it will be to their disadvantage.

- **A**uthority – I will have checked in private that the decision makers come with authority to settle and I will repeat that and remind them that if they need to speak with anyone before signing the deal (note the positive language – there is an assumption that a deal will happen) to make sure lines are open out-of-hours. The last thing we would want is for a deal to be on the table but that the necessary authority cannot be obtained because someone has gone home. People never admit to limited authority but it is a reality and the mediator must work with it.

- **V**oluntary – that is, the parties are there voluntarily (although the courts may have strongly encouraged them to come) and can leave at any time. I rarely say this. The last thing I want is to sow seeds of potential failure, therefore I may say that I don't want anyone to feel disadvantaged so they can call a break at any time.

- **N**eutrality – the mediator's role is to effectively manage the process and so is there to give the parties the best opportunity to achieve a settlement. It is a neutral role, and therefore:
- **N**o imposed settlement – it is the parties' decision. The mediator is not there to tell them the answer.
- **N**on-binding – parties are not committed to any deal until it is put in writing and then signed. Up to then they have the freedom to try anything without being committed, but once in writing and signed it becomes a legally binding contract.

CAVNNN is a mental mnemonic that I check during the first open session – it doesn't have to be all at once but all the points need to be covered before the session is over. I also mention:

- Idle time – there will be times when I am with one party and will not have left a task with the other. I will always try to say the time that I will return (and get the assistant to time-keep for me) and encourage the idle party to go for a walk or be usefully occupied. I do not want them to get bored and detach from the aim of achieving a solution to their dispute. Timekeeping is also important so that each party knows what is happening and also to create a momentum and assurance that this is all with a purpose.
- Refreshments – water, coffee, tea and biscuits should be on constant supply. I usually arrange for lunch to be served into the rooms so that we work through lunch. Having said that, one of the best experiences I have had was with a communal food table where people helped themselves and chatted whilst they ate. Even better was the time I mentioned in Chapter 4 (under 'Venue') when I was mediating overseas and several people in the mediation were staying at the same hotel. I invited everyone to join me at dinner on the understanding that no one talked about the case. Fourteen of us dined together and the mediation next day started in a very relaxed and friendly atmosphere; the case settled mid-afternoon.
- Time constraints – sometimes people have time constraints at the mediation. Often these are randomly imposed as a tactic and most fall away as a deal get closer to their deadline. I always ask in the first open session if anyone has constraints and then add that I am there as long as they want me but on overtime from 7pm – it is amazing how many mediations settle before that time.
- No interruptions – if, during the opening statements, a party wants to react, they should make a note and do so once the statements are concluded. The same courtesy will be afforded to everyone – there will be plenty of time to raise questions before we break.
- Outline of the day – this may have been covered during the first private meeting but may still be worth repeating. It would cover the purpose of the first Open Session, the breaking into private meetings, the possibility of lawyer or expert meetings and the certainty that the decision makers will meet together to settle the deal (again, note the positive language). I mentioned in Chapter 2 (Time Management) that at times I have given people headlines for a typical mediation day: 'Assuming that you would like to finish in normal working hours, for you to be signing a deal at 6pm you need to be shaking hands at 4pm as the lawyers usually need a couple of hours to get the wording right. That means you should be in serious negotiation by 2pm so you need to get all the detail (issues) out

Opening Stage

of the way by then.' It provides a sort of route map to settlement, which some people like, and it always surprises me when some people take it seriously, to the point where they might say 'it's 2pm – we should be in serious negotiation by now!'.

Opening statements

The opening statements by the parties set the tone for the rest of the meeting. They are therefore very important, although few use the opportunity to best advantage. The best statements do not repeat the pleadings or the written summaries provided before the mediation day, but are from the heart. Normally the claimant will start (although occasionally a counter-claimant may do so, or a party who is highly emotional) and the lawyer will lead. Ideally the lawyer's statement will be brief, may include their concerns about the other side's interpretation of the relevant law, but will also emphasise the fact that they are attending with the honest intention of achieving a settlement to which both parties can agree.

Telling their stories

Next is the decision maker. Having encouraged them, in the initial private meeting, to tell their story, I hope that they will do so from the heart and with emotion. Often they don't because it is too early and they are fearful of saying something that will upset their lawyer. That is another reason for having a longer meeting, because they will tell their story eventually, usually because something said by the other side has provoked them. Ideally though they should tell it at the beginning. I will then always go down the team to ensure everyone is included and can add to what has already been said if they wish.

Stimulating dialogue

The next stage, after the opening statements have been made, is a challenge. How do you keep everyone there and generate an opportunity for dialogue that is not contrived? This can be the most important part of the day, where posturing and adversarial attitudes can be replaced by real communication.

When I am reading-in for the mediation, I will usually note several questions in preparation for this moment, so that I can stimulate the early conversation. Prior to that I may well use the flipchart to note the issues to be resolved and/or matters of concern. I can then point to one and say 'Tell me more about ...'.

Using the flipchart

I mentioned in Chapter 2 ('Using visual aids') that I now view the flipchart as an essential tool for the mediator. Like most others who are not familiar or comfortable with it, I initially resisted using the flipchart, but once I became confident it was always in use. It is a great tool for diverting attention – it becomes a neutral focus for everyone. It is also great for reframing, for neutralising challenging statements, for summarising (particularly figures), for mind-mapping, drawing site plans or using graphics. I often use it for noting the various elements of a deal so that people not only see progress and that their needs are gradually being met, but also as a checklist for when the deal is written up by the lawyers. A few words of advice (other than to urge its use whenever possible):

- Use chisel-pointed pens (and check that they work before the mediation starts). It is best to take your own.
- Don't use yellow (it can't be seen beyond a metre).
- Unless your writing is clear and bold, use upper case letters. In any case write large.
- Unless requested, don't number the items (it may indicate an assumed priority).
- Vary the colour (one colour can looked cramped and seem boring).
- Try writing in 'balloons' rather than lists. Random shapes can be more arresting than straight-line listing.
- Stand to the side whilst writing.
- Make sure the flipchart cannot be seen through windows, vision panels or glazed screens. This is particularly important when in private meetings.
- Consider inviting the speaker to use the flipchart – it is very empowering (which is probably why most mediators hold on to the pen at all costs).

In most cases I will also write down offers, check them with the party, and, with their agreement, take the flipchart sheet into the other room, often leaving it there after explaining the logic to the offer. It may well be that a counter-offer will be added to that same sheet.

Managing emotion

One of the biggest challenges to a mediator is emotional parties (or even lawyers). As mentioned in Chapter 2 ('Managing emotion'), the 'rule' is to allow, even encourage, people to show emotion and to let it go until it runs out of steam or becomes abusive or destructive. Knowing this, and knowing that to sit on it will only lead to problems later, the challenge for the mediator is to not intervene and yet still be seen to be properly managing the process (ie be 'in charge'). It is a very fine line, not least because it can be very uncomfortable for the listeners. I always have to resist intervening, at least twice, before I do (or it ends). Then I must remember to:

- acknowledge the emotion – the worst thing that the mediator can do is to ignore it as if it hadn't happened; and
- accept that, no matter how unreasonable the emotion may appear, it is genuine to the person speaking and so should be valued.

Having been acknowledged and valued, the speaker is much more likely to become co-operative and positive.

Opening Stage

Breaking up

The first open session may well have lasted two or more hours (although there is no rule about this) but once it has served its useful purpose, and the mediator having checked that no-one else wishes to speak, it is time to break into private sessions (sometime called caucuses). The mediator should say who will be visited first and the other party be told when the mediator will be with them. It is also an opportunity for the mediator to speak with the Assistant, checking reaction, any particular observations and discussing what happens next.

Opening stage – in a nutshell

- Create an atmosphere of confidence and safety;
- the mediator's role is to manage the process and get the parties to a deal as quickly and efficiently as possible;
- their problem, their solution;
- encourage the parties to tell their story;
- and give them time and space to do so;
- don't be frightened by parties showing emotion – acknowledge and value;
- use the flipchart; and
- confidentiality is the (only unbreakable) rule!

CASE STUDY

The first open session

Half-an-hour later, the parties assembled in the main room. David did not allocate seating as there were so few people, although he and Mags occupied the 'top' of the table, near the flipchart and the door.

Most people had met before but David welcomed everyone and went round the table asking people to introduce themselves and state their role in the mediation. He wrote a table plan as they spoke and checked that everyone was comfortable with first names. Quentin hesitated but as everyone else had agreed he also did so.

David: *A few ground rules – there are not many for this is a flexible and informal process. The main one is that this is a confidential process, at two levels; whatever is said round this table stays with us and, more importantly, whatever is said to Mags and I in your private room stays private unless you give us permission to pass it on. This is to give you confidence to speak openly with us, knowing that it will never be used against you or weaken your position. Also, whatever is said or produced within this mediation is without prejudice, and so cannot be used in court if you do not achieve a settlement today. But most mediations settle – 80–90 per cent – so hang onto the fact that you have a really good chance of getting this sorted today. It won't be easy – if it was you wouldn't need Mags and me I – but most do settle. And when you do, it will be put down in writing for you to sign – up to that moment you are not committed to anything, but once you sign the Settlement Agreement then this becomes a contract that can be enforced in court.*

It is important for each of you to make full use of this. I am trying to paint a picture here of a safe environment and confidential process. You are not committed to anything until it is set in writing and signed. Up to that moment you can try anything and, if it doesn't work, try something else.

You have all signed an Agreement to Mediate, which confirms that you have authority to settle and that you come in good faith to negotiate a deal. Just remember that for a deal to be agreed both sides have to say 'yes'. There is no deal unless both sides say 'yes' and so part of our job is to ask you if what you propose is likely to get a 'yes' from the other side; and if it won't then to ask 'what will?'

I did check earlier if any of you have time constraints and I know Quentin wants to be away by 5pm. Most of my mediations settle in normal working hours so that should be possible but remember that, once you have agreed a deal, it will take a couple of hours to get it written up and for Chris and Jo to check it with their lawyer.

There was a murmur of disapproval from Harry's team when David said this but nothing was said.

David: *A quick outline of the day – the purpose of this meeting is for both sides to tell their story and for the other side to listen and raise questions. I will invite everyone to speak. Please don't interrupt – if you want to respond to a point someone has made, make a note as there will be plenty of time to raise questions when each side has spoken. I don't want anyone to feel disadvantaged by this – it is quite in order for you to request a break if you want to check something or just clear your thoughts.*

When this meeting has ceased to be useful we will break into private sessions and Mags and I will visit you in your rooms. Our sole aim is to help you get to a settlement so we are very open to any suggestions about lawyers or parties meeting together – I will certainly expect to have Harry, Chris and Jo together at the end to agree the details of any settlement.

Any questions?

Right, then we will start. I have asked Harry's team to kick-off as they are the claimants and I guess Quentin will start.

David was right, Quentin did start and he spent quite a long time laying out the legal issues that had to be addressed, his client's rights under the relevant law and the advisability of Jo and Chris avoiding the cost of going to court by reaching a settlement within the mediation. Angela had nothing to add. Harry said his 'lawyer had said it all' (which he hadn't) and Charles Pugh-Smith declined to comment but added that he was 'here to assist' as needed.

David didn't press Harry to say something, recognising that it was probably too early in the process for him to be relaxed enough to speak about how he truly felt. He was undoubtedly under instruction not to say anything that may help his siblings. David invited Chris and Jo to speak and Jo unfolded a prepared script. She apologised and said that both Chris and she were worried about the whole thing

Opening Stage

and had to write down how they felt. Most of it was about their concerns over the division in their family that went beyond the three siblings, about how the village was in danger of taking sides, about their concern for the farm (and their continued ownership) and how upset they were and wanted to end the misery that had taken over their lives.

Harry: *Then sign the mortgage deed!*

Quentin put a restraining hand on Harry's arm.

When Jo had finished and Chris confirmed that she had nothing further to add, David invited Stephen to speak but before he could do so, Quentin, with Harry's 'hear, hear', asked, quite aggressively:

Before you speak, just why are you here – do you have an interest in this? Are you in a relationship with one of Harry's sisters? Or do you just like interfering in other people's business?

David intervened:

Quentin, I must ask you to be more courteous – you were informed of Stephen's attendance and role before the mediation and, if there is an issue, you should have raised it then. This is not a forum for cross-examination; we should all be here with the same intention – seeking a solution to Harry and Chris and Jo's problem – your role is supporting your client in getting there.

Quentin: *I'm sorry – have your say.*

Stephen said very little – he just wanted to be a friend and supporter to the 'girls'.

David then invited questions and for a time the two sides exchanged information quite courteously. When the exchange subsided, David said:

I have a few more questions to ask but I think they may be best left for when we are in private. However, there is one matter – amongst the bundle I received were plans for a second scheme, which included houses in the paddock. Where does that sit in all this?

Quentin looked at Angela with a fierce expression. Angela stirred and confirmed that she had included the papers in the bundle, and that Chris and Jo's lawyer had a copy.

Quentin asked for a break.

David: *OK, we will take a break. I'll have a quick chat with the other side then join your team Quentin, say in five minutes?*

Quentin: *Make it ten.*

So they went to their rooms and David asked Mags what she made of the opening session.

And so the exploring stage began.

Mediator challenges

Opening stage

1 **Participants**

A mediation involved the claim of an ex-partner in a gay relationship claiming an equal share in a business created by his ex-partner. The ex-partner arrived at the mediation with his new partner, without having informed the other side. What do you do?

2 **Joint session**

A very bullish solicitor says: 'Let's miss out the open session. We know their case, let's get down to the figures'. Do you agree, resist or what?

3 **No honest intent**

In the first private meeting before the open session, the lawyer for one side says: 'We are only here to avoid a costs penalty. There is no chance of us doing a deal today.' How do you react? This could be a short day and an easy way of earning a fee!

4 **Counsel**

Counsel on one side completely controls his team. He makes the opening statement, will not allow his client to speak and insists that the mediator addresses all questions to the party through him. How do you handle this without creating an enemy?

5 **Decision maker**

The decision maker has not arrived and is likely to be at least an hour late. He tells his team to start without him. You are very concerned that he will not be present when the other side gives their statements, nor be party to the subsequent discussions. Do you delay the joint opening session and have a series of private meetings until he arrives or carry on regardless?

6 **Room allocation**

Host party have commandeered the main room and are well settled. Guest party have an inferior room and the mediator has been allocated a cupboard. Your principle is normally to allocate the worst room to the host, and allow them to use the main room after the opening session. Do you move everyone around, put up with it and say nothing, or something else?

7 **Key document**

Barrister asserts during the opening statements that the other side had no right to build 'anything at all' but you, the mediator, have a letter in the bundle provided for the mediation, written by his instructing solicitor, which clearly states that their client gives permission for the building work to proceed. Yet the other side don't seem to have remembered the letter and certainly have not corrected the barrister. It seems that neither side have come fully prepared. What do you do?

8 **Brown envelope**

A cheery party bounces into the main room and says to the mediator: 'It is really important for me to get a deal today. Here is a bonus if you can get one for me'. Tempting?

Opening Stage

9 **Demonised party**

One party refuses to meet with the other and has built them up to be the most crooked, scheming, unreasonable party that ever walked the earth. Your experience of this demonised party is very different and you feel strongly that settlement would be more likely if the parties were to meet up. How do you manage this?

10 **Crowd control**

One party is alone in his room when the other turns up with ten members of her family. You had not been able to make contact with either party before the mediation so this was not expected. How will you manage this situation?

11 **Urgent text**

You are in an open session and a text arrives on your mobile. Embarrassed because you had forgotten to turn it off, you see it is from one of the parties from a very difficult mediation that you had two days ago. The deal struck then is about to unravel and that they urgently need you to intervene. What do you do?

Chapter 6

Exploring Stage

Purpose of the exploring stage

The exploration stage is probably the key stage of any mediation. It is where the mediator establishes what the real issues are (as opposed to those presented) and helps the parties start to shape the eventual settlement. The biggest danger is the temptation to go straight to the figures – after all, most commercial disputes are about money and most deals involve a payment of some sort. However, the thing to bear in mind (and even to say to the impatient parties) is that going straight to the money is no different to what they were doing (and failed) before the mediation, so trust the process – this is different.

The basic premise of negotiation is that if a party's needs are met, the deal will be done. A good negotiator will establish what the other party needs and will construct an offer where those needs are recognised and met (in part anyway). Meeting the other party's needs is likely to make them (the other party) want to do the deal and so in turn meet the other side's needs. The exploration stage is therefore all about the mediator further building on the rapport already in place (hopefully), reinforcing the parties' trust and establishing their real interests and needs.

Private (caucus) sessions

Transformative mediation is about focussing on the relationships and the parties' stories, not the problem. It sees commercial mediation as problem solving, ignoring the underlying relationships, and there is a lot to be said for commercial mediators spending more time on exploring parties' relationships, rather than going straight to the issues. After all, behind most disputes is a broken relationship.

The problem is that transformative mediation does not generally believe in the value of private meetings and, in commercial mediation, the reality is that one party is not going to reveal sensitive information in front of the other party, especially information that may weaken its negotiating position. So meetings between the mediator and a party in the privacy of their own room are essential if the mediator is to learn what the real drivers in a party's case are.

It is important to be realistic about timing. The early private meetings inevitably take longer than the later ones because they are information gathering. This is where open questioning by the mediator reaps great rewards. Getting a party to speak and demonstrating that they are being heard are both key skills for the

Exploring Stage

effective mediator. Using the flipchart (usually at a later stage of the mediation) is another way of showing a party that they have been heard and their important issues noted.

Mediation is a flexible process and it is quite possible to have a variety of meetings during the day – lawyer/lawyer, expert/expert and so on. However, the mediator needs to be sure about the justification for such meetings. The best are either the open sessions, where everyone can hear first-hand what has been said and done, or private meetings with the whole team. That way knowledge is first-hand and not filtered through those who have been part of a smaller meeting. Having smaller meetings is tempting for the mediator, because it can make managing the process easier and the parties more likely to be influenced by the mediator, but it should always be remembered that the purpose is not to make the mediator's life easier. The only purpose should be: 'What helps the parties move towards settlement?'

When organising a side meeting, it is important that the mediator warns the parties, gets their permission and gives them time to prepare. And once the small group is gathered, the mediator should restate the purpose of the meeting and give permission for it to be ended if anyone is unhappy or needs to consult other team members. No one should feel disadvantaged by the mediator's actions.

There is another downside of side meetings, and a (manipulative) upside. The downside is that what happens in such a meeting will be reported back differently in each room. The mediator cannot be in both rooms at the same time, and so cannot ensure that the report to the rest of the team is accurate. One way round this is to call an open session and have a joint report.

The other upside is that the mediator may be able to have 'off the record' chats with the remnants of the team, especially if the mediator's assistant is competent enough to referee the side meeting. I suggest that this is manipulative but have to conclude that a lot of what the mediator does is manipulative, although for the best reasons. Parties come to mediation in deadlock and the mediator helps them find ways out of it and into communicating effectively.

Saving face

A common reason for deadlock is that parties have been backed into a corner and cannot find a route out. The mediator is able to help deflect the focus on the party's position and allow them to negotiate with dignity. 'Deals with dignity' is a common term of mine and mediation should help parties reach a settlement and walk away with their head held high. This is covered further in Chapter 8 ('Deals with dignity').

The mediator must also head off the likelihood of a party putting themselves in a corner during the negotiations. Bottom lines, last offers, matters of principle and threatened walk-outs should be deflected so that parties have the maximum flexibility to reach a settlement. How do you do it? Most often by reality testing – asking them: 'If your purpose in this mediation is to reach a settlement, does this get you closer? If not, then how about trying something different?'

Topping and tailing

Whenever I enter a party's room I will always ask them to bring me up to date with their thinking. I need to catch up because they will have been chatting, hopefully about the case, whilst I have been elsewhere. I will also remind them that whatever we talk about is in confidence. That's what I call 'topping'.

The 'tailing' is, as I leave the room:

- to summarise and check what is confidential and what is not;
- to leave a task (if I can);
- to ask if there is anything else before I leave – this last-minute invitation, my hand on the door handle, can often prompt a gem of information; and
- to confirm how long I will be before I return.

These are good habits to adopt for every mediation.

Positions and interests

Generally, the Western style of negotiation is to pitch high and give little slowly. This is positional bargaining – build the best possible case so there is room to move. The belief is also that the party may get a better deal, especially if the other side is not as good at negotiation. Anything else is soft and not manly! The trouble is that this can alienate the other side, encourage them to be equally 'tough' and lead to deadlock, if not outright failure. Or, if there is a 'winner', it may create bad feeling, even enmity, with the 'loser'.

Mediation gives space for parties to try something different – principled negotiation. It is based upon the premise of this being a joint problem which is best solved by a joint solution. That is, co-operation. In mediation there is no deal unless all parties can say 'Yes', so the best deals come from a joint approach. Not everyone responds to the opportunity but they still do deals. It is my experience that the best deals are possible if the parties co-operate, or at least take responsibility for addressing the other party's needs as well as their own. That's a challenge because it is often counter-intuitive, but mediation provides a different negotiation forum and those that recognise and embrace it get the best outcomes.

Principled negotiation focuses on needs, not the claims. Often they can be very different. I mentioned in Chapter 1 ('Why the only route to justice?') that if I ask a party, 'What do you need to be able to do a deal today?' (and I usually do), the most common answer is 'to put an end to this misery'. The dispute has taken over their life, affected both work and personal relationships and often been financially challenging. It is understandable. If a business has a conflict that cannot be negotiated out by the people involved, the next thought is to go to a lawyer. The trouble is it then ceases to be a commercial argument but becomes a legal one. The lawyer (rightly, because that is the lawyer's skill) reframes the problem in legal terms, builds a case based upon the relevant law, and the parties' rights under that law, and does battle with the other side. The party ceases to be the front line, loses control and pays the legal bills. Mediation allows the parties to step away from the legal battlefield and to regain control for a day.

Exploring Stage

Sometimes even the party doesn't know their needs because they are so focussed on their pain and feeling of injustice. The mediator needs to be patient and explore what lies behind the claims, what is driving them and what the key factors are in any settlement. Because the legal arguments are so restricting, often the non-financial possibilities of a settlement have not been considered. The fact is anything (legal) can be considered. More than once I have had a contract, which was the basis of the dispute, 'ripped up' and a new (workable) contract agreed. I even had one case which was clinched by an annual season ticket to a Premiership football club – nothing to do with legal rights but everything to do with common sense. Spending time in exploring needs (of both/all sides) is crucial to constructing the best settlements.

If it doesn't settle, the legal arguments start the next day, but most mediations do settle, so there is a really good chance that a deal will be done and the parties can regain their lives the next day. Even those that come reluctantly to mediation respond to the common sense opportunity that mediation offers and are invariably seduced by the process to become active participants.

Of course, many disputes are settled before a mediator gets involved. Lawyers should, and do, negotiate deals in the majority of cases, so mediators tend to get the difficult ones.

Relationships v problem solving

I mentioned earlier that commercial mediation is a solution-based process and there is a danger of commercial mediators ignoring the relationship issues in disputes because their focus is on getting a deal. The fact is that behind most disputes there is a broken relationship and it is important that the mediator acknowledges this. It has taken me some time to remember this because mediations have become harder and I have gradually realised that if I spend more time with the person and less with their problem, the solutions tend to emerge more easily. Spending more time on relationships usually results in the party's needs becoming more evident and the movement towards settlement tends to become smoother and more co-operative. If a party feels heard, if their pain is recognised, if their emotion is valued, they are more likely to move on. That doesn't mean that problem solving is inappropriate, just that taking time with relationships should precede solutions. This is particularly so with irrational or unreasonable people because the temptation is to ignore, dismiss or even resist them. It is even more important to spend time exploring why the person feels so strongly and is taking such an apparently extreme position.

Moving on

Once parties' needs are known, the shaping of a deal can begin. That takes us to the negotiating stage.

Exploring stage – in a nutshell

- Keep the problem and the solution with the parties.
- Encourage co-operation – there is no deal unless all parties say 'Yes'.

Exploring Stage

- Be patient – spend time on establishing needs and drivers, don't rush to solutions.
- Relationships are an important part of exploration.
- Open questions are good!
- Top and tail private meetings.
- Use small meetings/working groups but always be clear about the reason for doing so (and tell the parties).
- Constantly reassure about confidentiality to encourage parties to be frank and open.
- Help parties avoid situations where loss of face could become an issue.

CASE STUDY

Private meetings

Following a quick chat alone, David and Mags spent a few minutes with Chris, Jo and Stephen.

David: *First of all, let me remind you that all of this is confidential. OK, any comments about that opening session?*

All of them commented about being despondent about achieving a settlement, given the other side's intransigence.

David: *Just hang on to the fact that they are here and that most mediations settle. You've a very good chance of bringing this to a conclusion today and getting on with life tomorrow. As you know, I'm going into the other room in a few minutes; what do you know about the development schemes?*

Jo: *Not a lot. We were aware of the second, larger, scheme but it is typical Harry – grand schemes but totally unrealistic. Even the smaller scheme is pie in the sky – he just doesn't have the skill, stamina or resources to make a success of it.*

Chris: *I agree. What should be done is for us to sell the barns in their current state but with the planning permission. There is money in that and no risk. Someone else can take the risk. We are farmers, and have been for generations.*

David: *Can I mention that – sell as they are with planning?*

Chris: *Sure – we suggested that a long time ago, but he just sees the potential profit in the completed scheme. And, given the current housing market, let alone the future, there can be no certainty about selling the completed scheme, let alone make a profit.*

David: *Thanks. I will only mention it if I think it is appropriate. I realise that I am running out of time, so when I am with you next I would like to talk about your family relationships, if that is OK. They obviously aren't good at the moment but I would like to know what is behind that. Anything else before I go? OK, it will probably be about 40 minutes before we get back to you.*

David and Mags returned to the main room.

Exploring Stage

David: *Any comments?*

Mags: *You didn't check confidentiality when you left.*

David: *No. I was happy that they gave permission to use the sale of properties as existing and felt there was nothing else of importance.*

Mags: *So you don't treat everything as confidential?*

David: *No. One of the key skills of an effective mediator is the strategic use of information – what to use, when to use it (or not), when to reframe. I always check anything that may be sensitive, but never everything. It may be that is what you were taught, which is the safe foundation, but in practice you need the flexibility. Of course, that comes with experience and you need to err on the safe side in the early days. By the way, let me know when the 40 minutes are up, please.*

They went into Harry's room.

David: *Before we start I just want to remind you that this is confidential.*

Quentin: *Good. We have talked about the second scheme that you mentioned. We don't see a problem with it being known. It is Harry's preferred option but, although the planning authority has indicated that they would not object, it has yet to go to them for formal approval.*

David (to Harry): *Thanks. If the second scheme did get approval, how would you manage it?*

Quentin: *This is not to be shared with the other side but Harry has a joint venture partner who would manage the scheme.*

David (to Harry): *Harry, tell me why that needs to be confidential – one of your sister's concerns is the fact that you are not experienced in housing development and so they see the risk as being too much.*

Quentin: *We just don't want to share that information at the moment.*

David (to Quentin): *Quentin, I understand your concern and of course I will respect it if you want me to keep the information confidential. But in the end, Harry is the decision maker and I would like him to respond.*

Harry: *The girls have missed their opportunity to be part of this and so I don't see why they should be told what they are missing.*

David: *OK, I understand. My only thought was that if they were reassured by your professional approach, they might be more amenable to signing up.*

Quentin: *Leave that for us to discuss whilst you are with them.*

David spent some time discussing the schemes and the valuations with Charles, their valuation expert, then turned to Harry.

David: *Harry, tell me a bit about the farm. It's mainly arable isn't it?*

Exploring Stage

Harry talked about the farm, how it had been in the family for several generations, how he had run it with his father, and how his father had left it to his children on a 40/30/30 split, and how it had been really hard over these past several years (due to the economy, cheap imported grain from the former communist countries and atrocious weather).

David: *I see from what you are saying that it is hard work. Did the 40/30/30 split surprise you?*

Harry: *Yes. It is traditional for the farm to pass to the eldest boy, so I would have expected it all to come to me – the land that is, not the buildings.*

David: *Has that caused some difficulty between you and your sisters?*

Harry: *Of course. They are just a teacher and a shopkeeper, have little or nothing to do with the farm. Yet here I am seeking their permission to invest in what should have been mine in the first place.*

David: *Thanks for telling me. I can see that you feel very strongly about it.*

Mags indicated the time.

David: *OK, I did say to the others that I would be back to them by now, but I don't want to stop you sharing anything else whilst we are with you. Is there anything? OK. So I can talk to the others about the second scheme but, not at present anyway, that you have a potential development partner. What else is confidential? Well, I'll be about 40 minutes with the others. If you want to stretch your legs or have a comfort break, do so. I'll be back at 12.15.*

David and Mags went to the main room.

David: *Any comments?*

Mags: *Two things, both about body language. Harry's when he was talking about the split. He was really wound up and obviously feels very hurt by it. The other was Quentin's as Harry was talking, particularly about the scheme. He was really on edge and unhappy that he was not doing the talking.*

David: *Yes. It is very difficult because this should be party-focused but lawyers often find it very difficult to let their client speak freely. On the other hand, it is a delicate matter bypassing the lawyer to get their client to speak, without alienating them. I think we are OK although I do wonder why Angela is there! She has not said a word.*

Mags: *There is another thing – the fact that Angela seems to have released a sensitive document without Quentin knowing. How would you deal with that?*

David: *I often say, 'you can only work with what you've got'. Sensitive or not, it is now public. Let's see how they are dealing with it.*

David and Mags continued private meetings through lunch, talking further about their relationships, a little about the legal positions and then, in a meeting in Harry's room, Peter said:

Exploring Stage

Harry, *I can't remember when it was but at some stage the statement was made, 'the future of the farm depends upon it' – it being the signing of the mortgage deeds. This is of course in absolute confidence, but what did that mean?*

Long pause and Harry looked at Quentin to get his approval before responding.

Harry: *To be absolutely honest with you, the farm business in the past few years has made a loss and the bank is threatening to call in the overdraft. Usually the overdraft is underwritten by the future crop sales but they are not happy with that any more. So they want a £250,000 mortgage on the land. The rest is for the development. I must get the girls to sign, otherwise the bank will foreclose and we will lose everything.*

David: *Gosh, that's serious. But do the girls know about this?*

Harry: *No, although they may suspect. They are involved round the edges so don't really know what goes on.*

David: *So the situation is that you own and run the farm business, which has the overdraft, but 60 per cent of the land and property is owned by Chris and Jo and the bank will only continue the working overdraft if all the land is mortgaged with them.*

Harry: *Yes. It is totally unreasonable of the bank because my 40 per cent would cover the overdraft several times over.*

Charles: *The bank obviously wants an unencumbered asset in case it has to sell. We are looking for other funding sources but farming is not seen as a very safe investment at the moment and time is running out for Harry.*

David: *So your prime need is to get the overdraft covered?* (David looks at Angela and Quentin.) *How comfortable are you that Harry's sisters are being asked to sign the mortgage deeds under a misapprehension that it is for the development?*

Quentin: *Not very, although the money will be paid into the development company and then half of it loaned back, so it is legal.*

David: *But how do you think Chris and Jo will feel when they hear about this?*

Harry: *Probably cross, but they aren't part of the business or the development so why should they care where the money goes?*

David: *Put yourself in their shoes Harry. How would you feel if you had signed up to a mortgage for a development scheme and find that half is going to pay farm debts?*

Harry stayed silent.

David: *Look, part of my role is to oversee a deal that will stick. I suspect this deal, whatever its form, won't stick if this remains confidential. Quentin and Angela, I know you are looking after Harry's legal rights and interests in a professional way but there are family and relationship issues relating to trust here, which need exploration. In my experience this is more effectively managed with the siblings alone. I suggest that we have a meeting with Harry and the girls, no lawyers, so that Harry can explain the situation. Mags and I will be there but in the background.*

Quentin: *We need to talk about that.*

David: *And I need to prepare Chris and Jo on the assumption that it will happen, so I will spend a few minutes with them without going into any detail. Anything else? I will treat it all as confidential for the moment.*

Peter and Mags went to the main room.

David: *Well?*

Mags: *I am gobsmacked. How devious can you get?*

David: *I can see how it would happen. Harry feeling that the land should be his, the girls not doing what he wants, the bank pressing him for security. I can see that pride, if nothing else, would make him want to cover up what is effectively a failure. Let's go next door.*

They went into Chris and Jo's room and explained about the possibility of a meeting with Harry. David resisted their questions as to the reason and said:

I don't want anyone to feel disadvantaged by this. Just call a halt if you are not happy. I will be there to manage the process and make sure you feel safe.

Chris: *Good, because he is a bully and once he starts, we are out of here.*

The meeting took place and Harry was not at all the bully. In fact, after the initial tension, by the end all three of them were quite sombre and even kindly towards each other.

They returned to their rooms and David and Mags joined Chris, Jo and Stephen.

David: *Well, how do you feel, both of you?*

Chris: *Initially very angry but then sad.*

David: *Sad?*

Chris: *Yes, because he is our brother and he has no one else to share the burden with now that Dad is gone.*

Jo: *And we have been concerned about the poor harvests but not taken the trouble to speak with him, to see how he is coping.*

David: *Tell me what you really need to be able to give him what he is looking for – that is to sign the mortgage deeds.*

Jo: *He needs more than that. If the farm business has lost money for the last few years, he needs a consultant to advise on how to make the farm profitable again. That makes the development scheme even less important – it is no good Harry seeing that as saving the situation. Once that is done and sold, he will be back losing money on the farm again.*

Exploring Stage

David: *OK – I understand what you are saying and the eventual deal can cover whatever you want, so long as you all agree. That is the beauty of a mediated settlement – it can include anything, so long as it is legal. But what do you two need?*

Jo: *An end to the misery.*

Stephen: *And the cottages and farmhouse ring-fenced so that they are not included in the mortgage or the development. And they want to have the confidence that the development is being done properly, not in Harry's usual bodged manner.*

Chris: *And I need some security with the farm shop. It is my livelihood and I don't want to lose it because of Harry's bad management or risky development schemes.*

David: *So can I tell Harry that in principle you are prepared to sign the deeds but that there are several important details that need to be sorted first? Don't forget, there is no deal unless you all say 'yes' and you are not committed to anything until it is in writing and you all sign.*

Chris and Jo: *Yes.*

Mediator challenges

Exploring stage

1   **Assertive lawyer**

    Throughout the mediation one side's lawyer has been saying to you: 'What you must do now is....'. Not only does it aggravate you (although you have concealed it well) but most of it you were going to do anyway and now it looks as though you are incompetent and need guidance from the lawyer. How do you retrieve the situation?

2   **Needs**

    'Needs!' the party shouted. 'My need is to crush him. The bastard had an affair with my wife whilst we were in business together and I want to crush him'. Yet this was just at the start of the exploring stage. How do you react?

3   **Arithmetical error**

    In private, one party's lawyer points out that there is an arithmetical error in the other sides' computation of their claim, which benefits her client by some £500,000. You are sworn to secrecy, the lawyer stating that she is under no obligation to tell her opposite number of their error. Do you see an ethical issue here? What do you say?

4   **No money**

    In confidence, in the first private meeting, the defendant party tells the mediator that she knows she must pay some money but she has none. No assets, very little in the bank. If the case goes to court and she loses (which she accepts she will) the little she has will have been spent on legal fees and it will be nothing but a pyrrhic victory for the claimant. What do you do with this information?

Exploring Stage

5 **Unrepresented party**

One side has lawyers present but the other is unrepresented. There is a point of law that the lawyer has mentioned, and which you are sure is relevant, but of which the unrepresented party seems to be unaware. It could significantly increase the likely settlement figure. What do you do?

Chapter 7

Negotiating Stage

This chapter deals with getting the shape of the deal worked out, seeing needs being recognised and met and developing a co-operative approach to problem solving. It covers negotiation styles and tactics, overcoming blockages, reality testing, power imbalances and cultural aspects.

Shaping the deal

I strongly believe that spending time on exploration, establishing parties' needs and exploring relationships, is the best investment for a successful negotiation. Having laid these foundations, the parties are more likely to co-operate in achieving a solution. Even so, I still avoid figures until late into the negotiation if I can because I want the first offer and counteroffer to be in the ZOPA (zone of probable agreement) and for that to happen the negotiators need to be confident about the seriousness of the other side. I try, often with the use of the flipchart, to start shaping the deal, noting the key needs to be included and how they may be met. I note just general headings to start with (eg, payment, warranties, legal costs, future work) and then add key points (eg, staged payments, discounts), leaving the detail for later – like pieces of a jigsaw gradually fitting together. When parties see a shape that suits them they are most likely to be sensible about the detail, because they won't want to lose the deal. First offers are then likely to be in the zone, sending a message that 'we are here to do a deal and you can see we are being reasonable'. Usually the other side reciprocates and a settlement occurs, often within three moves.

Negotiation styles, techniques and strategies

Shaping the deal as described above does need the mediator to be tough at times and to manage the process firmly. It is a matter of confidence, knowing that this works and resisting the temptation of parties to regress to extreme positions, but it does work, and it is one of the areas of mediation where the mediator can really add value to the negotiation.

Pepperdine University in the United States categorised negotiation offers in four groups – insult, extreme, credible and reasonable, the latter being the ZOPA. The mediator's aim must be to get first offers pitched in the reasonable zone, or failing that, at least in the credible zone. Outside that and there are problems!

Of course, some people are poor negotiators. Usually they don't realise it and often consider that they are really good. Many times I have been tempted to give them

Negotiating Stage

my business card and say 'I run a really good negotiation course ... you should be on it!' There is no doubt in my mind that the best deals arise from parties co-operating, but as mentioned before, it can be counterintuitive to the more natural Western style of negotiation, which is adversarial and based upon a 'winner' and a 'loser'. Some less effective techniques are set out below.

First and final offer

This is usually preceded by 'I don't want to play around giving a little here and there, so this is it.' No matter how reasonable the offer may be, it will not be well received. This is a negotiation, and a first and final offer comes over as an ultimatum. The offering party appears to be bullying and the response will inevitably be one of resistance and/or resentment. There is no dignity in such a negotiation. So I will always reality test a first and final offer, exploring the likely response and suggesting that something is kept back to allow another stage of negotiation. If that fails and the party insists on sticking to a first and final offer, I will suggest a reframe along the lines of 'I (the mediator) have encouraged the other side not to "salami-slice" and so to place their best offer first. This is it and I don't think there is anything more'. That way it comes from a neutral source and avoids the perception of bullying.

Salami slicing

This is starting from an extreme position and giving little, slowly, probably with the hope of wearing the other side down. This is most likely to happen if the mediator goes to the money too early. If time has been spent on establishing needs and shaping the deal, it is very unlikely that negotiations will start here. There is too much at risk. The likely response will be that the offering party is not at the mediation in good faith and/or has no intention of reaching a deal and/or is just playing silly games. So again I will reality-test. What are they trying to achieve? How is the other side likely to react? Does it get you to a deal? Does it encourage the other side to be reasonable? What happens if they respond with a similar counter-offer? There is a danger of me, the mediator, appearing to be judgmental about such an offer and so I may well precede any comment with repeating what I said in the first Open Session: 'My role is to give you the best chance of doing a deal .....so...'. It is so important for the mediator to be seen as even-handed and unbiased.

Low offer

This is similar to salami slicing, where the opening offer is in the insult zone. Again, this is most likely to happen because figures are being considered too early and the mediator's reaction should be to challenge and reality test. If it persists, I would normally invite the person making the low offer to do so in person to the other side. At least I am distanced from the reaction and can pick up the pieces afterwards.

Mediator's advice

Sometimes parties will ask the mediator for advice on the level of offer. This may well be the result of poor preparation and/or lack of proper risk analysis. Parties should always come to a mediation fully aware of their exposure, their chances if the matter goes to court and the upside and downside of their case. They should do this, but don't always do so. If they don't, it puts the mediator in a very difficult position because usually by this time in the mediation the mediator has a pretty good idea of where the case is likely to settle. It can be very tempting to give a steer to a party or even push them towards the mediator's solution rather than allow them to find their own. However, the rule is to avoid advising the parties. Help them to analyse their situation, discuss parameters but don't pitch figures (yet).

There is an issue over potential incompatibility of negotiation styles and reaction to insulting offers. It takes nerve to maintain a co-operative and principled negotiating strategy if the other side are being positional and trying to 'win'. The mediator can discuss the options open to the principled party:

- refuse to play the positional game, and say so; or
- reciprocate reluctantly, and say so.

Part of the mediator's role is to keep the responsibility for the problem, and for the solution, with the parties. If a party is a poor negotiator, it is their responsibility. If they insist on an un-cooperative approach they are in danger of not achieving the best deal, but that is their responsibility.

Having said that, there is nothing wrong with the mediator coaching a party on presenting an offer in a way that will achieve a positive response.

Coaching

It was mentioned in Chapter 2 ('Core skills') that reframing is one of the important skills for the mediator, whether it be changing a negative statement into a positive one, or reframing an offer so that it will be better received. The mediator's role is to give the parties their best opportunity of getting a deal. Helping the parties to frame an offer is part of that role. After all, the mediator knows what is going on in the other party's room and will have a real sense of the mood, the needs and the zone of the likely deal – without giving away any confidences, all of that knowledge can be used to help a party pitch an offer that is sensible and likely to be well received. The fact is that a sensible offer is likely to have a sensible counter-offer in return.

However, despite the mediator urging a party to make a sensible offer, their instincts for positional negotiation may prevail and an offer in the insult or extreme zone be made. There is no reason why the mediator shouldn't challenge that, reality testing being another key skill of the effective mediator.

Reality testing

Reality testing is what it says – the mediator testing how realistic the statement/ position that has just been expressed is. It is part of managing the expectations of the parties and of keeping those expectations grounded, rather than in fantasy, and is the time when optimistic expectations are usually abandoned and the realistic

Negotiating Stage

shape of a deal hits home. It is the time when 'win-win' becomes 'pain-pain'! Sometimes it is the time when a party's solicitor breathes a sigh of relief because what they have been advising an unaccepting client suddenly gets accepted.

Techniques commonly used in reality-testing include;

- risk assessment (or reassessment in the light of what has emerged in the mediation);
- challenging assumptions upon which a party may be making an assessment;
- predicting the outcome in court (or arbitration);
- calculating the cost, including management time, of proceeding through court;
- exploring the reasoning behind settlement offers; and/or
- standing in the other's shoes.

Questions posed may include:

- Why (do you want/say that)?
- How will the other side react to that?
- Would you make that offer in person?
- What would a court say to that?
- What do you think the other side's walk-away figure is?
- If you're right, can you live with that?
- What happens next if you don't settle today?
- What's the worst-case scenario if you lose in court?

I have to say that the last question is one I keep as a last resort. It can so easily be misinterpreted as a form of bullying by the mediator, but it is undoubtedly a reality and should be tested. You will see these are a mixture of open and closed questions. The later the stage of the mediation, the more likely it is that closed questions become appropriate.

There is a potential danger with reality testing. The questions may well be challenging and there is a danger that a party may feel the mediator is taking sides. It is sensible to preempt this by starting with words like, 'I did warn you earlier on that I may ask you difficult questions,' or, 'I'm going to ask you the same questions that I have been asking the other side,' or, 'It's not my role to argue the other side's case, but ….'.

Because the mediator knows what the thinking is in both/all rooms, they are likely to have more knowledge about respective positions and negotiating range than either party. They are therefore in a unique position to guide the parties to a deal. This can be a sensitive issue, partly because of information given in confidence and partly because the deal must be theirs, not the mediator's. It is not unusual for a party, towards the end of the negotiations, to ask the mediator, 'Is that their best offer?' or, 'They say this is their final offer, do you believe them?' I always respond with: 'It may be, but you need to test it to extinction, then decide if it is the best you can do.' Or, as mentioned in Chapter 2 ('Modelling other's behaviour') I may say, 'I believe everything that I am told in a mediation, but I know some people do not tell me the truth.' That can be taken either way.

Overcoming deadlock

Most parties come to mediation because they are in deadlock. They have reached a point from which they can find no way out – or, if they can, they will lose face. So the mediator offers a way out where deals can be done with dignity. There are several techniques for doing this – not least because the mediation process is very different to the litigation process in which they are generally immersed, and so it provides a more flexible forum for negotiation. The opening statements also offer an opportunity for the dispute to be reframed in commercial terms and for the key issues to be redefined. That alone may give momentum to the settlement discussions. However, the bald fact is that by introducing a neutral third party, communication can be started in an unthreatening (and uncommitted) way using a trusted person who will show no favour to either party. Very often this will eventually lead to the parties communicating directly with each other.

There are, however, some techniques that the mediator may use if deadlock occurs during the mediation:

- Take a break. It is amazing what a bit of fresh air can do for people spending the day in a stuffy, air-conditioned room. Going for a walk can change the dynamic. Even better, sending the decision makers out for a walk together can have a dramatic (usually beneficial) effect on their positions. However, sometimes parties come to mediation unprepared or too early, or something arises during the mediation that requires further information, so breaking off the mediation and rearranging another date may be the prudent thing. It is difficult though, and the parties need to be the ones who decide on this, because parties will often press on for a deal despite the risk or uncertainty, just to achieve finality.

- Have some food, especially if the mediation goes into the evening. I find blood sugar levels plunge around 4.30 pm (so biscuits are useful) and, come 6.30 pm, pizzas are essential. The last thing a mediator wants is for the final negotiations to be prejudiced by parties getting fractious through lack of food.

- Break the problem down, or, more likely, drop the detail and look at the big picture. Sometimes taking one smaller item and working on that can create a momentum for other 'jigsaw pieces' to take shape and be fitted. More often though, people are deadlocked because they are stuck in the details whereas most mediations settle on hitting a figure to which both sides can say 'Yes'. However, sometimes it is necessary to allow them to wallow in detail first so that they can be faced with the futility before accepting that it won't work and allowing the big picture to take over.

- Change the groups. If deadlock has occurred because individuals (eg experts or lawyers) have become stuck, then try another grouping – even bringing everyone back together and saying, 'that didn't work, what else shall we try?'

- Identify an emotional blockage, and encourage it to be expressed, either in private or to the other party.

- Identify a tactical deadlock and work with the cause to understand and examine the reason and its effect. Some parties just have bad negotiating techniques!

Negotiating Stage

- Say 'I've run out of ideas, you're still stuck, what do you suggest?' You can only say that once in a mediation, otherwise your credibility may be challenged, but it does keep the responsibility with those who are causing the deadlock.
- Bring everyone together and summarise the progress made and make them face the reality that the mediation may not settle unless they change positions. Again this is a once and final tactic, but it is an effective reality test if parties are faced with going home and will often lead to them coming off positions to rescue the deal.

Whatever the reason for deadlock, and the technique for breaking it, it is important to always remember that the parties are responsible – it is their problem and their solution. The mediator is there to give them the best chance of a deal. It they mess up, despite the mediator's best efforts, that has to be their problem!

Power imbalance

Not all parties have equal power in mediations – indeed most do not. Some mediators, particularly those in family and community mediation, have major concerns about this but I have rarely found it to be an issue. Of course, a wealthy person or business may not be bothered (or admit to being bothered) about the cost of going to court, but it is the waste of time and resources (and money) that affects everyone. So the finality that mediation offers is usually of tangible benefit to all parties. And when someone does express concern about unequal power, I always respond that both or all parties have the power to say 'No' to a deal. There is no deal unless everyone says 'Yes'. There is equality in that.

Cultural aspects

When we use the word 'cultural' we all have different explanations as to what we mean. Most people immediately think of nationality and ethnic background but it actually embraces a multitude of characteristics – education, age, gender, religion, profession (or not), traditions, principles, values and so on. And all of those have regional differences. In reality I think culture is best defined as 'the way we do it here'.

This means that all mediations have a cultural dimension, although some may be totally complementary to those attached to the mediator. This is a big issue, and is the subject of much deeper examination in Part 2 of this book, but what follows are a few pointers:

- NEVER make assumptions. If you are in danger of making them, turn them into facts. Check them out, and ask if you are not sure. Assumptions can lead to disaster.
- Check where the authority lies. It might not be with the obvious person – in some cultures it is the quietest person, in others it might be the person not present (that might be an insurer, or the business owner, or the decision maker's spouse).
- Accept that time has different relevance to different cultures. In the United States and Europe, decisions are generally made quickly, time is of the essence; Asian

and Eastern cultures can be very different, leaving time for matters to evolve. Having written that, beware of making stereotypes – there are many people of other ethnic origins who have adopted Western styles of living and negotiating. It can become very confusing so NEVER make assumptions.

- Recognise that some cultures need detail and others only bother with the big picture. This may only emerge as the mediation develops.
- We all have common needs and values (eg, food, water, shelter, love, family, respect, dignity). It may be that identifying what is common and building from there will create the foundations for bridging differences and creating a commonality.

Negotiating stage – in a nutshell

- Try to shape the deal first, then add the detail.
- Usually, delay figures until the shape of the deal can be seen.
- Avoid bottom lines.
- Keep the problem and the solution with the parties.
- Be prepared to coach parties to give offers a better chance of a good response.
- When deadlock occurs, take time to explore the reason and establish the effective key.
- Precede challenges and reality testing with a 'neutrality' reinforcement.
- Culture is 'how we do it here'.
- NEVER make assumptions. Ask, check out, turn into fact.
- Be prepared to take risks and follow instinct.

CASE STUDY

More private meetings

David and Mags reviewed the situation in the main room and decided to meet with Jo and Chris and Stephen. Mags told Harry's team that they would be with them in half an hour.

David: *So on the assumption that you will sign the mortgage deed, what else needs to be in the Settlement Agreement?*

Stephen: *As I said before, all the properties need to be excluded from the deed and then the cottages, farmhouse and the shop need to be ring-fenced, with the barns and paddock allocated to the development (assuming that it goes ahead). If it does go ahead Chris and Jo want to have a say in the way it is done – consultants, contractor and so on. After all, they own 60 per cent of the assets, which we value at £400,000 as they stand with planning permission – more if the second scheme goes ahead. And they want half Harry's profit.*

David: *How do you think Harry will react to that? Chris and Jo's agreement – he only owns 40 per cent of the assets.*

Negotiating Stage

Jo: *And there are other conditions. I want to own the pair of cottages that are unoccupied and do my own renovation scheme when I can afford it. I am prepared to swap my share of the barns for his share of the cottages.*

David: *This is getting complicated. I need to use the flipchart.*

David did a mind-map style of summary of all the issues:

- Ownership of land (with mortgage deed linked to it)
- Ownership of barns and paddock
- Development scheme (with profit-share and consultants linked to it)
- Ownership of cottages (with occupied pair and derelict pair linked to it)
- Ownership of shop (and Chris' security linked to it together with 10 acres of market garden that serves the shop)
- Ownership of the farmhouse, currently occupied by their mother and Chris

David: *anything else?*

Jo: *Yes – the management of the farm. Harry needs to get some consultancy help to make sure it is profitable.*

David: *How do you think he will react to that?*

Jo: *Not very well, but he needs it, especially as we own 60 per cent of the land.*

David: *You mention owning the land. How important is that to you? Have you ever thought about doing a land/property swap?*

Silence.

Stephen: *You mean the girls take the properties and Harry has 100 per cent of the land?*

David: *Well, it was just a thought as Harry needs the land and you have expressed interest in the buildings – some of them anyway. I don't know how the figures stack up but you have the valuations. Perhaps, if it interests you, you could do some work on the figures whilst I am in the other room.*

Mags mentioned that they had run well over the half hour.

David: *Then let me go to the others now. What can I use and what is confidential?*

Chris and Jo agreed that the flipchart sheet with the mind-map display could be taken to the other room. The rest would stay confidential.

David and Mags went into the main room.

David: *Well?*

Mags: *I thought your idea was brilliant – swapping land and property. It will overcome a lot of difficulties, both now and in the future.*

David: Maybe, but it needs to be their idea, not mine. They need to own it.

They went to Harry's room, apologised for the delay and talked through the flipchart. Although David did not mention the land/property swap suggestion, he did ask Harry how important the buildings (other than the barns and paddock) were to him.

Harry: *Not much. The farmhouse is because Mum and Chris are living there and Mum has the rights of occupation until she dies. After that, who knows? It is too old and expensive for me to live there. I prefer new houses, which are fuel-efficient and smarter. In fact I have my eye on one of the new ones in the paddock scheme.*

David: *Let's talk about the paddock scheme. Chris and Jo still favour selling the properties as they stand with planning permission, rather than do the development. Do you think this might be the time to tell them about the joint venture? Quentin, I notice you have been quiet of late, what are your thoughts?*

Quentin: *I suppose so. I don't see any reason not to. Come to that I don't see any real advantage in telling them either.*

David: *Am I right in saying that they still own 60 per cent of the paddock and barns?*

Quentin: *Yes.*

David: *So how confident are you that you can go ahead without them having a say?*

Harry: *Before today I would have just gone ahead and to hell with what they thought. I can see that won't work today at least.*

David: *The best deals in mediation are always through co-operative negotiation. Joint problem, joint solution. Principled rather than positional. Positional bargaining invariably gets the minimum solution rather than the best.*

Quentin: *I haven't a clue what you are talking about, but, Harry, it's your call.*

Harry: *OK, I am happy for you to tell them about the joint venture. It will go ahead whether or not the second scheme is approved.*

David: *I don't need to know the details but what's the deal over money in and profit share?*

Harry: *50:50 on both.*

David: *If Chris and Jo own 60 per cent of the barns and paddock, where does that place them on profit share?*

Harry: *I hadn't thought of it. I'd probably go to 10 per cent.*

David: *We're heading into detail and I would rather stay with the principles at this stage. Perhaps you would talk about it whilst I am in the other room – put yourself in their shoes and think about how you can construct something which will get them to say 'Yes'. Anything else? OK. I shall be about half an hour. Quentin, how are we for time?*

Negotiating Stage

Quentin: *I still need to leave at 5pm but Angela will be able to draft a Settlement Agreement, assuming a deal is done.*

David: *So is your work done then?*

Quentin: *Absolutely not! There is still a lot to be done.*

David and Mags went back to the main room.

David: *I shouldn't have made that last remark.*

Mags: *Perhaps not. He took it well though.*

David: *Some pieces of the jigsaw are on the table – the mortgage deed and the development. Still a lot of detail but I like people to see the shape of the deal before we fill in the detail. It usually means that they are more sensible about the detail if they can see a shape that meets their needs.*

Mags: *What next?*

David: *We seem to be running two parallel solutions, with several variables. If there is a land/property swap, that is very different to picking off each issue. Let's see what the girls are thinking.*

They went into Chris and Jo and Stephen's room. They had obviously been working hard as there were several flipchart sheets on the table with lots of figures and notes. Jo was in teacher mode.

Jo: *OK. Here is one possibility. We give Harry our shares in the barns and paddock and he gives me his share of the derelict cottages and Chris his share in the shop and smallholding. Chris and I will then swap each other's shares in the shop and cottages, so that we each own outright the property that we want. That means he gets any profit (or loss) from the development and we are not at risk with the properties that are important to us.*

David: *How do the respective figures work out?*

Stephen: *On my valuations, he gains on the shop and is about equal on the cottages.*

David: *Would you go through the figures with Charles if they ask?*

Stephen: *Sure. I've tried to be sensible, although some of the properties are difficult to value.*

David: *Great, well done. Thank you for working so hard whilst we have been in the other room. I presume that means the property/land swap is not an option?*

Jo: *We feel it is a step too far at the moment. Our father left the land split for a reason and we feel we need to ensure it stays in the family. So we are more likely to influence Harry over making the farm a viable concern if we have an interest in the land. Eventually, perhaps, when our mother dies and the farmhouse is unencumbered, we will consider it again.*

David: *That's fine. Now what can I take into the other room?*

Jo: *The lot!*

David: *Thanks. I think any discussion about farm consultants needs to be between you and your brother. Probably not part of a Settlement Agreement, just an understanding.*

Chris: *Whatever you feel best.*

David: *Good. Anything else?*

David and Mags go to the main room.

David: *I think this might work. I can see the advantages for Harry and for his sisters.*

Mags: *I am not sure Harry will accept it coming from the girls.*

David: *You might be right. Let's see how things are in the other room.*

David and Mags join Harry and his team in their room.

David: *Perhaps you would bring me up to date with what you have been doing before I start.*

Quentin: *We feel strongly about the development scheme. Harry doesn't want his sisters looking over his shoulder all the time. It is his scheme, he will be doing a lot of the work and he wants the profit. The most we will give his sisters is 10 per cent, otherwise it is not worth his while.*

David: *Ten per cent of the overall profit of Harry's share?*

Quentin: *Of Harry's share, we can't speak for his partner.*

David: *How do you think his sisters will respond?*

Quentin: *They can take it or leave it.*

David: *But does that get you the deal? [silence] Harry, this may not be the only solution. Hang on to the fact that your prime need is getting the mortgage deed signed. Your sisters have agreed to entertain this as a reality and so it is what goes with it that needs to be sorted. I'm going to throw out a 'what if ...' now. There is no commitment, just a possibility. What if the girls were to sign over ownership of the barns and paddock to you so that you are free to do with them as you wish, without reference to them? And you keep the profit.*

Harry: *Great! How much do they want for them?*

David: *This is just an idea at the moment. No figures have been tabled.*

Harry: *Well, as you know, and so should they, I don't have the cash. That's the whole point of the mortgage. That's the whole reason why we are here.*

Negotiating Stage

David: *OK. I hear that. But if that could be sorted, is the idea attractive?*

Harry: *Of course. It would suit me very well to get on with the development without them breathing down my neck all the time.*

David: *Then can I discuss it with them?*

Harry: *Sure.*

David: *So I won't mention, unless it becomes relevant, about profit-share. Just ownership. Anything else before I go?*

David and Mags go to the main room.

Mags: *Why didn't you table the full offer?*

David: *I felt Harry needed to let the idea sink in first, especially as Quentin was being assertive. Just let him see another piece of the jigsaw of the deal ready to put into place. Let's go and see the girls.*

David and Mags went into the sisters' room and reported that Harry was amenable to the idea of taking ownership of the barns and paddock but not for money. After a little while, David asked Stephen if he would be happy to meet with Charles to see if there was agreement on property values. Stephen was happy to do so and David and Mags returned to Harry's room to relay Chris' offer of her share in return for the shop and smallholding, and Jo's share in return for the two derelict cottages.

Harry: *I am OK with Jo's offer but I need to check figures on the shop.*

David: *But you agree the principle?*

Harry: *Yes. I need to speak with Charles.*

David: *And Stephen is happy to go through their figures with Charles.*

Quentin: *Leave it with us for a few minutes.*

David: *How long?*

Quentin: *Five minutes.*

David: *Is that a lawyer's five minutes, or a QS's?* [David's background was quantity surveying]

Quentin (actually laughing): *Just five.*

Five minutes later they told David that the proposal was agreed and that Charles did not need to meet with Stephen.

And so the concluding stage began.

Mediator challenges

Negotiating Stage

1 **Key information**

   There is a record drawing, recently discovered by the defendant and which has not been revealed to the claimant, that completely justifies its claim but disclosure has not happened yet so they do not know of its existence. You, the mediator, are told to keep this information confidential. It looks as though the claimant is going to settle at a much lower figure than it would if they knew that the drawing existed. What do you do?

2 **First and final**

   One party tells you that they are about to give you their first and final offer. There will be no moving from it and the other side had better believe them because if they don't accept they are 'out of here'. How do you respond?

3 **Giving a steer**

   One party has been dithering over what offer to make in settlement. You have a good feel of what figure will succeed. They ask you: 'What do you think we should settle at?' Do you tell them? If not, how do you respond?

4 **Bug**

   After several private meetings and just as the negotiations are under way, one party greets you as you enter their room with 'look what we've just found'. It looks like a pen and it was in a container on their table, but in actual fact it is a bugging device. How do you react?

5 **Mediator not wanted**

   The mediator is asked to leave the room whilst parties talk about offer strategy. You suspect that they are going to make a silly offer and feel that, having been part of the discussions with the other party, you could be a useful contributor to this party's conversation. Do you object, leave without saying a word, explain that you could be useful, or something else?

6 **Relaying offer**

   The mediator relays an offer from the defendant of £9m to the claimant (who turns it down). The mediator reports back to the defendant that £9m not accepted, and the defendant's lawyer explodes and asserts that instruction was to relay £8m. Lawyer angry to the point of abusive. How do you react?

7 **Walk out**

   The claimants are three sisters and they are constantly arguing. You return to their private room with an offer from the other side only to find that one of the sisters has left without letting you know. In checking with the other two, she has not left them with authority to settle on her behalf. How do you retrieve the situation?

Chapter 8

Concluding Stage

This chapter is about putting the detail on the shape of the deal, putting it in writing and following up afterwards.

Getting the deal

Once the shape of the settlement can be seen and the detail has been added, I always bring the decision makers together to seal the deal. There are two reasons for this:

- a good negotiator needs to look the other negotiator in the eye to be sure that the best deal is on the table; and
- by sealing the deal and shaking hands, the decision makers own it. That is why it is so rare for mediated settlements to unravel.

The third of the two reasons is that it humanises the settlement. There is a danger that, with most of the negotiation being done through the mediator shuttling between parties, bad feeling can return and parties become demonised again. That is especially so if there is an incompatibility of negotiating style and/or one side has been particularly difficult. Face-to-face, the decision makers take responsibility for the outcome and can express their feelings to the other side.

Deals with dignity

The ideal scenario is that the parties do a deal, shake hands and become friends again. And that happens in many cases. Parties leave the venue with heads held high and recognising that, although the outcome may not be as they had hoped, honours are even and both/neither won. No-one was crushed, it was a deal with dignity.

When that is so, I usually suggest we break out the alcohol! Most mediations take place in lawyer's offices and, even when times are tough, there is certain to be some drink in the office or a wine store somewhere in the building. My policy is to get the parties back into the main room to have a drink whilst the lawyers are writing up the Settlement Agreement (they are allowed a glass when the settlement has been agreed and signed). It is very rewarding for the mediator to see parties who were once at war, chatting socially together. Indeed, I have witnessed new deals being done – even a joint venture agreed – during the couple of hours which it normally takes for the Settlement Agreement to be finalised. But a word of warning:

everyone, but particularly the mediator, needs to keep a clear head because issues often arise during the drafting,

Pain-pain

Unfortunately not all mediations settle with good humour. Sometimes, especially when high emotion is involved (and perhaps not properly expressed during the mediation) bad feeling prevails to the end. The fact is that mediation being sold as 'win-win' is a misconception because it happens very rarely. I always warn the parties that it is more likely to be 'pain-pain', but most parties can cope with that if they feel the pain is shared. If they don't (and it is really the mediator's job to ensure both sides know that each are suffering, because neither knows what is going on in the other room) and one party feels the pain is all theirs, then, even if a settlement is reached, there will be a feeling of it being unfair and not a 'deal with dignity'. It may also be a reason for a settlement not being reached on the day.

Mediator recommendation

Sometimes, when the parties cannot agree but are wanting to find a settlement, they will ask the mediator to make a recommendation. It is a risky business and one for the mediator to avoid if at all possible. The obvious danger is the potential perceived loss of neutrality plus the additional danger of pleasing only one, or none, of the parties, and so losing the ability, as a neutral, to follow up after the mediation. Also, if there is any indication early on that the mediator may do this if the mediation doesn't settle, parties may have that in mind throughout the mediation and be very selective in the information passed to the mediator. It potentially affects the whole mediation (and reduces the chances of it settling). I have succumbed three times over twenty years to making a recommendation – once was a disaster, once a success and the third time I heard nothing (so I presume it pleased nobody). One question to ask is: 'Why would the mediator do it anyway?'. My answer in the three occasions was that the poor souls had got themselves into a mess and didn't know how to get out of, so I rode to their aid. It was a mediator's ego trip really.

There is a big difference between a (usually non-binding – but it doesn't have to be) mediator's recommendation and a mediator being evaluative. The latter is the mediator expressing an opinion (whether requested by the parties or not) on the relevant law, the chances if the case goes to court or the 'correct' solution. A recommendation is the mediator's sense of a just outcome given the information provided in the mediation. It may have nothing to do with the relevant law (and in my case, being a non-lawyer, it couldn't).

If the mediator agrees to make a recommendation it must be at the request of both or all parties, delivered to them in writing (very important, as people are selective in what they remember) to both or all at the same time and with a clear caveat on the fact that it has been based upon the information provided during the mediation. Of course, that information will have been very selective – the mediator doesn't know if they had 95 per cent or 5 per cent of the information – so the recommendation may be very flawed.

Recommendations should be avoided and the parties should be made to take responsibility for their own solution.

Having said all that, there are some parties who need the mediator's support in 'selling the deal back at the ranch'. This is most likely with a government department or local authority, where a deal needs to be ratified by a committee or senior officer. I see no problem in recording the deal that the parties have reached and endorsing it as the independent mediator. That is very different to it being the mediator's deal.

Settlement Agreements

Most mediators will start the day by saying: 'You are not committed to anything until it is put into writing and you have signed it'. So writing it down is really important.

However, the common wisdom for commercial mediators with Settlement Agreements in mediated disputes is NOT TO WRITE THEM. The main, rather negative, reason for this is that it is one of the few areas where a commercial mediator is potentially vulnerable for a negligence claim. Writing up a deal that does not work, or which omits something vital, could lead to a claim. It needs to be tested in court, but it is best that you – or I – are not the subject of the test.

I am never one for acting out of fear so for me the main reason for not recording the deal is that there are others (usually more competent than me) present who can do the writing. Most commercial mediations have lawyers present or at the end of an email. They are the ones that should do it.

If lawyers are not present and you, the mediator, is the only independent third party present, then writing the Settlement Agreement may be unavoidable. If that is the case, it needs to be done in the presence of the parties and with their agreement to every word. It is their deal – you are just the scribe.

So the rule is that the mediator is the custodian of the spirit of the deal. Generally, the mediator supervises others writing it, makes suggestions, keeps them focussed and asks the questions. The mediator's role is to 'keep the spirit' and make sure that the deal will stick.

The appropriate Settlement Agreement depends on whether or not legal action has commenced. If proceedings have not commenced then a simple Heads of Agreement (HoA) will probably suffice.

Heads of Agreement would normally include:

- reference to the dispute;
- parties in dispute; and
- terms of settlement – how much? When? Who to? In full and final settlement and in relation to any conflict arising out of the litigation case or the dispute.

Note that it is always better to state the date for payment rather than x days. Check public holiday dates. Is the money to be paid to the solicitor or the party? Should the bank details be included in the agreement? Are there terms (ie, staged payments, payment subject to certain action by a party?) What are the VAT/income tax/inheritance tax/corporation tax/capital gains tax implications?

Concluding Stage

Note also that 'full and final settlement' may not be as straightforward as it seems. What about defects (patent or latent), warranties, retention monies, defects liability periods?

- Costs – both sides pay own costs? Settlement inclusive of costs?
- Default provisions? (Interest for late payment. Reference to the mediator if the settlement terms are not met.)

Note that if subsequent matters are referred to the mediator, is it for comment or a decision or for a further mediation?

- Confidentiality provision? (Except for the purposes of fulfilling the agreement.)
- Period of grace?
- Mediator not to be called as a witness?

Note that this would normally be a clause in the Agreement to Mediate, so is probably not needed in the Settlement Agreement.

- Governing law?

Plus any specific provisions agreed by the parties.

Both or all parties sign (but not the mediator).

In addition to the above, a Consent Order refers to the Court in which the dispute is to be heard, the Claim Number and the fact that the parties have agreed to compromise their action 'on the following terms...' and ending with: 'The Action will be dismissed with no order as to costs'. The Settlement Agreement then has to be registered (usually by the claimant's solicitor) with the Court for ratification.

A Tomlin Order is all the above but the settlement terms are attached as a schedule. This maintains confidentiality of the settlement terms. The Tomlin Order (face sheet) uses such wording as:

'BY CONSENT

IT IS ORDERED THAT:

1. All further proceedings in the action be stayed upon the terms set out in the Schedule attached to this order, except for the purpose of enforcing and giving effect to those terms, and
2. Each party be permitted to apply to the court for that purpose without the need to bring a new claim.'

Both the front sheet (the Consent Order) and the attachment (the Schedule) are signed by the parties.

The key to an effective Settlement Agreement, which is often drafted late in the day/evening/night/early hours (when no one is at their best), is to keep it simple. If necessary (although this rarely happens), the lawyers can enlarge the Settlement Agreement on another day – and the mediator can be available to settle any resultant disagreements. The lawyers invariably disagree over something – they are protecting their client's interests and so every word becomes important. That's why it usually takes two hours to write.

It is very rare for a Settlement Agreement to fail because it is the parties' deal – they have worked at constructing it, they have negotiated the details and they have said 'Yes' to it. They have invested in it and they are usually just pleased to put the dispute behind them and get on with life without the aggravation.

One final point – it is worth the mediator asking one of the party's representatives (probably the claimant) to bring a precedent and laptop to the mediation, ahead of time, or having a template for a Settlement Agreement on a laptop or memory stick. Some lawyers do so and most will be sensible about it, but many templates grow with obscure clauses based upon some irrelevant past experience and become cumbersome and often controversial. So the mediator having one that is 'clean', unbiased and simple may be well received.

Settling, or not

The final theoretical stage of a mediation is termed 'concluding' (rather than 'settling') because not all mediations settle on the day. Most do, especially the lower value disputes where the cost of going to court is high and disproportionate to the claim, but some don't. Of those that don't, some settle soon after because the momentum of settlement has continued and/or, in some cases, the sheer horror of returning to the litigation battle causes a party to settle on terms that were unpalatable on the day.

If the mediation does not settle on the day, it is good practice to bring the parties back together in an open session and for the mediator to:

- review the progress made from the start of the day;
- summarise the stage now reached, identifying the remaining differences;
- list what needs to be done to bridge the gap;
- agree an action plan to settlement; and
- ensure everyone has contact details in case the mediator may be of future use.

It may be valuable for the mediator to record this in a follow-up email but it is wise to get parties agreement to this as it could potentially breach confidentiality (everything that is said and produced in the mediation being confidential and without prejudice).

Aftercare

Whether or not the mediation settles, the mediator should follow-up. If it settled, it is an opportunity to build on the goodwill generated, thanking the lawyers and expressing the hope that you may work together again. If it didn't settle (and fortunately that doesn't happen very often) then it will probably have been agreed that the mediator make contact after a short period and in any case is on hand as a neutral third party if needed. Unless a new day (or half-day) of mediation has been agreed, then this follow-up work would normally not be charged.

In workplace, family or community mediations, there will always be a follow up session to review how the parties are getting along. These may be further meetings or, in community cases, a follow up call by the case manager.

Concluding Stage

Generally though, in commercial mediations, the mediator may never know what happens after the mediation day because they are history, a reminder of past miseries. The fact that the miseries have ended because of the efforts of the mediator seems to be forgotten. The parties have what they want – to end the misery and get on with their lives (and never see or need the mediator again). I often say to the parties 'I hope I never see you again,' usually following with a reframe: 'Or rather, that you never have need of me again'. However, I say the opposite to the lawyers: 'I hope I do see you again – soon!'

Concluding stage – in a nutshell

- Keep the problem and the solution with the parties.
- Encourage the decision makers to meet and agree the final deal.
- If it doesn't settle, record the progress made and agree an action plan to achieve settlement.
- Avoid making a recommendation, if at all possible.
- Avoid writing up the Settlement Agreement. If there is no-one else, make sure it is the party's wording.
- Keep the Settlement Agreement short and simple.
- Follow-up, whether or not it settled.

CASE STUDY

Open meeting

David: *I've brought us together to summarise what you have agreed and to make sure there is nothing else to sort out before Angela puts it all in writing* [Referring to the earlier flipchart sheet].

- *Chris and Jo will sign the mortgage deed.*
- *All the properties will be ringfenced, so the mortgage applies only to the land.*
- *Chris and Jo will sign over their part of the paddock and barns to Harry.*
- *Harry will sign over his share of the shop and smallholding to Chris.*
- *Harry will sign over his share of the pair of derelict cottages to Jo.*
- *Jo will sign over her share of the shop and smallholding to Chris.*
- *Chris will sign over her share of the derelict cottages to Jo.*
- *This means that Harry owns the paddock and barns outright, Chris owns the shop and smallholding outright and Jo owns the pair of derelict cottages outright.*
- *Nothing else changes. The land, farmhouse and rented cottages remain in the 40/30/30 ownership.*

Agreed?

Let me thank you for your positive approach to this – all of you. Is there anything else?

Concluding Stage

Angela: *I need to include timescales and dates.*

Harry: *I need the deed to be signed by the end of this month (that is in seven days) and the paddock and barns within a month. The rest can happen whenever.*

Chris (cross): *Oh no. It all happens at the same time. You need the deed signed in seven days, everything else happens in seven days.*

Quentin: *But you have Land Registry and other formalities to go through for the transfer of property. It will take much longer than seven days.*

Chris: *Then so will the deed signing.*

Silence. An atmosphere of resentment takes over.

David: *Harry, will the bank accept a statement of intent from Chris and Jo, so that all the paperwork can coincide?*

Harry: *I don't know. It's not ideal but I can ask it.*

David: *Can you ring them now please? It would give everyone a breathing space to get it right. All we can do today is have a Heads of Agreement which the lawyers will convert into the various contracts.*

Harry: *OK, I'll ring it now.*

Jo: *When you've done that, Chris and I need to speak with you.*

Harry: *That sounds serious.*

Jo: *Nothing that will change what we have agreed, but still important.*

David: *Right, Angela will get on with the Heads of Agreement, Harry will phone the bank. Quentin, it's 4pm, you could catch the early train!*

Quentin: *Oh no. I'm here to the end.*

David: *It will take a good half-hour for Angela to get this down in writing. I suggest you get some fresh air, go for a walk, whatever. Just be back here at 4.30pm. Chris, Jo and Harry can then have a chat. Mags and I will be in the main room if you need us. Angela – please keep it simple and let me have a copy of the draft before you circulate it. Chris and Jo – please contact your solicitor and make sure he is available for you to check the wording of the Settlement Agreement.*

Everyone returned to their rooms, David and Mags stayed in the main room.

David: *Well done Mags. Thank you for your support.*

Mags: *This has been a real privilege. Thank you. Why did you ask for a copy of the draft before it is circulated?*

David: *Writing up the deal is such a responsible job and I just want to make sure there are no nasties slipped in. If there are, I want to challenge them before they are seen by the other side, otherwise it could sabotage the deal.*

Concluding Stage

Mags: *What happens next?*

David: *I will keep an eye on Angela and the time, but our work is done really. I will check that there are no hitches over the next couple of weeks but really we are history. They want to move on and we are a reminder of the painful past. Let's spend the next half hour having a debrief.*

There weren't any nasties, except for a few minor changes, the wording was approved by Chris and Jo's solicitor and signed by Chris, Jo and Harry. The three siblings met, but no-one knows what was said. And they all left at 5pm! And would you believe it, Chris, Jo and Harry went to the pub. For some reason the lawyers and the mediator were not invited!

Mediator challenges

Concluding stage

1 **Authority**

    The deal is done and being written up by the lawyers. One party takes you aside and says that the deal exceeds his authority (he got carried away by the moment of doing a deal) and he is worried that he is going to be slaughtered when he returns to the office tomorrow. Any thoughts?

2 **Ratification**

    The deal is done but one party says that he needs to present it to the Board next week for ratification. Nothing was said about this at the start – everyone said that they had authority to settle.

    Worse, the party says, in public, that he had explained this to you before the mediation started, but you have no recollection of anything other than him saying that he was representing the Board – so what do you do?

3 **Second thoughts**

    The deal is done and the settlement ready for signing. One of the decision makers becomes very agitated and disappears into a room with her lawyer. You are called in to the room and they explain that the decision maker is having second thoughts. What do you say?

4 **Tears**

    The deal is done, but not signed. You go into one party's room and find both father and son in tears. You realise that they have been rather bullied by their lawyer into doing a deal that they feel gives no justice. You tell them that it is not too late, they haven't signed anything. Through the tears they say that they need to bring the matter to a close and want to sign anyway. Do you give them some tissues, tell them to go for a walk or open a bottle of champagne (or none of these)?

5 **CFA**

    You are aware of one party's lawyer browbeating his client into agreeing to the final offer from the other side. The lawyer is on a CFA and you suspect that he has his own agenda in getting settlement. What do you do?

Concluding Stage

6 **Better deal**

One side's lawyer, despite his conviction to the contrary, is a poor negotiator. His client has taken a back seat in the negotiations and trusts his lawyer to get him a good deal. You know that his client can get a better deal, indeed you could get an increased offer from the other side even though the lawyer is ready to accept one that is much lower. What do you do?

7 **Counsel**

Despite your efforts to the contrary, counsel is still speaking on behalf of his party. It looks as though the mediation is not going to settle but you sense that, if you can get her away from counsel, his client would be more flexible and likely to be able to achieve a settlement. You ask to see her alone but counsel says: 'No. What do you want to say to my client that you don't want to say in front of me?' How do you get out of that one?

8 **Deals with dignity**

Mediation usually enables parties to do deals with dignity. You have said to a very hard-nosed party in a negotiation that is deadlocked at £40,000/£50,000: 'If you'll split the difference I will do my best to persuade the other side without telling them that you will' (but already knowing that the other side will). He thinks for a moment and then says: 'Alright, I'll go to £42,500'. His lawyer looks shocked, expecting him to split the difference, but he is one who likes to win. Next step?

9 **VAT**

As the deal was being written up, I said: 'What about VAT?'. One side said, 'It's included,' the other side, 'No, it's not'. Suddenly the deal was 20 per cent out. How do you retrieve the situation?

10 **Too late to do the deal**

Parties are close to a deal, but it's late at night and the venue is closing. They decide to meet to conclude things the following morning, but you can't make it. By the evening the next day, you hear that the claimant's barrister (who was NOT present at the mediation) has criticised the terms reached the previous day and as a result the claimant is pulling out. What do you do?

11 **Full and final settlement**

Lawyers are drafting the Settlement Agreement and one party insists on the wording: 'full and final settlement of ALL claims, known or unknown'. The other party refuses because, they tell you in private, there is another claim surfacing, which they have not been able to finalise. Even if this had not been the case, they would not have signed up to the deal on this basis. The deal looks as though it is broken – what next?

12 **Serial user**

A lawyer who has proposed and used you for several mediations writes to you saying: 'We seem to be giving you a lot of work. What can you do for us?' How do you respond?

Chapter 9

Setting up a Mediation Practice

Introduction

Being well trained and obtaining accreditation is only the first step to becoming a successful commercial mediator. There are a lot of accredited mediators out there who have little or no work. Those that do have work usually have a 'day job' with mediations as a happy 'bolt-on'. Very few are able to generate enough income from commercial mediation to be self-supporting. But some do, and this paper is to try to help everyone get into that select and happy band.

What have you got to offer?

The first thing is to really work out what makes you different from the many other mediators looking for work. Start with the general, work up to the specific and end with the personal. General is gender, age, lawyer/non-lawyer, etc, specific is work experience, areas of expertise, qualifications, interests, any particular specialism or niche, etc, and personal is what you are good at (numbers, chairing meetings, facilitating others, rapport-building, etc). Identify your USPs (unique selling points). If nothing else this will give you the basis of a mediator profile that is much more appealing than a conventional CV. And when you write that profile, summarise your USPs at the start, so that the reader will know you are different from the other mediators being considered for work.

Create experience

No one wants to employ an inexperienced mediator, so getting experience is the first challenge. The best way is through assistantships (or 'pupillages') – accompanying lead mediators on real mediations. Most mediators mediate alone and every time that happens it is a missed opportunity. So find out the names of the established commercial mediators (Chamber's Directory is a good start) and woo them. Work out what they have to offer (specialisms, etc) and highlight your added value without appearing to be pushy (non-lawyer to a lawyer mediator, male/female to their female/male, specialist knowledge, etc). The essential requirement is availability (being prepared to go on a mediation at short notice) and making life easy for the mediator. Meeting up with them is a good move – it helps to reassure the mediator that you are safe and could be good company; the downside is that the mediator will anticipate the reason for meeting up is to get work and so you

Setting up a Mediation Practice

may meet resistance from some of the busier mediators. Cornering one at a social event is probably the best strategy! Most of us are more malleable with a drink in our hand.

A well-known American mediator was once asked: 'How did you convince people to use you when you had little or no experience?' 'I lied,' he replied. I don't advocate that but you can be creative with the extent of your experience. Every assistantship is a case to go on your profile. More than that, most cases span more than one sector (an architect's professional negligence case is, at the very least, insurance and construction and may also be property and partnership sectors) so you can be (truthfully) creative about your areas of experience.

Some newly trained commercial mediators join local community mediation groups, partly because these groups are always in need of good quality volunteers and partly because it is a way of keeping the essential mediator skills polished and effective. It is also a very rewarding (and challenging) area of work.

Personal network

The people most likely to use you as a mediator are those that already know you. So draw up a comprehensive list of contacts (business and social), grade them from 'hot' prospects to 'tepid' and make them fully aware of what mediation is and what you have to offer. Use these contacts to make more – ask them for names of people they know who might be interested. If they are willing, get them to introduce you so that your approach is not 'cold'. Every contact you make has the potential of more contacts and your personal network can rapidly grow. But don't lose sight of the fact that the best contacts are the 'hot' ones that know you – so keep them hot.

Joining mediator groups/panels

There are several mediator groupings in the UK, the most established being the Association of Northern Mediators and the Association of Midland Mediators. These are groupings set up primarily for mutual support, the sharing of experience and the development of mediation as a profession. Whether or not they lead to work, they are a very worthwhile source of meeting other people who operate in what is generally a very solitary profession.

At the time of writing, there are just over 60 mediation providers (bodies offering the services of mediators) in the United Kingdom accredited with the Civil Mediation Council. Accreditation gives the providers access to the court schemes, which is where most inexperienced mediators get their first cases. With so many mediators (and providers) around, most providers are now stipulating an entry level for their panel of mediators and so it can be quite hard to get accepted. Even being on the panel does not guarantee getting any cases and so it can take some time to gather a body of experience, and therefore confidence. But it is one of several possible routes to getting appointments.

Setting up a Mediation Practice

Marketing

Aside from your own network of contacts, there is a huge body of potential users of mediation that are ignorant and in need of knowing the benefits that mediation offers. The problem is reaching them. Most commercial cases are controlled by lawyers and so they are the gatekeepers to appointments. Law firms generally have their own 'pet' mediator list and it can be quite difficult to break through that barrier. The obvious target is therefore business itself – after all, it is business that stands the most to gain from mediating disputes, not the lawyers. Breakfast/lunchtime/early evening awareness seminars to businesses, Chambers of Commerce and professional institute branches can spread the message and your name. The best form of awareness event is a commentated demonstration,[1] although it is very difficult to fit one into an hour.

As far as marketing materials are concerned, hard copy materials (other than business cards) rarely justify their cost but having an attractive one-page electronic information sheet is a useful follow-up for any contact. A smart, quality business card is always an asset, especially if it includes a photograph (no-one recalls a face from a card received six months ago). This can be the most effective way of getting your name known most widely.

A lot of people use the writing of articles for professional journals as a way of getting their name known. The trouble is that general articles on mediation have already been written and so editors are now looking for more focussed or specialised articles which are only really possible with experience.

Conclusion

As with most new businesses, it takes a lot of time, patience and determination to get a mediation practice established. It is a long-term project, probably (unless you are lucky or have a ready-made market) requiring at least two years before the investment yields return. Your best strategy is to:

- capitalise on your USP;
- work your personal network;
- sweet-talk an experienced lead mediator (or two) for assistantships;
- design an attractive information sheet and quality business card; and
- join an active mediator association.

And remember – mediation is a life-changing experience, both for the party and for you. It is a privilege to be involved, and worth the frustration and cost of getting there.

Good luck!

---

1   See www.mata.org.uk for a library of roleplay case studies.

Chapter 10

An Overview of the English Legal System[1]

The purpose of this chapter is to provide a brief guide to English law and legal procedures for the assistance of mediators who are not legally qualified or who are not normally involved in dispute resolution.

It is a general explanation of certain legal principles which may frequently be encountered by mediators. It is intended to assist non-lawyer and non-contentious lawyer mediators in a better understanding of legal points which may arise in a mediation, particularly where parties are unrepresented.

Note: This chapter is believed to contain an accurate statement of the issues it covers at the time of writing. However, by its general nature, and its purpose, it does not purport to be a detailed exposition of the law on any particular topic, or to be exhaustive, and should not be relied upon as such.

The court system

With some exceptions, mediations tend to involve parties to disputes which, if not settled by agreement, are potentially the subject of legal proceedings in the civil courts (High Court or County Court) or, if the subject of the dispute arises from a relationship between an employer and an employee (or prospective or former employee) the employment tribunal.

The County Court or, in cases of complexity or high value, the High Court, has the jurisdiction to determine most types of dispute. Most disputes before the County Courts or High Courts are brought in respect of a claimed breach of contract (failure to comply with a legally binding agreement) or tort (an action or inaction regarded by the law as amounting to a civil wrong giving rise to an entitlement to compensation, referred to in legal terms as 'damages'). Both of these are discussed below.

Claims in employment tribunals are brought in respect of a number of specific types of claim where the tribunal is given jurisdiction to deal with a work related dispute such as unfair dismissal or discrimination on certain prohibited grounds.

---

1 © Grant Goodlad February 2008, revised June 2013 With additions from Jane Gunn and David Richbell.

Generally speaking, the types of case which can be dealt with in the court system and the tribunal system are separate and distinct each from the other. In other words, claims which can be brought in the courts cannot be brought in the tribunals, and vice versa. There are some exceptions to this: claims for breach of a contract of employment or outstanding salary at termination of employment, can be brought in either the court system or the tribunal system, although in the latter compensation is currently limited to £25,000.

As a result of these differences in jurisdiction, a dispute may involve both systems. For example it is not uncommon for a dispute to involve dismissal with allegations harmful to a person's reputation. In such a case the fairness or otherwise of the dismissal would fall to be decided by an employment tribunal. The claim for defamation (a tort) would be dealt with by the court system.

The distinction between the two systems is of particular importance so far as costs are concerned. 'Costs' is the concept of the successful party recovering all or most of its legal fees from the unsuccessful party. This is covered in more detail below but in general terms, the successful party is likely to recover costs in a case brought in the court system, whereas in an employment tribunal, each side normally pays its own costs irrespective of the outcome.

Prior to July 2013 there was a further financial distinction between the two systems. In a court case, fees are payable to the Court Service by a party bringing a claim. On 29 July 2013 new legislation took effect providing for fees to be payable to bring a claim in the employment tribunal.

The Court Rules

Civil courts and employment tribunals have their own separate rules of procedure. In the case of the civil courts these are the Civil Procedure Rules 1998 (CPR). The equivalent in the employment tribunals is the Employment Tribunals (Constitution and Rules of Procedure) Regulations 2004.

The Civil Procedure Rules came into force on 1 April 1999. They were intended as a shake up of the previous system, which was thought to be expensive and to permit delays, or at least not to be sufficiently robust as to deter delays. To an extent they have succeeded in reducing delay. Cases are now being dealt with more quickly, at least at the lower value end where there is no particular complexity or reason why the case should not be heard sooner rather than later.

Similarly, the Rules are now designed to reduce expense, particularly in lower value cases. Thus:

- cases are now allocated by the court to one of three tracks;
- the track largely depends upon the likely value of the case, although there is discretion to take into account complexity in addition to value; and
- the court will allocate more time and resources to the higher value and more complex cases and, in terms of the costs allowed to the successful party, will expect the litigants and their lawyers to do the same.

The three tracks are:

(1) The small claims track – this is for cases where the sum in issue does not exceed £10,000, or if it includes a claim for personal injury, the value of the compensation for the injury itself (as opposed to resulting financial losses) does not exceed £1,000.

(2) The fast track – this is for claims between £10,000 and £25,000.

(3) The multi track for higher value and more complex claims.

Allocation of the court's resources and costs varies depending on which track is followed.

In the small claims track (up to £10,000), there is frequently no appearance at court to deal with preliminary issues. A district judge usually considers the claim and defence on paper and specifies the steps to be taken by the parties to prepare for a hearing. The hearing itself may last only 90 minutes and is often relatively informal, and the successful party is not usually awarded costs against the other party (unless that party, exceptionally, has acted unreasonably in the conduct of the case) but may recover a limited amount of fixed fees, court fees and witness expenses.

In a fast track case (from £10,000–£25,000), there may be a case management conference at which the parties have the opportunity to discuss with a judge what steps are necessary to prepare for trial. Nevertheless, the Court will be concerned to limit the time committed to the case. For example, if expert evidence is required, it may be limited to one expert in total rather than one for each side. This is on the basis that expert witnesses are now required to be impartial. Further, the parties have the opportunity to jointly appoint an expert witness. Alternatively, each party has the chance to put questions to an expert witness, irrespective of who appointed the expert. The successful party usually recovers costs from the losing party. However, those costs are normally assessed summarily on the day of the hearing and there are limits on what can be recovered.

In multi track cases, the procedure is more flexible to cater for the circumstances of the particular case. There may be several case management conferences to track the progress of the case, and expert evidence is likely to be permitted from both sides, with different experts from different disciplines where this is necessary. The trial hearing, when reached, is less likely to be so limited in time. It may last several days, or more, depending upon the circumstances of the case. The successful party is likely to recover costs against the loser. However, the issue of what costs are recovered against whom can be complex. When there are several issues and one party succeeds on some and the other on others, the situation becomes even more complex, and there are specialist costs judges who deal with these issues. Preparing for that also adds to expense, risk and so a party's incentive to settle.

In all cases, albeit to the different degrees and timetables the court might fix, the minimum parties will have to do to prepare for a court trial are:

- set out their cases in 'pleadings' – formal statements of their claim or defence, as the case may be;
- attend court to discuss, or at least receive on paper court orders to follow, the steps to be taken to ensure that the case is ready for hearing when timetabled;

- disclose documents relevant to the issues in the case (whether or not they help the case of the party in whose possession they are); and

- exchange signed statements of the witnesses of fact to be relied on.

The court also has specific powers to control proceedings in the case of disobedience of its rules or orders, or where one party or the other has a hopeless case. In the case of one party's failure to comply with a rule or order of the court, the other may apply for an order that the case of the party in default be struck out. The court may impose sanctions, including a strike-out, for failure to comply. In so doing, the court must act in a way that is proportionate to the default. Such sanctions normally include an order for the defaulting party to pay the legal costs wasted by the other party by reason of the default. It is not usual for the court to immediately strike out the party concerned; normally it would give that party the opportunity to correct the default. A party that has been struck out or had some other sanction applied is entitled to apply to the court for relief from sanctions. The Court Rules also give the court power to strike out a case that has no reasonable prospect of success, on the application of the other party. So, a claimant may apply to strike out a defence or a defendant may apply to strike-out a claim. A claimant may make such an application even before a defence is served.

All applications of these types are made by way of application notice supported by evidence (a witness statement or affidavit, and any relevant documents).

Redress through the court system

Most, but not all, claims are for damages (payment of monetary compensation). However there are other remedies available through the court system.

Damages are regarded as a legal remedy; other remedies are 'equitable'. The distinction is historic based on an archaic distinction between the courts of law and the courts of equity, which were merged many years ago. Damages are calculated in accordance with specific legal principles. Whilst there may be a dispute as to the amount of damages, and competing evidence from both sides, the court must come to a finding as to the amount and award damages to a party who has established liability against the other. The principles by which damages are calculated in claims for breach of contract and in claims for negligence are set out in later sections of this paper which deal with those specific types of claim.

The most common type of equitable remedy sought is an injunction. That is, an order made by the court requiring a party to refrain from doing (or less usually, to do) a particular act. Such orders are commonly sought, for example, to restrain a trespass (unlawful entry onto another's land) or to enforce restrictive covenants (terms of a contract of employment preventing a departing employee from soliciting his former employer's clients). As these are equitable remedies, the court has a discretion whether or not to grant them and will take into account factors such as:

- whether the party seeking the remedy has acted promptly; and

- whether granting the remedy sought would affect the rights of third parties not involved in the litigation.

An Overview of the English Legal System

The Court has jurisdiction to grant a number of other remedies, for example it can review the decisions of public bodies on the application of a properly interested party or pronounce on the validity of a will. Detailed discussion of those matters is, however, outside of the general nature of this chapter.

Limitation periods

There are time limits for bringing a claim before the court. The rules can be complex in the way that they are applied and the description below attempts to give a general guide.

The time limit will depend upon the type of claim that is being brought. It will also depend upon the status of the person wishing to bring the claim, in that time does not run against a person who is regarded by the court as 'under a disability'. This means that time does not begin to run against a child until he or she reaches the age of majority, and it does not run against a person whilst that person is regarded as a 'patient' (ie, lacks mental capacity). The time limits referred to in the following paragraphs are therefore subject to those points.

In the case of a claim for personal injury:

- the limitation period is three years;
- the three years run from the date upon which the claimant knew or ought to have known that he or she had suffered injury for which the defendant is liable;
- that date is readily identifiable in simple cases, such as a road traffic accident causing immediate injury. However it may be an issue in more complex cases such as those involving clinical negligence; and
- the court has discretion to allow a claim to be brought late and there is a checklist of factors to be taken into account in deciding whether to exercise that discretion. Most important is whether or not a fair trial is still possible notwithstanding the late issue of proceedings.

In the case of claims for breach of contract, or for negligence other than that causing personal injury:

- the limitation period is six years;
- in a breach of contract case, the six years run from the date of the breach;
- in a negligence case, the six years run from the date upon which damage (loss) was caused by the negligence complained of;
- this again can cause difficulty in cases where the damage is latent, such as the negligent design of a building that initially appears sound but later deteriorates; and
- in cases of such latent damage there is an extension of time such that the limitation period does not start to run until the damage ought reasonably to have been apparent, but subject to an overall 'longstop' period of 15 years.

In the case of a claim brought under the terms of a deed (a document executed under seal such as a lease or a mortgage), the limitation period is 12 years from the date upon which the claim arose.

Other rules apply in cases of fraud, or where the party has fraudulently concealed information. Those are complex and beyond the general nature of this chapter.

Costs and funding

In cases other than those dealt with under the small claims track, the usual rule is that 'costs follow the event', that is that the loser pays the winner's costs reasonably incurred in bringing the case. Because costs are in the discretion of the Court there are some exceptions to this, such as:

- the possibility that the court may deprive the successful party of all or some of its costs if that party has unreasonably refused mediation or other attempts at ADR;
- in cases where there are several issues, a costs order based upon the parties' respective success on each issue may be considered as opposed to the overall outcome, particularly where a party succeeds on limited issues of low value compared to the totality of the claim brought; and
- where a claimant has failed to do better at trial than that claimant would have done by accepting an offer of settlement made by the defendant pursuant to Pt 36 CPR (as to which see more below).

If an award of costs is made, it is usually made on the 'standard' rather than the 'indemnity' basis. If the court's order as to costs is silent as to which basis is to apply, then it is deemed to be the standard basis. The difference between the two affects how the court approaches the assessment of the costs to be paid. If costs are assessed on the standard basis then any doubt as to whether the costs incurred by the receiving party were reasonably incurred is to be resolved in favour of the paying party. If costs are assessed on the indemnity basis, then any doubt as to whether the costs incurred by the receiving party were reasonably incurred is to be resolved in favour of the receiving party. In other words, an award of costs on the indemnity basis is more generous than an award on the standard basis. Such an award is also somewhat punitive in nature.

When and how the costs are assessed will usually depend upon whether the claim is dealt with at a fast track trial or a multi-track trial. At a fast track trial, the costs of the successful party are usually summarily assessed there and then at the end of the trial. The parties are therefore required to exchange schedules giving a breakdown of costs no later than the day before trial, and they are expected to be in a position to deal with costs arguments at the conclusion of the trial. In the case of a multi-track trial, issues of costs are likely to be more complex and the usual order is for there to be a detailed assessment. The question of costs is therefore adjourned to a later hearing, possibly conducted by a specialist costs judge. the party receiving the costs is then required to serve a bill of costs giving a detailed breakdown of the costs claimed. The party paying the costs is required to serve points of objection to which the receiving party responds. The Court then carries out an assessment at a further hearing.

Whether costs are assessed by way of summary or detailed assessment, the court will take into account the same factors in assessing whether the costs are reasonable. Those factors are:

- the time spent in working on the case;
- the grade of the fee earner who carried out the work. This is based on the assessment by the court of the degree of qualification and experience required to conduct the case;
- the hourly rate charged. The court looks at guideline rates for each court location;
- whether disbursements (other expenses incurred such as expert's fees) are reasonable; and
- having considered those other factors, whether the costs incurred are proportionate to amounts in issue.

Notwithstanding this last factor, in lower value cases (particularly on the fast track) costs can exceed the amount in dispute. Even in higher value cases, costs can be a significant figure in relation to the amount in dispute.

The position on costs can be affected by settlement offers made prior to trial. Whilst the court cannot be informed of without prejudice discussions (see the section on 'without prejudice' later), the court rules make provision for specific settlement offers to be taken into account where costs are concerned. Those provisions are contained in Pt 36 of the CPR and are referred to as Part 36 offers. Prior to the CPR there was provision for a defendant to make a payment into court. Part 36 is the equivalent under the new rules. Either party may make a Part 36 offer, open for acceptance for 21 days, and each has consequences if not accepted by the other and not beaten at court. If a claimant fails to recover at trial more than a defendant's Part 36 offer then the consequences are that the claimant will not recover from the defendant costs incurred from the last date on which the offer could have been accepted, and the claimant will be required to pay the costs incurred by the defendant since that date.

If the claimant recovers more at trial than was offered to be accepted in a claimant's Part 36 offer then the consequences are that the defendant is required to pay indemnity costs from the last date upon which the offer could have been accepted, and the defendant is required to pay enhanced interest on the amount awarded to the claimant and interest on the claimant's costs incurred from the same date.

The way in which a party is funded can also be relevant. If a party is not personally paying its own costs than this can affect the approach of both the party and its representatives at a mediation. If a party is not privately paying for legal representation, the most usual alternatives are funding by:

- legal expenses Insurance;
- public funding by the Legal Services Commission (formerly known as Legal Aid);
- a Conditional Fee Agreement (prior to 1 April 2013); or
- a Damages Based Agreement (since 1 April 2013).

In the case of legal expenses insurance, the insurer will usually only support the case as long as the party's legal representative (often chosen by the insurer) advises a better than 50 per cent chance of success. The party is unlikely to be personally at risk regarding costs of either side as the insurer will meet these. The opposing party is likely to be aware that any adverse costs order against the insured party will be met by the insurers. The insurance premium is normally an allowable cost if the claimant succeeds or settles. Problems may arise because the claimant feels that there is no pressure to settle as the costs are insured if the claim does not succeed. Alternatively, because the insurer will have a say in the eventual settlement, there may be more pressure to settle.

In the case of a publicly funded party, that party is likely to be relatively impecunious as public funding is a means-tested benefit, so the prospects of that party having to pay costs personally are remote. That party's legal advisers will be under a duty to the Legal Services Commission to report if that party is abusing public funding and upon prospects of success. The opposing party is likely to be aware that the prospects of recovering costs from the publicly funded party are remote; they must be informed of the fact that the party has public funding. If the funded party settles, the legal costs covered by the funding must be repaid from the settlement figure. Problems may arise because the funded party is not under pressure to settle. However, its lawyer has a responsibility to avoid additional legal costs if a settlement is reasonable, and so the party may be strongly influenced by its lawyer to agree a reasonable deal.

In the case of a conditional fee agreement, there is an agreement between a party and its legal representatives whereby the representative will not be paid if the case is not successful but will be paid an uplift on usual fees if the case succeeds. It is important to define 'succeeds' as it may influence settlement within a mediation. There will also be an insurance taken out on behalf of the party concerned against any adverse costs order. On an assessment of costs, the court will be entitled to increase the base costs to reflect a reasonable success fee. In some cases the court has no discretion and is required to allow a 100 per cent success fee. The success fee is meant to reward the lawyer for taking the risk on the case. The lower the perceived risk, the lower the enhancement – so a low risk case may have an enhancement of 25 per cent on the lawyer's basic rate, a high risk case may be 100 per cent. Hence lawyers do not want the other side to know the percentage as it would reveal their risk assessment. Problems arise because the threat of litigation is less incentive to settle in the mediation and so the lawyer may put pressure on their client to settle – in other words, the lawyer has an interest in the outcome. Also, opposing lawyers love to challenge the level of fees and uplift, endangering the other side's lawyer/client relationship.

In the case of a damages based agreement, this type of agreement has replaced a conditional fee agreement where the funding agreement is entered into on or after 1 April 2013. Like a CFA, the lawyer will not be paid if the claim does not succeed; however, if the claim does succeed, the unsuccessful party will only be liable for the basic legal costs incurred by the successful party, The unsuccessful party will not be responsible for the uplift or success fee charged by the lawyers for the successful party. That will be payable by the successful party from his or her damages, subject to a maximum percentage of the damages recovered, and limited to certain elements of the damages award (in personal injury cases, 25 per cent of damages, excluding those awarded for future care and loss, in employment tribunal cases, 35 per cent of awards). In personal injury cases, general damages are to be increased by 10 per cent as a quid pro quo for this change. In such cases 'qualified one way costs shifting' is to apply. This means that a costs order in favour of a defendant will not usually be enforceable against an unsuccessful claimant, and will only be enforceable against a claimant who is successful but fails to beat a defendant's Part 36 settlement offer, to the extent of the damages he or she is awarded.

Employment tribunals

The Employment Tribunal Rules of Procedure are less detailed or prescriptive than those of the courts, but there is still some formality and common features.

The employment tribunal has its equivalent of pleadings in that the claimant must set out his claim in a claim form (which must contain certain prescribed information) and the respondent must set out its defence in a response form.

Awards by tribunals are limited in certain cases:

- an award for breach of contract is limited to £25,000;
- awards for unfair dismissal consist of two elements, a basic award and a compensatory award;
- the basic award is calculated in a similar fashion to a statutory redundancy payment and is a function of length of service (maximum 20 years taken into account), age (factor of 0.5 for service under 21, 1 for service between 21 and 41 and 1.5 for service over 41) and gross week's pay (maximum £450 for dismissals on or after 1 February 2013) – thus the maximum basic award is £13,500 (i.e. 20 years service x age factor 1.5 × £450);
- the compensatory award is to compensate for financial losses suffered as a result of the employee being unfairly dismissed and is subject to a maximum of £74,200, again for dismissals taking effect from 1 February 2013;
- the tribunal also has the power to order an employer to reinstate or re-engage the employee. If the employer fails to comply further compensation can amount to a minimum of 26 weeks and a maximum of 52 weeks' pay. This is again subject to a maximum, currently £450 per week;
- the limits on a week's pay and the compensatory award are increased annually with effect from 1 February in each year;
- the applicable limit in unfair dismissal cases is that applicable at the time the dismissal was effective, not the later date of the employment tribunal hearing giving rise to the award; and
- awards for unlawful discrimination are uncapped. They frequently include not only financial losses but also awards for injury to feelings and personal injury (usually psychiatric injury caused by the discrimination).

There are time limits for the bringing of a claim and the lodging of a response. Compared to the limitation periods for court proceedings, the time limits in the employment tribunal are relatively short. For most types of claim, the time limit is three months from the date of the act complained of (or date of termination of employment in unfair dismissal cases).

Employment tribunals have the power to make orders requiring disclosure of documents and exchange of witness statements in a similar fashion to the civil courts, and frequently exercise that power. Tribunals also have the power to strike out a party's case at an early stage, if that case stands no reasonable prospect of success. There is also power to strike out for non-compliance with orders made by the tribunal, in similar fashion to the civil courts.

Each party normally bears its own legal costs of representation in the employment tribunal, irrespective of the outcome. However, the tribunal has the power to award costs if a party or its representative has acted unreasonably in the bringing or conduct of its claim or defence. For the purpose of awarding costs, acting unreasonably includes bringing a claim or raising a defence that has no reasonable prospect of success.

Contract

A contract is a legally enforceable bargain between two or more parties. In the event of breach of its terms by one party, the other frequently seeks damages in the form of money compensation. For a contract to be legally enforceable there must be:

- an offer by one party (for example to supply goods and/or services);
- acceptance by the other party;
- supported by 'consideration'. Consideration is what is provided by the second party in return for that supplied by the first. An example would be the price for goods and/or services. Whilst the law will only recognise a legally binding contract if there is consideration, the law is not concerned with the adequacy of that consideration. In other words, the fact that the agreed price may be unreasonably low is not a reason to refuse to perform the contract – even a token £1 can constitute sufficient consideration;
- certainty, which means that the terms of the contract can be identified sufficiently to understand and enforce the bargain made between the parties; and
- an intention to create contractual relations. This will invariably be the case in a commercial situation but the issue might also arise, for example, in contractual disputes within a family.

Contracts may be oral or written. Commercial contracts are frequently reduced to writing, often with very detailed specifications as to what is to be performed, and terms as to how and when payment is to be made. Whilst in general, parties are free to contract on whatever terms they wish, there are some restrictions, for example:

- the Unfair Contract Terms Act 1977 renders void any attempt by contractual term to exclude liability for death or personal injury caused by the negligence of the person seeking to rely upon that term; and
- consumer protection legislation contains provisions protecting individuals who contract as a consumer, for example by requiring a company relying upon standard forms to show that its terms are reasonable, or by providing for a 'cooling off' period.

The 'measure of damages' (calculation of compensation) for breach of contract is the sum required to put the innocent party in the position it would have been in had the contract been performed in accordance with its terms.

Negligence and personal injury

Negligence is one category of what the law describes as a 'tort'. That is a legal wrong done by one party to another, which entitles that other to bring a claim for legal redress. Other examples of torts are trespass (unlawful presence on another's land) or battery (physical assault).

To establish a claim in negligence, a claimant must show that:

- the defendant owed to the claimant a duty of care (normally a duty to act to a reasonable standard within the relevant field);
- the defendant was in breach of that duty; and
- the claimant suffered loss caused by the breach, provided that loss is not too 'remote'.

In some instances, there may be concurrent claims for breach of contract and for negligence. This is common in claims against professionals for breach of both a contractual and a tortious duty of care.

Personal injury claims are frequently brought in negligence, often arising out of road traffic or workplace accidents but also in clinical negligence cases. In each of those cases it is long established that a driver, employer, or doctor owes a duty of care to other road users, employees or patients respectively.

Breach of the duty causing loss gives rise to a claim for damages. The measure of damages is the sum required to put the innocent party in the position s/he would have been in had the negligence not occurred. In the case of negligence causing purely financial losses, this is simply a monetary calculation. In the case of negligence causing personal injuries, losses incurred may include either or both financial losses and compensation for the injuries themselves.

Financial losses may include losses incurred to date of trial or settlement and losses projected into the future. Those losses typically include loss of earnings, costs of care, travel expenses etc.

Compensation for injuries themselves is referred to as 'general damages' for pain, suffering and loss of amenity. Quantification of this is not an exact science but is by reference to guidelines published by the Judicial Studies Board and to previous cases involving similar injuries.

Confidentiality and without prejudice

There are two aspects whereby courts may be asked to uphold a legal duty of confidentiality:

(1) by refusing to admit in evidence before the court matters which are confidential; or
(2) by granting an injunction – a court order restraining a breach of confidentiality.

A legal right of confidentiality may arise by contractual agreement, whereby a term of a contract between the parties requires one or both to keep certain matters confidential, or by reason of the relationship between the parties. In certain relationships, a duty of confidentiality is recognised to exist, for example:

- between doctor and patient, the doctor's professional duties including a duty of medical confidentiality; and
- between qualified lawyer (solicitor or barrister) and the client, there being a duty of confidentiality referred to as 'legal privilege'.

Whilst these various types of confidentiality prevent disclosure of confidential information to third parties, different considerations apply where there are legal duties of disclosure of information to public bodies (such as the police) or to the courts.

English law does not regard contractual or medical confidentiality as absolute. So, for example, a party subject to contractual or medical confidentiality may be required to break that confidentiality and disclose information to the police or to the courts to comply with legislation or a court order. Legal privilege affords greater protection to confidential information because it is recognised that as a matter of public policy individuals should be free to seek legal advice without risk of adverse consequences. Legal privilege cannot be broken by court order or to comply with legislation save in exceptional circumstances such as those involving terrorism and money laundering.

Without prejudice discussions and correspondence enjoy a particular form of confidentiality. Without prejudice discussions or communications are those entered into for the purpose of seeking to resolve a dispute out of court. Again, this is a matter of public policy, as it is recognised to be in the public interest that parties should be free to explore settlement of disputes without the risk that this will be held against them if that exploration is unsuccessful and the dispute is heard in court. If a discussion or communication is without prejudice, properly so called, then it may not be referred to before the court hearing the case has come to a decision (otherwise than subsequently in respect of costs).

An offer may be made by either party to settle a case 'without prejudice save as to costs'. There is a particular mechanism within the Civil Procedure Rules (Pt 36) which specifies how such an offer should be made. A Part 36 offer, or offer in similar terms in other proceedings, may be revealed to the court after a decision has been made but before the issue of costs is dealt with. If the successful party at court had been made a Part 36 or similar offer which was not accepted but which is equal to or better than the court's award, then that party may be penalised in costs incurred since the date by which that offer could have been accepted.

Communications in the course of mediation are confidential, both contractually (there should be a confidentiality provision in the Agreement to Mediate) and under the without prejudice rule, as the purpose of mediation is to facilitate an out-of-court settlement.

Appendix 1

Responses to Mediator Challenges

Note: I have experienced all the following challenges, except one. The responses are what happened in the real situation – they are not necessarily the right one or the only one, just the real one as I lived it.

Preparing stage

1 Conflict of interest

The rule should be 'if in doubt, disclose'. As a non-lawyer mediator I have rarely encountered possible conflicts. On one occasion I felt that repeat business from an insurer might be an issue but the other party accepted it – possibly because the insurer was paying the full mediation fee. In fact, it was a long time before I was appointed by them again, so it ceased to be a possible issue.

2 Papers

In each case we agreed to go ahead. No matter who has caused the delay, mediators can 'only work with what they've got'. If that means no papers, and the parties still want the mediation to go ahead, then so be it. A good mediator should be able to mediate a case with no papers or foreknowledge of the case, although it is not ideal.

I now send reminders to the lawyers a few days before the date I have said I would be preparing, and again the night before if they haven't arrived. The sad fact is, many lawyers – barristers particularly – tend to ignore the mediator's timetable and consider their own to be more important.

3 Support documents

This is particularly common with construction disputes. After checking what is there, I telephone the lawyer who compiled the documents (or both if there were separate bundles), tell them that there is at least a day's reading involved and ask them to prioritise the order in which I (slowly) read them or agree to pay for the extra hours of preparation. It is their problem, not the mediators.

4 Inflammatory summary

In this case I persuaded the lawyer that the mediation should continue as everyone was prepared for it and had set the time aside. I did agree to speak with the lawyer and explain the fact that the summary had not been well received by the other side. His response was 'That's Bill [the counsel] for you – he's just like that in court'. I responded that this was not a court and I expected a bit of courtesy and co-operation on the day.

Not that my comments made any difference. Counsel was just as provocative in person and, although the mediation settled, he made it a very uncomfortable experience.

Opening stage

1 Participants

On the face of it, this was a very provocative move on the part of the ex-partner and it caused real consternation at the start. He denied that was his intention and asked me to take a message to the other side apologising and saying that he had brought his 'new' partner for support as he was worried about the mediation and meeting again with his former partner. It was agreed that the new partner would remain in the private room and not be a part of the open session.

In a similar case where one side turned up to the mediation with a former employee of the other side, unannounced, the mediation was almost sabotaged until it was agreed that the former employee should leave and be obtainable by phone if needed.

2 Joint session

I succumbed on two occasions and regretted it both times. The mediation soon deadlocked and we had to go back to having an open session, but three hours later.

I now respond by saying that mediation is a different forum to litigation, not least because it is party-centred. It is a process that works – and then I mention the two occasions when I succumbed and it failed. They have always agreed to have an open session, albeit reluctantly, and it has always worked.

3 No honest intent

I never believe them. Mediation is a seductive process and many times a reluctant party has grabbed the opportunity of doing a deal and ending their legal battle. If it turns out to be true, it is the parties who decide not to continue, not the mediator. The mediator should always be the last to leave.

4 Counsel

Whenever counsel are present they invariably assume the role of spokesperson, negotiator and deal-maker. Some are more controlling than others but it always changes the dynamic from a party-centred process to a lawyer-centred one. I try to explain in the initial private meeting before the open session that this is an opportunity for the parties to be in control, supported by the lawyers. It rarely has any effect!

In this case, having done all that, I had a private word with counsel (who is a renowned and expensive QC), explaining that I needed to speak with his client direct and not through him. It made little difference and it became obvious that counsel had his own agenda and it was not to settle in mediation. The case did eventually settle six months, and £1 million more in legal fees, later.

5 Decision maker

A missing or absent (ie not intending to be present at all) decision maker makes settlement in mediation so much harder. In this case I had private meetings with each side until he arrived and then, after he had been briefed, had the open session with him present.

6 Room allocation

This is not an unusual experience, though sometimes it is purely a thoughtless act, and it more than justifies me getting to the venue an hour before the mediation starts so that such things can be sorted, preferably before anyone else arrives. I always talk through the problem with the host lawyer, asking them why they have allocated the rooms as they have. Whatever their reason I will say that it is to their advantage to have the other side as comfortable and relaxed as possible, not overheated and frayed by lunchtime. I will also explain the disadvantage of their 'private' room also being the one for the open sessions and that there is a potential loss of confidentiality. If all else fails I will (charmingly) badger their receptionist or facilities manager for an allocation of better rooms. It is so important to start the mediation well and a welcoming, well-provided room with natural light is part of that.

7 Key document

Difficult one. In the end the parties have to be responsible for what they do and how well they prepare. Right or not, I didn't feel able to remind the building owner's team of the letter but I did draw the barrister's attention to it in their private room. He was shocked by its existence and he changed to a much more conciliatory approach for the rest of the mediation. Not sure if I would do the same thing if it happened again.

8 Brown envelope

This is the one that did not happen to me – although I await the situation with interest! I cannot see any situation where it would be acceptable – the question really is whether to tell the other side about the offer, or not. I don't think I would tell them because it was done in confidence and anyway would be likely to affect the other side's perception on the offering party.

Responses to Mediator Challenges

In the early days a mediation organisation tried a success-fee model whereby the organisation received no fee (although the mediator did) if the mediation did not settle. It folded in less than a year. Even though the mediator received a fee, there was huge pressure on getting a deal and so the mediator had a vested interest in the outcome anyway. Not a good situation in which to be a neutral.

9 Demonised party

Again, not an unusual situation. One of the great advantages of the initial open session is that parties face each other and have to accept they are both human and have emotions. On the other hand, the mediator cannot force a party into attending an open session so I usually explain the benefits and, if they are still adamant, I will agree but suggest we have one later in the day. That usually does happen because the party has settled into the process and feels comfortable with the mediator. I always say: 'I don't want anyone to feel disadvantaged by this – you all have the right to bring the meeting to an end if you are unhappy. Just say you want a break or need to discuss something in private.'

10 Crowd control

There were three issues in this case – one party being unrepresented, the second being the unexpected crowd and the third that one party was alone. In fact in this case both parties were unrepresented, so I had spoken with both beforehand about the possible downside and suggested that they had their solicitor's contact details in case they needed to check anything. The fact that one party was alone was an issue I had addressed before the mediation. I urged the party to bring a companion because it was likely to be a long day and there would be idle times. He responded that he was happy with his own company and would bring some work to do. It was the unexpected crowd that was the main issue. The party explained that they were there to support her. I explained the surprise and imbalance of the teams and that I needed to check with the solitary party. In the event he wasn't worried and thought it rather funny. When I went back to the other party she said that they had decided only three of them would meet with the solitary party, the others would stay in their private room. It worked.

The problem with this sort of situation is that the supporters tend to 'wind up' the party and so become a potential blockage to settlement, especially if they are not involved in all the meetings. In this case the parties acted sensibly and they achieved a settlement.

11 Urgent text

It should be an absolute rule that the mediator's phone be turned off during the mediation. The mediator's attention should be totally focussed on that day's mediation and not be distracted by anything, urgent or not. I realise that not every mediator has the same strict policy. In fact I ask that everyone's phones be turned off whenever I am in a meeting with them.

In this case I apologised and switched the phone off. However, there is a big difference in having the phone off all day, and therefore being in ignorance of any issue, and knowing that there is an urgent problem. I actually asked permission to respond to the text, and they agreed.

Exploring stage

1 Assertive lawyer

I hate being told what to do, especially by someone who is less experienced than me, and not a mediator at that. I realised that I was starting to show my irritation, so I asked for a quiet word in private. I thanked him for being so helpful but requested that he now focussed his energies on getting the best deal for his client whilst I focussed my energies on managing the process. He did, and I did!

2 Needs

This was a case of the party not telling his story in the initial open session. He was silent and said' 'My solicitor has said it all'. His solicitor hadn't and I was getting it unadulterated in the private session. There was a whole mixture of emotion – broken trust (both friend and wife), failed business, desire for revenge, wanting the other guy to suffer. We spent a lot of time talking through all these issues – the strongest being revenge. His former business partner showed no sign of remorse at what had happened, both with the wife and the business. Eventually the aggrieved party accepted that his greatest need was to bring the whole sad affair (pun intended!) to an end, as he was close to a nervous breakdown, and to move on. The final deal was painful for both of them.

3 Arithmetical error

My first reaction was to say 'Part of my role is to oversee a deal that will stick. What will happen if they find out after signing a Settlement Agreement?' I then thought 'What will happen if they then realise that I knew about the error?' Neither response was very commendable. The fact is a mediator should not condone, let alone participate in, underhand tactics by a party. The lawyer relented and agreed that the other side should be told. When I did, they said that they already knew about the error and it just meant that their negotiating margin was much smaller!

4 No money

I challenged her wish to keep the information confidential but she asked for some other issues to be addressed first. I asked in the other room if they had done a credit check on the defendant's business (normal practice for the claimant lawyer). They said they had and that she had nothing. Their purpose in investing in the mediation was to be sure that she was genuine and that she had nothing outside the United Kingdom. If they were sure, then they wanted to make a proposal for some consultancy in lieu of payment. If they hadn't known about her situation, I would have urged her to reveal the information rather than allow the other side's to negotiate a deal in ignorance. I think that would have been bad faith and would not have worked.

5 Unrepresented party

My experience is that it is rare in commercial mediation for a party to be unrepresented. When it does happen (probably because the party doesn't have the money or the claim value is so low that it doesn't justify a lawyer being present), I always talk through the implication with the party and explore the possible downside – this case being an example. I also say in the first opening session that I will encourage the party to check the Settlement Agreement with a lawyer before signing. I can see that it could be a particular challenge for a lawyer-mediator who knows the relevant law and could be tempted to advise the unrepresented party.

In this case I asked the unrepresented party if they wished to check the Settlement Agreement with a lawyer before signing. They said not as they were happy with the deal. So he signed.

Negotiating stage

1 Key information

As with the arithmetical error above (under 'Exploring'), once the mediator knows, they cannot condone underhand tactics. I do wonder why the defendant revealed the information to me in the first place – if I had been ignorant of the existence of the record drawing, it would not have become an issue. In this case the defendant was a utility company and their action would have conflicted with their stated policy of openness with the public. After discussion, their decision maker took the record drawing into the other party's room and apologised. It was painful for the defendant because the settlement was much higher than they had expected, but would have been even higher and more damaging to them if they had gone to court.

2 First and final

The excuse for a first and final offer is usually that the offering party does not want to enter into salami-slicing (small steps from extreme positions). In a way that is commendable, but it is not likely to be well received by the other side. It could easily come over as bullying (especially if it also has the message 'accept or I am out of here') and will certainly deny the other side the opportunity to negotiate their deal. I always suggest to the offering party that they keep a bit back so that the other party can negotiate something a bit better.

The only situation where I have encouraged a party to give their best offer first is when they are talking in settlement areas that are so far away from the claimant's. This is a reality test (on both sides).

3 Giving a steer

Parties in negotiation should always have prepared and worked out their strategy and walk-away point. If they don't then they are all at sea. This has got to be their deal, so all I feel able to do is to suggest they test the other side, pitch a figure and see how the other side reacts. At worst, invite the other side to pitch a figure (although in my view that gives them an advantage in the negotiation). In the end I say they must do what is best for them.

4 Bug

I have had a party do a security sweep of the mediation rooms before the mediation started, but this was a one off! The mediation venue was the offices of the other side and my instinct was to immediately confront them with the bug. Unfortunately the offended party said that they didn't believe they had said anything that might weaken their negotiating position and that they needed to get a deal so they would continue, having disabled the device. They did a deal, but it was much worse than they had anticipated. Next morning I had a call from the offended party to say they felt that, after all, their discussions had been heard and they had been compromised by the bug. My response was 'too late!' the defendants would say this was a ploy by the claimants to break the deal – which is exactly the reaction that they did have. The defendants denied all knowledge of the device and suggested that the claimants planted it in the first place! They had to live with the deal they made on the day.

I think now that I should have gone with my instinct and confronted the defendant at the time. There might have been a very simple answer to the issue that would not have compromised the mediation.

5 Mediator not wanted

This is a reality and now seems to happen in most mediations but I wouldn't insist on staying with them (although I might suggest that I could be of help). It is probably because the party wants to keep their real position secret from the mediator in the hopes that they can get a better deal. The fact is that more often than not they spend an hour or more discussing their offer, with the other side (and the mediator) getting frustrated, and then hit a figure that stands no chance of being accepted. I then have to spend more time with them sorting out a more realistic offer.

6 Relaying offer

I now write every offer down and read it back before taking it to the other side. In this case, I had to apologise but the fact was £8 million or £9 million was not an acceptable offer, so my 'error' made little difference to the negotiations. Afterwards my assistant stated to me in private that the offer was definitely £9 million – it was as well my assistant said that to me in private rather than to the lawyer, otherwise I could see an argument resulting and further loss of confidence in my role.

7 Walk-out

Threatened walk-outs are not unusual in mediations. They tend to be either posturing, or a frustrated attempt by one side to make the other side 'come to their senses'. It usually is not a good move because it is rarely taken seriously and so can undermine the credibility of the 'walking' side.

In this case it had been the result of an argument between the three sisters and the walk-out had been real. I spoke with the absent sister on the phone and she insisted that she would not return. In the end the agreement was that the negotiations would continue and she would be kept informed over the telephone, either by her sisters or by me, and that, in any case, I would speak with her to be sure of her agreement to the final deal. She ended up by faxing her agreement to the settlement.

It would have been so much easier if they had a lawyer, or even an independent person, present. I should have realised that three sisters who did not get on and who were unaccompanied, was not an ideal scenario.

Concluding stage

1 Authority

First thought was for him to get the authority. I always say to parties to ensure there is an open line, especially out of hours, in case they need to speak to someone before signing the Settlement Agreement. But in this case he hadn't made the arrangement and his boss was not answering his mobile phone. There being no other alternative, I called a joint meeting where the situation was explained. The other party were livid, making comments about authority and good faith and so on. I then had a private meeting with the first party, making my usual comment: 'You can only work with what you've got — in this case an uncertain deal'. They had two options – wait and see if the deal on the table would be ratified or change the deal to be within his authority. They opted for the second.

2 Ratification

This is almost always the situation with government, local authorities and health and other trusts. Sometimes it is being part of the blame culture where people are reluctant to take responsibility in case they are criticised. Often it is because it is in the rules of the trust or other body. In all cases it should be 'on the table' from the start and the eventual settlement can take that into account. In this case it wasn't and it came as a surprise (to me as well as the other party).

There was quite a heated discussion but, again, this was a reality and we had to work with it. The Board representative explained the procedures, agreed a timetable and undertook to advocate the Board's acceptance. He was totally confident that this would be a formality and that the Board would nod it through. They did.

3 Second thoughts

The deal is that there is no deal until it is put into writing and signed by the parties. The deal had been put into writing but not yet signed, so there was no deal (yet). I explained the situation to the other side and had a private meeting with the wavering party. I try to resist the temptation to press a party to sign the deal – thus achieving another 'success'. This is the party's solution and if they are unsure then it is best for the mediator to support them. I suggested a cooling-off period of a few days. The other side agreed and the Settlement Agreement was signed on that basis. Three days later the deal was confirmed.

4 Tears

In this case the claimants were so overwhelmed by the dispute that they were falling apart. Their lawyer, rather than being supportive, was telling them not to lose the chance of settlement. The other sides' counsel had really gone for them in the initial open session, to the point where I had to intervene and bring the meeting to a close.

They did go for a walk, and signed the Settlement Agreement when they returned but left feeling that there was no justice in the deal. It was not a very satisfactory outcome. However, their burning need was to bring finality to the matter, not least because their health was suffering but also because their family life and business were affected. I do wonder how they are a few years later.

5 CFA

This case was mediated before the Jackson reforms, although I don't think it would be very different now. Most settlements are lump sum and it is left to the party and lawyer to sort out their share. I could see in this case that the lawyer feared the amount of time involved in taking the case to court would be disproportionate to the eventual award. Either that or he had too much other work on and wanted to get this one out of the way. In the end it was their responsibility and I spoke with the party to be sure that he was happy with the deal – he said he was and signed the Settlement Agreement.

6 Better deal

Their problem, their solution. The mediator's role is to give them the best chance of doing a deal. It would be good if that was the best deal, but I see some awful negotiation styles and tactics in mediation. In the end the mediator can do everything for them to get the best deal but if they mess up it has to be their problem, not the mediator's.

7 Counsel

Separating a party from their lawyer can sometimes be difficult. I do say at the start of the mediation that it is a flexible process with a variety of meetings including just decision makers on their own. I also ask myself why I want to see the party on their own – if it is to make my life easier that is not a good reason. After all, I know that the more people there involved in a meeting the less the chances of mixed or edited messages.

In this case I was up front and told them that I thought there was a chance that his client may lose a deal that would be acceptable because he (counsel) was being too protective of his client. I did a hypothetical – 'if they were to offer you £xx might that be acceptable?' Counsel said: 'Is that what they are offering?' I said: 'No, this is hypothetical, but what if they did?'. Counsel said he would certainly consider it. I looked at his client and asked her – she said it was a figure she would accept. Two steps later there was a deal – not exactly at the hypothetical figure but very close. The conversation had opened up what was becoming an entrenched position.

8 Deals with dignity

I responded by saying, 'That is not what I said,' and he said, 'No, but that is what I said'. The other side were disappointed but reluctantly agreed. I told the hard-nosed party and he raised his arms in triumph and said: 'You see, I told you I am a good negotiator'. Rightly or wrongly, I said 'No, you just like winning'. For the sake of £2,500 he robbed the other side of doing a deal with dignity.

9 VAT

I should have mentioned it earlier! In most business cases VAT is an in-out transaction but in some it is an expense that cannot be recovered. All figures in this particular mediation were exclusive of VAT and so it was assumed that the end deal was also. It took a long time, and a bit of compromise, to eventually hit an inclusive figure. When damages are involved they can be VAT-free. The lawyers need to be in control of this and agree, or even take advice, on what is applicable.

10 Too late for the deal

The common wisdom is that you keep at it on the day and get the deal signed up before people go home and in most cases that happens. I do wonder, however, about the sense of persevering late into the night when people are tired and perhaps not thinking clearly. The danger of not signing is as in this case, made worse because the barrister had not been party to the negotiations. In the end though, it is the parties responsibility and there had not been a signed deal, so nobody was committed. Despite my efforts to retrieve the situation, the deal fell through and they went to court.

11 Full and final settlement

My experience is that the 'known or unknown' wording is a try-on by the lawyer doing the drafting. If it is unchallenged, then great for their client. Usually it is challenged and the wording removed. This case was complicated because of a possible future claim that was not known by the defendant. I spoke with the claimant about how serious they were about the second claim and, if they were, how would they respond to the defendant questioning why they wanted the wording removed. They responded that they wanted to keep their options open and admitted to the possible additional claim when challenged by the defendant. I had a meeting with the defendant and they decided that they were not worried by the second claim and so removed the wording from the Settlement Agreement. I don't know if the second claim was made – I was certainly not asked to mediate it!

12 Serial user

I didn't respond!

Appendix 2

Recommended Reading List

The following publications are worthy of a read.

Books

A F Acland, *Perfect People Skills*, Random House Business Books, 2003.

R A.B Bush and J P Folger, *The Promise of Mediation*, San Francisco: Jossey-Bass Publishers, 1994.

K Cloke, *Mediating Dangerously*, San Francisco, Jossey-Bass Publishers, 2001.

K Cloke, *Conflict Revolution*, Janis Publications Inc., 2008.

R Fisher, W Ury, and B Patton, *Getting to Yes*, 2nd edn, London: Penguin Books, 1991.

R Fisher and D Shapiro, *Beyond Reason*, London: Penguin Books 2005.

G T Furlong, *The Conflict Resolution Toolbox*. Mississauga: John Wiley & Sons, 2005.

J Gunn, *How to Beat Bedlam in the Boardroom and Boredom in the Bedroom*. Prime Publishers, 2010.

R H Mnookin, S Peppet, and A Tulumello, *Beyond Winning* Cambridge, MA: Harvard University Press, 2000.

C Newmark, and A Monaghan, *Butterworths Mediators on Mediation*, Tottel Publishing Ltd, 2005.

K Patterson, J Grenny, R McMillan and A Switzler, *Crucial Conversations: Tools for Talking When Stakes are High*, McGraw-Hill, 2011.

S Roberts and M Palmer, *Dispute Processes*, 2nd edn, Cambridge: Cambridge University Press, 2005.

D Richbell, *Mediation of Construction Disputes*, Blackwell Publishing, 2008.

D Stone, B Patton and S Heen, *Difficult Conversations*, London: Penguin Books, 2000.

F Strasser and P Randolph, *Mediation – A Psychological Insight into Conflict Resolution*, London: Bloomsbury Continuum, 2004.

W Ury, *The Third Side*, London: Penguin Books, 1999,

Recommended Reading List

Articles

R L Riskin, 'Understanding Mediators' Orientations, Strategies, and Techniques: A Grid for the Perplexed' 1 Harv Negot L Rev 7.

R L Riskin, 'Decisionmaking in Mediation: The New Old Grid and the New New Grid System' 79 Notre Dame L Rev 1 (2003).

Part 2
Maturing

Contents

	Page No.
Chapter 1 Introduction	119
Chapter 2 Psychology in Mediation (Paul Randolph)	121
Chapter 3 It's All About Relationships (David Richbell and Henry Brown)	129
Chapter 4 Intercultural Mediation: The Fundamentals (Joanna Kalowski)	145
Chapter 5 Further Communications Skills (Jane Walmsley)	157
Chapter 6 Sector Specialisms	165
Mediating farming and rural disputes (Anthony Glaister)	165
Mediating disputes in the Armed Forces (Susan Morgan MBE)	167
Mediating banking and financial services disputes (Charles Flint QC)	170
Mediating charity sector disputes (David Richbell)	173
Mediating clinical negligence disputes (Tony Allen)	175
Mediating competition disputes (William Wood QC)	178
Mediating construction/engineering disputes (David Richbell)	180
Mediating employment disputes (Liz Rivers)	183
Mediating energy disputes (Jane Player)	187
Mediating entertainment and media sector disputes (Andrew Hildebrand)	190
Mediating franchise disputes (Michael Cover)	194
Mediating insolvency disputes (Chris Fitton)	196
Mediating insurance/reinsurance disputes (Jane Andrewartha)	200
Mediating intellectual property and IT disputes (Jon Lang)	205
Mediating partnership and family business disputes (David Richbell)	208
Mediating personal injury claims (Neil Goodrum)	211
Mediating planning related disputes (John Pugh-Smith)	214
Mediating probate and trust disputes (Beverly-Ann Rogers)	218
Mediating professional indemnity disputes (Nicholas Pryor)	220
Mediating property disputes (Mark Jackson-Stops and Michael Wyldebore-Smith)	224
Mediating public sector disputes (Jon Lang)	229
Mediating shareholder disputes and post-transaction warranty claims (Stephen Walker)	231
Mediating shipping disputes (Silas Taylor)	237
Mediating sports disputes (Quentin Smith)	240
Chapter 7 Learning from Other Mediation Disciplines	243
Transformative mediation (Jane Gunn)	243
Evaluative mediation (Andrew Goodman)	247
Community mediation (Eve Pienaar)	255
Family mediation (Mary Banham-Hall)	262
Workplace mediation (Clive Lewis OBE DL)	272
Peer mediation in schools (Chris Seaton)	282
Storytelling (Geoffrey Corry)	285
Mediating in faith communities (David Richbell with Zaza Elsheikh)	288
Environmental and public policy mediation (Andrew Floyer Acland)	292
Restorative Justice (Lawrence Kershen QC)	297
Co-mediation (Eve Pienaar)	304
Assistantships (David Richbell)	309

Part 2 Maturing

Chapter 8 Analysing Risk (Elizabeth Jones QC and John Clark)   313
Chapter 9 Mediation Ethics (Michel Kallipetis QC)   325
Chapter 10 Achieving Excellence – a Delicate Balance (Heather Allen) 341
Chapter 11 Conclusion (David Richbell)   347

Chapter 1

Introduction

The purpose of Part 2 is to build upon the basic skills and process covered in Part 1. This is for Commercial mediators who have trained, been accredited and are now out in the world effectively resolving disputes. Unlike Part 1, it includes contributions, including some chapters, by other mediators who are also out there making the world a better place. So the style varies and, in a few cases, what has been written differs from my vision of commercial mediation, but that is the richness of the mediation world and I have to accept that my way (although it is the right one!) is not necessarily everyone's way.

I thank all the many contributors to Part 2. I have been very touched by the fact that all willingly agreed to write something and most of their contributions are included without alteration or significant editing on my part. I salute their generosity and support in making this book possible.

The thinking behind Part 2 is partly to cover what may have been left out of the basic training, or to cover it in more depth (for example, Chapter 2, 'Psychology in Mediation' and Chapter 5, 'Further Communication Skills'), partly to anchor us in good practice (for example, Chapter 3, 'It's All About Relationships'), partly to expand the skill-set (for example, Chapter 4, 'Intercultural Mediation' and Chapter 8, 'Analysing Risk'), and partly to expand the horizons of a newly accredited commercial mediator (for example, Chapter 6, 'Sector Specialisms' and Chapter 7, 'Learning from Other Mediation Disciplines'). The final two chapters offer a warning (Chapter 9, 'Mediation Ethics') and lead us into Part 3, 'Mastery' (Chapter 10, 'Achieving Excellence').

My wish is that every mediation is a good mediation, that the mediator gives the parties the best opportunity to find a settlement to their dispute and that the mediator helps the parties use that opportunity to the best of their ability. That is a two-way process, one internal, one external. Internally, the mediator should be totally focussed on the case and on the parties' needs, making this mediation the most important thing in the mediator's life for that day (or more). Externally, this means managing the mediation process efficiently and using skills to ensure the parties are relaxed and able to make the very best of the opportunity given to them by the mediator. I am confident that most of the time that is what most practising mediators achieve. I think some of the time some mediators are on auto-pilot and not giving of their best (a subject covered in Part 3), and sometimes I fear there are cases that settle despite the mediator. Good, bad or indifferent, this book should help.

I should mention copyright. Most of the contributors have gifted their piece to the book and some have licensed the inclusion of their piece in the book. I thank all who have contributed, regardless of the arrangement, and, in recognition of this, the royalties from the book are being donated to a mediation charity.

Chapter 2

Psychology in Mediation

Paul Randolph

Paul Randolph trains mediators, as I did, but his approach is different. He starts with the psychology of conflict and builds the skills and process from there. So, for those he has not trained, I asked him to write this chapter. (DR)

> 'It is madness to incur the considerable expense of litigation – usually disproportionate to the amount at stake – without making a determined attempt to reach an amicable settlement. The idea that there is only one just result of every dispute, which only the court can deliver is, I believe, often illusory ... Parties should be given strong encouragement to attempt mediation before resorting to litigation.'
>
> Lord Phillips of Worth Matravers
India, 29 March 2008

Many of us mediators have come to mediation through litigation – either directly, having been litigation lawyers, or indirectly as non-lawyers, through watching from the sidelines as others have squandered time, money, and energy on protracted court warfare. Mediators are only too aware of the madness represented by the rush to litigation; we know it is commercially indefensible for commercial entities to be in dispute with each other for any length of time. To enter into a commercial dispute resists economic analysis, and to remain in or prolong the conflict with each other defies rational scrutiny. Any dispute, however grave or petty, will deprive the parties of the three essential elements needed by any commercial enterprise: time, money, and energy. The dispute will lower morale, adversely affect productivity, and is bound to translate at some point into loss of profit. In a major survey undertaken in 2003, the American Arbitration Association (AAA) examined the attitudes towards alternative dispute resolution processes by 250 companies, from the 'Fortune 1000', to mid-size public companies, and privately held businesses. The survey results showed that ADR 'dispute-wise' business management practices were associated with positive business outcomes. The most dispute-wise companies were more likely to have stronger relationships with customers, suppliers, employees and partners, they had lower legal department budgets and, perhaps most importantly, their price/earnings ratios (a good indicator of shareholder confidence) averaged 68 per cent higher than the average for companies in the least dispute-wise category.

It can thus rarely, if ever, be in the commercial or practical interests of either party to remain in dispute. Most outcomes achievable through litigation can be equally – and more economically – secured through negotiation and agreement. So even where, for example, one party seeks to protect its intellectual property rights through the deterrent quality of visible litigation, it could just as effectively be achieved by finding a suitable formula for a solution through collaboration.

Yet despite all this, commercial parties seem averse to resolving their disputes reasonably, rationally – and economically. Why are so many hard-nosed, business-orientated, profit-conscious executives prepared to drag their companies and their families endlessly through the courts?

The answer lies not in our lawyers, but in ourselves. For centuries, we have proved ourselves to be a species wholly incompetent at resolving our disputes. In our competitive, combative, and adversarial ways, we strive not only to win, but we go further in wanting utterly to crush and humiliate our opponents: we want to see blood on the walls. Traditionally there has been only one alternative to an amicable or negotiated settlement – that was war. Historically, this was conducted fairly crudely, with armies of soldiers on the battlefield. In more modern times, we have evolved a little by attempting more sophisticated forms of warfare, with cohorts of lawyers in court. Both models of warfare may *end* the dispute, but neither is effective at truly resolving the conflict. Both will invariably leave the underlying conflict to fester, and neither will address its root causes. What is more, protracted litigation can be as socially destructive as war, forcing businesses into liquidation, driving marriages onto the rocks, and devastating the health of all involved.

Yet conflict will always be with us: we cannot eliminate it. Prayers for peace are offered up on a daily basis by millions across the globe, yet there has not been a single day of peace throughout our existence. It is therefore vital that we appreciate that there may be a positive purpose to the conflict in our everyday lives. If we can accept the importance of conflict, then we can begin to work with it.

Many philosophers and psychologists have identified conflict as having a constructive role in our everyday lives. When well managed, conflict can in fact prove valuable, by creating a cycle of conflict and reconciliation, which brings with it greater mutual understanding, as well as progress and advancement, and significant changes for the better. Hegel, the 18th century German philosopher, identified the cycle of *thesis, antithesis and synthesis*, where *thesis* represents the status quo, *antithesis* is the challenge to that status quo, and *synthesis* the new product resulting from the conflict. Louis Coser, a 20th century American psychologist, born in Berlin, pointed out that conflict also had a unifying function, a group-bonding character, creating stronger associations and greater cohesiveness amongst diverse groups.

Mediation can address many of these aspects. By actively facilitating reconciliation, the mediator gives a small nudge to that cycle of *thesis-antithesis-synthesis*, and by promoting real and true resolution of the dispute, the mediator helps to create a more collaborative atmosphere in which cohesion and bonding can be given a sporting chance.

So how does the mediator achieve this? I propose to examine four psychological elements that drive conflict: emotions, self-esteem, values, and perceptions.

Emotions

All disputes will have a common thread running through them: one party demands something and the other party is unwilling to give it. This will invariably involve a commercial element as well as an emotional element: the demand will be driven partly by commercial criteria, and partly by emotional factors. Similarly the refusal to give in to the demand will be driven by both commercial and emotional components. Few disputes are without significant emotional content. If every dispute were approached from a purely rational, practical, pragmatic or commercial standpoint, very few disputes would continue in existence: they would be resolved mathematically, geometrically, geographically – or simply logically.

Any allegation of 'fault' is highly emotive and inevitably involves considerable injury to feelings. To allege a breach of contract or an act of negligence creates deep feelings of hurt and anger; similarly, when that fault is denied, it can result in yet greater irritation and upset, by 'adding insult to injury'. So the first principle with which the psychologically-informed mediator must grapple, is that when parties are in conflict, they do not think or behave *rationally* but rather are driven by their emotions. Frequently, they may not even recognise their own underlying emotions. They may believe that their demand for 'damages in compensation' is utterly logical – simply a desire for proper redress or recompense – whereas in fact the demand for money may be driven by anger, hurt, or a desire to punish or humiliate.

Emotions are not the monopoly only of the parties in dispute: the emotions can often spill over into the psyche of their legal advisers. A 2007 survey by solicitors Field Fisher Waterhouse, showed that 47 per cent of company executives and in-house lawyers admitted that a personal dislike of the other side had led them into expensive litigation.

We mediators need to gain an understanding of the strength of influence upon behaviour that emotions represent; we should accept that those in dispute are likely to be driven, not by reason, but by emotions. We may then more readily see that it is wholly futile for us as mediators – or for the parties' legal advisers – to seek to persuade the party to change their position, whether through logic or rational legalistic argument. This may explain the frequent exasperation of lawyers with their clients: 'they just don't seem to be able to see sense,' or 'I can't seem to get through to them that …'.

Aristotle, the Greek philosopher, expressed one of the most enduring metaphors of conflict: the eternal battle between reason and emotion. To Aristotle, emotions were primitive, unintelligent, and bestial expressions of behaviour; rationality on the other hand, was pure and good. The two, however, were always in conflict. This notion evolved as Aristotle's 'master and slave' theory, whereby, in a proper world, logic should be the master and emotion the slave. Unfortunately in conflict, the reverse seems to be true: passions overwhelm logic. What is more, the greater the stakes and the more critical the outcome, the greater is the emotion and the scarcer the logic.

There is an anatomical and neurological explanation for the fact that when we are in dispute, our ability to think rationally seems to diminish, or occasionally disappears completely. It may explain that feeling when 'the red mist descends' and one is heard to say: 'I'm so angry I can't think straight'. It may also explain that sudden loss of temper, or behaviour described as being out of character, or even why when we sleep on it we feel differently the following day.

The explanation lies in the amygdala, a small almond-shaped part of the brain, which governs our instinctive 'fight or flight' responses. In moments of perceived danger or attack, the amygdala blocks the neurological pathways to the cortex, the 'thinking' part of the brain, thereby taking control of the reasoning brain. Hence it is sometimes referred to as an 'amygdala hijack'. At the same time, the amygdala precipitates chemical reactions in the body, by stimulating the production of adrenalin and other hormones, whilst helping to pump oxygen through the blood to support and aid the muscles. This neurological function was clearly vital for the survival of the species. When facing an attack by a wild animal, it would have been fatal to man to conduct a cerebral analysis of the options available: 'jump to the left, or jump to the right, or retreat, or fight back'. The amygdala thus served to prevent 'paralysis through analysis'.

It is this 'hijacking' of the rational mind that so frequently occurs in the high emotional state of a bitter dispute, and creates an emotional barrier to settlement. Of course, nowadays, we are rarely faced with a similar type of attack in the wild – even when in a commercial dispute. Yet an attack that is represented by an allegation of fault, or of a breach of contract, can be perceived to be just as threatening and equally dangerous and frightening, for it is an attack upon our integrity and upon our self-esteem, which can produce the most violent of defensive instincts – and so trigger an amygdala hijack.

Self-esteem

Self-esteem is one of the most powerful deciding factors in mediation. It can create the strongest emotions when people are in conflict. We all have self-esteem. We all harbour a need to think well of ourselves, and for others to think well of us. Our self-esteem governs most of what we do each and every day. The entire cosmetic and fashion industries, for instance, are built upon our self-esteem, and they demonstrate how important it is for many of us to project the way we would wish to be seen and experienced by others. Equally our behaviour and conduct towards others is governed by the way we wish to be perceived by them.

The problem with self-esteem is that it is not static: it can go up, and it can very easily go down. Consequently we expend considerable time, effort and energy in maintaining and protecting our self-worth, and in seeking the approval of others. This is particularly so by parties in a mediation: the approval of others, including the mediator, is a goal to strive towards, whereas disapproval by others, especially of those whose opinions matter, is strictly to be avoided. Manipulation or exploitation by others, which can be perceived as being held in contempt, is total anathema to the self-esteem of parties in dispute.

There can be little more damaging to self-esteem than to be on the receiving end of allegations – and denials – of negligence or breach of contract, or still worse, of criminal or dishonest conduct. Yet these types of allegations populate pre-action correspondence and pleadings. They are often accusations of *failure*, a failure to act in a way that all other reasonable persons would act, or accusations of failure to abide by previous agreement. At their extreme, they can be assertions of fraudulent, dishonest or deceptive behaviour. Many of these will be perceived as a form of personal betrayal.

Self-esteem is not confined to individuals about themselves: it can also manifest itself in corporations. Corporate self esteem, felt through the injury to feelings of the executives in relation to their organisation, can be as powerful a driver as it is to an individual: 'What do they take us for?' or 'What sort of a company do they think they are dealing with?'

Most parties at a mediation will have some other person or persons in the background, whose approval is important to them. They may be a board of directors, trustees, an employer or boss, a spouse or a partner, a relative or simply a friend. Being able to demonstrate to these people that the party has secured a 'good' outcome at the mediation, or at least one which will be seen by those others as a 'good' outcome, can become a crucial need for that party's self-esteem.

Thus the psychologically informed mediator will be aware that the conduct of parties in dispute may be governed at the mediation entirely by the desire for approval, in order to *maintain* their self-esteem, or by the need to *protect* it against the fear of manipulation, or exploitation, or even worse, humiliation. This will translate itself into a variety of curious behavioural strategies, no doubt familiar to many experienced mediators:

- parties constantly seeking to persuade the mediator that they are 'the angels' in the dispute, and that the party in the other room are 'the devils';
- the question as to who makes the first move: neither party is prepared to 'go first' when making offers or proposals – not for any sound commercial reason, but for fear of getting it wrong (ie pitching too high or too low);
- 'keeping cards close to the chest': the fear that disclosure will be used against them for manipulation or exploitation purposes; and
- having the 'last word': the need to be seen as having 'won' will often result in the mediator being asked by one party to try and squeeze one more small and inconsequential sum or concession out of the other, immediately prior to settlement.

With the knowledge that this often child-like behaviour is precipitated by a need to protect or maintain self esteem, the mediator will be able to address it with empathy and understanding, rather than incredulous condemnation.

The need to be heard

An important aspect of self-esteem is the need to be heard. One of the existential 'givens' that we all share is a need for self-expression. This is most aptly demonstrated by the growth of social media, where we constantly express ourselves, whether on our mobile phones, or through Twitter, Facebook, LinkedIn, and other social networks. However, with the desire for self-expression comes a corresponding need to be heard.

Being heard translates into being valued, appreciated, and understood. Many disputes are the result of parties feeling undervalued, ignored, misunderstood, or misrepresented: 'They are not listening, so I have no alternative but to litigate – that will make them listen.' However, the need to be heard is one that can most readily be addressed in mediation. By investing a little time in 'active listening', the mediator can demonstrate to the parties, not only that they have been heard (possibly for the first time in their lives) but that they have also been understood and accepted – without judgment, even if not 'agreed with'. It is for these reasons that the skills of listening are such vital tools in the mediator's tool box: the use of techniques such as reflecting back, paraphrasing and summarising, as indicated by Carl Rogers, the 20th century American psychologist, in his rhetorical approach to 'person-centred' therapy, represent important tools for active and effective listening. Although they may be termed 'techniques', if and when used naturally and non-mechanistically they can be the most powerful skills for *proving* to a party, beyond doubt, that they have been truly heard. Once heard, the party is disarmed, and points of resistance are removed; the party's anger is assuaged and there is nothing more to rail against. Their self esteem is restored.

Values

Our values are linked to our self esteem, for it is when these values – particularly those which we hold dear – are challenged or abused by others that we find our self-esteem under attack, and we become angered and in conflict. Values are the principles by which we all live. We create them in order to carry us through life in some ordered manner.

The level of emotions created by an attack upon our self-esteem will vary from person to person. What may anger one party may leave another totally unmoved. This is because they will have differing values and value systems. If the attack is upon values that we do not hold strongly, we will be less troubled by an incursion upon them. If, for example, one person's values consist of being ever-punctual, they will feel abused if the other side is consistently unpunctual. On the other hand, persistent lateness may have no effect upon someone who views punctuality as unimportant or irrelevant.

Frequently values and value systems become sedimented – in other words, so rigid as to be impervious to rationalisation. To parties with such sedimented values, it is wholly counterproductive to try to persuade them that a minor transgression (as for instance, being a few minutes late) should be of little consequence 'in the greater scheme of things'. It is the rigid adherence to sedimented values that often prevents parties from reaching a settlement. 'This is a matter of principle,' say the parties, seeking to justify their entrenched positions (cue mediator's silent groan – this is the last thing we want to hear), but it is precisely when the parties stand firm 'on principle', that the mediator needs to understand and work with these values, so as to secure that vital shift of attitude necessary for a satisfactory resolution.

Shared values, on the other hand, can be a useful concept for a mediator to utilise in order to secure an attitude shift. When parties in a dispute are made to realise that the dispute throws up values which are common to both of them, and which they share, it can have a beneficial affect upon parties holding entrenched positions. For example, if business executives in a partnership dispute can see that the dispute has arisen because they both share a passionate desire to secure the success or survival of a business, and merely have opposing views as to how this is to be achieved, the bitter sting of emotions can be taken out of the dispute. Similarly, if warring parents In a divorce were able to appreciate that they both have the best interests of the children at heart, but simply cannot agree as to how this is best achieved, they may more readily be able to temper their animosity towards each other. In this way, the mediator might succeed in reducing the dispute from a fiercely hostile battle to a mere 'difference of opinion'.

In all such situations, the mediator will need properly to understand the parties' respective value systems, in order to know whether it is worthwhile trying to change them, or simply to work with them. In other words, the mediator must ascertain whether values are so sedimented as to be incapable of change or whether they are such that, with a little gentle 'stirring', they can nevertheless be worked with.

Perceptions

Finally, we turn to perceptions – yet another important driving force in conflicts. In fact, what is actually under consideration here are *misperceptions*. Misperceptions are assumptions that we all make – about the people we meet, their appearance, their intellect, their behaviour, and their motivations. Invariably, these assumptions are incorrect, but when allowed to fester for any period of time, these assumptions can become fixed in the mind as established facts. Emails are notorious for creating misperceptions, as people will read into them tones of voice and meanings that simply do not exist or are wholly unintentional. Many disputes are founded upon an assumption about the conduct or motivations of another: one party will assume that they know why the other did or said something or why they conducted themselves in a certain manner. The more tenuous the relationship, the less prospect there is of one party giving the other the 'benefit of the doubt'.

Parties therefore proceed headlong deeper into conflict, harbouring grudges based upon assumptions created historically and re-enforced over periods of weeks, months or even years. Thus, for example, one company may make sinister assumptions as to why a supplier continually delivers goods late, or a family member will speculate as to why 'Uncle Bill never came to Granny's funeral', or the CEO will smart under the belief that his wife 'was snubbed by the Sales Director at the office party'. These assumptions will often be very far from the truth. A skilled mediator can use the mediation process as an excellent forum for identifying these misperceptions and helping the parties dispel them.

Conclusion

With some knowledge of these various human traits and the part they play in creating psychological blockages to settlement, a mediator may be better able to facilitate conflict resolution. Without such understanding of human interactions, mediators will simply find themselves scratching their heads in bewilderment at the unfathomable antics of the parties before them.

Chapter 3

It's All About Relationships

David Richbell

I am a red-blooded commercial mediator. I get settlements. Indeed I tell the parties: 'My role is to give you the best chance of getting a deal'. But I try to be nice when I am doing it! I still measure my performance against settlement rates, despite saying that all I can do is to give the parties their best chance, and if they foul it up that is their responsibility. But settlement is key to me and if they don't settle, whatever the reason, I still beat myself up – what could I have done better? What could I have said/done that would have made the difference? Should I have spent more time exploring or, perhaps more important, talking with the parties about their relationships, how they were, why they fractured?

After 20 years of mediating commercial dispute, nearly half of which have been in the construction industry, I have been examining what I do and realise that I have gone far, probably too far, from the model that we used to teach. The temptation is to spend less time on exploration – establishing parties' needs rather than wants – and much more time on negotiation. And I realise this is one reason why it seems to have become harder. I have realised that if I spent more time with the person and less with their problem, the solutions would emerge more easily. It is about relationships, and I realise that if I spend more time on the damaged or broken relationships, the parties' needs would be more evident and their movement towards settlement would be potentially easier and more co-operative. I believe that behind every dispute lies a damaged relationship. Even in the most dispassionate insurer/insurer case, relationships still exist, and it is not just party to party, but lawyer to lawyer, expert to expert and a mix-up of all of them. It is (or should be) all about relationships.

Having said that, I now call myself a non-evaluative commercial mediator. One year, Chambers Directory included the comment 'laid back'. I felt outraged. Here I am working myself to a frazzle helping others solve their problems and I am described as laid back! Calm – yes. Persistent – yes. Patient – yes. Laid back – NO! Especially as I have heard stories about one mediator who had the habit of taking a book with him to read whilst the parties were in their rooms, and another who was seen shopping – twice – having left the parties some tasks. That is the same mediator who is purported to have run two mediations in the same building at the same time – neither knowing about the other until a lawyer from each mediation met in the toilet and asked each other who was mediating – and found it was the same person. I don't know what happened next but stamina is a vital quality of an effective mediator and that particular mediator must have had it in spades!

So I'm no longer a facilitative mediator. It's a shame because it is a very unthreatening term but I don't want to risk being seen as a 'laid back, touchy-feely nice person', rather, an emotionally intelligent nice person who is prepared to bang heads together if necessary. Although, now I think of it, banging heads together might be seen as being a bit evaluative. I want to give the impression of a mediator who is active, alert, vibrant, engaged, energetic and dynamic as opposed to demonstrating a more laid-back, let-them-get on-with-it style suggested by the term facilitative mediator. I want the parties to feel they have had their money's worth and if I can engender some sympathy as I sag exhausted beneath the table as they sign the settlement agreement, then all the better.

The non-evaluative mediator

What do I mean by the non-evaluative mediator? I am comfortable with pitching figures, coaching parties, challenging and reframing but I won't advise, express views on merits (not that I could, being a non-lawyer mediator) or recommend settlements. And I do say at the beginning: 'My role is to give you (the parties) the best opportunity of reaching a settlement – and most do'.

I would guess that most mediators would identify with that. But as I mentioned earlier, 20 years of experience does not mean I am at my best. I have increasingly realised that I hit the figures earlier than I used to, yet I know the best results come from leaving the figures until quite late. If I concentrate on the parties' needs so that, when they can see those needs are valued and likely to be met, they are much more positive and co-operative when the figures start. They see the shape of the deal and so want it to work – and it usually does. However, I don't go much further than saying to the parties: 'What do you need to be able to do a deal today?' I often then have to explain what I mean by 'need', but eventually they will tell me what their real drivers are. What I don't do, until recently anyway, is talk about their relationships and feelings. I suppose to a certain extent that is because it became a bit of a joke when we were training mediators: 'Tell me how you feel about that,' 'That must have made you feel angry,' and so on.

A (good) example

I say until recently. Some time ago I mediated a case which involved a small building company, which had a term contract with a housing authority, being suspended after someone had made a passing remark over lunch that they suspected collusion between the company and a housing authority manager. Three months later the company was cleared of any wrongdoing but by then their reputation had been tarnished and the work had been placed with competitors. Three years later their claim for lost profits and other headings came to mediation. During the initial open meeting I said to the builder, 'I can see you are still upset at being suspended,' and he absolutely broke down in front of the other party and talked about the way this one action had ruined his business, his marriage and life in general. Ironically the person who had made the original accusation was on the other side of the table. Later the builder's lawyer said to me that being given the recognition, and therefore permission, to say how he felt to the person he felt most responsible had transformed the builder. I think we too often shy away from emotional situations – probably because they make us feel uncomfortable – and forget that this is a party-centred process and it is not our comfort that we should be thinking about.

A (not so good) example

Another experience had the opposite effect. It was a right of way dispute across a neighbour's garden. The husband worked shifts and sometimes that meant that he returned home in the early hours of the morning and, wheeling his motorbike into his garden, woke his neighbour's dogs, which in turn woke his neighbour and her children. She blocked off his gate and he took legal action. In gathering evidence, he photographed the blocked gate from his neighbour's side. During the mediation his neighbour, in a constantly hysterical state, accused him of taking photographs, which could have been of her teenage daughter. From the start I found myself resisting her apparently increasingly unreasonable behaviour and at one stage I had a private conversation with her in the corridor on her way back from the toilet, asking her why she was so negative in her attitude. The mediation went downhill faster than before, and although, despite all odds, the parties agreed a very elegant solution, she refused to sign the Settlement Agreement. Later, the feedback on the mediator (me) was that I was unsympathetic, one-sided in my approach and a poor manager of the process. I offered another half-day mediation without cost but she refused. My lesson was that I should have sat down with her and talked about what had happened, why she was so upset, to explore the effect she was having on the other party, they being equally upset (but, in my neutral and unbiased view, much more rational), and to show that I heard and valued her position. I didn't and it was a salutary lesson for me.

Transformative mediation

Jane Gunn writes later about transformative mediation, but the learning for me was that, besides the process being spread over several meetings on separate days, transformative mediation focuses on the relationship rather than problem solving. Getting the relationship on a better level usually enables the parties to find their own solution.

Conclusion

I think we commercial mediators can learn from the transformative process. Spending more time on the damaged relationship helps parties to move on and co-operate in finding a solution. So in the exploring phase we should be making time to talk about the relationship behind the dispute, why and how it became damaged and to give value to the emotions that attach to it. Whilst the end result may be no different to a more 'conventional' mediation, it is far more satisfactory because it has become a human, as well as a commercial, discussion. It takes some determination and preparedness to do it justice, but if the mediator's role is to help the parties get the BEST deal, then the human dimension must not be ignored.

Having difficult conversations

I don't like it, but I am a flier. When it comes to conflict, when I have to face a difficult conversation, I duck the issue. It is silly because trying to avoid the discomfort leaves me with the feeling of being taken advantage of, disliking myself because I am a coward, and creates an environment where the feelings fester and the situation gets worse. It also robs the 'offender' of the opportunity to understand how and why I feel as I do and so be able to put things right (whether 'right' means being sorry or making me realise that my feelings are unjustified). This helps nobody and what makes it worse is that I know better. I know that talking about the problem and how it makes me feel is the right approach and honours the other person. I know that tackling the problem (I don't mean fighting – as in 'fight or flight' – but facing up to the problem) is the honourable way and it is not acceptable to say that sometimes prevarication sorts things out and the problem goes away. The trouble is I am beginning to realise that perhaps I like to have someone to aim all my bad feelings towards; I want a demon in my life so that I can be nice to everyone else.

So what good is that to me as a mediator? Despite being an avoider, the strange thing is that I can help other people have difficult conversations – and I do, often – and I don't feel that I am being a hypocrite. It really does seem to be a matter of 'don't do as I do, do as I say'! Actually, it is basic stuff – listening, understanding, valuing, turning from history to future, helping people to move on, saving face.

There are two sorts of difficult conversations that face the mediator. One is mediator to party, where the mediator is almost a party; the other is party to party, where the mediator is a facilitator, and occasionally a coach. Both can be complicated by the fact that most parties have lawyers present and most lawyers feel the need to protect their part. So there is a potential barrier to be overcome before these conversations can take place. That can be overcome by successfully building rapport and trust (with lawyer and party – and all the others in their team) and creating a safe space where it is felt to be acceptable to be vulnerable and potentially weak. The results, however, can be transforming; it can break a deadlock situation, it can totally change one party's perception of the other's position. Even if it doesn't transform, it might well prompt them both to realise that neither is likely to back down and so working towards a settlement rather than going to trial would be in both their interests!

There are several key points to having or facilitating a difficult conversation. Most are mentioned elsewhere in this book, some several times because they are so important:

- different stories;
- conflict can be positive;
- separate people from the problem;
- step into others' shoes;
- face the demon;
- turn assumptions into facts;
- look to the future, not back at the past;
- save face;
- prepare and rehearse;
- end positively; and
- look out for ... and avoid ...

Different stories

This is a statement that was in my first book, in Part 1 and will probably be repeated in Part 3. Everyone sees the same facts and events differently. It may be because of age, gender, ethnicity, education, religion, politics, wealth, power, marital status, community and so many other things; it doesn't necessarily mean they are any more right or wrong, *just different*. We are unique and we interpret things in our own unique way. If parties can understand that then they are on the way to understanding that their truth is not the only one.

The other 'truth' is that all parties are part of, and probably contribute to, the problem. All parties have a responsibility both for the problem and for the outcome.

Conflict can be positive

If people are prepared to listen, to try to understand why there is more than one truth, to value the fact that the other party's truth is genuinely felt, despite being different from their own, then the opportunity is there to co-operate in finding a solution. People rarely change unless they feel understood – they will stick and become entrenched if they feel unheard or ignored. So the mediator is in a position to coach people into listening and accepting (though not necessarily be changed by) that the other side's 'truth' is genuinely felt.

Separate people from the problem

This is a common phrase in mediator training but not so easily explained. It is really about recognising the emotions involved and separately identifying the facts of the problem. Almost always the emotion clouds, if not blots out the facts. So it is important for the mediator to help unravel the facts from the emotion whilst not devaluing either. Both are a reality and both need to be acknowledged.

Step into other's shoes

Whilst not actually swapping shoes, it is a good and accepted technique for mediators to ask parties to step into the other's shoes, or see the situation through the other's eyes, or even sit in their chair. It can be a powerful reality test, although many people resist such a suggestion as it means that the other party becomes human to them again.

Face the demon

So often one party demonises the other – or both each other. This person becomes the sole reason for their current misfortune – sometimes even for all misfortune since birth. Although it is often resisted – particularly by an over-protective lawyer – I know that putting the parties in the same room together will prick the demon balloon and make them see the other as fellow humans with feeling and emotions. Popping the demon is an essential step in helping parties towards a co-operative approach to their problem and its solution.

Turn assumptions into facts

Part of demonising is making assumptions (sometimes the most outrageous assumptions) about the other party, both of facts ('they don't have any money') or emotions ('he doesn't care about our mother's wishes'). It is a vital mediator's tool to ask: 'Is that an assumption or fact? If it is an assumption you need to turn it into fact. What questions can you ask of the other side to do that?' This is particularly important in the negotiation (or bargaining) phase of a mediation. I have experienced countless examples of poor negotiating based upon assumptions rather than fact. The more certain the facts, the sounder and more confident the negotiation – and the better the eventual settlement.

Look to the future, not back at the past

I would think that at some time in every mediation I am heard to say 'You can't change the past but you can influence/control the future'. It is not something to say early on in the mediation but there comes a time when looking back at the history of the dispute needs to change to looking ahead towards how this may be settled for the better. Most people know they have to let go of the past – it is done, out of their control, to be learned from – and often they need the mediator to provide an excuse to turn and face the future.

Save face

I have used the term 'deals with dignity' elsewhere in this book. It is very important for the mediator to be able to help parties avoid losing face (by heading off any corner that they are about to enter) and to achieve a solution which means that they can leave with their head high. If the mediator has done their job properly, one party's need to crush the other, or for revenge, or to be seen to 'win', will have been replaced by the recognition that the best deals come from co-operation and meeting the other's needs.

Prepare and rehearse

Most difficult conversations need to have a 'dry run' before they take place. The way a message is received depends so much on the delivery. The mediator may well need to do some significant coaching, probably with both sides, to ensure that the eventual conversation is productive. It needs to be well delivered and well received. The deliverer needs to be clear about the points s/he wants to make, anticipate how they will be received, use words that are non-judgemental and are not seeking to blame or exact punishment. There needs to be a clear end-goal in mind.

The receiver needs to accept what is said as information, not criticism, and to seek to understand, and be clear about, what the delivered is trying to say. That may mean asking questions or it may mean taking time to consider a response. The mediator has a role in both because both parties are likely to be concerned, probably anxious, about the conversation, and the mediator's role is to help both parties give the situation their best shot.

End positively

The best outcome of the conversation is that both parties feel better informed, that they understand what has driven the other side to the position they are in, and that they are able to move on to start shaping a settlement. If that is not the result then the likelihood is that the deliverer will have removed a blockage and can move on to more positive things, whilst the receiver may not have been able to accept what has been said and may even feel aggrieved and the process set back. The worst outcome would be for the conversation to backfire, be badly delivered (despite the mediator's coaching) and badly received (despite the mediator's coaching). That could be the end of the mediation – or the signal for preparing another difficult conversation!

Look out for... and avoid...

When the difficult conversation takes place, look out for:

- inconsistencies from both deliverer and receiver in words, expression and body language. That will challenge the authenticity of what is being said;
- switching off by the receiver, and, even more importantly, the deliverer when receiving a response; and
- hints or markers that suggest underlying issues that have not been revealed to the mediator (or the deliverer/receiver);

and avoid:

- advising rather than coaching. Keep the responsibility for the conversation with the parties;
- pointing out their mistakes. So often we mediators see that 'if only' a party had done/not done something, they wouldn't be here in a mediation. The fact is they are, and history can't be changed. However, at the end of the mediation it could be appropriate for the mediator to ask what lessons had been learned that means they won't be back needing a mediator again. However, if they do, give them your business card;
- expecting forgiveness. For me this is a particular challenge. As a Christian, forgiveness is part of the message. So I want people to put their differences behind them and to be nice to each other again. They have sorted the dispute, achieved a settlement, can see the future without conflict, can move on, learn from the problems and forgive each other. If only! Sometimes, rarely, it happens. When it does it is great to witness. I just need not to expect it every time.

Finally

The mediator is in an incredibly important position in conducting or facilitating difficult conversations. By describing their stories in a way that is true for both at the same time, by reframing, by summarising, by modelling their behaviour, the mediator can transform a situation of high conflict to one of understanding and co-operation. It is a big responsibility by one that can bring big rewards. It just needs the mediator to be an acceptor rather than an avoider, of difficult situations and transform them into productive dialogue.

High conflict disputes

Henry Brown

There will be times when a party in a mediation seems to defy all logic, common sense and common understanding. My experience is that I have become increasingly frustrated, pulling out what hair I have left and coming away from the (usually unsettled) mediation feeling we didn't even get past first base. So I asked Henry Brown to explain why. (DR)

In 2001, I established a training programme for family mediators jointly with two psychotherapist-mediators, Neil Dawson and Brenda McHugh, based on our view that there was a link between attachment issues in childhood and high conflict in adulthood. These views were developed in a book and DVD we created in 2006, entitled *Managing Difficult Divorce Relationships*, in which, stimulated by a contribution from Professor Peter Fonagy, we extended the link to refer to disorganised attachment. In 2011, Arthur Marriott and I incorporated a chapter on this subject into the third edition of our book *ADR Principles and Practice*, extending these ideas in two ways. First, we realised that the principles applicable to matrimonial issues applied equally to all kinds of disputes; secondly, we recognised that the personality traits that manifested themselves in high conflict were not exclusively attributable to attachment disorder, but also arose in other kinds of personality – as observed by Bill Eddy and the High Conflict Institute in the United States.

High conflict parties require special attention because some of the approaches and strategies that may be appropriate for addressing conflictual situations will not necessarily be right for high conflict cases and may be counter-productive.

The special meaning of 'high conflict'

The common perception of high conflict is that it is manifested by anger and hostility. While this may occur, it does not of itself indicate high conflict. Rather, high conflict in a dispute context exists where either or both parties behave in a way that maintains rigid, polarised positions, inhibits progress and keeps resolution frustratingly out of reach, leaving a sense that no solution will be good enough to end the dispute.

The main attributes of high conflict are a significant combination of the following indicators:

- highly polarised positions with no shades of grey;
- negotiations are ineffectual, leaving agreement frustratingly out of reach;
- a party maintains a rigid 'world view', which, albeit reasonably presented, is likely to contain some element of distorted or misconceived thinking;
- there is a tendency to blame other(s) for the problem or issue;
- although communication may be extensive, there is no 'hearing' of the other's position;
- emotions (possibly covert) may prevail over reason;

- third parties' and professional vindication is sought;
- any agreements reached break down easily or are ambiguous or difficult to follow;
- there is a strong belief that the legal system will support and vindicate a party's case;
- each process (such as mediation, counselling or the court) feels like a new forum to retell the story rather than a place to seek resolution;
- there is an aggressive, exhausting energy with a sense that the conflict could continue until everyone is totally exhausted, physically, emotionally and financially; and
- for a professional, the effect is stressful, exhausting, challenging and draining.

Distinguishing high conflict from other factors

Impasse is not of itself an indicator of high conflict. There may be different reasons for deadlock, including differing views as to fairness and justice, with different perceptions as to entitlement. There may be differences of fundamental and non-negotiable values and beliefs, or there may be commercial or personal imperatives that do not allow a party to accept the terms under consideration. Nor does being 'difficult' necessarily indicate a high conflict personality. There are many ways of being difficult including being passive aggressive (for example not carrying out responsibilities effectively, or subtly disrupting plans, or confusing issues through ambiguity, misunderstanding and misstatements), being unable to make a decision and permanently hovering 'on the fence', or being persistently negative.

The mere fact that a person may be angry or emotional does not of itself indicate high conflict (though if combined with other indicators, it might). Some emotional responses are almost inevitable in most disputes where people have strong feelings.

High conflict personalities

There seems to be a clear link between high conflict and personality – that is to say, there is a category of people who may be said to have high conflict personalities. Three personality backgrounds, which overlap one another, are linked to high conflict:

- attachment disorganisation;
- personality disorder;
- maladaptive traits of either or both.

Attachment disorganisation

The foundation for this concept is attachment theory, a concept formulated by psychoanalyst John Bowlby that the infant is in effect programmed to seek closeness to a parent or carer who provides comfort and protection. That provides a secure base from which to develop greater emotional security as a child and adult. If, however, the carer cannot attune effectively to the infant, then the infant is likely to have later insecurity problems.

For most people, levels of attachment may vary between secure and insecure but will be more or less adequate. However, for perhaps 5–10 per cent or less of people, the attachment system breaks down and becomes disorganised and dysfunctional. In such cases, trust, a critical component of secure attachment, may co-exist alongside its polarised opposite, not just mistrust, but paranoia. Someone with disorganised attachment may for example initially regard their lawyer, mediator or other professional adviser as an attachment figure and 'the best in the world', but at some stage that professional will fail to live up to the person's needs and become the object of criticism, with potential allegations of negligence.

This brings us to reflective function, empathy and mirror neurons. Professor Peter Fonagy describes the reflective function as the way in which people:

> 'try to understand each other's mental states: their thoughts and feelings, beliefs and desires in order to make sense of and, even more important, to anticipate each other's actions'.

This is closely related to empathy, which the Penguin *Dictionary of Psychology* defines as:

> 'a cognitive awareness and understanding of the emotions and feelings of another person....a vicarious affective response to the emotional experiences of another person that mirrors or mimics that emotion'.

From the perspective of neuroscience, this relates to the brain's mirror neurons. A neuron is a cell that processes and transmits information through electrical and chemical signals. Mirror neurons are able to represent the intentional states of others and provide fundamental emotional resonance. An individual's attunement experience may be key to an ability to empathise with and attune effectively to the intentional states of others.

The malfunctioning of the reflective function and of mirror neurons may be one of the manifestations of high conflict personalities.

Personality disorders and maladaptive traits

The Royal College of Psychiatrists defines 'personality' as the collection of characteristics or traits that make each of us an individual, including the ways that we think, feel and behave. Where someone's personality develops in a way that makes it difficult to live with themselves and/or other people and to change those ways of thinking, feeling and behaving, resulting in unwanted consequences such as difficulty in making or keeping relationships and/or controlling feelings or behaviour, the person may have a personality disorder. People with personality disorders tend to have a narrow and inflexible range of attitudes, behaviours and coping mechanisms.

Psychiatric diagnoses are widely based on the American Psychiatric Association's Diagnostic and Statistical Manual of Mental Disorders, currently DSM-5. There are various categories of disorders, those most closely linked with high conflict being:

- anti-social (which may include deceit, manipulativeness, callousness, hostility and irresponsible or disruptive behaviour);
- borderline (characterised by significant instability of interpersonal and social relationships, self-image and mood, and impulsive behaviour); and
- narcissistic (characterised by an exaggerated sense of their own importance, with limited capacity for appreciating the perspectives of others).

A dispute resolution professional would not dream of making any diagnosis or 'labelling' anyone, but some basic understanding of relevant personality disorders provides a background to these traits that may have such an influence on high conflict.

It may be preferable for a dispute resolution professional to view all people as having a collection of personality traits on a range of spectrums, some of which may be maladaptive, rather than thinking in terms of disorder categorisation.

Cautions and reservations

This subject is not one in which there can be dogmatic assertions or absolute certainties: the whole field is too new and tentative for that. Dispute resolution professionals should not probe into personal histories to establish whether a party might perhaps have had difficult attachment issues in their childhood. Nor is it appropriate to share insights about psychological causes of high conflict with the parties or their representatives. This is likely to be resisted and met with defensive and possibly hostile reactions. It may be more helpful to maintain any insights as one's own working hypotheses.

Strategies for working with high conflict

The following are particularly relevant to high conflict disputes:

Boundaried empathy

One feature of disorganised attachment, personality disorders and maladaptive traits is a tendency to ignore boundaries and to try to get the mediator to go beyond his or her ordinary professional limits, whether by seductive, manipulative, demanding or bullying conduct.

Professor Fonagy's advice is to make one's professional role clear at the outset: 'I can do A, B and C, but I can't do E, F and G'. Then if a situation arises where one is pressed beyond one's proper limits, one is able to remind the party specifically about these limits.

The risk of poor boundaries is that the party may view the mediator as a new attachment 'carer', with high hopes for his or her needs to be met, but with little prospect of this being achieved. Boundaries and limits are important to maintain, but this should not be at the cost of empathy, which remains critical. The keywords here might be 'boundaried empathy'.

It's All About Relationships

Structure and records

With high conflict parties it is also necessary to avoid misunderstandings and to provide a structured framework. This may for example include being clear about process and having and maintaining ground rules about the conduct of the mediation, being specific about how costs will be calculated and charged and keeping parties up to date with these, maintaining relevant notes and providing parties with summaries and notes of any relevant matters.

Small incremental steps may be necessary

Huge leaps are unlikely, so mediators should encourage patience and plan the process to allow for the possibility of small incremental steps. There should not be an automatic expectation that the dispute will necessarily be resolved in one session. While a single session might be planned, parties' expectations might be prepared for the possibility of this being extended to a series of meetings and/or other interim communications.

Directiveness and proactivity

The conventional wisdom for mediators is to avoid being directive. However, this is less likely to be effective with high conflict disputes, where parties are inclined to be reactive rather than proactive. The mediator may need to be robustly proactive in proposing procedural ways of dealing with matters. This should not be confused with heavy handedness, nor should it interfere with maintaining a sensitive working relationship with the parties. There may well be some resistance to the mediator's directive and proactive role, so it would need to be deft, sensitive and supportive, while also clear, reasonable and firm. This should not become a contest with the parties.

Dealing with a party's 'world view'

A very challenging task when working with high conflict parties is to manage their world views, even those that appear to be based on cognitive distortions, in a way that is both respectful and appropriate and neither accepts nor criticises those views.

Professor Fonagy cautions against trying to sort out problems based on paranoia as if they were rational, though he considers that it may be necessary to treat the information as true and reasonable and see what the consequences would be if that were the case. The mediator would not however suspend critical judgment. There is an inherent paradoxical aspect to this. Bill Eddy says: 'Don't argue with their logic. Try to understand it.'

This involves listening with attention, respect and empathy and taking the party's views seriously, without losing objectivity, surrendering judgment or acknowledging that these views are correct. It does not preclude an element of objective reality testing.

Help personal and analytical responses

High conflict parties commonly have difficulty in appreciating the views and thinking of the other, with poor reflective functioning. The implications and consequences of attitudes and proposals may not be understood and in the privacy of separate confidential meetings the mediator may need to help a party to appreciate these better by way of informal coaching.

The mediator can help parties with risk analysis by providing material and guidance. The mediator can also help parties express themselves to one another more effectively by getting to the essence of each communication, reframing appropriately and ensuring that substantive messages are not obscured by emotional or repetitive overtones.

Further relevant strategies

The following further considerations are relevant to high conflict personalities:
- Formality trumps trying to be likeable when working with high conflict personalities, to avoid being adopted as a new attachment figure.
- It is better for the mediator to maintain a rather more professional stance, with empathy and some informality as appropriate. The aim would be for 'empathetic objectivity'.
- Symbolic measures may be especially relevant to high conflict personalities, especially when looking for a face-saving outcome, which may also be important.

High conflict dispute endings

It is in the nature of high conflict disputes that they may not be resolved by agreement. The mediator should not regard it as a failure if the issues have to be resolved by adjudication. That may well be the right way for matters to be decided. If in such event there are any recriminations against the mediator, these should be dealt with briefly, courteously, professionally and non-contentiously, in such a way as to not invite a contentious reply. Fallout from high conflict disputes may be regarded as an occupational hazard.

Who is at the centre of mediation?

David Richbell

As commercial mediation has 'matured' it is worth considering again who is, and who should be, at the centre. Is it:
- the party?
- the lawyer (solicitor, barrister, judge)?
- the mediator?
- the providers?
- the Civil Mediation Council (CMC)?

The party

It is said that mediation is a party-focused process. It is the party who is at the centre. It is their problem, their solution, their process. This is the opportunity for the party to really have a day in court – a far better day than being in a real court. Here a party can say what they want, with all the feeling and conviction that they have, the only restriction being time and courtesy (ie non-abusive) – and that it is free of bloodshed.

Unfortunately the theory rarely works in practise. Too often the party is put in the background, sometimes by choice, and others speak (and negotiate) on their behalf. Which is a tragedy, for mediation provides the opportunity for each of the parties to tell their story – their story (not someone else's version) – to the other side(s) and to then hear their version of the same story. Done well it can help parties change position and provide reasons for them to become flexible in their approach to a solution.

So why does it happen so rarely? Well, it may be too early in the process. A party is inevitably cautious of the process (it is, after all, usually the first and only time that they experience mediation). They don't want to say something that will be used against them in the future, or which may upset their lawyer. Too often a party, when invited to speak after their lawyer has made an opening statement, will say 'no, my lawyer has said it all'. They haven't! The lawyer has given the legal argument – there is a much more powerful one to be said by the party for it is, after all, their money (payer or receiver), their emotions, their life, which is why many good mediators have a fairly lengthy opening session, to give time for a party to settle down, feel confident about the process and then be stirred into speaking.

Similarly, the party should be the one to negotiate the deal. It is their problem, and their solution. Everyone else should be in support but the deal should be theirs. At the very least, the parties should be the ones to seal the deal, to agree the final details and shake hands. They need to own the outcome – that is the most powerful reason why mediated deals stick.

The lawyer

Given the above, that mediation is a party-focused process, the lawyer is cast in a supportive role. The theory goes that the lawyer takes more and more of a back seat as the party leads the pathway to solution.

For the solicitor, this means preparing the party, encouraging them to take a full part in the process, advising on legal merits, undertaking and reviewing risk analysis and supporting her/his party in their quest for a solution. This may be a challenge for someone who is normally a problem-solver and a fighter for the best deal.

For a barrister this is even more of a challenge. Instinctively a leader, spokesperson and assumed negotiator, most find it difficult to allow others (preferably the party) to lead and for them to be adviser, supporter and encourager. Indeed, it may be difficult to justify a barrister's fee in such circumstances. The worst thing that a barrister can do is muffle the party, grandstand the opening session and highjack the deal. Perhaps it would be better not to attend at all.

The judge may well be a significant player in a mediation: instigating the mediation in the first place; threatening sanctions if parties do not mediate or do not mediate in good faith; being the final arbiter if it doesn't settle. Stories of dead-cert cases that went the wrong way because the judge got out of the right bed the wrong way (or the wrong bed the right way) are always an incentive for even the strongest cases to settle in mediation. Whilst not present, or in the centre, the judge's shadow is always cast on the mediation proceedings.

The mediator

The best mediators are unnoticed most of the time. They are firm but discrete managers of the process whose function is to give the parties the best chance of finding a solution to their dispute. This involves getting parties talking, and the more they talk, the more the mediator recedes into the background. It involves the strategic use of information (what to give, what to hold, what to reframe) without being overbearing or the central focus. A good mediator retrains the ego, demonstrates humility and takes no credit for the solution.

There are some big egos in commercial mediation and it must be quite difficult for their owners to avoid the feeling of self-importance, especially when they are constantly in demand and where most of their mediations settle. But even the best mediators must never forget that mediation is a party-focused process and that the mediator is just a means to helping that party achieve a solution. One advantage of mediation is that it brings finality, removes risk and lets the parties get on with life the next day. That same next day, the mediator is usually history.

The providers

Whist mediator providers may not be at the centre on the day, they have a huge influence on the development of individual mediators and on the profession as a whole. Collectively (which strangely is not a word normally used in connection with ADR organisations) they are a body which could have a strong voice in the promotion of mediation and in the development of common standards for the accreditation and development of commercial mediators. To a certain extent this is achieved through the Civil Mediation Council, although that body has other interested parties who have their own voice. It is the providers who have a collective interest in expanding the market, in offering a variety of specialisms and skills and who can bring a commercial as well as professional aspect to mediation. Unfortunately there is no indication (yet) of the many mediator providers in the United Kingdom showing anything other than a precious defence of their own 'territory' and they still seem a long way from speaking with a united voice. Mediation is the poorer for it.

The Civil Mediation Council (CMC)

The CMC is probably the most representative of all mediation organisations, having many individual as well as company members. As I write, it is in the process of change, becoming a charity with a board of individual practitioners, providers and trainers, and having an advisory board of interested, and influential parties including academics and representatives from the Ministries of Justice and Business, which gives it some claim and authority to be at the centre of commercial mediation. In its time it has moved from being an advocate for the increasing use of mediation to moving towards being the standard-setter (and regulator?) of civil, commercial and workplace (and other?) mediator disciplines. One day it will drop the 'Civil' from its title and become the Mediation Council. Unquestionably, the CMC already provides a valuable bridge between the government and the practitioner and that will become increasingly important as the move towards regulation gains strength. Whether or not it is at the centre of mediation, it will always be a centre of influence.

Conclusion

Of all the influences that prevail on commercial mediation the most important is that it is a party-focused process and all else should be subsidiary. It is their problem and their solution and the mediator and all the others are there help them get the best deal possible.

Chapter 4

Intercultural Mediation: The Fundamentals

Joanna Kalowski

Joanna Kalowski is an extraordinary person. She is a trainer of great humour, communication skills and knowledge. She has mediated some exceptional cases, advised government, both central and state, on mediation and its related processes and has still had time to write books. I count myself lucky to be her friend. (DR)

Mediators all cherish the fond hope that it is the process, carefully and skilfully managed and applied, which will take parties from conflict to settlement, whoever they might be. Maturing mediators find themselves looking beyond process, even beyond techniques, in the search for ways to manage particular dynamics.

The intercultural dynamic requires such a search. In the preface to his book, *The Dynamics of Conflict Resolution*,[1] Bernie Mayer writes:

> 'What makes a successful peacemaker or conflict resolver is not a set of processes, methodologies, or tactics; it is a way of thinking, a set of values, an array of analytical and interpersonal skills, and a clear focus.'

With this as a starting point, mediating in an intercultural setting moves from problem to challenge, challenging mediators to move beyond stereotypes towards understanding something of the people at the table, not merely the issue that brought them there. Intercultural mediation is an opportunity to expand our understanding of self and other, to be fully engaged in the role of mediator both personally and professionally. Whatever professional experience we have gained, whatever life has taught us, we bring to the moment in which parties need us to guide their thinking, to untangle the 'what' from the 'how', and fact from assumption.

The question facing mediators is how to do this, where to begin.

Knowing what 'intercultural' signifies – and what it does not

Across the English-speaking world, intercultural and cross-cultural are used interchangeably: it can be helpful if mediators understand some subtle differences.

---

1 B Mayer, *The Dynamics of Conflict Resolution: A Practitioner's Guide* (Jossey Bass, 2000).

The intercultural is best defined as 'contact between people of different backgrounds where one enters the other's society for a time-defined stay, for a defined purpose.'

The cross-cultural, on the other hand, defines 'an interaction between people of different backgrounds living in long-term, open-ended contact with one another in the same society, where that society's rhetoric is multiculturalism, bi-culturalism or equality.'[2]

For the purposes of mediation, these definitions matter. They allow mediators to consider in advance whether the parties to a dispute are foreign nationals whose major contact has been commercial and who have come together in this place to attempt settlement. This scenario typifies the intercultural business dispute between companies whose representatives live and operate in different countries. It will be an intercultural mediation in the truest sense.

While the corporate and business environment are unifiers, similar even in very different countries, once a dispute breaks out mediators can expect language and cultural assumptions, values and differences to play a role in exacerbating the conflict – or at the very least, to affect the flow of communication and understanding between the parties, even where they are speaking the same language. Certainly language is an issue if one party is a native speaker of a language and the other speaks it as a second language, but well beyond language, the parties' assumptions and expectations are worth examining in order to ensure that there is a shared understanding of the problems, the issues, the options and any agreement that emerges. This is an iterative process, and in an intercultural mediation, wise mediators check regularly. How and when is a matter for the individual mediator.

Intercultural mediation presents complexities and challenges, but they differ in nature from the challenges facing parties and the mediator in a cross-cultural setting where parties are citizens of the same society.

As the societies in which mediators operate become ever more diverse, it is likely that while the parties to a dispute might all be English[3] citizens, they will be from different backgrounds or different countries of birth. Those backgrounds bring with them sets of assumptions which may not be shared and, just as in the intercultural setting described above, the existence of a dispute will cause those assumptions and approaches to complicate the issues and affect communication between the parties.

The difference between the two is that the first, the intercultural, is a better known phenomenon: everyone has travelled and had advice along the lines of 'when in Rome' – a list of things to do and avoid which will supposedly keep them out of trouble. The problem this presents is that there is a tendency to apply the same principle to the cross-cultural setting, which is more nuanced, more complex and where power relations are likely to play a role. Even if it were possible in the intercultural situation to find reliable (and not stereotyped) information about different countries' values, assumptions and approaches, it would be risky to apply that willy-nilly to individuals in dispute. It might, however, prove a useful starting point.

---

2   Ibid.
3   English is used throughout to illustrate the cross-cultural example of a citizen born elsewhere but living and operating in the society of which they are a citizen.

In the cross-cultural situation, it is next to impossible. This is because cultural adaptation is on a kind of continuum, and it can be extremely difficult to work out to what extent, for instance, an overseas-born party has adapted to the society of which they are a citizen, and therefore to what extent attitudes and values encountered in a mediation are personality-based, cultural, or a mix of the two. Parties themselves are often unable to tell because adaptation to the host culture happens unconsciously and imperceptibly, and it is not until a person returns 'home' that they realise how much they have changed. In this context change means the unwitting abandonment of certain behaviours or beliefs, or the addition of elements of the new culture, often without conscious awareness. Grief can accompany the abandonment of key cultural behaviours if it is conscious, and resentment can flare if that person is now treated as if they were still 'traditional' rather than 'English', when they feel they have given up so much. The parties' perceptions of one another affect the cross-cultural setting in a way which differs from the intercultural, because if they are all 'English', parties may expect their own worldview to be shared, and will be at best surprised and at worst surprised and dismissive if it is not.

Case study

A Sikh doctor who had been living and practising medicine in the same hospital in Australia for a decade made the painful decision to cut his own hair short and stop wearing a turban when he and his wife decided things would be easier for their young son if he did not have to wear one.

Some time later, in a mediation between the doctor and colleagues over rostering and 'collegiate relations', the doctor discovered his colleagues did not remember he was a Sikh, nor that he had ever worn a turban. He was deeply offended, and said so.

'Why?' they asked, incredulous. 'Aren't you just one of us?'

The doctor turned to them and said his decision to remove his turban had been very painful; having never had to make a similar decision, his colleagues simply did not understand 'what all the fuss is about.'

It was left to the mediator to find a way to describe the situation from both perspectives. The mediator stated simply that it seemed the doctor's gesture had been a conscious move towards his colleagues and towards the society he lived in, but now that his hair was no different from anyone else's, his 'gift' was invisible, except to him. This statement enabled his colleagues to see things differently and to acknowledge his gesture; it also allowed the doctor to forgive them for seeing him through the prism of the majority culture.

Cross-cultural mediation also differs at the level of rights and power, particularly where change is under discussion, as it so often is. Where parties meet as equals, as citizens of the same state, but assert strongly differing views on what should happen in particular circumstances, those who have traditionally been more powerful can resent assumptions of equality and seek to 'educate' the others and impose their (time-honoured) views. Whether the parties are contributors to a workplace, a neighbourhood, a company or the task of nation-building in a democratic society, their views on ways to tackle a problem merit equal consideration, even if certain views are later discarded in favour of views the parties can all agree to.

It falls to the mediator to make this plain in a way that will not cause embarrassment to either party. 'It's not about agreeing, it's about listening to one another's views. You never know what you might discover you agree with.'

Which approach to take?

Mediation requires professional and personal training and development; mediating across cultures requires no less development, and quite possibly more, yet it does not often feature in mainstream mediation training. There are many approaches to operating across cultures, including the ethno-specific and its opposite, the broad cultural approach. No single approach provides the perfect answer, though all offer insights. Other approaches developed to provide awareness of culture are the psychological, interpersonal, linguistic, socio-historical and normative-legal.

The ethno-specific approach emphasises differences at the expense of similarities between groups and is facts-based. In describing cultural groups in these terms, it can descend into stereotyping: the Dutch are clean; the Koreans are hard-working; Australians will bet on a raindrop rolling down a windowpane, and so on.

Given the complexity of working with individuals in a dispute setting, this approach has limited value, since forces other than culture are operating on individuals to make them behave as they do: personality, gender, life experience, age and social status, for instance, all play a part.

It is no use studying the 'exotic other' and ending up with a series of stereotypes; to understand others, it is essential to understand the way culture works on the mediator as an individual. Absent such knowledge, they can unintentionally appear to side with the party whose culture most resembles her or his own, and so alienate others.

What matters here is that mediators are aware of the impact on parties and the process of the beliefs they, the mediators, hold.

The broad cultural approach

The 'broad cultural approach' of Paul Pedersen[4] tends to be useful. It sets out to define what a cultural perspective aims to achieve:

> 'The cultural perspective seeks to provide a framework for understanding the complex diversity of a plural society while identifying bridges of shared concern which bind culturally different persons to one another.'[5]

It also provides clues to why we are baffled by behaviour:

---

4   P Pedersen, *Culture-Centred Counselling Interventions* (Sage Publications,1997).
5   P Pedersen, *Counselling across Cultures* (Sage Publications, 2007).

'Similar behaviours can have different meanings and different behaviours can have the same meaning.'[6]

'Behaviour is not data until and unless the cultural assumptions underlying it are properly understood.'[7]

Pedersen's search for a way of understanding the gap between expectations and behaviour is particularly useful when applied to mediating across cultures. He demonstrates how 'obvious differences in behaviour across cultures are typically overemphasised while the more difficult to discover similarities in expectation are overlooked or underemphasised'. This is a useful tool for mediators working in an intercultural setting: find out what parties expect; make no assumptions about the meaning behind what they are doing. Presume nothing, question everything.

Self-awareness is essential for intercultural mediators. Mediators need to be aware of their own preferences and culturally influenced approaches, perspectives and choices. This requires insight and tolerance of discomfort, such as when parties or their representatives behave in ways mediators find challenging, unexpected or 'unhelpful'. It is at such junctures that intercultural exchanges are taking place – even if imperceptibly. If mediators adopt this view, private session/caucus becomes a valuable tool, and protects mediators from the dogma of all-caucus or no-caucus thinking. Success in intercultural mediation demands mediators use every available avenue to assist parties towards understanding and resolution.

A key role of intercultural mediators is to demystify what is taking place and debrief parties who may be baffled by the responses or reactions of others. That is not to say that mediators necessarily have to know the reasons, cultural or otherwise, which underlie certain behaviours. They simply have to be aware there is a need to intervene and manage the moment in which doubt, frustration or hesitation emerges.

Intercultural insights can help overcome impasses which result from culturally different expectations and behaviours, and which parties may express in emotional terms: 'Why are they so stubborn? Why won't they just admit their errors?'

They may also express frustration and confusion in procedural terms:

> 'We are ready to walk out. They are taking so much time to make decisions that we are beginning to suspect they aren't genuinely seeking settlement.'

In order to have access to a range of process responses, it is important for intercultural mediators not to be dogmatic about preferred models of mediation, to be prepared to incorporate every tool available, to use private and joint sessions flexibly, and to structure processes which meet parties' needs, not those dictated by mediator comfort or discomfort. Non-caucus models of mediation will cause particular problems, particularly when parties need the opportunity to withdraw with dignity, understand what is happening for themselves and the others, and prepare to meet again once they are able to do so.

---

6   Ibid.
7   Ibid.

The importance of understanding high and low context communication

Edward T Hall, an American anthropologist, wrote *The Silent Language* in 1959, and worked in the area of cross-cultural research until his death in 2009. His contribution to the field was to categorise cultures as being either 'low' or 'high' context in communication terms:

> 'In *low context cultures*, the circumstances of an event warrant little attention, and the focus in communication is on objective facts conveyed. Surrounding circumstances are filtered out.'[8]

Low context communicators think of themselves as open, direct, frank and sincere. The Angles, Saxons, Jutes and Danes are all examples of low context communication, so most English, German, Dutch and Danish speakers tend to be lower context than, for instance, speakers of Latin languages. Even in low-context communication settings, women tend to be higher context communicators than men, and English speakers would all be aware of the difference in style (context) between Australian, American and British speakers of the English language.

> 'In *high context cultures*, surrounding circumstances play a key role in interpreting data. Factors such as gesture, posture, tone of voice, and the social status of the speaker and the social setting of the interaction are used to interpret spoken words.'[9]

It is instructive to examine what high and low context communicators think of one another, and to recognise the scope for irritation and conflict arising out of two very different styles.

High context communicators think of themselves as polite, cautious and respectful and have a preference for illustrating what they are saying with story and metaphor.

But...

Low context communicators see high context communicators as time wasters, verbose, indirect and hard to fathom.

While...

High context communicators see low context communicators as rude, abrupt, insensitive, overly direct and even insulting.

Since such differences are exacerbated in a dispute, this is fertile ground for mediators and can provide the basis for bridging otherwise intractable misunderstanding and miscommunication.

Hall's definitions still galvanise readers and are of great value to mediators working across cultures. Where one group anticipates facts and filters out anything 'irrelevant' (think of lawyers' comments in this context) and the other supplies

---

8   E T Hall, *The Silent Language* (Doubleday, 1959).
9   Ibid.

endless detail which illustrates their grasp of a topic and their personal importance, conflict can arise merely from the exasperation each party feels faced with the other's style and reactions.

More emphasis is placed on parties' communication style than on mediators', and mediators are at an advantage when they understand how *they* come across when communicating with parties. They may unknowingly be adding to the difficulties of high context parties by speaking very directly, asking direct questions and expecting direct answers, hallmarks of a low context style, without a full appreciation that it is up to mediators to adjust their communication style to facilitate optimal information exchange between the parties.

Similarly, if mediators are high context communicators but unaware of the fact, they may irritate and frustrate low context parties by appearing to draw the process out, allowing too much time for certain elements of the mediation process and letting 'unclear' (indirect) communication – metaphors, stories and hints – pile up until the low context communicators in the room feel uneasy and uncertain of precisely what is being said. Unable to 'read between the lines' and temperamentally unprepared to do so, low context communicators can feel they are being disadvantaged by the capacity of the other party to engage with the mediator.

If mediators intervene to 'speed things up', high context communicators can begin to feel pressured by time or by overly direct communication, and may fall silent or withdraw altogether, ultimately unhelpful to both sides and to reaching settlement.

Once mediators realise the mismatch in styles is to some extent the result of low or high culture style, they can intervene to manage it. Whether they do so in joint or in private session, it is up to mediators to make what is happening explicit: to name the reactions and normalise the discomfort parties may be feeling.

Case study

Take the following example, drawn from a real situation.

Recognising the gulf in approaches taken by a Japanese and an American party, the mediator had to create opportunities for breaks that let the impatient Americans (far lower context than the Japanese) out of the room while the Japanese (much higher context communicators) took time to work though options and alternatives without feeling pressured. Once both parties were released from the pressure to behave in ways each found 'inappropriate' in their own terms, the atmosphere changed, and the emphasis returned to finding a mutually satisfactory solution – a shared goal, even if the behaviours being pursued to reach that goal were not shared. Had the mediator not intervened, a walkout was very likely, with a poor prognosis for reaching settlement. Both parties had begun to feel irritated by the other, and were showing it non-verbally. The Americans were drumming on the table during long silences and looking questioningly at one another while the Japanese were avoiding eye contact with them and increasingly talking to one another in undertones in Japanese, even though the parties had agreed English would be used and no interpreter was necessary.

The mediator spoke about the need for breaks to consider the ideas on the table, making this the pretext for inviting the parties to return to their own rooms. Moving between them to talk and clarify issues, the mediator saved face for both.

The comfort of familiarity with one or more cultural frameworks

Geert Hofstede's Five Dimensions of National Culture

Multiple frameworks exist[10] and intercultural mediators benefit greatly by being familiar with one or more. Hofstede's model is useful because it has been frequently replicated and has wide application. Like all models, it has imperfections, but remains a useful guide and one source of valuable information for mediators.

The five dimensions Hofstede identifies are:

(1) **Power distance (PDI)**

Defined as the extent to which the less powerful members of society accept that power is distributed unequally (eg, use of titles v given names at the first meeting).

(2) **Individualism (IDV) and its counterpart, collectivism**

Defined as the extent to which people in a given society believe that you look after yourself and your immediate family; collectivism as the extent to which people see themselves as belonging to groups (family, clan or organisation) which take care of them in return for loyalty. (eg, explaining to one party planning to send a single representative and its legal adviser to mediation why the other side will be represented by three or more – or even a whole clan group).

(3) **Masculinity (MAS) and its counterpart femininity (or tough v tender)**

The extent to which the dominant values in a society are achievement and success; femininity as the extent to which dominant values are about quality of life and caring for others. (The combination of IDV and MAS is interesting in this regard and frequently emerges in commercial mediations and negotiations; one side is concerned for the future of a committed workforce, the other with shareholder value.)

(4) **Uncertainty avoidance (UAI)**

The extent to which people feel threatened by ambiguity and uncertainty and try to avoid such situations by creating rules to be followed in those situations. High uncertainty avoidance cultures appear rule-bound and inflexible to low uncertainty avoidance cultures. ('Why wait, let's just do it,' versus 'That's not the way we go about things, and it would be disastrous if we didn't have regard to

---

10 Cf F Trompenaars and P Wooliams, *Business across Cultures* (Capstone, 2004), C Kluckhohn and F Strodtbeck, *Variations in value orientations* (Row Peterson, 1961), E Hall, *The Silent Language* (Doubleday, 1959), M Minkov, *What makes us different and similar: A New Interpretation of the World Values Survey and Other Cross-Cultural Data* (Klasika y Stil Publishing, 2007), J DiStefano and M Maznevski, 'Culture in International Management: Mapping the Impact', IMD Perspectives for Managers, 104, November 2003, D Moïsi, *The Geopolitics of Emotion: How Cultures of Fear, Humiliation, and Hope are Reshaping the World* (Anchor, 2010).

protocol/expectations/public reaction', etc. Even walking into a cocktail party as a guest and introducing yourself to people without waiting for your hosts to take you around could give unintended offence, and is a common example of low v high UAI.)

(5) **Long-term orientation (LTO) and its counterpart, short-term orientation.**

The extent to which a society favours a future-oriented perspective rather than a conventional historical or short-term perspective. In this context, international intercultural disputes are often complicated by Western powers' preference for final and binding agreements, while other countries insist you can't bind future generations because the future is not foreseeable.

Some insights for mediators based on Hofstede's model

- Hofstede does not set out to apply the dimensions to or describe individuals, whose behaviour is influenced by multiple factors such as gender, personality, age and life experience; but the dimensions often prove helpful as a guide to what may be creating blocks and hesitation in an intercultural or cross-cultural mediation and provide mediators with a lead as to how they might intervene, what they might say to overcome a problem.
- In all societies you will find both elements of all five dimensions, but one predominates.
- All societies are in flux, so no single aspect of any of these dimensions is fixed for all time. Indeed, mediators will recognise in one culture, behaviours and attitudes that once characterised their own, particularly where gendered behaviour and gender relations are concerned.
- Conflict within groups will often arise from currents related to changes in one dimension, which a sub-group in that society is seeking to promote. Intergenerational conflict is one such example: freedom to experiment with lifestyles and relationships versus respect for one's elders, the community and its standards and expectations.
- Conflict between groups such as international corporations may exacerbate tensions around dominant orientations/dimensions which the mediator will need skills to address and normalise.

Hofstede also identifies four unasked questions that influence cross- and intercultural dialogue. They are:

(1) How personal should I be?

(2) How direct should I be?

(3) How do I get a turn to speak here?

(4) How are good relations made and kept here?

The way we answer these questions is influenced by a number of factors of which culture is but one. Personality, gender, life experiences and social status all play a part, but children of any culture unconsciously know the answers in their own cultural setting by about the age of eight.

If, for instance, one party's expectation is for strict turntaking and the other feels it natural to speak whenever they want to comment, it will not be long before an intercultural mediation is adversely affected. The party which thinks its representatives are 'doing the right thing' by hanging back will be offended by the other's failure to do so.

How should intercultural mediators speak?

If mediators have prepared for an intercultural mediation by giving due weight to the parties' communication styles, they can, in certain circumstances, indicate at the outset that since only so much time has been set aside for these negotiations, it might be best if parties were free to engage in a kind of conversation with one another, with the exception of the opening statements, which parties should be allowed to finish before the others comment or ask questions.

In other circumstances, where parties are both more inclined to formality, or at least more accepting of it, the mediator might propose another format for communication at the mediation, one in which parties speak one after the other, ping pong style, until later in the mediation when issues have been clarified and key information exchanged.

Once again, this calls on intercultural mediators to have a wide repertoire of communication styles with which they are comfortable, rather than a favoured style to which they default almost unconsciously. Only in this way can mediators guarantee the comfort of parties in an intercultural mediation.

Hofstede's framework and his four unasked questions provide a way of legitimising the intercultural mediator's suite of interventions and are far more palatable to adults than the ground rules or guidelines usually asserted. They provide a context within which to intervene which makes sense to the parties because its intention is to facilitate the unimpeded flow of communication between *them*, rather than impose rules on the parties which often make little sense, and can seem patronising when they appear to be more about the mediator's sense of what is polite and courteous – another phenomenon unlikely to be shared.

Intercultural mediators need also to be highly self-aware, and aware of their use of language. The notion of interrupting is a critical one in this context because not in all cultures is it impolite to interject: quite the contrary – it shows interest and keenness to engage. For that reason, intercultural mediators need to develop a neutral language, one which favours neither side, and to state that they will intervene only if there is a risk neither the parties nor the mediator can follow or hear parties' exchanges because 'all are speaking at once'. Reframing in this way enables all parties to feel comfortable and is at the heart of intercultural mediators' effectiveness. Mediators should not only be focussed on reframing what parties say, but what they themselves say.

Beyond behaviour: assumptions, expectations and intentions

If behaviour is not data, then doubt creation and reality testing are key tools in intercultural mediation. The mediator's most useful question may just be: 'Could what they say possibly mean something other than you are assuming?' Equally useful in a moment of misunderstanding is asking one party what they understood the other to be saying, and then asking the other what they meant and sensitively handling the different assumptions that emerge.

An excellent guide for intercultural mediators is Pedersen's finding:

> '[O]bvious differences in behaviour across cultures are typically overemphasised while the more difficult to discover similarities in expectation are overlooked or underemphasised.'

Case study

Take the following example drawn from the author's experience in mediating native title claims by Aboriginal communities to their ancestral lands, known as 'country'.[11]

I was driven to meet an Aboriginal community in a remote part of Australia in preparation for the next day's mediation with representatives of government. It is common in remote communities for people to crowd onto the back of a truck, and it is an unwritten rule in the outback that you leave gates as you find them. As this truck arrived at a locked gate and I was close to the tail of the truck, I hopped off, swung open the gate, held it open while it drove through and then closed it again and hopped back on board.

Barely arrived in the community, I was told by my very skilful case manager that the community had let her know they didn't want to work with me. Astounded, I asked why, only to be told I had offended them. She wouldn't say how, and possibly didn't know, so I asked her if I could meet the senior women and try to find out what had caused the problem and, if possible, put it right.

The case manager set up a meeting and I went alone to meet a group of women, full of trepidation. After a time, I said I understood I had given offence and would like the chance to make it right. (I didn't ask a direct question about what I had done wrong, because I know Australian indigenous culture is high context and direct questions are poor form.)

One of the women got slowly up, came over to me and said: 'You come here as a guest, but you behaved like the host' (note the use of indirect communication). Baffled, I waited for her to say more (long silences are a normal part of the exchange). 'You opened the gate to the only place on the planet we can call ours.' I was horrified, but recognised instantly that we had the same expectation, the same intention, but different behaviours, and replied: 'And when I did, I intended to show my respect for you because in my culture you don't allow older people to do something which it is easier for you to do yourself.' Looking into my eyes, she said: 'All we saw was just another presumptuous white woman', and held out her hand. I took it and the others smiled. The moment had passed; we were reconciled.

---

11 Expressions like 'my country', 'my mother's/father's country', 'on country', and the use of the word without the definite article, 'ceremonies on country' are now Aboriginal English terms in common use in mainstream Australian English, considered correct and preferable.

What happened here was a classic case of shared intention around courtesy and respect with entirely different expectations of the behaviour that ought to accompany the intention. The indigenous women expected me to stay where I was and let them struggle on and off the truck in a display of welcome, and I expected to open the gate myself to demonstrate respect for their age and high status in the community.

While this can happen in far more mundane settings, this event dramatically underlined the fact that, however much we think we know, we will get it wrong when working across cultures. One of the few ways to overcome such a faux pas is to explain at the level of intention, and that confers on mediators the responsibility to be clear about their intentions and able to state them. Then, if we are lucky, and Pedersen is right, we might just find that despite assumptions of rudeness and inappropriate/different behaviours, we have much in common at the level of shared expectations and intentions.

Chapter 5

Further Communication Skills

Jane Walmsley

Jane is a great facilitator and trainer. We devised and ran my last mediator training course in the United Kingdom together and I am so pleased that she is able to continue that through this chapter. (DR)

The mediator's role is to give the parties the best shot at doing a deal. Good communication skills are recognised as being crucial to any mediator's ability to do that. This chapter builds upon the basic skills of an effective mediator covered in Part 1. They can be defined as 'the ability successfully to make known or to tell others about ideas and feelings'.

As mediators, that means:

- conveying how we feel and think about ourselves and others;
- conveying information directly from, to and between others; and
- enabling the development of an atmosphere and environment in which the parties and their advisers can concentrate their efforts on their commercial negotiations.

When I sat down to write this chapter, a number of questions sprang to my mind. On the basis of this definition, are good communication skills not sufficient? How might a set of skills that already meets that definition be developed and improved? What would be different about those skills? I spent a few minutes with a dictionary and constructed for myself a definition for advanced communication skills:

'the ability successfully to make known or to tell others about ideas and feelings *in a more careful and thorough way than is generally done.*'

So, the next question I asked myself was, what raises the level of our core communication skills from good to the next level – what makes us more careful and thorough? In my opinion, it is greater awareness of and flexibility in the nuances of behaviour patterns and techniques, and how, why and when we use them. What follows are some ideas about and techniques for developing awareness and flexibility that I have found to be helpful and effective. They relate to communicating presence and self-confidence, establishing and developing high levels of rapport and fostering an atmosphere conducive to robust and respectful negotiation. They are relatively straightforward to describe and understand; they can be more tricky to embed as attitudes or habits.

The foundations: presence, self-awareness and self-confidence

The ability to develop a fine attunement to the nuances of communication behaviour patterns and techniques is seen readily in people who have a strong sense of their own preferences, prejudices, strengths, weaknesses and values. Such self-awareness provides a secure footing from which to explore others' perspectives. It removes the need to prove anything to anyone and establishes the foundations for demonstrating genuine interest in others. You can be genuinely interested in others as equals because you have confidence in yourself.

In the context of mediation, the heart of this lies in the mediator's ability to balance and demonstrate in equal measure:

- thorough preparation;
- good planning;
- self-confidence (not arrogance);
- genuine interest in everyone present;
- genuine interest in facilitating the parties in finding their own solution;
- taking, retaining and ceding control, as appropriate; and
- being comfortable with the unknown.

An imbalance of focus or priority in any of these areas will be apparent to the parties, whether we like it or not, and could be interpreted as, at best nerves and at worst incompetence, fear or interest in our own settlement record rather than their dispute.

Prepare and plan

Thorough preparation is a given. A mediator whose focus from the outset is on proving to the parties how much they have read into their case and how well they have memorised documents, page numbers, etc demonstrates more interest in self than in them. A mediator who has confidence in the quality of their preparation and planning and in their ability to demonstrate that quality when required can concentrate more readily on communicating a calm, confident and safe presence which will, in turn, have a beneficial effect on others' responses.

Challenge your own assumptions and judgements

Assumptions and judgements impede openness, exploration and understanding. They can be about the parties, their advisers and their advice, what is and is not important and relevant, whether and how the dispute might settle, etc. Often, we can take quite a long time to notice that we're making them, by which time there may be misunderstandings creeping in that might take a while to clear up. To develop a greater awareness of your assumptions and judgements keep these questions in mind:

- What assumption(s) or judgment(s) am I making here?

- What are my reasons for making them?
- What evidence is there to support them?
- What evidence is there to refute them?
- If I were to act as if this assumption or judgement is correct, what would I do and what might be the outcome?
- If I were to act as if this assumption or judgement is incorrect, what would I do and what might be the outcome?

Your responses to these questions will increase your self-awareness and enable you to open up and deepen communication from the outset.

Self-confidence

Communicating a confident presence is both simple and challenging. It is simple in that it is best achieved by allowing others to see less rather than more. It is challenging in that it can be difficult to accept that allowing others to see less rather than more is effective. Sound planning and preparation and high levels of self-awareness are the starting point that allow for everything else to follow. Other things that help are:

- *Breathing* – pay attention to the speed and depth of your breathing. To calm yourself, slow your breathing down and deepen it into at least two thirds of your lungs.
- *Eye contact* – establish eye contact with others and maintain it well. It makes more difference than anything else.
- *Posture* – in a virtuous cycle, good posture that suggests a relaxed and confident attitude will in itself generate a more relaxed and confident attitude. So, pay regular attention to your posture and adjust it as necessary. Aim for a straight back, relaxed shoulders and level chin. Keep your hands in view (to reinforce your trustworthiness) and make sure that they are not distracting when they move – so don't fiddle! When seated and you want to make a point, to interrupt an unhelpful exchange or to ensure that you are heard, lean forwards by moving from your hips not your waist and form a triangle on the table top with your forearms and fingers.
- *Being still* – fidgeting, taking notes (or at worst, dictation) or evidently waiting to speak are distracting and suggest a focus on self rather than an openness to and interest in the other person. Quieten the inner commentator and these intrusive tics will diminish.
- *Sounding confident* – your voice should be well projected and at an appropriate volume. It is possible to project your voice without shouting. Speak at a moderate pace and in sentences that are shorter rather than longer. Use the power of silence.
- *Dress and grooming* – wear something that is both comfortable and smart to boost confidence levels immediately. Ensure that the colour(s) of your outfit enhance and brighten your appearance. For example, if I wear navy or grey with pink, purple or emerald green, I tend to look healthier and more energetic than if I wear a black suit and white blouse. I only need to stand close to shades of

apricot, coral, baby blue or primrose yellow to look washed out and as if I've had the 'flu for a fortnight! Most importantly, wear clothes that fit.

These foundations are significant. A mediator who is at ease with themselves and who can demonstrate from the outset that they are confident and interested in others will allow the parties to relax in the knowledge that they are in safe hands in that process on that day.

Establishing and developing rapport

Strong rapport eases the flow of communication. We seek to build rapport by, or infer it from, speech, body language and gaze. More specifically, when strong rapport has developed, what is visible between people is well maintained eye contact, acute listening, matching body language, matching phrasing patterns and turntaking in conversation. The foundation stone of rapport is genuine interest in and openness to others, which needs room to develop.

Openness: make mental space for everything

Keeping an open mind is often a difficult task and particularly in a mediation context when there is so much going on. We all form opinions about the people we're working with on the day, the strengths and weaknesses of their respective positions, how we think the dispute should be resolved, whether we like them or not. While listening, I can find it tricky to stop my internal commentary and quieten my mind. I find that telling myself not to think about my own views and to concentrate on the parties doesn't help me. If you tell yourself not to think of an elephant, what happens? When my internal commentator pipes up, I have found it to be more beneficial to notice the thought and then let it go and sit quietly in a corner of my mind. That way, there is still plenty of room for what I'm listening to. My thoughts have their own space and can wait there until I'm ready for them. I find that if I try to dismiss them until later, they keep coming back like a persistent and annoying mosquito.

Show them that you are listening and are interested

The quality of a listener's eye contact is significant in influencing the depth of rapport and quality of communication between people in conversation. Eye contact tells us that we have the other's full attention. So, no matter how infrequently the other person looks at you while they're speaking, it is vital that you continue to look at their face and eyes so that whenever they do look for you, you are there, giving them your full attention; you're there to catch them. This does more than anything else to enhance and develop the quality and depth of rapport that we establish with our parties. There is a difference between well-maintained, interested eye contact and staring that becomes competitive or persecutory. An obvious point, that, but it wanted to be written!

Match their language

Do this so that you sound more like them. They will hear you more easily and feel more comfortable with you. So, pay attention to how they phrase what they say.

Do they use visual, auditory or kinaesthetic language: 'They can't see the wood for the trees,' 'He really likes to blow his own trumpet,' 'Their argument is so woolly'. When you paraphrase to demonstrate that you are listening and understanding, make sure you use their preferred form or a combination of two or three, for example: 'It looks like…', 'It sounds like…', 'It feels like…'.

Match their body language

Then, if necessary, lead it. If their body language is positive and energetic, match in equal measure. If it is either aggressive or withdrawn then your matching needs to be a moderated version of theirs, the balance shifting quickly to you demonstrating the calm, confident body language described above. Once someone's emotional state is acknowledged non-verbally, they will more readily respond to signals to adjust their behaviour, which will have an impact on their mood and the clarity of their thinking.

Fostering a conducive atmosphere

Again, the starting point here is listening: the willingness to listen with genuine interest and an open mind; the ability to listen acutely and with concentration and patience to everything being said; the ability to let others know unambiguously that and what you have heard and understood. Giving people a really good listening to, in my experience, fosters the development of rapport, demonstrates empathy, reduces the emotional temperature of a conversation or situation and allows reason and pragmatism to come to the fore. By communicating to the parties a non-judgmental attitude coupled with sincere interest in them, their situation and their story an environment can be developed in which open exploration can take place. So, listen for, and help others to listen for, the right stuff. By 'the right stuff', I mean everything rather than something in particular over and above anything else. Listening for everything enables everything that is pertinent to be given attention and avoids incorrect assumptions being made.

Tell people that and what you have heard and understood

You might be hearing and understanding everything that one of your parties is saying about their take on the factual matrix, their emotional state and what they want to offer and would like the outcome to be. However, even if you understand, it doesn't necessarily follow that everyone else in the room does. So, providing a précis serves several purposes:

- you check out and confirm or correct your understanding;
- you enable others in the room to hear again what has been said, repeated by a different voice;
- you provide the reassurance to the speaker that they have been heard and understood accurately so that they can move you and give the speaker the opportunity to reframe what they said if it seems unclear; and
- by acknowledging everything they have communicated, you validate (not necessarily agree with) their perspective. This, too, allows people to move on.

Further Communication Skills

The ingredients for a good précis are a summary of the facts, a labelling of the emotions being communicated, either in words or non-verbally, and a checking out of the person's needs or intention as they have expressed them, again either in words or non-verbally. You can do it with a heavy hand or with a light touch. It need not be long and can be adjusted according to the amount of information you're dealing with. There's little worse than someone who does this too often and in tedious detail. If you are making mental space for everything and genuinely giving your full attention to the other person, you will be able to judge when is the right time and what the combination of ingredients should be.

Basic mediator training reinforces the importance of exploring beyond facts and paying attention to emotions. When acknowledging emotion, there can be a fine line between being empathetic and respectful and being patronising or paying lip service. Much depends on phrasing patterns, tone of voice and timing:

- *'I can see that/it's clear that you feel angry/frustrated/irritated/unsure about...'* delivered in a tone of voice that implies a statement of fact can be effective when there's a danger of the process beginning to indulge the parties in dwelling on the past and you want to move it on. Earlier in the process, it could be interpreted as a platitude uttered by the mediator to buy themselves airtime.

- *'So, you're feeling angry/irritated/nervous/excited about...?'* delivered tentatively, as a question and with a genuine intention to acknowledge their feelings can be just the thing to do to let the other person know that you are fully engaged with what they're saying and to allow them either to feel fully and deeply understood or to correct your understanding. A sense of empathy between you will be the result. If your attention is full and genuine and you use a label that doesn't quite hit the spot for them, they will give you a correct one with no loss of rapport. Genuine engagement and the desire to understand are the key here.

More about phrasing patterns

As well as ensuring their own understanding, a mediator must also make it easy for the parties to hear and understand both each other and the mediator. Wittgenstein said: 'The limits of my language mean the limits of my world.'[1] In the context of mediation, as long as the parties continue to blame the other side and reinforce their own position, there is little room for progress. In altering the language being used by and between them, the mediator can be very effective in shifting the parties' perceptions: shifting the limits of their world in and of the dispute. So, the mediator's awareness of and ability to fine-tune their own phrasing patterns are significant, particularly in relation to asking questions, paraphrasing and summarising.

Some techniques that can help here are:

- *Ask why without using the word 'why'*. A question beginning with why can have the immediate effect of making somebody feel that they want or ought to explain, justify or defend themselves. Their focus remains on themselves and on the past or on saving face in the realisation that their perspective has been challenged. There is a fine balance to strike, it seems to me, between challenging parties' positions and perspectives yet avoiding interrogating them or backing

---

1 The *Tractatus Logico-Philosophicus* (1922).

them into a corner, especially as the process progresses, people are getting entrenched, or the mediator is getting frustrated. The following examples are of 'why' questions that use a few more words yet mean the same thing. They can serve to loosen thinking and enable exploration of alternative ideas:

- o what is your thinking about...?
- o what are the reasons for....?
- o please tell me about the background to...
- o what are your conclusions about...?
- o how is [x] different from what you're looking/asking for?

- Depersonalise to defuse

  It is not uncommon for parties and their advisers to make confrontational, blaming, self-justifying and sometimes downright rude statements, in both joint and private sessions. Again, unless challenged, those phrasing patterns can strengthen the parties' limited perspectives rather than opening up and shedding light on the issues to be resolved. So, the mediator's role is to challenge without being confrontational and so open up the landscape of the discussions. One of the most effective ways of doing this is by paraphrasing and summarising, aiming to take the sting out of as much of what is said as you can. For example:

If they say...	... you might say something like...
'What you've/they've got to understand is...'	'There appears to be confusion about...'
'You've/they've got it wrong...'	There is a difference of opinion between you about...'
'It's obvious that/everybody knows that...'	'A perspective that many people share is...; many people might agree/take the view that...'
'They keep contradicting yourselves...'	'A few minutes ago I heard [x]; I think I've just heard you say [y]
'They're talking complete rubbish'	'So, there is disagreement about...'

It takes concentration to pay such close attention to precise phrasing patterns, noticing the actual or potential impact and acting to defuse the situation immediately. Any internal chatter gets in the way and dulls the senses. Again, creating mental space is key in being able to use these skills appropriately and at the right time. Well-judged and well-framed statements by the mediator, phrased and pitched in the right way for the parties can ease tension, minimise confrontation and begin to open up mental space for the parties and their advisers too.

Match their language, continued....

Again, paying attention to phrasing patterns will alert you to the sorts of things that influence your parties in their thinking and decision making. Using the same patterns as theirs will enable them to hear more clearly and feel more secure in their understanding of the deal they are working towards. For example:

a party that says ...	... will hear most clearly
'I want/need x and y'	'They want to give you...'
'This will be resolved when x and y happen'	'For them, a solution incorporates x, y and z'
'If we can get x and y in place, then we could consider z'	'If you could offer them z, they might be able to consider x and y'
'It would help me hugely if we could agree x and y'	'A really helpful starting point for this might be to consider x and y'

Conclusion

The ideas and techniques that I have described are the ones that I find most helpful. I find them effective in opening up and maintaining clear, constructive communication even in the most fractious or high-temperature mediations, and in improving the quality and depth of communication during the process. They are founded on core communication skills, adjusting and elaborating on them to give a range of approaches that are sometimes more subtle, sometimes more precisely-focused. Used with awareness and lightness of touch, they can fine-tune, broaden and enhance a mediator's style and help to generate the atmosphere for open, constructive, robust negotiations.

Chapter 6

Sector Specialisms

Although I have mediated in many of these sectors, it is a real pleasure to have contributions from other mediators who have built a reputation in their field. Their brief was to assume the basic skills and process had be learned and that the mediator was now out in the world, eager to practise. What extra should they know about your particular sector? There are several common threads in these contributions, not least having to manage emotion and showing endless patience and tenacity.

Mediating farming and rural disputes

Anthony Glaister

> 'The land is the only thing in the world worth working for, worth fighting for, worth dying for, because it's the only thing that lasts'
>
> Gerald O'Hara, in Margaret Mitchell, *Gone With The Wind*

Farming disputes produce some of the most challenging mediations. Deepseated differences nurtured and built up over time, and often over and between generations, explode into an almost intractable breakdown of communications mired in prejudice and self-righteousness. Many farming-related disputes tend to involve families, as they struggle to run a business together or to simply live next to each other without coming to blows. There are then the disputes between the landlord and the tenant farmer over access, rights of way, mineral extraction, lease renewals, and even management of game where it is perceived as an activity that detrimentally affects the farming activities on the land. The last category is farming-related disputes with third parties who have no direct interest in the land, with suppliers of feed and machinery, with builders, and with external bodies such as DEFRA, utility suppliers, local authorities and the like. The common denominator in most of these disputes is the use and occupation of land.

Variety volatility and volume

From a mediators' stance, how do we deal with the sort of family at war scenario in the first category. Will they agree to mediate at all? Will they accept the others' presence in the same building, let alone the same room? Will they accept the advice and guidance of their representatives, if they have one? Will they trust the mediator to be impartial and independent, particularly when their behaviour may be, shall we say, challenging? It's vitally important to get some idea before the mediation of what one might expect. You can get this from the documents, or from the answers made by the representatives to the tactful and carefully crafted questions put over the phone to the representatives.

The following list of factors are amongst those that make farming disputes more challenging:

- The time scale of disputes between family members or neighbours often makes them rather like divorce cases where historic perspectives of hurt and offence run deep.

- Given the emotive extremes, it is likely that one or all parties have either resorted to retributive actions or even violence. Family, neighbour and business relationships become dysfunctional. As one mediator put it: 'In Yorkshire the sport of getting the better of someone seems to be ingrained in farmers'.

- There may be a lack of an audit trail where agreements were done with a handshake and without any record. There is a greater likelihood that oral evidence will be relied on, with witnesses required to give evidence and hence greater cost.

- There may be a lack of liquidity and flexibility in the options. Carving up a small family farm probably renders the farm(s) unviable.

- Changes in agricultural practice over the years create new friction points where land is shared or effects neighbouring land. A dispute can easily develop out of the joint use of a private drive and the greater wear and tear of modern, larger agricultural machinery. Similarly you often get involved in situations where new money and new aspirations about living in the countryside conflict with the business requirements of farming. If a farmer plans to erect a large industrial-sized cattle shed or a wind turbine well in excess of domiciliary usage, it is going to create friction with the neighbours.

- The variety of competing interests in on or over rural land make it that much more likely that disputes arise between farmers and other non-occupational parties; footpaths and the ramblers, shooting syndicates, hunts, flying clubs, local planning authorities, DEFRA and utility companies all come to mind.

Looking back at the rural disputes the writer has mediated, I entirely subscribe to what Peter Coleman said about responding to difficult relationships:

> 'Making matters worse are conditions of prolonged conflict, high tension, threat, polarisation, all of which serve to exacerbate the problem. In high stress situations our capacity for thorough, effective decision making becomes increasingly impaired by perceptual distortions, anxiety. And inflexible thinking.'[1]

Conditioned as we are to handling some quite difficult relationships in mediations how are we to handle ones with these rural peculiarities?

The mediator's perspective

Mediators receive documents and perhaps a position statement before the mediation begins. The factual recitals may tell you each side's story from different

---

1   Peter Coleman, *The Five Percent: Finding Solutions to Seemingly Impossible Conflicts* (New York: Public Affairs, 2011), p 42.

perspectives; but it often misses out in informing you why events happened. In a family farming dispute you need to understand some pretty complex characters and absorb the dynamics behind actions taken on the ground. You can't begin to design how the mediation might be conducted until you understand and appreciate the emotional undercurrents. So you may need to make some enquires of the representatives over the phone, perhaps probing them to give you a lead. The chances are that they have lived and breathed the dispute for some time, and they may be able to give you an insight into why their clients behaved as they did.

Your initial private meeting with each party may take rather longer than usual. The oral history related can be a bit like painting by numbers, where you need to fill in the gaps to get a better picture. Feelings need acknowledging whist some initial venting takes place. This can be quite disconcerting as now you have moved to base camp you are much more able to appreciate the mountain that you are about to climb; the high emotion, high resentment and the extent of resistance to face-to-face engagement makes it much more of a challenge to get them to agree on some sensible way to interact in the future and within such a tight time frame.

All mediators need to have plenty of patience – and high emotion rural disputes perhaps need a little more than usual. Having heard the story and got a better handle on why relationships had deteriorated, all those negative assumptions, beliefs and feelings need a bit of redirecting towards something a little more constructive. If the mediator simply absorbs more of each side's story, and then assumes that the joint meeting might begin positively, he either hasn't got the a typical rural dispute or he hasn't worked on the parties so that they can really appreciate that the meeting with the other party might provide an opportunity to say something positive and that ultimately a mediated solution just might address some of their needs.

Mediating disputes in the Armed Forces

Susan Morgan MBE

The military environment has a reputation for strict discipline, unswerving obedience to orders and a clearly defined chain of command. At one end of the spectrum, this may manifest itself at ceremonial events with the barking out of commands on a parade square to deliver precision of drill and uniformity of response. At the other, it may be evidenced by the unhesitating response of subordinates to robust orders delivered by their superiors in the heat of operations, where life and limb may be at stake. Against that backdrop, what place, might you ask, does mediation have in a military environment?

My personal experience is that mediation has firmly taken root as a management process in the Armed Forces, and I think it has done so because of the confluence of a number of factors over the past decade. In particular, following the deaths of four young trainees at the Army training depot at Deepcut, both Sir Nicholas Blake's Deepcut Review and the House of Commons Defence Committee's Duty of Care report in 2004–05 shone spotlights on bullying and harassment in the Armed Forces.

In the years that followed, I witnessed the Armed Forces responding to these concerns with both cultural change and structural reform. First, the Ministry of Defence adopted a comprehensive policy for investigating complaints of bullying and harassment, articulated in a handbook known as Joint Service Publication 763.[2] It identifies mediation as a potential tool for dealing with such complaints, and offers specific guidance on when and how it might be employed.

Other significant reforms in the Armed Forces also helped to promote the place of workplace mediation in resolving complaints. The Armed Forces Act 2006 (AFA 2006) made extensive changes to the statutory grievance procedures (known as the Service complaint system) in the Armed Forces. This resulted in the creation of a policy document, Joint Service Publication 831.[3] It too advocates the approach that whilst every complaint must be taken seriously, many can be swiftly and satisfactorily resolved informally. In particular, it states: 'Mediation can prove to be a powerful tool in seeking informal resolution.'[4] Amongst the reforms made by AFA 2006 was the establishment of a Service Complaints Commissioner (SCC) to help inject further independence into the Service complaint system administered by the chain of command. Amongst her responsibilities, the SCC is under a statutory duty to make annual reports on the fairness, effectiveness and efficiency of the Service Complaints system.

It was against this backdrop of reform that workplace mediation within the Armed Forces was born. The climate of reform created fertile conditions in which mediation could grow and prosper. For example, in her 2013 report (at p 37), when reporting on the performance of the Royal Navy, the SCC observed that:

> '... nearly a third of cases which were closed at Level 1[5] were resolved before formal decision, either because they were informally resolved or withdrawn. This represents a significant efficiency saving. If complainants are satisfied with the informal resolution, it also marks a significant effectiveness and fairness saving.'

So techniques of informal resolution such as mediation have been championed by an independent statutory watchdog too.

Also, from my perspective, the reason mediation has been embraced by the Armed Forces is, at its heart, very simple. Mediation is a method of restoring operational effectiveness. So, just as orders can deliver operationally effective Armed Forces, so can mediation. It is one of the many services in the management kitbag that, dependent on the requirement, may be utilised in restoring unit cohesion. Operational effectiveness is the military equivalent of the business need. In this respect, the Armed Forces and businesses are no different. It is all about supporting business outputs, and an effective, motivated and happy workforce supports that outcome.

---

2   JSP 763: The MOD Bullying and Harassment Complaints Procedures.
3   JSP 831: Redress of Individual Grievances: Service Complaints.
4   JSP 831, p 7.
5   Level 1 is the first stage at which a Service complaint is considered under AFA 06 procedures. Level 1 is at unit (ie Commanding Officer) level. There are two other levels at which a Service complaint may be considered (Levels 2 and 3). These are at Headquarters (ie Superior Officer) and Defence Council (ie Service Board) level.

Although new policy can be written and laid down, this can be meaningless if there is no commitment to its successful implementation. In the Royal Navy, an organisation of approximately 35,000 people, where I was a member of the Navy Headquarters Equality and Diversity Team, life was breathed into mediation as a new management technique. How was this done?

First, the Royal Navy significantly invested in my training and accreditation; I am qualified as an Advanced Workplace Mediator, delivering one-to-one mediation, group mediations (up to groups of 25) and subsequently, supervision for newly trained mediators. In addition an in-depth understanding of the different types of grievance processes, which could lead to an employment tribunal, was also provided, with bespoke training. I had complete access to our qualified Naval barrister specialising in employment law who was key in providing advice on the legalities of the processes.

Having completed over 50 successful mediations, travelling worldwide (Jordan, Key West and Cyprus to name a few destinations), the Royal Navy had its 'proof' and again invested in training an additional 24 mediators.

Mediation acquired credibility because senior officers became champions for the cause. An internal communications campaign helped to spread the message throughout the Naval Service, for example through leaflets and briefing key managers such as those on courses preparing to become commanding officers of ships at sea.

Organisational changes helped to ensure that mediation did not wither on the vine. A small designated team of Service mediators, which I led, was established to provide a dedicated, on-call core of expertise, ready to be deployed 24/7, 365 days a year. The cadre of professional complaints managers, including the Royal Navy's lawyers, also promoted mediation when advising the chain of command on how to deal with complaints. They too saw the value of mediation as a potential tool for facilitating the early resolution of complaints, which would otherwise require time-consuming and resource-intensive investigations to satisfy legal and policy requirements under AFA 2006. This resulted in a professional engine room and a highly integrated approach, which laid the foundations for the SCC's observations already noted above.

Notwithstanding this helpful umbrella of organisational support, so much was to depend on delivering results on the ground. In setting the conditions for success, a key task for the Navy's specialist mediators was to explain to the affected parties beforehand the benefits of mediation before it was employed as a management technique. This secured their 'buy-in' rather than as it being seen as a solution imposed by management to sweep issues under the carpet.

The Royal Navy, in common with the other Armed Forces, is a hierarchical organisation where people are very rank conscious. This had the potential to undermine mediations, so as mediators we adopted a methodology where all parties would refer to each other by their first names and would not wear uniform. Together with the approach of conducting mediations off-site and the confidentiality surrounding the process, this broke down barriers and contributed to the success of the mediations conducted. In effect, it allowed for an arena where an apology could be made without losing face – perhaps a particularly pertinent issue in a military environment where the rank divide is so clear.

Sector Specialisms

If mediation is to work, personality also has to play a part. The mediator needs to be credible, both in the eyes of the employer (which is buying in to mediation as a tool for resolving workplace disputes) and also in the eyes of the employees who are parties to the mediation. I was fortunate that I was well known, experienced and, with a Service police background, was from a profession that projected trust and integrity.

So what is the value of workplace mediation in the Armed Forces? Well, these days we tend to live in a results-driven environment. Against that yardstick, during my time in the Royal Navy, over 90 per cent of mediations were successful. That, in turn, meant a rebuilding of working relationships, a restoration of team cohesion and a return of operational effectiveness. For me, that statistic speaks for itself. It burns brightly as a beacon for the value of mediation in the workplace, whether that happens to be in a military or civilian environment.

Mediating banking and financial services disputes

Charles Flint QC

In 1983 90 per cent of the British public regarded banks as well run institutions; in 2012 that figure had dropped to 19 per cent.[6] Regulatory, political and media criticism of the banking industry has taken its toll not only on the reputational standing of financial institutions but also on the willingness of customers to bring claims. So is it any surprise that claims by customers against banks, spurred on by regulatory action in respect of mis-selling, are now such a substantial element of financial litigation?

Are bankers and banking disputes different from any other commercial disputants, with their own arcane practices and language, but at heart with similar problems? Are bankers harder negotiators, or immune to the attrition of litigation?

Well to start with it would be a mistake to assume that banks or financial institutions – or those responsible for the transaction which has given rise to the dispute – are immune to emotional or personal factors affecting the decision-making process. It may appear surprising to hear a hedge fund invoke considerations of fairness or commercial morality in challenging the conduct of its counterparty, but in the context of a mediation it can happen. My most dispiriting start to a bank lending fraud case was when the senior in-house counsel of the bank lent across the table, pointed his finger at the defendants, assured them that his bank had high ethical standards (a claim that would look rather hollow when the LIBOR scandal broke a few years later), would never tolerate sharp practice, and would ensure that the defendants were prosecuted for fraud and sent to prison. Was this calculated posturing or did it reflect genuine anger within the bank, which had discovered that its manager had been suborned into waving through dishonestly high property valuations? Of course we settled the dispute and nobody was sent to prison, but not after considerable effort to neutralise the emotional undercurrent on both sides.

---

6   British Social Attitudes Survey 2013.

As a mediator I see very different types of banking and financial services disputes. Disputes between banks and other financial institutions usually raise issues about misrepresentation, mistake or the terms of trading on a specialised market. Claims by customers against banks will more often be for mis-selling of financial products, usually derivatives (a contract which derives its value from the performance of an asset, index or interest rate) or swaps. These are not confined to claims by retail customers, but may be brought by large corporations or even governmental bodies. Most claims by retail customers of banks are likely to fall within the remit of the Financial Ombudsman Service (FOS), which now has the power to award compensation of £150,000. The FOS operates an informal system of dispute resolution, free of cost to the consumer, which may lead to an enforceable award against the bank. So these claims should normally not lead to court proceedings, or require mediation.

In previous recessions, banks have tended to be the claimants, seeking to enforce loan obligations. In the recession following the 2008 crash the banks were as often the defendants to claims brought by retail and commercial customers claiming to have been mis-sold financial products, the claims primarily being based upon breaches of the conduct of business rules made by the regulator under the Financial Services and Markets Act 2000, rather than upon the common law. These mis-selling claims raise particular challenges for settlement by mediation. Rarely were the parties interested in a continuing relationship, unless driven to it in order to unwind their transaction. The customer believed they were induced to enter into the swap or derivative by misrepresentation, or at least without a fair and clear explanation of the risk. With hindsight the risk, for example of interest base rates falling to 300-year lows, appeared theoretically clear, but to the business customer in the world before Lehman Brothers (the financial services firm that went bankrupt in 2008) this was not at all obvious. The customer felt let down and wished to have nothing more to do with the bank that tricked them into the deal. All the energy in the mediation was devoted to extracting the parties from the embittered relationship.

From the point of view of the bank there are wider interests at stake, beyond those directly affecting the transaction with its customer. The financial product may well have been the subject of adverse media or regulatory criticism. claimant lawyers may have acquired a portfolio of cases, often on conditional fee agreements. It is then an interesting question whether the individual claimant is best advised to commence proceedings, thus incurring the costs and risk of being the first mover, or wait to see if other litigants, or the regulator, take action which eventually requires the bank to offer settlement terms. In the case of the mis-selling of interest rate swaps to business customers they could reasonably have expected that the action of the Financial Services Authority (FSA) in 2012 in requiring banks to review their sales of interest rate hedging products would have led to speedy offers of compensation. But the FSA mandated review has been very slow in producing settlement offers and some businesses are threatened by insolvency. In the meantime the first such claim litigated by commercial property developers against a bank, based on alleged breaches of the conduct of business rules, failed in the Court of Appeal.[7] So customers would probably have been best advised to delay issuing proceedings, but many have an urgent need for compensation.

---

7   *Green & Rowley v RBS* [2013] EWCA 1197.

In any of these mis-selling cases the bank will be very concerned not to set a benchmark for future settlements. The bank is unlikely to be prepared to offer substantial compensation without having fully assessed the scale of exposure on its entire book of business. Although the mediation process, and any settlement, will be protected by confidentiality there is a clear risk of establishing a precedent for other claims of the same type. If the claimants' solicitors are acting, or proposing to act, for other claimants then it may be impractical to prevent the fact that the bank was prepared to pay out on such claims from becoming known to other claimants.

One particular group of claims illustrates this problem. In the early 2000s, Italian regional governments were persuaded by investment banks to hedge their exposure to interest rate increases and currency movements by entering into derivative hedging products. As interest rates fell and the dollar rose against the euro these contracts proved extremely uncomfortable for the public authorities which had taken them out, and litigation and threats of criminal prosecution followed. Several of these claims have been mediated, some successfully, but the political aspect of these cases raises a real barrier to settlement. The banks are unwilling to make any substantial concessions on these derivative contracts, not only because they view the contracts as clear, but also because the disputes have high political visibility. Any agreement to unwind the transaction would be broadcast by the administration which secured the concession, thus placing pressure on the banks to offer the same terms to other regional governments.

Inter-bank transactional disputes raise different issues. In these cases, such as a disputed transaction on a financial market, mediation offers all of its recognised benefits. The parties may actually value their relationship well beyond the store they set on being proved right on the issue in dispute. The resolution can be confidential and flexible. The parties may agree to reverse or adjust the terms of the transaction, remedies which are unlikely to be available from the court. There may be an unwillingness to jeopardise accepted market practices in court, or to test the meaning of market rules before a judge who may not be familiar with the ramifications of an unexpected decision. The avoidance of reputational risk still has some value, even after all the political and regulatory criticism of the last few years. Equally important in driving a consensual resolution may be the reluctance to expose in public trading strategies, or, even worse, mistakes in executing them.

The commercial valuation of the claim by the bank is not the only factor in play. A trader or manager will be well aware that the outcome of the dispute may have an immediate impact on the profit and loss account of the department, and thus on the pool available for bonus distribution at the end of the year. On the other hand the removal of an excessive provision in the accounts could provide a real benefit, not only to the institution but also to the trading team responsible for the transaction.

So what does one need as a mediator to be best placed to settle these disputes? I would emphasise the need to *understand the transaction*, not just its legal form but its commercial aim and how it was designed and intended to operate. I may not begin to understand the mathematical equations underlying the product, but at least I try to *understand the factors* operating and the *risk* that the transaction was designed to manage or to pass on to a counterparty. Only with that understanding can you *gain the confidence* of the parties, *speak their language* and be best placed to guide them to a solution. Preparation is all.

Mediating charity sector disputes

David Richbell

A considerable number of other sectors in this chapter have a connection to charities. They employ people, do business, provide services and commission work. They range from small community groups to major health and education bodies. All have workers of some sort, have trustees with statutory duties and manage money. Often they own buildings, some of which will be historic with precious contents. The legal limitations, reliance on volunteers and/or low-paid workers and the almost inevitable lack of funds brings added complications to 'normal' commercial disputes. Often charities are formed for commercial reasons.

Disputes often involve:

- volunteers and/or low-paid workers v management;
- management v trustee responsibilities;
- fundraising v fiduciary duties;
- profit v principles; and
- service v trade.

Volunteers and management

Most people get involved with a charity because they identify with its purposes and principles. Sometimes their involvement is by way of donation, maybe even as a benefactor; sometimes it is by giving their time. Whatever their involvement there is a serious difference in their relationship to the body when compared with a 'normal' business. They are there by choice and they can withhold their involvement by choice. It can almost be a case of 'the charity owes me as I am giving my time/money'. It is therefore often difficult to get reliable commitment so that credible plans can be made and it can make managing the charity very difficult. I have mediated several cases where:

- voluntary staff refuse direction from a manager;
- a volunteer has been disruptive but won't leave;
- intermittent help has had a negative influence;
- a key funder has 'blackmailed' the charity into a course of action for fear of losing their support; or
- a manager has been heavy-handed and caused a walk-out.

Disputes are often caused by people being in roles for which they have the time but not necessarily the skills or the sensitivities needed. All these cases emphasise the need to have clear guidelines, responsibilities and procedures so that staff and management can be confident in their work. Of course, many charities have that. We mediators only see the ones that don't (or, if they have, are not working). So much depends on people feeling valued and that their contribution is worthwhile, the more so because they are giving freely of their time/money.

Sector Specialisms

Management v trustees

Whether large or small, charities need managers. They may be paid, or not, but they have a responsibility to run the charity for its stated purposes and within the legal requirements. That can be tough, the more so if management is by committee rather than an individual. Managers often have ideas, see opportunities, especially for raising funds, that may well be good but not necessarily in compliance with the principles of the charity. That can cause real tension, not least because management are usually tasked with the financial viability of the charity, but the trustees are personally liable in law. So one may be quite entrepreneurial, the other risk-averse. One very successful charity shop ran a café at the rear of their shop and the trustees were threatened with closure, and worse, by the local authority because the shop was for retail only. The manager was sacked and sued the trustees for wrongful dismissal.

Sometimes there can be a power struggle between management and trustees. One classic mediation dealt with a dispute where the founders of a religious charity, who were the trustees (and elderly), were constantly being challenged by a much younger and energetic management committee who saw the trustees as dinosaurs who were inhibiting the potential of the charity. As is so often the case, the underlying problem was the lack of meaningful communication and the embedding of presumptions of motive and intention. This was much more a series of facilitated conversations, than 'proper' mediation.

Fundraising v fiduciary duties

Almost all charities are short of money and it is a constant worry to discharge the purposes of the charity and balance the budget. Trustees worry about being liable for debt and workers get frustrated with being inhibited in their work because of insufficient money. One fundraiser did a deal with a contractor to overcharge a wealthy client and pay the surplus to the charity. It was well received by the charity until the deceit (if not fraud) was discovered (by accident). The mediation was about how the situation could be rectified with the minimum of publicity and damage to the charity and to the unintentional donor.

Profit v principles

The public do not expect charities to make a profit, nor do they expect staff to be paid big salaries. Both happen. The challenge is to ensure that the purposes and principles of the charity are not compromised and that the need for money does not rule everything else. One mediation involved a challenge to the salary paid to the chief executive. The underlying issue was division within the board of management, where a minority considered their colleagues to be in the control of the CE, most of whom had been appointed at the CE's suggestion. The salary was not altered but the balance of the board was.

Service v trade

Most charities exist for the benefit of the public. There is an obvious need, a person or persons form a charity to meet that need, and the people involved are inspired and fulfilled by making it happen. As the charity matures and the first flush of enthusiasm wanes, or as it grows and has to be run more as a business, the sense of service and fulfilment can fade. One growing educational charity which was known for its person-centred style of management, saw the need to employ a full-time accountant. Gradually the emphasis changed to a budget-driven business with financial targets for its various activities. Staff became de-motivated and there was division within the director's meeting. One director called for a mediation and the eventual settlement was that two directors left the charity (and started up another) – both are still in existence.

A similar case involved a community sports facility. One group of volunteers, on whom the running of the facility depended, clashed with the management who were trying to adopt more business-based processes. As so often happens it seems, the founders of the charity were losing control to 'the suits', who insisted on more efficient accounting and on imposing new regulations. All the founders wanted to do was serve the community, as they had done for many years. It became an amateur v professional conflict, not helped by government and local authority interference. The founders eventually resigned the charity.

Conclusion

Charity sector disputes usually involve significant emotion, and often the feeling of betrayal and challenge to principles. Legislation and regulation have made life more difficult and often cause resentment, especially when those most involved find themselves unable, or not prepared to meet the standards now regulated. It is often hard for the mediator not to feel some sympathy for people in that situation, who often feel their reason for being is being taken from them. Sympathy is not a mediation word, but we are also human.

Mediating clinical negligence disputes

Tony Allen

Claims against healthcare professionals (whether as individuals or, more often, within an entity like a an NHS Trust) involve a potent and characteristic mix of complication, which to an extent spills over into mediation of such claims. The facts emerge from an occasion when a person placed trust in the hands of experts to care for their health, an essential part of their being, and alleges they were professionally let down. Such situations inevitably engender strong emotion, felt either directly or vicariously where the patient was a close relative. This perceived failure may have led to permanent damage to health, to a failure to prevent shortening of life, or even to death, and such sad outcomes are hard to accept without anger.

Yet frustration often results when complaints and claims of clinical negligence are made. They are technical, and dependent for success on expert opinion, since the leading test for whether negligence is made out depends upon the opinion of a 'reasonable body of practitioners'; in other words the healthcare profession sets its own standards. claimants will, except in self-evidently disastrous cases like operating on the wrong limb or organ or administering the wrong drug dose, have to enlist supportive expert opinion before their claim can be advanced at all. Furthermore, unlike some other negligence claims, there is almost always an additional hurdle to overcome even when breach of duty is proved or admitted, in that to prove that damage was caused by that breach, or the extent of damage as claimed, can be difficult. If a patient was doomed anyway, a late diagnosis of disease may have done little to delay the inevitable. Besides these difficulties remain the ordinary ones typical of all injury claims of proving the heads of damage.

Difficulty and pain is not the exclusive preserve of claimants, however. As any professional who has been accused of negligence will testify, such allegations are extremely painful and distracting, disturbing sleep and endangering concentration on continuing work. Affected claimants may have little sympathy for this aspect of the clinical claims equation, but mediators who ignore it may be overlooking their responsibility to all parties, as well as missing a normal personal dynamic, which exists in most cases, even if it quite often does not emerge because of the absence of the relevant healthcare professional from the mediation itself.

This background gives a strong steer to the importance of preparing properly for such mediations. Prior contact will normally be with the lawyers for each party, and apart from the usual questions about their previous mediation experience, any explanations to supplement their knowledge and checking practical matters like venue, time, the terms of the mediation agreement, and what settlement attempts if any have been made so far, it is always important to look at the human factors behind the claim. Checking what contact there has been hitherto between claimant and family and the healthcare professionals is important. Was any formal complaints procedure invoked and how did that turn out? Is there any unfinished business? Has there been any explanation of what went wrong, or any reassurance of changed practice? Has anyone apologised and if not would this still be appreciated? If so, who needs to attend that mediation? Who does the claimant need to hear from, if this can be set up? Is the mediation the best place for this to happen? Will the claimant and family feel able or want to encounter relevant healthcare professionals, or conversely will they be angry if those professionals do not propose to attend? Careful consideration by the mediator from the earliest stage to these issues is needed and careful diplomacy to achieve what each party wants or fears. Special arrangements may be necessary to enable a professional to escape from their busy schedule. It may be necessary to offer to talk to the doctor in advance in the event of reluctance to meet.

Is it appropriate for healthcare professionals to attend such mediations, and how should it be managed on the day? There is an inescapable risk of an outburst during such an encounter. But it is rarely inauthentic, and may well be an integral part of the value of the mediation. I have seen many honest and painful expressions of feeling on both sides when they meet, leading to a sense of closure for both claimant and defendant. Often this will have been the first meeting of patient and family with the professional involved since the claim was brought, litigation being the distancing force that it always is. So the opening meeting must be carefully prepared and managed on the mediation day. Time spent in each room gauging the mood is essential, remembering that each party is entitled to have their emotional state treated confidentially as much as their assertions of fact or opinion. It is important both to suggest conveying strength of feeling from either party to the other and specifically to obtain permission to do so. Such a meeting does not necessarily need to take place during the opening session. I have seen doctors keen to meet their erstwhile patient but who had to wait until late in the day before the claimant could bring themselves to do so. However, my repeated experience is that there is enormous potential value in the parties meeting face to face to exchange views, information and feelings. Not infrequently, there is a real sense of resolution on both sides by the end of the mediation.

What of the technicality of clinical claims? This too requires preparation by the mediator. It is necessary to understand the medical as well as the legal and medico-legal issues involved. Access to anatomical diagrams, medical dictionaries, learned articles, etc is easily arranged. Lawyers in this sector are usually specialists and do such preparation work themselves and are often extremely well informed. They expect any mediator to cope with both the relevant concepts and vocabulary, understanding the implications of the expert reports that lie at the heart of such cases. There is also the question of understanding how damages are calculated. The Judicial Studies Board guidelines are occasionally of assistance in quantifying damages for pain and suffering although they were mainly designed for personal injury trauma cases rather than clinical conditions, so are often used by way of analogy, rather than being directly relevant. Damages for past and future loss broadly follow the same pattern as for personal injury claims, so will be daunting for a mediator inexperienced in these sectors.

Unlike in the commercial sector, there is a degree of specialisation among the legal profession in clinical negligence in England and Wales. Solicitors' firms almost always only act for claimants or defendants, and this can colour their approach to their own clients and to their opponents, though because both specialist groups are relatively small, there is a good deal of respect for each other as well among top law firms. However, there can be suspicion of opponents and defensiveness and protectiveness for clients as well. Barristers assign themselves only to one or other side less exclusively, though some only act for one or other. A Google search will usually reveal all that needs to be known.

Despite the positive views taken of mediation in clinical negligence claims which emerged from the Mulcahy Report in the late 1990s, mediation has not been taken up in this sector as much as might have been expected, despite occasional positive opinions being expressed by practitioners. I have heard it said that claimant lawyers, perhaps encouraged by the zeal which led to the founding of AvMA (Action against Medical Accidents) by Arnold Simanowitz, feel unhappy at the prospect of having to compromise their client's genuine needs for damages within a mediation. But if ever there was a risky area of law with uncertain prospects of success it is clinical claims. Is going to court and losing preferable to settling at a sensible discounted value and getting something, even if not everything? Maybe claimant lawyers somehow fear surrendering control over their client's case to a neutral. As this is what initiating proceedings at all involves (to an adjudicative judge) it is hard to understand this fear, especially as mediators emphatically value the expert representation and advice which lawyers tender to their clients at a mediation. On this and the earlier objection, it must be remembered that no one is compelled to settle at mediation; the lawyers are there to advise whether a better outcome at trial is worth pursuing, and if so and the client agrees, they can walk away from the mediation without penalty.

As to the technicality of whether breach of duty or causation is made out sufficiently to justify a full or discounted offer, there seems no reason why discussion of the relative merits of each expert opinion cannot generate enough appreciation of the risks that each side faces on this to lead to settlement. An under-used option is to

Sector Specialisms

try to get the experts to attend at the mediation and have the debate that they are ordinarily required to have under CPR Part35 with the parties present to assess the respective persuasiveness of each.

Clinical negligence mediations have a high rate of settlement, at least 90 per cent in my experience, and they can be settled before issue of proceedings, much earlier than usual in litigation. Where they do not settle on the day, it may prove necessary to adjourn or decline to settle until further evidence is sought. Then at a later stage further discussions very often lead to settlement after adjustment of each side's risk analysis, usually through direct discussions, though I always offer to help further. If an unsettled case proceeds to trial, one or other party finds that their assessment of their prospects of success was seriously wrong.

Clinical mediations also very often lead to a sense of business done at a personal level for both claimant and clinician, hard to obtain if a claim is settled by the arms-length acceptance of a Part 36 offer with its threat of costs sanctions if rejected and misjudged. The mediator's role from start to finish is to enable difficult conversations to take place, both face to face and in private, about both (literally) painful past events and also the chances of success for each side and the risks of failure. The mediator is there to prolong discussions rather than allowing parties to make a dramatic withdrawal, and to coach the parties in what offers might attract the other party towards possible settlement (though in clinical cases with the extra element of both monetary and non-monetary outcomes). Above all, the mediator is there to promote the lay parties back into the centre of their case, when so often excluded by the nature of the litigation process, and indeed by the joint settlement meetings chosen frequently as the settlement process by lawyers in the clinical sector.

Mediating competition disputes

William Wood QC

Typically, commercial mediators will come across two main types of competition dispute. In a sense these correspond roughly to our old legal friends liability and causation. In the first type of case (the liability dispute) the main issue is as to the existence (or the threat) of an anti-competitive arrangement of some kind. The second type of case ('the follow-on dispute') deals with the damages claims that can follow where a third-party claims to have suffered loss because of a cartel or other anti-competitive behaviour. Follow-on cases typically occur when a domestic or European regulator has found that there has been unlawful anti-competitive behaviour. The background is therefore very often that the liability issue has already been disposed of.

Two examples of mediations of liability disputes are in the public domain. As the *Racing Post* reported at the time,[8] a mediation took place in the dispute between bookmakers and racecourses over television rights. The bookmakers contended that the concerted action by the racecourses in grouping together to exploit the broadcasting rights of the sport of racing was anti-competitive. In a second case,

---

8   *Racing Post,* 17 March 2008.

private marina operators on the inland waterways sued the British Waterways Board alleging anti-competitive conduct by virtue of the BWB's own private marina operations. In relation to these BWB was said to hold a dominant position, an unfair and anti-competitive advantage. In both of these mediations the focus of the endeavour will have been to map out constructively a future means of co-existence for the parties rather than simply to concentrate on the issue of the illegality of past conduct.

Mediations in follow-on cases have not to date been referred to in the public domain and no examples are available. But this emphasises that the importance of mediation is that it provides a private as well as an effective and inexpensive way of resolving matters of considerable potential embarrassment.

Mediators need to bear in mind that both types of dispute are likely to be being handled by extremely bright specialist lawyers from the major firms of solicitors. They are likely to impose a very analytical framework on the process and on any negotiations that may take place. Clients tend not to feel empowered to speak when faced with specialised matters of this complexity. The mediator has to be aware of this and deal with it.

Mediators also need to be aware that these cases will often be dominated not just by lawyers but by experts as well, usually accountants and economists. They may well attend any mediation. It is not uncommon for the parties to seek a multi-day mediation so that there can be 'special subject' conferences attended by experts from each side to deal with specific issues. A mediator may feel that these tend too much towards the mini-trial. But they do offer a useful and cost-effective way of ensuring that the issues are fleshed out and expressed leaving the parties free then to explore their real interests.

Issues in a liability dispute will often revolve around the definition of a relevant economic market (because the definition of the relevant market will often determine whether or not the particular piece of commercial conduct is lawful or anti-competitive).

Issues in a follow-on case are likely to revolve around causation, with the cartellists typically contending that no real increase in prices was achieved so as to overcharge the claimant and indeed that the cartel was inefficient, badly run and poorly policed! The cartellist will also allege typically that any overcharge was passed on by the claimant to his own customers; this allegation brings up the perennial legal problem of the 'pass-through' defence. It is an inevitable part of a mediation of this kind that the mediator is updated by the parties on the latest twists and turns of this debate.

Many competition cases, particularly of the liability kind, crucially concern the future relationship of the parties, parties who are usually going to be co-existing within the relevant industry for the foreseeable future. Mediations of this kind are therefore challenging, creative and immensely worthwhile. A court will only be able decide that at a particular moment in time a party or parties were or were not acting illegally. At the mediation the parties can if they wish discuss the legality or otherwise of what has happened in the past. But if they are well advised they will want to work on finding a lawful method of co-existing to their mutual benefit in the future.

Sector Specialisms

This is not always easy. But the mediator can usually observe with justification that the issues as to future coexistence are not going to go away. Even if the parties leave the mediation and fight the case they will merely get a verdict on past conduct and will still have to return in due course, probably to the negotiating table or to another mediation, to map out the future.

A mediator's great allies in competition disputes are the cost and the unpredictability of the formal legal process. This may be true of all complex commercial litigation but it is especially true of competition cases.

Cost estimates in competition cases are frequently absolutely eye watering. I have seen estimated final cost figures for one party of $10 million and more in follow-on cases. This is usually because the fees charged by the expert accountants and economists dwarf even those of the magic circle lawyers who typically try these cases.

The unpredictability of competition cases lies partly in the complexity of the battle of wits in which the lawyers engage and partly in the broad discretions that ultimately reside with the court in deciding whether or not to condemn a particular course of conduct as unfair or illegal. As is widely reported, the financial implications for the major software companies in their various competition law battles are enormous. Huge economic advantages follow from success and disaster accompanies defeat. Of course these are the extreme examples. But few managements can afford to ignore these kinds of volatility and they are well advised to use mediation to bring some control and certainty to bear.

Finally, one aspect of follow-on claims concerns group mediating with action groups. Current proposals exist for competition cases, and follow-on cases in particular, to be the first area for the application in England and Wales of opt-out class actions. This will allow the courts to designate certain class actions in which the claimant lawyers will be taken to be acting for the entire affected group against the cartellists, save to the extent that any particular victims opt out of the group. Mediating these cases will require a mediator, as ever, to get a proper understanding of the dynamics within the group and the authority and representative capacity of those taking direct part in the mediation.

Mediating construction/engineering disputes

David Richbell

Introduction

Back in 2008 I wrote *Mediation of Construction Disputes*. It didn't top the bestseller list but it has been an asset in getting the world of construction interested in a better form of resolving disputes than arbitration, adjudication and particularly litigation. I started the book by saying how creative the construction and engineering industries are, particularly in creating disputes. They continue to be so – which is good for the mediator.

Construction and engineering are complex industries. There is a lot of detail in building a hotel, or a ship or an oil-rig. There are a lot of processes involved in the preparation, design and construction of the finished article. A lot of people are involved and there will be serious time and budget constraints. All have the opportunity of mistakes, lack of co-ordination, and miscommunication.

Construction and engineering mediations

There seem to be several peculiarities with construction and engineering mediations:

- there are inevitably a huge quantities of documents, which go into excessive detail and are overflowing with numbers;
- crowds of people are in attendance, particularly with multi-party cases; and
- there is surprisingly high emotion.

Smaller cases

Of course, some disputes, such as a building owner being in dispute with the builder over defects or time or cost overruns, are likely to have just a handful of people attending the mediation. It is easy to assume that these smaller disputes are simpler to mediate but my experience is that they are still very detailed and the emotions run high. Most commonly, the building owner has lived in the premises and tolerated the dust, noise and disruption, usually for a far longer period than originally expected. They also have to live with the results and any serious defect, wrong detail or unfulfilled expectation can become a major issue as they are confronted with it every day. This generally leads to high emotion at the mediation and quite often the undeserved demonising of the builder or consultant.

Larger cases

Larger disputes often involve an element of crowd control, especially if there are more than two parties, which is often the case (building owner v developer v consultant/designer v contractor v sub-contractor, with insurers and funders also in the mix). This requires very clear and firm management of the process so that everyone stays focussed on the purpose of the mediation.

There is a real need for the mediator to be involved well before the appointed dates, so that they may influence who attends and discuss the format of the mediation day(s). It is not unusual to have a bespoke process, so that the mediation is structured to the particular case and the people involved.

Bespoke process

Larger cases often warrant a purpose-designed process, especially if there are several parties and/or some parties are from outside the United Kingdom. If site visits are involved, their purpose needs to be clear and agreement made as to who attends and all parties must be invited to participate. On the day(s) of mediation one option is for most people to attend for only part of the mediation and that the eventual settlement negotiations involve only a few key people. An alternative is

Sector Specialisms

to have one day of 'coal face' people (those actually involved in the construction) and for another day to have just the decision-makers and their legal advisers. That way the people who 'owned' the works, and experienced it day-by-day, can have their say, and be seen to be heard, but the potential of them becoming blockages to the eventual settlement, because of their emotional commitment to their version of the 'truth', is removed. Mediation is a flexible process and the mediator needs to determine what process best suits the dispute.

Experts and expert mediators

Experts almost always attend mediations, but it is rare for them to contribute much to the outcome. The main reason is that they will have made their report before the mediation and should have met to agree common ground. What is left is 'uncommon' ground where they disagree and it is very unlikely that they will change their position during the mediation. There is a real chance therefore that they become a blockage to settlement as they persuade their client that their version of the case is the right one. The trouble is no one knows beforehand if their expert will be needed at any time during the mediation, so they are invariably asked to attend (and spend the day(s) bored and idle).

The choice of commercial mediators is now vast and so it is normal for lawyers to select a sector-specialist mediator for their case. Whilst that is understandable, experience and reputation should still be paramount. Unfortunately, some of the most suited specialist mediators are non-lawyers but they are rarely selected because of their perceived (but unnecessary) lack of relevant law.

Co-mediation

There is a section in Chapter 7 on co-mediation, but multi-party cases are very suited to having two experienced mediators working harmoniously together. Because I advocate it, I have several established pairings, usually with a female lawyer (to cover as many permutations of need and situation as possible). I strongly believe that an established pairing which works comfortably and harmoniously together offers a great deal to the parties. Not only is there a second experienced mind at work, but the work can be shared and the time used more efficiently. Unfortunately co-mediation is rare in commercial mediation, probably for no other reason than the fact that it is perceived to be double the cost.

Papers and numbers

There is no doubt that the amount of documents provided for the mediator is often huge and so can be a real challenge when preparing for a mediation. The mediator must be confident about the case and parties must feel sure that the mediator understands their problems and has a full grasp of the key issues in dispute, but, in the end, the mediator's role is to manage the mediation process as efficiently and effectively as possible and so give the parties the best chance of reaching a settlement. Detailed knowledge of the case is not necessary; indeed one of the skills of an effective mediator is to help parties get out of the detail and grasp a bigger picture. So the mediator has to be selective and prioritise the reading-in, if necessary with the help of the solicitors involved in the case. But the level of preparation is up to the mediator – they need to be confident and feel well prepared.

Most commercial mediations settle on money and construction/engineering disputes are no different. However, the volume of information that goes behind the financial claims is usually vast and parties, including the lawyers, are often quite overwhelmed by it. A mediator who is comfortable with figures and who can group, adjust and reframe figures can add a lot of value to the negotiation process. As in other issues, being able to simplify the financial claims can be a real benefit and help the parties to believe that the task is manageable and a settlement possible after all.

Summary

In addition to the fundamental skills of an effective mediator, those involved in construction and engineering mediations need to be:

- a firm, if not assertive, manager of the process. It is likely that there will be a lot of people attending at the mediation, most of who will want their view to be heard and to feel their attendance is worthwhile;
- creative with the process – that is avoid imposing the 'normal' one-day format with open and private meetings and to give time to working on what best suits the case and the people involved;
- prepared to include site visits, which can put the dispute into context and enable the mediator to ask informed questions; and
- comfortable with numbers – that is not to be overwhelmed by their volume and to be able to manipulate them to help the parties and their advisers' clarity and effectiveness.

Mediating employment disputes

Liz Rivers

Employment mediation is *always* personal. For most of us, our performance at work is core to our self-esteem and self identity, so when things go wrong it can be stressful and painful. Likewise for a manager, to be accused of bullying or discrimination is often very distressing. As mediators we have the opportunity to help people navigate what might be one of the most stressful events of their lives and get their career back on track.

To clarify, by the term 'employment mediation' I mean disputes:

- between employees and employers;
- where the employee has already left or will be leaving;
- where lawyers are involved and the settlement involves a compromise agreement; and
- where if the claim does not settle it is likely to end up in an employment tribunal or possibly the courts.

Sector Specialisms

The aim of employment mediation is to bring to an end a working relationship which has broken down, allowing all concerned to move on rather than being tied to the past. This should be distinguished from 'workplace mediation' which takes place:

- between two or more employees working in an organisation;
- lawyers are not involved; and
- the aim is to improve a working relationship that is in crisis.

It is helpful to understand some of the differences between employment tribunal claims and ordinary commercial disputes:

- Each party usually pays their own costs so the claimant is not at risk of paying costs if they lose. Conversely, if the claimant get's compensation they cannot recover their costs so they have to deduct these from any amount awarded. The employer will have to fork out costs for a tribunal hearing whether they win or lose. This gives a greater incentive to both parties to settle before a hearing than the High Court position where the winner can recover the majority of their costs.

- At the moment here is an upper limit of £87,700 on compensation in the employment tribunal. This can only be exceeded if the claimant proves discrimination. In practice most claimants want to claim more than this cap so they will frame their claim in discrimination terms. This has a distorting effect in that the facts need to be tweaked to fit the discrimination categories such as sex, race, age, disability and sexual orientation. Another typical discrimination claim is 'whistleblowing', technically known as protected disclosure, which I have heard referred to as the 'white, male, middle-class discrimination claim'.

- The other way to recover a substantial amount in an employment case is to bring a personal injury claim in the County or High Court. Typically this would be framed as 'I was bullied/overworked and my health broke down as a result' (usually the health issue is a mental health diagnosis such as depression). Substantial damages can follow from this.

Tips for handling the practicalities of employment mediations

Before the day

- Make sure the claimant's lawyers provide a schedule of loss before the mediation, ie setting out what they are claiming and how the figures are calculated.

- Make sure both parties have access to tax advice throughout the day – sometimes this can be crucial for the claimant to understand how much money they will actually receive after tax has been paid, and to structure the settlement as tax efficiently as possible.

- Get the employer to send their standard compromise agreement to the claimant's lawyer in advance of the mediation so they can review the standard clauses in advance and just need to slot in the key provisions once agreed (eg amount of compensation and the wording of the reference). This can really speed up the drafting phase.

- Sometimes claimant lawyers are on a very tight budget to prepare the mediation (especially where it is trade union funded) so the preparation and prior information is rather limited. Be prepared for this – it does not mean they are incompetent.

On the day

- At the opening joint session make a list of all the elements that need to go into a compromise agreement so that there are no surprises later on. Helpfully, these items are fairly standard, such as:
  — agreed factual reference;
  — named person who will deal with any reference enquiries;
  — mutual 'non-disparagement' clause, ie neither party will publicly criticise the other;
  — confidentiality as to the content of the settlement terms;
  — outplacement support;
  — agreed reason for departure (eg resignation or redundancy rather than dismissal).

  Ask the parties in joint session if there is anything more they need to add to the list.

- Always talk in figures that are gross of tax and leave the claimant to work out what their net figure will be. There is nothing worse than discovering late in the day that the gap is much wider than you thought because one party is talking net figures and the other gross.

- Steer people in the direction of purely factual references, as far as possible. It is fairly standard practice now to provide references that just state the dates of employment and the position of the employee. These are much easier to agree than qualitative references about what the employee was like, which are usually much more contentious.

- Mitigation is a big factor in valuing claims. The employee has a duty to look for another job to replace their loss of earnings and if they are in a strong job market where it is relatively easy to get another job this will reduce their claim, however strong their claim might be.

- Don't be thrown by huge initial claims. Typically an employee will start with an argument such as: 'My career has been ruined, I'll never work again so I'm entitled to 20 years' loss of earnings'. In reality, employment tribunals rarely award more than two years' loss of earnings as compensation so initial figures from the claimant usually reduce quite substantially during the course of the negotiations.

In general it is helpful to have a working knowledge of employment law and how employment tribunals typically value claims. This particularly comes in handy when reality testing offers and demands.

Handling the emotional and relational aspects of the dispute

The employee perspective

Work relationships can be very powerful and we invest a lot in them. When they break down it is hard to shrug your shoulders and walk away. As well as dealing with

Sector Specialisms

the practical aspects of the negotiation, you need to be working with the emotional and relational aspects. Often people are not ready to move on, to accept what is on paper a good offer, until these aspects have been addressed. For example, Jane worked for Tim and things were fine until she came back from maternity leave. From her perspective she was excluded from things and could not understand what had gone wrong. Tim was unhappy with aspects of her performance but found it very difficult to give her straight feedback (a very common scenario). It became clear in the course of the mediation that he had not been straight with her and given her the opportunity to address her performance issues. Having this acknowledged was very validating and allowed her to accept an offer and move on, rather than hanging on for an explanation to make sense of the difficult experience she had had.

An employment lawyer commented to me that it is only the disputes that have a strong emotional and/or relational aspect which go to mediation – the rest they can settle themselves, so always be prepared to address these aspects.

The employer perspective

Recognise that the employer will have feelings about the dispute too. To be accused of bullying or discrimination is very uncomfortable and the manager is likely to be experiencing strong feelings. Also recognise the differing agendas and tensions within the employer team. There may be tensions between line management and HR, and a conflict between the organisation's stated values about how it treats its employees and the facts of the case. This can have reputational implications.

Tips for handling these aspects

- Speak to both the claimant and the employer representative before the mediation to put them at ease and start building rapport. I'm a great believer in speaking to lawyers *and their clients* before the mediation. I explain how the day will run, give them a chance to ask questions, find out how they feel about the day and ask some gentle questions about the case. I find this makes a big difference on the day as to how settled and at ease people are when they arrive. Remember that for the employee, this will probably be the most significant thing happening in their life at this time.

- Make sure the claimant has enough support to make a good decision. Ask them if they want to bring a friend or family member to the mediation as well as their legal advisers.

- It can be helpful to acknowledge the power imbalance in these cases – it is almost always more significant for the claimant than the employer.

- Where appropriate, create an opportunity for the employer and employee to sit down together one-to-one and acknowledge any hurts or, lessons learnt so that they can each move on emotionally. Keep this entirely separate from the negotiations about the terms of settlement

- Helping people to mourn the past and move on is crucial. I often find people are still attached to the trajectory they had been on (salary, bonuses, career prospects) before things went wrong. Helping them come to terms with this loss, grieve it and then be open to a new path is vital.

The power of a good ending

Mediation can bring about a good ending rather than a bad ending to a relationship that has not worked out. This is something that is not particularly recognised or valued in our culture, yet is very important. In one sex discrimination claim I helped the claimant devise a ritual for herself where she decided to have a bonfire to burn all the papers associated with her claim, and have a dinner for all the friends who had supported her through it. Rituals can be very powerful as a way to manage important transitions.

Managing your own responses

Be prepared to manage your own responses to the issues that come up. We have all had bosses, many of us have had workers reporting to us, and we all have our own history and pattern of how we deal with authority. Issues around discrimination, stress, abuse of authority and mental health may trigger painful memories in us that can impact on our impartiality. Mediator impartiality does not mean neutrality. We *should* have a response when we encounter bullying or injustice. Impartiality means that we are aware of our responses and able to put them to one side sufficiently while in the mediation, then go and work on it elsewhere, eg in peer supervision.

When is mediation not appropriate?

There is a tension between individual and organisational needs to get closure and move on, and society's need for openness and accountability. Most compromise agreements contain a confidentiality clause that the employee will not talk about the circumstances of their departure. Generally this is helpful but overuse can be counterproductive, for example in the case of NHS whistleblowers where gagging clauses were overused with the effect that important information in the public interest did not come out.

And finally.....

As mediators we have an opportunity to help create both more humane organisations and more self-aware employees by helping both parties reflect on the causes of the dispute and unpick themselves from a relationship which is no longer working. It is a privilege to be able to support people through these difficult phases in their lives.

Mediating energy disputes

Jane Player

Whether energy disputes revolve around traditional oil and gas projects or 'new' energy resources, more often than not they invite multi-parties and cross cultural issues. Because of the resources required, these collaborations see sophisticated large energy corporations together with large finance houses involved in projects in challenging jurisdictions with state or public parties and increasingly environmental interests. Local regulatory controls further complicate matters together with the consequences of international funding and investment interests. The governing laws relating to the different agreements at play are often multiple and conflicting. The jurisdictional implications when disputes arise, whether it is arbitration under the various contractual clauses or tort and contract claims under relevant governing laws, further complicate issues. Disputes inevitably involve large sums of money, a lot of people and have significant cross-cultural implications. Finally, potential claims that could arise under energy treaties and bilateral state investment treaties lead anyone involved in energy disputes to know that resolving them is a legal, logistical and commercial minefield.

Energy projects are also, by their nature, long term. Multi-year commitments are sought by states, investors and contractors due to the heavy and expensive initial investment required both in the infrastructure at the location and for the extraction, maintenance and transportation post-extraction. For this reason, complicated contractual provisions are set out in an attempt to have a clear road map to dispute resolution.

Nevertheless, negotiators and draftspersons of modern investment treaties and project documentation rarely include a mandatory mediation mechanism, including a cooling-off period that you might find in some treaties (for example tax disputes in the Energy Charter Treaty). If mediation has not been provided for in the contracts themselves it is much more difficult to suggest mediation once a dispute has arisen. Some will oppose it if their professional interests are more specialised in litigation (eg in-house governmental lawyers) and a mediation proposal may be seen as a weakness in a climate that is often characterised by tough talking business people and lawyers. But it is clear that mediation could avoid a number of risks evident in litigation and/or arbitration, whether investor state arbitration or commercial arbitration. Thomas Wälde in his article on mediation/alternative dispute resolution in oil and gas and energy transactions[9] talks of these advantages in the following terms:

- *Sovereignty problem* States are not happy to be dragged into public disputes. Mediation has the ability to resolve issues arising out of collaborations and projects in a discreet and private manner.
- *Third party involvement* Where you need third parties to be involved to get a satisfactory global settlement, mediation is a sufficiently flexible process to allow all relevant parties to be at the table. Arbitration, by its contractual nature, cannot easily do this without consent.
- *Costs* Costs of mediation are approximately 10–15 per cent of any full blown arbitration or litigation and this is a particular attraction for states and less well funded public bodies.
- *Enforcement* A mediated settlement achieved by consent and upon the efforts of the parties themselves is more easily enforced.
- *Loss of face* In the mediation context this provides a huge advantage over other forms of ADR.

---

9   Thomas Walde 'Mediation/Alternative Dispute Resolution in Oil, Gas and Energy Transactions: Superior to Arbitration/Litigation from a Commercial and Management perspective', available at: http://www.ogel.org/article.asp?key=65.

I would add a further advantage of mediation in such complicated projects. This is the creativity that the mediation forum provides to the parties, giving them greater opportunity to find a workable, pragmatic and commercial solution to a dispute. Settlement agreements can include everything from apologies (or at least an acceptance of responsibility for outcomes) to future promises of work/investment in new projects and the reworking of profit shares in existing collaborations. This is in contrast to judge-imposed decisions which will be contract or reasonable damages based, or arbitration where the arbitrator or panel is bound by the remit of its authority in the arbitration agreement itself. Where you have complicated environmental issues, multi-party interests and changing economics in long-term energy projects, this flexibility should be welcomed. Mediation also retains the ability to find a solution that suits the very business partners whose business interests are best served by a swift ADR process with the other business partners, so that projects can continue without the paralysis that litigation or arbitration can bring to a project.

Experience of energy disputes show that when issues arise business executives, instead of running their business, become irritated at requests by the in-house and external legal teams of both them and the other side to devote increasing attention to the dispute. To make matters worse, once engaged, their emotional needs in the dispute get in the way of rational judgment. As Thomas Wälde comments in his article:

> 'The fear of losing and thus losing face and credit in a competitive corporate environment full of detractors looking for their competitors' weaknesses will compel executives to get engaged in the dispute much more than the dispute warrants'.

A dispute leads to hardening of positions, the inevitable polarising of views by lawyers setting out their 'best' position and the lock-in of bargaining positions. The trust that may still be available arising out of the project itself is fast eroded and just when all parties should be sitting down and saying, 'Is this dispute really necessary or can it be settled?' the train towards litigation or arbitration leaves the station.

A further complication in these long-term projects is that the executives who first put the collaboration together and instructed the lawyers to draft the agreements may have left their position or even worse, the company. As a consequence, the initial intentions of the parties are often lost. Overlay onto that the potential for cross-cultural misunderstandings and it is easy to understand why these disputes can get out of hand so quickly. It might therefore be useful to remind ourselves that the main objectives distinguishing mediation from litigation or arbitration are as follows:

- Mediation allows the parties to come to an agreement rather than have one imposed on them by an outside authority.
- The objective in mediation is to either maintain a relationship or end the commercial relationship in a pragmatic and efficient manner. In large-scale energy contracts where there are complicated and inextricably linked contracts and corporate relationships, it is almost always better to try to maintain the existing relationships than reinvest in alternatives. Further, those companies, whose reputation to work well with partners and resolve issues amicably rather than litigate them into submission or play unnecessary power games, win a

worldwide reputation that makes it easier for them to build new commercially productive relationships elsewhere.

- Costs and time required to solve the issues at hand can be dramatically minimised and the emotional focus of senior executives involved in the dispute avoided. The distraction that a dispute can cause to those whose energies are best focussed on finding a creative solution can be immense.

- Finally it is worth mentioning that in my experience when you mediate a dispute there is a 'magic' dynamic within the process itself; once you get over the hurdle of having all the parties in the room agree that it is better to stick together than to fight to the death, then during the process of working through a solution the parties find themselves brought back towards a common purpose. This dynamic is priceless when you are looking to repair a valuable long-term relationship. Indeed where you are working in practice to find a solution, you may find that the value that one party puts on a particular preferred solution is not the same as another. This enables the mediator, with his or her unique informed knowledge working in private with all parties, to devise a compromise package or a new deal which covers the needs of both parties but does not necessarily 'cost' in the same way as a finding of liability might.

Many other industry sectors will recognise the features of an energy dispute described above as features common to their industry. The advantages of mediation will apply with equal force. Even if a fully worked-through solution isn't found at first, experience shows sub-issues are often resolved and the main areas of dispute minimised, which either leads to an ultimate settlement, or, at worst, reduced cost in a subsequent arbitration or litigation process. Indeed, one differentiating factor in energy disputes may be that in the truly large projects, the amount at stake means that the costs of litigation and/or arbitration will not be the determining factor in deciding the best form of resolution. In reality what happens is that most of these disputes do not start with mediation. The business tries to resolve the issues as they arise through negotiation and, if that fails, dispute resolution provisions provided for in the contract are triggered. If a mediation does happen it is often after significant expense has already been incurred in other Dispute Resolution processes. Whilst mediation, as we know, always adds value no matter when it is used, you do wonder whether, if thought about earlier or provided for in the contract as a prerequisite, when positions were less entrenched, how much more value the mediation process could have provided.

Mediating entertainment and media sector disputes

Andrew Hildebrand

A man goes to a doctor for a rash on his arm.

'What do you do for a living?' the doctor asks him.

'I work at the circus, giving enemas to the elephants,' he replies.

'Quit doing that and your rash will clear up,' the doctor says.

The man looks horrified: 'What? And give up show business?'

If mediating is about dealing with people as well as problems, understanding typical personality types can be helpful. This is especially true in the entertainment sector. With apologies upfront for the odd generalisation, here are some quirks to look out for.

The entertainment industry

As a sector, the focus is distinctly international. This reflects both the nature of the industry's economic market and the fact that it originated in the United States, from where we have inherited many of our customs, working practices, terminology and even behaviour.

'Creatives', invariably highly skilled perfectionists, tend to be pre-occupied with artistic concerns. In addition to the normal panoply of IP rights designed to protect against unauthorised economic exploitation, 'moral' rights exist to protect creators against reputational abuses. These include the right to have authorship properly identified and to protect against derogatory treatment of one's work. This reflects the fact that the artistic currency can often be about reputations, not money. To an outsider the pre-occupation with 'credits' might seem excessive but these can have a significant bearing on a creator's next job. Creatives can appear relatively unsophisticated when considering business ramifications and, at a more extreme level, possibly disparaging towards both the 'Money' (ie the financiers) and the 'Suits', ie the lawyers and finance managers.

'Suits' tend to be more pre-occupied with commercial aspects, ie how a project is 'exploited' (a phrase that hints at the latent tensions between divergent creative and business needs). Most commercial aspects, even down to the minutiae of how projects get financed and receipts get calculated and divided, tend to be handled primarily by in-house lawyers rather than finance teams, especially in film and television. This is a throwback to early Hollywood studio practices, as is the industry parlance for calling in-house counsel 'business affairs', a phrase designed to make them appear more accommodating and proactive than traditional lawyers, while massaging egos to make individuals feel that they are running the business.

Egos are not entirely foreign to the entertainment industry and people can appear somewhat self-regarding. It isn't always apparent from people's behaviour which side of the camera they think they are on, even on the business side where, compared to other industries, negotiations can be somewhat aggressive. That said (and this is equally true in the various individual areas, like film, television, music, gaming, theatre, and advertising), within each grouping there is invariably a real sense of community, with companies regularly conducting business with one another and relationships and reputations (both individual and corporate) often being key.

For a mediator, working with dysfunctional and fairly vocal people who take things personally may be not be unusual but the show business side invariably needs to feel that you 'get' them and their idiosyncrasies (and, equally, that none of it fazes you).

Terminology, often US originated and invariably catchy, can be confusing to outsiders, not least because it may have been designed to be confusing to insiders. Profit definitions, for example, are notoriously convoluted. Don't be afraid to

Sector Specialisms

ask what anything means but ask too many questions and you may get the cold shoulder.

The industry's attitude towards litigation

Compared to other sectors, the entertainment industry is not litigious. There are a number of reasons for this. First, people in the business often know each other. Relationships can be key and people tend to be wary of unwinding them. As I mentioned, transactions tend to be conducted by in-house teams. They are there to make deals work and problems disappear, if necessary by cobbling together whatever they feel works. Production-based companies tend to be reticent about taking on commissioning entities, while the commissioners (often financiers or broadcasters) like to be seen as 'talent' friendly. Suing the talent sends the wrong message.

The industry is also less litigious than it used to be. While this is mainly because litigation is now considerably more expensive, some entertainment businesses fell foul of technological developments and now generate significantly less revenues. This is most noticeable in the music industry, added to which there seem to be considerably fewer 'adviser abuse' cases or band splits. If anything, reunions appear to be in vogue. (After years of artists citing 'irreconcilable music differences', I long for the day when they mention 'commercial similarities').

The industry's attitude towards mediation

As a sector the entertainment industry is finally using mediation more regularly, though compared to Californian companies, businesses still appear relatively unfamiliar with it. This is probably because, before the relatively recent advent of mediation, the industry had already adopted a raft of alternative (again, often US based) procedures to resolve specific disputes and it is probably a case of 'If it ain't broke...'.

Film industry disputes historically tend to be referred to arbitration, often in Los Angeles, with film title disputes (such as 'The Butler') being referred to the Motion Picture Association of America (MPAA), credit disputes to the various guilds or unions, and independent film or television distribution contract disputes to the Independent Film & Television Alliance (IFTA), for instance.

In TV, the main broadcasters commission producers in accordance with 'terms of trade'. These are pre-agreed with the relevant trade bodies and, bar odd exceptions, rarely stipulate resolution by mediation.

As a result, contractual dispute resolution clauses feature low on the entertainment industry business affairs radar, as opposed, say to discussions about choice of law and forum.

Typical industry disputes

These tend to be about three things, money, divergent practices and content.

Money

The old adage 'Where there's a hit, there's a writ' isn't far off. Claims tend to come from people purporting to be key 'originators', or who have been unlawfully or inappropriately depicted, or from profit participants who haven't received proper accountings. Dormant claims sometimes re-surface years later, say where a new means of delivery evolves through technological advances, or because of a successful adaptation, like *Spamalot* (based on the film *Monty Python and the Holy Grail*).

The film industry also attracts occasional disputes over various financing schemes. Fifteen years ago there was a rash of 'insurance backed' disputes and we are currently experiencing a flurry of tax avoidance/IFA mis-selling disputes.

Content

These fall into three categories:

- unauthorised exploitation;
- defamation/privacy/confidentiality; and
- licensing disputes, generally over a licensor's infraction or a licensee's rights handling or royalty accounting (or lack of it).

Divergent practices or laws

Typically these arise where:

- there could be significant economic ramifications if an individual exercises a personal creative right, eg where a director threatens to take his or her name off a film;
- collaborators from tangential industries, or different countries, have difficulties adapting to each other's practices. On films, for example, one often sees problems with music specialists over soundtrack or music publishing practicalities, with brands over commercial tie-ins, or with distributors in foreign territories; and
- the international aspect of the business is a further complication as copyright-related laws often differ between jurisdictions, creating unforeseen difficulties. Moral rights, for instance, are inalienable (ie incapable of being waived or assigned contractually) in many civil code jurisdictions. In some US states, 'publicity' rights (ie an individual's right to control the commercial use of their name, image or likeness) can survive an individual's death. In France, privacy laws tend to be unusually restrictive.

The suitability of mediation

Litigation may well be the preferred option for an 'unauthorised infringement' dispute where an infringer deliberately intended to harm a rights owner's business, not least 'pour encourager les autres'. Mediation should otherwise be suitable for most other types of industry disputes. It can also be the only effective way of saving a project from greater problems, not least because most films, programmes and commercials are made on tight timeframes and need to hit vital distribution deals or release/campaign windows. Where international partners are involved, it is also likely to be rather more effective than suing abroad. The fact that negotiations take place away from any media glare can appeal to broadcasters, publishers, licensors and public figures worried about damaging projects or brands, or alienating talent or business partners. The ability to agree settlements on a non-precedential basis can be particularly helpful for newspapers in defamation/privacy cases and for defendants concerned about possible third party satellite claims.

That said, and despite the much vaunted success rates, UK businesses often seem unaware of mediation and the entertainment sector is no different. People seem to be less cynical about the process than in some other sectors and they tend to respond well to the experience. The informality suits them, as well as the flexibility of being able to create tailor-made solutions. The sector is, after all, inherently creative and relatively unregulated.

What does the sector want from their mediator and what is unusual about the people at a mediation

Finally, like many sectors, parties often want a mediator who they feel will 'get them' and who will understand the intricacies of the business well enough to be able to generate practical solutions or give incisive reality tests (invariably to the other side). In content-related disputes, for example, understanding the art of framing an appropriate apology is likely to be key. A preference for a credible industry 'insider' is also likely where parties aren't already familiar with mediation, where a dispute involves technicalities, or say, on cross-border disputes where knowing the parties could be an advantage.

Mediating franchise disputes

Michael Cover

Franchising is a vibrant and growing sector. According to the annual NatWest/ British Franchise Association Survey in 2012, the annual turnover of the sector in the United Kingdom was around £13 billion, there were nearly 1,000 franchises (franchisors) and approximately 40,000 franchisees in the United Kingdom. This means that the average franchisee had an annual turnover of about £325,000. Another source, Franchise Development Services, reported in 2014 that the combined potential future investment in franchising in the United Kingdom, when bank lending was included, could amount to as much as £15 billion. In the same report, Franchise Development Services also noted that Subway, one of the leading franchises in the United Kingdom and Ireland, was planning to expand from 1,500 to 2,000 outlets over the next five years. Franchising is thus big business, involving many multinationals and other entities right down to a multitude of SMEs.

Franchises will typically involve a licence of intellectual property of the franchisor, generally a trade mark or trade marks, together with an agreement of provide know-how and a system of operating, and perhaps also with an agreement to supply goods for use or sale in the franchise outlet. There may be a structure which involves a head franchisee, who may, for example, have been granted the rights for a particular territory, such as the United Kingdom, and then a layer of sub-franchisees. There will also be a significant property (in the sense of real estate) element. The British Franchise Association (BFA) – already mentioned – is the main voluntary, self-regulatory body for the industry.[10]

So much for the commercial background – what about the law in this area? Franchising is seen by many as a specialist area of law and there are lawyers and other advisers that are experts in it. However, the main structure of a franchise agreement will generally involve intellectual property, contract law and company law and, as there will be a property or properties from which to trade, property law. There is also something of an enhanced regulatory environment and competition law considerations will almost certainly be present. As such, the disputes that arise out of franchising tend to occur in those areas, and often have the addition of employment. These may be disputes up or down the chain of franchisor and franchisee or disputes within, for example, franchisees themselves. There may also be disputes about the renewal or assignment of franchise agreements, recovery of debts and breaches of the franchise agreement itself.

The disputes that come up within the franchise area tend to involve a mix of some or all of these points. By definition, the parties will already know each other well, perhaps too well, and they may even be part of the same family. There may be a need for a clean break or else the imperative may be to keep the business going and the money flowing. In any event, emotions may well be running high and the parties may not even be prepared to go into the same room for the opening general session.

More specifically, the mediator may have to deal with a franchisor that is a company and where two shareholders have fallen out. There may be no shareholders' agreement and there may be no mechanism for dealing with the shareholdings, in circumstances where one of the parties allegedly is not pulling his or her weight. The situation may be complicated by the supposedly defaulting party being a shareholder in one of the franchisees. Bank accounts and financial reporting are also fertile areas for disputes on franchises, where one party complains that he or she is getting no or inadequate or inaccurate financial information.

Last but not least, there is the vital element of the intellectual property. This may take the form of registered trade marks for the brand that is the subject of the franchise through to copyright in the manuals that go with the operation of the franchise. There may be a dispute about the ownership of the intellectual property or action may be involved to enforce the intellectual property after the franchise agreement has been terminated. This intellectual property may be of great value, with the potential franchisees' banks more willing to lend on a business which is founded on the ability to use an established brand name or trade mark.

Disputes between franchisors and franchisees may arise after a change of control or reorganisation at the franchisor. This might result from changes to the franchisee network, amendments to the manual or changes to the requirements for financial reporting, with plenty of opportunities for breach of contract claims in each direction. This is not all bad news, as there may also be opportunities for added-value solutions for settlement, which might involve the franchisee remaining in

---

10 www.thebfa.org.

the franchise network on different or enhanced terms. In all this, the overarching confidential nature of the mediation process, and the likely confidential nature of any settlement achieved, is a huge advantage. This may be a particular advantage where the dispute is between a franchisor and a number or group of its franchisees. Mediation of franchise disputes is well suited to the needs of seeking commercial solutions in what are generally relatively long-term relationships.

The BFA has a Code of Conduct and also an independent mediation service, on whose panel are solicitor mediators experienced in franchise matters. There may be some tendency on the part of the parties to franchise disputes to appoint through or from the BFA Panel, so there may already be some knowledge of or familiarity with both mediation and the sector. This is mirrored in other jurisdictions, for example Australia, where there is the Office of the Franchising Mediation Adviser that has a panel of mediators who are available to resolve franchise disputes there.

Franchise disputes lend themselves to mediation, because there will generally be an established business relationship which either needs to be stabilised or made the subject of a clean break. The business may need to be kept afloat in both the short and medium term, whatever the outcome.

Finally, there are a number of other sections of this book which should be read in conjunction with this section on franchises, including those on intellectual property, cross-border (for many franchises extend across borders), shareholders and mergers and acquisitions and partnerships and family businesses.

Mediating insolvency disputes

Chris Fitton

Introduction and scope

There is no doubt that there are particular issues arising in disputes where there is an insolvency aspect of some sort, and very important that any mediator tasked with helping the parties is alive to those issues. In this short piece I highlight some of the peculiarities that I have come across in my mediating of insolvency cases over the past decade or so, pointing out along the way some actions the mediator might take to possibly minimise/smooth out those issues in practice. Our aim, as always, is to give the parties the best opportunity to make as much progress towards resolution as possible. I hope to further that cause a little, by sharing with other mediators what I have learned – tips I wish someone had listed for me before I started all those years ago.

Types of insolvency dispute

The insolvency of an individual or organisation almost always gives rise to a loss to some constituency or another, and where there is a loss – particularly an unexpected loss – a dispute often follows. Sometimes the insolvent entity is the claimant, for example a liquidator or administrator alleging misfeasance against a former director or officer, or an action against a third party who received some preference or similar, or an allegation that some pre-insolvency transfer was transacted at an undervalue.

In other cases the insolvency issue is with the defendant – perhaps the director who guaranteed the bank's lending to the company (and now pleads poverty), or a liquidator inheriting conduct of the defence of a claim started pre-liquidation. In all such cases, peculiar legal issues/tensions can come into play, some of which I address below. Thinking about how these peculiarities affect the negotiations in a mediation – the challenges they pose to the mediator – will hopefully improve the quality of mediation provision for such cases, whether by what is said and done on the day of the mediation itself, or in influencing/directing the parties' better preparation for that day.

Some issues typically arising at insolvency dispute mediations

The authority question

We all know the importance of having the right people at the mediation – as a minimum, individuals with the necessary legal authority to negotiate and ultimately bind the parties to the dispute. In corporate insolvency situations that generally means the liquidator or the administrator. It is in the nature of insolvency cases, however, that the settlement of a dispute almost always has a knock-on effect on the interests of other parties who are not directly party to the mediation. So for example, a liquidator accepting in settlement a sum less than that which might be recovered from a third party at trial may affect the amount of other creditors' dividend at final distribution. Or a personal guarantor paying the bank all they say they can realistically afford will very likely affect their spouse and family. Although these non-party interests are irrelevant in a strict legal sense (since, in the first example, the liquidator's signature creates a legally binding settlement), this common characteristic of insolvency disputes often profoundly affects the negotiations: it can define the parameters within which those attending the mediation are able to negotiate settlement. A prompt from the mediator to the parties' solicitors in advance, suggesting, for example, that their client's spouse attend the mediation – even though they are not a party – may be a helpful intervention.

Another issue impacting decision-making is the fact that the liquidator/administrator has a professional duty as officeholder only to act in the interests of the creditors. They should only be prepared to make concessions on points/figures if they are satisfied that those concessions can reasonably be justified. What that can lead to in practice is the legal representatives being 'put on the spot' during a mediation – sometimes a surprise for them – to give advice on the merits or otherwise of some proposed settlement structure: if the liquidator anticipates that thei decision to compromise may be challenged in the future by individuals who are not party to the mediation, then they may want the comfort of being able to point to legal advice they received in justifying that decision. Again, if the mediator spots in advance that that situation may arise, then that can greatly reduce the risk of the mediation having to be 'paused' (or even adjourned to another day) whilst the liquidator's lawyers consider or document that advice, or get counsel involved over the phone, hastily briefed from the mediation room.

That advice will usually be obtained only so that the new proposal can be compared to the alternative, allowing the litigation to continue (costs, uncertainty, delay etc). It is of course the case that that alternative (continuing the litigation to trial) is

Sector Specialisms

something the mediator can encourage the liquidator's legal team to have already assessed and advised on well in advance of the mediation day, so as to save the time needed for that side of the comparison.

Valuation issues

At the heart of an insolvency dispute there is very often an issue of valuation. If it is an avoidance action – liquidator seeking to set aside a transaction at an undervalue – then the true value of the asset dissipated will of course be central to liability. The alleged extent of the undervalue will also be central to quantum. Where a director's misfeasance is alleged, it is the loss the company is alleged to have suffered as a result that will be most hotly disputed. That dispute may include allegations as to:

- secret profits;
- damage to the company's trading performance; or
- misappropriation of client lists or price lists, sales figures, etc.

Although making these valuation assessments will often be difficult, the parties can only have a meaningful negotiation if each side knows how the other side assesses the alleged financial consequence caused by the wrongdoing. So it is essential, in my view, for these valuations to have been attempted (and communicated!) in good time before the mediation, however much they may need to be qualified/caveated with assumptions/subjectivities: there is little credibility in alleging a loss without quantifying it, yet that is surprisingly common in my experience.

Statement of affairs

What assets and liabilities there are in a company in administration or liquidation is obviously of great significance to a party pursuing a claim against that company (or, indeed, a party being sued by the administrator/liquidator). It is therefore important at a mediation to have as clear a picture of that as possible – typically a statement of affairs from the liquidator, or equivalent summary. There may be no harm in the mediator canvassing the need for such a summary to be prepared and circulated in appropriate cases, or for any such document that already exists being brought up to date for the mediation. Also for the position on costs to be made clear.

Timing of the mediation

Insolvency disputes tend to be mediated at an earlier stage than other cases, the parties recognising that the scope for settlement/realisation of any recovery is greater if the pot has not been depleted by lawyers' costs or the costs of the insolvency practitioner. This brings its own problems – the allegations can lack detail/proper particularisation, or be unquantified, or be vague when it comes to legally tricky issues like causation or remoteness. Many such disputes are mediated before proceedings have been issued and so rely on pre-action protocol correspondence only. Rarely will full disclosure have taken place or witness evidence been exchanged. It is a consequence of having to conduct the dispute in this way – on a shoestring – that one party or the other (often both) may be having to make judgments or take important decisions at the mediation on the basis of very limited information/paperwork, sometimes doing little more than guessing how certain issues may come out at trial. This can lead to some rather rough justice taking place in my experience, particularly in lower-value cases where the imperative to minimise costs is strongest. It is worth noting, however, that in liquidator v director type cases, the director will himself be present at the mediation. So if they wants to, they can say in person what their witness evidence would be – whether directly to the liquidator in the joint session/other session convened specifically for that purpose, or indirectly through the mediator in the course of the day's discussions. Some preparation for that may be worthwhile on both sides.

Costs

A liquidator will be an insolvency practitioner whose fees will be due from the assets of the liquidating company, and paid in priority to creditors. This can make for some interesting dynamics at the mediation, depending on the balance of company assets/secured debtors. For example, in modest liquidations it may well be the case that the liquidator will not be paid anything unless a realisation is made on the disputed claim currently in issue. This may in practice impact the liquidator's decision making (akin to the claimant solicitor on a no win/no fee arrangement) – and it is as well for the mediator to appreciate that. This is in contrast to the position with an LPA Administration (a Fixed Charge Receivership), where the Administrator (whilst still owing duties to others) will generally be acting in the interests of the secured lender - typically a bank - and being paid by that lender on an ongoing basis, whether or not a recovery is made.

Another costs-related peculiarity of bank-led recovery litigation is in relation to the costs of the mediation. Often the defendant debtor's position is that if their pleaded defence fails, they have no cash to pay the claim anyway. If the bank believes there is nevertheless some equity in the debtor's property, it is not uncommon, in my experience, for the bank to offer to fund the whole of the mediator's fees themselves, rather than the fees being agreed to be paid on the usual 50:50 basis. The rationale for this apparent generosity by the bank is that achieving a mediated (therefore consensual) outcome to the dispute may give the bank a better net recovery position than traditional court-based action (possession proceedings). However, it will frequently be the case that such defendants are acting in person (no legal representation), so will have no costs of their own in attending the mediation. Obviously, if that is so, then one issue the mediator may want to be satisfied about is the extent to which that defendant is properly committed to the mediation process: it may be that their commitment to the mediation is low given that it is, in effect, costing nothing.

Conclusions

I have attempted to list here some of the insolvency-related mediation issues I have found in my practice – there will certainly be many more that I have not yet encountered. Where I can, I have offered my own view on how the mediator might handle or head-off some of these issues, so as to maximise the parties' opportunity to find settlement. Of course, that can only happen if the papers are sent to the mediator early enough for their suggestions to be considered.

I have been generally impressed with how readily insolvency practitioners, banks, etc have embraced mediation, no doubt frustrated by the expensive, drawn-out alternative – court proceedings. I have seen many cases where the assets within the liquidation would certainly be depleted by litigation costs long before the proceedings reached trial.

So in this particular sector – insolvency – mediation has an important role and a bright future. The challenge now is to find ways in which these cases can continue to be mediated as early as possible, and in the same relatively low-cost way, but with better-informed outcomes, reached less stressfully. Part of the solution there, in many cases, may be for more targeted, early work on the quantification of alleged losses, and an early appreciation – on both sides – of the value in settling early, before substantial costs are incurred.

Mediating insurance/reinsurance disputes

Jane Andrewartha

It is, of course, highly likely that there may be some form of insurance involvement in most of the different specialist sectors covered by this chapter.[11] This section addresses those disputes in which it might be said that, whatever the relevant industry affected, insurers play a dominant (or at least a major) part. Those who work directly in the insurance and reinsurance sectors (and different considerations may apply to each) demonstrate, generally, a high level of awareness of mediation. On the insurer side of the claim, the mediator is often dealing with highly experienced claims handlers, many of whom have responsibility for extensive litigation and arbitration caseloads; such parties, therefore, are frequently well practised in the use of ADR generally and specifically mediation. The same will not necessarily be true of their opponents who may range from equally experienced risk managers representing blue chip companies to first time litigators, whether corporate or individual. As such the mediator may be faced with an immediate imbalance between participants.

An historic view

My first experience of mediation was in the early 1990s when Philip Naughton QC successfully mediated a (then) extremely large tri-partite dispute between various London underwriters and an underwriting agent. It was, to my knowledge, the first major insurance mediation held in England but it did not represent the first London (insurance) market[12] experience of mediation. Many London market insurance practitioners of the 1990s, having participated in mediation in the United States for a decade or more, had considerably more mediation experience than most English

---

11 The range is extensive covering first party and third party claims, life, accident and health, aviation, marine, energy, contingency, financial guarantee, political risks, credit risks, terrorism, war and many other classes of business.
12 References in this section to the London market are made to distinguish between the writer's international dispute resolution experience in this country and elsewhere. Much of what is said as to the London market will be equally applicable to the UK insurance market generally (although international claims handling experience is most likely to be found in those entities based in London).

mediators. Not all were wholly impressed by their Stateside experience. Today it remains the case that some insurance representatives will have a wider experience of mediation than those they select to mediate their disputes. The claims handler's experience may extend to managing multiparty claims (class actions abroad or litigation brought under group litigation orders[13] in this country), transnational disputes (with more than one set of related litigation, often in several different jurisdictions), court ordered mediations (in one case with which I was concerned the London insurer was ordered to attend mediation in the United States while not even being a party to the US litigation!) and staggered settlement timetables (where the parties have already set their own schedule for handling different aspects of liability or catastrophe claims). This breadth and depth of experience can greatly enhance the skills and approach of those mediators chosen to assist the industry. Certainly working directly in this sector is always a mutual learning experience.

Direct insurance as opposed to reinsurance

There is a distinction to be drawn between claims involving insurance, of which there are many variations as discussed below, and those involving reinsurance where the insurer is himself insured by others, thus laying off part of his own risk.

Many claims will be perceived as having a direct insurance involvement. The industry has limited control over the jurisdiction or forum in which such claims arise, or are resolved. In the case of liability policies, for example, that choice may be in the hands of the third party claimant who will select what he considers to be the most advantageous jurisdiction open to him. Reinsurance disputes, on the other hand, are more easily channelled by the industry into their chosen dispute resolution process (normally arbitration). It should be noted also that reinsurance considerations may give rise to their own issues when it comes to compromise settlements of direct claims.[14] Whatever the commercial factors motivating the direct insurer, they could conclude that where there are genuine coverage issues they may be better served by an adverse court judgement than a mediated settlement.

Insurance

I consider insurance related mediations to fall into three broad categories – others may identify many more.[15] Most obviously, there are coverage disputes (where the insurer has a disagreement with the insured; normally, the former becomes the defendant and the latter, the claimant). Next are disputes invoking the insured's liability cover (product liability, professional indemnity, public or employers liability

---

13 A group litigation order (GLO) allows the court to procedurally manage a number of separate claims which give rise to 'common or related issues of fact or law'. See CPR Rule 19.10–19.15.
14 See *Commercial Union Assurance Co. Plc v NRG Victory Reinsurance Ltd* [1998] Lloyd's Rep IR 439 (Court of Appeal).
15 The international (US/UK) mediator, Mike Holland, who has kindly reviewed this writer's contribution and whose background lies in insurance in both the United States and in England, identifies disputes between insurers and their agents, brokers, other insurers, their actuaries, investment managers, escrow agents and service providers as matters he has personally dealt with.

and the like), where the insured is the defendant to third party litigation (and the involvement of insurers in the defence of the claim may or may not be disclosed). Finally there are subrogated actions (where insurers seek recovery of their outlay to their insured by way of an action, normally brought in the name of the insured, against the responsible party). These disputes each have their own distinctive features and there may be reinsurance implications attached to each of them.

Direct insurance claims, therefore, present themselves in many forms. They can involve the interests (not always aligned) of both insured and insurer in one room with the opposing party (who may also have insurers involved) in the other. The mediated claim may be the defence of the insured under a liability policy or a third party recovery pursued in the insured's name through a subrogation action. The mediator needs to be aware of the possibility of the insured only having partial insurance cover and, hence retaining (in addition to any reputational risks involved) a significant monetary interest in the outcome of the litigation and its accompanying mediation. More complex still are those cases that proceed where the insurer (usually due to unresolved coverage issues) has reserved its position as to the existence or extent of insurance cover available (often undisclosed to opposing parties). That situation may give rise to real tension between the parties in the same room. On occasions the mediator is required to mediate between those parties as to their respective contribution to any proposed settlement. Similarly, in subrogation actions (where the insurer/insured are the claimants against a third party) there may be unresolved issues concerning the allocation of the proceeds of litigation between insured and insurer as well as further issues surrounding the costs of continuing with the litigation (uninsured losses often prove more costly to pursue through remoteness or lack of foreseeability).

Brokers

In all of this there looms large the figure of the broker, the individual or company who acts as the intermediary between the insured and the insurer or the cedant and his reinsurer. Brokers are generally diligent in their pursuit of the claims service they offer their insureds; many will wish to see their clients through to the resolution of their claim, which may include the broker's attendance at the mediation. Where, however, there are coverage issues between insurer and insured, the broker's presence (or absence) may hold a different significance. Many years ago I was told, as mediator, that the insured's broker would be in attendance at the mediation in a separate room; the other side were not to be advised of that fact. It became plain to me in the mediation that the broker was to be an undisclosed contributor to the final settlement. Matters did not go to plan, however, as the fire alarm sounded in the middle of the process and the occupants of all three rooms were ushered indiscriminately down the same staircase! (I would handle that situation very differently these days.) More recently a mediator colleague in the United States advised that he had urged the adjournment of an insurance mediation because of the obvious empty chair in the room – that of the broker. He suggested to the parties that the broker be invited to attend; a tri-partite solution was concluded on the second day with the brokers acknowledging their own contribution to the problem and bridging the ultimate gap between insurer and insured. It is the task of the mediator to sense, and deal appropriately with, the complexities of the insurance mediation.

Reinsurance and retrocession[16]

The industry prefers to keep its own disputes to itself and, for that reason, many reinsurance contracts contain arbitration clauses providing for confidential resolution of disputes before a (usually three arbitrator) tribunal specified as requiring experience in the industry. That, of course, can prove extremely expensive and slow especially where all three arbitrators are lawyers. While there exists an established body of good, experienced arbitrators available to handle such disputes, the arbitration clause can sometimes be drawn so narrowly as to severely limit the choice of arbitrators (sometimes excluding lawyers). Whether the selected arbitrators are busy, full-time arbitrators or those who receive only the occasional appointment, it is rarely in the interests of the tribunal to urge the parties to consider referring the case to mediation.[17] To do so would deprive the arbitrators of their living.

There is, therefore, no discernable equivalent of the Court pressure[18] that exists in England (and other jurisdictions) for the parties to reinsurance disputes to consider mediation before proceeding to a costly hearing. As a result there are not presently a very great number of reinsurance mediations taking place; those that do occur can result from a well-intentioned, but not necessarily well-informed, cedant or reinsurer drafting their own mediation clause. Such clauses are sometimes modelled on arbitration clauses and do not always make for an easy process. They often provide for compulsory mediation (which always has its difficulties). I have myself encountered one clause that demanded three mediators! A further provision, as a pre-condition to arbitration, required mediation and called for a mediator with 10 years' direct experience in the insurance industry (at the time an impossible provision to fulfil). It resulted in a largely wasted trip to a nonetheless very pleasant island where an arbitrator with no mediation experience whatsoever wandered from room to room predicting (inaccurately as events transpired) that, regardless of the merits of the claim, the arbitrators would *'split the baby'* and the parties to the mediation should do likewise. No settlement resulted.

The insurers

Nor are all insurers the same. Major litigation and arbitration cases may involve a substantial market of different entities (whether company or Lloyd's market[19]) not all of whom are of the same mind. This may give rise to authority issues and to the presence of multiple insurer representatives at the mediation. Each insurer writes the risk on a several basis (that is, solely in respect of their own participation without any liability for the involvement of others). There can sometimes even be

---

16 Reinsurers do, themselves, lay off some part of their exposure and, when they do, the contracts under which they do so are called retrocession contracts.
17 Although, to their credit, the LMAA (London Maritime Arbitrators Association) now includes, in its questionnaire due 14 days after close of submissions, the question 'Have the parties considered whether mediation might be worthwhile?'. This is a milder version of the requirements that result from the court's overriding directive as particularised in Pt 1 of CPR.
18 Part A of the Directions Questionnaire specifies that the parties must inform the court if they want to attempt to settle and draws attention to the costs consequences of failing to attempt to do so.
19 In addition to involving numerous insurance companies, the insurance industry worldwide is served by the infinitely flexible and entrepreneurial market of underwriters who are, together, referred to as Lloyd's of London. As a marketplace for insurance, Lloyd's has its own regulatory regime and codes of practice.

different terms applicable to the different insurers on the risk. It will not therefore necessarily follow that all insurers are willing to settle at the same level. That can be more markedly the case where one or more of the insurers are in run-off[20] and, no longer having a relationship to protect, may assume a wholly different approach to commercial settlement. Insolvent markets introduce their own problems as they result in shortfalls in cover that must somehow be accommodated in the settlement. Insurer participation is also often written in layers; issues may arise as to what may or may not be read into the presence or absence of those representing higher layers of cover in the mediation.

The very existence (or lack) of insurance cover may, in England, be a matter of intense interest to claimant parties but is very often something that a defendant is reluctant to disclose for fear of raising expectations. The same is true of the limits on cover where it is known that insurance cover does exist.[21] In the United States, I understand, claimants are generally entitled to know the details of any relevant cover; this may lead to a mismatch of expectations (and therefore some mistrust or at least dissatisfaction) if an American claimant is pursuing a claim before the English courts. In addition to issues that arise from complex insurance placings at different levels among a number of companies or Lloyd's Syndicates, there are many risks that are covered by mutual associations. Examples of such bodies include the P&I clubs in the marine industry and professional mutuals such as the Bar Mutual and the (now defunct) Solicitors Indemnity Fund in the legal profession. The dynamics in a mediation where the losses that result from litigation are shared between the members of the mutual are different again, if only because the negotiators on behalf of such associations believe, or assert, that they are.

Summary

These, therefore, are some of the complexities of the insurance and reinsurance industries which ensure that every mediation that is touched by their involvement will have many, often unspoken, considerations that extend far beyond the pure legal merits of the underlying dispute. That is true in whatever area the dispute arises (and, of course, the London insurance market has a reputation for covering every conceivable risk from Angolan energy risks to Zimbabwean political risks). The mediator needs to be extremely well prepared and alert to all possible issues in play whilst making no assumptions. This is a truly rewarding sector in which to mediate as often the parties on both sides of the case have a real and sophisticated appreciation of the process. The mediator must, however, always be sensitive to potential imbalances between the parties such as may exist where the non-insurance party has not been involved in litigation previously.

Accordingly my tips for those appointed as mediators in this sector are as follows:

- thoroughly prepare in respect of the technical issues involved in the underlying case as well as those insurance aspects which overlay it;
- ask appropriate questions where the role or involvement of certain parties is not clear;

---

20 That is, they are no longer writing fresh business.
21 Sometimes, of course, low levels of cover are disclosed precisely to manage expectations.

- learn what the parties and insurers real interests are – they may not be obvious or necessarily aligned;

- be ready for unexpected responses from the insurance interests present and test whether apparent limiting factors (eg reserving or reinsurance considerations) have real relevance to the dispute in hand;

- be aware of the possible imbalance of negotiating skills between the parties; and

- finally, as mediator, avoid any element of predictability in the handling of mediations for repeat users – consider carefully whether impartiality or effectiveness is threatened by multiple appointments by the same party or representative.

Mediating intellectual property and IT disputes

Jon Lang

This contribution is intended for the mediator who does not have an IP or IT background but who may become involved in IP and IT disputes as their careers develop.

Given the suitability of mediation for the resolution of IP and IT disputes, not least because of the far greater range of solutions available than if before a court or arbitrator, the ability to deal with common issues across several jurisdictions, speed and low cost, mediation has been flourishing in these areas for a number of years.

But the sectors are very different, albeit there is often an overlap. IT is an industry sector and what are commonly described as IT disputes usually involve licensing, product development, service agreements and the like. In other words, at the heart of IT disputes is usually a contract, which of course means that the parties are usually in a pre-existing relationship. This may be the case in an IP dispute as well, but usually they arise because an IP owner alleges infringement of an IP right against an unrelated third party, albeit commonly a competitor. Thus there needn't be, and often isn't, a pre-existing relationship in an IP dispute. There are of course cases that could be described as either IT or IP related (or both) – an allegation that use of a patent is outside the scope of a licence granted, or a patent entitlement claim arising out of a product development project.

Each sector will be considered separately, but it is not intended to provide a full analysis of either. That would require something far more weighty which I covered in my book in 2006. Much has changed since that book was written, but the basic challenges in each field remain: in IP mediation, the complex and dynamic nature of the law, the high degree of expertise of the clients, their advisers and the mediator, and the huge range of settlement options to choose from; in IT, the factual complexity of the disputes, the volume of material relevant to the dispute (not necessarily the mediation) and the common use of experts.

Finally, in terms of this introduction, and to help put some of what follows in context, the buying market in these sectors, like specialist mediators!

Sector Specialisms

Intellectual property mediation

This is an area of mediation where some knowledge of the law is important. It is also important to understand and appreciate the actual IP parties are arguing about. Intellectual property in any of its forms represents the labours of the human mind. Parties get very upset if they feel that the fruits of their creative or intellectual endeavour are not appreciated or understood. So know the law and love the product (trade mark, design, invention …).

Know the law

The law in this area can be complex. There is often a European dimension to it. Whilst parties do not expect or want a detailed legal analysis of the dispute (but rather, for instance, the infringement to stop or a commercial arrangement struck without the risk of losing or having cut back a registered right which would have ramifications far beyond the dispute being mediated), they will expect a little more than basic knowledge. Without that, it will be very difficult for a mediator to properly articulate one side's position in the other room, or effectively reality test with each party their position, or offer meaningful suggestions as to how matters may be resolved.

Mediators in IP mediations are typically instructed by specialist practitioners, be they solicitors, trade mark attorneys or patent attorneys. If a more general practitioner is instructed by the underlying client, they are likely to use specialist counsel. The mediator needs to be able to follow the discussion and understand the 'shorthand' used, and thus investment in understanding the relevant law is important. The specific area of IP will usually be apparent from the pre-action correspondence or statements of case. Once you have a handle on this, a worthwhile starting point is the Intellectual Property Office website and, in particular, the 'Types of IP' page.[22] Also, have a look at some articles. Most solicitors active in IP, as well as trade mark and patent attorneys, publish articles that are readily available online.

The Intellectual Property Office also contains useful information on the various types of IP related proceedings available outwith the courts, for example, where one party challenges another's trade mark. You may well end up mediating trade mark registry proceedings and a basic understanding of what is involved will be helpful.

Love the product (trade mark…)

You might be mediating a design right dispute concerning a bathroom fitting, or a trade mark dispute concerning the packaging design of a product or the logo used on a fashion accessory, or a patent dispute concerning a method for extruding a particular substance. Get to know the subject of the dispute. Look at websites. Look at brochures. Look at what others in the same market are doing. This may not be so easy with a patent dispute but quite often there will, somewhere in the papers, be an explanation of what it is all about. If there isn't, ask. There is no shame in

---

22   http://www.ipo.gov.uk/types/patent.htm.

this. Sometimes experienced High Court IP judges will be provided with a 'primer' explaining the invention that is the subject of a patent.

Where appropriate, suggest that samples be brought along to the mediation. Many cases have been settled with parties looking over products bearing an allegedly infringing trade mark, or which are said to infringe another's design right, with parties suggesting changes that could be made to resolve the dispute. Maybe organise a separate room at the mediation where products that are the subject of the dispute can be viewed throughout the day. Note that it's much easier to work with colour copies where colour is important!

IT mediation

Often, mediation in the IT field bears considerable similarity with mediation in the construction and engineering fields – they can be highly detailed and argument can descend to incredible levels of granularity. Experts are commonly present at the mediation (unlike in the IP field where the clients and primary advisers tend to be the 'experts'). I usually have in my mind in an IT mediation whether there is going to be an orderly disengagement between the parties, or a re-engagement on varied terms, the latter being a far easier path to settlement given the obvious value creation (as opposed to mere distribution) opportunities, but often all options need to be kept open.

For me, management of experts and time and process design are key in the successful mediation of IT disputes.

Experts

It is worth making a preliminary point here. Some mediators hold strong views about the presence of experts at a mediation. In an IT dispute, there is often a mismatch in the level of IT expertise, with one side feeling that it is appropriate for an expert to be with them every step of the way. Don't push back! The parties and their advisers know more about it all than you do.

Experts, by their nature, will be opinionated. They will have strong views. The strength of view will depend on the basis of their instruction, whether a report has been signed and the purpose for which it is to be used (court as well as the mediation or just the mediation). The further experts are from nailing their colours to the mast, the less strident they will often be in their views. In any event, if experts are at the mediation, they need to be used as a force for good. In other words, they need to buy into the notion that they are there to help their clients do a deal, not win the argument.

For this and other reasons, it can be helpful to have pre-mediation meetings at which experts are present. Easing them into the process before the day of mediation, so that it is seen as a value-building, pain-sharing exercise, rather than a zero sum game, will be important, and it will help with a key question in most IT disputes, as already mentioned – is there to be a re-engagement or an orderly disengagement? Here trust is a key issue and experts can help.

Sector Specialisms

In mediations where the parties are going to want employ experts, it can be helpful for their reports to be provided consecutively so that each side has an opportunity of addressing the other's arguments. The last thing that one wants at a mediation are experts who have been asked to consider different questions. A pre-mediation meeting at which at least the legal advisers of the parties are present, can be helpful to make sure each side is on the same page in terms of the areas it would be useful to debate and, importantly, when and how and the time to be allowed.

Time management and process design

There is likely to be an abundance of material to read. Read it! Get a feel for the product. Again look at websites and get a real feel for the parties. The lawyers and clients will be on top of the detail. You don't need to know as much as they do about the case but you do need to build rapport and trust fast. The best way of doing so is to show that you have put in the effort and time to have a good working knowledge of the case.

Time is the common enemy at an IT mediation. Before you know it, the sandwiches will arrive and you will only be on point 6 of a 50-point defects list. Plan the day in advance. It is not unusual for IT mediations to be spread over two days and, very occasionally three, but if you are having to get everything resolved in just one day, working fast is essential. There is little time for a 'get the drains up' approach, but at the same time parties need to know that their points are being taken on board. Suggest that the party with the list of 50 defects talk only about a few that illustrate the key points they wish to make. It might be that that type of discussion can be dispensed with completely if there is to be a disengagement, or a recovery plan is already on the table. The more all of this can be worked out in advance, the better.

I have mentioned pre-mediation meetings to discuss making the best use of the day. Usually, more 'process' focused meeting are with the parties' legal representatives jointly. It can also be useful, however, to have more 'merits'-based discussions with the parties separately. For these types of meetings, the presence of the parties themselves, and any experts, is important. They will welcome the opportunity of explaining their view of life without the time pressure that the day of mediation inevitably brings, and you will have an opportunity to float some ideas that will have time to be 'slept on'.

Mediating partnership and family business disputes

David Richbell

Of all the areas of dispute that I have mediated, the most difficult and challenging (for me) is contested probate. Next is partnership and family business. I realise that part of that is because I am an only child and, in my mind, having siblings would have led to a less lonely and more complete childhood. Of course, the reality may well have been very different! But it does affect my approach to these disputes because it pains me to see families at war. Partnership disputes are as bad because they are like divorce – the shattering of parties' hopes and expectations despite, often, many years of working closely together. So I recognise that I come to these disputes with 'baggage' that may affect my neutrality, and that I need to be aware of that as I prepare for and conduct the mediation.

Although these are not unique to this particular sector, there are a few characteristics that are always present in partnership and family business disputes:

- high emotion – betrayal, suspicion, demonisation, revenge;
- historic, if not lifetime, relationships often defy common sense;
- the need for 'justice'– equal division of the 'spoils', no one gets a better deal than another; and
- attachment to particular items (property, clients, memorabilia) that transcends monetary value.

I have mentioned elsewhere that behind every dispute lies a broken relationship. Never more so than in partnership and family business disputes, where it is usually the broken relationship that actually causes the dispute. It is therefore important that the mediator spends time exploring the relationships, when they were good, what caused them to fracture, why they are driving the positions in the dispute.

Separating people and problem

This is a stock phrase in mediation, but not so easy to practise. I had a case that clearly demonstrated what this meant – it was a workplace dispute where a new director had a long-serving manager to work with and supervise. There was a lot of good feeling between them at the start and the director threw himself into his role with great enthusiasm. Unfortunately their relationship soured and the manager became obstructive. I was asked to help sort the problem and it became clear that the manager felt devalued because the new director was raking away some of her work and not talking to her about it. The problem was that there had been no clear allocation or tasks and responsibilities and the manager had no experience of talking to a director about how she was feeling. The *problem* was no clear boundaries or task allocation, the *person* was the feelings this created. Once they understood this, the director (and the manager) were able to recognise and value each other's feelings and then they were able to deal with the problems jointly, and co-operatively.

So with the partnership and family business disputes. Helping parties to separate personal feelings from the practical issues is a major step to helping them work out mutual solutions. Ignore that and it becomes a permanent blockage to co-operation and finding settlement.

High emotion

The more personal the problem, the more emotional it becomes. Even siblings will demonise the others, believing them to be the sole cause of all their misfortune, probably since birth. This creates suspicion and the belief that the others cannot be trusted. Hurt, especially if their partner and/or children are affected, must be revenged.

My view is that parties must take responsibility for these, often unjustified, positions. One of the benefits of the initial joint meeting is that parties have to recognize, and accept, that their 'foe' is also human and has human emotions. The balloon of demonising is pricked and the 'injured' party has to recognise that their 'foe' deserves a reasonable response.

This is covered elsewhere but the mediator spending time listening to, valuing and showing that, whatever is said, it is recognised as important to the person speaking, is vital to helping them move on.

Historic relationships

Of course, siblings have known each other all their lives (and their parents even longer!) and the relationship of older to younger, sister to brother, parent to child is almost unchangeable. Seniority of elder siblings, authority of parent and so on will have a serious effect on the way a business is run. Senior partners tend to assume that the firm is still theirs despite having partners of often equal status. It is difficult to let go of authority and status. I have mediated several cases where a bullying elder brother has created such tension within the family business that his, often more talented, siblings have rebelled and brought the business into real crisis. Similarly, a founding partner may run the partnership as his personal fiefdom, completely ignoring the need for regular partners' meetings and fair treatment of travel and other business expenses. It can be a very difficult task for such parties to change their lifetime habits.

Justice

Of course, every litigant wants justice – even more so when siblings or partners are concerned. The trouble is that mediation is not necessarily about justice, or even fairness, because everyone sees both justice and fairness differently. What mediation does is to give the parties the opportunity of achieving a settlement, which is just and/or fair in their eyes. If the business is to be split, or the partnership dissolved, there needs to be the feeling that there is no 'winner', in particular that the perceived cause of the dispute does not benefit more from the outcome than the others – in fact the general feeling is usually that they should benefit less. The mediator's role can be vital in helping parties achieve a 'fair' outcome whilst helping to ensure that the settlement is both realistic and workable. Trusted neutrality creates the bridge for overcoming historic differences and suspicions.

Attachment

Not all cases involve the emotional attachment to something but I have mediated cases where a disproportionate value has been attached to a property (whether building, picture or even a desk!), memorabilia (rug, photograph or even a coffee mug!) or a client (personal friend, particular project or personal attachment). In one case a sibling desperately wanted a small cottage on the farm that was being broken up, valued by the experts at much less than her share of the main farmhouse. Her explanation at the end was that she had been born in that cottage and so wanted to maintain a continuity for her children. It may have seemed irrational to others but to her it was very important.

Law

In many cases, particularly with the division and ownership of property and dissolution of partnership, there are particular legal requirements attached to any settlement. The lawyers representing parties at the mediation should know the relevant law but, as in all mediations, it is still incumbent upon the mediator to ask the relevant questions and ensure that the settlement will stick.

Mediating personal injury claims

Neil Goodrum

Introduction

Mediation is particularly suited to personal injury cases. Frequently, they involve a claimant who is a one-time user of the judicial system and a defendant who is a frequent and sophisticated user. Even supported by counsel and solicitors the claimant is unfamiliar with the legal situation in which they find themselves, in circumstances where they are under significant stress and uncertain of what to expect.

In any dispute the people are central and what I particularly like about mediating in personal injury cases is that both parties get to work within a process that enables them to communicate more as people and less as actors in a drama for which they do not have the whole script. Claimants are able to communicate in their own terms with defendants, frequently defendant insurers. Defendants are able to have a dialogue with claimants and explain their approach to a case in terms that would get lost in the litigation process and the language that accompanies it.

More personal injury cases should mediate than presently find their way into this process. We all know that the vast majority of personal injury cases settle at some point before trial. It is not certain that this does not hide unsatisfactory elements in the settlement process that mediation can address.

Some aspects of all litigation are particularly evident in personal injury cases including the stress and emotional upset for the claimant. Also present is the belief sometimes that the case must be virtually ready for trial before the time is right to discuss settlement. The particular costs arrangements that apply to these types of cases can also make settlement more difficult.

It's about the people

I have found that part of my role in these mediations is managing the dialogue between the parties when they are seeking to move at different speeds. The defendant insurer's representative will usually be an experienced claims manager who is there to get things sorted out quickly. While appreciating any sensitivities of the claimant, this manager is not likely to be particularly interested in spending a lot of time in exploration and may become frustrated at the lack of progress. Establishing rapport with the defendant's representatives, as well as their lawyers, is an important aspect and enables you, as mediator, to normalise the delays that might take place as the claimant prepares to discuss resolution.

I have seen many cases where the claimant is anxious and in some circumstances distressed about the case and about the meeting. They arrive not quite knowing what to expect. It is particularly important that the mediator works to establish rapport as quickly and effectively as possible. To help achieve this it is very helpful, if possible, to include the claimant themselves in the pre-mediation contact, either in a joint conference call with their solicitor, or, if everyone is comfortable with it, in an initial direct conversation. If I can, I tend to try and speak to the claimant personally before the day, if for no other reason than that I am not then a complete stranger to them when the day starts.

The work that the mediator does with the claimant in the early part of the mediation exploring, so far as is appropriate to the individuals concerned, the background and impact of the case, is the foundation of an effective negotiating phase.

Balance is vital. The claimant may need attention to ensure that they are not intimidated or alienated by the process. The defendant will need to feel that the mediator, while paying proper attention to the sensitivities of the claimant, remains impartial and engaged with them.

Early process management

Frequently, an early discussion is about whether or not the claimant attends an opening joint meeting. I have often spent time with both parties negotiating who should attend the opening meeting and how it is going to be conducted. It is increasingly common, in my experience, for lawyers for both parties to suggest that an opening meeting be dispensed with in these types of cases. My view is that to acquiesce to this suggestion is a serious error. Clearly, as mediators, we cannot force parties into a joint meeting, but as managers of the process we should make every effort to encourage them to meet at this stage, without radically damaging rapport. It may be the only occasion during the day when they do meet and it is the best opportunity for the parties to see that nature and character of the people they are dealing with. It makes a difference if a party speaks in the presence of the other party to the dispute. Furthermore, later in the day, when things get a little more difficult, it is harder for the parties to overlook the personal aspects of the case and that they are dealing with individuals.

Who should be there?

In pre-mediation contact, I always discuss with the defendant's lawyer whether or not a decision maker from the insurers, assuming an insurer is involved, will be attending. Hard experience teaches that there are few things as frustrating in mediation as being on the verge of a settlement only for this to be vetoed by a claims manager who is absent and contacted by telephone 'for instructions' at 5pm. Mediation is a dynamic process and the absent claims manager has not been involved in the changes that have occurred as the mediation has progressed. If possible, get them to the meeting. If not, I try and speak to them on the telephone early in the day so that contact has been made and a basis for further contact is established before things start moving.

When speaking to the claimant or their lawyer prior to the mediation, I encourage the claimant to have a supporter with them. They need someone who is a trusted family member or close friend who can be their companion; it is unlikely that their lawyer can play this role.

Sometimes it is helpful to have key experts or counsel contactable, if not present. Thinking ahead as mediator, I try to avoid a situation where the mediation gets stalled because some crucial piece of information or vital opinion cannot be obtained.

It's a negotiation, isn't it?

Perhaps linked to my point above about the claimant and the defendant moving at different speeds, ultimately, I want to get the parties into the negotiating phase and this means managing the process to bring them to the point where they are both ready to engage with this. The groundwork needs to be laid before the day. First, it is important to understand the point reached in the case. Do the parties have all the information they need to make a decision, or are they able to 'take a view' so that they can reach an agreement. I have had one case where it transpired that one party was not ready to resolve the matter until they received a further expert's report and in another there was a difficulty over the CRU (Compensation Recovery Unit) certificate which was discovered to be out of date.

Secondly, I find myself frequently acting as a 'negotiation coach' in these cases, particularly seeking to normalise the bargaining process to a claimant who may not be as commercially sophisticated as the defendant, even with the benefit of legal advice. This may involve working with the defendants on the timing, format and manner of presentation of any offers that they wish to make.

The costs mediation

On 1 April 2013 the position on costs in civil cases changed significantly and this has had a major impact in personal injury cases. Prior to 1 April 2013, cases of this type were generally funded by conditional fee agreements (CFA) and after the event insurance (ATE). A major stumbling block to settlement at mediation often arose just at the point when the parties thought they were approaching settlement. The claimant's lawyers would say that they were entitled to a success fee, often of 100 per cent of their costs. Additionally, where the case was funded by ATE insurance, settlement would mean that the insurance premium would be recoverable from the defendants. In these circumstances, what then ensues is a mediation over the costs, not infrequently involving a mediation between the claimant and their lawyer. At this point the settlement can break down even though the parties are near agreement on the claim itself.

Although the rules changed in April 2013, CFAs with success fees and funding arrangements entered into prior to that date are valid and recoverable as before. Because of the timescales involved in litigation, as mediators we are likely to be dealing with cases under the old rules for some time and so we need to be familiar with how they work and understand the negotiation dynamic that results.

Under the new arrangements, as mediators, we need to understand the changed funding provisions for these types of cases. These can still involve CFAs, but without the recovery of the success fee from the defendants. The reforms mean that mediators must now be familiar with how success fees payable by the claimant impact on the settlement. They will need to understand the uses and impact of Damages Based Agreements and costs insurance where premiums are not recoverable from the defendants. Also to be noted is the impact of qualified one way costs shifting (QOCS). These change the negotiating dynamic as in most personal injury cases the defendant will not recover their costs from an unsuccessful claimant. There are exceptions to QOCS, particularly regarding the impact of settlement offers under Pt 36 of the Civil Procedure Rules. Familiarity with these exceptions will be essential for mediators.

More personal injury mediations?

The changes in April 2013 may have far-reaching implications for case management by the court. While doing little directly to push more cases to mediation, the impact may be that there is greater encouragement to the parties to go to mediation from judges. The perception has been that few cases of this type mediate, with a lot of use being made of joint settlement meetings (JSM). In one authoritative survey ,only 1.8 per cent of personal injury cases went to mediation, although the indication is that of cases that are mediated around 88 per cent settle. Mediation offers something more to the parties than provided by JSMs, at marginal, if any, additional cost.

The author of the reforms to the civil justice system, Lord Justice Jackson, stated in his final report:

> 'There is a widespread belief that mediation is not suitable for personal injury cases. This belief is incorrect. Mediation is capable of arriving at a reasonable outcome in many personal injury cases...'

Conclusion

Mediators have a lot to offer personal injury parties. One of the big advantages is getting two parties with differing outlooks and experiences to work together, actively engaged, to resolve the dispute. For this reason, my feeling is that as mediators in these cases we can help, particularly in the early phases including preparation, to lay the groundwork for a successful outcome which is seen by both parties as better than the alternative.

Mediating planning related disputes

John Pugh-Smith

Mediating a planning issue, outside litigation, differs from most other kinds of dispute resolution due to the requirements of governance, the need for transparency, the requirement for consultation with different parties, the democratic process that has to be followed and the wider expectations of 'the public interest'. Accordingly, the degree of flexibility and confidentiality within the 'mediation exercise' has to be balanced against achieving a lawful decision-making process.

Rapport building is particularly important at the outset, given that most of the participants are likely to be unfamiliar with mediation in its various forms. This is particularly the case with local government officers and civil servants. Their understanding and consequent co-operation will be a key to ultimate success. Indeed, if the political will can be obtained from the councillors (and/or sponsoring MP) then the necessary buy in to the process is more likely to take place. Without it, then the mediator will probably struggle against the unequal odds of political agenda and the tight timescales imposed by central government on the planning decision-making process, as the concept of civil litigation's stay of proceedings and costs sanctions for failing to embrace alternative dispute resolution are, at present, unknowns to the planning system.

It also needs to be borne in mind that third parties (members of local interest groups, local politicians) may lack the desire to be committed to a process where trust and confidentiality are so desirable. Indeed, in the world of localism, leaks, and the end justifying the means, a workable mediation agreement or protocol will need to be drawn up near to the outset of the process if respectful conversations are to take place and if tangible progress is to be made. The mediator will need to counsel the participants of their duties and obligations as well as draw upon the deepest reservoirs of patience and optimism. At its most basic, the protocol may be no more than achieving a commitment to respect and work with the process. A more formalised mediation agreement may subsequently emerge, but do not expect the same level of formal commitment as with a commercial mediation. So long as the scope of the mediation, the level of participation, and, the structure of the outcome are clearly defined then the mediation process will usually be good to go. However, this consensus to commit to constructive participation may only emerge over several individual and group sessions. Therefore, it should be borne in mind that the administration of the process may be quite intensive, particularly in the early days with the need to set up initial appointments, site visits and rooms for meetings. As this can be challenging for sole traders without the back office support to which larger firms may have access, the use of a mediation provider or other agency may be necessary. The mediator should also include within the fee estimate a budget scale covering the potential for several meetings. There should also be no expectation that matters will be resolved by one or two plenary sessions – although miracles do happen!

Given the need for reality testing, it is highly desirable, too, that the proposed mediator is sufficiently familiar with the workings of the planning system and of local government procedures to be able to give appropriate guidance, or, have ready access to a good independent source of advice. The mediator may also need to encourage the parties to seek their own specialist legal advice for the drafting of any revised s 106 planning agreement or deed of variation.[23]

The continuing management of expectations will also be a necessary part of the mediation process. The mediator should be alive to and respond to the realities of what can be achieved. For example, will the process just be a consensus building exercise or is the intention to resolve a specific dispute (or part of one)? Either way,

---

23 Section 106 of the Town and Country Planning Act 1990 as amended – planning obligations.

the mediator will need to make clear how matters are to be recorded and then reported if agreement is reached. Indeed, unless the local authority participants have specific delegated authority, the outcome will need to be reported to elected members, and, a decision published. As a mechanism to help build compromise, the use of an independent adviser may assist, eg the District Valuation Service (for the local planning authority), or a reputable firm of chartered surveyors. However, the personality and credibility of the individual mediator will remain key to the overall success, but they should not underestimate the time and effort it may take to achieve a solution.

Whilst information produced during the mediation process itself can be protected from disclosure under the Freedom of Information Act 2000 (FOIA 2000), the local authority's reporting process itself will require particular care. If trust is to be maintained and the release of commercially sensitive material (eg viability assumptions) is to be carefully managed then the mediator must be alive to the challenges and solutions for this stage of the process. As it may well require a continuing monitoring role the mediator, as well as the parties, will need to be aware that everybody within the mediation will have to work together on the resolution of this aspect. Indeed, it is a balancing exercise, with s 41 of FOIA 2000, in essence, seeking answers to the following questions:

- Is the information actually commercially confidential?
- Is there really likely to be prejudice?
- Is there an overriding public interest?

Therefore, all involved need to appreciate that disclosure may be required even where there is harm. For example, in *Bristol City Council v Information Commissioner & Portland & Brunswick Squares Association* (EA/2010/0012), a local authority's own viability information, as landowner as well as planning authority, was discloseable upon the basis that the public interest required such disclosure. Nevertheless, where the outcome of the mediation is being reported to Council Members, for example where a s 106 agreement is to be modified or discharged (under s 106A or s 106BA of the Act), the reporting officer is entitled to take a more measured and proportionate response by, for example, only providing summary data for public disclosure. This approach was endorsed by the High Court in *R (English) v East Staffordshire Borough Council* [2010] EWHC 2744 (Admin).

Despite these constraints, mediation and the use of mediation techniques still have a significant role to play and there are a growing number of examples. Taken at its most basic form of facilitating conversations and rapport building, it has helped members of the local public and planning officers to formulate a neighbourhood plan through the use of neutral chairing. It has also been undertaken so as to enable confidential exploration of individuals' positions without infringing public law/third party rights. It has worked well with negotiations on financial obligations, and the variation of existing s 106 planning agreements. This role may require further help from an independent surveyor or other technical adviser and it is essential that the viability appraisals are prepared on a common and recognised basis, eg the development appraisal tool (DAT) used by the Homes and Communities Agency. Mediation has also been used, successfully, in the field of enforcement in securing a programme of remedial works. Other uses, within the development management process have embraced discussions over alternative design and layout solutions and the use mix of the development.

Finally, there is the question: 'Who pays'? Currently, there is no formal mechanism in place or common practice. This may have to fall to one of the principal parties due to funding constraints or other considerations as well as the incentives for the parties involved. Again, care will be needed to ensure that the bearing of this responsibility is appropriately explained to the other participants.

The above summary deals with non-litigation planning disputes. Where High Court proceedings may be contemplated then the Judicial Review Pre-Action Protocol (paras 3.1 and 3.2) specifically encourages alternative dispute resolution including early neutral evaluation by an independent third party (for example, a lawyer experienced in the field of administrative law or an individual experienced in the subject matter of the claim) or mediation. However, time will be short, and no stays or extensions of time are currently permissible; Pt 54 of the Civil Procedure Rules (amended since 1 July 2013) now only allow six weeks to elapse from the date of the decision before proceedings must be commenced in cases of planning judicial reviews. Indeed, with the Government's commitment to a specialist planning and environment court, within the Administrative Division of the High Court, to achieve a fast track determination of planning cases, the ADR seeking party will have their work cut out to try and effect a mediated solution before the trial date. Accordingly, a paper trail should be created as soon as possible so that the costs position can, at least, be protected.

If it is a compensation or related issue then the Upper Tribunal (Lands Chamber) (formerly known as the Lands Tribunal) follows a similar approach. Indeed, the procedures in the Lands Chamber in large part reflect the rules, practice directions and protocols that govern civil cases in the High Court. Thus, Rule 2(1) of the 2010 Rules provides: 'The overriding objective of these Rules is to enable the Tribunal to deal with cases fairly and justly'. Rule 3 encourages the tribunal to seek, where appropriate:

'(a) to bring to the attention of the parties the availability of any appropriate alternative procedure for the resolution of the dispute; and

(b) if the parties wish and provided that it is compatible with the overriding objective, to facilitate the use of the procedure.'

The Practice Directions, supplementing the 2010 Rules, state at para 2.1:

'(1) Parties may apply at any time for a short stay in the proceedings to attempt to resolve their differences, in whole or in part, outside the Tribunal process ...'.

Paragraph 2.2 relates to costs in the context of the ability of the tribunal to allow the parties time to settle disputes by ADR, and para 12.2 of the Practice Directions provides that:

'The conduct of a party will include conduct during and before the proceedings; whether a party has acted unreasonably in pursuing or contesting an issue ...'.

The tribunal will automatically allow a six-week period for mediation, though the parties may apply for a longer stay. While such 'mediations' (including early neutral evaluations) will tend to be the province of specialist surveyors and lawyers, the potential benefits of mediation in compensation cases have already been identified as being significant. Like commercial mediation, the dispute can usually be resolved in a very short time (most mediations taking no more than one day) and can avoid the costs of a trial of the issue before the tribunal (which might take several days). Even if the dispute is not finally resolved, the mediation may yet serve to reduce the differences between the parties. It is to be hoped that such benefits will be recognised in the wider planning field.

Further background reading can be sourced from the following:

- A Guide to the Use of Mediation in the Planning System in Scotland (Scottish Government, 2009)
- Mediation in Planning: Report commissioned by the National Planning Forum and the Planning Inspectorate (2010)
- Mediation in Planning: A Short Guide: National Planning Forum and others (2011) (2nd edition proposed 2014)
- Mediation Delivery Programme Closure Report (March 2014)

Mediating probate and trust disputes

Beverly-Ann Rogers

One of the pleasures and challenges in mediating probate and trust disputes is the opportunity that the process presents to foster emotional closure as well as commercial closure. So many mediation clients say to me: 'I can't really mourn my father/sister/partner whilst I am locked in this dispute,' or: 'The challenge to her ability to make a will means I keep re-running in my mind the last painful months of her life.' I suspect that people in a dispute arising from a death become stuck in the anger phase of the grieving cycle and indeed the dispute may be a manifestation of that anger. The end of the dispute is, in itself, a powerful factor in helping parties move on but the mediation process can enhance the effectiveness of the closure.

I set out below some of the approaches I have found helpful in weaving together the commercial and personal resolution and some of the challenges in doing so. I do see the personal and the commercial as complementary strands: the prospect of commercial resolution loosens the emotional tangle and the loosening of the emotional tangle facilitates the commercial resolution.

People in conflict tend to be confused, fearful, angry, blaming and also uncomfortable and guilty about feeling those emotions. They also want to behave well. I find empathy, deep attention and respect for participants are like a magic balm; it defuses the negative emotions and enables them to access the best within them. I try to connect with them and acknowledge their key feelings at the initial meeting. Occasionally I encounter someone who seems to be consumed with hatred and a desire for vengeance coupled with a complete sense of self-righteousness. I find that difficult. My natural reaction is a combination of disapproval and a desire to shift them emotionally, and yet I know that you can only help someone shift if you are standing alongside them with complete acceptance. I ask myself the great Ken Cloke question: 'What would have had to have happened to me to make me behave like this?' I also remind myself how painful it must be for them to live with those poisoning thoughts and emotions scouring a rut in their mind. I am not pretending that it completely overrides my initial reaction but it usually helps me to be with them with some compassion.

It is only when a party feels that their position has been fully heard and appreciated that they might be receptive to the perceptions of the other party. We all tell ourselves stories to justify our bad behaviour. It inclines 'us' to assume the worst about 'them' and explains the saying: 'It is not our differences that divide us; it is our judgments about each other.' If our negative feelings are accepted without judgment, it frees us up from having to justify them. I try to identify any misperceptions about what happened or about motives and feelings and exchange information that might at least open up the possibility that the judgments about the other are wrong. Sometimes it helps parties to hear from the mediator that their assumptions or fears are wrong. I will never forget a bitter dispute between mother and daughter. In the daughter's private room, her worst fear suddenly surfaced: 'She doesn't love me; she loves Mary!' She needed to hear from me, as a neutral, that my perception from talking to her mother was that her mother loved her very much.

I encourage the parties to look at and try to identify common ground in the possible structure of settlement, very early. This may seem contrary to the received wisdom that exploration must precede negotiation. However, my experience is that, even though the parties know that the discussion about figures will be difficult, the agreement of a structure and hence a framework for that discussion creates relief, a sense that resolution is possible and a constructive platform for exploration. Typically, after the initial joint meeting or, if a joint meeting is not feasible, in lieu of it, I invite the parties' lawyers to a meeting with me to identify any further information needed, for instance information about the current value of the estate and to explore possible structures for settlement. By way of example, in the case of a dispute about the validity of a will, typically we will discuss which of the competing wills will be admitted to probate as a vehicle for administration of the estate, who will administer the estate, the likely costs of administration, how the legal costs of the parties might be borne as part of a settlement, what legacies can be agreed and tax considerations and possible savings. In a dispute under the Inheritance (Provision for Family and Dependants) Act 1975, in addition to information to be exchanged and tax considerations, we will discuss the elements and possible structure of financial provision, for example life interest or lump sum or a combination of both.

Part of the benefit of bringing the parties' lawyers together early on, particularly where the parties themselves are not willing to meet, is the creation of a more direct line of communication than shuttle diplomacy by me. It is far more powerful for a party's lawyer, rather than me, to report to his client from direct experience that the other party is taking a constructive approach towards resolution. Sometimes, but you do have to know and trust the lawyer in question for this, I will take the lawyer from Party A into Party B's room to discuss a particular issue. In one case, this was highly effective is discussing the restoration of visits between a grandson and his grandmother as part of an overall settlement. Having talked directly to the grandson's mother, her lawyer was able to reassure the grandmother that the mother was sincere in wanting to arrange renewed contact and visits, despite their cessation for well over two years because of a dispute over the father's estate.

Between families there are always sensitive issues. I am conscious that my primary brief is to help the parties resolve the external conflict and sometimes it feels like I am walking a tightrope between asking the difficult questions and not losing the rapport which underpins my role. However, I also know that it is the questions I ask with my heart in my mouth which are the ones that can lead to extraordinary grace and generosity. In a recent bitter dispute between a widower and his stepdaughter about their late wife/mother's estate, the stepdaughter asked me to raise the question of the disposal of her mother's ashes. I asked the widower if he had any plans for his late wife's ashes and he described them to me in detail. I listened and then I said: 'And if it was really important to Jane to have them?' There was a long silence and finally he responded: 'If it is important to her, she can have them.' A little later they bumped into each other in the corridor and had their first conversation since the funeral. For reasons that, as a non-petrolhead, I have never understood, when it comes to negotiating sensitive matters, cherished number plates appear to be on a par with the ashes!

At particularly difficult moments in the mediation I may borrow something called 'break state' from neuro-linguistic programming, by chatting to a party about something they enjoy or an area in which they have expertise. It is simply a way of helping parties move from the uncomfortable feeling of uncertainty associated with the dispute into a better frame of mind and a more competent one for making decisions.

Parties usually come to mediation having re-run their story for many years and imagining a particular ending. It is likely they will leave the mediation with a very different ending. I believe it helps them reach a difficult decision and live with it comfortably if we can offer them the resources to justify it to themselves and others. Sometimes it helps to set the resolution in a larger frame than the narrow confines of the dispute by looking at the impact of the dispute on their life or other family members. Without making any comment on the merits, it is also possible as mediator to affirm their decision. The particular affirmation will vary from client to client; it may be reassurance that that they have got the best deal they could get on the day or simply that they have behaved with dignity.

Finally, if we are working completely with the participants in mediation, we also need to maintain boundaries and disengage, both for our benefit and theirs. As someone expressed it beautifully, we give the participants and the process our all and, at the end of the process, we erase ourselves gracefully.

Mediating professional indemnity disputes

Nicholas Pryor

Professional indemnity disputes have been a ripe source of work for mediators over recent years. Indemnity insurers such as ITT London & Edinburgh and the Solicitors' Indemnity Fund were amongst the earliest adopters, and mediation quickly proved itself an effective tool for the settlement of the mass of claims against property professionals arising out of the early 1990s property slump. This included several mediations where large numbers of claims by an individual mortgage lender against numerous law firms were mediated in one process. Today mediation has become a standard part of the process for claims from every professional background and a wide range both of complexity and value.

Sector Specialisms

There are a number of issues particular to mediating disputes within this class of insurance, which I try to identify in this contribution.

This insurance was known initially as errors and omissions cover. It is important to remember that it covers precisely that, ie losses arising from errors or omissions of judgment in the handling of professional affairs. The requirement on any professional is not that they necessarily be right or that they measure up to the highest professional standards. Negligence is judged against the standard of the reasonably competent practitioner holding himself out as having the same level of expertise. What must be shown is that the professional either did something that would not have done, or failed to do something that would have been done by a reasonably competent practitioner. The test is not whether the advice proved to be wrong or whether different advice might have led to some different result, but whether what was done could have reasonably been done in the circumstances.

This principle is not always in the minds of claimants and their advisers, who come to mediation with unrealistic views as to how straightforward it will be to establish their case. Claims are frequently fact sensitive and court decisions will often turn on the facts rather than law, and will strike a careful balance between fair compensation for those who have lost as a result of professional error and the protection of professions from unrealistic levels of liability. Claims may be rejected because the alleged duty of care is seen as extending the concept to unreasonable levels.

A mediator will benefit from splitting the claim back into its component parts and reviewing each separately. Every one of the four elements of scope of duty, breach, causation and quantum is essential to the making of the case. Too often a claim is presented based on a number of untested assumptions, where a duty of care or retainer is alleged in tenuous circumstances. Little thought may be given to whether a duty actually exists to take the steps said to avoid the loss. Many claimants assume that the professional's duty is to insulate them from any form of loss. Claims are traced back from the loss, rather than built up from the duty.

The two key elements most frequently neglected and where claims most frequently stumble are causation and quantum. Claims are littered with *post hoc* arguments that appear to ignore basic rules of reasonable foreseeability and direct and proximate causation by the breach, or which give little consideration to what heads of loss can realistically be traced back to the breach.

Regarding the issue of quantum, it is often left to claimants themselves to say what they consider they have lost without any real intervention, guidance or analysis by their advisers. This raises unrealistic expectations of the amount the claimant is likely to recover, and tends to consolidate the total figure in their mind, making it harder to get them to value their claim realistically. Figures may be left as estimates until a very late stage, making the exercise of valuing the claim for settlement very difficult. To appraise the risk, an insurer needs an informed view of likely litigation risk and recoverable quantum. Where figures are put forward with little rationale, this becomes difficult.

A common feature is a marked imbalance in the levels of specialisation and experience between claimant and defendant and their respective advisers. This is a highly specialised sector of the insurance market, and many of the claims professionals have wide experience over many years, against which they can reality check the claim in hand. That experience is invaluable when valuing a claim for settlement.

It is rare to find a similar level of experience on the claimant side. Save for multiple repeat claimants such as the secured lenders or banks, most claimants will be bringing a claim for the first time and will be novices in the arts of presenting, prosecuting and settling such claims.

Amongst advisers, the defence is usually represented by one of a small number of panel firms with departments specialising in the defence of claims against specific professions. They too have wide experience of similar claims over the years. Such expertise is very much less concentrated on the claimant side, and it is rare for there to be parity of experience and expertise on both sides. One task for the mediator is to try to even out this imbalance.

Novice claimants need help with the process of analysing a claim to find a value for settlement. It will be their first experience of trying to put a figure to a sense of grievance. It is worth explaining to them that the question in insurers' mind will be: 'What is the chance that this claimant will succeed in pinning a claim on my insured and how big is that claim likely to be and what will it all cost going forward?' From that, the insurer can start to put a price to the value of settling the claim. Insurers are sensitive to issues of their insured's reputation, and will generally seek to create a fair settlement for a fair claim. Any settlement will, however, need to be reasoned and capable of rationalising against the objective merits of the claim.

Claimants should be encouraged to explain how they propose to deal with the issues the defence have raised, rather than in ridiculing them or restating their own sense of certainty about their claim. Insurers settle claims on the basis of an assessment of risk and the value of avoiding that risk. An insurer who feels that the claimant doesn't understand or give adequate weight to the points raised against them is much less likely to want to engage in negotiation.

The greater part of the mediator's task generally lies in the claimant's room. Claimants usually have a strong sense of grievance arising from the loss they have suffered. They feel badly let down by their adviser, whose duty they see as to protect them from loss. The response to this should be to recognise and acknowledge the grievance, and allow the claimant to feel validated in their sense of having been let down.

This sense of grievance is very real to many claimants and quite often entirely understandable. Where possible, try to persuade the defendants to consider using the early stages of the day to recognise the claimant's feelings. Giving the impression that they are considered misplaced should be avoided.

The grievance may flavour the claimant's views of the strength of his case. It can be difficult to see that the justice system could do anything other than make him or her whole. They trusted a professional and had been let down. Surely the result cannot be anything other than in their favour. They will see the points made in defence as being merely obfuscation and delay, but success in litigation comes not from convincing yourself, but from convincing others. Within the context of the mediation, that means convincing the defendants they may be at risk.

There is a need to be aware of the dynamics within the defendant's room. Defendants too can feel a strong sense of unfairness. Many will have been in practice for years and be experiencing their first claim. Others will have gone out of their way to assist a client in difficulties and feel sorely treated when all goes wrong and they are held responsible. There may be discord between insured and insurer, as each may have slightly differing underlying agendas. An insured may see any attempt at compromise as a tacit acceptance of wrongdoing. There is also the economic effect of any settlement on their practice and on their claims' record and future premiums.

Insurers may be more attuned to the commercial considerations encouraging settlement. The mediator may have to intervene to enable agreement on negotiation positions or settlement terms. In an extreme case, insurers may exercise or threaten to exercise the claims control provision in the policy entitling them to take control of the claim and settle despite their insured's view. Insurers are understandably reluctant to do this lightly.

These difficulties are multiplied where there are claims against different defendants (with different insurers) in respect of a single loss. There will be a complex process trying to persuade them all into a single position with an agreed apportionment between them. Often the various insurers are agreed how the claim ought to be settled, but not on how that should be apportioned between them. The most difficult position is where each insurer is determined that they will make the smallest contribution and resists any attempt to allocate the payment equally or agree any other division. Such resistance can sometimes continue to the point that the entire mediation collapses simply because it proves impossible to get a unanimous agreement on apportionment.

A material factor may be the existence of a coverage dispute between insured and insurer. This may arise where the insurer considers there has been a significant breach of policy terms and conditions, such as a failure to disclose material information at inception or renewal, or a failure to notify relevant circumstances likely to give rise to a claim in timely manner. The actions complained of may be alleged to be deliberate or fraudulent and thus potentially lie outside the scope of cover. In such circumstances insurers may, depending on the seriousness of the breach, avoid cover altogether, or retain contact and involvement in the dispute but with their rights to decline cover expressly reserved.

In such cases, the mediator will find more than one dispute to be resolved, and will need to separate discussions on the main claim and the coverage issue. Generally, unless the defendant and their insurers have been able to reach agreement on a common front for the purposes of the mediation, the mediation will have to proceed on the basis that all the disputes are discussed in parallel with the aim of all of them concluding simultaneously. Insurers will often wait to see whether there is a possibility of an overall settlement on terms they could accept before resolving the coverage issues.

While the claimant will often be aware of these issues, they will not be involved in their resolution. The mediator will usually not be permitted to discuss any aspect of the coverage issue with the claimant. Most claimants will resist allowing coverage issues to affect their negotiating position, even though its relevance to their likely recovery is self-evident.

Settlement is an attempt to balance off risk and find something that on the whole is better than losing, without losing more of the chance of winning than is bearable. Many claimants pick this up quickly and become quite proficient in working out where the number might lie. The old truth that good settlements leave no one party happy and all parties equally unhappy is validated time and again.

Mediation of property disputes

Mark Jackson-Stops

As a one-time chartered surveyor, I'm often called upon to help people sort out their property disputes. The first thing I want to know is whether this is a dispute involving domestic property owned or occupied by at least one of the warring parties, or a matter involving business or investment properties. If it is the former, I know that the challenges will be considerable. If it is the latter, perhaps there will be a better chance of an objective approach to risk assessment as the prelude to negotiation.

The domestic property dispute

It's not just the Englishman who treats his home as his castle. It is human nature to protect the place in which we live and the family within and we all have need of clearly defined boundaries (the castle wall); many people like to pull up the drawbridge and keep trespassers at bay. But it's as well to remember that, when confronted with, for example, a boundary dispute involving a few millimetres of land either side of a hedge, it's often not so much about the disputed land per se, but more likely to be the symptom of a relationship breakdown – or even the failure of the parties ever to have tried to build a relationship in the first place.

We are all in some senses still tribal. If the new neighbours are perceived not to be of our 'tribe', we will tend to find fault in their conduct. From small beginnings annoyance and irritation grows until there is a trigger – perhaps the erection of a new fence as part of a general upgrading of the house. There will, of course, have been no dialogue and the tape measure will be out to assess by how much there has been encroachment. The Land Registry plan may be of little assistance at this scale, so then historic maps and photographs are sought. Other neighbours are recruited for corroboration going back to their childhood days and affidavits are sworn. Solicitors are retained, they recommend an expert should report, and costs rack up.

There will probably be some evidence of inappropriate behaviour. There may have been angry words, threats, offending fences may have been demolished or claimed rights of access blocked. There may even have been vandalism and the police will often have been called.

How is the mediator to deal with this? Where solicitors are retained, I will telephone a day or two before. I will want to find out whether there is mutual respect between legal teams or not; if so, the solicitors can become allies in the search for a negotiated outcome. I will want to know about their clients, the type of people and whether their advice to the client is being heeded. Sometimes it becomes clear that a solicitor would welcome support from the mediator in steering their client towards a solution that they believe is in the client's interest. What is the character of the clients? Will it be profitable to get them together or will it be better to keep them apart? My default position is to bring people together, but with neighbours this is often better deferred.

Where should the mediation be held? Where the problem is a right of way, a right of light, a boundary or similar, access to the site for an inspection is essential. Sometimes I have moved from one house to the other; in other cases the better solution is to hire rooms in a local hotel allowing quick access to the properties if we need to check anything on site during the day. It must be borne in mind that it is rarely appropriate to get parties together in the house of one of them. 'Roundtable' meetings must either be in hired rooms or in the open air.

In order to manage expectations, I always warn disputants and their advisers in the run-up to a mediation of a neighbour dispute that neither party should expect to recover costs as part of the settlement. If neighbours are to settle their differences by negotiation, there can never be a winner or a loser – only a compromise outcome that both can live with. The demand for recovery of costs inevitably says 'I win, you lose' and this is usually an insuperable impediment to settlement.

Claims for possession of domestic property often disguise much deeper relationship breakdown. A man was seeking possession of a house from a woman and her teenage daughter. The counter-claim was based on an alleged promise of a tenancy for life. The negotiation involved many tens of thousands of pounds for possession of the house and the return of a case containing sexually explicit photos. The parties didn't meet during the day, but once the settlement was signed, they parted with a kiss.

On another occasion, what seemed like a simple possession action turned out in reality to be the negotiation of the 'divorce' settlement of a celebrity couple who had never married but had been in a relationship for several years. One of the pair, realising that possession being nine-tenths of the law, was not going to move out of the other's property until a comprehensive settlement was agreed involving other assets too.

As mediators we know that things aren't always quite what they seem. We have to pick up quickly the information that is not in the pleadings and be alert for the true needs and interests of the parties.

Neighbour disputes in multi-occupied buildings

I have boundless admiration for the community mediators who work in socially deprived areas to make peace between fractious families in tenements and tower blocks. In the leafy squares of London's West End, tempers can get equally frayed in the defence or assertion of property rights. The fashionable taste for wood strip flooring has recently spawned many disputes relating to noise transmission nuisance to add to the plethora of other nuisance claims where people live cheek-by-jowl. Landlords get dragged into the dispute as the complaining party requires them to take enforcement action or not to allow alienation of a leasehold interest while the alleged nuisance persists. Even when a nuisance is ameliorated, the complainant often becomes over-sensitised to an extent that can appear irrational to the passing observer.

I believe the mediator's role in these types of cases is to offer a sympathetic ear, to give the parties, especially the complainant, the chance to air the grievance and know they are being listened to, but to remain doggedly non-judgemental. Once the parties feel they have been heard, there is the chance to come up with pragmatic solutions from the perspective of the informed man in the street.

In almost all neighbour dispute cases, the resolution achieved by the parties with the help of a mediator is such that a judge could never offer. In the case of the noisy wood floor, the outcome was an agreement by reference to a floor plan of those parts of the flat above which would be covered by rugs of a certain minimum specification. The landlord was relieved not to have to take enforcement action on the tenant's covenant to have close fitted carpets throughout the flat and the owner of the upper flat retained his prized hardwood floors.

Landlord/tenant disputes – residential properties

Landlords, as we have seen above, can get dragged into what are essentially neighbour disputes. Mediation is also naturally suited to resolving disputes directly between landlords and tenants, for example where service charges are disputed. Recovery of costs of repair is a minefield for landlords who must follow complex statutory procedures as well as comply with lease terms. Lessees will often challenge whether the works are repair or improvement, whether there has been fair apportionment in accordance with lease terms, and whether proper tendering procedures have been followed. Likewise the complexities of leasehold entranchisement – the purchase by the lessee of a freehold interest or an extended leasehold term by virtue of a statutory right – is a fruitful area for disputes, whether as to the service of notices or the valuation of interests.

Non-domestic property disputes

In the field of landlord and tenant, I have seen an increase in dilapidations claims and rent reviews coming to mediation. The vast majority of such cases are settled by negotiation between respective surveyors. Perhaps in the economic environment of the past few years, with both landlords and tenants under increased financial pressures, these are harder to settle and mediation offers the opportunity of widening the scope of the negotiated outcome. For example, a lower review rental might be traded for a longer lease term (or the converse), outcomes which no arbitration can achieve.

In the public realm, I have seen at first hand the value of mediation in cases of compulsory purchase and compensation, reducing the uncertainties and considerable expense of pursuing matters to the Lands Chamber of the Upper Tribunal. There is an increasing awareness that planning issues can be handled in the same way (dealt with elsewhere), although with proper consideration of public interest and consultation.

In my own mediation practice the majority of property cases involve claims of professional negligence (also dealt with elsewhere), Errors by solicitors in conveyancing, by surveyors in carrying out valuations or structural surveys, architects, project mangers or engineers in design or monitoring, all impact on the value of a real estate asset.

A significant proportion of property cases involve subrogated claims by insurers, stepping into the shoes of their insured, to claim for property liability losses. Where a fire, a flood or subsidence for example can be forensically traced to the negligence other parties, mediation can be the ideal forum for settlement especially where there are multiple defendants and the biggest issue is often the apportionment between defendants.

Choice of mediator for property cases

I am not a believer in specialist mediators, that is to say mediators who have detailed subject matter expertise. The important thing is that the mediator should understand and speak the 'language' of the dispute with reasonable fluency as well as being familiar with the dispute resolution process in the event that there is no agreement – whether before an arbitrator, the Lands Chamber or the High Court. Suitable mediators might come from a surveying background or from the perspective of practice in property law. But above all, a mediator needs the sensitivity and the authority to win the respect of all parties necessary for him or her to steer them towards a resolution they can all prefer to the uncertainty of a judgment handed down over which they have very limited control.

*[In addition to Mark's contribution what follows is a contribution from **Michael Wyldbore-Smith**, a mediator who has specialised in boundary and rights of way disputes – and survived!]*

Boundary disputes can strike fear, bewilderment and disappointment into all those involved. It is one area of litigation where emotions as well as costs run particularly high.

Given the uncertainties involved in disputes of this type, alternative forms of resolution should be a party's preferred choice. Mediation should be at the top of their list. They then remain in control of the process and will avoid the dangers which litigation involves – huge costs, an inability to predict the outcome and destroyed relationships. The mediator dealing with a boundary dispute will need great patience, a degree in diplomacy, and the ability to hold back from banging the party's heads together as they fight over a few millimetres of land which has no value.

Inevitably, the parties are at war – they may once have been friends and neighbours but now they are at loggerheads. They cannot stand the sight of one another and will either do their best to avoid each other or possibly do their best to annoy one another – loud music, car engines revving, doors banging. As a result, boundary dispute mediations seldom start with a joint session. They usually start on site and then either move to a lawyer's offices or require the mediator to shuffle from one side of the disputed boundary to the other. What the mediator needs (in spades) is the patience of Job.

The preliminary documents will reveal the strength of each party's case –title deeds and plans, historic photos, aerial photos, witness statements from former owners.

Sector Specialisms

There will be a reliance on plans which have no worth – Land Registry plans do not determine the lines of a boundary nor do plans produced by the Ordnance Survey. Developers' plans are notoriously unreliable and in any event builders do not follow them to any great degree of accuracy.

There are some instances where the dispute is worth the party's efforts to fight their corner: a blocked access; the loss of sufficient space to extend their kitchen; an invasive hedge. But more often than not one wonders (and despairs) at the sheer folly of the two contestants. A strip of land a few millimetres wide and 20 metres long rarely has much value, particularly in Lower Slaughter (where surprisingly not a single villager lost their life in either the First or Second World Wars) or the suburbs of any town. There might be some excuse for worrying about a narrow strip in Kensington or Chelsea but the cost of the fight will probably outweigh any gain.

So why do these disputes arise? Most commonly heard reasons include: 'An Englishman's home etc,' 'It's a matter of principle,' and 'My solicitor thinks my case is watertight'.

As almost the first words any mediator dealing with a boundary dispute will say to the parties are 'if you are expecting to win outright you are likely to be disappointed,' they should probably have come to a sensible compromise some time earlier. You do not need to be an expert on boundaries to mediate a boundary dispute but a basic knowledge will help, for example the hedge and ditch rule, whether the boundary is marked by an overhanging gutter or the wall of the house; the rules about adverse possession.

The mediator will have to be careful to avoid displaying any preference for one party's version of events over the other. There will be accusations of harassment and a whole history of blame. Solicitors' letters will have been going backwards and forwards for months, litigation will have been threatened, and opinion from expert surveyors and counsel obtained. Each side is convinced their stance is justified. Neither side is going to back down, costs are mounting and mediation is a last resort.

Pity the poor mediator who now has to unlock this chaos.

Begin with the conveyance and (hopefully) the plan attached. If it has measurements, you are off to a good start. If the plan is to a small scale and has no measurements then you need to look for features on the ground which may provide evidence of an original boundary line – old fence posts, concrete footings, the edge of paving. After that you are relying on old photos, witness statements, and your own intuition.

The private sessions will be lengthy and tiring – emotions will run high and you have to work hard to find a chink of hope. For hours there is no movement on either side and then unexpectedly you sense a slight shift of position – perhaps a realisation that if a settlement is not achieved costs will escalate and that each side faces a long and gruelling progress to court. One of the lawyers may begin to show a loss of confidence. The parties need to be reminded constantly that while the dispute persists they cannot sell the property concerned. They also need to be reminded that they have to continue to live side by side or to settle and sell. They will need to be challenged yet encouraged. They must be reminded that some sort of compromise is essential and gently persuaded to put forward an offer. The other side will regard it with derision but at least you have something to work with and slowly but steadily you may be able to bring the two sides closer to one another.

An offer of cash is one obvious way of trying to find terms of settlement but others which sometimes succeed are an offer to replace or reconstruct; to exchange the area in dispute for an equivalent area, to provide a new access to an area which is otherwise land locked, to divert an existing access or to allow an easement for services.

A person remains entitled in law to protect and preserve that which is theirs. A good mediator will help towards that aim.

Mediating public sector disputes

Jon Lang

There can be few more challenging areas in which to mediate than the public sector. Often, there is not just a contractual issue to resolve, but a statutory backdrop and political dimension to contend with too. Not surprisingly, the range of disputes that are mediated is far broader than in other sectors, from multi-million pound procurement contracts to far more localised issues such as the investigation into conduct of employees at a state-run entity.

Mediation in the public sector has, in the past, been characterised by a mismatch between the high percentage of public bodies that regard the process as a sensible alternative to litigation, and the considerably lower percentage that actually use mediation as their preferred method of resolving disputes. That mismatch is becoming a little less marked, with mediation being used more and more to resolve the full range of disputes that arise within and concerning public bodies. Indeed, the results of CEDR's fifth mediation audit published in May 2012, noted that mediators who had been asked to identify sectors that would see most growth in mediation usage over the next two years included the public sector in their list.

The reasons for increased usage of mediation in the public sector is beyond this short contribution which instead focuses on some of the challenges mediators might face when mediating in this area.

Despite the vast array of disputes one mediates in the public sector, there are often certain shared characteristics necessitating considerable versatility and skill on the part of the mediator and, importantly, careful pre-mediation groundwork on the part of all involved.

Appreciation of statutory framework

Public bodies usually act within a statutory framework and often contract with third parties to assist in meeting their statutory obligations. Funding reviews, economic cutbacks and changes in the statutory framework within which public bodies function can often be the root cause of a dispute. An understanding of both the statutory framework and political dimension within which a dispute has arisen is often essential, not just for fully understanding the dispute, but also for finding solutions. So spend some time understanding the full context of the dispute.

Public accountability

Public bodies are subject to varying degrees of public accountability. It makes 'throwing in the last £50,000 to settle the deal' very unlikely. Thus, whilst public bodies will attend a mediation under the cloak of confidentiality and privilege, the outcome of a mediation may well need to be made public (at least to some extent). Sometimes, the outcome of a mediation will also need to be justified publicly, eg where monies paid or not recovered raise issues of public accounting. Depending on the nature and size of a dispute, and the political climate at the time it is resolved by mediation, it may be the case that a mediated outcome is used as a political 'football'. A parliamentary or local government debate about alleged mismanagement of a public budget springs to mind. Thus, post-mediation matters require careful consideration, pre-mediation, so that parties properly understand whatever constraints might exist in preserving the confidentiality of an outcome. Issues of confidentiality, especially when agreeing something other than the norm, can be tricky and a degree of forward planning in this regard is always a good idea given that it is by no means unusual to discuss, during a mediation, what can and cannot be said post-mediation, in the form of press releases, Q & A scripts for press departments or otherwise. This may be no more than a discussion with one or more of the parties about the issues that could arise in this regard on settlement and perhaps a suggestion that they have a chat with their press departments. It may be that the mediator, for fear of tempting fate, says nothing to the parties about issues that could arise on settlement, but be prepared for issues around confidentiality to arise, particularly if there is press interest in the dispute and/or political interest in the manner of its resolution.

Decision-making and authority

Decision-making within a public body will be structured, maybe by committee, and will often be more complex than within a commercial entity. Moreover, the authority of negotiators to bind the public body they represent will usually be limited in some way. This will often be the case with commercial entities too, but the process by which sanction can be obtained for additional authority can be more challenging in the public sector. Accordingly, decision-making mechanics and issues of authority will often require a little additional thought, pre-mediation. Neither factor will prevent a public body from actively participating in a mediation, but the ease and manner in which decisions can be made and further authority obtained in 'real-time' needs careful thought and planning.

Moreover, it is sometimes the case that, because of the scope of settlement, input from several different departments across one public body is required, making pre-mediation preparation more crucial than ever. The simple suggestion of ensuring out of office contact numbers are exchanged pre-mediation can save hours and the mediation itself. Suggesting that all possible stakeholders are available can also save the day. A full pre-mediation discussion with the public body prior to the mediation about the simple mechanics of 'getting it done' is essential.

Post-mediation approval

If it is likely to be the case that a particular settlement can only be formerly approved and executed post-mediation (having been hammered out and agreed in principle at the mediation by those officers of the public body present on the day), that should be made clear to all pre-mediation. No one likes surprises, particularly after a hard day of negotiation. The party negotiating with the public body will not welcome their hope and expectation of absolute finality being dashed at the last stage of the process. However, if the procedure is described in advance and it is explained that it would be unusual for a settlement recommended by those present at the mediation not to be approved (which is usually the case), the element of surprise is removed and any concern is likely to be minimised.

Attendees

Given the nature of the public sector, securing the attendance of those who, at first blush, appear to be the 'right' people (as in the most senior), can be something of a challenge. A Minister of State is unlikely to attend. A chief executive of a public body might be in attendance for a mediation of a very significant dispute, but the reality is that sometimes the people that the mediator and/or the other side would really like to be in attendance won't be. Explore this in advance. If it occurs to the mediator that, without a specific dialogue having taken place, settlement may be difficult to achieve, think about telephone conversations. A chief executive could perhaps be asked to be on the end of a phone at a specific time to have a conversation with the other side during the mediation if, for instance, a specific and self-contained dialogue needs to take place. Not ideal, but usually preferable to there being no conversation at all.

Despite the difficulties just described, there should always be individuals present at a sufficiently senior level such that the other side are comfortable that the public body 'means business', comfortable that if calls need to be made to other stakeholders impacted by any potential settlement or further authority sought those calls will be answered (whatever time of day or night it is), and comfortable that any deal will be 'carried' back at HQ.

Mediating shareholder disputes and post-transaction warranty claims

Stephen Walker

This section deals with two types of disputes involving private companies:

(1) disputes between shareholders; and

(2) disputes between vendors and purchasers after a share or asset sale.

Shareholder disputes

These, like partnership or joint ventures disputes, are commercial divorces. Most are either between

Sector Specialisms

- majority and minority shareholders complaining about being prejudiced; or
- shareholders in deadlock, usually in quasi partnership companies.

Essential law

Companies Act 2006, s 994: unfair prejudice

This provides the statutory remedy for minority shareholders claiming unfair prejudice. Their petition must show that there are grounds for believing that the affairs of the company are being conducted in a way, which is unfairly prejudicial to the members as a whole or a class of member, which includes the petitioner. Petitioners do not normally ask the court to wind-up the company: they want it to continue. Instead they ask to be bought out or for the Board to be ordered to act in a particular way.

Insolvency Act 1986, s 122(1)(g): just and equitable

A parallel remedy is a winding-up order on just and equitable grounds. These can include where a minority shareholder has been excluded from the management of the company which can also be a ground for an unfair prejudice petition But the applicant must be able to show that they have clean hands ie they have not been guilty of improper conduct and that there will be a surplus for distribution to members after the winding- up.

Companies Act 2006, ss 260–264: derivative action

A minority shareholder who claims that they have been prejudiced by a wrong done by the majority shareholder to the company rather than to them personally can apply to the court to bring an action against that shareholder in the company's name. Any financial award is for the benefit of the company not the individual shareholder.

Remedies

The remedies available under s 994 are wider than those available under s 122 but the usual one is for a clean break under which the majority shareholder buys out the minority shareholder. There is always argument about the time and methods of valuation.

Particular features of shareholder dispute mediations

The golden goose paradox

Shareholder disputes damage the company. This is not because company assets are spent on the litigation – company law prohibits this – but because attention and effort are diverted away from the business. Also, a majority shareholder can be tempted not to increase the value of the company if there is a risk that he may have to buy out the minority shareholder.

Mediators can use this danger of killing the golden goose to bring a dose of commercial reality.

Winning can be worse than losing

If the majority shareholder defeats the minority shareholder's petition they do not have to buy out this shareholding. But they are left with a disaffected shareholder and the threat of further unfair prejudice proceedings.

If the minority shareholder wins and obtains an order that the majority shareholder buys their shares, they are often disappointed. The company has suffered. The majority shareholders whose wealth is dependent on the health of the company cannot pay the price decided by the court. Pyrrhic victories are common.

The dominance of accountancy evidence

The key question is: What is the company worth?

Valuations are carried out by accountants and often by the company's auditors. Usually both sides have their own valuation. Valuation is said to be an art not a science, ie there is a lot of room for disagreement. Knowing the language if not the mechanics of valuation is helpful. The main valuation methods are:

- **Earnings**

    Used when valuing either the whole issued share capital or a controlling interest where there is a going concern. Two key acronyms are:

    — **EBITDA** – earnings before interest, taxes, depreciation and amortisation. It is a measure of the value of the business of the company before taking into account how it is financed; and

    — **P/E ratio** – price/earnings ratio. This reflects the value of the equity of the company as a ratio of earnings post-tax. P/E ratios are used as comparators in valuations.

- **Net assets**

    This is the breakup value.

- **Turnover**

    Used for new companies that are trading well but are not yet profitable.

- **Market value**

    Often used in shareholders agreements that stipulate how shares should be valued. Arguments arise over what discount, if any, should be applied for a minority shareholding.

- **Fair value**

    This is not the same as market value. Minority shareholders usually prefer a fair value basis. There is no generally accepted definition but it incorporates the concepts of fairness and equity for both buyer and seller, which the market value basis does not.

Sector Specialisms

NOTE : You will find that accountancy evidence while necessary is not sufficient to achieve settlement.

Managing experts

Be prepared for a duel between the accountants. Despite avowed adherence to CPR Practice Direction 35 they are often partisan and adversarial. But private meetings with them usually reveal a surprising amount of common ground compared with the hostility and differences displayed in their reports.

Thinking outside the box

The opportunity for parties at mediation to create their own solutions and achieve outcomes that no court could give them is particularly relevant

Often one party cannot afford to buy out the other even if it wants to. Instead businesses are restructured, properties and assets transferred and payment plans secured by charges over a diverse range of company assets are devised. Structuring such settlements requires detailed preparation, ideally before and not at the mediation.

In particular consider:

- Tax advice on how best to structure payments and receipts cannot all be taken from the same accountant. Both the payer and receiver need to know their net position after tax.

- Where assets are going to be transferred or charged, the consents of prior charges holders and debenture holders must be obtained. Often they are not.

Help the parties by reminding them of these preparatory steps. Most parties come to mediation wanting to settle. Finality is valuable. Most mediation agreements provide that there is no legally binding agreement until all the parties have signed a document recording the settlement. So if they want finality on the day they have to sign on the day.

If all the advice and consents have not been obtained, conditional agreements, heads of agreement and agreements in principle are the order of the day with all their inherent difficulties.

O' Neill letters

These are a way a majority shareholder can put pressure on minority shareholders who are claiming unfair prejudice. If the majority shareholder makes a reasonable offer to purchase the minority shareholder's shares this might prevent the conduct complained of from being unfairly prejudicial. They emerged as a distinctive feature of s 994 litigation as a result of judicial encouragement from Lord Hoffmann in the case of *O'Neill v Phillips* [1999] 2 BLC 1 16d.

Date of valuation

This is important. The general rule it is that the court will order valuation at the date that it makes the order. If the proceedings have been going for some time it can mean that valuation at the date of trial is on a company whose financial standing is very different from what it was at the date of the petition or the prejudicial conduct.

Post-transaction warranty claims

The origins of warranty claims

In asset or share sales in private companies both vendors and purchasers give warranties. They have to be read together with the disclosure letter. Most claims are for breach of vendor warranties.

Essential law

Claims are either for a breach of warranty ie a breach of contract claim, or misrepresentation under the Misrepresentation Act 1967.

A misrepresentation is a statement of fact or law as opposed to an opinion or estimate of future events, which is false and induces the recipient to enter into a contract. The recipient must prove reliance. They will not be able to do this if they were unaware of the false statement or the agent checked the truth of the statement.

There are three types of misrepresentation: fraudulent, negligent and innocent. The remedies vary. Rescission, ie restoring the parties to their pre- contractual position is available for all three. For fraudulent and negligent, damages on the tort basis can be awarded as well as rescission. For innocent it is one or the other. Damages on the contract basis are usually awarded.

In contract the purchaser is compensated for their loss of bargain, ie the difference in value for what they paid and the actual value. In tort, the purchaser is restored to the position they would have been in if the misrepresentation had not been made.

Warrantors' liability is usually limited in the sale agreement by:
- limiting the amount of damages payable to the amount of the purchase price that they received;
- setting time limits by which claims must be made – normally six years for tax warranties and two years for all others; or
- stipulating that claims cannot be brought in respect of matters that have been disclosed against.

Particular features of warranty claims

The importance of accounting evidence

Most claims allege that the financial information provided was misleading, eg profits have been overstated. The purchaser's accountants calculate and evidence

Sector Specialisms

the loss. Often they cannot, despite pre-contract due diligence, really examine the figures until they have full access to the information after completion of the purchase. The vendor's accountants invariably dispute their findings.

The ambiguous position of advisers

Both purchasers and vendors will have received specialist advice from tax advisers, accountants, surveyors, financiers and lawyers. When a claim is made the parties either:

- tell the advisers to sort it out; or
- go straight to new advisers and seek advice on both the warranty claim and the liability of advisers.

Mediators have to be alive to hidden agendas, with the parties wanting to preserve their rights against advisers. Parallel mediations between a party and its advisers may be required.

Be prepared to ask an adviser early on if there is any professional embarrassment. Do it in private. Advisors are usually open and realistic. There is no point in humiliating anyone.

Reputational risk

Parties are often anxious to avoid publicity. Even if a purchaser takes a warranty claim to court and wins, there will be always be the risk of some shortcoming being exposed which can discourage funders or future targets from dealing with them. Purchasers are often alerted to irregularities by disgruntled employees of the target business who may want to air dirty laundry. Mediators need to encourage parties and their advisers to look at the bigger picture.

Tax advice

The tax implications of undoing a deal in whole or in part or making payments can be crucial. Parties need to compare their actual post-transaction balance sheets with their 'as if' ones, depending on what settlement structure is adopted.

It is depressing how little analysis is often done before the mediation. Mediators should encourage the parties to seek tax advice on possible settlement structures before the mediation. Increasingly frantic early evening calls to accountants and tax counsel are a feature of this type of mediation.

Joint and several liability

Under the sale agreement, the warrantors are often jointly and severally liable for breaches of warranty. Joint liability gives rise to disputes about who is really to blame for the breach. Parallel mediations amongst the warrantors are often needed.

A warrantor's liability is usually limited to his share of the sale price. Even where there is several rather than joint liability a warrantor who is having to pay out for something that he thinks is the responsibility of another warrantor can create the need for a parallel mediation.

Remorse

After completion, buyers and sellers can feel remorse – buyers because they think that they have overpaid and need to find a scapegoat, and sellers, if they are still part of the business, because they regret the loss of control. This can be aggravated by family members who are affected by the vendor's decision to sell. It is an advantage if they are present.

Mediating shipping disputes

Silas Taylor

Mediation has become well established as an alternative means of settling maritime disputes. Many of the leading marine Insurers are based in the United Kingdom, which also has the world's greatest concentration of marine lawyers, and it is commonplace for International shipping contracts to provide for English law and jurisdiction to cover disputes arising. Accordingly the majority of the world's shipping disputes are dealt with in London, either by way of litigation in the Specialist Admiralty or Commercial Courts or by arbitration, often involving tribunals such as the London Maritime Arbitrators Association. Mediation usually takes place between parties already involved in such a process who see the benefit of a compromise solution to achieve certainty and avoid unnecessary costs being incurred. International shipping disputes tend to involve large sums of money but costs can and do reach $1 million or more per side to conclude heavyweight cases. The incentive to explore settlement options by way of mediation is obvious.

A shipping or maritime dispute is essentially any dispute that involves in some way the operation of a ship. Obvious examples would be a collision, or salvage, or hijack, or disputes in respect of a charter party (hire) contract. The actual spectrum is huge, for example differences arising in respect of repair, construction, towage, pilotage, loading stowage, and specifications of cargo, supply of fuel oil, personal injury, safe operation of ports, surveyor negligence, insurance coverage, etc. Some of these disputes involve specialist areas of maritime law, but many are simply contractual or tortious issues which can only be distinguished from general commercial disputes by the fact that they in some way involve a ship. Whilst the mediator of these varied matters would be expected to have experience of maritime law, perhaps the more important attribute is an understanding of commercial ship management and operation. Shipping has perhaps more than its fair share of technical phrases and abbreviations.

There are some particular benefits in shipping disputes being resolved by way of mediation but at the same time, as I shall seek to explain, maritime mediation poses some particular challenges to the mediator.

I have always felt that one of the main advantages of maritime mediation is the preservation of relationships. Ship operation is a complex business that can only function with the involvement of a long chain of intermediaries. If an owner is to charter their ship for a voyage, many parties are going to become involved in the exercise beyond the charterer, for example, placing brokers, insurance brokers, insurers, port operators, tug companies, bunker (fuel) suppliers, surveyors, repairers, shippers, classification societies, managers, stevedores, lawyers, ships agents, mooring agents – to name but a few! Although shipping is perhaps the best example of a truly global business, those involved in it represent a fairly tight knit community and the system, of necessity, has to operate with a significant element of trust. When things go wrong essential relationships are threatened. Mediation works well in bringing people together to achieve an often painful solution which nevertheless enables trade to continue. Those involved in the chain are all dependant upon each other.

As a simple example, I mediated a case between a tug owner and a repairer in respect of a dry dock accident. The dispute was very acrimonious and set to go to a lengthy trial where only one side could win. However both parties operated in the same port. The owner would have to divert his vessels hundreds of miles to get them repaired elsewhere. The repairer was dependent on the tug owner for the bulk of his trade. Litigation, whichever way it went, would probably have ended the relationship. After a tough, but successful mediation both parties are still trading.

Fortunately, now that many marine operators and their insurers have gained experience of the process there is a greater understanding of the benefits of a mediated solution and awareness of the importance of considering commercial relationships alongside the cold analysis of litigation risk.

The potential for success is enhanced by the fact that those coming to maritime mediations are usually some way down the track of litigation or arbitration. So the key issues (and risks) are already clear.

Typically, those engaging in maritime mediation are being advised by experienced specialist maritime solicitors, often with technical experts involved and supported by experienced insurance claim handlers all familiar with the mediation process.

The Admiralty and Commercial Courts will encourage, and sometimes require mediation and even arbitrators these days will often promote mediation as a sensible option to explore. However, most come to maritime mediation because they accept the potential positive advantage of at least giving it a try.

All these factors work together in achieving a greater settlement rate in mediation than is perhaps the case elsewhere – in my experience, something in excess of 80 per cent.

Perhaps the biggest challenge facing a maritime mediator is that mediations tend to be overpopulated – 12 or 15 or even more people attending for each party is not unusual. Solicitors usually attend with a team of two or three and then there will be others such as owners, managers, brokers, insurers, experts, etc. This is far removed from mediations involving just those with the personal problem and one or two advisers. Also, whilst risks are appreciated and the need for relationships acknowledged these are hard-nosed business people, so the emotional element is reduced, or at least camouflaged.

Nevertheless the need to develop a rapport and understanding remains paramount, it just requires more time and patience when one is dealing with a 'committee'. It is essential to work out what everybody's role is and more importantly who it is who ultimately carries the financial risk. This is far from straightforward and simply asking the question is not enough as any answer is likely at best to be ambiguous. A complicating factor here is often the involvement of protection and indemnity associations (P & I Clubs) who are mutual insurers providing liability insurance to their insured 'members'. P & I Clubs will usually try and do everything they can to support their member. They often insure the liabilities that are the subject of the mediation if their member is a defendant, or will underwrite costs and expenses (sometimes of both sides) if supporting their member as a claimant under 'defence cover'. However, that defence cover is discretionary. The influence of the member or the P & I Club will usually depend on the member's size and record. So when one gets beyond the posturing there is often tension between member and club. Sometimes the club want to settle a liability but the member (although it is not his financial risk) wants the club to take a hard line and fight. Sometimes the member is running a claim with defence cover whilst the Club is concerned about the situation and anxious to find a settlement rather than face the difficult option of withdrawing cover. People are understandably reluctant to be open about these issues but an experienced mediator can usually work out where the ground lies.

Working out exactly who has the ultimate problem is essential. First, this enables the mediator to concentrate his energies and questions with the person who counts. Beyond that, in my experience, breaking down the 'committee' approach on both sides is particularly important and sooner or later in the proceedings a face-to-face meeting between the people who count on each side is usually invaluable. From an early stage it is important to consider who the candidates for such a meeting should be.

Experienced shipping lawyers often come to mediation with a detailed strategy agreed with their clients and will seek to manipulate the mediator and the process. They will seek to distance their clients from the mediator and deflect direct questioning, something not easy anyway in a room full of people all wanting to butt in. This problem is compounded by the fact that there is little scope for the mediator to have sensible contact with the parties themselves prior to the mediation. The identity of those attending is usually kept guarded until just before the mediation day and the parties will almost always be based overseas, only flying in the day before, a day spent in meetings with their lawyers.

I believe patient persistence is the answer to this problem in that the actual person with a problem will usually actually want to talk to the mediator, so it is a question of politely bypassing the lawyers and continuing to address the key person. As for manipulation of the process then, it is a question of being robust. At least with shipping mediations there is rarely an imbalance of power.

One of the most interesting features of shipping mediations, but one that the mediator has to be sensitive to, is that the parties are invariably from different countries, and rarely from the United Kingdom. Those involved in shipping come from all over the world, but with an emphasis on Greece, Asia, Scandinavia and America. It is important to appreciate that different nationals have a different approach to negotiation, and often a different cultural attitude to the mediation process. Of course, in addition individuals vary and do not always follow the national trait. It is, however, essential to get a feel for what people's attitude to negotiation is before the serious bargaining begins. Within the constraints of confidentiality it can be helpful to suggest to the other side where a problem might lie, and how it might best be approached. Everybody is usually keen to give the process the best chance of success and to modify their own approach accordingly.

In some countries bartering is a way of life, approached with enthusiasm. For others it is very difficult and to be approached with caution. Some people are only comfortable with a salami-slicing approach to negotiation, whilst others want to get straight to the 'zone'. More importantly from the mediator's point of view, some nationalities feel an overwhelming need for all offers to have a considered justification. This may well mean that more time needs to be spent before embarking on offers and also maintaining a dialogue and argument between the parties rather than allowing a simple horse trade on numbers to develop. Cultural concern for the settlement itself should also be considered, especially if there is hope of a maintained relationship. Settlement usually hurts and for some it is important to maintain a dignified, almost solemn approach after the deal has been struck. On the other hand, in some countries a settlement would be expected to be met by everybody hugging each other rather than the more normal handshake and smile!

Despite its particular challenges, maritime mediation is an increasingly popular option which I believe gives the parties the best opportunity to find a settlement to their dispute and I am sure this trend will continue.

Mediating sports disputes

Quentin Smith

There are several reasons why mediating sports disputes might justify its own section.

Sport is an industry that, whilst necessarily incorporating all aspects of commercial activity, is largely 'insolvent', relying upon the largesse of benefactors, funding from government and charitable donations, and underpinned by the guarantee of goodwill. It means that, in addressing conflicts within, it frequently defies conventional forms of negotiation and resolution.

A multi-million pound owner of a top club recently stated to me, in an opening/ plenary meeting: 'Some people do drugs – I do football'.

The relatively few in sport who can afford litigation can also afford to lose, which invites a nihilistic approach, as they tend to 'know the price of everything and the value of nothing' (Oscar Wilde). The much larger proportion of the industry's population know the value of everything but cannot afford the price of anything.

I have successfully mediated disputes, in most major sports, involving players/ athletes, agents, clubs, governing bodies, referees, funding agencies, sponsors and broadcasters. The issues have included severe injuries, dismissals, walkouts, corporate structures, transfers, insolvencies, property, event management, shareholdings, funding arrangements, commercial contracts, defamation and, of course, whistleblowing. Perhaps only match/competition (and drugs) results are beyond negotiation?

A critical feature of sports disputes is the familiar mantra of mediation: concentrate on parties' interest and not their positions. This requires a three-dimensional analysis of the parties' history, presence and purpose. Thereafter, understanding how they see themselves can be essential in unlocking difficulties. For example, wealthy club owners invariably need acknowledgement of their contributions to the(ir) community, their benefaction/self-sacrifice and reparation for anything that might impugn their integrity/status.

An owner of a premier rugby club was astounded that when he bought a construction company for over £70m it was barely mentioned in the *Financial Times*. Around the same time, a guitar-playing international in his rugby club (which had a turnover well below £10m) released a CD and received a whole page feature in the *Sunday Times*. He (the owner) was not pleased! Incidentally, I know he would have traded his super-yacht to have been a rugby international!

Players/athletes are invariably anxious about the fragility of their careers, which can easily be ended abruptly/prematurely whilst earning at levels in their youth which are most unlikely to even be approached in subsequent years. Their need for respect can be clouded by the public's adulation or derision. For some, their image rights can equal, even eclipse, their earnings from playing.

Governing bodies, funding agencies and charities have political pressures and social responsibilities that need to be taken into account; international corporations, as sponsors, have also been profoundly concerned/affected by sports not matching their corporate standards in such areas.

Therefore, the commercial and social imperative is for swift outcomes that provide elegant exits for parties whose instinctive desire is to win in the competitive environment in which they operate. Security, stability and a restoration of confidence are frequently critical to survival. Mediation, with its inherent flexibility, creativity and collective endeavour in achieving an agreed (rather than imposed) outcome, is their salvation.

Here are some observations, infused with some guidance, from my experience:

- Everyone is aware of sport – we grow up with it and its reach is extensive. Its disputes occur in amateur and professional environments and there appears to be a greater expectation amongst the parties that a mediator will have some familiarity. There does not seem to be the same level of expectation in other industries. This does not mean that there need be intimacy with idiosyncrasies but more a sympathy (occasionally empathy) with circumstances. There is an encouragement for an emotional connection in addition to an intellectual/commercial one.
- Research on the backgrounds of the parties can be rewarding in understanding context. It can also assist in establishing rapport and credibility early on in a mediation. However, it is important to remain detached and to make clear that sport may not be more exciting than pensions or IT disputes.
- Sport is entertainment and publicity is its life-blood. Therefore, its disputes are almost always in the public domain – the media coverage will have affected the parties and infected their outlook. It is most unlikely that a mediator will be unaware of a high profile dispute which will often migrate from the back to the front pages of newspapers and add spice to broadcast news. The pervasive effects of the internet/social media also magnify the significance and commercial

implications with the consequent impacts on, for example, the outlook of sponsors, the value of image rights and customer confidence. Confidentiality (or the lack of it) is a frequent feature to be addressed.

- Sport has a surprisingly high level of self-containment and self-referral. Many participants and adversaries know each other, which can create patterns – exploring them is usually revealing and helpful in defining, or determining, the structure of a negotiation and giving the mediator some insight into how to change 'the pattern of play'.

- Many of the legal advisers will be 'fans', sometimes with Board positions and possibly working with enthusiasm/devoted support rather than with detached reason/rationale. The mediator needs to establish agendas and balance interest in each room, in addition to between rooms.

- This may affect the extent of a mediator's pre-mediation involvement when considering and, perhaps, making suggestions on team selection, ie who should attend the mediation.

- Those working in sport, tend to be 'straight-talkers' – a predictable feature of a pressured, competitive and fragile industry. After all, using a rugby club as an example, how precarious is a business that relies, principally, on what 15 people do for 80 minutes, once per week, for 40 weeks of the year? Much more than in any other type of dispute, I am asked: 'What do you think?' Parties usually expect the mediator to 'get stuck in' – it requires a different level of engagement, but, I believe, a strict adherence to the principle of impartiality. Referees should never seek popularity or be a feature of the match.

- A key aspect to bear in mind, and often exploit in mediations, is that the business of sport moves fast and with a relentless momentum. It means that there is an attraction in outcomes which are both economic and expedient. Evidence is usually 'front-loaded', accessible and capable of swift assessment, which means that cases can be mediated very early in their life with satisfaction. Despite bravado, posturing and an abundance of testosterone, parties are uncomfortable in the uncertain/unfamiliar arena of litigation and the consequent delays.

- It can be helpful and important to remind parties of their public responsibilities. They may be role models, custodians of a community's wellbeing, providing the opportunity for sport to demonstrate the virtues and values of society. The business is multi-dimensional and those in disputes are inclined to a limited outlook.

Thank you for your indulgence of the sporting metaphors above – please feel free to sprinkle more into whatever mediations you are undertaking – it's about: the parties playing-through; seeing how they are configured on the pitch; moving the ball around in midfield; (not) scoring early; pulling stumps; playing to the whistle; not falling at the first; playing the wicket; going off-piste; dropping for an eight count; spinning the ball out wide; taking the game to them....

Chapter 7

Learning from Other Mediation Disciplines

Most of us practise a form of facilitative, or non-evaluative mediation. We help people do deals. And whilst most of us consider it is the best form for commercial mediations, there are other mediation strands, or disciplines, that are successfully practiced in the United Kingdom, and which can offer insights and skills to mediators who are on a journey, seeking to learn and perfect their skills. What follows are tasters of these other disciplines.

Transformative mediation

Jane Gunn

Two business partners Jim and David arrive at the mediation. Each has with them a legal team comprising their solicitors who have been working on this case for some time and barristers instructed especially for the mediation. They are in dispute about the terms of their partnership agreement, as David wants to retire from the business and move to France. In addition, there are claims relating to drawings and expenses and who owns the property that the business is run from.

Scenario 1

The mediation begins with the mediator's opening speech, outlining the process (usually a progression from joint to private meetings) and ground rules such as confidentiality, the without prejudice nature of the mediation and highlighting the mediator's role which is to help the parties to get to a deal as soon as possible.

Position statements and case papers have already been exchanged and shared with the mediator but each barrister makes a speech emphasising their client's position. The mediator asks a few (open) questions to clarify understanding and asks if anyone else wants to speak at this stage. No one does. The solicitors have already indicated that their clients do not want to spend time in the same room and neither do they. They would rather use the mediator to negotiate with the other party.

The mediator suggests that perhaps they should break the joint meeting and retire to their private rooms. The mediator then spends time with both Jim and David separately seeking to understand their stories in more detail. Not surprisingly, each has a completely different version of events as to the history of the partnership and in particular who owns the property.

The mediator works privately with each party and their legal team discussing the shape of a possible deal and outlining on the flip chart three options that might deal with the various issues raised. Who will own the property? How will Jim continue the business? What money, if any, will be paid?

David's solicitor states that there is 'no point' in continuing with the mediation unless they can agree the basic concept that money will be passing from Jim to David and not vice versa. They'd like the mediator to convey that message to the other side and see what proposal they have to make.

The mediation develops into a 'shuttle negotiation' with the mediator conveying messages and offers to each of the parties. The mediator 'reality tests' each offer with the parties in the context of their real needs and costs of continuing legal action. Eventually, when the parties seem to have reached a deadlock, the mediator suggests a figure and structure that might provide an acceptable solution.

Scenario 2

The mediation begins and the mediator emphasises that the mediation is an opportunity for the parties to have a different kind of conversation than has perhaps been possible so far. The mediator's job is to support the parties in having the best conversation that they can – that's it. The parties get to make all the decisions.

The mediator invites the parties to open the conversation with what they feel is important. David's barrister says a few words about his client's case and the mediator reflects back what was said and checks who else would like to speak. David immediately jumps in and becomes quite angry as he describes how he feels about Jim's behaviour. Jim responds with equal passion and the mediator waits for a break before summarizing the key points on which they disagree and checking where they would like the conversation to go.

Eventually Jim's solicitor suggests that they would like some time to reflect on what they have heard so far. The mediator checks to see if each party would value a private session and joins them in their rooms.

Jim's solicitor wants to make an opening offer. The mediator checks how they would like to convey that message and reminds everyone that it is not the mediator's role to become either parties 'voice'. Jim and David decide that they would prefer to meet face-to-face with the mediator's support. During this meeting Jim and David begin to acknowledge where the other is coming from and as they do so, the conversation becomes less heated. An hour later, after consulting with their lawyers, they have reached an agreement and the mediation is concluded.

What exactly is transformative mediation and what has it got to teach commercial mediators?

Transformative mediation is often misunderstood. To some people the term 'transformative' suggests a psychodynamic process that will seek to change the parties to a mediation or attempt to heal them or their broken relationship. For this reason transformative mediation has been treated with some suspicion and often

Learning from Other Mediation Disciplines

avoided by lawyers and parties to commercial disputes on the basis that the parties' relationship is not at the heart of the dispute and/or does not need fixing.

The problem – destructive dialogue

Have you ever been in a mediation where the parties and or their representatives did not want to sit in the same room as the other side? I mediated such a case recently. Both parties were represented by lawyers who saw the mediation as an exercise in reinforcing their legal positions in a short joint meeting and then participating in shuttle negotiation. Their idea of mediation was that the mediator would run up and down the corridor with messages passed from one to the other in an attempt to broker a deal. If you can call this dialogue at all, it was extremely dysfunctional. The parties and their lawyers remained wedded to their view of the case and firmly attached to their legal positions. They did not wish to listen to anything that the other party might have to say and were thus unable to learn anything new to help them move towards a different outcome.

Commercial mediations often follow this kind of pattern, with the mediator acting either as a shuttle or, when that doesn't work, being asked to reality test and/or evaluate to encourage the parties to reach a settlement.

The solution – constructive dialogue

Most commercial mediations are conducted according to a problem-solving approach, based on the theory that conflict is a problem of how to meet incompatible needs with limited resources. The mediator's role is to help the parties in solving that problem and reaching an acceptable settlement. The transformative approach however, is based on the alternative theory that conflict is a crisis in human interaction and that what the parties most need help with is enabling a constructive dialogue to take place between them. What they do not need is for the mediator to attempt to solve the problem for them, either by being explicitly evaluative or by controlling the way the mediation process unfolds and so directing what is discussed and when.

The primary goal of transformative mediation is to enable the parties to have a more constructive dialogue than they have had thus far. First, the mediator seeks to *empower* the disputing parties. In other words, to strengthen their capacity to analyse situations and make effective decisions *for themselves*. Secondly, the mediator seeks to enhance each party's *recognition* of the other. In other words, to enable them to see and consider each other's perspectives and so to be more open and responsive to the other.

Self determination

The belief of transformative mediators is that the parties (and/or their representatives) have both the ability and the desire to decide for themselves how the conversation should be conducted and what a good outcome for them would be.

A mediator with a 'transformative' orientation starts from a relational perspective and believes that his or her job is primarily to help the parties to *transform their interaction* with each other from destructive to constructive, while they explore various topics and possibilities for resolution. If the mediator does this job well, the parties are likely to make positive changes in their interaction and, as a result, find acceptable terms of resolution for *themselves*, when and where such genuine terms exist.

Client centred

Unlike the mediation mentioned in Scenario 1, where the focus of the mediation was solely on legal positions and on the lawyers' negotiations based on those positions, the focus of transformative mediation is the clients themselves. The parties to the dispute are at the centre of the mediation, making their own decisions about both the content and the process of the mediation. The mediator's job is to help them to reach a clearer understanding of their own interests and options and, if they so choose, to reach a better understanding of their opponent. The role of lawyers and advisers is to support their clients in this quest but not to take control of the proceedings.

The mediator does not seek to control or direct the mediation process or content believing that the parties are best placed to fulfil both these roles.

Skills and tools

The goal of third-party intervention in facilitative mediation is to encourage interest-based bargaining and moves towards a settlement that resolves the parties' issues. The mediator uses skills such as rapport building, open questions, listening and reality testing to help the parties to discover underlying needs and interests as a basis for principled rather than positional-based negotiation. The focus of the mediation is very much on the 'problem' and shape of any settlement terms and a successful outcome is a settlement agreement that solves the problem on fair and realistic terms.

By contrast, the goal of third-party intervention in transformative mediation is to enhance the parties' own decision-making and communication by helping them to shift from destructive to constructive interactions. Listening remains an important skill but instead of listening with macro-focus and trying to understand the parties' problem, the mediator adopts a micro-focus concentrating on the interaction between the parties and looking for opportunities for them to become more empowered and thus able to better analyse the dispute and also better able to understand and acknowledge the other party's situation.

The mediator uses a repertoire of skills and responses, namely reflecting, summarising, checking-in and staying out. Checking-in is the way the mediator asks questions that help the parties make decisions about the mediation process as well as the content being discussed; staying out is when the mediator withdraws from direct involvement in the conversation and allows the parties to talk directly to each other without interruption. A successful outcome is when the conversation becomes more constructive and the parties' capacity for decision-making is enhanced.

Lessons for commercial mediators

Most commercial mediations follow a similar pattern focusing on problem solving, issue analysis, reality testing and negotiation. Lawyers representing the parties frequently speak and act on their client's behalf and negotiations are conducted based upon the perceived legal positions and chances of success at trial. Mediators are expected to take control of the mediation process, determining when and how the issues should be addressed and dealt with.

The parties themselves are often marginalised by this approach, remaining silent or saying little and there is little if any opportunity for direct conversation with the other party.

The transformative approach, on the other hand, teaches us that if we have the courage to put the clients at the centre of the mediation and use our skills in such a way to empower them to think and act more clearly, we may be surprised at their capacity to make their own decisions about how the issues are addressed and resolved.

Evaluative mediation

Andrew Goodman

This is a challenge for me. It is a great disappointment that the market is moving towards an evaluative form of mediation and that a lot of mediators are prepared to condone it. I passionately believe that a non-evaluative form of commercial mediation is unquestionably the best but, through laziness on the part of the lawyers (or indeed the mediator) or the wish to have the mediator on their side, the UK market has gradually followed that of the United States towards evaluation. Therefore, with some trepidation, I asked Andrew Goodman, a firm believer in the merits of evaluative mediation, to make this contribution (DR).

In this jurisdiction, for the most part, mediators are selected because at least one of their attributes is the ability to appraise, either at the outset or through the first part of the process, the parties' respective positions, whether as lawyers or technical experts or as specialists. However they don't. Typically, civil-commercial mediators in the United Kingdom are trained to work under a self-imposed constraint: in the United Kingdom, mediators are taught and expected to deliver facilitated mediation in which the mediator is prevented from expressing his or her opinion on the merits of the dispute, even if the parties ask directly for it. This is in direct contrast to mediation traditions in the United States and Pacific Rim countries, where mediators, particularly judicial mediators, will commonly offer when asked a non-binding view of the likely outcome of proceedings as an impetus to negotiation. Sometimes more forceful mediators will give an opinion whether asked for or not. Yet offering a view is seen as an anathema by a healthy majority of UK practitioners who have been trained in the facilitative model.

This section is intended to ask, why? What is the problem, and can it be overcome? Can using evaluative techniques, simply meaning where the mediator expresses a non-binding opinion on the merits of the dispute, make better, more prescient and more commercially minded mediators who are more aligned with client expectation? After all, an evaluation by the mediator does not determine the outcome, even if it risks endangering settlement – it offers a non-binding opinion at best, otherwise it would be an arbitral methodology.

As to outcome, it is merely a different approach, namely to allow the parties a qualified neutral outsider's view of their positions in the context of themselves considering all their interests.

To examine these questions it is necessary to introduce evaluative mediation in its proper context, or more specifically in its two proper contexts – first as a working, but hidden, part of standard form facilitative mediation procedure, and second as a specially commissioned mediation process. To do so let us ask what does evaluation mean in practice? Where and how is it used in UK alternative dispute resolution? Whether prejudice against its use is justified? Whether, having identified the difficulties associated with evaluation as well as the benefits, these can be overcome?

Mediation and decision making

Orthodoxy in mediation training and practice is based on two fundamental principles that have impeded the development of a more evaluative style of mediation in the United Kingdom since the inception of the presently accepted facilitative commercial model here, in 1989. From the outset we are taught the mediator should be, and should be seen to be, neutral. Any perceived bias is viewed as potentially a fatal flaw in the process, either propelling one or more disputant parties to leave or creating a risk that may happen. In addition, the outcome to the dispute must remain within the exclusive remit of the parties as a matter of ownership:the mediator must not be seen as imposing a solution – whether because his or her professional background engenders a mind-set used to operating in an arbitral way, or because they think a strong suggestion will lead to settlement, or even because they genuinely think there is a 'right answer' to the problem at hand. Even the suggestion of a proposed genus of outcome tends to be frowned upon unless it originates from a party as a contribution to the process, for example during brainstorming.

These two needs have driven the view that mediators cannot offer opinions on the merits because the process does not permit them to be decision makers (a suggestion which cannot be so, since the mediator manages the entire process, in terms of participation, order of events, inter-party and party-mediator dynamics, timetable, and influence – all of which makes the mediator in fact a key decision maker).

Part of the difficulty may be laid at the door of the lawyers, who remain the principal gatekeepers of disputes, and the way in which, as a professional body, lawyers have developed civil-commercial mediation to remain under their dominating influence.

Lawyer mediators and lawyer mediation advocates tend to have great difficulty in avoiding an evaluative style, even where the facilitative process demands they do so. Often it is more a matter of suppression than abandonment. Legal training and practice is dependent on the structure of procedural and substantive rules, rules of professional responsibility, rules of logic and rules of legal thinking, all of which seep into an analytical approach to rights-based dispute resolution. In truth most of these rules came about historically, as much to help protect professional monopolies in dispute resolution as to help their disputant clients.

As distinguished international mediators Greg Relyea and Roy Cheng point out:[1]

> 'Rules may bring a degree of certainty but they also restrict possibilities. Rules may produce some defined standards but they also tend to result in generalised outcomes and remedies instead of individualised agreements. Rules, however arbitrary and ill-defined, may engender feelings of comfort, order and predictability. Working within the rules and also outside traditional boundaries of litigation, remedies and legalistic problem-solving may engender feelings of a loss of structure and loss of direction.'

But their impact is clear. Lawyers approach mediation from the springboard of litigation, or what otherwise would become litigation. The starting point is dealing with a 'case to be determined' rather than a 'problem to be solved'. This approach makes it extremely difficult to escape consideration of the merits while trying to move open-mindedly into the realm of wider party interests. And it gives rise to the idea that the mediator should be a participant in the decision-making process since they are regarded by the parties as a quasi-tribunal.

This is exemplified in two mediation scenarios. First, in the opening plenary session, the lawyer acting as mediation advocate will typically anchor his client's negotiating position upon the merits of the legal case. A mediator will hardly interrupt an opening statement to suggest the merits are irrelevant. This will be because of lack of confidence, the need to give an appearance of even-handedness, a recognition that the dispute will stem from such legal issues anyway, or the need simply to get underway and get the process moving.

Secondly, should the mediator chose to deal privately with lawyers or other representatives absent the lay parties, all participants in such a 'professional' caucus will have a tendency to stray back to an evaluation of the merits, even if not overtly expressed by the mediator. Sometimes even recent authorities in the particular field of law are discussed between opposing lawyers and the mediator.

It is hardly surprising, since most mediations take place not just in the 'shadow of the law', as many commentators have described it, but with a real prospect of existing litigation continuing, or legal process being issued. In the negotiation stage, professional advisers come into their own by weighing what is on the table against their perceived view of the merits of the case – in order to advise what will happen in the event the mediation terminates without resolution. Participants measure their positions against traditional rights, remedies and norms that provide the initial framework for some mediations.

Why then, should we not simply recognise that evaluation can have a valuable role to play within mediation, and that even a facilitative mediator can learn to engage with and benefit from training in and experience of a more evaluative approach?

There are two aspects to utilising evaluation in mediation; both as a genuine and important though secondary (almost subliminal) part of the structured but flexible

---

[1] Greg Relyea and Roy Cheng, 'From Gladiator to Mediator: The challenges for lawyers who become mediators', www.mediate.com, April 2010.

approach which we regard as facilitative in terms of outcome, and commissioning an evaluation from the outset as the intended primary approach – using the process to build a consensual solution around an expression of non-binding opinion by the mediator as to the likely outcome of litigation or some other tribunal determination.

Using evaluation within facilitative mediation

There are a number of areas within the facilitative model which permit the use of evaluation to good effect, some without the mediator endangering his position of neutrality, others where such a risk may emerge but the circumstances justify it.

Merits and reality testing

Mediators are generally hired for their subject matter expertise. If the dispute centres on an issue of legal or technical principle, the mediator should reasonably familiarise himself or herself with that principle and recent learning on the subject as part of their preparation, if they do not already know it. Even without wishing to express an opinion, the mediator might conclude that in an argument on the merits, one party is simply wrong. They may have misconstrued, misinterpreted, omitted an essential ingredient of the principle, or may have been advised erroneously as to the state of current law, or current technical specification. If that matter can be clearly and easily demonstrated, privately in caucus, or privately in 'professional caucus', with that side, why shouldn't the mediator do so? On any view it is a facet of reality testing, the only difference being the method of communication: the facilitative model only permits the use of adroit questioning to cause the party introspection. The evaluative approach enables the nettle to be grasped more directly. And if the defect is obvious, it can be presented as fact rather than opinion.

Whether it is a distinction of language or approach, the mediator should not permit the reality of the situation to be clouded by a party's self-delusion. Mediators must continually use their discretion, skill and judgment during a mediation process that is unfolding, changing direction and raising unexpected twists and turns.[2] That should extend to the use of evaluation in reality testing. Gagging the mediator in such circumstances will be extremely frustrating for him or her, and may influence the mediator's position in the negotiation phase.

Dealing privately with lawyers or technical experts

Let us examine the premise that there is a separate and slightly different dynamic between the mediator and the lay disputant, and between the mediator and that client's professional advocate or technical expert. This stems from the impact of co-professionalism, or the fraternity between the lawyer mediator and the lawyer representative, or the expert mediator and the party expert. It concerns a shared familiarity with rules, process, ethics, the nature of professional instruction and retainer, the business of a profession, and experience, and this familiarity manifests itself in shared language and professional jargon, exchanging war stories, and typically the informality of professional relationships – even otherwise adversarial

---

2 Op.cit.

relationships – in the physical absence of the lay client. However, it may give rise to the leakage of pertinent, confidential information to the mediator (wrongly, or apparently wrongly) disclosed by the professional as his own 'true' opinion on the merits, on his or her client, or on a previously unspoken agenda.

In such circumstances how should the mediator respond to receiving information from a professional that he or she might not expect to receive directly from the lay disputant? Can the mediator respond with an informal evaluation in such circumstances? Orthodoxy would suggest no, or at least not without using extreme caution. The answer may be the vehicle chosen for an expression of opinion which is intended to introduce momentum into the proceedings towards the end of the exploration phase. Rather than being concerned with the stricture of process, this problem could simply be viewed as a matter of language, and its use in conveying any particular message. For example a mediator could properly carry appoint to the professionals in a fraternal, objective, academic overview of the current law in an area, or the current state of established professional thinking among specialists or experts.

Overcoming deadlock

There may well come a point where the parties have arrived at deadlock during the negotiation phase. This normally occurs when the parties, while recognising the value and convenience of an interest-based solution, are drawn into a retreat towards entrenched positions. There are well-known techniques for the mediator to cope with this situation, including retracing steps, considering other options, calling for a joint meeting or specific small-scale joint meetings of the decision-makers, seeking permission to reveal additional information, brain-storming, and visiting older, more successful ground.

One technique is to cause parties to re-evaluate their BATNA (Best Alternative To a Negotiated Agreement) in order to get them to shift there position, principally by highlighting risk. In the United States this is known in some circles as BATNA-bashing, and is, in effect, a process of evaluation. Even a facilitative mediator can work through the detail of a party's BATNA to look at risk assessment, litigation cost, time cost, reputational and relationship damage, and hidden items that a party or its professional advisers may have overlooked. The question then becomes whether the mediator should express an opinion on the BATNA. With the use of careful language, this can be done without damage to the mediator's perceived neutrality. It may not be enough to simply allow the party to remain introspective.

Appraising a technical solution

Even a facilitative process should not prevent mediators who are legal or technical experts from appraising the value of a proposed solution to the dispute. Nobody is suggesting that the outcome must be regulated by the mediator, or that it should be seen as objectively fail, but the mediator is entitled to evaluate the intended agreement by reference to settled legal principles – the outcome must be sufficiently certain, lawful, workable and enforceable to stand the scrutiny of the court as a valid contract. If the mediator is a lawyer and they consider that the settlement agreement is flawed in law, that opinion should be given, together with an indication of what the problem is and, without negating the parties' intentions, how to fix it. If the mediator is a technical expert, one would reasonably expect him or her to raise issues of practicality or workability with the parties if the matter was in doubt. To do so, the mediator is entitled to express an opinion on the merits of the intended solution, and should.

The expression of opinion by the mediator at these various junctures in the broadly facilitative process can, I hope, be seen as a benefit. The parties are simply exploiting the knowledge, skills and experience of their appointed problem solver. The fluidity of the process and flexibility of outcome surely demands that mediators should not restrict the use of these attributes, or worse, leave them outside the process altogether. As is a well-known aphorism in this subject, the mediator may be neutral, but he is not neutered. Mediators should use their opinions to challenge party pre-conceptions and force them to be open to reality, as much as any other aspect of the communication and negotiation skills and abilities which they bring to the table.

Commissioning evaluative mediation

In an evaluative mediation process the same issues and much the same process arise but the environment is open. The parties understand from the outset that the mediator may, on request or otherwise, express a personal view of the strengths and weaknesses of the parties' legal cases and a prediction of the likely outcome should the matter go to determination by an arbitral tribunal. This openness gives rise to its own problems, which I now turn to.

In the standard UK facilitative model the mediator may give an impression that implies to the parties that he or she holds an opinion as to the merits, which often appears to be the case in reality-testing, but which the process does not permit to surface. The parties may assume that the implied opinion is either based upon the mediator's actual knowledge of the law, the arguments of the mediation advocates, or his or her own experience or common sense view of the matter. However, once that opinion is expressed in the course of an evaluative mediation, the mediator will have to know how that opinion has been formed or influenced, and may well have to explain that to the parties.

This gives rise to a number of problems, which the evaluative mediator will need to address, some in preparation, some during the course of the mediation.

Preparation

Like any other decision-making process involving two or more parties, it is important to establish ground rules. When, in what circumstances, how and to whom will the mediator express and deliver his or her opinion, and in respect of what?

These questions may properly be dealt with between the parties upon the mediator's appointment, and should be reduced to writing and contained in the Mediation Agreement, subject to such flexibility as the mediator may need, consistent with minimising his or her risk of the additional professional liability which might lie for giving an uninformed or erroneous opinion which a party relies upon subsequently to their foreseeable detriment.

The scope for opinion giving is wide: on the law; on areas of technical expertise, such as valuation, tax application, or levels of recoverable damage; on the merits, in terms of liability; on settlement issues. Once the mediator is empowered by the agreement to offer such view, they may have to undertake serious research between delivery of the mediation bundles and position statements, and the mediation appointment itself. There will be both cost and time implications, principally because the mediator will need to know the extent of the information available upon which his or her views are expected to be based.

Even an experienced evaluative mediator needs to be wary of giving a view based on limited information. It almost goes without saying that a mediator is highly unlikely to have access to the same material as a trial judge. On the other hand, there may be much more material available on the parties' wider interests, the sort of information a judge would never need to consider. And therefore it is possible to have a more balanced view about such concerns.

It is important for both the mediator and the parties to recognise and reduce to the Mediation Agreement the scope of the mediator's ability to be evaluative, and any limit on the extent of the material which the parties will make available. The mediator must manage party expectations in this regard from the outset, or the process will run into trouble.

It may be that, the parties having agreed that an evaluation should be made, it should be made as late as possible after all non-evaluative alternatives have been exhausted and to ensure that the mediator's knowledge of the case is by then at its greatest.

Form

Having prepared the ground, and having agreed whether the evaluation be verbal or in writing, the mediator should introduce a number of caveats which are necessary to protect the mediation process. The parties need to be aware of the implications, particularly the dangers, of an evaluation being given since it will undoubtedly affect their attitude to the process and most likely, to the mediator. Particularly in the context of considering BATNAs, a reassessment of the strengths and weaknesses and the no-settlement alternatives should be made with each party in private.

The mediator will need to protect his or her position by emphasising the neutrality of his or her status: just because an opinion is expressed, that does not change the function of the mediator.

The evaluation should be delivered in private to each party, and each side should be told the same thing, using the same words. In the United Kingdom it is entirely sensible that evaluation should never be given in joint session, although in jurisdictions where caucusing is unknown in mediation, that must be the practice. The mediator should reiterate that his or her view is non-binding, and is given only to stimulate settlement negotiations.

For one side the evaluation is likely to come as a blow – potentially, but not always, unexpected. Under those circumstances it needs to be married with an explanation perhaps relayed as the best commercial solution, given the limit of the facts and opinions revealed in the mediation.

For the other side, latching on to the mediator's opinion should not be used as a device with which to beat a disputant towards a predisposed position. Although an identical opinion should be given to both parties, a difference of emphasis may be a useful tool with which to hold the parties in the process: the mediator ought to explain that the evaluation is made and published to both sides:

- without blame or judgement;
- mindful of potential injury to the party/lawyer relationship (and particularly should be worded so as to avoid embarrassment, or reduce loss of face to the party or advisers); and
- accompanied by, as appropriate, a settlement range, or consequential proposals, to encourage further negotiation.

There is a significant risk that the parties will have their attention diverted towards discussion of how, why and upon what basis the mediator formed his or her view. Presupposing the mediator is acting honestly and has considered the merits objectively, this risk gives rise to the question of how much explanation should the parties be given. Ultimately that does not matter, since the mediator is not making a decision. He or she is merely expressing an opinion, which, though coming from an authority figure, the parties are free to accept or reject.

Consequences

A mediator should not deliver an evaluation without having a reasonably clear idea of the consequences. This is likely to require a view to be formed of the likely reaction of both lay and professional members of the disputants, particularly of the party's case against whose merits s/he is going to opine.

At the very least, having given his or her evaluation the mediator needs to allow the parties time to consider and reassess their position; that may be a relatively long period. It may require an adjournment.

The mediator needs to have prepared in advance a strategy that avoids entrenchment on the one side, and loss of face, including the lawyer's or other professionals' loss of face, on the other. This can be done by encouraging the parties into a co-operative problem-solving mode by seeing the mediator's opinion as nothing more than impartial data for them to use as one of the foundations for settlement.

It follows from the potential consequences of evaluation that the mediator is taking a calculated risk and the process will be fatally undermined. This requires his or her proper consideration of all the issues, and also that of the personalities involved in the dispute – clients, supporters, decision makers, professional advisers. Many commentators, including the author of this book,[3] have argued that the risk is not worth it. They point out that:

---

3   David Richbell, 'Non-lawyers make the best mediators', CMC Debate 18 January 2012.

- the perceived loss of neutrality after giving an opinion may make the mediator's position untenable;
- the evaluation may be derived in part from confidential material gained only through private caucuses, leading to a loss of confidence that the mediator can be trusted to preserve privacy;
- in any event there will be feelings of loss of ownership or control by the parties, the danger of entrenchment by one party, and the worry of collusion between the mediator and that party whose merits s/he favours; and
- the loss of face may be sufficiently significant to cause a party to flee the process, at least for a while.

The latter may be a reflection of the potentially significant damage that might be done to the lawyer/own client relationship.

These are entirely realistic concerns. But any such risk should be met by the professionalism of the mediator. An evaluation will not be given lightly. Even the decision to make one will not be taken lightly in view of the risks described. Before doing so the evaluative mediator will have some regard for the mechanics of forming the view to be delivered, this based on the mechanics of fact finding, evidential values and the receiving and weighing evidence, the impact of impression, and the adequacy or paucity of materials used in an interim analysis. The mediator's view of the merits may alter, and he or she must be alive to that possibility.

A lawyer mediator will already be imbued with these concepts as a result of orthodox training, since the law encourages judges and lawyers to be critical about the facts, the law, and the credibility of witnesses and parties. They understand decision making based on authority, transparency and the proper exercise of discretion. They are predisposed to focused analysis and judging people. It is for this reason that lawyers find facilitative mediation a challenge to their intellect and to their mindset, and require training and time to break such a difficult habit. Evaluative mediation returns them to a comfort zone offering the security of their rules and their world, integrity and applied ethics. How can that not be a benefit to the client?

Community mediation

Eve Pienaar

'My neighbours are abusive and frighten my wife and children. They pour bleach on our clothes on the line, don't maintain the fence so my children are too scared to play outside with their dogs close by and they scratched my car only last week...' After listening to this party in private session, the other might offer: 'That family have no respect for my partner and me. Their kids are up until 10pm or later every night, screaming and running up and down the flat. I work shifts and am off sick right now, suffering from depression with sleep deprivation...'.

Community mediation operates in a wide spectrum of activity, from multi-party social change projects to neighbour- and community-based conflict. This section gives an overview of the latter, with particular emphasis on the differences between community and commercial mediation, from the practitioner's perspective.

The example given above is based on a real case, where both sets of neighbours had strong reservations even about meeting one another, given how acrimonious emotions had spiralled out of control. They had not spoken directly for months, complaining to their social landlord and the police on so many occasions they were eventually referred to mediation. The mediation was successful, in that the parties were able to speak again, dispel negative assumptions and made a real effort to understand one another. They worked through their issues to reach agreement on how they would live alongside one another without conflict.[4]

Community mediation is a powerful tool for effecting social change and managing conflict effectively, on very little resource. It operates mostly in the more deprived elements of society, often in urban settings where competition for basic amenity is felt acutely. It is accessible, free of stigma and empowers parties to regain control over a part of their lives that has been lost to anger, stress and hurt. It deserves higher status and better resource, as an investment in managing the cost of conflict, but sadly it is all too often low on the list of demands for government funding.

In the words of Bush and Folger:

'Mediation offers an effective means of organising individuals around common interests and thereby building stronger community ties and structures. This is important because unaffiliated individuals are especially subject to exploitation in this society and because more effective community organisation can limit such exploitation and create more social justice.'[5]

Overview of the community mediation process

Community mediation has been part of the fabric of society for generations in certain cultures, such as the Australian aborigine or parts of Africa. It became widespread in Western society in the United States, only as far back as the Arbitration Act 1888 and became properly entrenched in labour disputes from the 1960s. It migrated to a wider, social conflict dimension in the 1990s and began to reach into the United Kingdom at that time.

Community mediation services were set up around the United Kingdom from around 1990. Sadly, their offering has since shrunk with the tightening of public funding and dismantling of the Quality Mark assurance scheme of the Legal Services Commission in 2008 and the National Mediation Helpline in 2011. Community mediation service providers carry out awareness training and work closely with key stakeholders to raise funding for their limited resources and embed their offering into the community they serve. They would typically seek funding from the police, their local Council, social landlords and other statutory agencies who have to handle high levels of social conflict, particularly in low income social groups.

Community mediation shares the fundamental attributes of commercial mediation, with some very significant differences. These could be summarised as:

---

4 The case was co-mediated for Ealing Mediation Service (EMS), by Eve Pienaar. EMS systematically check in with the parties a month after the mediation, to check whether further intervention is needed. In this case, no further intervention was requested.
5 Robert A Baruch Bush and Joseph P Folger, *The Promise of Mediation – the Transformative Approach to Conflict* (Jossey-Bass, 2005).

Community mediation	Commercial mediation
• Service provider allocates cases	• Parties agree choice of mediator
• Mediators selected for compatibility with parties	• Parties select the mediator
• Mediators have little background to the dispute and don't contact the parties before the mediation (although the office does)	• Pre-mediation contact with the parties and preparation is essential
	• Co-mediation is rare
	• Parties are usually represented by lawyers and experts
• Co-mediation the norm	• Parties share cost of mediation
• Parties are not professionally represented	• Mediator selected for expertise
• Free to the user	• Parties often never meet again (litigation comes to an end)
• Mediators are not expert – varied professional background	• Confidentiality key to the process as a whole
• Parties likely to have on-going relationship (neighbour)	• Without prejudice is a key driver
• Confidentiality primarily relevant to private meetings, given on-going relationship of parties	• Often a contained dispute, ends with the mediation
	• Mediation ethos is directive and sometimes evaluative
• Without prejudice unlikely to be a driver	• Settlement agreement is a binding contract
• Conflict management, not an isolated dispute	
• Mediation ethos is narrative, transformative, never directive or evaluative	
• Settlement agreement is non-binding	

The main difference between community and commercial mediation is the ethos the mediators bring to the process. In community mediation, typically co-mediated by two mediators who will have the same practice standards but very different backgrounds, the approach is narrative and even transformative.[6] It is about enabling parties to move from a place of deeply felt negative emotion and vulnerability, to finding compassion in their hearts. This takes time, validation of feelings and respectful listening by the mediators. It is entirely inappropriate, for instance for the mediators to make any suggestion as to possible solutions or to give advice of any nature.

---

6   In very broad terms, a 'narrative' mediation approach relies on the parties finding a better understanding of their situation through narrating their story, describing how they came to be in conflict, which it is felt enables them to then see a path out of the conflict without any intervention from the mediator other than to guide the story-telling. A 'transformative' approach takes this one step further, in the belief people change fundamentally through the empowering process of understanding how they came to be in conflict and how they will better handle similar situations in the future.

Learning from Other Mediation Disciplines

Process outline

Cases are referred directly from the clients or, more often, from statutory agencies such as the police or social landlord. The case manager will match a pairing of mediators who present some affinity with the parties, either in terms of gender, age or cultural background. Co-mediation enables a better chance of at least one mediator gaining the trust of the parties in the little time afforded to the mediation (generally no more than four hours and sometimes shorter).

The process and approach will vary from one community service offering to another. Generally, the mediation format is the 'all-in-one' approach, where the mediators meet the parties individually in separate, private sessions, and then brings them together for the joint session for the rest of the period allocated to the mediation. 'Shuttle' mediation is used where there is such tension between the parties (or vulnerability) as to make it unsafe to hold a joint session. Shuttle mediation is usually less effective as there isn't the scope for emotional change at a deeper, visceral level. Joint meetings are a powerful means of enabling change, as the parties, facing one another sometimes for the first time in ages, see for themselves the impact of their behaviour and can put their own hurt into words.

The venue is usually pretty sparse, maybe a few chairs in a community centre and a plastic cup of water if one is lucky. It is helpful to arrive a little early, debrief with the co-mediator partner to ensure the pairing models neutrality and constructive communication, for instance agreeing who will open and how questions will be shared, taking care to model equal airtime between the mediators at least.

The mediators will manage the introductions and transitions between meetings carefully, when there has been a history of violence or abuse. Always bring tissues and prepare for the unexpected, keeping an open mind at all times. One party may turn up with a 'friend' likely to intimidate the other side, or may turn up with young children if childcare plans fell apart. Provided the other party is given the choice to accept or not, it is generally best to accommodate the parties' approach so that they don't put up resistance to the process from the outset.

Tools for the mediators

The Mediation Service Providers operate to a high quality standard of service, both to clients and the community they serve. Their mediators are trained, assessed and accredited and are supervised regularly. More often than not the mediations are shadowed by a less experienced mediator and feedback and practice reflection are built into the process at the end of the mediation.[7]

There will be a handbook for the mediators to refer to, with policies on how to handle tricky issues such as child safety or mental health matters. The mediators are required to commit to working on a certain number of mediations per annum and to attend support group meetings where difficult cases are reviewed in a supportive

---

7 At Ealing Mediation Service, the mediators will send a copy of the agreement reached by the parties back to the office, with a case report on economic and cultural traits of the parties for diversity monitoring. The Service tracks numbers of cases referred per annum, those which convert to mediation and then the percentage which settle/require follow-up work, on a regular basis.

Learning from Other Mediation Disciplines

environment. It is a rewarding and fulfilling manner of giving back to society, with the support of the wider community mediation environment.

Within the process itself, key tools are neutral, compassionate communication,[8] modelling constructive exchanges for the parties, and ground rules. It is vital to agree with the parties at the outset that either side has the right to a period of 'uninterrupted time' and that everyone will adopt respectful communication, avoiding name-calling or character assassination. This is no panacea, and many a meeting has to go through a few 'time outs', but it helps the mediators moderate the exchanges and engage with the parties to look to the future rather than dwell on past misdemeanours.

The mediation 'agreement' has the role of Settlement Agreement, by analogy with commercial mediation. It is a non-binding record of the mediation meeting and is usually drawn up by the mediators. It captures the essence of the agreements the parties reach to regulate their conduct as respectful neighbours. It is couched in positive obligation terms, rather than vague statements as to what 'should not be done'. It is always balanced, neutral and not personal in nature. The kind of statements it might contain could be:

- Sue and Faisal will each place their bins out on Monday mornings rather than Sunday nights, to avoid the dogs messing the common areas;
- Sue will keep the landing free of the buggy and children's shoes;
- Faisal will knock on Sue's door if the children are making noise after 9pm;
- Sue will try and get her children to bed by 9pm;
- If Faisal is planning a family reunion, he agrees to let Sue know in advance so she can bring the children to her mother's for the evening; and
- If either Sue or Faisal have an issue with one another, they agree to text one another or put a note through the letterbox, before complaining to the Landlord.

Above all, the agreement should be straightforward, workable and carry provision for how the parties will communicate if the relationship becomes strained again. Generally, the risk of not reaching agreement, for the parties, is likely to have a bearing on issues like eviction and securing the right to move to another council property. In either case, the disruption to individuals and to families can have devastating effects and there will usually be a genuine desire to reach agreement with the other side to avoid these.

Who are the parties?

Community mediation should not be confused with restorative justice or family mediation. It is a process best suited to help ordinary people, living in close proximity, for whom the strain of poor amenity and quality of housing have led to intensely stressful conditions. The overwhelming cause of such disputes is around noise, but may also include issues of harassment, abuse or difficult behaviour.

---

8   For those interested in taking this further, the notion of 'clean language', developed by Rosenberg, is worth exploring. Essentially, the premise is to seek to avoid 'tainting' language with one's assumptions, to allow the other a blank canvas to express themselves.

Noise pollution is one of the highest causes of stress, with insidious consequences. The television blaring until late at night, the kids' stereo or the sound of children playing and fighting on laminated flooring directly above the head of someone needing sleep before setting off for work early the following morning can lead to what would otherwise be seen as highly aggressive behaviour. The person suffering the noise will bang on the door or hit the ceiling with a broom, in turn frightening the children above who then cry and make more noise. The parent demonises the neighbour below, the children then taunt and make fun of the neighbour, etc. it all escalates and soon brings friends, relatives and others living on the estate into polarised factions. Conflict which is allowed to feed on itself is hugely destructive for the families involved and the community at large.

The parties are generally from the lower end of the spectrum in terms of earning power and education. They may not share a common language and almost certainly will not share cultural values and ways of living. One party may well present mental health issues and vulnerability, and the mediators have to be careful to work within their remit and not stray into counselling or advice mode.

Case study

In one case, mediated for Ealing Mediation Service, a young Rastafarian man was at risk of eviction if the mediation with his neighbour, an older, Irish woman, didn't succeed. At first the man resisted meeting his neighbour in joint session, explaining the anger he felt made it almost impossible to control if in her presence. He described the 'red hot anger' which would overwhelm him when she made a noise over his head, under the influence of alcohol.

The mediators were aware that the man was under the influence of drugs and the woman had alcohol on her breath but decided to go ahead with the mediation, given that the parties had turned up and wanted to proceed. Once the parties did meet in joint session and the man explained to his neighbour how he believed the Council were urging her to complain in order to give them grounds to evict him, the relationship dynamic shifted dramatically and the parties were able to find settlement on all presenting issues – in fact, they left for the pub together!

Some particular features of community mediation

The parties will will have fairly equal bargaining power, albeit low in value. The stakes may seem low in comparison to commercial mediation cases involving expensive litigation – in fact they are often higher in terms of personal freedom, peaceful amenity and mental anguish. There is no price to broken sleep or fear of violence from the other side of a partition wall. The consequences of either can be hugely destructive, leading to being signed off on long-term sick leave with little pay, depression and mental health issues. The level of resource expended by the community and statutory agencies, directly stemming from poor noise insulation in social housing, for instance, is quite remarkable, yet the root cause is not tackled.

Although the parties may appear broadly of equal power, this 'equality' is qualified. Mental health issues, addiction, poverty and vulnerability can tip the scales heavily. In one case, again involving noise,[9] the Irish catholic family living above a complainant explained they had four children, in two-bedroom council social housing, but had to devote one room exclusively to their seventeen-year-old son who was deeply autistic, on instruction from the Council, or risk losing the benefits they received to care for him. The opportunity mediation presents in such cases is to transform feelings of aggrieved righteousness to compassionate understanding – not an easy task but one that is surprisingly often forthcoming.

Research has shown complainants to be in a somewhat stronger position than the other side.[10] Whether they put their position forward more forcefully, believe they are in the right more than the other side or simply are more competitive than the party they are complaining about, research shows they will get their demands met more frequently than the other side. The mediators will be sensitive to these power imbalances and compensate, where necessary, by suggesting the other side bring a friend or have 'time out' to consider demands placed on them. It is very important, in the community mediation context, that the parties come out of the process feeling they have been heard and the process was fair, even if they have had to make difficult concessions.

Conclusion

Devoting some time to pro-bono community mediation is demanding, often emotionally draining but on the whole very fulfilling. Seeing two neighbours, who have not spoken sometimes for years, finally look at one another and begin the process of forgiveness and compassion, does restore one's faith in humanity. Ultimately, it is a lot easier to live in ignorance, assumption and hate, than cross that Rubicon of allowing the heart to reach out and share in the difficulties the other person cannot escape.

Further reading

Karen Grover Duffy, James W. Grosch and Paul V Olczak (eds), *Community Mediation – A Handbook for Practitioners and Researchers* (Guildford Press 1991).

Robert A Baruch Bush and Joseph P Folger, *The Promise of Mediation – The Transformative Approach to Conflict* (Jossey-Bass, 2005).

John Winslade and Gerald D Monk, *Narrative Mediation: a New Approach to to Conflict Resolution* (Jossey Bass Inc., 2000).

Wendy Sullivan and Judy Rees, *Clean Language: Revealing Metaphors and Opening Minds* (Crown House Publishing, 2008).

---

9   Case mediated for Ealing Mediation Service in Northolt, 2012.
10 Castrianno, Pruitt, Nochajski and Zubeck, 'Community mediation – complainant/respondent differentiation', paper given at the annual.meeting of the Eastern Psychological Association, Buffalo, NY (1988).

Family mediation

Mary Banham-Hall

Family mediation is a process where a mediator or co-mediators help a couple resolve the issues arising on their separation or divorce. The mediator is impartial and the process is voluntary – requiring commitment and active participation to work. Family mediation is facilitative, forward looking and problem solving.

Family mediation differs in several key respects from civil mediation. It starts with a mediation information and assessment meeting ('MIAM' or Intake) with both clients together or separately; there then follows a series of sessions over a period of weeks or months – usually between one and five sessions of about an hour and a half each. Mediators do not hold confidences as between the clients and normally the couple is together with the mediator, who will give neutral legal information to help inform their decision-making. A significant proportion of family mediators are lawyers, but a good many are from a therapeutic background.

Family mediation can accommodate the couple's relationship and history, as they bring it with them into the room. If there are children, parents may need help with communication. Mediators try to help couples move from dysfunctional couple boundaries to functional parenting boundaries, vital if there are children. Often at the beginning of mediation, ground rules will be set with the mediator's help, such as how the couple is going to interact inside and outside of mediation and in relation to each other and their children. What goes on outside of the room between sessions has to be managed by the mediator too. It has to be safe and power imbalances have to be addressed. The dominated party if there is one, has to be empowered to function within the process without the dominant party feeling the mediator is biased.

Usually both parties are going to get a share of the assets and time with the children. The range of probable outcomes is much narrower than with civil litigation, without winners and losers in the conventional sense. Although the family court has a wide discretion, outcomes are within an average range. This means that in a vast number of financial cases legal costs can exceed the value of the difference between the parties and people have a strong motive to use mediation if they can and if they know about it.

The history of family mediation

In the 1990s there were only 600 to 800 family mediations a year for private clients only in England and Wales. Then in 1999 the Legal Services Commission (LSC) introduced compulsory referral to an LSC-accredited mediator to hear about mediation, prior to the grant of legal aid for court proceedings. Couples did not have to mediate – just hear about mediation. In one year, the number of family mediations where one or more clients was legally aided grew to about 14,500 per year and stayed about the same for well over a decade. Compulsory legal aid referrals formed about 85 per cent of all referrals to mediation by solicitors, not because private clients were unsuitable for mediation, just that there was no legal requirement to refer them to a mediator, so they were not for the most part referred.

The LSC set the Legal Aid Quality Assurance Standard (LAFQAS) – determining in great detail exactly what mediators were required to do in a legal aid mediation. Services were then audited against this quality mark, which provided a clear template for family mediation. Subsequently, the revised quality mark – the Mediation Quality Mark or MQM – replaced LAFQAS, but the key features of family mediation today originate in the original legal aid quality template and legal aid services are still audited against this. By contrast, non-legal aid mediators are not audited or regulated in the same way and standards and experience are more variable.

In 2007 the National Audit Office (NAO) Report on Family Mediation was published. It concluded that mediation was much better for families, producing better outcomes, less stress, was faster and cost much less than the conventional legal route or court proceedings. The report also concluded lawyers had a contrary interest to their clients to earn fees, were routinely diverting clients from mediation to keep work and were over-using the domestic violence exception to retain business. Shortly after this, screening for domestic violence was shifted to family mediators, as some of those cases were suitable for mediation.

One-third of clients interviewed by the NAO had not been told about mediation by lawyers – of which 40 per cent said they would have tried it. The following table shows average costs and timescales of mediated and non-mediated cases from that report:

	Mediated L/A case	**Non mediated L/A case**
Average cost	£754	£1,682
Duration	110 days	435 days

The NAO concluded the LSC should promote mediation. Legal Aid for family private law cases cost the taxpayer £360m per annum (until it was stopped in April 2013). Legal aid mediations cost about £15m–£18m per annum. The LSC expects couples to mediate where possible, but clients interviewed by the NAO said:

> 'My solicitor never mentioned mediation. I got a letter saying I'd declined it – when I asked about it I was told it was another standard letter and to ignore it.'

> 'My solicitor wrote to my partner's solicitor asking for mediation but they refused and said it would not work.'

The next big change came in April 2011 with the introduction of the MIAM, whereby all would-be applicants to court – privately paying, as well as legal aid – would have to hear about mediation from a mediator before issuing proceedings. This started to capture some private clients, but rapidly fell into disuse, as courts were not insisting on the filing of the FM1 form showing a MIAM had taken place or mediation had broken down, and by 2013 MIAMs were not working as intended and indeed were rarely taking place at all.

Family mediation only became mainstream once disputants had to hear about mediation from a mediator – then many chose to mediate. This is the critical difference between family and civil mediation and explains why family mediation has taken off and civil has not. On 31 March 2013, the funding code referrals of legal aid applicants to mediation stopped, following withdrawal of legal aid for most private law family proceedings, unless a very substantial domestic violence threshold was met with significant evidence. On 1 April 2013, referrals to mediation dropped sharply as a direct result of the end of compulsory referral to mediation of legal aid applicants, with lawyer referrals sitting at roughly a third to a half of the original compulsory referral level and legal aid payments to services shadowing that drop. Without the pre-issue filter of a MIAM and some of those cases mediating, court applications in England and Wales have risen (depending on which court and month) by 25 per cent to 50 per cent and although some of these, initially, were the last wave of legal aid certificated cases working through the system, very many are litigants in person and other cases that could have been mediated had there been effective compulsion to hear about mediation from a mediator.

Compulsory referral to hear about mediation from a mediator – increases mediation take up

The 1999 requirement that would-be applicants for legal aid for family proceedings had to hear about mediation from a mediator before getting legal aid for court proceedings started the process of making family mediation mainstream. Many people hearing about mediation from a mediator chose mediation and avoided court as a result.

In April 2013 whilst legal aid was kept for family mediation, it was stopped for all private law family proceedings and legal advice, unless there is domestic violence with a specific level of evidence. As a result all legal aid funding code referrals to mediation stopped too. The effect was immediate. Despite the government setting aside an additional £10m for extra family mediation to help private family law disputants who could no longer get legal aid for lawyers, those clients did not find their way into mediation; they went to court in great numbers, both in person and with lawyers paid for however they could manage. The figures, released under Freedom of Information searches, have been staggering. Legal aid mediations are down by 30-100 per cent and court applications up commensurately. At court, cases cost the tax payer a lot more than the small savings made on mediation legal aid. Welfare reports and court costs are expensive and those families suffer additional and avoidable stress by becoming conflicted and litigating. The extra £10m made available by a generous government was not spent – nor was about half of the pre-existing spend of £15m–£18m. It will be surprising if as much as £10m (just over half the pre-existing spend) was spent on legal aid for family mediation in the tax year ending April 2014. One of the problems is capital eligibility cuts. Also, everyone thinks there is no legal aid for family mediation and that it stopped with legal aid for family law. They do not know there is still legal aid for family mediation. Without the compulsory referral to mediators, people do not hear about mediation and cannot and do not choose to mediate. If any further evidence was needed of the absolute necessity of a compulsory referral to a mediator to hear about mediation, this is it.

The Children and Families Act 2014

The Children and Families Act 2014 introduced compulsory referral to a mediator to hear about mediation at assessment with a ticketed MIAMs mediator, before anyone can bring a private law court application – not just legal aid clients, but anyone at all. This started on 22 April 2014. This change as expected massively increased mediation assessments and increased mediation starts, thus proving beyond any shadow of a doubt what mediators have always said: if people hear about mediation from a mediator, many will choose to mediate; if they do not, they will not find their way to mediation. This is a critical issue for all disputants and for the future of dispute resolution and specifically the uptake of all mediation, family and civil, which needs to be embedded in our DR system as a standard part of the resolution process. Our solicitor referrals have doubled since April, and our referrals over all are up over 60 per cent. Whilst the conversion rate to mediation starts has also fallen, our starts are up too, though not as much as we had hoped. Interestingly some of the comments of clients at assessment are quite revealing:

- 'I don't want to mediate and my solicitor says I don't have to.'
- 'I just want the form for court and don't want to hear about mediation.'

You have to wonder what has been said to people to make them so opposed to hearing about mediation, as these are mostly people who, when you do their MIAMs, really don't understand the first thing about it. Mostly they come and listen. Many then want to mediate. Engaging the other party may be a different matter; they can be evasive. The MIAMs is still valuable. It tells people they can still agree things even after court proceedings start. There is an escape route. Besides, the culture is changing and there is a more positive attitude to mediation. MIAMs help with that. What we also need is a compulsory MIAMs for the respondent party, which would make a real difference.

Family mediation models

Originally much family mediation was co-mediation with two mediators working together, often one legal and one therapeutic. This can help resolve harder cases and produce better success rates. However, the LSC as it then was (now the Legal Aid Agency or LAA) yet again influenced the development of the model, by refusing to pay for co-mediation unless it could be justified on audit by them. The extra payment for co-mediation was minimal and sole mediation has evolved as the primary model of mediation in most cases. Good services will still use co-mediation in difficult or higher risk cases and it is a valuable resource, with two mediators working together on an equal basis.

Lawyers are not usually present in family mediation, but advise clients between sessions and, where necessary, make the settlement binding after the end of mediation, usually in a consent order on or after decree nisi in divorce financial cases. They can provide a valuable reality check for clients with advice about best and worst alternatives to a mediated outcome – just as very positional legal advice, un-tempered and at both ends of the spectrum, can torpedo mediation.

Training, accreditation and legal aid agency recognition

Family mediation foundation training takes eight full days and usually takes place in three blocks with training exercises between. Once the mediator has completed the core training they have effectively done their driving theory test, but still have a great deal to learn to drive the car. The gold standard for qualifying as a family mediator is becoming a recognised legal aid mediator, which takes at least a year of part-time, practical, supervised on-the-job mediating and training. The membership organisations (including the Family Mediators Association, Resolution, ADRg and National Family Mediation) run their own accreditation schemes requiring the preparation of a similar portfolio, and it seems likely there will be a single portfolio accreditation to legal aid standard under the aegis of the Family Mediation Council (FMC) before long. The FMC is the over-arching council responsible for family mediation standards and its committee is made up of representatives of membership organisations, the LAA and the MoJ.

All family mediators must have a professional practice consultant (PPC), undertake regular supervision with that PPC and continued professional development and training, be insured, and belong to a recognised membership organisation in order to practice.

The family mediation process

All family mediations start with an assessment meeting – MIAM, which can be joint or separate, as the clients prefer. At assessment the mediator hears the clients' story, checks if there has been domestic violence and if so whether it makes mediation unsuitable – this is a big subject on its own. The mediator also screens for child protection issues, as the one circumstance where confidentiality may be breached is to make a child protection referral. The mediator is assessing the issues to be resolved and whether the client has the capacity to mediate. They will explain the principles and process of mediation. Surprisingly, many clients still think mediation is about reconciliation, counselling and saving the marriage, but of course it is not. The mediator explains that clients can take legal advice, reflect and explore the practicalities of options between sessions.

Types of mediation and direct consultation with children

Family mediations are generally categorised into three types – children only, property and finance (where there are no children issues) and all issues. Some mediators specialise, for example, doing only children mediation, though most qualify as general family mediators. Some qualify to conduct direct consultation with children (DCC), which is two or three days' extra training combined with a CRB check at higher level.

Most children mediations consist of a mediator helping the couple to focus on their children and helping them to separate their own feelings from those of the children. Shared ground rules will often be set for co-parenting and often methods of communication may need to be mediated. For example, text messages if running late and a book going to and from with the child, setting out essential information for the other parent on handover, such as when medication was given, what children have eaten, lost, broken, etc. The mediator has to start where the parents are, then work with them to improve their situation with action plans between sessions and holding them to task.

Increasing numbers of children cases are now involving parents who have never lived together and often fathers who have had no relationship with the child from birth. The initial contact may often take place at a contact centre and may be supervised or supported at the centre. The mediator is starting from scratch, developing the parenting of two almost complete strangers. Some couples will move onto functional parenting relationships and need no further help, but many will constantly run into difficulties and return to mediation. Some couples may be in and out of mediation over a period of years – but those couples may otherwise have been in and out of court, becoming entrenched and implacable opponents. Mediation definitely anchors them in a better place and improves longer term outcomes for children.

Children often say they feel like parcels and nobody cares what they think. It's common for them to tell each parent what they want to hear, then the parents think the other parent is lying. It becomes clear in mediation that the children are appeasing the parents. So parents may wish to give their children the opportunity for their wishes and feelings to inform their decision-making via the mediator. Both parents have to consent to a Direct Consultation with Children (DCC) and the children have to want to come. If the children say anything is to be held confidential, then the mediator cannot feed it back. Children are mostly honest in their approach. The most common plea is that their parents stop arguing, and yes, they do usually say what they want, as it is what they have come for. It is best to forewarn parents that they may or may not like what the children say, but they should respect it if they can, as they have raised expectations by asking children to speak and ignoring them could be damaging to their relationship with them. Generally, DCC supports and restores children's relationships with their parents, where this is possible.

After the feedback session, parents can make decisions which reflect their children's wishes and feelings. The whole process is far less intrusive than a court application. It is also faster and cheaper. However, DCC only happens in a minority of cases and the LAA pays nothing extra for it despite the extra sessions and time taken. DCC it is a huge specialist topic on its own.

Property and financial mediations

The mediator is required to ensure full and frank financial disclosure prior to mediating. In practical terms this usually means giving the clients the court Form E (the financial disclosure form used in court proceedings) and asking them to complete this and to supply the same documentation, proving the value of all assets, liabilities and income, as they would provide for court. If the lawyers have already performed this task (not often) then the mediator can work with what has been done. The fact that financial disclosure is completed by one mediator at shared cost saves couples time and money. Normally the mediator prepares a joint asset schedule on the flipchart during the mediation, together with the clients. Frequently one party will have a lot more financial information than the other and one of the mediator's tasks is ensure that they have an equal understanding of their financial situation. Disclosure has to be full and complete and is 'open' even if mediation breaks down, so all of the documents and the Form E are transferred to the lawyers if it goes to court. Whilst mediation is not forensic, parties are able to ask each other questions and get answers and the mediator helps clients to get to the bottom of things. If an actuary's report is required to facilitate discussions on pension sharing, then it can be obtained on a joint instruction. An accountant can also be jointly instructed to calculate capital gains tax or the value of a company. Some mediators will want the lawyers or clients to organise these instructions and some mediators may help clients do it themselves. Family mediation needs similar information to any other resolution process – it's just faster and less adversarial.

The mediator will prepare an open financial statement (OFS) which is a full and clear summary of the basic family financial information, an asset schedule and information about their income. In most cases financial documents are attached to the OFS or have been shared between the parties during mediation. Once there is financial clarity based on the financial documents, then the mediator will start looking at options with the couple.

A competent mediator will refuse to proceed unless financial disclosure is complete. So, for example, if a policeman refuses to provide his pension information after a 20-year marriage, the mediator has to stop the mediation until he does, even if the wife is not asserting herself on the issue. This addresses power and information imbalances. The court won't approve settlements that are unfair or incomplete and so the mediator should not preside over such; it is unethical. Ideas will be challenged by the mediator and reality checked, then an action plan will be put together to help evaluate the options. For example, clients may be asked to find out what it will cost to re-house, what they can borrow on mortgage and what their new budget on a new home would be. There is a highly practical focus and the question asked most often is: 'How will it work for you both?' 'In this way focus is diverted from 'How much can I get for me?' to consideration of both parties' futures and the children. Thinking is less positional and impossible ideas are ruled out.

At the end of a successful mediation the mediator drafts a without prejudice, non-binding memorandum of understanding (MOU) setting out the proposals for settlement. This should include details of the agreement on all issues, so that the solicitors can advise and readily convert to a binding consent order for approval by the court on or after decree nisi of divorce, if the parties were married or in other cases a separation deed. Only at that point, once the consent order has been signed by the parties and approved by the court is there a binding unassailable agreement.

So a key distinction between family and civil mediation is the fact that in family mediation mediators do not hold confidential positions between the parties, all is open. Also, the outcome of a family mediation isn't binding at the end until the lawyers have made it so. This is an important protection for some vulnerable clients. The mediator should ensure the weaker party is not disadvantaged. However, the mediator is not outside the room; some couples are still living separately in the family home and some people will agree to anything. It is critical to the success of family mediation that there are safeguards in place to prevent unfair, unworkable and abusive mediation settlements being approved and becoming binding. The requirement for legal advice and lawyers to draw up the agreement is an important protection, as is the judge's scrutiny of the final agreement and rejection where appropriate. These important safety nets need to be retained, because families are not like civil disputants and more protection is required. It greatly assists the mediator to be able to say judges don't rubberstamp any old agreement. If that safeguard was breached, the floodgates could open to unfair unworkable agreements and this would bring mediation into disrepute. We must avoid that. There should be a fair settlement for both parties within the normal discretionary goal posts of a court adjudicated decision. It is important to ensure that mediation does not become a route to grave injustice and hardship.

The couple

The selection of couples for mediation is important. Some couples and cases are unsuitable for mediation. People have to have capacity to mediate, so, for example, people with serious mental health issues or addictions often do not have the capacity to mediate. If there has been systematic violence and one party is frightened of the other, mediation is probably unsuitable, though if the couple is living apart at undisclosed addresses and there are children – and mediation can be made safe – and if both parties wish to mediate and will agree to abide by the ground rules, then it may be very helpful. Indeed, the writer has been told by more than one battered wife, that they found mediation an empowering experience. The subject of screening and suitability is a big one and beyond the remit of this contribution, but by and large people who appear to have capacity and to want to sort matters out in mediation should usually be allowed to try it.

Managing the process of family mediation

The mediator has to manage the mediation at two levels. They carry out a practical functional management of the process such as collection of information and listening to the clients, working out what the issues are about, re-framing, challenging, reality testing – all the usual mediation skills. However, in family mediation especially, the mediator has to be aware of the sub-text of what is going on between the couple, as this will often have an impact on the mediation itself. For example, a couple may be locked into a 'crossed transaction'.[11] One of them may be a controlling/approving parent and the other might respond as an adaptive/rebellious child. This may be the pattern of communication established over many years and it can take over in mediation. The couple will only be able to mediate when in their adult state and the mediator will almost certainly have to separate them and shuttle between them in separate rooms to get them thinking as adults and make progress. Similarly, the mediator will need to have a working knowledge of neuro-linguistic programming (NLP). If one party seems to be programmed to do what the other tells them, with little sense of self-preservation, then again shuttle mediation may be needed. It is vital the mediator sits where they can see both faces and gauge reactions. They will see long before they hear when they need to intervene to head-off major meltdown. One person may light the other's blue touch-paper – the temptation may be irresistible – but once the adrenalin is released, reason is dispelled and the mediator will need to intervene quickly to prevent the process descending into chaos.

Shuttle mediation

Shuttle mediation is the norm for civil cases, but not in family cases. Everything in family mediation has to be shared and everything said has to be fed back, albeit in re-framed form, to ensure everyone remains fully and equally informed. Shuttle mediation normally takes longer, but sometimes little or no progress can be made when in the same room. The mediator must decide whether and how much to shuttle mediate. There is nothing more infuriating than a client insisting on shuttle mediation where there are children, and parental communication is 90 per cent of the problem.

---

11 See the seminal work on transactional analysis by Eric Berne, *Games People Play: The Psychology of Human Relationships* (Penguin, 2010).

Learning from Other Mediation Disciplines

Mediation at court

In about 2003, in Milton Keynes county court there were virtually no CAFCASS (Court Welfare) officers and private children cases were not progressing. At that time there were three mediation services offering legal aid in Milton Keynes and court asked them to set up a court rota to mediate first appointments of private law Children Act applications at court. The services ran in court mediation every week for over seven years. The number of welfare reports ordered fell dramatically, settlement rates increased; many cases were taken back to the services and mediated in a calmer environment. The court saw what mediation could do for parents and families – and the court. The mediators worked harmoniously with district judges and CAFCASS, but were only paid if a client was eligible for legal aid *and* produced an increasingly impossible level of proof of income rarely available at court, but required by the LSC as it then was. The scheme was not properly funded or viable. Services were then told that they could charge private clients at court – but no clients wanted to pay for mediation, as they had paid their court fee and often their lawyers too and although the mediator was doing the work at court, they did not want to pay them. Some people were avoiding pre-issue mediation, as it would be free at court! One service closed, another withdrew and by March 2013 the court found six months' funding to re-establish the 'pilot' when it continued to have the beneficial effects it had always had. The money ran out, and although in court mediation assessments and pilots have been started in many courts, they are foundering and stopping, as mediators are unable to work for nothing. These cases that could have been mediated make their sorrowful way through the courts, spending on CAFCASS reports increases and more contested cases proceed to trial – a false 'economy' that costs much more than mediation, if ever there was one.

Some of the cases mediated at court have been litigating on and off for years, with repeated court applications. Mediation can be transformative. Clients at court are usually highly emotional, stressed and very positional. However, the judges' homilies asking them to try mediation and handing the problem back to them, combined with the realisation that the opportunity for them to influence what happens is slipping out of their grasp, often helps them to mediate successfully, when they might not have done before.

Mediation at court can be extremely effective and the agreement to mediate is amended to allow a case summary to be placed on the court file. The case is often adjourned and re-listed for review to check if further help is needed and this will hold a recalcitrant party to task. Court mediation should be embedded and funded properly; the work is extremely hard and requires a very high skill level, but it is better for families and takes huge pressure off court resources.

The right time to mediate

There's no universal right time to mediate – it varies between couples and that is why referral should take place at different points before and during court proceedings. For some it will be pre-issue and that gives the greatest savings. For others the second party (respondent) may have no reason to participate, for example because they are sitting on all the assets or they have the children and the other party has nothing. Once court proceedings are under way is a better time to mediate those cases, as they then realise they do have to give ground or risk having it cut from underneath them

Facilitative mediation versus evaluative mediation

This debate will go on forever. Many mediators, particularly from a therapeutic non-legal background, will say the purity of mediation is imperilled by any form of evaluation. Realistically, with the demise of legal aid for family law and the tiny amount of legal aid available for advice during the course of mediation, many clients will be without legal advice or worse still one will be advised to the teeth and the other not at all. The mediator is charged with addressing power and information imbalances between clients and with giving legal information. Family mediators cannot mediate without giving clients information about the issues that have to be resolved and the background legal framework within which they are operating. The key here is in the preparation of clients at assessment, where the mediator explains that legal information has to be given and that it may or may not feel impartial, for example, the couple that came to mediation saying: 'We've agreed the pensions and the children – I'm having the pensions, she's having the children!' The mediator has to explain this is not a viable deal. Most couples know that this is ridiculous, but they get the point.

Also, many clients will be paying for mediation and will want a settlement that will work and pass judicial scrutiny, they can be rejected by judges and this is an important protection for vulnerable parties. So yes, family mediation can be quite evaluative and in the writer's opinion, necessarily so.

What civil and family mediation might learn from each other

The key lesson for civil mediation is that without compulsory referral points to hear about mediation from a mediator, there will be no significant growth in civil mediation. Despite the Jackson reforms, the CEDR Report of 2014 showed the rate of increase in mediation has slowed down. If the referral points do not exist or once they disappear – the number of mediations reduces dramatically and court applications increase. This equation is simple and has been borne out in family mediation over the years by every change in the rules about compulsory mediation assessment (or not) of disputants by a mediator. Why do people not choose mediation without compulsory assessment? Primarily because they don't know about it, think it won't work for them or believe court is the only answer, or are discouraged from attempting it by some lawyers who prefer clients to litigate. The comments of some clients in the 2007 National Audit Report and now after the 22 April 2014 changes mean that factor can simply be ignored no longer.

Civil and family mediators might with appropriate training consider using the other's model, so long as the clients make an informed choice and sign the right agreement to mediate. Mediators have become very inflexible about which model they use: whether confidences are held or not, whether it takes place in one day or over time, and whether the outcome is binding. The writer feels that in high conflict family cases the agreement really needs to be made binding on the day, as with civil mediation. Otherwise the couple's conflict re-asserts itself and so often the deal falls apart or another six months is spent salami-slicing via the lawyers. It's disturbing to hear from clients their cases are still not finally binding six or even twelve months after a family mediation ended, despite a mediated conclusion. For a binding agreement on the day their lawyers would need to be present as a protection for more vulnerable clients and to meet the family law conventions with regards to a binding agreement.

Civil mediators might usefully work with the family model in non-nuclear/couple family cases, such as probate cases. The civil model is exhausting and misses the opportunity for real movement between sessions as with the family model, where clients have time to reflect between sessions and outcomes often benefit from that. It really isn't always about the money. Relationships in families are often the problem – and dealing with the relationships in mediation is often part of the solution.

The grey area is Trustees of Land Act (TOLATA) cases – which are civil cases, but for unmarried couples with property disputes. The writer has used both models in such cases. If one client is legally aided, the conventional family model only can be used because of the LAA mediation quality mark requirements – but if the clients are both private the civil model works well too.

Conclusion

Family mediation has been shaped by its funding – by the LSC, now known as the LAA. It was legal aid referrals that made family mediation grow and the quality mark that specified how it would be done. It resulted in something clear and of a high standard, if unduly prescriptive and not adaptable to meet differing client needs. Civil mediation has not received the same financial impetus and has not grown significantly. There is more room for debate with civil mediation and for mediators to design their own accreditation and a detailed specification of how their process works, a regulatory framework and professional standards, but this may produce as many problems as it does opportunities. However, unless the take up of civil mediation is increased very substantially, there are not enough cases to train mediators on, or for them to prepare a portfolio for a qualifying assessment procedure or even to hone their skills. Only a small number of civil mediators can currently make a living at the work – contrast the vast numbers who litigate. Until this balance is shifted massively towards mediation, it will continue a minority activity by the privileged few and disputes will continue to go to court on auto-pilot and the court costs will often be the biggest issue by the end.

Our justice system should deal with all the disputants' motivations, legal, emotional and psychological. Until it does, lawyers and judges will continue to argue about the legal narrative of cases – while the parties often argue about what is important to them (their beliefs, feelings and principles) – even though none of that is dealt with at court or by the lawyers representing the parties. Mediation deals with the non-legal conflict and dispute drivers – and the writer's forecast is that in the near future common sense will have prevailed and we will have equality of status for legal and mediated resolutions for both family and civil cases, simply because this is an idea whose time is now long overdue. Disputants will have to hear about mediation from a mediator in civil cases as well as family cases. Then we can expect the shift towards the more balanced resolution system that any cost benefit analysis or common sense analysis of dispute resolution demands.

Workplace mediation

Clive Lewis OBE DL

The historical context

There has been a mood swing across organisations in the United Kingdom relating to how conflict and its related elements are managed. This has been developing for a number of years and can be particularly attributed to some notable happenings such as:

- more data about the costs associated with conflict;
- staff, line managers and HR professionals feeling increasingly stressed;
- companies' increasing accountability to shareholders;
- the spread of success stories relating to alternative dispute resolution;
- people's unwillingness to give a significant portion of their lives to conflict situations;
- a revised ACAS Code of Practice;
- rising legal fees;
- government encouragement; and
- most recently, the introduction of Employment Tribunal fees

The uptake of mediation and conflict resolution practices in the United Kingdom has been slow, although to date the public sector has picked it up much more quickly than the private sector. One of the possible reasons for this is, arguably, the willingness of some sections of the private sector to throw money at problems to make them go away through things such as compromise agreements. Whilst this provides a temporary reprieve, it is unlikely to unearth and provide a solution for what might be ingrained cultural issues within an organisation. There is also a high likelihood of damage, possibly worse than before, being sustained at some future stage. This method encourages the rewarding of poor management and systems, and in the most extreme cases leads to problems such as those faced by Enron in 2002. Documents show that at Enron, simply talking about what was going on was off limits. Organisations that fail to support open communications are doomed to fail. With the emergence of more and more data on the costs of conflict and the increased government focus on this area, organisations are likely to embrace conflict resolution strategies more swiftly over the next few years. Mediation is useful in a wide variety of conflicts, particularly in the aftermath of an incident when emotions have eased enough that the parties can begin to negotiate.

Few of us want to be in conflict or involved in some form of litigation procedure. Mediation is not intended to be positioned as the be all and end all of dispute resolution tools and it is just one of a number of alternative dispute resolution (ADR) options. It is however probably the most flexible. The human dimension of alternative dispute resolution is the real difference between ADR processes and traditional processes. It is mediation's response to the human dimensions of conflict that make it really special.[12]

Until recently, it has been the legal profession that has done the most to raise the profile and extol the virtues of mediation. In a commercial context, the use of mediation has grown phenomenally due to the pressure being put on established courts to adopt it as part of the reforms recommended some years ago by Lord Woolfe. These reforms mean that in many cases parties are being compelled to attempt mediation prior to going to trial.

---

12 A F Acland, *Resolving Disputes without Going to Court: A Consumer Guide to Alternative Dispute Resolution* (Company Business Books, 1995).

The organisational background

We can all learn something about how to manage conflict and relationships better. At the centre of all conflicts are human needs. People engage in conflict either because they have needs that are met by the conflict process or because they have (or believe they have) needs that are inconsistent with those of others.[13]

Until recently, the number of disputes being encountered in UK places of work was building at a staggering rate. Cases going to employment tribunal rose from under 50,000 in 1988 to a peak of 236,000 in 2009. This rate of increase has proven to be unsustainable with the numbers of new cases stagnating over the last few years. However, around 600,000 cases are lodged in the UK employment tribunal system at any one time. The introduction of employment tribunal fees in July 2013 should go some way to reducing the number of legal claims. In June, prior to the fees' introduction, new claims soared to 25,000; in August new claims plummeted to 7,000, and edged up to just 14,000 in September. The lasting impact of the fees remains to be seen, but the fact remains that the statutory dispute resolution system wasn't designed to cope with such high levels of fall out and is cracking under the pressure. The financial cost of our collective industrial relations failure is running to nearly £30 billion per year, with the cost to our health and emotions likely to be just as substantial. Something has to change. It is unlikely that the human race can go on living this way without running the risk of engendering some irreversible and irreparable damage at some point in the future. Thousands of working people are watching their lives slip by whilst conflict, turmoil, tension and anguish takes its toll.

Part of the impact of globalisation, the information age, constant change, higher unemployment, increasing longevity and employment legislation has been the proliferation in the complexity of issues related to managing the workforce. The world of work has changed beyond all recognition in the last 20 years, with the concept of a 'job for life' becoming redundant. The phrase 'work until you drop' is becoming much more prescient and multi-national workforces have become the norm. The United Kingdom, along with most other countries in the developed world, is still recovering from one of the worst periods of recession in the post-war era. The recovery period has brought uncertainty and paranoia as cuts, particularly in the public sector, start to bite. The tough economic conditions that developed towards the end of the first decade of the 21st century have brought:

- higher unemployment, with around 7.7 per cent of the UK working population out of work;
- more people claiming job seekers' allowance;
- a 220 per cent increase in the number of companies going bust; and
- a 19 per cent increase in the number of personal bankruptcies.

The combination of these aspects and others not listed is that the workplace is increasingly becoming an arena where employees arrive each morning weighed down with concerns about their families and loved ones. This also puts pressure on management level staff to become more attuned and aware of employees'

---

13   B Mayer, *The Dynamics of Conflict Resolution: A Practitioner's Guide* (Jossey-Bass Inc, 2000).

personal pressures, requiring increased levels of people skills and sensitivity in order to keep positive employee relations intact.

In recent times, there has been a shift in employee relations thinking across three eras.

The post-war era

The nation recognised the need to work collectively to rebuild the country's infrastructure and get the economy back on its feet. Most people acknowledged a sense of sharing responsibility in doing what was necessary to recover and recuperate from years of collateral damage. During this period, trade unions served their members well to protect employment rights and prevent manipulation and exploitation as businesses competed for market share or greater efficiencies.

Political and economic change of the 1980s and beyond

The Government worked hard and fast to promote capitalism and secure Britain's future as a major player on the global economic field. We began to see a rise in collective disputes and the Government clashed with unions as it tried to pursue change quicker and faster. As privatisation emerged, we saw employees revolt where executives were awarded double digit increases in remuneration packages. At the same time, the impact of European legislation began to come forth with the signing of the Maastricht Treaty, which opened the floodgates for numerous types of employment rights.

Post-recession period

We are now witnessing the effects of the increases in both individual and collective rights. Again, there is a need to help get the United Kingdom back on its feet, but this time the war we are recovering from is one based on the collapse of the financial markets and loss of confidence. We are living and working in a period not only created by the recession but tested by it. One of the ways employees are coping is to accept short-term sacrifices in return for long term security. Periods of austerity bring with them a reduction or absence of choices for many people. As psychologist Abraham Maslow postulated, we must first attempt to satisfy survival-based physiological needs, and only afterwards do we seem to satisfy higher level personal and social needs, such as aesthetics and self-fulfilment.

In order to surface successfully from this current period the labour market must pursue employee relations strategies based on:

- consensus rather than conflict;
- developing positive attitudes towards change;
- building transparency, communication, honesty and reliability;
- encouraging openness from line managers;
- a willingness to promote employee flexibility;
- clearing the way for the employee voice to be heard; and
- promoting a fair balance between employees, trade unions and employers;

It is not possible to simply mandate good employee relations. To support the above it will also be important to develop a legal framework where the law and market work in harmony and common sense solutions are favoured.

Why mediation in the workplace works

Mediation works because, unlike other dispute resolution processes, it fully addresses emotional needs. Whilst the opportunity might be given to discuss aspects such as injury to feelings in the litigation or grievance process, the opportunity is rarely given for the disputing parties to discuss emotional issues in detail with each other. In an Employment Tribunal, for example, where the employee wins the tribunal claim, although a judgment may take account of the emotional effect that the dispute has had on someone, such as injury to feelings, it is unlikely to result in full closure for the 'winner'. Issues probably still exist between them and their former employer about how they felt as a result of the way they were treated.

Workplace or employment mediation?

Often these two terms are used interchangeably for mediating disputes at work. The two terms, however, have different meanings:

- Workplace mediation refers to a dispute where, at the commencement of the mediation, there is an ongoing working relationship between the parties.
- Employment mediation refers to a dispute where, at the commencement of the mediation, the working relationship between the parties is in the past.

It is important to note however that workplace mediation could also turn into an employment mediation midway through the process. This would happen as a result of one or more parties' indicating a desire to sever the working relationship and seeking to negotiate mutually agreeable terms for settlement.

The difference is important to note as there are some issues a mediator will experience when conducting an employment mediation that they may not experience when undertaking a workplace or internal mediation. Three examples of this are interaction with lawyers or other representatives, issues about legal costs and arrangements for a party leaving an organisation as part of a settlement. In employment mediation cases, the mediation commissioner is much more likely to be an employment lawyer.

Employment mediation is often more commercially focused and leans more towards negotiation. The mediator will have to work with both the parties and their legal representatives, and will have to understand issues around potential compensation. When reality checking, the mediator may also refer to case law. Arrangements for compromise agreements to be drafted and signed off will also have to be made.

In workplace mediation there is much more of a requirement to work with people's emotions and consider potential cultural issues for the organisation. Mediators will often have to display large amounts of patience when dealing with the parties and will also have to think about potential flaws in the organisational structure that may have led or contributed to the dispute in the first place. In this sense, the mediator can also become a trusted adviser to the organisation.

The business case for workplace mediation

Intractable conflict is depicted as a zero-sum conflict, which is exhausting and costly in human and material terms.[14]

Conflict costs money. Costs might be seen through the impact on management time, poor health, a breakdown in customer relationships leading to a loss in revenue, or projects running over time and budget. Some reading this text may have the impression that mediation and other conflict resolution tools are soft and fluffy. Nothing could be further from the truth. Mediation sessions are tough, but have measureable business benefits. Below I provide some solid examples that I hope will help demonstrate the business case for conflict resolution principles.

A survey conducted several years ago by the American Management Association, responded to by 258 managers, including 116 chief executive offices, 76 vice-presidents and 66 middle managers, indicated that they spent 24 per cent of their time resolving conflicts. Applied to the United Kingdom and assuming an average base salary of £70,000 per manager, this translates to £16,800 per individual per year and over £4m per year for the whole group. There are, of course, many additional costs outside of base salary, such as lost revenue, lost bonus, employee turnover, management time, sickness and absence costs, impact on customer service and so on. Whichever way the maths is done, conflict is expensive.[15]

In another study of 1600 employees it was found that:

- 22 per cent of employees said they had actually decreased their work efforts as a result of the conflict;
- Over 50 per cent reported that they lost work time because they worried about whether the instigator of the conflict would do it again; and
- 12 per cent reported that they changed jobs in order to get away from the instigator.

There are examples of organisations that have realised significant cost savings by the strategic management of conflict resolution. Most data on this topic is US based, but it transfers well so it is worth using. Karl Slaikeu and Ralph Hasson, in *Controlling the Costs of Conflict*, list these examples:

- In the first year of comparison, Brown and Root reported an 80 per cent reduction in outside litigation expenses by introducing a systematic approach to collaboration and conflict resolution regarding employment issues.
- Motorola Corporation reported a reduction in outside litigation expenses of up to 75 per cent per year over six years by using a systematic approach to conflict management in its legal department and including a mediation clause in its contracts with suppliers.
- National Cash Register Corporation reported a reduction in outside litigation expenses of 50 per cent and a drop in its number of pending lawsuits from 263 to 28 between 1984 and 1993 following the systematic use of alternative dispute resolution.

---

14 E Newman and O Richmond (Eds) *Challenges to Peacebuilding: Managing Spoilers During Conflict Resolution* (United Nations University Press, 2006).
15 K W Thomas and W H Schmidt 'A Survey of Managerial Interests with Respect to Conflict' (1976) 19(2) The Academy of Management Journal 315.

- The US Air Force reported that by taking a collaborative approach to conflict management in a construction project, it completed the project 144 days ahead of schedule and $12m under budget.[16]

The business case for dispute resolution methods in the workplace is sound and is gradually becoming underpinned by more and more evidence. An additional benefit of mediation is that people who voluntarily settle their cases are less likely to return to court or initiate additional actions.[17]

As change continues to be a constant, all companies will need to address the structures that keep the organisation on its feet. Ken Cloke refers to the sounds that are made by the cracks in organisational systems. The challenge to line managers and HR professionals is to hear these cracks as they develop and not to have selective hearing or become tone deaf with the application of appropriate solutions. For example, an organisation may be aware of a department leader who may cause relationship breakdowns amongst some colleagues. The response the organisation may take is to undertake an organisational restructure to try and fix the problem. Whilst this might address the issue of personality clashes, a bigger problem may emerge. This could be that the organisation now has a weaker structure to deliver against its corporate objectives. The perpetrator may also leave after some time, exposing the weakness in the fudged organisation structure. Although sometimes harder, it is always better to concentrate on the primary needs of the organisation rather than fit personalities into boxes. It may take time, money, energy and effort to resolve conflicts, but it takes much more time, money, energy and effort not to resolve them.

Cost savings that organisations can derive from strategic conflict resolution programmes probably represent the biggest current untapped opportunity for competitive advantage and organisational effectiveness.

Return on investment

In a period where organisations are thinking of creative ways to save money, commissioning mediation is a great investment. The table below highlights the areas impacted when conflict exists.

Conflict impact areas	
Increases	**Decreases**
• Customer complaints	• Productivity
• Employee turnover	• Project delivery
• Sickness	• Employee attraction
• Absence	• Employee engagement
• Legal fees	• Health and well-being
• Risk	• Certainty

---

16 K A Slaikeu and R H Hasson *Controlling the Costs of Conflict: How to Design a System for Your Organization* (Jossey-Bass Inc, 1998).
17 J Pearson, P Munson and N Thoennes 'Legal Change and Child Custody Awards' (1982) 3(1) Journal of Family Issues 5.

I have a few thoughts on why the mediation and conflict resolution industry has failed to persuade business leaders on the business case for conflict resolution at work and why there continues to be a degree of reluctance. Here are some of them:

- It can be easy to ignore, avoid or simply put off dealing with conflict. It is one of those matters that require a large amount of energy and effort to deal with. It is often much more convenient to do something else.
- Acknowledging that conflict is present can be seen as recognition of failure. Few people, if any, want to be associated with failure.
- Some problems can go away quickly if you throw money at them. This is far easier to do in the private sector and probably explains why the public sector accounts for around 75 per cent of revenue related to the workplace mediation market. It also probably demonstrates why 75 per cent of disputes going to employment tribunals are linked to the private sector.
- There is a lack of understanding in the boardroom about how the impact of conflict affects the bottom line.
- Conflict situations are not always identified as a risk and included in the risk register alongside issues such as health and safety.

The table below begins to show how the tool of mediation can be utilised at both operational and strategic levels.

Mediation at the operational and strategic level	
Operational level	**Strategic level**
• Solves disputes • Gives line managers their time back • Improves customer service • Reduces absence • Improves team work • Focuses on wealth creation, productivity	• Helps organisational learning • Helps form succession planning • Improves productivity savings • Increases the likelihood of achieving organisation objectives • Enhances competitiveness • Improves employee engagement • Improves organisational health and well-being • Can be linked to operational and financial reviews • Compelling business case for corporate and social responsibility • Reduces business risk

Tension exists at board level too. It can be a prerequisite that part of the criteria for becoming a boardroom member is that individuals aren't reticent in coming forward. The added dimension about conflict in the boardroom is that it can spill over and affect various parts of the organisation. For example, if team members get wind of the fact that their boss is engaged in conflict with a colleague it can mean that they take sides with their leader. In extreme cases, silos may develop as whole functions may refuse to collaborate with each other out of a sense of loyalty. At board level, there are so many exciting developments that can happen linked to managing conflict, for example the summarisation of the outputs of a year of mediation cases could be used as a framework for organisation learning. Conflicts mark the frontiers, the places where we weaken and divide. Yet these same frontiers embody the forces that transform us and dissipate our differences. Conflicts probe both our innermost natures and the outermost limits of our being. They provoke cruelty and compassion, competition and collaboration, revenge and reconciliation. Mediation is the *dangerous magic* that helps us move from one to the other.[18]

Case study

Pursar Technologies is a FTSE 250 global business. A dispute had developed between its marketing director, customer service director and chief technology officer regarding an email sent by the customer service director to the chief executive with a proposal on direction for the company. The marketing director and chief technology officer were also copied in to the email. The marketing director replied to all parties asking the customer service director to explain why he had proposed an idea about how the company should be adjusting its marketing strategy without discussing it with him first. The situation was then made worse when the chief technology officer indicated that he wanted to adopt an alternative marketing strategy to the other two. There followed a big falling out, which the chief executive decided was best left to the three of them to sort out.

This decision backfired, and eventually relations became so strained between the three that not only did they stop talking to each other but also stopped making joint visits to customers and collaborating on organisational initiatives. Customers then began to be negatively impacted by this turn of events and the sales pipeline started to slow down. Three months of this led to the chief executive realising that something needed to be done and engaged the services of a mediator. The mediator was locked in a room with the three executives for three hours and by the time the parties emerged they had agreed to put the dispute behind them. Apologies had been exchanged and it was back to business as usual. The chief executive was astonished that three months of stand-off could be settled with a three-hour conversation. He also realised that the organisation had paid a huge price for pontificating over a dispute that could have been settled as soon as the original email had been sent.

Mediation in this instance, as with many, served a double purpose. Not only did it achieve its direct aim of getting the senior executives talking again but it also had a knock-on effect of allowing them to build organisational capability, reduce organisational risk and increase competitive advantage. Mediation in any organisation is unlikely to be highly successful unless members of the board understand its benefits and are willing to engage in mediation themselves when trouble strikes.

---

18   K Cloke, *Mediating Dangerously: The Frontiers of Conflict Resolution* (Jossey-Bass Inc, 2001).

The future of mediation at work

Human conflict – from family feuds to labour strikes, to international warfare – is an ever-present and universal social problem, and the methods to manage it are a challenge for everyone.[19] We are living in an interesting period. As I write (2014), for the first time in 70 years the United Kingdom has a peacetime coalition government. As an observer, this seems to be presenting both challenges and learning opportunities for comrades on the front and back benches. Those that once traded blows from opposite sides of the House are now forced to work together collaboratively and jointly in the nation's interest. This agreement is symbolic of a new beginning in so many ways. It shows how previous enemies can work on putting their past battles behind them (or at least to one side) and shows what can happen when there are shared interests at stake. In the transformative mediation process, parties can recapture their sense of competence and connection, reverse the negative conflict cycle, re-establish a constructive (or at least neutral) interaction, and move forward on a positive footing, with the mediator's help.[20]

Successful political decision-making and conflict resolution requires speech over silence, collaboration over aggression and creative contention over accommodation. Dr Martin Luther King Jr said: 'Our lives begin to end the day we become silent about things that matter.' A working premise of mediation is that disputing parties have a connection with each other on some level. In business disputes where it is likely that there will be some form of ongoing relationship the injured party/ies want some acknowledgement of their suffering. A good mediator will instinctively know the right sort of questions to ask to bring the parties closer together. The political landscape provides an interesting philosophical backdrop for the implied direction the rest country should be taking.[21]

Mediation has the ability to touch on both the strategic and operational, the transformational and the transactional machinery of government at both the macro and micro levels. Mediation can have a far-reaching impact to help the UK economy get back on its feet following one of the worst periods of recession for many years. The business case is compelling.

As government cuts start to bite and organisations seek new pragmatic ways to solve problems and strengthen relationships, mediation has the potential to perform on the national stage.

The types of areas in which mediation can make an impact are:

- taking on a major role in restorative justice;
- helping organisations mitigate and reduce risk in line with the David Walker's report to government;
- helping to lower insurance premiums when mediation provision is in place;
- supporting the government's initiative to measure general wellbeing;

---

19 O J Bartos and P Wehr *Using Conflict Theory* (Cambridge University Press, 2002).
20 R A Baroch Bush and J P Folger *The Promise of Mediation: The Transformative Approach* (Jossey-Bass Inc, 2005).
21 D Bowling and D Hoffman (Eds) *Bringing Peace into the Room: How the Personal Qualities of the Mediator Impact the Process of Conflict Resolution* (Jossey-Bass Inc, 2003).

- helping the Coalition to find it easier to work together;
- facilitating conflict resolution principles across the political spectrum;
- supporting the Government's plan to overhaul employments laws as part of the employers charter;
- improving the nation's health and wellbeing in line with the publication of the Health report led by Dame Carol Black;
- increasing UK skill and key competency levels;
- supporting the UK's objective to secure its place as a leading global player by 2020 in line with the Leitch report;
- increasing the engagement levels of employees across the nation in line with the McLeod Report;
- increasing trust;
- helping to reduce the 175 million working days lost every year to sickness;
- helping to reduce the £1.7bn annual cost of absence in the NHS;
- proactively managing the employee relations issues that will surface with the removal of the default retirement age;
- supporting the Office for Equalities predicted increase in tribunal cases that arise as a result of the introduction of the Equality Act;
- providing a method to manage disputes that emerge following the proposed increase in claims for unfair dismissal rising from one to two years;
- becoming a major tool for the potential increase in class action cases;
- helping to stem the flow of the 25 per cent year on year increase in legal fees leading to an average of £5.8m being spent by every major employer each year; and
- helping small businesses with limited cash flow find a quicker and cheaper alternative to litigation.

Peer mediation in schools

David Richbell with Chris Seaton (Peaceworks)

I think one of the greatest areas of mediation work is in schools mediation. Teaching children to resolve conflict in a non-violent way must be one of the best legacies for the next generation and could change the world. Peaceworks has been involved in this area for a decade, working in over 90 schools, training hundreds of teachers and thousands of children and young people. Chris gave me permission to take the following extracts from the Peaceworks High School Peer Mediation Coordinator's Manual (DR)

Peer Mediation is a tool that can be used to address conflict situations if the people involved are willing to engage with it. It is one form of conflict resolution and not necessarily the right one for every conflict. In both primary and secondary schools, peer mediators are trained to deal with low-level conflicts such as playground squabbles. More complex situations such as those involving violence or involving issues that started outside the school environment are not suitable for this level of intervention.

A team of volunteer peer mediators or peer supporters are trained and supported and are available on the school playground and around the school to offer interventions in low-level conflicts that may occur. In our experience, the lunchtime break is the one where most conflicts occur and it is best to start the team operating at this time. Students should not be asked to be on duty for more than one session a week and should not be expected to mediate students older than themselves. It cannot be emphasised enough that mediation is a voluntary process and peer mediators should be encouraged to volunteer for this position and not appointed. Also those taking part in the mediation should only do so on a voluntary basis. Lastly, peer mediators must be reminded in their training that they cannot mediate their best friends or their siblings, as impartiality is impossible in this situation.

We have found that the most effective teams will in some form be 'student-led'. This may involve them having had some input into the formation of the service such as the name of the team, how they are to be identified and how they are to make themselves known to the rest of the school. They will take responsibility for being in the right place at the right time with the right resources and also supporting peer evaluation of the service. The school has the responsibility for providing adequate training and on-going support and for keeping the profile of the team high among the adults in the school so that the service is well used. A teacher or school leader also needs to be accessible should the peer mediators come across any issues of a safeguarding or criminal nature or which are causing the peer mediators any other concerns.

A peer mediator can be anyone who is willing to undertake training in mediation skills and to make a commitment to taking responsibility for conflicts and their resolution in constructive ways. We have trained primary school children from as young as six years old through to university undergraduates and beyond in a simple mediation process. This process focuses on the needs and priorities of the disputants and empowers them to manage the outcomes of their own disputes. The by-product of this commitment to training and participation in an on-going peer mediation programme will usually be:

- improved communication skills;
- increased ability to cooperate with others;
- improved relationships and self-esteem;
- positive behaviour patterns;
- self-discipline and the positive management of emotions.

At the heart of conflict resolution is the premise that conflict is an integral and normal part of life and learning. The absence of conflict does not necessarily indicate a vibrant, creative, learning environment. The eclectic mix of human beings of many different personality types, cultural belief systems and backgrounds within school communities almost necessitates conflict as ideas and ways of doing things find a workable common level. Thus, schools that insist they have no conflict or bullying may well be unable to view what is certainly going on below the radar.

Conflict can be described as, a difference, which impacts people in a significant way by challenging a perceived need or belief system.

Within school communities this can be present in the minutia of playground squabbles right through to policy-making decisions affecting the future of the organisation itself. How adults manage conflict will no doubt be reflected in how pupils manage their own conflicts. A hierarchical system which imposes sanctions and directions from the main power brokers in the organisation, whilst ensuring the smooth running of the school community, will not necessarily equip young people to manage their own conflicts in a creative and pro-active way.

Training young people in the skills of conflict resolution is one step on this journey, but our experience within many school communities has demonstrated that this alone is not sufficient to make a difference. We make the case for training across the whole school community for peer mediation schemes to become effective and a real resource for schools.

In the secondary school sector, different models of introducing peer mediation have been used. These include small-scale or taster approaches that just involve training a small group of selected students in the relevant skills to help their peers. However the gold standard is usually accepted to be the whole school approach, which is the norm when we work with primary schools. This approach involves the whole school community – teachers, support staff, governors and parents – in learning the basic concepts of conflict resolution and mediation, as well as students throughout the school community. This enables the culture of the school's management of conflict to reflect the principles that the students are being taught to model.

In secondary schools peer mediation is more commonly introduced as part of a wider curriculum of conflict resolution. Different agencies have approached peer mediation training in different ways but all with the same aim, to teach children and young people how to resolve conflict by using basic mediation skills and taking on board the concepts of making healthy choices about the future rather than appropriating blame for the past.

Some schools have taken the non-retributive approach to conflict further and have incorporated the concepts into behaviour management and disciplinary policies. Thus peer mediation is sometimes framed as one of a number of 'restorative practices' used in schools. These sometimes include restorative justice conferences, where victims and offenders are brought round a table with others affected by the conflict and behaviour. A skilled conference facilitator seeks to enable all parties to participate and find resolution, closure or healing from an issue arising from poor behaviour or conflict. There is much work still to be done in researching the impact and value of peer mediation but several studies demonstrate the positive effects of well run and thought through peer mediation programmes. These studies demonstrate that where the key ingredients of adequate training, a culture of cooperation and empowerment, sufficient time and resources and on-going mentoring and support are in place, such schemes lead to more peaceful playgrounds and the impartation of key life skills in the area of conflict resolution.

The Peaceworks programme introduces three core skills at the heart of the curriculum inputs. These are:

- active listening – a key listening skill;
- i-messaging – a key communication skill; and
- brainstorming – a solution-focused problem-solving skill.

The premise is that by introducing simple, transferable skills to students to be used in a disciplined format, the work of peer mediation can be easily sustained. We have deliberately chosen to focus on three areas where we all need to shape when we are trying to manage conflicts well: the listening, the speaking and communication and the problem solving.

The mediation process is distilled into four simple steps for young peer mediators. They are encouraged to set the scene and lay down some ground rules then take students through:

A. Ask for the story – the story-telling stage with each story reflected back by the mediator.

B. Brainstorm some solutions – get input from the parties on how to solve it.

C. Choose the best one – evaluate the ideas and put a package together.

D. Do it – close the session and everyone confirms what they are going to do..

In summary, peer mediation involves the use of key mediation skills that are common to all mediation processes. It is usually done with co-mediators who are older than those involved in the conflict. It involves quite specific training and requires a greater network of support than adult mediation. As with community mediation, its spread is hampered by lack of funding and inconsistent recognition of its' true value by the relevant authorities. Where it has been adopted the results have been truly amazing.

Storytelling

Geoffrey Corry

I first came across the concept of storytelling in the late 1980s when Ron Kraybill of the Mennonite Conciliation came to Dublin to talk about community mediation centres in the United States.[22] He named storytelling as the second stage of the mediation process in stark contrast to data gathering, the term used by Haynes.[23] Coming from a southern Irish relational culture where the art of telling your story – the *scéil* – is part of everyday life in the family, the shop, at work and in the pub, it just struck me as making eminent sense that people in conflict need to be able to tell their story to the other about what happened in the incident(s), what they experienced, their memory of the event and how they are seeing it now with the benefit of hindsight.

---

22 Ronald S Kraybill, *Repairing the Breach: Ministering in Community Conflict* (Herald Press, 1980).
23 John M Haynes, Gretchen L Haynes and Larry Fong, *Mediation: Positive Conflict Management* (SUNY, 2004).

Learning from Other Mediation Disciplines

Diagram 1: The Storytelling Mediation Process

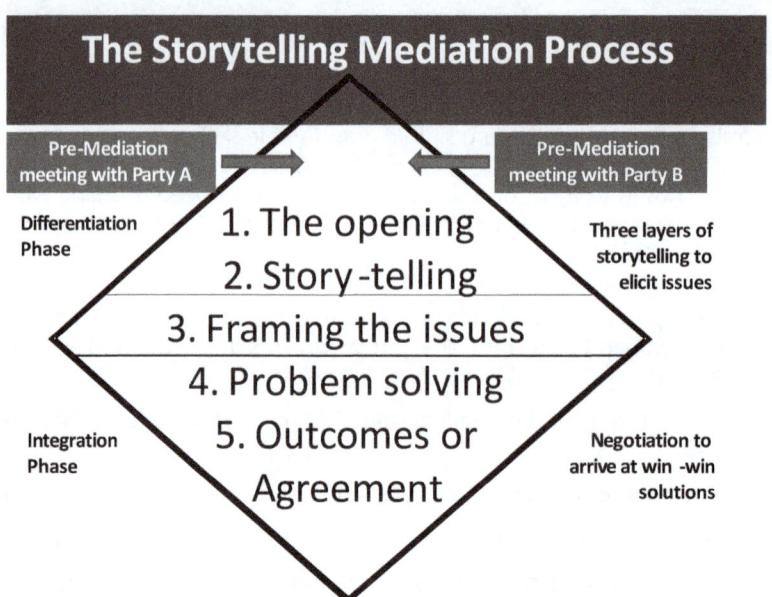

The story probably is not the whole truth but embedded in the 'narrative truth' is the stuff of what matters to them. Dismissing it as spin or a rehearsed story is profoundly disrespectful and undermines the building of a relationship of trust between the mediator and the disputant. If it is a 'saturated story' as named by narrative mediation,[24] then we need to be ready as facilitators to hold the dripping sponge before us and let the water pour out in the presence of the other at the same time as having a go at dissolving the toxicity.

If the shuttle go-between is the essence of 'normal' facilitative mediation, then managing the telling and hearing of the story in a face-to-face interactive process in the joint session is the essence of storytelling. It is not like a tribunal where the story is told uninterrupted but is heard in bite sizes as disputants take turns in revealing the layers of each of their stories.

Known for their tradition of talking circles, the indigenous American Indians have a saying: 'You talk and talk and then the talk begins' (Ellinor and Gerard 1998). This dynamic of three layers of talking needs to be held in tension with: 'You listen and listen and then the listening begins'. Diagram 2 below attempts to visualise this positive talking and listening process, a kind of DNA helix dialogue process with its own integrity, if only we could discover its internal properties! My mediation experience points to three layers of a virtuous cycle from estranged misunderstanding to mutual understanding.

Layer 1 When disputants open up, it can go very fast and all the issues come out in rapid succession. Many generalisations are made and much blaming occurs. The task of the mediator is to listen, reflect back what they have heard, acknowledge the emotional content and reframe the toxicity.

---

24 John Winslade and Gerald Monk, Narrative Mediation: *A New Approach to Conflict Resolution* (Jossey-Bass, 2000).

Diagram 2: The DNA of storytelling

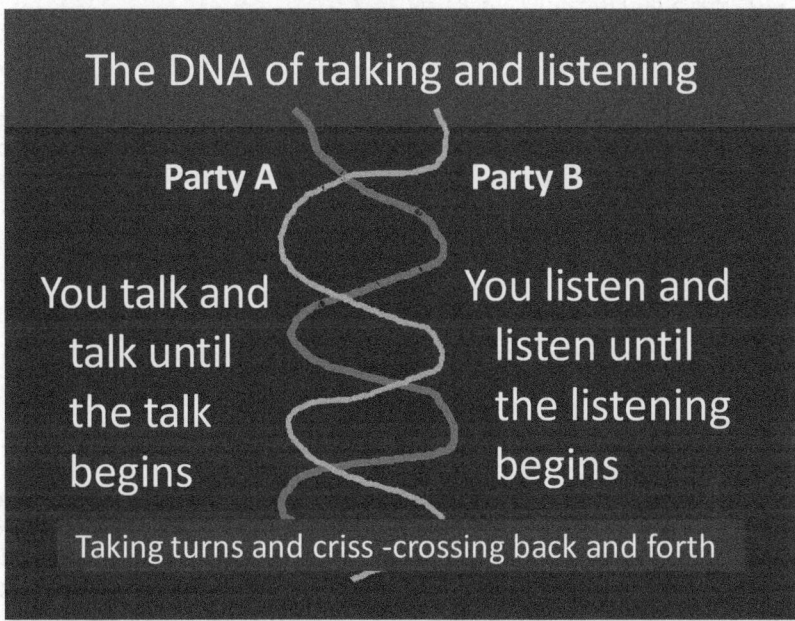

Layer 2 Each disputant takes turns in talking and hearing about what happened in the different incidents. It takes time and patience for each to talk it out fully until they feel heard and understood, first by the mediator and then by the other disputant. It is amazing when someone has the courage to speak personally of their own experience, with all of the emotion expressed and acknowledged, how it opens up the space for themselves and for others.

The mediator's task is to acknowledge the efforts made by each party in telling their story and to help them to name the bits they want heard and understood. When a party says the same thing a second or third time, the instinctive reaction of the facilitator is to wish they would stop repeating themselves. However, this is actually a cue telling you that's the bit they want heard! Once it is heard, acknowledged and understood, the person is likely to move on. By drawing the hot emotion, frustration, annoyance and anger to yourself as facilitator through reflective listening, you can ensure the attack does not land on the other party. This party-to-facilitator dialogue is crucial for de-escalation and pre-empting a possible walkout.

Layer 3 The breakthrough into layer three comes as party-to-party dialogue gets off the ground and one party reaches out beyond their own suffering to engage the other so as to really talk it through. You can see it coming when one party actually shifts in their seat and turns their body to hear the other, asks them a question or responds reflectively to a point already made. Weingarten identifies it as the point when one party is able to listen carefully to the other without defensiveness.[25] For Bush and Folger, it is the moment of recognition 'of *letting go* – however briefly or partially – of one's focus on self and becoming interested in the perspective of the

---

25   Kaethe Weingarten, *Common Shock: Witnessing Violence Every Day: How we are harmed, How we can heal* (Dutton, 2003).

other party'.[26] The disputant is no longer using the moment to score points but wants to understand the other's perspective.

At this moment, the mediator needs to step back from controlling the dialogue and pass it back to the disputants to work with the difficult questions they want to ask of the other that have been going around in their mind for some time. The use of bilateral questions can help to consolidate new party-to-party understandings and insights:

- What do you think Ann does not yet fully understand about your situation?
- Which bit does James not yet fully appreciate?

These relational transactions create the platform for humanisation and open the door to forgiveness and apology. Disputants regain their self-respect: 'We are now meeting each other at an equal level.'

The storytelling process changes the perceptions of the other and allows disputants to see the situation differently: that the conflict has multiple truths and not as fixed as once perceived. It is unclear the chemistry of these change moments and whether the relational change comes about by the cognitive or the affective. Does a person's thinking change by *affective empathy* when they have been touched by the emotion in the other's story: 'I am feeling what it must have been like for you.'? Or does a person feel warmer towards another when they have understood in some new way (through *cognitive empathy*) what the other is saying: 'I can understand better why you had to take that course of action.'? Maybe it is contingent on personal style and whether a person is mainly a left-brain logical thinker or has a right-brain relational capacity.

In conclusion, for effective mediators, it may not be a question of choosing either shuttle mediation or storytelling as your preferred approach but rather that we are equally proficient in both processes. Hybrid process models that combine both elements are a possible way forward.

Mediating in faith communities

David Richbell with Zaza Elsheikh

Introduction

Before identifying what faith community mediation has to offer commercial mediators, it is worth noting the main differences to 'conventional' commercial mediation, typically:

- Usually everyone involved has the certainty of being right because their faith (or their interpretation of their faith) tell them so.
- So, being challenged by a different faith (or different interpretation of their faith), it becomes a threat that their faith is being challenged.

---

26 Robert A Baruch Bush and Joseph P Folger, *The Promise of Mediation: The Transformative Approach to Conflict* (Jossey-Bass, 2005).

- There are a large numbers of diverse views and positions because most people have a personal belief.
- Often those views can seem to be completely irrational to an objective 'outsider'.
- The needs of the wider faith community invariably impact on the outcome.
- There is a need for keeping face and reaching agreements with dignity (although that applies to most commercial mediations as well).
- It is difficult being peacemakers in their own community.
- Because of all the above, time and many meetings are needed because they are never sorted in a day.
- Being paid a fee is very unlikely!

Many of these are dealt with in more detail later.

Most of the major religious faiths in the world have a teaching of peacemaking and reconciliation. The irony is also that many, if not most, major conflicts in the world have been 'justified' by differences in religious belief, notwithstanding that peace and love for others are their cornerstones. Because of this, faith disputes are more challenging than relatively monochromatic secular disputes.

Issues commonly in dispute

The issues in dispute involve the most deep-seated internal conflicts about spiritual versus secular identity, the search and right to justice, attribution of blame (and forgiveness), and ultimately drafting a settlement where the overriding objective is that all the terms must be face-saving and faith-preserving. Needless to say, they are invariably highly emotional because a party's religious belief is often associated with an uncompromising sense of identity, belonging, security and immortality.

Many of the common areas of dispute in commercial mediations are to be found in faith community disputes:

- Governance: Allegations of abuse of power or lack of transparency about distribution of charitable funds by their leaders. Disagreements between Trustees and Management bodies.
- Property: Ownership and disposal of property, particularly following schism within the community. Dissolution of partnership assets is a common feature too.
- Business relationships, particularly family businesses: Breakdown of relationships, dependence on unwritten agreements and the basis of trading and funding.
- Personal: Polarising of the community following breakdown of relationships, particularly involving the faith leader and/or other officers.
- Workplace: Dysfunctional team dynamics, exacerbated by differences in attitudes, behaviours and interpretation of scriptural directives about worship. Polarisation and isolation within a group can lead to a rift spreading throughout the community.

Issues behind the disputes

There are some issues that are particularly specific to faith mediation:

- Orthodoxy and liberal: Often the challenge to what is traditional and the wish to 'progress' and 'modernise'. In commercial disputes this may be reflected more in regulation and authorities than parent organisations or communities.

- Prayer and process: Depending on the wishes of the parties in the mediation, some religious observance, including prayer, may well be included in the mediation process.

- Outcomes: 'Success' is not always easy to measure. Reopening fractured lines of communication may in itself be a success.

- Consensus-building: Very often much of the preparation in faith disputes is finding commonality in diverse groupings so that crowd control becomes manageable and productive.

- Seniority: Not necessarily 'authority'. Traditions in various ethnic groups often dictate that those who lead are not necessarily the ones who make the decisions. In faith groups that can be even more pronounced as religious seniority may hold sway over the parties who are in dispute.

- Time: Most disputes in and between faith groups take months, and many meetings, to resolve. The actual mediation process is likely to be designed specifically to suit the dispute and the people involved. Preparing people for the mediation often takes a long time. Indeed, parties may not even know that they need mediation, let alone what it actually is!

Expectations and needs

It is ironic that few faith communities have a tradition of mediation either within or between communities. Most deal with disputes either by ignoring them or resorting to a form of adjudication (whether that be arbitration or judgment). It is not surprising then that many faith disputes end up with a med-arb process, so that the parties are able to compromise without fearing reprehension or disappointment about the terms of settlement by the group they are representing at the mediation. Indeed, authority to settle may be an issue. Actually identifying who the parties are in the dispute and then ensuring that they have the authority to settle on behalf of the larger community (or groups within it) can in itself be a time-consuming challenge for the mediator. Any settlement that is reached generally must have regard to preserving the dignity of the disputants (which is often why the parties have chosen to mediate rather than litigate).

Choice of mediator

Co-mediation is by far the best route for helping parties to resolve disputes in faith communities. That usually means at least one mediator from the relevant faith background (although this may be a challenge, given the many sects and groupings within most faiths), and a co-mediator, probably of a different gender and offering a different perspective. However, some parties insist on mediators from their own faith, probably in the belief that their community problems should stay within their community or just that their problems will be more readily understood. The fact

Learning from Other Mediation Disciplines

that the whole mediation process is confidential, regardless of who mediates, is often not fully appreciated or understood by all parties.

In many cases the mediator will need to be familiar with all the relevant doctrinal sources (which the parties will readily provide) as well as the historical background of the matters in dispute. Although a good mediator will no doubt be sensitive to the parties, their beliefs and the sensitivity of the dispute, faith mediation can be a minefield for those unfamiliar with the principles, beliefs and customs of a particular religion. It can be a minefield even for those of the particular religion!

On some occasions and in some communities, if settlement cannot be reached or the parties prefer to have a declaratory award to be written rather than an agreement reached through compromise, a pre-agreed and separate individual replaces the mediator and acts as arbitrator.

The mediation process

The mediator may well have to design and adapt the mediation process to suit the circumstances. It is rare for such disputes to be resolved in a day; indeed it may take many weeks and many meetings just to prepare for the mediation proper. This may be to help people move to a psychological state where they enter into mediation with realistic expectations of what is required of them and what the possible outcomes may be. It may be to 'corral' many different positions into similar groupings so that the mediation process is manageable. Consensus building may well be necessary so that there is a clear understanding of the majority will and needs.

It may even be that time is needed for the real problem to be defined.

What mediation in faith communities may offer commercial mediators

Having identified the differences and peculiarities found in faith disputes, what would enhance the practice of the effective commercial mediator?

- **Bespoke process** Most faith community mediations have a process designed specifically for the dispute. It is so easy for a commercial mediator to use the tried and tested one-day format for all mediations whereas starting with a blank sheet and asking 'what is the best process for this dispute and these people?' may be a far better approach. It may be that having two half-days with a break between could help parties to move from entrenched positions. Or one day for several people to have their say and another with just decision-makers and their advisers. Mediation is spoken of as a flexible process but is often used quite rigidly. 'Slow mediation' may be better.

- **Extended preparation** Most commercial mediators make contact with the lawyers before the day of the mediation and then assume that those lawyers will properly brief and coach their client. Sometimes that happens but often the parties come to the mediation in ignorance, and fear, of what is ahead of them. Early contact, even by conference call with the lawyers involved, can greatly aid the process on the mediation day.

- **Facilitating conversations** Very often faith community mediation is about opening effective lines of communication, of having an impartial person help people to have a conversation. Sometimes that is all that is necessary. So often commercial mediation is all about settlement, getting deals, and the real needs of the parties are forgotten. Success is not necessarily defined by a settlement being reached. A cease-fire may be all that can be achieved in the short term with an effort to improve the parties' resilience to withstand conflict.

- **Relationships** These are paramount in faith community mediation. Not only high emotion but people's core beliefs can be challenged, so much time is often spent in listening and valuing sometimes the most extreme opinions before helping people to move on. Commercial mediation often gives little time to party's relationships even though they are probably broken by the dispute. More time on relationships may well make the path to a solution much smoother.

- **Patience** A quality that should be seen in any mediator, no matter what type or sector. The mediator cannot be seen to be irritated by unreasonable people, and this can be tested to extreme at times.

Conclusion

Although the commercial mediation model is successful and to be trusted it is important for mediators to be open to the needs of each case and to be prepared to adapt the process and skills to suit particular situations. Commercial practice can be enriched by the experience of mediation in faith communities.

Environmental and public policy mediation

Andrew Floyer Acland

One of the aspects of mediation that first intrigued me, nearly 30 years ago now, was the idea that broadly similar processes seem to work in widely different circumstances. All mediation has certain constants: the importance of deep listening, the need to create a shared story of what has happened even if the parties choose to interpret it quite differently, the value of building clarity and structure into how a situation is discussed. These are basic to all mediation and need no rehearsal here.

Third-party involvement in public issues such as environmental situations, however, does have dimensions that may be absent from mediation in other contexts. For a start, while it is recognisably part of the ADR canon, what is it an alternative to? Often it does not involve a 'case' as such, unless it is the mediation of a legal dispute that happens to involve environmental issues, which is certainly one strand of environmental mediation, although not perhaps the most interesting one. Most of my work arises because a business or a government department or a local council recognises that something it wants to do is likely to be contentious and, rather than bulldozing through the decision and taking the flak, it invests time and effort in trying to understand the likely objections, exploring how the negative effects of the decision may be mitigated, and adjusting direction accordingly. Sometimes the point of making a decision has not been reached, but the political radar has picked up icebergs to be avoided; sometimes the policy is still in conceptual form and the aim is preventing even having to switch on the radar.

In recent years this is increasingly the case as government and business alike see the value of collaboration and partnership, sometimes across unlikely divides, both to reduce opposition and to spread risks, costs and responsibilities. In fact, with the advent of 'partnership brokering' we are seeing a new type of third party entering the scene, directing skills familiar to any legal or commercial mediator to managing the creation, rather than the preservation or dissolution, of shared interests and relationships.[27]

While there are certainly many similarities between what I do and what a commercial mediator does, there are also differences between 'mediation' as it is understood in the bulk of the ADR world and its use to address public issues. For a start, most people probably think of mediation as small numbers of people closeted in separate rooms with an individual shuttling between them. My work usually involves fairly large numbers of people, and is frequently as much about the technicalities of running a large and complex meeting as it is about the assisting of negotiation or the resolving of conflict.

For this reason it tends to get described as 'facilitation' rather than mediation as the task of the third party is usually as much to get the parties themselves to make the running as it is to intervene and pick up the pieces. Facilitation's sense of making things easier, helping people to get out of their own way, provides a more rounded feeling for the role than mediation with its connotation of being mainly concerned with working through confrontation and conflict. The difference in language can conceal the fact that third party intervention in situations of public conflict is also about helping people to understand their differences and explore areas of common ground and potential solutions even if the immediate working processes are somewhat different.[28]

Perhaps it is also worth describing further the type of contexts within which public issues mediation/facilitation takes place. In most situations, a number of bodies – any number from a handful to several dozen, and ranging from large corporations, through central and local government, to non-government organisations such as community groups and campaigners – are coming at the same issues from different perspectives and bringing with them different needs and interests, values, political, cultural or religious beliefs, fears and concerns. Because of this the issues are massively clouded, surrounded by uncertainty, distorted by widely differing perceptions of past, present and future. The challenge is usually not to find a 'solution' as such – assuming one even exists – but to ensure there is real understanding of the decisions that need to be made and the consequences of the various choices available for different stakeholders. You will notice how often the word 'difference' appears here – this is because much of this work is about helping people to appreciate the range, ramifications and consequences of difference.

This raises another contrast with legal and commercial mediation. Often it is more about the future than the past: from pipelines that need to be decommissioned, waste that must be disposed of, and roads or reservoirs that may be built to problems that may arise as the consequence of new technology, industrial development, loss of biodiversity or climate change. Sometimes the focus is the management of multiple uncertainties, the commissioning of research that needs

---

27 See, for example, www.partnershipbrokers.org.
28 There are occasions, especially when working with members of the public, when it is better to avoid using 'mediation' and its implications of deep and irresolvable conflict; terms such as 'facilitation' or 'facilitated dialogue' can be less alarming.

to precede development, or the gradual evolution of policy that must take account of many factors. Sometimes processes last not a day or two, as in the world of legal ADR, but roll over into months and years.

For all these reasons our methods have to be different and this puts a premium on the skills of process design. A legal mediator can, more or less, stick to the well-trodden pattern of a joint session to hear initial presentations followed by separate caucus sessions in which the parties consider their real interests, contemplate the balance of cost and risk, and test out possible grounds for settlement. In my world, each meeting, and in fact each session of each meeting, has to be designed from the ground up often long before any meeting. The first 'meetings', indeed, may be emails and telephone calls to establish who should be involved, what the scope of the meeting should be, and what ground rules need to be in place before people will participate. Then the overall purpose of the process needs to be hammered out: is it to increase mutual understanding, for example, or to build relationships, or to make decisions? Does there need to be a review of the history and background, who exactly the stakeholders are, or what process agreements need to be in place, before any substantive progress can be made? Again, this is not so unlike a commercial mediation, but usually more driven by ideology, values and politics rather than self-interest or hard cash.

Once these preliminary points have been agreed there comes the detailed process design. *How* to get this group of people to discuss these issues in a way that results in that type of result (note *type* of result: we are talking about *process* results here, of course, not *content* results)? What is the sequence of big public meetings, small working group meetings, expert research results, independent consultancy reports, external policy decisions and so on, that will get everyone from where they are to where they want to be? Who needs to have what sort of conversation with whom about what, and when? It means working out how a particular combination of people with their varying interests and concerns, professional backgrounds, cultural differences and political sympathies can most usefully discuss complex issues in a way that lays the foundations for the next stage in the process. Juggling all these interdependent variables is like creating a piece of theatre with highly opinionated actors, but no script, no prompter, and constantly shifting scenery. Sometimes one's only ambition is to get agreement to a further meeting without a change of cast.

Eventually experience teaches how long it will take a dozen people to identify and prioritise a range of issues, or whether 100 people with deep divisions should discuss their differences in a plenary meeting or work in small groups to do so. And when the careful design, honed over weeks of drafting and re-drafting, falls apart in the first half an hour because people are too angry, or too scared, or simply want to start somewhere else—then the mark of experience is not to panic, but to take a deep breath, re-design on the hoof, canvas agreement to a new process, and to keep doing so for as long as necessary. Mediators certainly need stamina, but at least they get to sit down occasionally: facilitating a large meeting can mean preparation starts before dawn and the work ends only after a dozen or more hours on one's feet.

The logistics of such processes are also very different from those of other streams of ADR. The numbers of people involved often dictate the use of methods that enable the rapid and transparent sharing of ideas. Sometimes the humble flipchart can visibly capture progress as it is made, or allow people to draw diagrams or pictures to explain ideas or relationships; in very large meetings it may mean using a laptop computer and data projector to ensure that progress can be followed and recorded.

Learning from Other Mediation Disciplines

In one meeting, I remember a bank of video cameras being used to relay the results of small breakout meetings to a larger gathering. In this environment Post-it Notes and sticky dots advance from being irritating reminders of tasks undone to versatile tools that allow one to collect, collate and structure ideas quickly and visibly. Facilitators can easily turn into stationery fetishists.

Such processes also draw on one's imagination and inventiveness as well as on more traditional mediation skills. A colleague, for example, faced with helping a community of Amazonian Indians to communicate to an energy company their concerns about gas exploration near their village, came up with the idea of a 'mind map' on which they could use images to express, structure and communicate their thoughts and feelings.[29]

In all this the third party becomes both master of ceremonies and choreographer of reluctant dancers. Those fundamental mediation skills are still the irreducible starting point and, like all mediators, we also need the ability to create a sense of calm and confidence when progress seems impossible and breakdown imminent: nervous and reluctant participation can turn into outright rebellion if the participants do not believe the facilitator can control the process and keep them safe. The old image of the swan – serene on the surface but paddling like hell underneath – often comes to mind.

We are, however, spared the debate about whether mediators should be 'evaluative' or merely 'facilitative'. Raise so much as a sceptical eyebrow in my world and your career can come to a speedy end: for us the independence of the third party means the absolute separation of process and content. If independent opinion is likely to be required it becomes a design issue.[30] In the case of a long dialogue process about the future of the nuclear industry, for example, it was supplied by a panel of independent scientists.

In the early days of my work, 20 years ago, much of it was fairly private and more akin to legal and commercial mediation than is the case now. People from a business and a pressure group, say, and a local council or government department, would gather to discuss their differences and the conclusions reached might be shared only among a small number of people. Some meetings were always public, either because the participants demanded that everything should be a matter of public record, or because there was media interest: it was difficult, for example, to hold meetings about the Newbury bypass without television cameras on hand to record any bloodletting.[31] In recent years the demand for transparency and accountability has become increasingly powerful and these days it is rare to have a meeting whose record is not openly available, although the use of the Chatham House Rule, for example, enables people, especially public officials, to speak freely.[32]

As the nature of this involvement in public issues has evolved, so also has the relationship with other public processes, and the final and probably most dramatic divergence of public issues mediation from the rest of ADR. The language of

---

29 http://en.wikipedia.org/wiki/Mind_map.
30 Through a long dialogue process reviewing the future of the nuclear industry this role was played by a number of independent scientists hired for the purpose.
31 The cameras would always leave when it became apparent that properly run meetings need not entail violence, however controversial the topic.
32 'When a meeting, or part thereof, is held under the Chatham House Rule, participants are free to use the information received, but neither the identity nor the affiliation of the speaker(s), nor that of any other participants, may be revealed.'

mediation, conflict resolution, consensus building and stakeholder dialogue has begun to intermingle with the language of 'public engagement', 'public dialogue' and 'public consultation'. It has gradually become apparent that much public issues mediation is similar in function, if not in the methods used, to some of that carried out under the traditional heading of 'public consultation'. The word 'engagement' is a useful halfway house, denoting something more active and, literally, 'engaging' compared with the dry and lugubriously official-sounding 'consultation'. As an alternative it also has the merit of not being saddled with the baggage of consultation and connotations of sham efforts to consult the public when everyone knows the critical decision has already been made.

In discovering engagement, however, we have also discovered that what we had previously considered to be stand-alone processes are in reality part of a spectrum of methods through which people can be connected to those making the decisions that affect their lives. Just as legal mediation can be put on a spectrum of dispute resolution methods stretching from partnering, prevention and negotiation at one end to arbitration, adjudication and judgment at the other, so methods of engagement are part of a wider spectrum.

The point is that the skills needed to design and run public engagement processes, or to broker and manage partnerships between the public and private sectors, are powerfully similar to those used by every mediator with a flair for process design. So the mediation methods used, exceptionally at the time, to help nudge forward a solution to the *Brent Spar*, Shell's infamous oil storage buoy that was the subject of one of the first high profile facilitated dialogue processes, are now used up and down the country by every type and level of government and organisation to help make meetings more amicable, manageable and productive.

This takes us a long way from what is usually considered ADR. Or does it? My vision of ADR is that it can help us respond positively to the challenges of human conflict, wherever and in whatever context they occur. The sad fact is that we are still pathetically bad at resolving this most basic of human problems. Human conflict prevents or complicates the resolution of so many other problems, whether it is famine in Africa, the situation in the Middle East, or the dilemmas of multiculturalism or high-speed rail at home. You can see this every day: an issue erupts, generates acres of newsprint and hours of airtime. Every interest group leaps into the fray and the columnists and the television pundits enjoy new opportunities to voice their opinions and prejudices. At no time, all too frequently, is any real effort made to set out the various arguments systematically, to examine how the language used is preventing or assisting effective communication, to analyse what different parties are trying to achieve, or to look for how different points of view might be reconciled. Opinions are easily polarised, errors of fact or reportage constantly reproduced and differences gleefully exacerbated in a culture that values sound bites more than sound arguments.

The trenches are dug, the factions take up residence, and nobody really explores the validity of different points of view; nobody sits down with the various protagonists and helps them to listen to each other, to understand why people think the way they do. It is very easy to forget that the lessons mediators learn on their first day of training are unknown country to many in positions of authority or influence. It may be that the most important task of our first generation of mediators, whether legal, commercial, family, community or environmental, is to teach as well as practise, proclaiming methods of effective negotiation and dispute resolution.

Learning from Other Mediation Disciplines

ADR is a broad church and one that can shelter many different approaches to conflict. I have tried to set out here my own sense of the relationship between legal and commercial ADR and mediation in the context of environmental and other public disputes. For the last 20 or so years we have been working hard to bring ADR into the mainstream of legal life; it would be so good if it could also be brought into the mainstream of public life.

Restorative justice and mediation

Lawrence Kershen QC

The limits of adjudication

I'd been practising at the Bar for more than a quarter of a century when I first heard about mediation. Or rather, when I first understood that it wasn't meditation or even medication, but meant helping people to resolve their disputes themselves.

My litigation work covered both civil and commercial as well as criminal cases. And it seemed to me that the litigants were often dissatisfied with the outcomes of the court cases – even when they won. Not only did winners sometimes feel like losers, but the binary outcomes that were either win or lose often did not reflect the underlying issues and needs of the disputants.

So the concept of mediation, and a process where the outcomes could be put together by those involved, had an immediate appeal for me. In 1994 I was accredited as a mediator by CEDR. Within five years I had ended my legal practice to work full time in mediation and training of mediators.

From retribution to restoration

I started to imagine how the principles of dispute resolution by dialogue might apply in criminal cases. Not so much to resolve guilt but once guilt had been established, in dealing with the fallout from the crime for all those involved.

Experience in criminal practice suggested that many of those who committed crimes had little awareness of the consequences of their actions. Their ability to empathise with the other at the receiving end of their harmful acts was in the majority of cases blunted by circumstances or upbringing, and in rare cases absent. It seemed to me that hearing face-to-face the effect of what they had done offered a chance of waking up that sense of connectedness, that at some level their conscience could be touched.

And any sense of remorse – always a key element for judges to consider in sentencing – offered the possibility that next time they would be less likely to repeat the offence.

Equally I wanted some victims of crime to be able see those who had harmed them, and hear the circumstances that had led to the delinquent behaviour. Perhaps they would recognise that the offender was not some monster who had targeted them, but a demoralised youth who had himself been a victim. I felt sure that the aura of fear and trauma that endured after the event would be reduced by telling the offender the consequences of what he had done, and asking: 'Why me?'

Then I discovered that victim offender mediation existed and was being carried out in isolated pockets across the country. I felt obliged to work to support

Learning from Other Mediation Disciplines

its development, and became a member of the fledgling Restorative Justice Consortium. I did my best to promote it in the legal world, including meetings with two successive Lord Chief Justices who turned out to be far more knowledgeable about restorative justice (RJ) than I expected.

Restorative principles

From the stalwarts who were practising RJ, I began to understand that there were different applications of restorative principles and process. As well as victim offender mediation, there were meetings where all those affected by a harmful act came together in a facilitated meeting or 'conference'. As well as victim and offender, participants routinely included partners, close family members, neighbours, workmates and respected community members and sometimes the arresting police officer.

As well as conferencing I learnt that applications could include indirect communication between parties, sentencing circles facilitated by a judge, even 'circles of support' for sexual offenders. Restorative processes were being used in schools to address conflicts that arise in the playground, the classroom, between teachers and so on. In the criminal justice context, not only were there pre-sentence RJ schemes but diversion schemes, conditional cautions and 'restorative policing'.

The results of the Government's own research showed that these restorative processes achieved more than any other court-based disposal, both in enabling victims to move on from a crime – to escape victimhood in fact – and offenders to connect with the consequences of their actions on others, and to develop empathy. Reoffending was reduced by 27 per cent, and 85 per cent of victims reported satisfaction with their RJ experience.[33]

Giving the harmed and the harmer opportunity to enter into dialogue is shown to be hugely effective in satisfying victims' needs, and awakening a realisation in the perpetrator of the consequences of their actions. Indeed the effect is often to elicit empathy in one party for their 'adversary'. Furthermore those who have caused harm are often able to return to the community having understood – perhaps for the first time – the effect of their behaviour, having been given a way to make amends, and having some self-esteem restored.

The experience of transformation that is inherently possible in any such meeting could fairly be described as miraculous. Individuals may approach it filled with anger, fear and grief, maybe built up over a long time – yet emerge on the other side with empathy or compassion or even a desire to help the other. The process of 'meeting and talking' may even offer ways to find forgiveness for the other.

Shared values

So at the heart of both mediation and restorative processes is the value of dialogue between disputants as a path to resolving differences. Both approaches grow from the same roots, and there are obvious shared principles that underlie them.

Both disciplines have a process and structure that aims to create a safe space for effective dialogue to take place. In practice RJ is more structured than mediation,

---

33   http://www.smith-institute.org.uk/file/RestorativeJusticeTheEvidenceFullreport.pdf.

perhaps reflecting the greater need for safety in that context and to avoid re-victimising the person harmed.

In both there is a protagonist-antagonist relationship, whether it is victim/offender or claimant/defendant – although the parties in mediation don't necessarily agree who has which role. Indeed the parties in RJ may find that the differences between their roles may not be as clear-cut as they seemed.

The approach of the facilitator is non-judgmental, just as that of the mediator is facilitative rather than evaluative. As in mediation, the consent of all parties to engage with an RJ process, freely given and without a promise of reward, is fundamental. However the Crime and Courts Act 2013 provides that the judge may adjourn sentence for a restorative conference. If so, there is plainly a question as to how freely a defendant might give his consent.

That said, the key skills which are fundamental to the effectiveness of both processes are the same – empathy, listening, questioning, making sure the parties have the best opportunity to be heard, and guiding them towards the construction of an agreement about what needs to be done to bring about settlement or closure.

Like a settlement agreement in a mediation, the concluding phase of a restorative process – certainly in a criminal justice context – requires an outcome agreement or accord. This sets out the mutually agreed steps that will be taken to repair the harm. In both disciplines there is a wide, indeed infinite, range of possibilities for what might constitute this restoring of the status quo.

Restorative Justice and commercial mediation compared

There are however significant differences between the two disciplines. Some very broad distinctions can be drawn between civil/commercial mediation and RJ in the criminal justice context – always bearing in mind the imperfect nature of generalisations as follows:

Restorative Justice	**Mediation**
Where no civil legal action initiated	Where civil action initiated (often)
Criminal proceedings initiated (often)	Not applied in criminal cases (save Victim/Offender)
Acknowledged wrongdoing	Responsibility for harm not accepted (often)
Primary focus on harm and emotional	Primary focus on economic consequences
Often follows clearly structured	Structure adaptable to process process, eg 'script', eg changing groupings
Content may be confidential	Without prejudice and confidential but not legally privileged
Break-out meetings rarely used	Generally private meetings/caucuses
Outcomes non-binding legally	Legally enforceable as contracts and/or eg accord court order
Aim to repair harm	Aim to resolve dispute

Distinctions

Some of these distinctions are inherent in the different nature of each process, eg a pre-condition in most RJ processes is an admission of guilt, or acceptance of responsibility for the harm caused. In mediation liability may never be admitted – indeed it may be a term of settlement that no such admission is made. The effect of this on the resolution of underlying causes may be obvious.

Nevertheless a restorative process can also be effective where there is no accepted wrongdoer. Sometimes members of a group are perceived as jointly responsible without the individual wrongdoer ever being identified. In some circumstances both parties may regard themselves as victims, and so on. Yet it is still possible to explore how the harm can be repaired and find resolution.

The complementarity of the RJ process is also key. In most serious crimes, RJ can rarely be an alternative to the established criminal justice system. If serious wrongdoing could be excused by an apology, victims may feel, as was sometimes the case in South Africa's Truth and Reconciliation Commission, that the perpetrators had 'got away with it'. As was said there, justice and reconciliation are not alternatives, but go hand in hand.

The agreed outcome in RJ may be as straightforward (and challenging) as an apology. Or it may be some activity that will repair the harm done, literally or symbolically. For an individual, it may be s/he undertakes to carry out some sort of personal work that will help them develop or change their behaviour, eg rehabilitation programmes. Sometimes it will be systemic, organisational or procedural changes to avoid the same events happening in the future. It is key that these actions are agreed by all involved.

What can Restorative Justice offer commercial mediation?

Some of these different practices can inform and enrich the process and practice of mediation.

Safety through preparation

Government research showed that restorative process is most effective when it is done face to face. The heart of the RJ process is this restorative meeting between victim and offender and the dialogue that can take place. For example the victim needs an opportunity to seek answers to questions like: 'Why did you do it?', 'Do you realise the effect of what you did?', 'What are you going to do to put it right?' The offender is given an opportunity not only to explain themselves and the context of the events, but to hear first-hand from the person harmed. For this dialogue to take place, a safe environment has to be created and maintained.

So a hallmark of effective restorative process is thorough preparation of the parties. Only when the facilitator is satisfied that an individual feels ready to meet the other will they come together. If that happens before they are fully prepared there are real risks not only of disappointed expectations, but of re-victimisation. It is plainly unacceptable that an RJ process should risk more harm being done to someone who has already been harmed by another's actions.

This preparatory work may be to help clarify what a party wants to say. Some of it may be to manage expectations of what they want from the other – what they want to hear, and what the consequences might be if those expectations are not met – to prepare them for possible disappointments and strong feelings.

It may also entail ensuring that the right people are going to be present. They may be people who have been indirectly harmed by the crime such as family members or co-workers. They may include people who will enable the party, whether victim or offender, to feel safer in the face-to-face meeting. Certainly the facilitator will have developed a solid trust between him or herself and the participants.

Timing

The 'up-front' investment of time in RJ, with several preparatory sessions of an hour or so with individuals, can mean that the actual meeting between them may only take two or three hours, as compared with the day or more of typical commercial mediations.

Forming a relationship of trust with the parties is of course fundamental for a successful commercial mediation, and the earlier the better. Detailed preparation of the parties seems to be less common, particularly directly with the parties. Not many mediators aim – or budget – for even a single preliminary meeting with the parties.

Pre-mediation telephone calls are more usual, so they may have to be seized on as the opportunity to focus on building rapport. It may be helpful to ask a party's representative how the mediator can help them, opening up a space where they can talk about what's important to them, and even how they think it might resolve.

An opportunity for the mediator to speak directly with the party may be helpful, particularly if s/he is not familiar with the process. And it can pay huge dividends to discuss whether the key people will be at the table, such as the insurer or a figure senior enough to give an apology or expression of regret that is meaningful to the other.

Focus on relationship

Commercial mediations are often presented by the parties as being all about money, and it can be seductive for the mediator to believe that that is the whole story. It can be tempting to sideline or ignore the fractured relationships that lie behind many disputes. The effectiveness of RJ lies in part in its focus on relationships between the parties, and the importance of valuing and spending time on them. That is not to say that outcomes are not important, but that they grow out of the initial exploration of the emotional harm.

Of course the contract the mediator makes with the parties may seem to preclude the expression of feelings. However an exploration of the emotional impact of damaged relations may be critical in unlocking the dispute, particularly where there is a personal element to the dispute.

'Personal' issues seem to include where a party perceives his identity to be under threat – eg allegations of professional negligence or dishonesty, damage to

Learning from Other Mediation Disciplines

reputation or confidentiality – or where there is a sense of identification with or ownership of the subject matter, like the MD who founded the company and regards it as his 'baby', or a land or boundary dispute.

However strongly legal and other advisers may advocate their clients' positions, they will not have the personal, emotional connection that can be addressed in this way. Even managing directors, CEOs and finance directors will only rarely have the sense of being harmed that is at the heart of what RJ can address.

The healing of damaged relationships is partly encouraged by the act of listening, which in itself can validate the individual's experience. Appropriately timed questions can also be hugely effective. Timing is of course key, to ensure that the mediator has built sufficient rapport with the party. Questions such as:

- 'How do you feel about what has happened?'
- 'How has this affected you – and others?'
- 'What needs to happen for trust to be restored?'

can help the parties to address and resolve not only the dispute but the deeper sources of conflict between them.

Personal engagement

Implicit in such an exploration of the emotional dimension is that the disputants themselves have the opportunity to speak, as distinct from representatives or advisers. Victims are empowered by being able to ask questions, challenge, articulate their experience. Their input and participation is vital in determining needs and outcomes, as indeed is that of the offenders. Both are involved in the repair of the harm so far as is possible.

So giving all disputants the opportunity to speak, and the assurance that they will have that opportunity, is vital. This provides a helpful antidote to the interruptions and outbursts that can erupt in a mediation. It helps to create a safe framework that promotes the work of recovery and healing that is ultimately the domain of the individuals at the centre of the dispute. It is this willingness to engage with the personal and emotional that offers the opportunity to address not merely the dispute but the conflict that underlies it.

Part of the reason this is difficult to achieve in mediation is that we are not employed to do more than dispute resolution. Partly we tend to be problem solvers by background, and delving into the emotional or, heaven forbid, the touchy feely, may not come naturally, or feel safe.

To caucus or not to caucus

Thorough preparation also means there is less need for breakout meetings and virtually all communications in RJ are conducted face-to-face. Of course in the negotiation phase of a commercial mediation there is a different emphasis. It may involve questions of sensitive information, resources and strategic steps in the bargaining process. There may be a degree of coaching which happens between mediator and party. Certainly exploration can take place far more freely and openly in private meeting.

Nevertheless there is much to be said for a non-caucus approach to commercial mediation – or at least enabling parties to keep talking beyond the 'safe' point, where the mediator would normally break into private session. Relations between parties who work through strong feelings may be improved by it. This seems particularly important where they have a relationship to resume, eg as neighbours or members of the same community, when the mediation is over and the mediator has disappeared into the sunset. Of course, in community, neighbour and workplace mediation the facilitator will follow-up, so the parties know he or she will be in contact after an agreed period.

Standards for practitioners

In dealing with the aftermath of crime the safety of the victim is a priority. Those involved and the community at large have to feel confident that the facilitator can ensure at least that no further harm will be done, and at best the process is managed with integrity in a way that is secure and effective. Because of this core need for safe process, the Restorative Justice Council in conjunction with its membership has created:

- a Best Practice Guide;
- a Practitioners Register;
- a national Trainers Register;
- a Code of Practice for Practitioners;
- a Code of Practice for Trainers; and
- a Restorative Service Quality Mark for agencies.

It has also created a Practitioner Accreditation programme.

It may be a source of some surprise that commercial mediators have not as yet agreed on a Best Practice Guide for practitioners, nor offered the public accreditation of practitioners to an agreed standard, or the Register of Accredited Practitioners that would follow. It is fair to say however that all accredited mediators are obliged to follow the EU Code of Conduct for Mediators. Furthermore all mediation providers on the Ministry of Justice civil online directory have to be accredited by the Civil Mediation Council, which is moving towards a registration system.

Enhancing commercial mediation

Contests between different 'schools' of mediation to be practitioners of the pure form are interesting but ultimately unhelpful. Different techniques are appropriate to different mediation contexts and times. Each approach to mediation – facilitative, transformative, narrative and so on – has its own truth and value, and a flexible mediator will draw on them as appropriate. The key question, of course, is when are they appropriate?

Some of the elements that make up a restorative process can inform general commercial mediation practice. For example, starting preparation early enables a commercial mediator to encourage the 'right people' to be at the table, and to start the initial phases before the mediation day. Ensuring all participants have a voice will help to engage them and any issues they may have. There may be occasions when several shorter meetings are preferable to one long one. Additionally, the time is coming when standards and a Register of Practitioners, through the good offices of the CMC, will provide a measure of quality assurance for the greater good.

However, since restorative justice and processes focus in particular on the personal harm caused by conflict, they suggest some specific approaches in commercial disputes where there is a personal element. For example, preparation in such cases might include making contact with parties who feel they have been harmed. Allowing sufficient exploration of personal feelings and needs can be crucial in loosening strongly held positions. And any process that aims to restore will ask the question 'What are the lessons to be learned?', to ensure as far as possible that the harmful events do not recur.

By integrating these techniques into commercial disputes I believe it is possible to address the sources of conflict and achieve more systemic and durable settlements. They could be described – as I am starting to – as restorative mediations.

What is common to all these approaches to conflict resolution is that they seek to address human differences in a people-centric way, looking to empower individuals to find resolutions for themselves. Of course this journey from a blame-based, retributive system to one that is more restorative, from third-party resolution of disputes to self-determination, requires a shift in attitudes – and that takes time. However this changing culture suggests to me that in resolving our differences and managing conflict for ourselves, humankind is evolving to be more responsible, and response-able.

Co-mediation

Eve Pienaar

Introduction

Co-mediation is the pairing of two professionals to facilitate the mediation process. It is most commonly understood as two experienced mediators but can take many forms and is of value in many different settings. Arguably, it is under-used in commercial disputes and is reserved for multi-party or some complex, multi-issue disputes. In other models, its value is recognised and co-mediation is the norm in community mediation and in family mediation, often pairing a mediator with a therapist or child expert. It is used more extensively in certain jurisdictions with a more developed history of mediation, whether tribal or in the United States, and is used in multi-stakeholder mediations such as environmental or large planning disputes. Co-mediation opens wide the opportunity of creative problem solving, yet its value has yet to be exploited to the full.

This section will look at the benefits of co-mediation and also the challenges it presents. It will then follow the order of Part 1, highlighting the factors that distinguish it from the more widely used solo commercial mediator model, through the stages of mediation. I have co-mediated a number of disputes in the commercial, workplace and community fields, including (on commercial disputes) with David Richbell, for whom I have great respect.

In this country, experienced commercial mediators will frequently work with an assistant, to provide practical experience to newly trained mediators. Whilst this is useful in terms of practice development, it is not co-mediation and the assistant will usually shadow the lead mediator without engaging directly with the parties to any significant extent.

Benefits of co-mediation

Key benefits of co-mediation include:

- **Two heads are better than one** Provided they are attuned to one another, two mediators will afford a broader approach to tackle the issues. However experienced, a mediator cannot avoid bringing his or her cultural 'filters' to interpret and analyse the dispute.
- **Feedback during the mediation** Working in partnership enables one mediator to draw to the other's attention, outside earshot of the parties, any blind side or unintentional bias.
- **Dividing tasks** Multi-party or multi-issue cases lend themselves particularly well to co-mediations and will be explored more fully below. But at a deeper level, mediators can complement one another with one taking notes while the other focuses their entire attention on exploration, or one mediator can provide an empathic ear while the other focuses on the numbers. We all have different skill sets and some of us will necessarily be more attuned to the underlying tensions a party is hiding, including from themselves – it can be demanding to offer the full spectrum of active listening and exploration.
- **Wider spectrum for matching parties** Co-mediation allows for a richer match for the needs of the parties, for instance in terms of gender mix or professional backgrounds (lawyer and surveyor). This aspect is sometimes crucial in community mediation or family mediation, where a party from a different ethnic background or gender cannot overcome their fear of perpetuated injustice, without some ability to affiliate with one of the mediators. In commercial co-mediation, the pairing is generally of two, experienced commercial mediators; one might be a specialist in the field of the dispute (eg surveyor) and the other a 'big name', or better known mediator. Unfortunately, on large cases for which the parties select the co-mediation pairing, there is a tendency to select two mediators from different backgrounds but who have not worked together before and are not aligned in their approach on the day. These ad hoc pairings can be counterproductive if one or both co-mediators are used to working solo and find sharing airtime and decision making a challenge.
- **Accelerating the process** In multi-party or multi-issue cases, time is the enemy for the mediator. The need to explore and hear each party's story is at odds with the limited time (typically one or maybe two days) afforded to the process. Two mediators can work in parallel in different rooms, or can divide tasks in a complementary manner. On one case, my colleague and I co-mediated over two days, involving a number of utility service providers with competing claims against a developer, we were able to work in parallel exploring and assessing quantum issues for the different joined claimants, allowing the whole of the second day for the negotiation stage.

Learning from Other Mediation Disciplines

- **Co-mediation models collaborative problem solving** Mediators who work harmoniously together present a powerful example of thoughtful conflict management and this can influence the parties to reflect back such an approach, consciously or at a deeper level. It is harder to behave unreasonably when continually faced with thoughtful and respectful interaction from the mediator pairing.
- **Quality control** Mediation is a demanding task and it can be a challenge to listen attentively, take unobtrusive notes, manage the process and develop a strategy for a potential route to settlement. Co-mediation should provide mutual support for the mediators as well as higher quality service delivery.

To illustrate these points, I am reminded of a three-party mediation between two owners of long leases in a luxurious mansion block in Kensington, and the beleaguered Landlord Association, dragged into the vicious dispute between them. The Landlord Association was concerned that the litigation was draining the tenants' property maintenance funds. The claimant would not drop her war of attrition against the young Italian family living below her flat, whose children's noise disrupted her need for peace. The defendants couldn't sell their flat and escape back to children-friendly Italy while the dispute hung over their property. The judge had sent them to mediation in despair over the self-destructive conflict. I was paired up with a newly-qualified mediator who was a psychologist by training. She helped unravel the underlying resentment of the claimant against the family below, following her bereavement from her husband before they had been able to start a family. It was only when we could start exploring what her life would look like with the family below able to put their property on the market that she could begin to let go of her feelings of anger and desire to punish. The dual mediator/psychologist approach was hugely beneficial on the day and recognised as such by the parties when it finally settled in the small hours.

Challenges of co-mediation

Later in this section we will look at the practical issues co-mediators need to keep in mind on the day. Conceptually, the two biggest challenges are convincing parties that co-mediation can be more effective and faster than solo mediation (as well as value for money), and finding a co-mediator with whom you not only work well, but where both of you 'up' the other's game.

There is understandable resistance by parties to appoint co-mediators on grounds of cost, selection and because most commercial mediations are settled successfully by one mediator. I don't deny that the majority of disputes heading for court or already in litigation do not require co-mediation. Multi-party cases will almost always benefit from co-mediation if they are to be handled in a single chunk of time rather than spread over various days for the different caucus meetings. Multi-issue cases may be suitable for co-mediation, although not always. Unfortunately, the lawyers who select and suggest mediation to their clients will rarely put co-mediation forward for economic reasons, even though the mediator(s) is/are paid a relatively small amount when compared to the costs of the mediation day (partners and associates from law firms, experts, client management time and so on).

From a practitioners' point of view, the main difficulty (after promoting the concept) is finding a co-mediator you trust and with whom you share core practice beliefs. It also has to be someone with whom you know you work effectively and who enhances your skills, whether complementing them or simply because they have a different analytical spectrum to yours, which enables the pairing to offer a far broader mediation practitioner angle than either one of you could offer alone. I have had unsuccessful attempts at co-mediation, where I felt my partner railroaded the mediation and largely ignored me, which was irritating personally but also detrimental to the mediation process as it projected an autocratic approach which the parties emulated by remaining positional and confrontational. In the majority of cases, however, co-mediation has been very rewarding. Mixing gender and professional backgrounds ensures a wider spectrum of how my colleague and I interpret information at every level. This affords a different and richer problem-solving tool for the parties to work with. I meet those colleagues I co-mediate with regularly to discuss our respective experiences and ongoing practice development and to ensure we are closely attuned to one another when working together.

Co-mediation is not easy; it requires twice the attention of solo mediation as it requires each mediator remaining vigilant to their mediator colleague as well as to all the parties and the process. However, it also provides mutual support and effective analysis in deadlock, in a process that is otherwise often lonely and emotionally draining. Done well, co-mediation also affords a unique opportunity to learn from an experienced colleague and debrief honestly and constructively following the mediation, a great source of practice development.

Co-mediation in practice – process stages

Preparing

Preparation is critical. The mediator pairing should agree who will contact the parties and how, ideally together by conference call but if this isn't practical, then at least ensure both are copied on all emails and receive all the papers. It is important the parties feel the co-mediators are a unit from the outset, to avoid an imbalance in perception of who is leading on the day.

Co-mediation is mostly used for multi-party mediations. Crowd control is the first issue to address. Ensuring only those individuals who will truly add to the problem solving are present pays dividends on the day, as time has to be managed carefully. If the mediators can reduce numbers at the joint meetings, by meeting some parties separately, either in advance or in parallel, this will save time and help with logistics on the day.

The fee may be a blended rate or not, depending on the value and complexity of the dispute. The parties needn't know how the pairing work the fee out by themselves.

When I co-mediate a case, my colleague and I speak over the phone after reading the papers and then meet to discuss how we will share tasks and even script how we divide airtime in the opening joint session, as it is so important that we come across as naturally attuned and experienced as working as a pairing. This is less important as the day progresses, when the dynamics of the day can't be predicted and the initial impression has been set. In complex cases likely to take more than a day, it would be appropriate for the mediators to hold pre-meetings with the parties individually, to design the process and begin to consolidate the working relationship.

Learning from Other Mediation Disciplines

It is more important than ever for there to be a 'mediator own room', so the pairing can meet – the mediator pairing might agree with the parties in open session that they will meet alone every hour, on the hour, to debrief and agree a strategy going forward.

Opening – the joint session

The mediators should meet all the parties together, be careful to always include the other in their communication ('we' rather than 'I' at all times) and never close a meeting without checking in with the other.

The mediators should share equal airtime if possible, as agreed beforehand. Not only does this project their strength as a complementary pairing, it models collaborative communication and sets the scene for a constructive discussion.

The mediators can divide up roles, one questioning and the other summarising or using the flipchart. The parties begin to see that they are getting twice the value in terms of skills, experience and attention to their issues.

Exploring

Arguably the stage where co-mediation is most effective, at least from the parties' view, is during exploration. Two mediators working in parallel (and remaining in close communication) can save considerable time, keep all the parties engaged and reduce costs on the day.

The challenge is to avoid the parties feeling that each mediator is aligned to a party, or for them to drive a wedge between the pairing. I recall one situation where one of the parties became visibly distressed and withdrawn. Upon asking her in private what was troubling her, she said she felt my co-mediator (a psychologist who took extensive notes and held an impersonal, inscrutable expression) was 'judging' her and the disapproval she imagined froze her ability to think beyond a desire to leave. Fortunately, we were able to redesign the process so that she no longer felt threatened.

Negotiating and concluding

By the negotiating stage, the parties should be seeing the value of the pairing in helping them find a route to settlement. One may be more numerate and the other might be working on structuring a package of all the different issues that need to be addressed . The co-mediators will come from different angles to help the parties look at the issues in fresh light and a deal will usually emerge sooner than would otherwise have been possible.

In the words of Bianca Keys, an experienced US co-mediation practitioner:

> 'the dynamics and teamwork of the two co-mediators can have the greatest of impacts on the progress of the mediation through the comfort levels and trust of the parties involved.'

With twice the level of attention, skill and energy, co-mediation does afford the parties a better chance to find that path to settlement.

Conclusion

As practitioners, we have a role to play in building and promoting co-mediation in the commercial field, where it lags behind some of the more progressive practice areas such as community or family mediation. Co-mediation, where it is done well, is a cost- and time-effective process enabling a richer solution to parties' conflict.

I believe there is a broader and little explored opportunity for co-mediation in the United Kingdom, bringing professionals from different backgrounds together to better help the parties work constructively through conflict. On many occasions I have come out of a workplace mediation feeling my work was done but one or both parties would derive huge value from the ongoing support of a coach to help them build on the work done during the mediation.

Bringing together the skill set of a mediator and a psychologist, coach or other professional could add a whole new dimension to the process. Mediation is an emotionally laden process for the parties and one from which they learn a lot about the other side but also themselves. Even commercial mediations involve hurt, broken dreams and loss at a deeper level than purely financial. Family business feuds, estate management, elder care, partnerships and loss of trust in the workplace – all of these involve hurt individuals who may benefit from some follow up and support by a professional other than the mediator, whose job is done. What an opportunity this is to build on this with tools to take this learning forward and take some life-long learning with them as well as settlement of their dispute.

Suggested further reading

Bernard S Mayer, *Beyond Neutrality: Confronting the Crisis in Conflict Resolution* (Jossey Bass, 2004).

Kenneth Cloke, *Mediating Dangerously: The Frontiers of Conflict Resolution* (Jossey Bass, 2001).

Marian Liebmann, *Community and Neighbour Mediation* (Cavendish Publishing Limited, 1998).

Robert A Baruch Bush and Joseph P Folger, *The Promise of Mediation: The Transformative Approach to Conflict* (Jossey Bass)

Assistantships

David Richbell

Assistantships/pupillages/observations is a subject close to my heart. I feel very strongly about them and I believe any practising mediator has a responsibility to offer newly-qualified mediators an opportunity to experience the real thing.

Why?

Why should practising commercial mediators have such a responsibility?

- It is very difficult for newly-qualified mediators to get started.
- Few, if any, mediator training providers offer assistantships.
- The Civil Mediation Council (CMC) registration scheme requires at least two assistantships before members are eligible for registration.
- All mediator providers require prior experience before accepting new mediators onto their panel.
- It is good for the mediator to have a companion who can also observe, hear and see what goes on.
- It is good for the mediator to have a companion who can give feedback and help unwind at the end of the mediation day.
- It is good for the newly-qualified mediator to see different mediators in action, their different styles and techniques and the different sectors in which they work.
- There could be added benefit to both mediator and parties if the assistant has sector expertise, or has a different background to the mediator (eg lawyer/non-lawyer, male/female).

To me, this is a win-win situation and I see no downsides if the assistant is properly briefed.

Appointment

The CMC encourages (but does not require) accredited providers to offer assistantships. Unfortunately those that do rarely offer assistantships to non-panel members. So there is a desperate need for all practising mediators to offer opportunities. Some do when approached by the newly-qualified mediator direct, and there is a case for mediators being reactive rather than pro-active in this matter – the newly-qualified should make the effort to contact mediators to request assistantships, rather than the mediator actively offering them. Of course, I am in the position of having trained many mediators in the United Kingdom and beyond, so there has never been a shortage of people requesting assistantships. It may be expecting too much to expect mediators to make a training provider aware of assistantships, or to mention it on LinkedIn or social media. But it doesn't have to be a burden.

What I do

This is not to suggest this is the only, or even the best, way but it works for me and makes no demand upon my time or attention. I gather 20 or so names of people wishing to have an assistantship and put them on a group email. They have either contacted me or I have trained them and the list is reviewed at the beginning of each year. The deal is that I send out an email when I have a mediation appointment and the first response gets the booking. The only exception to this rule is if an overseas mediator wants the booking or if the first response had the last booking (and there are others who responded later). I already have their profiles on the

Learning from Other Mediation Disciplines

database so I include their details in my email to the parties confirming my booking as their mediator. The email ends:

> 'Finally, I will have an assistant with me at the mediation. xxx name is xxx and xxx is attending mainly to gain experience. Of course, xxx attends without cost and will be bound by the confidentiality provisions. I attach xxx profile for your information.'

The assistant gets no fee although I offer to contribute towards expenses if they cannot be reclaimed.

Only once has there been an objection, and that was because the proposed assistant was a competitor to one of the parties' lawyers. As in that case, any objection should be respected and another assistant booked.

Role of the assistant

I do not like observers. It indicates detachment and being sat in the corner like a naughty child. It gives no benefit to the parties or the mediator. The main fears for mediators are:

- the assistant will speak, say something inappropriate and/or sabotage what the mediator is doing; and
- the assistant will persistently ask what is happening, why the mediator is doing/saying what they are doing and being a distraction to the mediator.

I have to say that neither has been my experience, except for one infamous occasion when someone I had trained persistently requested an opportunity to accompany me. He had by then some mediation experience. I had been trying to get my assistants to be more involved and had gone from saying 'if you want to ask a question do. If it is inappropriate I will just suggest you park it' to 'I reckon I can get us out of any mess you get us into, so feel free to comment or ask a question'. It may sound very risky, but it did result in assistants making a more positive contribution. Until this occasion, when the assistant more than took me at my word and gradually took over a private meeting with a virtual cross-examination. I took him to the plenary room to pull him back when one of the lawyers followed us and said 'David, I am not happy with the way you are conducting this mediation. I don't feel you are being even-handed'. This was serious – it is vital that any mediator is seen to be evenhanded. I said to her 'This is serious...' but was interrupted by my assistant saying 'B*******! [a word yet to enter my mediator's vocabulary] You don't know how hard we have been working in the other room to get them to ....'. I interrupted and then the lawyer said they were concerned about whether the mediation should continue. There was an eruption behind me and my assistant said (using the same jargon): 'B*******! The trouble with you is your case is crap!'. OK, so I asked for it. The mediation did continue, and settled, but he didn't speak again. He did ring me the next day to say how much he had enjoyed the experience and that he would be happy to help me again. I haven't taken him up on this!

That experience aside, I find most assistants to be very sensitive to their role. I ask them to be another pair of eyes and ears, and that we will always speak together between private meetings. I ask them to time-keep and run errands but most of all I ask them to make brief notes that can be used in a debrief (if we have time). In particular any learning points, anything that I do that is different to their training, anything that I do that they have been told not to do, and so on. I want it to be a good learning experience for them, and there is a possibility that it will be a good learning experience for me as well.

Prior to the mediation, I arrange for copies of the electronic documents to be sent to the assistant – I will also have hard copies of the agreed bundle but I rarely arrange for those to be sent to the assistant – and I will speak to them after my telephone contact with the parties' lawyers a few days before the mediation date, mainly to update them following my preparation.

Debriefing

If time permits I will have a debrief with the assistant, usually in a pub or wine bar but sometimes in the period between the deal being done and the Settlement Agreement being signed. My preference is that the period between shaking hands and signing the paper is spent with the parties coming into the plenary room and having a drink with me (most law offices have a wine cellar), because it can be a really beneficial experience. The dispute is over, they have agreed a deal (their deal) and often they are able to relax and socialise together. This is particularly possible when the parties have co-operated in achieving the deal. So that is a much better use of the time, but when that is not possible, I will debrief with the assistant. The assistant's (brief) notes are invaluable, because we will have both forgotten what happened early on in the mediation. So we rewind the day, pick up on significant points and I will give some, limited, feedback on the assistant's performance, and they will do so on mine, although it is very difficult to get any useful feedback from a novice mediator unless they are used to coaching or doing peer reviews.

Conclusion

I always have an assistant. I find them invaluable as a sounding board, as a mate for the day and as a timekeeper/runner. On the rare occasions when it hasn't happened I have felt quite isolated. Mediating is a solitary profession and the mediator can feel lonely at times, so having a companion makes a lot of difference.

I should mention co-mediation. It is common knowledge that I am a fan of co-mediation, especially for multi-party cases. Eve has written a piece on it in this chapter. It is very different to having an assistant. Proper co-mediation is a team of equals, not Lead and another, but many 'co-mediations' are just that two unequal lead mediators. I mention it because this is not 'proper' co-mediation.

Chapter 8

Analysing Risk

Elizabeth Jones QC and John Clark

Liz Jones and John Clark are a formidable team. Not only because of their obvious intellectual powers but also their preparedness to share their experience and knowledge with others. (DR)

When David Richbell asked us to write this chapter, he said that this topic probably needed a book. He was right. The following is a brief introduction to the topic of risk analysis. At the end of the chapter we recommend some books that you may like to follow up if you would like to know more.

Why analyse risk in mediation?

Risk is everywhere. Deciding to settle requires risk analysis.

Risk is uncertainty. More specifically, risk exists when you take an action for which there is an uncertain outcome. Tossing a coin or throwing dice are obvious examples. Investing in the stock market has risk – will your investment pay off? Choosing a school for your children has risk – you hope it will be the right one, but you can't be sure. Crossing a busy road is a decision you take with an uncertain outcome. Should we take action on the possibility of global warming or not take action? Pretty much everything we do involves decision taking with future uncertainty, with risks of a greater or lesser magnitude. You need to decide which way to go when the road ahead is foggy and unclear. Mediation is no different.

The core decision a mediation party must make is whether or not to accept or make an offer without knowing exactly what might happen in the future. Usually, the value of the offer you are deciding whether to make or accept is a reasonably well-known quantity; on the other hand, the costs and benefits of continuing a dispute can be highly uncertain. Yet you need to compare, on the one hand, the settlement offer (whether making or accepting) and, on the other hand, continuing the dispute. You have to decide now, in the face of uncertainty.

So dealing with risk and helping parties understand and get comfortable with making decisions under conditions of uncertainty is central to successful mediation, but how do you value your alternative to settlement? How do you assess the risks?

Parties and advisers are usually well acquainted with the central risk in mediation, namely litigation risk. What will the outcome of the litigation be if you do not settle, and go to court? This outcome is obviously uncertain. Our experience, however, is that parties and their advisers often don't take full account of all the risks they face, for example, reputation risk – the uncertainty parties face about the effect on their reputation if they settle, or indeed if they don't – or payment risk – the risk that a paying party might not properly abide by, or be able to abide by, the terms of an agreement. Litigation often involves having to make a substantial down-payment by way of funding your own costs, and may also require individuals who are important to a business to spend their time on litigation rather than their usual job; financial and human resources may need to be diverted to the litigation rather than the business. These items need to be included in the calculation of the costs and benefits of proceeding with litigation. If their magnitude is uncertain then they constitute a risk.

We believe a mediator's job is to help all parties make rational, informed decisions and see through the fog of uncertainty – whether or not they settle. To properly analyse the risks involved, the first task is to ensure that each party has fully thought through all the uncertainties that might affect them, ie they need a complete list of risks. The second task is a way of thinking about those future uncertain outcomes when a decision is needed today. A key problem here is that humans are not very good at handling uncertainty. Indeed, we tend to make fast, emotional decisions, rather than slow, rational choices, as we discuss next.

Barriers to rational risk analysis

'Man will become better when you show him what he is like.'

Chekhov

People tend to make decisions on the basis of heuristics – 'rules of thumb'. Heuristics are simple, efficient rules which people often use to form judgments and make decisions. They are mental shortcuts that usually involve focusing on one aspect of a complex problem and ignoring others. These biases work well under most circumstances and help us make speedy decisions when time is at a premium, but they can also lead to systematic and sub-optimal deviations from logical or rational choices.

For example, people are more easily swayed by a single, vivid story than by a large body of statistical evidence (known as the availability heuristic – the information is more readily available psychologically). Consider a child who has suffered brain damage as a result of hospital negligence. The child's mother, talking to another set of parents in a hospital waiting room, heard how they received only a small sum when they went to court, despite their needs and the strength of their case. Based on this vivid and available example, the mother accepts a much lower settlement than the hospital would be willing to offer, when a more dispassionate analysis based on a better understanding of the risks and what a larger sample of parents have achieved, might have had her hold out for more. Poor risk analysis led to her making a less than optimal decision.

Some other common biases encountered in mediation include the following.

Asymmetric attitudes to gains and losses

Consider a game in which a fair coin is tossed. If it is heads you get £20. If it is tails you get nothing. I'm offering you a deal: you can choose between playing the game or I give you a guaranteed £10. What do you do?

Most of you will already have done the 'risk analysis' in your head already. Tossing a fair coin gives you a 50 per cent chance of getting heads and winning £20. Your 'expected value' is therefore £10 (=50 per cent x £20). In other words, before you toss the coin your risk analysis tells you that you are choosing between a guaranteed £10 and an expected or risky £10. Most people would tend to go for the guaranteed £10, rather than toss the coin.

Now let's change the rules of the coin toss game. Now you either pay me £10 or you can toss the coin and pay nothing or £20. In these conditions, most people prefer to gamble. In other words we have asymmetric risk behaviour when considering gains and losses. We suffer from loss aversion. In mediation this means that a claimant might prefer a sure settlement over the risk of going to court, say. On the other hand, if a defendant has to pay they may prefer the gamble of going to court than the certainty of paying out now. Skilful mediators and parties will recognise these tendencies and adjust behaviour appropriately.

A particular example of loss aversion is known as the endowment effect. This often happens when claimants tend to think in terms of their rights. To take an example: a claimant has lost his property empire when the bank repossessed his properties during a property slump. The claimant is claiming damages equating to the value of his lost property. Although he is a claimant, he is fixated on a figure that he perceives as his own property – his right. He doesn't recognise that his choice is between the uncertain outcome of a court decision versus a settlement. Instead, he is averse to settling because he perceives that he will suffer a loss if he settles for less than the original property empire value. Helping him understand that what he has is a chance rather than a right can counter the endowment effect.

Anchoring

How many times in mediations does one party or the other become anchored to a wholly unrealistic opening bid? How many times do parties say: 'I've moved £x from my opening offer and he's only moved £y'? A lot. Simply explaining the phenomenon of anchoring (and also that most people will find the other side's opening bid laughable and/or insulting) can go a long way towards avoiding unnecessary conflict in many negotiations.

Overconfidence

Most people think they are a better than average driver. Similarly, most people think they will win when they go to court. Indeed, a US study once ascertained that most trial lawyers (68 per cent) advised their clients they would win. Most people are wrong. Overconfidence can lead to people turning down good settlement offers. Unrealistic optimism can lead parties to hold out for terms that the counterparty is unlikely to accept. For example, in a substantial dilapidations claim, the parties were many millions apart, separated by a significant difference in the rate per square foot advised by their respective experts, both of whom were intransigently confident that their figure was correct. There was no chance of settlement until both of them faced the possibility that they could be wrong. In this actual case, they were persuaded that they might be mistaken, met alone and solved the problem in a short time.

Confirmation bias

Linked to overconfidence, this is when we pick up on information that supports our case and ignore or discount evidence that works against us. This can lead to unrealistic assessments of the risks of going to court, for example.

Fundamental attribution error

We tend to blame internal motivation for other people's behaviour, but external circumstances for our own. So in mediation, the other side are evil liars and tricksters, whereas our (equally outrageous) opening bid was merely an attempt to get the ball rolling given the circumstances.

Groupthink

Groupthink is a psychological phenomenon that occurs within a group of people, in which the desire for harmony or conformity in the group results in an incorrect or deviant decision-making outcome. Often in mediations you will have teams on both sides. It can be hard for opinions outside the mainstream to be heard in such circumstances. Confirmation bias is reinforced, as is demonisation of the other side (fundamental attribution error discussed above). This is, in our experience, a very widespread phenomenon in mediation.

Sunk cost fallacy

It's no use crying over spilt milk. Some costs you are not going to get back. Some legal costs or management time spent in the run up to the mediation, for example, may well not be recoverable if you go ahead to trial. These costs are not going to change and you will suffer them whether or not you go to court. Therefore, you should ignore them in your decision making. Taking sunk costs into account when deciding what to do in the future is a fundamental error, and, again, one that is often made. The reason we go wrong is loss aversion. It's a loss; it won't change, but we don't like it. Often, even though the court won't give the party back their money, they would rather go to court than crystallise the loss by accepting a settlement.

These are just a few of the typical types of bias that can slip into decision making in the mediation process. The most straightforward way of overcoming them is to be aware of their existence. But a rigorous approach to risk analysis can also help identify and overcome them.

Approaches to risk analysis

Once you have identified all the risks, and are aware that you may be suffering from the various biases described above, how can you evaluate the risks while guarding against the biases?

Let's return to the basic game described above. If it is heads you get £20. If it is tails you get nothing. I'm offering you a deal: you can choose between playing the game or I give you a guaranteed £10. What do you do?

As already suggested, the way you think about this is to calculate an 'expected value'. This is the average of the uncertain outcomes weighted by the probability of them happening. Here the outcomes from the coin toss are £20 or £0, so the expected value is £20 × 50 per cent + £0 × 50 per cent = 10 + 0 = £10. *After* the coin is tossed, you will get £20 or nothing, rather than £10. But *before* the coin is tossed you need a way to think about valuing the uncertain outcome, and calculating an expected value is how you do this.

Analytically, there is not much difference between this and a simplified version of what we sometimes ask parties at mediation to do when we they need to decide between a settlement offer and going to court. The orders of magnitude might be different – the settlement offer might be £10m and winning in court might yield £20m versus nothing if you lose, for example. Lawyers might estimate the chances of winning in court are 50 per cent. So now the relevant party is being asked to consider a guaranteed £10m as against an 'expected' £10m.

Things are rarely as simple as this. First, litigation usually requires a down payment – there will be significant upfront costs to get to trial. You may get some of that money back if you win, but usually you will not get it all. The outcome numbers need to take into account recoverable costs, the time value of money and other complexities. Similarly, cases are rarely just one issue, win or lose. There will often be several interrelated issues, all of which affect the final 'expected value' of going to court. For example, a reasonably straightforward case might need to consider whether certain evidence is admissible or not. Was the party negligent? What were the actual damages? A judge may be asked to find on all of these issues, which in effect means there is a probability attached to each of these questions. The probabilities themselves are subjective assessments made by your lawyers and there may be a range of answers. When things start to get complicated like this, you need a tool to help you do the risk analysis. A useful tool in such circumstances is a *decision tree*.

An example of a decision tree is shown below. In this stylised example, a bank is accused of defrauding a client. They are in mediation. The bank has offered £8m to settle. If the case goes to court the client thinks he will get £16m if he wins, but may end up paying £2m if he loses (mainly as a result of legal costs). There is a complication around whether or not the judge will admit a certain piece of evidence; the chances are 80 per cent that she will not do so. If she does, the client's chances of winning are high (80 per cent); if not, they are reduced to 50 per cent.

Analysing Risk

Figure 1. Example decision tree

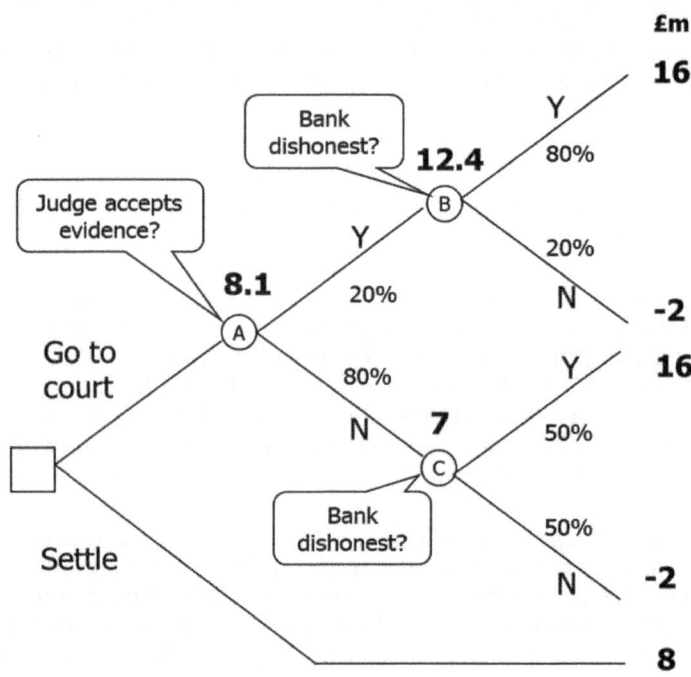

To be able to build a decision tree you need to know its structure, the probabilities and the value of different outcomes. Once you have set it up, you use it to determine the best decision.

Structure

The structure of the problem depends on what the decisions are, where the uncertainties or risks lie and the logical order of decisions and risks. Importantly you mustn't forget the possibility and cost of losing. It is really surprising how often parties in mediation do not take into account the downside. In mediations, as shown in this example, the prime decision is usually go to court or settle. If you settle you know you will get £8m, shown at the end of the settle branch. If you go to court, that branch has various uncertainties: will the judge accept the evidence (could be yes, could be no); will the judge find that the bank defrauded the client (could be yes, could be no)? Each uncertainty has a probability attached.

Probabilities

Probabilities are often subjective assessments and will depend on the merits and the knowledge and experience of legal advisers. This involves translating notions such as 'very good case' and 'chances are poor' into numbers. What advisers usually have in mind is in fact a range of probabilities (for example, from 60 per cent to 80 per cent) and these can be used at a later date to create scenarios of best case and worst case. (Probabilities at a node must always add up to 100 per cent – if they don't there's something wrong!) Here, the first uncertainty is whether or not the judge will accept the new evidence. The probability assessment of advisers is that the judge is likely to accept it only 20 per cent of the time. The next uncertainty is whether or not the judge will find the bank dishonest. This depends on whether or not the judge accepted the evidence in the prior uncertainty as can be seen from the different probabilities at each node. If the judge accepts the evidence, then the chance they will find the bank dishonest is 80 per cent. However, as can be seen on the branch where they do not accept the evidence, the chances of finding the bank dishonest are reduced to 50 per cent. At the end of each branch is an outcome value, which is what you will get/pay if that particular sequence of events takes place.

Outcome values

The numbers at the end of each branch must take into account all relevant costs and benefits. Some historical costs will not be recoverable so must be excluded (sunk costs, as discussed above). On the other hand, the future cost of management time (for example) will occur if the dispute continues, and should be included. Legal costs and taxes can both be pivotal and must not be omitted. The time value of money (interest) might also be an important consideration if the trial period is likely to be long. Here the outcomes are you get £16m if you win, but you pay £2m if you lose. If you settle, you get £8m.

Determine best decision

Once you have set up the decision tree, you need to calculate the expected value of your claim (or defence), in order to compare it with what is being offered in settlement. The way to read decision trees is from the end of the branches backwards. The *value* at the end of the line is multiplied by the *probability* on the line. This gives an *expected value*.

The first issue in this case is whether the judge accepts the evidence. The next issue is whether the bank is dishonest, and this issue appears on both the branches stemming from the node marked A. So both nodes B and C raise the issue of the bank's dishonesty, but the chances of whether the bank is held dishonest are different depending on whether the evidence has been admitted by the judge at A.

Figure 2. Expected value at B

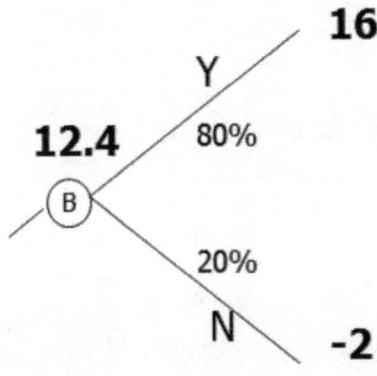

Analysing Risk

Take, therefore, the expected value at node B (which assumes that you have won on admitting the evidence at A). The expected value of the top branch is 80 per cent × £16m, or £12.8m. But from this has to be deducted the expected value at node B of losing on dishonesty. If you lost, you would have to pay £2m, the expected value of losing is -£2m × 20 per cent, or - £0.4m. (The negative figure is because you will be paying). So the expected value at node B is £12.4m (£12.8m – £0.4m). One way of thinking about this is to imagine the judge has decided in your favour on evidence, but has yet to decide the rest of the case. You take a break and the client says: 'Now we've won that, how much is this worth to me?' Your answer would be £12.4m, ie your chance of winning outright, reduced by a sum if you lose; all given you have won on evidence.

Now let us look what happens if the evidence is not admitted by the judge (node C).

Figure 3. Expected value at C

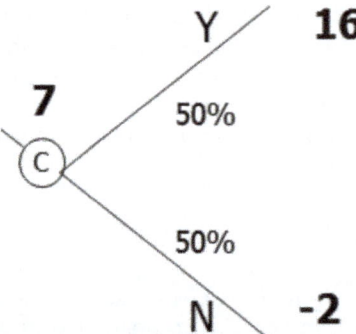

At C the chances of success are lower than the chances if the evidence is admitted (50:50 as against 80:20). With only a 50 per cent chance of winning the expected value at the node C is £7m (again adding the value of the two branches, so £16m × 50 per cent - £2m × 50 per cent). Obviously, this is lower than the case where the evidence is admitted. With these calculations in hand we can now do the thought experiment of asking what the case is worth before the judge has decided on admissibility of evidence, ie the expected value at node A.

Figure 4. Expected value at A

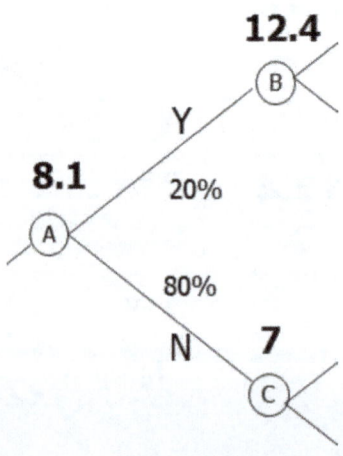

To get the expected value at A, we go through the same process of adding the expected value of winning on evidence to that of losing. In other words 12.4m × 20 per cent + 7m × 80 per cent = £8.1m (when rounded). So now we have an expected value for the whole case. This is like asking counsel, 'How much is this worth?' on the steps of the court, before the judge has decided anything.

In terms of the mediation it gives you something to compare a settlement offer with. In this particular case, the expected value is not far off the amount being offered in settlement. It is then up to the party to decide between accepting the offer and going to court (assuming the offer is final). In this case, it would be perfectly rational to accept the bank's offer of £8m. Despite the headline claim of £16m, and despite the very high prospect of success if the contested evidence were admitted, the substantial risk in relation to the admission of the evidence means that the offer correctly values the client's claim, but you have to go through the numbers to see this.

Let us now imagine that the offered settlement is £5m. In this case it seems rational not to accept the offer and to go to court. However, the mediator can use the decision tree to test why there is the difference in valuation between the paying party and the receiving party. Are the assumptions being used by the receiving party too optimistic? Are the assumptions being made by the paying party also too optimistic? The mediator can then test the assumptions and biases of all parties and see what can be changed to bring the parties closer together. It is not unusual in mediations to find that both sides are being advised they have a 70 per cent chance of success. The advisers are not both right.

Several numbers were thrown at you here, but the actual calculations were simple arithmetic and the complexity, if there is any, comes from the layers of probability presented by the structure of the problem. Putting these all together can lead to quite a complicated decision, which is precisely why this kind of tool can help demystify some of the features of decision making under conditions of uncertainty.

Let us give two real life examples of where this has helped. In one case, a bank was suing a number of individuals who had a common liability. Each individual had a number of defences; a debt had been increased without their knowledge, an agent had signed a document without authority, they were not a member of the particular group at the time and so on. The bank thought that they had an excellent prospect on each such issue. But each issue was an independent defence, and the defendants only had to succeed on one issue to win, while the bank had to win on every single one. The bank team were anchored to recovery of the sum claimed, were demonising the alleged debtors, and were demonstrating groupthink, as well as being overconfident. Setting out the probabilities in the form of a decision tree helped the bank understand that overall it had rather a low chance of succeeding, undid the groupthink, changed their attitude to the debtors and altered their anchor point.

In another case, a purchaser of a company was bringing an action for breach of warranty. They had an absolutely unanswerable case on liability. They had suffered very substantial damage – say £100m – and there was a great deal of personal animosity. But there was a contractual limitation of liability to £3m, and the defendants had a very good chance of succeeding on that defence. Again, drawing the decision tree helped the claimant work out that their real expected value was very low and that pursuing the claim because of how they felt was simply going to cause them more damage.

Pros and cons of risk analysis

There are both pros and cons to quantitative approaches to risk analysis. Pros include:

- **Increased clarity**

    Expected values and decision trees help parties understand the risks involved in the decision they face and help them decide between accepting an offer and not. Decision trees help unpack the uncertainties and focus on the advice being given. Sometimes they can help parties understand what is really going on. Sometimes it can be reassuring that a figure which a party wishes to take is in fact a realistic figure. Sometimes they can reassure parties that they are right to reject an offer – back to the lady with the injured child at the beginning of this chapter.

- **Communication tool**

    Never mind giving an answer, simply laying out the structure of the decision can help parties understand more clearly what the key issues are and also the strengths and weaknesses of their case. Vitally, such approaches can help mediation parties explain decisions to external authorities (eg company boards) after the event – why we accepted/offered or why we rejected.

- **Negotiation advantage**

    Doing the decision tree from the perspective of the other side is a very useful exercise in understanding where they are coming from and what sort of assumptions they must be making about outcomes and probabilities. This can be an important mechanism in bringing sides closer. It can highlight critical differences and allow reasoned debate about why advisers have differing probability assessments over certain issues for example.

- **Flexibility**

    Information may change or be revealed in the course of a mediation. It is easy to change numbers, play with the sensitivity of outcomes to certain key uncertainties and so on.

On the other hand, there can be issues with this kind of approach. Some of the cons are:

- **Numeracy requirement**

    It requires a minimal level of numeracy on the part of the parties and the mediator. Most commercial parties will be entirely comfortable with this approach because they will be using similar techniques in their investment analysis in the workplace. However, some will not, and mediators need to be able to communicate and explain to less numerate parties the indications such risk analyses give.

- **Garbage in, garbage out and anchoring**

    Without care, you risk the problem of 'garbage in, garbage out'. If the parties haven't structured the tree properly or haven't calculated the outcomes or probabilities correctly there is a risk of getting a misleading answer. Worse, it is a calculated answer of spurious precision. As we saw above, over-optimism and groupthink means that even the best lawyers can be optimistic with their probability assessments. Unfortunately, even if it is wrong, it might be an answer to which one party or the other becomes anchored. It is important, therefore, that the person preparing the decision tree knows what they are doing and emphasises that outcomes are entirely dependent on the subjective assessments made of the prospects of success. Advising parties in advance that their assumptions might change is almost always a useful technique in expectations management.

- **Quantifying qualitative results**

    When the outcomes are hard to quantify, for example, in the case of emotional costs and benefits, then decision trees and expected values can only help with the financial issues, leaving the parties to weigh these against the emotional pros and cons.

- **Risk neutral answers**

    Decision trees give a 'risk neutral' answer. They do not account for a party's appetite (or lack of it) for risk. Parties need to factor in their own attitude to risk on top of any answer a decision tree might give. So in the case shown in Figure 1, 'go to court' option is almost the same as the settlement option. However, 'go to court' has risk attached – the answer after the event could be higher or lower. Many risk averse parties will want to discount the £8.1m answer because of this. Bear in mind, of course, that you need to do a decision tree analysis first before you can then discount (or increase) the number according to your risk preferences.

Many parties and mediators do not use decision trees. Where the stakes are low, then it is not unreasonable to do a minimal risk analysis. However, we think that they are an essential part of the mediator's tool kit. We don't advocate a rigid adherence to the answers given by decision trees. We do recommend their use as at least an indicator and to help parties understand the true nature of the decision they are making. Otherwise, we (surprisingly) often find that the parties are comparing the most optimistic outcome with the settlement offer. At the end of the day, what else do parties do when faced with uncertainty? It is true that many claims settle without using decision trees, but are the parties making good decisions?

Summary

Finally, as we said at the outset, like many things in life, litigation is a gamble. Not only are the outcomes uncertain, in most cases you even have to pay money (in the form of costs to your lawyers to get to trial) in order to participate. Parties often tend to think in terms of rights. Parties will be significantly assisted in making decisions which they will recognise as good decisions after the deal is done (or not done) if they think in terms of chances, and recognise that they are making a decision where the outcomes if they do not settle are uncertain.

For the parties, our checklist for successful risk analysis in mediation is as follows:

- **Be prepared**

    It helps to take time before the mediation to think through all possible risks, and to get as much information as possible to inform the assessments of outcomes and their likelihood. This will enable parties to carry out a risk analysis before they get to the mediation. Of course, parties need to be prepared to be flexible if the information they have changes during the course of the mediation.

Analysing Risk

- **Determine the walkaway value**

    In our view it is essential to know what figure you will walk away from the negotiation at before you start negotiating (there's another book, or at least a chapter, in there). Using a decision tree to tease out thinking and analyse prospects dispassionately helps establish this figure. Again, parties need to be flexible if information changes during the mediation.

- **Avoid biases**

    It can be useful to have someone to play devil's advocate, ensuring that they know to check for hidden biases in assumptions and thinking. It's also worth using everyone in the team to contribute, and having as open a discussion as possible in order to avoid groupthink and confirmation bias.

- **Understand the other side**

    As suggested above, it is helpful to do the risk analysis from the opponent's point of view. This will help provide a sense of their walkaway value and hence the likely acceptability of any offers which might be made.

For mediators our checklist is similar:

- **Be prepared**

    Obviously the mediator should be on top of the case, its issues and the parties' positions on those issues. Mediators can encourage the parties to do their own risk analysis and at minimum gather the numbers required to do so (costs of going to court, probabilities of success etc). We always do a risk analysis as part of our preparation and deploy it if and when we deem appropriate.

- **Reduce biases**

    Biases won't be eliminated, but they can be reduced by explaining the possible hurdles to parties in advance. So, in our mediation preamble to both parties we say they are mediating ultimately to make a decision between accepting/making an offer or walking away and continuing the dispute. To make that decision they need to know the value of both options, including the gamble of going to court. We warn them of potential hiccoughs along the route to settlement. Telling both parties that the other side will find the initial offer insulting takes a lot of the sting out of what inevitably happens. Explaining how both sides will tend to demonise the other sides' motives can help. Explaining overconfidence, especially when it comes to assessments of how judges will perceive cases, is also sometimes useful.

- **Be bold**

    Many mediators don't use risk analysis. We think they should, while explaining all the caveats we have outlined.

The tools we have described here are at best a torch to shine through the fog of uncertain mediation decisions. They don't illuminate the whole road ahead and guarantee perfect mediation outcomes, but they do throw a little light on the way forward.[1]

1   For more illumination, we suggest the following: Howard Raiffa, *The Art & Science of Negotiation* (Harvard University Press, 1990); Daniel Kahneman *Thinking, Fast and Slow*, (Penguin, 2012); Belsky & Gilovich, *Why Smart People Make Big Money Mistakes and How to Correct Them* (Simon & Schuster, 2010).

Chapter 9

Mediation Ethics

Michel Kallipetis QC

No mediation book would be complete without a contribution from Michel. He is probably the busiest and most successful of all commercial mediators in the United Kingdom, yet, despite his fame, he remains a gracious and caring individual. He is also an entertaining speaker and opera singer. (DR)

Introduction

As all professionals know, and lawyers in particular appreciate, questions of ethics in the conduct of one's practice are seldom clear-cut. Everyone will agree that the basic principles themselves are fairly straightforward and can be expressed in simple terms. However the problem always arises when particular issues, usually unexpected, crop up which require the application of general principles to circumstances that are not black and white.

So it is with mediation. The ethical principles by which mediators are expected to act are not controversial but their application to situations that arise in mediation is not always the subject of agreement between mediators. Curiously, or perhaps inevitably, the more experienced mediators sometimes have greater difficulty giving a straight 'yes' or 'no' answer to any particular problem that may arise. This has been borne out in many conferences and seminars where particular problems have been posed to a group of mediators and there has rarely been unanimity on the approach to be adopted in terms of ethical conduct.

There are, of course, two issues to be considered: the ethical conduct of the mediator and the ethical conduct of the lawyers representing clients in mediation. Each issue merits its own chapter, if not a complete volume, but as far as this chapter is concerned I shall deal solely with the first issue – the ethical standards expected of mediators – and try to give some examples of problems which arise to which there could be more than one ethical answer. I shall also consider the possibility of regulation – an evergreen topic of conversation between mediators. In addition, thanks to my US colleague Larissa Lieberman, I will incorporate some of the attempts to create a regulatory regime in the United States, where mediation has been practiced for decades.

Why an ethical code?

Among mediators in the United Kingdom, particularly those who are engaged full time in mediation, there is a drive to establish mediation as a profession. A profession, to have credibility, needs an accepted code of ethics to which all mediators subscribe. Moreover, the trend by the courts towards persuading disputants to mediate rather than litigate by imposing severe costs sanctions upon those who unreasonably resist the persuasion, inevitably creates the impression in some that mediation is, for practical purposes, fairly compulsory. It would completely undermine that initiative if the disputants did not have confidence in the competence and ethical standards of those whom they feel obliged to appoint as mediators. Professor Parke of the University of Southern Queensland, along with many other academics, argues with some force that as mediation progresses towards becoming a recognised profession the need for a recognised minimum standards governing ethical behaviour by mediators becomes more and more necessary so as to give the requisite public confidence in the mediation process itself. Rather than submitting to a Code of Conduct drafted by those who theorise rather than practice mediation, the mediation community as a whole needs to assemble the accumulated wisdom and experience of those who mediate regularly and produce a set of ethical standards to which all mediators will subscribe and in which those who are required to use mediation can have confidence.

Some moves towards establishing an ethical code have been made in the United States, Australia and in Europe. The European Code of Conduct for mediators expresses in simple terms the basic requirements which the European Commission considered were necessary for the proper conduct of mediations. They are similar to those set out in the United States in the Model Standards for Conduct of Mediators. In summary they deal with impartiality, no conflict of interest, competence, confidentiality, quality of the process, advertising and solicitation, transparency over fees and charges, advancement of the mediation practice, and self determination. Many of these areas overlap but, in the main, they are universally accepted as the basic ethical requirements for any mediator.

Types of mediation

There is also the view that the type of mediation being conducted could influence the extent to which ethical principles may apply. Family mediations work on the basis that the interests of the children are paramount and therefore any information which may impact upon children's welfare would not be considered privileged from disclosure in any subsequent proceedings: similarly with mediations concerning the interests of a patient within the meaning of the Mental Health legislation. In community mediations, where the parties are seldom legally represented, it is difficult to impose an effective regime of confidentiality and the mediator's ethical duties are perhaps more difficult to determine with any rigidity.

The generally accepted classification is between facilitative, evaluative and transformative mediation. Facilitative mediation, which stresses the importance of the mediator's neutrality and party autonomy to help the parties develop their own problem-solving capacity, limits the ability of the mediator to steer or guide the parties towards a settlement. Evaluative mediation helps the parties to assess the strength of their position and their opponents and the potential settlements based upon law and practice and involves offering an evaluation. In California, a practice has developed among mediators to offer 'the mediator's proposal' at the end of a mediation, which the parties take away to consider. Any evaluative mediation creates a different problem for mediators as to how far they should push or steer the parties towards a particular settlement. Lastly, transformative mediation, which focuses on personal growth enabling the parties to develop a better recognition of their own goals, values and capacities and a greater empathy for the concerns of others, brings with it its own different applications of ethical standards as far as the mediator is concerned. This chapter is far too short to consider all the ramifications in respect of each of these mediation styles and therefore of necessity it will set out general principles and, in particular, consider the attempts made in the United States and Australia to regulate the process to see whether or not some form of regulation ought to be considered in the United Kingdom.

Regulation

Regulation is always a burning issue. Some attempt at regulation of standards has been promulgated, notably by the International Mediation Institute, but also by other countries in the European Union. The European Commission has toyed with regulation for some time but, as yet, has been unable to draft rules acceptable to all 27 Member States. The proselytisers of regulation argue that they want parties to have confidence in mediation, particularly in those countries where it is still a relatively new process, and perceive a need to hold mediators accountable in order to enable the consumers to have trust in the process. However, any attempt to standardise an ethical code for mediators creates its own difficulties and challenges. Any code has to take account of the interdisciplinary nature of the mediation and accommodate the flexibility of the process, which most mediators would consider absolutely essential for any successful mediation. There is an understandable reluctance to overburden mediators and the mediation process with regulation, but perhaps the most important and most difficult question is deciding which body should regulate mediators and what sanctions that organisation ought to apply. The cost of an effective organisation to regulate the conduct of mediators and adjudicate allegations of breaches of a Code is likely to prove prohibitive and raises an even more contentious issue as to how it should be funded. It is hardly likely that the mediators themselves would consider funding this and certainly it is not something that any government in the current economic climate would consider to be an essential part of public expenditure.

In Europe, various Member States have enacted codes of conduct applicable for mediators acting in their own jurisdiction. Most of these relate to court-appointed mediations, where different considerations may well apply in that if the courts are directing parties to mediation and a specific panel of mediators it will want to be certain that those mediators are competent and conform to the ethical standards of the court itself. Failure to do so, particularly if the reference to mediation is mandatory, would probably breach Art 6 of the European Convention on Human Rights.

The European Code of Conduct for Mediators

The European Code of Conduct for Mediators was promulgated by the EU Commission before the EU Directive on ADR was implemented by the European Parliament. This Code of Conduct sets out a number of principles to which individual mediators can voluntarily decide to commit, under their own responsibility. It was intended to be applicable to all kinds of mediation in civil and commercial matters. For the purposes of the Code, mediation was defined as:

> '... any process where two or more parties agree to the appointment of a third party – hereinafter "the mediator" – to help the parties to solve the dispute by reaching an agreement without adjudication and regardless of how that process may be called or commonly referred to in each Member State'.

Adherence to the Code is specifically without prejudice to national legislation or rules regulating individual professions. The Code itself deals with the usual basic principles that one would expect:

- independence and impartiality;
- the fairness of the process and the procedure;
- fees;
- confidentiality; and
- enforcement of any awards arrived at the conclusion of the mediation.

The Code itself is fairly basic, of necessity when one is dealing with 27 Member States, each with its own view about the effect or otherwise of mediation. Moreover, there is no compulsion about the Code and, as yet, no regulation to enforce it.

As already stated the real and most practical difficulty with any ethical code is enforcement. Most responsible mediation *providers* have some form of code with which they expect their panel of mediators to comply and, if one of its mediators fails to do so, then the mediation provider itself may take action against the mediator. In addition the mediation provider may be at risk of suit by the parties who have been disadvantaged as a result.

The United States Experience

In the United States there have been various attempts to set *standards*. It is instructive to consider what success such attempts have had. There is no clear regulation of mediator *ethics*. There is no state in the United States which licences mediators. No state has a binding ethical code for all mediators with a formal disciplinary board. However, regulation is increasing, with at least 27 states having statutory or judiciary-appointed standards of conduct and formal disciplinary boards for court-appointed mediators. Those rules often specify the qualifications necessary for such mediators. As with the United Kingdom, mediator organisations and private ADR providers have adopted their own standard. There are some specialised areas of mediation, for example, child custody, patients and those suffering with disabilities, where individual organisations have set their own standards for the mediators who mediate such disputes. All of the standards are either guidelines for mediators or model rules that act as guidance for states in creating standards. As such, none of them are actually enforceable unless a particular state has enacted them into law.

Moral Standards of Conduct for mediators was first promulgated in 1994 and revised in 2005 by the American Bar Association section of Dispute Resolution, The American Arbitration Association and the Association for Conflict Resolution. These serve as guidelines. The areas covered are self-determination, impartiality, conflicts of interest, competence, confidentiality, qualitative process, advertising and solicitation, fees and other charges and advancement of the mediation practice.

The Uniform Mediation Act (UMA), approved by the National Conference of Commissioners on Uniform State Laws and approved by the American Bar Association, provided guidelines for states in enacting laws pertaining to mediation. By 2011, ten states, plus the District of Columbia, had approved some version of the Uniform Mediation Act; this includes provisions regulating confidentiality and conflicts of interest.

The Model Rules for the Lawyer acting as a Third Party Neutral (2002) promulgated by the Georgetown Commission on Ethics and Standards of Practice in ADR provide model rules for states to adopt regarding ethical responsibility of lawyers serving as third party neutrals. These rules include rules on diligence and competence, confidentiality, impartiality, conflicts of interest, fees, fairness and integrity of the process.

Lastly, the ABA Model Rules of Professional Conduct, edited in 2005 to add two new rules expressly referring to mediators, provides for regulation as far as lawyers are concerned when mediating. In summary, it requires mediators to distinguish their role clearly from representing counsel. Rule 2.4 defines the distinction thus:

> '(a) a lawyer serves as a third party neutral when the lawyer assists two or more persons who are not clients of the lawyer to reach a solution of a dispute or other matter between them. Service as a third-party neutral may include service as an arbitrator, a mediator or in such other capacity as to enable the lawyer to assist the parties to resolve the matter.
>
> (b) A lawyer serving as a third party neutral should inform unrepresented parties that the lawyer is not representing them. When the lawyer knows or reasonably should know that the party does not understand the lawyer's role in the matter, the lawyer should explain the difference between the lawyer's role as a third-party neutral and a lawyer's role as one who represents a client.'

Rule 1.12 which applies to a former judge, arbitrator, mediator or other third party neutral provides guidance for mediators for resolving conflicts of interest that might arise from having previously served in a neutral capacity. The rule provides:

> '(a) Except as stated in paragraph (d), a lawyer shall not represent anyone in connection with the matter in which the lawyer participated personally and substantially as a judge or other adjudicative officer or law clerk to such person or as an arbitrator, mediator or other third party neutral, unless all parties to the proceeding give informed consent, confirmed in writing.
>
> (b) A lawyer shall not negotiate for employment with any person who is involved as a party or as a lawyer for a party in a matter in which the lawyer is participating personally and substantially as a judge or other adjudicative officer or as an arbitrator, mediator or other third party neutral. A lawyer serving as a law clerk to a judge or other adjudicative officer may negotiate for employment with a party or lawyer involved in a matter in which the clerk is participating personally and substantially but only after the lawyer has notified the judge or other adjudicative officer.

(c) If a lawyer is disqualified by paragraph (a) no lawyer in any firm with which the lawyer is associated may knowingly undertake or continue representation in a matter unless:
   (1) the disqualified lawyer is timely screened from any participation in the matter and is apportioned no part of the fee therefrom; and
   (2) written notice is promptly given to the parties and any appropriate tribunal to enable them to ascertain compliance within the provision of the law.
(d) An arbitrator selected as a partisan of a party in multimember arbitration panel is not prohibited from subsequently representing that party.'

Professor Menkel-Meadow's basic principles as set out in 'The Lawyer as a Consensus: Ethics for a New Practice'[1] provide a basic ethical framework for mediators, neutral consensus builders or facilitators. The rules are designed to ensure broad party and stakeholder participation and provide opportunities for participants to agree on procedural and ground rules, as well as on rules for agreements. They encourage participant recognition of both individual and joint interests and encourage parties to express reasons and justifications for their views, needs and offers. They facilitate creative and tailored solutions to meet the parties' needs and objectives, provide a place of fair hearing and respect for all parties. They also provide for the facilitation of capacity building and parties to negotiate on their own behalf.

Interestingly, they also provide for the consideration of the practicality and enforcement of agreements reached, provided of course that they must be free from bias and conflicts of interest and avoid unjust, unfair or unconscionable agreements wherever possible. The latter is an intriguing provision. When the European Commission working party was discussing the European Code of Conduct for Mediators there was a lengthy and quite heated debate (driven mainly by the European Consumer Association representative) as to whether or not there should be included within the Code a provision that a mediator should not allow the parties to enter into what was described as an 'unconscionable bargain'. Experienced mediators will readily appreciate that the difficulty with such a proposition is that frequently mediators are unaware of the full extent of the parties' reasons for entering any particular settlement. Once the mediator is put into the position of assuming an obligation to judge whether or not an agreement is 'fair or unconscionable', any challenge to the agreement after the mediation inevitably will involve the mediator him or herself. In my opinion this oversteps the universally accepted principle of an independent mediator whose task is to facilitate an agreement without actually imposing his/her own resolution.

Monitoring the settlement agreement

Most mediators will leave the drafting of any settlement agreement to the parties' lawyers. There is no ethical reason why this should be other than allowing the parties the freedom to contract as they wish. The difficulty arises if a mediation settlement agreement is patently unworkable or fails to include a term that has been agreed. In those circumstances it is generally accepted, and certainly my view,

---

1   C Menkel-Meadow, 'The Lawyer as a Consensus: Ethics for a New Practice' 70 Tenn L Rev 63–119 (2002).

that it is the mediator's obligation to point this out to the parties' representatives, and encourage the parties, if an agreement is patently unlawful, or breaches fiscal or other legislative provisions, to remedy the defect. In such circumstances it would be quite wrong for a mediator to ignore the problem, and his or her obligation is to make the parties' representatives aware of the potential difficulty and assist if he can in resolving it. In short, pointing out potential difficulties in a settlement agreement is a prudent and necessary part of a mediator's obligations to ensure that the parties are entering into the settlement with full knowledge and informed consent. This is a far cry from assessing the fairness of the agreed terms: allowing an agreement to be signed by the parties in the knowledge that, sooner or later, it could be open to challenge, not only does that not serve the parties' interests but it also inevitably will involve the mediator at some stage in the future in some form of suit, particularly if they are forced to acknowledge that they were aware of the difficulty and kept silent.

There are obviously ethical issues where a party is not represented by lawyers. The difficulty is assessing how much assistance a mediator can give without actually being considered to be advising the party. This is potentially one of the most difficult situations for a mediator. It is my practice to make arrangements with an unrepresented party for him or her to have access to a lawyer for advice by telephone, if necessary during the mediation, but in any event on the proposed mediation settlement. If the party concerned does not have a lawyer already, I have asked colleagues to assist on a pro bono basis and seldom have I been refused. Failing all else, it is prudent to suggest that the parties do not actually complete the agreement until the individual who is unrepresented has had the benefit of legal advice upon it. This is a far safer way to proceed and protects both parties and the mediator from any suggestion of coercion or lack of informed consent to any settlement.

Mediator's obligations

It is generally accepted that the mediator should explain his or her role and the process, discuss obligations concerning confidentiality and the ground rules for any sessions in private with one or other of the parties. It is also beyond doubt that a mediator should disclose any potential grounds of bias or conflict of interest that may give rise to questions about the mediator's impartiality. Often overlooked is the mediator's obligation to advise the parties that they may suspend or terminate the mediation in circumstances where they either conclude there is no useful purpose being served by continuing with it or if one or other party has said or done something which causes them to doubt the authenticity of the other. The mediator should also have reserved to him or herself the right to terminate the mediation if they learn of matters which make it impossible for them to continue. It is not only good practice but essential that all mediators should ensure that parties sign a mediation agreement which clearly establishes the contractual basis of the mediation. In the absence of any overriding Code of Ethics, it is good practice to include in the Mediation Agreement itself or in the general Terms and Conditions, any particular Code of Conduct to which the mediator has committed. In this way any breach of that Code would also be an enforceable breach of the mediation agreement.

One of the difficulties with the purist view of self-determination by the parties is that the primary role of the mediator is to facilitate a voluntary resolution of the dispute.

However, most experienced mediators will know that there are situations that arise when the parties do require and, indeed, some request assistance from the mediator to get them towards a settlement. In such a situation can it be right for a mediator to refuse? How the help is given, and to what extent, inevitably will depend upon the circumstances, the nature of the dispute, the mediator's relationship with the parties and the ability of their respective lawyers to assist. Most will agree that it would be quite wrong and unethical for a mediator to advise a client in the absence of their lawyer. In some instances, particularly court-appointed mediations, there is a pressure upon the parties and the mediator to achieve a settlement. Moreover, mediators on a personal level, whatever their protestations to the contrary may be, often like to be able to say that they have 'resolved a dispute'. Some parties may even choose mediators upon the basis of their settlement rate. This leads to another difficulty which I shall turn to later when dealing with ethical advertising.

The issue of self-determination raises the question: 'How far should a mediator use persuasive tactics to push the parties towards a negotiated settlement?' Other than in general terms, this is an impossible question to answer. No party should ever feel under inappropriate pressure from the mediator; on the other hand mediators have been criticised for failing to 'test us on our case'. Reality testing is a feature that is taught, and indeed practised by most mediators, but how far does this go? Like all ethical principles, it is a question of degree. If the mediator senses that there is resistance to a particular line then of course they should stop. On the other hand, there may be situations where they are unaware that their attempt to push the parties towards a settlement is becoming oppressive. A competent lawyer will be quick to 'call off' an overzealous mediator and protect their client from any undue pressure. Inevitably, however, there are situations beyond the control of the mediator in which parties are bound to feel pressurised in mediation. A party with no legal defence may well feel there is a pressure upon them to achieve a deal to avoid the inevitability of a judgment. There is hardly a mediation during which one party will not assert an intention to litigate in the absence of settlement. Almost as a matter of course the mediator will be asked to take a message accompanying 'a last and final offer' that failure to accept will precipitate an open or without prejudice offer in the litigation in similar or lesser terms. Is this coercion? Most of us would say obviously not because it reflects the reality of the situation. However, one person's reality is another person's pressure.

The quintessential rule is that a mediator should promote honesty and candour between and among participants and never knowingly misrepresent any material fact or circumstance in the course of a mediation. This is also a principle which is easily stated but more difficult to apply in a particular circumstance. Persuading parties often involves 'manipulating' information available to the parties and the mediator. 'Reframing' offers and presenting facts in a positive light are standard techniques that every mediator uses. More difficult yet is the situation, which quite often occurs, where one party says: 'I want to tell you this but I don't want you to pass it on to the other side'. One cannot erase the information from one's mind, and thus, in spite of every effort not to use it deliberately there is every possibility that one might inadvertently say or hint something which reveals the knowledge that has been given to you in confidence. Cynics might suggest that is precisely the reason why the information was given in the first place!

This gives rise to the next question as to what is adequate disclosure by the mediator to the parties. Most people would agree that a mediator should be totally open and frank. Usually the standards draw a distinction between an affirmative misrepresentation of material facts and passive non- disclosures. Some scholars would argue that it is unethical to condone passive non-disclosures by mediators; that again is a moot point. There are ways and means of indicating that one is in possession of knowledge that one cannot share. If the other side suspects that this is the position then, in my view, the best solution is for the mediator to tell the other party that for various reasons they believe that the other is aware of the fact of this information and, in the best interests of getting to a settlement, they ought to share it. Again, each circumstance is different and the mediator must just simply use his or her best judgement guided by the principles that they must not knowingly mislead.

Even evaluating a circumstance for parties is not without difficulty. Overzealous mediators often exaggerate the risks of non-settlement and over emphasise the benefits of settlement. If the parties are unrepresented, this is an area fraught with peril for the incautious mediator. It is good practice, as well as a prudent precaution, for any such messages to be given to both parties in plenary rather than in private and to be done in a non-directive fashion: do you know how much a trial will cost? Have you any idea of the difficulties involved in preparing for trial? Do you know what remedies are available to the court? Answers given by a mediator in such an environment, especially if couched in terms, 'I suggest that you seek advice as to… etc,' are less likely to give rise to a complaint of oppressive or coercive behaviour by the mediator. If the parties are represented by competent lawyers, they will be in a position to resist any of this overzealous interference by a mediator.

One of the issues raised by the principle of self-determination, frequently encountered by mediators, is the overzealous lawyer who is effectively 'calling the shots'. It is difficult to judge how far mediators should intervene between a client and his lawyer. It is even more difficult if one suspects that the lawyers' judgement is in fact unsound and even more difficult if they have simply got the law wrong. In the latter case, it is my practice to take the lawyer aside and have a quiet chat with him or her about the law, if necessary referring him or her to a particular authority or statute which gives me cause to doubt the accuracy of the advice being given. If the lawyer refuses to accept it there is not much one can do. I doubt whether anyone would consider that it would be ethical for a mediator to advise the client to seek advice from another lawyer. If a discussion with the lawyer in the presence of his client about the relevant legal principles fails to put the client on guard, then there is little else a mediator can properly do. In extreme circumstances, I have held a 'tutorial' with both sets of lawyers discussing the law in the presence of their respective clients, so that they can as far as possible make an informed judgement as to the risks of litigation. One of the ethics problems often posed in seminars is the dilemma facing a mediator who learns of a recent court decision that completely undermines one side's legal argument, of which both parties' lawyers are ignorant. Should the mediator keep the information to him or herself: generally the universal answer is 'no'. Should they inform one party and not the other: surprisingly this has never produced a uniform answer! Should the mediator in the opening plenary session reveal the decision without warning to the party who is disadvantaged by the case? Usually most mediators consider that would be unfair. The better approach is to inform the lawyers of the party who will be disadvantaged by the case and ask whether they are aware of it. If not it gives them an opportunity to rethink their client's position and advise their client on an appropriate stance to adopt.

Impartiality

The requirement of impartiality is generally interpreted as exercising neutrality towards all the participants and having no bias in relation to the subject matter. There is often a debate on how detached a mediator should be. There are two different views on mediation neutrality. Some commentators argue that neutrality means that mediators should prevent their own values from biasing the outcome. Others argue that neutrality requires a structuring of process that will ensure meaningful participation, informed decision making and a reasonable balance of power between the parties to promote fairness in the process. Whichever formulation is preferred, there are complications for creating ethical standards since most mediators tailor their approach to different mediations depending upon the nature of the dispute, the nature of the parties and perceived need for any mediator intervention at any particular time. Obviously a mediator will avoid actual and perceived bias and will ensure that there is a procedurally fair process. Most mediators will refuse to act if they perceive they are unable to be impartial, and most will withdraw if a situation arises where their impartiality is no longer beyond doubt. It is essential that mediators disclose any information that might lead to questions about their impartiality but provided they make a full disclosure and the parties give informed consent then there could be no criticism at all. One of the most difficult issues is the question of whether parties should refuse a mediator simply because that mediator has acted as mediator in a dispute with one of the other parties' representatives previously. There may be different considerations if they have acted in a dispute involving one of the parties themselves, but as far as the representatives are concerned, bearing in mind that most mediators will agree that their mediation practice depends upon referral, it would be inconceivable that having mediated once for a particular firm of lawyers, the mediator should never again be able to act in a mediation where that firm who is representing one of the parties. Nonetheless, some purists argue this is something that ought to be disclosed. In these days of legal directories which list and grade mediators on the basis of research garnered from those who have used them, inevitably people will be relying upon personal experience or comments from others when selecting a mediator. Thus it is not a question of impartiality but more a question of experience. Most research carried out in the legal community confirms that experience is one of the essential criteria when selecting a particular mediator. There is a related but separate question where the mediator has mediated previously with a particular party in a different dispute with a different other party. Is that something which should be disclosed? Prudence suggests that it is better to be sure that there is no objection to avoid any suggestion of apparent bias. However, it cannot be right that as a matter of ethical standards, a mediator may not act as mediator in any dispute with a party who was a party in a previous mediation conducted by him or her.

One of the other areas where there is considerable debate is the question of accepting gifts or items of 'kindness' from any party involved. This is a question practitioners in general have to deal with as a matter of professional conduct. After a successful representation of a client, would it be wrong for a lawyer to accept a bottle of wine or a bunch of flowers as 'thank you' from a grateful client. Most would say obviously not but where do you draw the line? If the client is extremely well off and proffers a case of very expensive and rare claret, does that overstep the mark? The variants are endless and the general guideline for advocates at the English and Welsh Bar is very broad: an advocate should accept nothing that might compromise his or her independence., In my opinion, mediators should follow a similar guideline. Is a mediator obliged to declare an expensive gift from a lawyer or their client for whom s/he has conducted a mediation, if that lawyer or the client appears in a subsequent mediation? The guiding rule should be whether or not accepting such gifts impairs the mediator's independence, and therefore his or her ability to act impartially. This is not a subjective test but an objective test: does such a situation create the appearance of bias?

The American Bar Association's Model Standard II provides that the mediator must conduct the mediation in an impartial manner and actually directs the mediator to withdraw from a mediation or terminate a mediation if the ability to act impartially is compromised and that could include situations, according to the Model Standard, where there is a party imbalance. Rule 4.5.3 of the American Bar Association's Model Rules for Third Party Neutrals seems to strike a balance between the different views of neutrality. In essence it boils down to this. Most mediators will accept that, as human beings, their feelings are bound to influence their view about the merits of a particular case. The importance of course is not to allow that to influence the way that they conduct their mediation. Expressing empathy with a claimant who has suffered terrible injuries is hardly compromising one's impartiality. Persuading insurers to make a sensible offer in such circumstances is hardly evidencing partiality. Most users would regard that as a mediator inculcating realism. Experienced litigators know that most judges will have empathy and sympathy with claimants who have suffered terrible injuries or damage, particularly if there is a dubious defence in law, and a mediator who challenges a party on a position which is tenuous, is doing what the parties have appointed him or her to do. Arguments as to causation or quantum of damages are everyday stuff for lawyers in court and, if raised in mediation, the fact that the mediator will engage vigorously in such a debate with one or other of the parties, does not in any way affect his or her impartiality. When one considers all these factors, I believe the equation is better expressed as 'the mediator is impartial as to the result but not neutral as to the facts'.

Conflicts of interest

The objective aspect of neutrality is that the parties must believe, based upon any disclosures the mediator makes, that they are neutral in the sense that they do not have any conflict of interest. Primarily most guidelines are concerned with the neutrality of the mediator towards participants and their advocates. Many enquiries focus upon mediators that were previously partners within a representative firm in the mediation or mediators providing other services to parties after the mediation. Most mediators who are still partners in a firm of solicitors or members of barristers' chambers will have difficulty in persuading parties that there is no conflict of interest (and certainly not the appearance of one) if they conduct a mediation in which one of their partners or fellow member of chambers may be representing one of the parties.

All the standards, including the European Code of Conduct, require the mediator to disclose any actual or potential conflict of interest. The UMA and Model Standards require reasonable investigation and disclosure of potential and actual conflicts. It is common practice for those representing clients to send details to the organisation or to the mediator of the parties and ask for a declaration that there is no conflict of interest. If the parties chose to engage the mediator after a full disclosure then clearly they waive any objection based upon the disclosed information and any attempt then to set the mediation aside on this ground is unlikely to succeed.

The American Bar Association's Model Standards III require mediators to disclose promptly any potential or actual conflicts of interest and seek the consent of the parties to continue in the face of any possible conflict. The rules also require the mediator to withdraw, even if a party consents, if the conflict of interest 'might reasonably be viewed as undermining the integrity of the mediation'. Model Standard III goes further than the Uniform Mediation Code because it has restrictions on what a mediator can do after the mediation. They cannot establish a relationship with any of the parties. This does not preclude a mediator from serving in another mediation with a party involved in the previous mediation but does prevent him or her acting for that party in any subsequent litigation, arguably in any subsequent litigation, but beyond argument in any subsequent litigation involving the same subject matter. This sensible distinction is probably uncontentious in most jurisdictions.

The universally accepted practice requires the mediator to make full disclosure of any actual or potential conflict and seek the parties' consent. Prudent practitioners will do this in writing. It is sensible that the mediator, when making a disclosure, has in mind the guidance, enshrined in both in the Model Standard and in the UMA, namely 'might the conflict of interest be reasonably viewed as undermining the integrity of the mediation'. Some commentators have argued that this approach undermines the parties' autonomy and freedom to choose a mediator, if the mediator refuses to act on this basis, even though the parties themselves may consent to his or her continuing. However, under the UMA, if a mediator fails to disclose a potential conflict the mediator is precluded from asserting privilege as to mediation communications made by the mediator.

An often-asked question is should the mediator withdraw from a mediation if they know one of the parties socially or professionally? The answer is straightforward: provided full disclosure of the nature of the relationship is given to the parties, it is a matter entirely for them. The greatest risk is that the mediated settlement agreement could be set aside for a mediator's failure to disclose an interest. In such a case, it is highly likely that the mediator would be personally liable for breach of in contract.

Competence

All mediators must comply with whatever standards are required for any particular organisation. Some mediators are asked in particular whether they are familiar with a particular area of law or subject matter. Should this be a matter for a Code of Conduct or regulation? Common sense dictates that it would be a foolish mediator who misrepresents his or her experience or competence to act in any particular dispute, not least because as far as the market place is concerned, that would be the end of his or her reputation as a mediator. That is sufficient safeguard for most practical purposes.

There is not such a clear line about a mediator having 'subject matter expertise'. Arguments against suggest that a mediator is less likely to be biased if they have less knowledge about the subject. On the other hand, those proponents who argue for a mediator with subject matter expertise consider the mediation is more likely to be successful because the mediator will more readily understand the complexities of the subject matter. The purist will say that a good mediator can mediate any dispute regardless of what the subject matter is. As a purist view this may be correct but in reality if parties want the mediator to have mediation experience of a particular subject matter then they should be entitled to have it and the mediator would be foolish to try to insist that he or she is able to conduct such a mediation if they don't possess the detailed knowledge that the parties consider they should require. Again this is more a matter of practicality than ethics.

Confidentiality

This subject alone is worthy of a book! I shall deal with it in general terms in this chapter given the limitations. There are several sources of confidentiality in mediation. In principle in the United Kingdom, the provisions are to be found in the mediation agreement, which is signed by the parties as a precursor to the mediation itself. As will be detailed later in this chapter, most European jurisdictions have enshrined the principles of confidentiality in statute. In the United States there are various federal and state rules for evidence, some based upon the Uniform Mediation Act, others upon local statutes which provide for the confidentiality of the dispute resolution process. In general terms, confidentiality must be maintained at all times unless both parties agree otherwise, or to the extent permitted by law. It is this latter qualification that has given rise to much difficulty in the United Kingdom. Courts in England and Wales have taken the view that the 'interests of justice' can justify judicial enquiry into what transpired in mediation (see *Farm Assist Limited (in liquidation) v The Secretary of State for Environment, Food and Rural affairs (No 2)* 2009 EWHC 1102 (TCC) and *Mrs AB and Mr AB v CD Limited* [2013] EWHC 1376 (TCC).

Courts in California, on the other hand, have set their face against any revelations as to what happened in mediation and there is an absolute bar upon evidence being adduced of what happened in mediation. There are various degrees in between these two extreme views. In general, most parties would expect that the process is confidential and that unless both parties agree to some aspect of that confidentiality being waived, they would expect that to be maintained. It is essential that the mediator explains the confidentiality provisions at the beginning of the mediation and reminds the parties throughout the mediation, if required, that these are the conditions under which everybody is operating. Whether a mediator, particularly in England and Wales, should go on to explain the complexities of the Court's decision in *Farm Assist* is a moot point. Personally I think not: it adds an unnecessary complication, and in any event there is far too much uncertainty as what the courts might do.

There are two aspects of a mediator's confidentiality obligations in the context of ethical standards that need to be addressed: the external and the internal confidentiality. The internal confidentiality is the mediator's obligation during the course of the mediation not to disclose to any party any confidential information provided by the other. Most mediators will make it a rule that whatever is disclosed to them in caucus remains private and confidential unless specifically authorised by that party for disclosure to the other side. It goes without saying that a mediator is, of course, under a general obligation not to disclose anything revealed to him or her in mediation by either party to any person outside. This is the external confidentiality and the requirement is not only upon the mediators but on the parties and all those present at the mediation in order to maintain the confidentiality of the mediation, even after the mediation session itself has been concluded. It is also self-evident that any documents, or other communications prepared specifically for the mediation, are covered by the same confidentiality. I would prefer to use the word privilege as this is much more meaningful as far as lawyers are concerned.

As far as the internal confidentiality is concerned, most UK mediators operate on the basis that information received from one party is confidential unless that party expressly authorises it to be disclosed to the other side. Some mediators, notably those in the United States, shift the burden to the parties by informing them that they will disclose all information they are given unless specifically requested not to. It is a question of culture and experience, but most mediators would agree that it is far safer to operate on the first principle and, if the message is at all controversial, prudence suggests reducing it to an agreed written form before it is taken to the other side.

The ethical dilemma for the mediator arises when he is in possession of knowledge from one party that, if imparted to the other party, may assist them to a settlement. They cannot, of course, leak the information itself (which would be a clear breach) but how far, if at all, may they impart by subtle means any important strategic information to the other side? Disabusing one party's misconceptions of the other, particularly where that is creating an impediment to settlement, is an essential role for the mediator. The question is how? Several authors quote Judge Richard Posner's comment in his speech on 8 July 2000 at the Eleventh Annual Frank Sanders Lecture for the American Bar Association's section of Dispute Resolution that a mediator, to help parties come to a common estimate of the outcome of a judgment on the dispute, must 'not only be a conduit of information between opposing sides but also an impediment to transparent communication between them'. This somewhat Delphic statement, I suspect, is really intended to convey the suggestion that a mediator, while encouraging complete openness between the parties, should also exercise discretion in the way they convey some information so that the manner of its delivery does not undermine the purpose of giving it. If removing an impediment requires disclosure of confidential information, the mediator must try to find a way. Most mediators, faced with such a dilemma, would explain to the party concerned the need to disclose the information to the other in the interests of correcting a misconception and moving both parties towards achieving a settlement.

There is no ethical difficulty where one party is seeking to use confidentiality as a cloak for fraud or for some criminal activity. As already stated, it is universally accepted that where the interests of children, patients and minors are involved, where the approval of a court is required for any settlement, confidentiality is no bar to informing the court of all relevant matters which may have occurred in mediation.

As far as external confidentiality, ie communications after the mediation session itself, is concerned, there is vast range of possibilities. In the United States there are several enactments which govern the position. Paragraph 2 of the Uniform Mediation Act provides a definition of mediation communications. The limitations imposed by the Federal Rule of Evidence 408 and the tier privilege structure used in the UMA, para 4 provide guidelines as to what can or cannot be disclosed after the mediation. The Model Standard V requires a mediator to maintain the reasonable expectation of the parties with regard to confidentiality. Section 8 of the Uniform Mediation Act and the Federal Rules of Evidence provide that offers to compromise, including settlement offers, and evidence of conduct or statements made in compromised discussions, including any admission of legal responsibility, are inadmissible in evidence in any federal court. It is not impossible for parties prior to the mediation to agree between themselves a confidentiality agreement that limits the extent to which information they are sharing may be used afterwards. In the United Kingdom, as the law stands at the moment, no private contract can create an enforceable privilege not to testify if a court decides that the evidence of a party or mediator is required at trial in the interest of justice. In Europe the position is not uniform. Part Three of this book explains how the EU countries have dealt with this issue when implementing the EU ADR Directive. It is self-evident that agreements between parties are not enforceable against non-signatories.

In the United States, nearly every state has some sort of legislation providing for some protection of mediation. Usually court-sponsored mediations are not protected to the same extent as private mediations. Protection for the state of the mediation, the type of information that can be imparted and who could invert the privilege – unfortunately there is no uniform approach and no uniform agreement between the Federal States in the United States as to the approach to be adopted. Similarly in England and Wales, the general view is that the mediation is totally confidential, but there are decisions where the courts have taken a different view in somewhat special circumstances. It is unfortunate that these decisions have yet to be reviewed with informed argument by an appellate court. Some argue that it would be far better to enact a mediation statute establishing mediation privilege, and provide for the same limited circumstances where the courts grant exceptions, as privilege is in common law which are well known to all practitioners.

Conclusion

Pursuant to the EU ADR Directive, most Member States have implemented the Directive itself in ways consistent with their respective legal system. However, not all have provided a Code of Conduct for mediators directed at the various ethical issues raised in this chapter, and those that have, have not applied a common approach to some of the core standards which should be standard, particularly if the cross-border provisions of the Directive are to be effective. An excellent guide to the scope of a mediation ethical code, which, in my view, could and should be adopted by all mediators worldwide, is to be found in The Mediators' Institute of Ireland's own Code of Ethics and Practice. I can do no better than quote from the sections entitled 'Scope':

> '4. We have attempted to cover as many aspects of mediation and the process as possible in this Code. However it must be understood that every mediation is unique and its very success depends on its retaining its flexibility. Every Mediator will mediate differently to every other Mediator and will mediate each of their cases differently depending on the type of mediation, the subject matter of the mediation and the interaction of all of the people in the Mediation Session and on their own training and experience.

Mediation Ethics

5. It is not possible to cover every scenario and, further, there may be occasions when the particular situation requires a different approach. Although, generally, a mediation will go through some or all of the steps below some mediations may not allow for that approach or may not allow for the steps to be gone through in that order. It is the Mediator's decision as to how the mediation should proceed taking all of the circumstances into account.

6. There is no 'right' process or 'right' way to mediate and, in the event of an issue arising in relation to a particular mediation, the totality of the mediation will have to be taken into account in assessing whether there was a breach of this Code of Ethics and Practice.'

The challenge for the mediation community in Europe is to agree upon a common Code of Ethical Conduct to which all professional mediators in Europe subscribe and thus present a uniform mediation standard of behaviour so that, regardless of the specific jurisdiction in which the mediation takes place, all parties will know that the same standard of excellence will be adhered to by any European mediator. This Code should not be drafted by the EU Commission, or indeed by any specific Member State's Justice Department, but ought be drawn up by practising mediators, who, from actual experience rather than theory, know the pitfalls, the temptations and the solutions. The Irish mediators have shown the way, and mediators in the rest of Europe should now take up the baton and produce a uniform Code of Ethics for European mediators. If we can succeed in this endeavour, we will have achieved something which even those jurisdictions which have been mediating for decades have yet to achieve. A piecemeal approach will not solve the problem, and the best thing that the EU Commission can do is to arrange a conference of practising professional mediators to start the task. The benefits will be enormous and perhaps the cross-border limitations of the ADR Directive will no longer be a bar to the adoption of mediation as a first choice for resolving all disputes in every Member State.

Chapter 10

Achieving Excellence – a Delicate Balance

Heather Allen

Heather Allen is a very experienced and successful mediator and has trained mediators worldwide since the mid-1990s. She draws on this wide experience to reflect on the kaleidoscope of demands and decisions facing the mediator and to describe some of the colours and patterns of excellence. It has been a real pleasure to work with her over so many years. (DR)

The excellent mediator responds to the challenges posed by the complexity of the case or situation, by any timing and other process constraints, and by the participants' behaviours. The focus and approach must be varied throughout the mediation with the mediator sometimes planning the next step and sometimes deploying intuition to make an almost instant response. The extent to which the right balance is created through intuition and intellect, in relation to a wide range of factors, determines effectiveness.

The following reflections seek to define and describe briefly some of those factors where the mediator makes choices to achieve the right balance for the benefit of the process and the parties. The word 'balance' in no way implies that the answer lies in the middle with the scales gently poised in equilibrium; in mediation, the need for a particular focus may be extreme in one situation and in another be absent entirely. The excellent mediator does not fall into one defined category of style but uses a panoply of techniques, skills and approaches to weave a way through the thicket of the parties' disagreement. The adage that no two mediations are the same is a good basis for rejecting any model that suggests that one approach might usefully fit all.

Each mediator, depending on experience, expertise and emotional and practical preferences, will feel more or less comfortable at different points on each spectrum. While reading this chapter, experienced mediators may recognise their natural preferences, and might reflect on those areas where their approach is more limited and those areas where they confidently use the full spectrum. The contrasting approaches within each aspect do not represent paradox or contradiction but rather a range of choices to be juggled, sampled and selected. Some of the identified ranges will be familiar from experience as a mediator or in other professional contexts, from training even if long ago, and from common sense; others might provide additional perspective and stimulate new ways of thinking about the complex job of being a mediator.

Much of the mediator's skill lies in the ability to be flexible, even to the extremes which lie outside our own zone of comfort, and helping the parties to be flexible, too. Thus, comfort and discomfort, for parties and for the mediator, can both contribute to progress. The comfort of the mediator may need to be sacrificed for the comfort, or necessary discomfort, of the parties. The balance between supporting and challenging an individual or team is a familiar management concept that has relevance in mediation, too: at any moment, too much support and the parties stand still, comfortable but making little progress; too much challenge and they lose hope and give up trying, or fight each other or the mediator rather than attacking the problem.

The mediator will, of course, work with the parties on the content of the dispute, in order to clarify their positions, what really matters to them and what they need from any settlement, discussing the risks and opportunities, the options for resolution and the practicalities and technicalities of any agreement. The mediator, as the primary manager of the process, must also discuss process issues with the parties, to keep them informed about what is happening, to consult and discuss the use of time consistent with progress, and to check and confront any possible challenges to the safety of the process, in terms of confidentiality, authority to settle and the preservation of the mediator's multi-partial role. A mediator should keep both content and process in view, and move the focus as required, being neither stuck immovably in the content nor hidebound by using the process rigidly or over-creatively.

In the mediation model espoused by most commercial and workplace mediators, the mediator is making process choices throughout the mediation, in particular about whether to work with the parties together or separately; to put or keep parties together, to meet privately with one or more members of a team, or to leave parties to work on their own. There are judgements to be made at every turn about the purpose of meetings and the likely dynamic created by varying the personnel in attendance, as well as time management considerations that can be eased by the use of a joint meeting, for example.

The mediator must also balance work on the issues with attention to the people. Those mediators with expertise in the sector or the issues in dispute might be the tempted to overuse that expertise at the expense of allowing the parties to work through the process fully and find solutions that fit their particular business or circumstances. Every mediator must draw a line professionally, of course, as they are not in this context working as advisers, therapists or judges. A mediator trained in psychology may bring useful insight to the personal dynamics, and will also need to work on the issues and the technical areas of the dispute, helping the parties to consider legal and business risks. Another mediator who brings technical expertise, in law, engineering, manufacturing or business, to assist the parties, will also need to take time to understand the people, their emotions and what drives them. Most of us have a preference for facts and figures or for feelings – the concrete or the sentient, as in the task and relationship axes of management theory. Each mediation demands a different balance of the mediator's attention to these aspects to meet the needs of the parties and the particulars of the dispute.

Jungian theory of type suggests that each of us has a preference for detail or big picture – awareness of this as a starting point helps a mediator to move appropriately between specific and global viewpoints, and to help the parties to do so. Thinking of a mediation as being in the shape of a kite, starting at a point,

Achieving Excellence – a Delicate Balance

opening up, then turning the corner and converging at a final point of agreement, the mediator helps the parties to open up and widen the discussion and then guides again in order to narrow the focus and funnel discussions towards agreement. The precise shape of the kite will vary from mediation to mediation, as more or less time is needed for expansion, explanation and discussion before the parties begin to finalise an outcome they can all sign up to.

In managing the process and in working with the views of the parties, enabling change to take place, the mediator treads a fine line between being accepting and exerting control. At times, the parties need the mediator to be exercising control with credibility and natural authority and, and at other times, as the servant of the parties, encouraging productive leadership to emerge from amongst the participants.

Part of the task of the mediator is to create momentum. Momentum is different from speed, and it is not one-paced. The mediator has an important role in assisting the parties to move through the mediation at a pace consistent with creating and sustaining progress. A mediator may find that working at a slower, measured pace works in one room, while in the other momentum is built faster. Particularly in the early stages, the mediator must help the parties to accept the varying levels of pace adopted by different parties that are probably appropriate to their needs. Where one party is ready to move forward much sooner than another, the mediator must help all parties to cope whether with irritation, boredom or despair, and to keep in view a horizon of settlement. Getting the right balance between driving forward or pulling back is demanding. There are occasions where the job of the mediator is to drive the process forward, to encourage the parties to develop ideas into agreements. At other times, such activity would be premature and would risk any progress stalling or even going into reverse, and the mediator must apply the brakes or tighten the reins. Mediation does not succeed on the basis of what the mediator wants but on what the parties need. Similarly, acknowledging or confronting a situation or bypassing a difficulty, by ignoring or changing the subject, all have their place in an effective process.

The mediator's behaviour affects the tone of the mediation: energising or calming – both are valuable. The mediator models the desired tone as a starting point for influencing somewhat the level of urgency or relaxation. More direct techniques than modelling may sometimes be needed to effect significant change: holding up a mirror to the party to describe and challenge the current approach, thus coaching them towards a change in attitude or style; or offering a break for refreshment or reflection to allow breathing space. Especially in cases where emotions are manifestly high, the mediator may need to be nurturing to provide the necessary comfort and security that allow the parties to participate effectively; on other occasions the primary task will be to help the parties to focus on the practicalities of settlement rather than on their emotions. If there is an inappropriate balance between the pastoral and the practical, the mediator might get in the way of resolution either by slowing down the process by overemphasis on the emotions associated with what has happened, or else by missing the fact that restorative processes need to be part of that particular settlement. The mediator will move between passionate, compassionate and dispassionate: all are appropriate at times.

Conversation in the early stages of mediation often begins with the parties adopting a narrow focus. Mediators need to live with a degree of uncertainly and discomfort, accepting that there is much they do not know or that do not understand, and to allow the parties to set the agenda. In this way, mediators can listen to what matters to the parties before helping them to widen their perspective. There are a number of models for developing a conversation in the context of mediation, and a range of prompts – hesitation, repetition, distraction and defensiveness - which alert a mediator to the need to move the conversation around and about. Facets such as legal, commercial and personal, may all impact on the dispute and its possible resolution. This trio provides a simple starting point for a wider ranging and more productive conversation that might lead to new areas for negotiation and that might even hold the key to settlement.

The mediator acts as a guide through time – the past, the present and the future all have significance in working out a resolution. Anger or despair can leave parties stuck in the past, yet there is usually some need to talk about what has happened to bring parties to this point; frustration or anxiety can lead parties to rush to seeking agreement before they have established what else needs to be resolved beyond the obvious, as a basis for detailed negotiation. With so much to think about it can be a challenge for a mediator to take seriously the maxim that 'what is happening right here and now is what matters,' encouraging a focus on the present and staying in the moment.

Clarity, precision and getting to the point are characteristics highly valued in some professional cultures and in some parts of the world more than others. There are moments in a mediation where crystallising and honing an idea, taking time to work in sharp focus and in depth on an aspect, are vital for progress. At other moments it is wise to leave things vague and fuzzy – words that often sit less easily in a western professional context; shading the edges of an idea or generalising to avoid the need for commitment can create freedom, scope and possibility. We sometimes need to abandon our own urges for the definitive to allow the best to emerge from mediation. Many mediators come from professional backgrounds where challenging apparent inconsistencies and contradictions is a daily activity; this can translate well into mediation, providing the parties with an opportunity to see a different reality and to reassess risk in a new light. Living with and working with the possibility that one or more of the parties is trying to deceive the mediator or is deceiving themselves, is important for a mediator, and, used sparingly and sensitively, the ability to challenge contributes to the mediator's effectiveness. However, spending too much time forensically searching for lies and deception will divert from progress, while looking for significant patterns in behaviour and conversation should lead to greater understanding about what drives the parties and might highlight possibilities for settlement.

Returning to a basic tenant of mediation, the importance of keeping the process safe and honouring promises in relation to confidentiality are paramount for a mediator. However, the effective mediator will be persuasive to enable the parties to expand their conversation and provide each other with additional material to inform their risk assessment, to create momentum and progress and to enhance their negotiations. The excellent mediator additionally knows when to encourage parties to give up their information, and how to work within the concept of confidentiality by providing a sense of what is needed and an indication of what might work for the benefit of all parties. In this and in other contexts, the mediator needs to be both a safe pair of hands and a risk taker.

The mediator makes choices between helping the parties to decide what to do and telling them how to proceed – offering flexibility and certainty in appropriate

Achieving Excellence – a Delicate Balance

measure, and taking calculated and considered risks. It is fairly uncontroversial to expect the mediator not only to offer suggestions about the process but to be firm, at least from time to time, in managing the process. The mediator has an active role in working with the content, too, and here the choice, expressed simply, will be between coaching and being directive. Coaching involves working with the parties on strategy, timing and presentation; in being directive regarding content and outcomes, the mediator might demonstrate a wish for the party or parties to comply with the mediator's thinking, and this is more problematic. There is sometimes a fine line between coaching and expressing a view about the level of an offer or the workability of a proposal, and in any group of experienced mediators there are likely to be differing views about where the line is placed. However, the motivation of the mediator must be unswerving, with all activities carried out from a perspective of non-bias, in line with the expressed interests of the parties, and with the integrity of the process unassailled.

Excellence, being the best that we can be each time we are invited into the fray to assist with the resolution of a dispute, requires good judgement, a mixture of well-informed analysis and powerful intuition. Intuition, although less easy to define and to teach, is not random or haphazard; it is the culmination of confidence and competence developed through experience. The mediator needs to be relaxed and attending to the 'here and now' in order to draw on and trust their intuition. Reasoned judgement is built in similar ways, through learning and experience, although using analytical skills to decide on action. Good judgement also demands courage and a letting go of ego. The excellent mediator exercises good judgement throughout, for the benefit of the parties and the process over any benefit for self. The mediator who can bring humour and a lightness of touch to the process will offer the parties a chance to relax for a while. Inappropriate light-heartedness in the face of anger, worry or despair will alienate the parties and create distrust of the mediator; whereas a well-judged change of atmosphere can help the parties tolerate each other's presence and can improve the prospects for successful negotiations.

The mediator is there to talk about the parties and their perspectives; 'don't talk about yourself' is generally good advice, especially for the new mediator. However, the mediator who knows how to pick the right moment to disclose authentically something of themselves – perhaps feelings, observations, hopes, frustration, or experience - adds a powerful dimension to the role. The challenge is to balance self-disclosure with being sufficiently detached and objective to be of equal use to all parties.

Even the familiar choices about whether the mediator is present or absent, silent or speaking, have an impact on progress. As with every aspect of balance touched on above, neither alternative is always wrong or always right. Certainly, the old distinction between facilitative or evaluative mediation fails to grasp the subtlety demanded of and delivered by highly competent mediators. Effectiveness is a complex weave of skills, personal qualities and knowledge – elusive and fragile, yet consistently offered by the excellent mediator.

Chapter 11

Conclusion

I hope that Part 2 has enhanced your knowledge, challenged and provoked you. It was intended to build on the basic skills and process contained in Part 1 and to fill some of the gaps left by covering some items only briefly. I hope that your mediation career, whether full-time or a bolt-on to your 'normal' profession, will continue to develop and become increasingly effective, so that mastery is within your grasp. Now to move on.

Part 3
Mastering

Contents

	Page No.
Chapter 1 Introduction	351
Chapter 2 The Route to Mastery	353
Chapter 3 From Mastery to incompetence	359
Chapter 4 Trust, Truth, Love and Forgiveness (or rather Greed, Lies, Hatred and Revenge)	365
Chapter 5 Mediator Bias (Paul Gibson)	369
Chapter 6 Intercultural Mediation: A Digest of Theory and Practice (Joanna Kalowski)	383
Chapter 7 One Continent, Many Methods (introduction by Bill Marsh)	393
Austria (with Thomas Kustor)	395
Belgium (Anna Doyle)	399
Bulgaria (Eliza Nikolova)	401
Croatia (Mladen Vukmir)	404
Cyprus (Christos Theodoulou)	409
Czech Republic (Tatjana Šišková)	410
Denmark (Gerd Sinding)	414
Estonia (with Triinu Hiob)	417
Finland (Petri Taivaloski)	419
France (Thierry Garby)	422
Germany (Renate Herrmann)	425
Greece	433
Hungary (Tibor Tajti)	435
Ireland (including Northern Ireland) (Jim Halley)	440
Italy (Carlo Mosca)	444
Latvia (Rada Matjušina)	450
Lithuania (Natalija Kaminskiene)	452
Luxembourg (with Alain Grosjean)	454
Malta (Austin Sammut)	456
Netherlands (with Manon Schonewille and Dr Fred Schonewille)	459
Norway (Anna Nyland)	463
Poland (Sylwester Pieckowski)	466
Portugal (Ana Maria Maia Gonçalves, François Bogacz and Thomas Gaultier)	471
Romania (Constantin-Adi Gavrilă and Luminita-Jana Trifan)	476
Slovakia (with Renata Dolanska and Slavka Karkoskova)	480
Slovenia (Simona Mlakar)	482
Spain (Mari-Cruz Taboada)	486
Sweden (Eric Runesson)	489
Switzerland (Jeremy Lack)	491
United Kingdom with Scotland (David Miles and Pamela Lyall)	497
Russia (Dr Tsisana Chamlikashvili)	505
Turkey (Deniz Artan Ilter and Samil Demir)	510
Chapter 8 Use of Interpreters in Mediation (Xiaohui Yuan)	517
Chapter 9 Enhancing the Political Process (John Sturrock)	527
Chapter 10 Beyond Mediation (Tony Willis)	533
Chapter 11 Standards and Regulation	539
Chapter 12 What We Do Changes the World (with Stephen Ruttle QC)	543

Chapter 1

Introduction

This is the reckoning. 'Part 3 Mastering' means that we are at the conclusion of the three-part book for mediators. We have trained, been moulded, done it and are now at, or near, the top. It is the most difficult part to write because you know the skills and process, you know what works and will have experienced the joy of helping people in dispute to put common sense back into the resolution process. So Part 3 is intended to keep you there. It looks at what mastery is like: the first few chapters take a deeper look at what it means to be there; the next take a look at the international scene – how mediation is being practiced in other European countries and what advanced skills might be used when mediating other cultures; and finally we see the potential of adopting a non-adversarial approach to politics and the significance of setting standards and the emerging mediator profession being regulated.

I should mention copyright again. Most of the contributors have gifted their piece to the book and some have licensed the inclusion of their piece in the book. I thank all who have contributed, regardless of the arrangement, and, in recognition of this, the royalties from the book are being donated to a mediation charity.

Chapter 2

The Route to Mastery

What is mastery?

I think mastery is:

> Doing the right thing, in the right way, in the right place, to the right person, for the right reason, with the right feeling, EVERY TIME.

It is doing it with a passion and humility that is infectious and inspiring.

In 2010 a group of around 60 people, probably half of whom were mediators, was asked: 'What makes a Master?' The words used included:

vision	childlike curiosity
self-awareness	being present
humility	instinctive
passion	able to improvise/innovate
compassion	transparent
tenacity	living the process
patience	dedication
from the soul	emotionally intelligent
fearless	focus
flexible	

Of course, many of these apply to mediators who have not (yet) attained the level of excellence that merits mastery. I would add the ability to critically reflect on each mediation, analyse what went well and what could have been done better. Mastery creates the competent convergence of knowledge, skill, experience, intuition and inspiration. I think it also comes from being in love with what we do.

As the discussion developed it became obvious that one set of words applied to the internal mediator (being rather than doing) and another to the external mediator (doing rather than being). The consumate mediator is a person who is centred, at peace with him or herself, unconsciously competent, instinctive in the use of skills and techniques, open and accepting of others and able to create a safe and nurturing environment in which people can be both vulnerable and positive. They will also be a person who does not rely on force of personality, charisma or position to be an effective mediator (although being charismatic may help!).

The route to mastery is a virtuous circle. Ultimately it involves those who have attained mastery passing on their knowledge and experience to others who will in turn become masters themselves and so pass their knowledge on to others. The circle will take many years and involve continual personal development, polishing of skills and techniques and a pile of experience. It unquestionably involves the sharing of experience and the giving back by the masters to 'younger' members of the profession of their wisdom and insights. At the moment, with the profession still in its infancy, the 'pioneer' masters have achieved that status by learning and sharing with each other.

The starting point is accreditation by a reputable body. I write later about standards and suggest that it is the assessment criteria, not the training courses, that should be regulated. Minimum standards breed mediocrity and we should be seeking to produce excellence.

Accreditation by a *reputable body* therefore means by a training organisation that has rigorous assessment of clear criteria that are accepted by the profession as standards that produce effective commercial mediators. The aim should always be for an accredited mediator to be good at mediating disputes and for those who are not good, or mediocre or uncertain, even borderline, to not be accredited. The aim should be to produce mediators who have the recognised potential qualities of the consummate mediator mentioned above.

It is recognised that one of the problems for newly-accredited mediators is getting experience and (paid) work. That is largely down to their own network of contacts, tenacity, determination and luck. Sometimes their training body can provide pupillages and, if they are lucky and the trainer is also a provider, some cases to mediate. This is key because there is nothing better than experience. But personal development and learning from others must go alongside, if not ahead of, experience.

Building on the foundations

Before a commercial mediator can polish their skills, the knowledge base needs to grow. No matter how many hours of training the foundation course comprises, it can only teach the safe principles. Such principles need to be expanded and made flexible. So part of this initial stage is taking those key areas on the foundation training into greater depth. For example, communication skills, understanding conflict, negotiation in mediation, managing the documents, settlement agreements, making confidentiality more fluid, risk-taking and so on. Building on the safe foundations, the new mediator is likely to need these areas of further training to obtain the flexibility in the skills and process of mediation to become most effective quickly. This has been covered in 'Part 1: Moulding'.

This is also where learning from the masters is most needed. Having the opportunity to soak up years of experience, challenges, skills and techniques is vital to grow in ability and confidence. Also, sharing and feeding off contemporaries helps not only in learning but also in building camaraderie in an otherwise solitary profession.

I mentioned earlier that the descriptions given for mastery split into two streams – internal and external. A master mediator would be expected to follow, and be competent in, both streams.

The internal mediator – being rather than doing

This is about what goes on inside you, the mediator – knowing yourself, understanding your values, principles and motivations so that you know how and why you react to conflict, challenges and relationships in the way you do. It is about understanding your own values, how they were formed, why other people may have different values and how that in turn causes them to react differently to you. It is about recognising how we deal with conflict and how our reaction may be different in different circumstances, and why other people will react differently to us. It is about understanding and managing our emotions in challenging situations and in having difficult conversations. It is about knowing that we are biased (see Chapter 5), have ingrained tribal instincts and unconscious allegiances. It is about recognising, and embracing, the paradoxical role of the mediator – how we need to be both strong and vulnerable, assertive yet be in the background, empathetic yet dispassionate, flexible yet structured, open-hearted yet manipulative, a risk-taker yet a safe pair of hands.

This is also about being instinctive, but recognising there are dangers as well as rewards; of being fearless but not reckless; of being centred and a peaceful presence that generates empathy and trust with other people, yet is a source of energy and creator of momentum.

We must learn and grow all the time. The internal mediator is about ultimate self-awareness.

The external mediator – doing rather than being

This is about using your skills, instincts and techniques to maximum effectiveness, and being challenged to go outside your comfort zones. It is also about:

- being open to techniques and processes of other mediation strands (transformative, community, family, etc);
- being prepared to abandon familiar processes and to design bespoke processes to suit the particular dispute;
- using visual aids, electronic programmes, conference and video communication and the like;
- being confident and knowledgeable about techniques for risk analysis, decision trees, etc and using them when appropriate;

- having a constant thirst for knowledge – finding trainings that expand knowledge and possibilities;
- ensuring that preparation for every mediation is complete and relevant so that parties are reassured by your knowledge and grasp of their problems;
- being aware of current legislation and thinking on the development of mediation as a profession and as an established part of the dispute resolution process;
- raising awareness by researching and speaking or writing on mediation-related subjects; and
- getting to the state in the mediation where knowledge, skill, experience, intuition and inspiration all beautifully converge.

Parties know if their mediator is under-prepared, ill-informed, operating on autopilot and/or unfamiliar with current systems and processes.

Achieving mastery

The internal mediator stream and external mediator stream go hand-in-hand. Both streams combined, the route to mastery is challenging, testing and rewarding, but not for everyone. The aim is for excellence, the golden standard. It is not just to provide another 'title', a long-service reward or to recognise services to the profession.

Having achieved mastery in both the internal and external mediator, the next chapter deals with what keeps the master at peak performance every they mediate. Amongst other things it should mean maintaining a log which is peer-reviewed, committing to peer reviews of actual mediations at least once a year, taking part in master classes and mentoring other mediators. All help to prevent the master from slipping from unconscious competence (doing it well without knowing you are doing it) to unconscious incompetence (not doing it well and not realising it) caused by over familiarity and assumption of success. The aim is for excellence; excellence that is continuous and on-going.

It is a disappointment that very few of these are common in commercial mediation in the United Kingdom. Few top mediators keep a log, let alone have it reviewed by a colleague, few offer assistantships (or pupillages), few mentor other mediators, and few undertake peer reviews. I just hope that, as the profession matures, these will become normal practice.

Peer review

Of all the suggestions for keeping mediators at the top, peer reviews are the most important, and the most useful (as well as the most scary). It should be common practice, whether the mediator is mediating a lot or infrequently, because the process is a solitary one and we mediators get very little feedback. At least once a year, another experienced mediator should sit in on and observe an actual mediation and then give the lead mediator honest and constructive feedback. Even if the mediator usually has an assistant at the mediation, such an assistant is likely to be inexperienced and therefore unlikely to give useful feedback. Useful feedback is, in my view, essential if busy mediators are to maintain a level of unconscious excellence.

The process should be simple. The mediator should select a reviewer, preferably an experienced colleague and then will do the following:

- Inform the parties. This is a sensitive matter. No party wants to feel that their chosen mediator is being 'inspected', so it needs to be 'sold' as part of a programme of excellence for commercial mediators.
- Agree reimbursement with the reviewer. Either a share of the fee or a reciprocal arrangement.
- Agree a date for debrief.

The review would be confidential and not shared with anyone else (unless both mediator and reviewer agree, and then only for clarification or assistance). The mediator should keep a record of the review, for use in their own logbook or feedback Digest. Of course, if a party objects then the suggestion should be withdrawn without any further discussion.

Role of reviewer

The role of the reviewer is to discreetly observe the mediator and to give honest and constructive feedback as a colleague (and friend) which will:

- debrief the actual mediation;
- give insights into style and techniques observed;
- identify unhelpful behaviours (if any);
- identify any significant differences from the CMC assessment criteria for commercial mediators; and
- discuss differences between the mediator's and the reviewer's normal practice.

This will ensure the reviewer should be familiar with the assessment criteria prior to the mediation.

Debrief

The mediator and reviewer should debrief face to face, if possible:

- on the day of the mediation; or, if that is not possible,
- would not normally last more than one hour.

Giving the review

Feedback should always be:

- Specific
- Helpful

- Kind
- Honest
- Respectful

Receiving feedback

As with any feedback, the mind can be selective and the mediator may remember only the good/bad bits out of context, so feedback should always be written down by the mediator and treated as learning, not criticism. It is repeated that this is a confidential process and so feedback is private to the mediator and reviewer.

Mentoring

Peer reviews should be part of a wider mentoring scheme, whereby experienced mediators take responsibility for supporting, encouraging and sharing experience with less experienced mediators. This may be in the form one or more of the of the following traits:

- Master classes. Experienced mediators share their knowledge with other, less experienced, mediators.
- Mediating with the masters' video-casts.
- The bi-monthly mediator breakfasts.
- Practice days. Some mediator providers already hold practice days. I would like to see experienced mediators demonstrate their skills and techniques at such events.
- One-to-one support sessions. Alongside the peer review scheme, I hope that a support network will develop that will allow 'wise heads' to be consulted if other mediators encounter difficulties.
- Offering assistantships. I believe that unaccompanied mediations are a missed opportunity for newly accredited mediators to gain first-hand experience. It should be seen as a duty for lead mediators to offer assistantships. It does not have to be a complicated matter and I am happy to guide anyone who wants to set up an assistant scheme.
- 'Top tips'. Experienced mediators sharing their wisdom with both users and practitioners.
- Sharing experience through talks, Practice sheets or specific papers on mediation practice.

I think it is a responsibility of experienced mediators to share their knowledge and give support to newer and less experienced mediators. My experience of the mediator community is that we are a friendly and open bunch, so all it needs is a willingness to make it happen. I hope sooner rather than later.

Chapter 3

From Mastery to Incompetence

Introduction

This chapter arises from my growing concern that familiarity breeds contempt – or more appropriately, familiarity breeds mediocrity. I say this having been a commercial mediator for over 20 years and recognising in myself the ease with which I slip comfortably into the mediation groove, using tried and tested techniques to help warring parties reach a deal. And most do reach a deal – over 80 per cent, and most of them because of me, not despite me. I think! But I aspire to mastery of my craft – I want to be the *best* every time, and so I am uncomfortable with my comfort at slipping into the familiar mediation groove.

It may seem audacious for me to write this. I am not a big name mediator who helps settle major, big-ticket disputes or who helps government resolve international embarrassments. I am not mediating three or four cases every week and I am not an eminent lawyer who helps frame European or other directives. I do not have the ear of politicians, nor do I guest at state or other banquets. But I have trained a lot of people in mediation skills and recognise that some, a precious minority, 'have it' and others don't. And sometimes when I am mediating, I experience the magic of being 'at one', when substance, process and relationships all come beautifully together – and that is something very special. It is also a great privilege.

When I trained commercial mediators (I don't any more, in the United Kingdom anyway, because there are so many who are losing their enthusiasm and becoming disenchanted because they have so little opportunity to use their skills) – we used the learning ladder:

- UNCONSCIOUS INCOMPETENCE – you can't do it but you don't know you can't do it. Peter Adler, an American mediator friend of mine, calls this 'dumb and happy'.

- CONSCIOUS INCOMPETENCE – you still can't do it but you know you can't do it

- CONSCIOUS COMPETENCE – now you can do it, but you are aware that you are doing it

- UNCONSCIOUS COMPETENCE – you can do it and you don't even notice you are doing it. Unintentional excellence.

My fear is that, over time, mediators, whether busy ones or ones that mediate rarely – but particularly the busy ones – slip from unconscious competence to unconscious incompetence. They don't even realise that they are no longer the best, but carry on in the familiar old mediation groove, believing that they are leaving the world a better place.

Horror stories

This fear is fuelled by a few horror stories:

- The mediator seen out shopping (twice) whilst mediating ('I left them with a couple of tasks'). *The focus of the mediator should be entirely on the mediation, to the exclusion of all else, even checking emails and messages.*
- The mediator found reading a book in the plenary room ('I was waiting for them to tell me what they wanted me to do'). *The mediator is the orchestrator of the process. They are there to give the parties the best opportunity to find a settlement.*
- The mediator who insisted on giving an opinion, even though he hadn't been asked. ('It's what they expect') *The parties, not the mediator, should be the centre of the mediation process.*
- The mediator who broke confidentiality (twice) in the same mediation ('They said it was confidential but I knew it wasn't really'). *Humility is a key quality of a master of any craft.*
- The mediator who said 'You're too far apart, I am bringing this mediation to an end'. *Tenacity is another key quality of an effective mediator.*
- The mediator who changed into his dinner jacket and told the parties he was off to the opera and 'would they please lock up when they left the building'. *The mediator should be the last to leave.*
- The mediator who had a stand-up argument with a difficult female party, telling her that she was totally unreasonable and that the whole mediation was a waste of his time. *A mediator should be open and accepting of everyone and never alienate anyone.*

All but one of these horror stories are about mediators who are in the UK top 20 – and one of them is about me!

There is a lot of talk in the United Kingdom about standards and regulation of mediators. A later chapter in Part 3 looks at both in more detail. The trouble is that, even if they existed, and had been agreed by all the interested parties, they would do little to avoid the horror stories mentioned above. As I write this, the Civil Mediation Council in the United Kingdom is moving towards being the standard-setter but at the moment all it does is set minimum hours of training (now 40), minimum hours of CPD (currently six) and a minimum of two mediations per year. In Ireland the MII accredit courses (usually 60 hours), lay down minimum points of education and reflective practice and also require three mediations a year. But we all know that a bad mediator will still be bad even after 100 hours training, and a 'natural' will be good after perhaps only 10. Minimum standards do just that, set minimum standards. There is no guarantee of excellence, certainly not of mastery.

Mediator's role

Before I attempt to identify what I mean by mastery, I think I need to remind everyone what a mediator is supposed to be, and do. I now concentrate on commercial mediators – I fully accept that other strands of mediation would frame this differently. The role of the commercial mediator is, crudely, to give the parties the best opportunity of achieving a settlement. There are certain skills attached to that, including:

- the efficient, if not instinctive, management of the mediation process;
- mediation being an assisted negotiation, the understanding of negotiation styles and tactics;
- building trusting relationships quickly, and respecting and keeping confidences;
- spending time on (their) relationships (with everyone involved);
- being open, honest and transparent, modelling behaviour to others;
- strategic use of information (what and when to give, when to hold, what to reframe and what to ignore);
- being a safe pair of hands;
- helping people have difficult conversations;
- de-demonising perceptions and widening parties views so that they can focus on the communication of needs and interests, not revenge and punishment;
- being able to challenge and reality test in an unthreatening way;
- being demonstrably even-handed in style and approach; and
- keeping going even when all seems over.

There are many more besides these.

The focus should always be on the parties, their needs both practical and emotional, and never on the mediator. The mediator should be the first to arrive and the last to leave.

All this should happen from the very start of the mediator's career and continuing throughout the whole of it!

The trouble is that it is very difficult to measure a mediator's performance. It is a solitary profession, as most mediators (unfortunately) work alone. Unlike lorry-driving or fighting a fire, it is less easy to identify bad results. I have a horrible suspicion that some lawyers regularly use poor and mediocre mediators because they know no better. They don't know that they could be using better mediators and get better results. Some would say that the market will sort the good from the bad but I don't agree. If experience is of poor practise, it becomes the expected norm. Perhaps even worse than that is the fact that, because we are in a solitary profession, good practise is difficult to verify and replicate. We don't even know that it is going on!

What are the dangers?

Sometimes I feel that the parties are at risk from the best of our intentions – are we deluding ourselves that we are doing something helpful, that our failures are harmless, and our successes great victories? Highest forms of proficiency and lowest forms of incompetence are two ends of the same curve, the majority of us falling somewhere in between. I think that, though we may strive for better, most of us, most of the time, are adequate and unexceptional. We get by.

The trouble is, the incompetent mediators are unaware that what they do doesn't work and tend to be supremely confident in their own abilities. Research shows that the incompetents, the bunglers and blunderers are actually more confident in themselves than the people who do things well. I know a mediator who epitomises this. He is a former partner in a large UK law firm and he is awful! I think people choose him because of his previously high status and it may be that his work will reduce as the lawyers recognise him for what he is. But in the meantime he is a very confident (and, he says, busy) individual.

There is a danger for the rest of us, in mediating a lot (I wish!) Repetition can lead to us limiting our approach, defaulting to a familiar process and so being on auto-pilot much of the time. I fear that really busy mediators cannot be on their toes every time, and that they slip into a comfortable routine that works for them, and probably for the parties much of the time. The irony is that repetition can also push us towards perfection, for the more a craftsman or artist practises, the better they can become. The difference is in awareness and intention – if we really want to be at our best then we must mediate often and be prepared to innovate and go beyond the familiar and focus what is best for the particular parties in that particular case.

What keeps masters masterly?

Having achieved mastery as a mediator, what keeps the master at peak performance every time they mediate? The trouble is, most of this is internal. It is about attitude and willingness, about humility and eagerness to learn no matter how experienced you are and about the constant seeking of perfection in an ever-changing and fluid dispute environment. A mediator must stay fresh, through:

- a constant quest for perfection;
- a willingness to evolve, to do something different;
- seeking review and criticism by maintaining a log or diary which is peer-reviewed, by committing to peer reviews of actual mediations at least once per year, by self reviewing after every mediation;
- sharing knowledge and experience through taking part in master classes, passing on experience and being open to being questioned and challenged;
- mentoring other less experienced mediators, and being mentored by others;
- having a thirst for knowledge by finding new training that can increase self-awareness and open the possibility of other techniques and processes.

These all help to prevent the master from slipping from unconscious competence to unconscious incompetence (caused by over familiarity and the assumption of success). The aim must always be for excellence; excellence that is continuous and on-going. Becoming a Master of the craft of mediation may not take a mediator very long – staying there is the challenge!

Acknowledgement

I have mentioned Peter Adler in this paper. Much of the stimulus for what I have written comes from our conversations and papers that he has written. I therefore wish to acknowledge that I may have consciously, or unconsciously, used his words in some places.

Chapter 4

Trust, Truth, Love and Forgiveness (or rather Greed, Lies, Hatred and Revenge)

There is a danger that this will become a sermon! As a practicing Christian, and probably for most non-Christians, this is a subject that reaches my soul and affects everything in my life. And as a practicing mediator this subject is also fundamental to my work, which makes me feel able to legitimately write this chapter on the subject.

Trust

In a later chapter on regulation, I write about trust being fundamental to the establishment of a credible profession. In this chapter I am focusing on the parties. Almost all the disputes we mediate involve broken trust, or at least the perception of broken trust, and that fuels suspicion, expecting the worst of the offending party which, as a consequence, makes co-operating to achieve the best outcome much more difficult. Our capacity to trust is precious. It profoundly matters when it is broken because it is the foundation of a functioning personality. It is also the bedrock of a healthy society. Broken trust is offensive, it is a personal affront and creates a lot of hurt. Rebuilding it is a long, careful and fragile process and it won't happen over the limited time of a mediation. The best we mediators can expect is that a few building blocks are created as we help mend fractured communication and rebuild broken relationships. Those building blocks can start with the first Open Session, as parties come face-to-face and have the opportunity to uncover the reasons for the trust being lost and the motivation of the offending party. It is an opportunity for assumptions to be tested and other truths to be recognised. Trust relies on the truth and it is important for the mediator to give time to exploring why parties see facts and events differently and why their truths differ. The skills are basic. Helping each party to listen to the other's story, recognising why the stories are different and encouraging them to value the other's story as being real (the 'truth') to them, reduces suspicion and makes space for acceptance and understanding. Trust may not be rebuilt, but acceptance and understanding are good steps towards it.

Truth

I wrote earlier that trust relies on the truth. But, sad to say, not everyone tells the truth. I don't know why, because not telling the truth complicates matters, avoids reality and usually results in pain. I suppose it may be through weakness, or greed, or temptation, or being easily swayed by another influence, or making a quick gain, but in mediation it invariably creates more complication and makes difficult situations more difficult. I am often asked in a mediation, when passing on a statement or a final offer: 'Do you believe them?' and I have to say: 'I believe everything I am told, but I know that not everyone tells the truth'. I think we have to believe what people tell us, no matter how unbelievable it is, otherwise we become suspicious of everything people say. I have written before that everyone sees facts and events through different eyes and interprets those facts and events differently. There are a lot of reasons for this – education, gender, age, ethnicity, sexual orientation, politics, community, peers and so on – and it doesn't necessarily mean that they are any more right or wrong, just different. So one of the mediator's roles, and a difficult one at that, is to get parties to see the truth through the other person's eyes. To understand the fact that their own truth is not necessarily the only, or even the right one. The trouble is that as time moves on, people filter out the uncertainties and uncomfortable bits and their truth becomes the only one, moulded to suit their belief and certainties. It therefore becomes much more difficult for the mediator to suggest that the other party's truth is worth considering

Love

Love makes us whole. I know that if people put love at the heart of what they do, it is life changing. In an ideal world, love would make laws unnecessary. Unfortunately, we are not in an ideal world and we mediators tend to get the unlovely rubbish – the ones left over because the easy disputes have been sorted before mediation is even contemplated. So we get the difficult ones, the ones that are deadlocked. With it come the people who are being downright horrible to each other. The worst, for me anyway, are the families at war. Siblings fighting over a deceased parent's will, family business break-up and division of property. Greed seems to become paramount and it brings the worst out of people: the determination that one person should not get a better deal and the complete disregard of the fact that these are blood relations. I suppose they are the worst because I am an only child and longed for a brother or sister when I was young. I want to say 'You don't know how lucky you are...,' but of course that is being idealistic because some families do not get on and what I expect to be shared love can become shared dislike, if not hatred.

As with so many other things, the mediator can only model how parties should behave. We cannot make the parties love each other, but we can be compassionate, open and accepting. We can model honesty and integrity, generosity and courage. We can help warring parties move to a respectful and co-operative approach which will help them achieve a better deal. And we can reopen lines of communication that have sometimes been fractured for many years. We can't make them love, but we can give a glimpse of a better way. Can't we?

Forgiveness

My belief is that if you love, you have to forgive. It is built in. It is therefore a disappointment to me that so few, if any, parties end a mediation forgiving the other for the pain they have caused. This disappointment comes partly from the knowledge that not forgiving means that the person carries a cloud, and usually a big black one, of resentment or hurt or blame that affects their continuing life. They have not let go. It also means that they remain a victim, often still influenced, if not controlled, by those who created the hurt. But I know that forgiveness, true forgiveness that comes freely from the heart, will break the spiral of hurt and revenge. In a society such as ours that breeds a blame culture, that is desperately needed.

Actually, I think that forgiveness is more important than justice. I accept that it does mean letting go of the right to recompense, to punishment, to balancing wrong with penalty, and it does take courage, but society is all the better for people who do not seek revenge, who forsake the eye-for-an-eye concept and adopt a more loving approach to 'justice'. This is not necessarily restorative justice (RJ, which was covered in Part 2). RJ may result in forgiveness but it is more about reconciliation – as in the Truth and Reconciliation process in South Africa. Forgiveness was not expected but often resulted from the process.

Of course, there are many levels of hurt and that affects the ability to forgive. An unintended sleight or miscommunication is much more easily forgiven than a vengeful act or a physical injury. The latter may take a long time to work itself out and that may never be concluded. Not many of us are like Gordon Wilson who immediately forgave the bomber that killed his daughter when a bomb went off at the Remembrance Day Parade in Enniskillen in 1987 (actually, what he said was 'I bear no ill will, carry no grudge'). Most of us need time to work forgiveness out.

But I do know that not being able to forgive can blight a life forever, and I would dearly love to help remove that blight. Yet it is probably arrogant of me to even suggest such a thing to the injured person. Actually, it is more than arrogant, for I recognise in myself the pleasure that I can take from having a focus for my bile. It is almost reassuring to have an outlet for my nastiness, so that I can be nice to everyone else! I suppose that means that I can understand why people often demonise the perpetrator of their hurt. It may be unreasonable and often irrational, but it turns the focus away from self (and therefore often reality) to the other, so it is less threatening and disturbing.

So what has that to do with being a mediator? Do we really have a role in encouraging forgiveness? First, I think we have a real role in pricking the balloon of demonisation. It is one of the undoubted benefits of the initial open session for the disputing parties to face each other and to realise that these are also human beings with emotions and feelings. It brings humanity back into the dispute. Secondly, we mediators know how powerful an apology can be and how releasing the acceptance of an apology is. Acceptance may well mean forgiveness and we do have a role in encouraging that because we know it will help the offended party to move on. Thirdly, when the deal is done, a discussion on how they feel/what happens next/have they let go/can they move on may well be appropriate. We know that parties often have to go through a grieving process when a settlement has been achieved, and forgiveness and letting go is part of that process.

Of course it is all about what is appropriate and a good mediator will instinctively know what is, and isn't, in the particular circumstances.

Chapter 5

Mediator Bias

Dr Paul Gibson

Paul is an Australian mediator and trainer of mediators. Our first contact was through the International Mediation Institute (IMI) but it was his paper on constructive disagreement that led me to ask him to write a chapter for this book. He is a non-lawyer mediator with a long history of resolving disputes using facilitation, negotiation and conciliation techniques. This is good stuff. (DR)

Mediators are required by their training and practice to be neutral (albeit with some conjecture over what the term neutral actually means). Further, the rules which govern the professional conduct of mediators require us to provide 'procedural fairness' for all parties in the mediation. The concept of procedural fairness takes us directly to considerations of neutrality and impartiality.

Some rules specifically mention that the mediator should be free from bias, but as mediators, are we free from bias? In this analysis, I will examine the effect of bias both on the conduct of mediation, and the practice of professional mediators, irrespective of whether the mediation methodology being used is considered as facilitative, evaluative, or transformative.

Introduction

Most of us would claim that we practice mediation free of bias – whether this is an attempt on our part to remain neutral, or to comply with the rules governing our professional practice.

The interesting and challenging point however is that mediators are not automatons – we are human beings. We bring our own baggage into the mediation room: cultural background, political and religious beliefs, gender perspectives, thoughts, perceptions, prejudices, emotions and feelings, history and professional training and experience (as lawyers, psychologists, engineers, social workers, business people, scientists, and so on). Some of this baggage we may understand, some we may not; some of it we may be aware of and much of it we won't.

We are constantly attempting to understand the minds of parties during mediation, but do we really understand our own minds at the same time? Most mediators would probably say that they do – but is that assertion actually true? We attempt to be logical and to follow due process, we try to be empathic and even-handed, but how much of what goes on inside our brain and mind do we really understand?

Mediator Bias

Advances in neuroscience and neurobiology challenge this assertion. We now know that our reactions and responses are driven by our relatively automatic thought processes (our biases) – some of which we are conscious of, but much of which we are unaware or unconscious of.

According to studies by John A Bargh, Professor of Psychology at Yale University, we don't give much conscious thought to a range of decision-making processes – from the day-to-day decisions about how we vote, what we buy, how we interact with service providers, and where we go on vacation, to the more complex and strategic decisions regarding life choices.[1] Bargh asserts that unconscious processes underlie the way we deliberate and plan our lives.[2]

The question for mediators is: 'Are we really conscious of our thought processes during mediation?' How do we perceive parties and their counsel during the whole mediation process? Whether we practice facilitative, evaluative or transformative mediation, the challenges for the mediator are to be constantly 'present' during the mediation and to be consciously aware of our own behaviour and the effect of our own personality and mindset.

These are not inconsequential challenges, as we will discover.

Bargh challenges us to better understand 'the tug that the unconscious exerts on us'.[3] We all act as a result of our unconscious self. We make judgements of people from first impressions (often before we have actually spoken to them), based on our observations of their race, gender, age, clothes, and other features (piercings, tattoos and the like). These observations and perceptions automatically derive from our internalised stereotypes of how members of a particular group, culture or subculture are likely to behave.

We evaluate parties' interests and naturally prefer options which they develop, based on our own deeply embedded attitudes. We find ourselves sympathising with one party more strongly than the other. Recently, I debriefed a mediator who had mediated a protracted bullying complaint by a female employee against her male manager. He found himself 'believing' the complainant's story more than her manager's story. When he became aware of this, he reflected on why this was so. Apparently for him, her allegation was so confronting, so painful, and had apparently continued for such a long time that he had thought 'this could be my daughter or wife'. His implicit bias had affected his thought process, even if only momentarily. He was aware that his neutrality had been unconsciously affected.

It is not uncommon for a mediator to find themselves in a position of sympathising with one side more strongly than another. Why is this? Is it because of our unconscious biases? Is it ok to be a mediator and still have unconscious biases? Do biases affect mediator neutrality? What can a mediator do to make themselves aware of these unconscious biases?

---

1 J Bargh, 'When Psychologists try to Understand' (2014) January, *Scientific America*, pp 32–37.
2 Ibid, p 33.
3 Ibid.

What is bias?

The concept of bias is familiar to the extent that many people no longer stop to consider what it means to be biased. Bias is most commonly referred to as an 'assortment of stereotypical beliefs and attitudes about social groups',[4] which is formed through a process of evaluation of that group, either by ourselves or others.[5] Therefore it can be argued that a bias is a tendency to favour a particular thing, person, belief and/or an act according to that tendency, even where it may seem illogical to do so.[6]

Bias is a kind of internal conflict of interest.[7] Biases are part of the mental model of an individual. Biases and mental models are derived from many different sources throughout the life of an individual such as: familial influences and socialisation; professional training and socialisation; and organisational culture and socialisation, the environment of your professional life.[8] In situations of dispute and conflict, often characterised by high levels of stress and emotion, personal biases often act in such a way as to hinder a mediator from being able to act according to the principles of neutrality. Amos Tversky and Daniel Kahneman argue that since biases have the potential to cause an individual to make illogical conclusions and decisions, these 'systematic errors' highlight the 'psychological process that underlie perception and judgment',[9] placing biases at the forefront of an individual's decision-making process.

The necessary purpose of bias

From an evolutionary perspective bias is our protection mechanism. As we encounter situations in our day-to-day life, and make decisions about what is safe or not, and what is appropriate or not, we rely on our inbuilt danger detector (a term coined by psychologist Joseph LeDoux). He has suggested that our unconscious danger detector determines whether something is safe or not to do, even before we begin any conscious decision making. The neuroscience bears this out.

We are generally convinced that our decisions are rational, but in reality most human decisions are made emotionally, and then we post-rationalise the facts to justify them. From a survival point of view this is a necessary trait. Where people are concerned, these decisions are hardwired into us.

In our pre-history, determining who or what was coming up the path towards us may have been a life or death decision. If it were a hostile animal or a member of a hostile tribe, you might die. Our minds evolved to make these decisions very quickly, often before we had even thought about it.

---

4   S Carpenter, 'Buried prejudice' (2008) 19 Scientific American Mind, p 33.
5   Dr Anthony Greenwald and Linda Krieger, 'Implicit Bias: Scientific foundations' (2006) 94 California Law Review, pp 945-967.
6   M G Haselton, D Nettle and P W Andrews 'The evolution of cognitive bias' in D M Buss (Ed), The Handbook of Evolutionary Psychology (Hoboken, NJ, US: John Wiley & Sons Inc., 2005) pp 724–746.
7   D Cain and A Detsky, 'Everyone's a Little Biased (Even Physicians)' (2008) 229 (24) JAMA, pp 2893–2895.
8   Prof Mario Patera 'Mental Models', (2013) KonfliktKultur.
9   D Kahneman and A Tversky, 'On the reality of cognitive illusions' (1996)103 Psychological Review 582.

Mediator Bias

The unconscious way we perceive people during the course of a day is a reflexive reaction. Why would it be any different in a mediation for the mediator? The challenge is to exert concentrated, wilful and conscious effort into being aware of and putting aside the unexplained and sometimes unwarranted negative feelings that we have towards others, be they parties, counsel, experts or support people involved in the mediation process.

So our default way of looking at and making sense of the world is driven by a hardwired pattern of making decisions about others based on what feels safe, normal, likeable, valuable and competent. Freud knew that the unconscious was far faster and more powerful than the conscious. He described consciousness as the tip of the mental iceberg.

The other purpose of bias is efficiency. In any given day we are required to process millions of pieces of information at any one time, but our brains can only functionally deal with many fewer pieces – probably less than 50. In order to manage the plethora of data, we have developed a perceptual lens that filters out unnecessary information and lets other information in. This lens uses certain perceptions, prejudices, preferences, interpretations that we have adapted through life from all of our experiences. These biases enable our brains to be efficient, the downside of which is that our brains become lazy.

As psychologists have shown time and again, our brains are wired to be lazy. In decision-making, we almost instantaneously form an opinion based on memories, experiences, patterns, and first impressions. This has an obvious survival value. Only when such decisions clash with our analytical faculties to the point where cognitive dissonance will not let us rest in peace do we have 'second thoughts'. Why would we challenge an assumption which has worked well for us in the past; for example, if the assumption that 'men who wear hats when driving are bad drivers' has been a reliable predictor for us in the past, why change it? If we can survive with a facile explanation, why look for a more complex one? After all, the brain is the main energy consumer in the body, so it makes biological sense that we should not burden it with difficult questions or decisions. It's a simple matter of conservation of energy. Unless our brains are challenged (consciously and mindfully) they continue to use well-trodden habitual neural pathways.

This perceptual lens enables us to see some things, and ignore others, depending upon the focus of our unconscious. It filters evidence that we collect, generally to support our already held points of view and to disapprove those points of view with which we disagree.

Conscious and unconscious bias

An individual may or may not be aware of their biases. Therefore, the impact and effect of the individual's biases on others may be deliberate or unintentional. Essentially, as it has been noted, biases involve a process of some kind of evaluation, either made by an individual or a predecessor who has a substantial impact on their 'mental model'. For example, an individual may be biased against a particular social group due to their own experience with that group or this bias may be learned from someone else's experience with that group. Such an evaluation or learning may lead to prejudices or judgements either for or against a particular social group.

The level of awareness an individual has of a potential bias will determine that bias as either 'conscious' or 'unconscious'; also often referred to as 'implicit' or 'explicit'. Unconscious or implicit biases are those which present negative mental attitudes towards a thing, person, group or belief at an unconscious level. Conversely, a conscious or explicit bias is an attitude that an individual is aware of having.[10] This seems simple enough. However, research has suggested that these biases have the potential to diverge. For example, it is possible for an individual to express a neutral or positive opinion about a social group which they actually have an unconscious negative opinion about.[11] Unconscious biases are built into the structure of our brain's neurons and are the result of the process by which the brain traditionally filters through information to perceive danger. Growing out of 'normal and adaptive features of human thinking',[12] unconscious biases are subtle and may result in unnoticeable behaviours such as being less empathetic towards people with whom we cannot identify directly from another social group.[13]

Awareness of what biases an individual has and the strength of those feelings will help an individual to better manage those unconscious biases and be more vigilant when they are in play in the mediation process.

Common personal biases

Personal biases, which are an 'assortment of stereotypical beliefs and attitudes about social groups',[14] have the potential to affect the actions and responses of an individual. Often, these personal biases arise out of the notion of 'in-group favouritism' or 'tribal bias' and aren't necessarily a choice, they are part of the individual's mental model, developed from a young age and shaped by many environmental and social factors. Sociologist William Sumner (1906) asserted that it is human nature to form groups or tribes (sometimes even referred to as gangs) to act as protective mechanisms or support.[15] Once such a group or tribe (or gang) has been formed, it is not uncommon for an individual to favour their own group or tribe over others, whether consciously or unconsciously, and make judgements according to those biases. This process of judgement based on an individual's own standards of culture from their own tribe or group is often referred to as 'ethnocentrism' or 'in-group bias'.

There are now hundreds of studies which have examined such personal tendencies – to associate positive characteristics with one's own in-group more easily than out-groups as well as to associate negative characteristics more easily with out-groups than one's own in-group.[16] Such studies have examined both attitudes (such as

---

10 Stanford Faculty of Medicine – Office of Faculty Development and Diversity (2014), *FAQ on Implicit Bias*, Stanford, viewed 28 June 2014 http://med.stanford.edu/diversity/FAQ_REDE.html.
11 Ibid.
12 H Ross, *Fighting the Bias in Your Brain* (Linkage – Cook Ross Inc., 2010) viewed 14 October 2014 at http://www.linkageinc.com/thinking/linkageleader/Documents/Howard_Ross_Fighting_the_Bias_in_Your_Brain.pdf.
13 T Cornish and P Jones *Unconscious Bias Factsheet*, (The University of Leicester, 2014), viewed 14 October 2014 at http://www2.le.ac.uk/departments/physics/people/equality/Documents/ub-fact-sheet.
14 Carpenter, above n 4.
15 Marilynn Brewer, 'Ingroup Bias in the Minimal Intergroup Situation: A Cognitive-Motivational Analysis' (1979) 86(2) Psychological Bulletin 307.
16 Nilanjana Dasgupta, 'Implicit Ingroup Favoritism, Outgroup Favoritism, and Their Behavioral Manifestations', (2004) 17(2) Social Justice Research 143.

automatic prejudices) and beliefs (associated with stereotypes) that an individual holds towards an out-group.[17] Nilanjana Dasgupta argues that these in-group biases work in such a way that an individual will tend to prefer groups with whom they can associate as 'confirmation of their positive self-esteem'[18] as well as to prefer groups which are valued more highly in mainstream culture as 'confirmation of the socio-political order in society'.[19] However, it would be misleading to suggest that such biases always result in outwardly discriminatory behaviour. Indeed, such personal in-group biases fall within the established category of unconscious or implicit biases and apply to multiple areas of everyday life and interpersonal relations and, for this reason, it is important for individuals to consider how such biases may impact on these relations, including those parties, their counsel and mediators involved in a mediation process.

There is no such thing as an exhaustive list of personal biases. Personal preferences for taste, colour, sound, familial associations and many other environmental and social factors affect our decisions and reactions to situations without our knowledge. However, it is often possible to place personal biases into categories. One of the most subtle biases is that of confirmation bias. Confirmation bias has been defined as meaning 'looking for the presence of what you expect, as opposed to what you do not expect'.[20] The argument is that, in seeking to answer a question or find a reason as to why something is the way it is, we are deliberately selective in the evidence we choose to use to support our arguments, disregarding other available information and hence creating a moral dilemma.

Other common biases include:

- status-quo bias – a preference for the current state of affairs, or existing conditions;
- negativity bias – a preference towards recalling unpleasant experiences compared with positive or pleasurable experiences;
- anchoring bias – the tendency to rely too heavily on the first piece of information offered (the 'anchor');
- projection bias – a feature in human thinking where one thinks that others have the same priority, attitude or belief that one harbours oneself, even if this is unlikely to be the case – for example, predicting that one's own views will stay the same over time even though this is statistically unlikely;
- observational selection bias – a statistical bias in which there is an error in choosing the individuals or groups to take part in a scientific study, sometimes referred to as the 'selection effect'; and
- bandwagon effect – the tendency to do (or believe) things because many other people do (or believe) the same thing.

---

17 Ibid.
18 Ibid, p.163.
19 Ibid.
20 Douglas Medin, Jerome Busemeye and Reid Hastie, 'Decision Making from a Cognitive Perspective: Advances in Research and Theory' (1995) 32 The Psychology of Learning and Motivation 386.

Identification of biases

Most commonly, difficulties will arise for an individual where they are not able to identify their own biases. The very phenomenon of implicit biases applies to situations where, although an individual may consciously believe something, such as racial equality, they may also act on subconscious prejudices, such as favouring white over black or Islamic (in-group biases).

One of the most effective tools available for testing one's own unconscious bias is the implicit association test (IAT) created and maintained by Project Implicit. Project Implicit is a joint research effort of Harvard University, the University of Washington and the University of Virginia which seeks to 'investigate thoughts and feelings that exist outside of conscious awareness or conscious control'[21] in examining these implicit biases. implicit association tests (IATs) are used to measure these unconscious biases and the results demonstrate several things, including the strength of an individual's in-group biases. The findings of these tests affirm the suggestions made by Nilanjana Dasgupta. first, it has been shown by the IATs that people are likely to show preference to a dominant social group, eg young over old as well as still asserting age-old stereotypes of men being breadwinners and women being the family carers (stereotype beliefs).[22] Secondly, it is mostly the case that people will prefer members of a similar social group to their own, and be wary of outsiders (automatic prejudices).

Rules and standards

As a starting point, any discussion regarding mediator bias needs to be placed into an appropriate professional practice framework. Two such frameworks are considered: mediation standards and rules, and mediator neutrality.

We might expect mediation practice standards and rules to contain elements of guidance regarding ethics (and ethical practice), as well as concepts of procedural fairness and natural justice. These areas (of ethical practice and procedural fairness) are fundamental to the philosophy of mediation and it is these areas where the impact of mediator bias would be most keenly observed and would arguably have the greatest impact.

Two such sources to which I will refer are the Australian National Mediator Standards (abbreviated as NMAS) and the ICC Mediation Rules. The Australian National Mediator Standards (NMAS) have been in place for Australian accredited mediators since 2007, while the ICC Mediation Rules came into force on 1 January 2014. These two reference points are at either end of a time continuum, NMAS being one of the earliest attempts anywhere in the world to standardise mediator competencies and practice, and the ICC being the latest to formulate standards of mediator practice.

---

21 Ibid.
22 Melody Finnemore, 'Prejudice May Exist Even When People Aren't Aware of Their Biases' (2010) Oregon State Bar Bulletin.

NMAS Practice Standards

In the NMAS Practice Standards[23] the word 'bias' is mentioned several times. It is first mentioned in relation to 'Impartial and Ethical Practice' where the Standards say that 'impartiality means freedom from favouritism or bias in word or action, or the omission of a word or action, that might give the appearance of such favouritism or bias'.[24] It goes on to instruct that 'a mediator will disclose actual and potential grounds of bias and conflicts of interest'.[25] The Standards provide guidance to the mediator as to whether they should continue with, or withdraw from the mediation, even with the express agreement of the parties to continue the mediation. There is a requirement for a mediator to 'identify and disclose any potential grounds of bias or conflicts of interest that emerge any time in the process'.

The essence of the meaning of bias in this context of the Standards is in direct reference to issue of partiality – proffering the interests of one party over those of the other party (or parties). Further, in the Standards the context of bias is extended to include both the process and the content (subject matter) of the mediation. Importantly, the onus for the identification of, communication of, and management of bias lies with the mediator.

It is self-evident that NMAS refers to conscious bias – that bias already known to the mediator.

ICC Mediation Rules

The ICC Rules[26] are silent regarding the word 'bias'; it is not mentioned once in the published document, or the accompanying Mediation Guidance Notes.[27] The Rules do however refer to the concept of neutrality in defining the term 'mediator':

> 'the term mediator shall be deemed to cover the neutral who conducts such settlement or procedures [mediation]'[28]

Additionally, the Rules also refer to the mediator signing a 'statement of acceptance, availability, impartiality and independence', as well as requiring the mediator to disclose in writing to the parties any circumstances which could question the mediator's independence, or give rise to reasonable doubts as to their impartiality.

The Rules allow parties to receive such a declaration and comment upon them. This mechanism of transparency seems key to dealing with these issues of the neutrality and impartiality of the prospective mediator.

---

23   Australian National Mediator Standards, *Practice Standards – For Mediators Operating Under the National Mediator Accreditation System* (September 2007).
24   Ibid, p 8.
25   Ibid.
26   International Chamber of Commerce, *Arbitration Rules – Mediation Rules* (International Court of Arbitration and International Centre for ADR, Paris, 2011, 2013).
27   International Chamber of Commerce, *Mediation Guidance Notes*, (Commission on Arbitration and ADR, Paris, 2013).
28   Mediation Rules, above n 25, p 72.

Mediator Bias

The Rules also require the mediator to be guided by the wishes of the parties and shall treat them with fairness and impartiality.[29] In these ways the ICC Rules place procedural obligations on the mediator, in such a way that 'procedural fairness' is maintained, without at any time attempting to define it or even use this precise form of words.

Again, the assumptions made by those who have formulated the rules are that the mediator is conscious of their potential partiality. This may be a dangerous assumption.

Mediator neutrality

Neutrality has been identified as a core concept of mediation.[30] As is recommended in most codes for mediators, as an independent third party in the dispute mediators must aspire to remain 'neutral and impartial' at all times,[31] and, whilst the importance of mediator neutrality appears to be largely undisputed,[32] it is difficult to accurately define what neutrality means, how to achieve neutrality, and the potential destructive effects of bias in the mediation process.

Gibson and Handy[33] take a different and broader view of the links between neutrality and impartiality. In their VISC model, they see 'neutrality' as a more fluid concept.

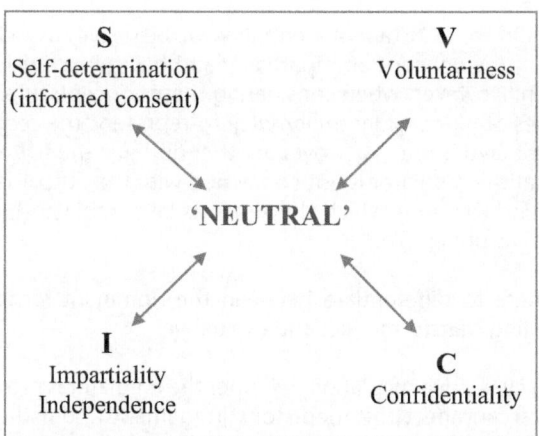

Gibson and Handy argue that neutrality affects a range of process and content decisions that mediators make throughout the mediation process, irrespective of whether it is facilitative, evaluative or transformative. They believe that bias affects both the process and content decisions, which occur through the duration of a mediation, and that the concept of neutrality is dynamic, changing as the mediation ebbs and flows.

---

29 Ibid, p 76.
30 Kimberlee K Kovach, *Mediation: Principles and Practice*, 3rd edn (West Publishing Co, 2004).
31 H Hung, 'Neutrality and impartiality in mediation' (2002) 5(3) ADR Bulletin 45.
32 C Izumi, 'Implicit Bias and the Illusion of mediator Neutrality' (2010) 34(71) Washington University Journal of Law & Policy 71.
33 P Gibson and F Handy, The Trillium Group (Unpublished, 2013).

They view bias as having an effect on all four dimensions of their model. Further, they see that directing attention to one dimension may bias direction away from other dimensions. In their view maintaining neutrality challenges the competing attention of the mediator.

The behaviour of the parties, their counsel, appointed experts and support people affect the mediator and therefore the process of mediation. How much of what a mediator does is automatic and how much of it is controlled?

As such, the research suggests that there is a direct conflict between notions of neutrality and impartiality and the inevitability of unconscious and implicit biases. The question which must be considered is that if all mediators are subject to implicit biases, is it possible for a mediator to be neutral? It is possible to suggest that there is a significant gap between the aspiration of mediator neutrality and scientific studies which demonstrate that all individuals are subject to unconscious and implicit biases.

However, comprehension of what mediator neutrality means and how it should look in practice is 'complicated by a lack of consistency in definitions',[34] and, as Carol Izumi (2010) argues:

> 'the dispute resolution lexicon is imprecise... there is no consensus within the dispute resolution community that neutrality and impartiality are terms of art or synonyms in the vernacular'.[35]

That is to say that in some instances, neutrality will be heavily associated with, even synonymous with, the concept of impartiality and being inactive in the process of conflict resolution. However, when considering these concepts in practice, Douglas Frenkel and James Stark consider *impartiality* to represent the requirement that a mediator does not favour one party over another during a mediation and *neutrality* to be the idea that the mediator is not concerned with the outcome of the process, that the parties find solutions which they view as favourable and not those which the mediator sees as preferable.[36]

It is important here to differentiate between the dominant forms of mediation: facilitative (including transformative) and evaluative.

Dealing first with evaluative mediation, whether the mediator is providing a binding evaluation, biases can affect the mediator's judgement about the determination of facts, the credibility of experts, the perceptions of the parties in dispute, the weighing of evidence, and the making of decisions themselves. The parties, and their counsel, demand and expect professional and ethical behaviour; they don't want the unintended consequences associated with the mediator's conscious or unconscious bias.

With facilitative mediation the mediator avoids any evaluation of the issues, and resists requests by the parties to provide opinions. Depending upon the attitude of the mediator, the parties will be more or less encouraged to determine the solution themselves and take responsibility for their own decision-making. They

---

34 Ibid, p 78.
35 Ibid.
36 D Frenkel and J Stark, *The Practice of Mediation: A Video-Integrated Text* (2008), 84.

may however be guided by a process determined by the mediator, designed by and managed by them to provide procedural fairness. It is possible however that the mediator may, in the course of the design and management of the process, be affected by their own biases.

In the purest sense, the mediator adopts a role of facilitating a discussion between parties in conflict.[37] This facilitative role is reliant upon the notion of neutrality, which is seen as a 'fundamental element of the mediator's role'.[38]

Transformative mediation takes this even further to the point of facilitating a conversation between the parties that encourages them to develop a process through which they can resolve their differences. The process of this mediation is to develop and restore the connection and relationship between the parties by empowering them in the decision-making processes, both in terms of process and content. This requires mediators to always be 'present', and to have high levels of self-awareness in terms of the implicit or unconscious bias.

Dealing with biases

Most research into the area considering the management of 'unconscious biases' suggests that the only way to combat these biases is to become aware of them in the first place.[39] Awareness requires self-assessment, reflection, and mindfulness. It also requires an openness and willingness to work to adjust engrained perceptions. There is no simple solution for combating unconscious and implicit biases – it takes time, hard work, conscious and disciplined effort, and a daily routine.

First, there must be an acknowledgement by mediators themselves that their professional practice may be affected by confirmation biases and tribal biases. Secondly, mediators must assess the impact which these biases are having on their practice irrespective of what methodology they are applying. Finally, measures must be implemented to consciously combat biases which are having a negative impact on the relationships with parties in particular as their behaviour will impact the mediator, and the mediator's behaviour will have an impact on the parties. It is a dynamic relationship.

Being absolutely neutral is a challenge for most mediators. It is no easy task to combat unconscious biases and indeed such behaviours are manifested in the actions of mediators in dealing with the parties.

The following provide some specific guidance to mediators in managing their own biases

---

[37] S Jacobs, 'Maintaining neutrality in dispute mediation: managing disagreement while managing not to disagree' 34 (10-11) *Journal of Pragmatics* 1403 at 1405.
[38] Cohen et al, 1999, 341: 347 (in S Jacobs, 'Maintaining neutrality in dispute mediation: managing disagreement while managing not to disagree' 34 (10-11) *Journal of Pragmatics,* 1403 at 1406.
[39] Howard Ross, 'Proven Strategies for Addressing Unconscious Bias in the Workplace' (2008) 2(5) *CDO Insights (Diversity Best Practices),* p 13.

Awareness

Primarily this involves feedback – from parties, spouses, business partners and respected professional colleagues, sporting partners and associates, siblings and adolescent and adult children. The reason for such a wide and diverse range of sources lies principally in a genuine attempt to receive accurate, insightful and helpful feedback from as many people as possible who have had the opportunity to witness your behaviour in as many and varied situations as possible.

Feedback may also include having parties and others involved in the mediation completing surveys and being involved in debriefings and discussions in relation to attempts at changing our mental models. Feedback aids an understanding and acknowledgement of unconscious biases.

You don't have to be captive to your unconscious biases. That is to say it is not possible to go back in time and change the upbringing, education and employment of an individual, which help to formulate established biases and mental models. However, taking the IATs would represent a practical first step in attempting to identify and increase awareness of individual 'unconscious biases'. The range of these tests enables a variety of insights to be gathered.

Acceptance

Receiving feedback is a necessary step, but it is only one step; acceptance of the feedback is often a more difficult step. The feedback, if honestly given, can often be confronting and difficult to accept because it challenges who we are; it questions those beliefs and prejudices which have sustained us, and presumably made us successful through life. Often these beliefs and prejudices are deeply engrained and tightly held – after all they have aided our survival and development. Moreover we have probably associated with people who have similar views, recalling that tribal bias is our primary bias (and most common).

The tricky part is that we will, unfortunately, seek out and probably only hear that feedback which already confirms our belief systems, recalling that confirmation bias is our secondary bias (probably the second most commonly encountered). It is a confronting process to discover our unconscious or implicit biases.

Mindfulness

The notion of being 'present' during mediation is a challenging prospect. Not because it is necessarily difficult; but because it requires exertion. The ability to concentrate not only on the words being used by parties, but also the meaning behind the words is mentally taxing and requires concentration. This is why many mindful mediators work in short sessions, often of not more than an hour. The brain consumes oxygen and glucose (much more than we credit) in order to maintain high levels of attention and concentration. This principle applies to both the mediator and the parties, recalling that the higher states of arousal and nervous energy associated with conflict call for even greater access to 'brain food' – oxygen and glucose.

Generally, our brains revert to our most ingrained attitudes when we are under pressure or stress. Mediation, particularly that involving high emotion and deeply embedded or protracted conflict, can be extremely stressful for all involved – the parties, the mediator, and others. The mediator in particular can feel the pressure of both the responsibility to positively assist the parties, as well as managing the process constructively and neutrally.

It is also why the breaks, when correctly managed, give the mediator and parties the opportunity to walk and breathe, replenishing the oxygen, and why access to sweets (glucose-laden) is also a good idea. All of this, however, only supports the brain as it is directed to focus, be alert, pay attention, remain neutral and suspend judgement. It is the suspension of judgement that can be the most taxing because the unconscious assumptions are ever present.

Increasing mindfulness involves the processes of reflection and training. Simple activities to increase the elasticity of our mental models may include keeping a diary or meditation, as well as changing established habits such as taking a different route to work in the morning. Trying new foods or wine, coupled with an understanding or study of where they came from will also help to increase mindfulness, an awareness of our surroundings and the present moment. More difficult and complex attempts to retain an elasticity of our mental models may include learning a new language or musical instrument or joining a society that challenges our traditional beliefs. Such practices will be rendered insignificant if they do not occur in tandem with the process of feedback.

Conclusion

Parties expect professional and ethical behaviour from mediators – that is what they pay for, and most rules of professional conduct lead parties and their counsel to believe that is what they will experience. What they don't want are the unintended consequences of mediator bias. The responsibility for maximising the former and eliminating the latter rests squarely with the mediator, irrespective of the mediation methodology applied. As mediators, our professional reputations depend upon this.

Chapter 6

Intercultural Mediation: A Digest of Theory and Practice

Joanna Kalowski

There is a note about Joanna in Chapter 4 of Part 2 of this book. She is a goldmine of knowledge and skills and I could sit at her feet for days and be entranced and entertained by her storytelling and her insights. She is a treasure. (DR)

> 'How did you get her to talk?' Culpeper asked as they set off together through the cold....
>
> 'I listened,' said Strike.
>
> Robert Galbraith, *The Silkworm*[1]

This simple exchange encapsulates much of the accumulated knowledge about cross- and inter-cultural communication. To gauge how people operate, it is necessary to put them at ease, get them talking and listen to the way they communicate, their different styles and preferences, if you are to have any hope of working with them in situations of tension and conflict, and if they are to have any hope whatsoever of working together.

Think of this chapter as an intercultural blog. It is intended to bring together learnings from many sources: practice, theory, experience, discussion with colleagues, writings from the field, and from failures and mistakes – a great source of instruction.

Someone once said that if a concept cannot readily be translated into another language – if there is quite literally no word for it in the other language – you have probably stumbled upon a cultural construct. So it is with mistakes: once you have made them and seen the effect they have in an intercultural setting, it is the effort to retrieve the situation which teaches you most surely what it was missing, what assumptions led you into error and what you might have done differently if only you had known what you know now.

Put simply, some of the techniques mediators in the Western world resort to more or less automatically are unlikely to work in intercultural settings unless adapted and sensitively applied. Mediation will fail if it is assumed to be culture-neutral, since that would predispose us to use standard approaches, stock phrases and set-piece mediations. Awareness is the intercultural mediator's ally, awareness not only of the other, but of the self.

---

1   Robert Galbraith, *The Silkworm* (Sphere, 2014), Chap 1, p 21.

Self-awareness has come to be viewed as the essential pre-requisite for intercultural mediators, and is identified as a key criterion of intercultural success in these terms:

Self awareness is the ability to:

- recognise one's own cultural influences and their possible effect on the mediation;
- recognise participants' culturally-shaped perspectives of behaviours or events;
- understand and appreciate participants' similar and different cultural perspectives, and possible imbalances between them;
- manage ambiguities and mistakes that may emerge in intercultural situations and settings;
- use the mediator's understandings of these differences and similarities to create a workable environment for all participants, including an environment that optimises communication;
- adjust one's own communication style to the styles of participants from other cultures, the goal being to help participants communicate optimally with each other, including establishing suitable processes to facilitate communication;
- prepare for a mediation by identifying possible cultural patterns and preferences likely to be relevant to particular mediations; and to design appropriate processes and prepare for a range of possible interventions.
- detect whether, when and how cultural considerations may be impacting on the mediation process as it progresses, including capacity to adapt the process accordingly and design appropriate interventions that also encompass any settlement and compliance phases and requirements.[2]

How people interact, argue, manage conflict and negotiate – and even whether they are prepared to speak up and describe a conflict and what lies behind it – is as varied as the settings in which the talk takes place. Taking account of that diversity is one thing: understanding its impact on interactions and the potential for collaboration is quite another.

> 'As human beings, we are constantly in search of an equilibrium between our identity and our relationship with those we encounter, and those encounters confront us with the wrenching awareness of our differences as well as reassurance that we are have similarities. That instability, that tension can be constructive or destructive, depending on context and the extent to which we are prepared and supported as we take risks.
>
> Viewed in that light, the intercultural can be seen as the lived experience of all that is strange. It changes us and our view of the world. It makes strangers of us all – hardly a comfortable place to find ourselves.
>
> All individuals and groups draw their identity from multiple cultural sources – if only we become aware of them. This tangle of sources of belongings can, if we permit it, lead to the possibility of multiple levels of affinity between people and groups, depending on the stakes and the context.

---

2   See http://www.imimediation.org/intercultural-certification-criteria.

Intercultural Mediation: A Digest of Theory and Practice

The goal of multi- or pluri-cultural policy has been an idealistic one: an attempt to live together with minimal friction, to work together despite our differences, to create a functional whole despite the disparity of the parts.

All of this requires individuals to transcend, not abandon, their own cultural systems, so that conflict and disagreements are seen not as threats but as challenges. Viewed that way, communication and interaction are not so much hampered by difference but can add a new dimension to the very idea of "different".

Intercultural experience is not just a phenomenon of national cultures and of ethnicity, but exists also at the level of generational, social, professional, philosophical, religious, political and economic differences. The promise of intercultural effectiveness is precisely to enlarge the capacity to engage and be effective at many levels of diversity.

Members of a heterogeneous group can proceed constructively together in a satisfactorily intercultural way if they can agree on a three-level framework:

1. To question and make adjustments as doubts and tensions arise;
2. To analyse similarities and differences in both cooperation and conflict;
3. To stand back and analyse communication to identify what created conflict and what created cooperation (meta-communication).

The goal of this framework is to foster mutual recognition, and to continually create the conditions for working together, on the understanding that the intercultural is learned by experience, and is circular and iterative:

Trial → Observation → Analysis → Conceptualisation →

This process leads to trialling new approaches, and group members become active learners, ultimately producing the very competencies they need.

Intercultural learning results from being constantly confronted with other points of view, with the reactions of people living the same experience in the same moment yet interpreting it differently. Conscious acceptance of undeniably different points of view is precisely what makes this learning intercultural.

Three indispensable conditions underpin the development of intercultural competence:

- Empathy
- Preparedness to work on differences and conflicts
- The will to cooperate.'[3]

This long exposition, more than any I have read, perfectly summarises the nature of intercultural learning and the sense of surprised satisfaction mediators report

---

[3] Adapted from the work of Marc Thomas, *Acquérir une compétence interculturelle*, Université de Nancy 2, 2000 and translated by Joanna Kalowski.

'when it somehow came together'. Asked to dissect and reflect on the mediation itself, mediators often talk about the time parties spent simply talking, even in tense situations, and reported their own ambivalence as they wondered whether this apparently aimless talk should be cut short. On further reflection and debrief, they are glad they did not.

What is happening here is what neurobiologists describe as priming.

> 'In addition to our emotional system, we are highly gregarious and social creatures, who have evolved to work in large groups. We have thus also developed a very rapid and unconscious socialisation system, which subconsciously assesses and judges whether other people are 'in our group' or "out of our group", "similar" or "different", and whether they are likely to try to dominate us or are trustworthy. These emotional and social systems share a common physiology, and the amygdala ... appear[s] to be involved in rapidly screening who is "safe" and "similar" ... [H]umans also naturally seek safety in building coalitions.

The impact of group identity on perception and cognition

There is an area in the prefrontal cortex of the brain associated with cognitive decision-making that classifies another person as being "similar" when consciously mentalising about them. This area has direct connections with another area of the brain, the anterior insula, where certain fundamental emotions, such as notions of fairness, are modulated. However, when a person is consciously classified as being "different", another part of the prefrontal cortex is activated. That area has no neural connections with the insula. By getting a person to focus on whether they are similar to or different from another person, a person is thus more or less likely to be able to empathise. Thus, group dynamics will impact the disputants' natural abilities to empathise, trust and bond, and how they will perceive what another person tells them. We not only tend to unconsciously categorise people as "us" versus "them", but we also seek to create comfortable social situations for ourselves.

Similarly, there are certain neurons in the brain, called mirror neurons, which are involved in non-verbal communication and empathy as well. They may become more or less sensitive depending on whether in-group or out-of-group recognition patterns are activated. Humans also secrete a simple neuropeptide called oxytocin, which is sometimes referred to as a "trust hormone". Production of oxytocin can drive close cooperation and bonding (eg between a mother and a new-born infant), but this same hormone can also drive adversarial behaviour and aggression if a person is perceived as dissimilar or out-of group.

A mediator's influence on group dynamics is therefore likely to greatly affect the parties' abilities to communicate and perceive effectively in a mediation. This relates to procedural issues as well as to substantive issues. A mediator can activate in-group patterns of social behaviour, generating empathy, collaboration and willingness to reciprocate, but a mediator can just as easily trigger out-of-group patterns, by priming parties to think in terms of "position papers", "the other side", "opening statements" and by seating them in separate rooms for much of the day. This may drive more adversarial behaviour, competition, aggression, loss of empathy, and an inability to communicate effectively non-verbally. Priming parties to prepare for a mediation by encouraging them to perceive one another as their "negotiation partner" rather than as the "other side", and helping them think in terms of mutual interests instead of positions, getting them [to] think through what their negotiation partner's interests and needs may be before they meet – [all this] can have a strong pro-social impact. This is something a mediator and the parties should think about and discuss carefully when setting up, designing and preparing for a mediation process.

Although it may be possible to lead the parties into a given style of mediation, this is ultimately a matter of ethics. Are the parties cognitively aware of the possible impacts of certain procedural choices on their relationships and social patterns? Being mindful means being cautious, about oneself and about the disputants' emotional and social patterns, and ensuring that there is a full understanding of potential impact on group dynamics by all participants whenever a procedural decision is made.'[4]

These insights operate as a brake on excessively goal-oriented approaches, especially in intercultural mediation settings. Mediators who question aloud the relevance of certain topics and the time wasted in 'small talk' (Let's return to the main issues... Is this relevant? Let's get back to business...) are at serious risk of cutting across the coalition-building and in-group scripts developing imperceptibly among parties to a mediation. They are also in a far better position themselves, as trusted others, to challenge or propose procedural decisions which they later perceive as threatening newly built levels of cooperation and collaboration.

As for separating the parties early and keeping them apart: the learnings of neurobiology should now suffice to throw such a tendency into serious question, especially in intercultural disputes where the need to build unconscious understanding can be greater even than in other mediations. This relates to a tendency, little discussed and undervalued, of the role culture plays in conflict situations:

- However apparently cordial previous relations between parties of different cultures might have been, the emergence of conflict hampers communication and can even shut it down completely. The risk of being seen as betraying one's own side limits the availability and choice of spokespersons, and those prepared to speak often lack credibility and status.

- As people search for reasons for the emergence of conflict, they assume it is due in greater or lesser degree to cultural differences, even when this is not (or only in part) the case.

- Communication style will get in the way, and may exacerbate the sense that 'we can't get through to them'. High and low context communicators will find one another more exasperating than ever, and risk talking past each other or switching off when the other speaks.

- Power differences, which once were background issues, will surface once again, with all the tension this can produce well beyond the issues in dispute ('You

---

4 Jeremy Lack, 'A mindful approach to evaluative mediation', Mfn Tijdschrift Conflicthantering (NL) No 3, 2014. This extract is quoted with the kind permission of the author.

only say this because you are playing victim' or 'We are tired of you pushing us around').

- People will attribute negative motives to one another. In conflict situations, or in situations that are strange, the first round of attributions is usually negative. If you walk into a room of strangers and everyone laughs, it is highly likely you will assume you are the butt of the joke.

- Old cultural resentments which have simmered beneath the surface may rise up again.

Mediators risk believing the conflict *is* cultural unless aware that culture often plays a convenient role in legitimising conflict whose sources lie elsewhere, in a place yet to be discovered and examined with skilled assistance.

Mediators working across cultures would do well to recall that while culture provides a structure and a basis for individuals and groups, it is not a straitjacket, and the identity of groups and individuals is affected by many other social and psychological phenomena.

In the settings in which many intercultural mediations take place, such as international commercial mediations or inter-communal conflicts in a given society, it is also as well to remember that one of the strongest forces acting on one group is prolonged contact with another. The cultural adaptation that results from such contact is frequently imperceptible to both; while one sees the other as clinging to old ways, they may in fact both have moved substantially towards one another without being consciously aware of the fact. Mediators report that uncovering this is another source of complexity. Once it surfaces, a group can begin to view adaptive behaviours in terms of loss: loss of identity, loss of important cultural values and virtues, and loss of contact with the country or culture of origin.

Prolonged contact, with its imperceptible effects on groups, means that the parties know more about each other and understand one another better than they assume. This insight, coupled with the learnings emerging from neurobiology, gives mediators a key role in working with parties in dispute to assist them to discover and acknowledge this for themselves.

At the heart of both conflict and its resolution is acknowledgment. Failure to acknowledge what underlies a dispute engenders conflict; acknowledgement, however belated, helps to resolve it.

Thinking back over many apparently intractable situations where parties had tried and failed to settle a dispute, mediators can all identify a moment when there was a shift. What happened that brought about change? What was said or done, what did the parties do which suddenly altered the climate and broke through the fog of circular discussions and put them on course to settle and resolve? On almost every occasion it is acknowledgment, directly or indirectly expressed. Stop for a moment and think about how it sounded in the moments before the breakthrough took place.

In commercial disputes, it might have been a party or their lawyer saying, however grudgingly, that things might have been different 'if only you'd disclosed this earlier', or 'if only we'd known about this document...'. In other kinds of disputes, the language might vary but the meaning is the same:

'In order for me to let go, to join with you in finding another way to bring an end to this situation, *there is something you have to do or say which you haven't done or said yet* ... something I can claim I didn't know. Then there can be movement.'

At that moment, the seeds of acknowledgment are planted. Parties can acknowledge that they would have acted differently, had they known; whatever the case, such knowledge is a pretext for saying something new, for moving on.

Quite early in a dispute it is possible to know what resolution might look like. It is not through a failure of imagination that the parties have not settled before this, quite the contrary. Most often the answer is staring everyone in the face, and mediators who think they have 'discovered' the outcome are sadly mistaken. Quite early parties get a glimpse of what shape the settlement might take: the problem is overcoming the obstacles that have prevented them from getting there themselves. Those obstacles are almost always about feelings – of resentment, anger, disappointment, even outrage. The businesswoman whose line of credit has been peremptorily stopped by her bank is indignant, and wants it restored. Restoration of the status quo is the goal; resentment is the obstacle that has limited communication to threats and descriptions of the impact of the bank's actions, most often written by parties' representatives in uncompromising terms and threatening legal action.

Mediators love attributing the shift in climate to the process of mediation itself, and it cannot be denied that providing a forum to air the issues is fundamental. But if the end of all our interventions is to bring about resolution, not merely to do deals, it is acknowledgement mediators need to pursue and model. Acknowledgement is an end in itself, because it opens the way to a quality of discussion not possible while disruptive feelings are in the air.

In mediation generally, acknowledgement is valuable; in the intercultural setting, acknowledgement is paramount. It is a pivotal moment and represents a shift in perception when one party's frame of references can unexpectedly encompass and embrace the very different response their negotiation partner had to an event or a circumstance. It is in this moment that intercultural learning takes place. The moment and the response also serve to free the responder. They quite literally did not and could not have known how something seemingly trivial in their eyes could seem so offensive to another.

Judges often assert that 'this is a just society' because their whole purpose is to dispense justice; in workshops on access to justice by minorities in their society, they learn to say instead that 'this society has been just to me'. This inter- (or cross-) cultural insight does not impede their capacity to work for just outcomes, it arguably expands it, and remains one of the most potent instances of the impact of considering the intercultural which I have experienced. It leaves space for a number of realities to exist side by side, without, as Pedersen says, 'one being right and the other being wrong.'[5]

Dialogue begins, not ends, with this expanding worldview; in intercultural terms, dialogue cannot succeed without it.

Mediators educated in the Western world are frequently given training in question techniques, the impact of open and closed questioning, and the place of both.

---

5   Paul Pedersen, *Culture-Centred Counselling Interventions* (Syracuse University, 1997).

If questioning is taken any further, it is into the realms of levels of questioning: from knowledge through application to problem-solving techniques (in ascending order). Certainly, it is most effective to ask problem-solving questions which enable parties to consider for themselves the advantages and disadvantages of certain options and alternatives. But the matter should not end there.

When mediators are working to build intercultural dialogue, asking questions, even in caucus, can be a dangerous business. Questions can have the effect of limiting the ambit of discussions to what the mediator knows, not expanding it to what the parties might now, unbeknown to the mediator or to one another.

Avoiding the impulse to ask questions until much later in an intercultural mediation, mediators would do better to 'cast a wide net', and invite parties to reflect on themes and issues on the principle that they don't know (yet) what the parties know, are unlikely to think the way the parties think or see things precisely as they do. It is only when mediators appreciate the worldview of parties, understand the way they filter information, what matters to them (and what doesn't) that they can be at their most useful.

The problem for mediators interculturally is that they don't know what they don't know; remaining self-aware and recognising with due humility that 'something is going on here, but I'm not sure what it is' is a call to action.

The choice of action and intervention is tempered if mediators recall that:

> 'a mediator's influence on group dynamics is ... likely to greatly affect the parties' abilities to communicate and perceive effectively in a mediation and ... relates to procedural ... as well as to substantive issues.'[6]

Consider the following invitation nets, some couched as quasi-questions, designed by a UK colleague for such intercultural dilemmas:

- 'There is something happening here that I don't understand and I am wondering if you might enlighten me.'
- 'It is always your choice what we talk about but is this something you need to explain to help me assist you?'
- 'Is there something about this interaction that you feel you cannot tell me about?'
- 'Have I said or done something that you find offensive in some way and if so, can I tell you now that I never mean to upset anyone?'
- 'Is there an unspeakable thing going on here? Is it something that really matters that you feel you can't talk about?'
- 'Sometimes I use some expressions and words that come from my culture which may not be in accordance with the way you deal with such things in your culture. If it concerns you, please tell me so I can understand better ways of doing things for you.'
- 'It seems like it is very important for them to talk about the past and that it is not for you. You would rather not talk about the past and they want to. How are we going to deal with this difference?'[7]

---

6 Jeremy Lack, op cit.
7 Unpublished: Jane Cooksey, mediator, lawyer, psychologist. Director, Berkeley Square Mediation Ltd. janecooksey@berkeleysquaremediation.com

The subtlety of these invitations to elucidate is striking, combining the need to understand a gap the mediator perceives (or a gap in the mediator's understanding) with a clarity about her or his role and purpose: to assist these parties to locate a durable outcome to their matter, a task they squarely see as being in their hands because they alone know 'what's really going on'.

The promise they make to the parties, contained in the statements above, represents a key stage in culturally synergistic problem-solving:[8]

- assume there are diverse cultural perspectives on the same matter;
- describe or learn about the situation from all cultural perspectives;
- find out what cultural assumptions underlie the parties' behaviour;
- identify cultural overlaps (if any);
- co-create options to fit the needs and interests of the parties, including at the cultural level;
- implement selected options;
- observe their impact over time in cross-cultural perspective; and
- refine solutions accordingly.

Implicit in the process outlined above is that the parties will remain in relationship for some time, perhaps forever, depending on the nature of the dispute.

An international study[9] found recently that conflict with local communities is costing oil, gas and mining companies billions of dollars. It found the single biggest hidden cost in projects of this magnitude is delay. Court cases, industrial action, environmental protests all hold up projects, so companies, the study asserts, are 'wrong to think they can bluff, bully or litigate their way out of trouble'. The study's most controversial finding, unsurprising to intercultural mediators, is that 'dialogue and community engagement' are best if projects are to succeed. They go on to state that 'contrary to popular belief, marginalised communities including indigenous people have huge clout', and that it makes no sense to try to proceed without engaging them.

Mediators in the intercultural arena ought not avoid the imperative to build relationship and a climate of communication which will enable talk to continue into the future, as the situation and perceptions evolve. In this climate, people are not only receptive to one another's viewpoints, but marvel at them; and perhaps also at the fact that while this may not have been something they knew at a conscious level, having heard it, it does not seem as strange as they might have feared.

---

[8] Adapted from the work of Nancy J Adler, 'A Typology of Management Studies Involving Culture' (1983) 14(2) (Autumn) Journal of International Business Studies, Special Issue on Cross-Cultural Management.

[9] Rachel Davis and Daniel M. Franks, *Corporate Social Responsibility Initiative Report 66*, 'Costs of Company-Community Conflict in the Extractive Sector' (Cambridge, MA: Harvard Kennedy School, 2014).

Chapter 7

One Continent, Many Methods

Bill Marsh is an ace mediator. He combines intelligent perception with humility, is articulate and humorous and has invested a huge amount of time and skill in helping the emerging countries of Eastern Europe to include mediation in their legal system. Much of what is written below by mediators in the various countries of Europe is due to his commitment to making this a better world. (DR)

Introduction

During the last 25 years, it has been my privilege to meet and work with mediators from right across Europe, and beyond. Some have been vastly experienced, other just embarking on a new discipline. We have discussed and debated the work we all love, often into the night. We have strategised, plotted and argued about how to mediate, how to develop mediation, and how to train mediators. We have certainly not always agreed. But all of them have taught me things, and given me fresh perspectives.

Even in my own mediation practice, when mediating between parties from very different countries and cultures, I have seen very different ideas of what the process is about, how mediators should behave, and what they should do. And when I have trained mediators around the world, they have by no means shared a homogenous view of what it is we all do. In fact, even amongst mediators from my own country there is a significant variety of practices and understandings.

Some may find this threatening and wish to defend 'their' way of doing things. But in reality, it should not surprise us. The expression of conflict – the way we fight and resolve things – is one expression of culture. The language we use, the processes we adopt, the assumptions and understandings we have all reflect our personal and cultural views of conflict. The subtler meanings of words such as 'truth', 'honour', 'transparency', 'winning' and 'losing' differ in different countries. Relationships to 'authority' – whether that be governments, judges, parents or mediators – vary widely as well, and with it, the understanding and practice of mediation.

Some of these differences derive from the way in which mediation has developed, and this is particularly true of commercial mediation. In the United Kingdom, for example, the early drivers for commercial mediation came from the business community, and especially in-house counsel. The same was true in the United States. It was the desire of business to find enhanced ways to resolve disputes that provided the early profile and momentum for mediation. The involvement of the courts and the state, in seeking to encourage the use of mediation and regulate its practice, came much later. It was a classic case of 'bottom up' development.

By contrast, many other European countries have adopted a 'top-down' approach. The initial focus of introducing mediation was through structural reform of the legal system, usually involving legislation to provide for and regulate mediation. Only once that was in place did attention turn to seeking to generate demand for mediation, and to involving the business community. It should be no surprise that such differing starting points have impacted heavily on the practice and understanding of mediation. For example, a demand-led, bottom-up approach will inevitably emphasise practicality and the needs and interests of consumers over regulation. A top-down approach will tend to regard mediation as an integral part of the delivery of the state's justice system, and hence reflect more the need for regulation and structures.

Some of the key areas of difference I have experienced, particularly in commercial mediation, have included the following:

- **The background of mediators**

    Some countries tend predominantly towards mediators with a legal and/or commercial background. Others give much greater overt profile to the place of psychology in the mediation process, and hence attract many mediators from that discipline or background.

- **Training**

    Training courses very widely in length (30 hours up to 400 hours) and in content (some include extensive academic input, while others focus purely on practical/skills related issues).

- **Focus of mediation discussions**

    Some commercial mediation processes focus heavily on legal issues as well as commercial ones. Others regard the legal issues as beyond the remit of the mediation discussions. For example, I was once informed by a Central European party in an international mediation that they were only prepared to discuss commercial issues at the mediation, and would not tolerate any discussion at all on the legal merits of the case.

- **Use of joint versus private meetings**

    This is a distinction not only between countries and cultures, but between individual mediators. To some extent it reflects differing understandings and practices of mediation, but to some extent it also points to the differing skills and comfort zones of each mediator.

- **The extent and nature of regulation**

    In some countries (for example, the United Kingdom) the practice of mediation is very lightly regulated. There is no single national accreditation standard, no single regulatory body for individual practitioners, and no national recognised qualification. In others, all those structures exist, and others beyond such as the requirement to register all mediations and agreements reached in mediation with the state or other body.

I could go on articulating a range of differences. Who is to say whether they matter, and which are right or wrong? In any event, no two mediators mediate the same way (If you doubt that, try co-mediating!), so at what point do we recognise and even encourage differences? And which are differences of substance, or merely differences of style? If we accept (as I believe we must) that conflict reflects culture, and cultures differ, then we should expect and welcome differences in the understanding and practice of mediation.

The real question, I suspect is what are the areas of similarity? For me, two stand out in particular.

The framework

There is a common recognition, throughout Europe (and beyond, in my experience) that a fundamental framework needs to be in place to enable mediation to happen and flourish. Perhaps most significantly, the confidentiality of the process needs to be protected in order for parties and mediators alike to engage confidently in the process. It is no surprise, therefore, that the EU Mediation Directive seeks to provide only for such a framework, leaving the detailed implementation up to each state to do as it sees fit.

The values

Mediators I have met right around the world seem to adhere strongly to a common set of values. These often include the desire to serve, a willingness to challenge the status quo, the preparedness to give centre stage to the parties and where necessary to go unnoticed, a recognition of the importance of people and compassion, and overall a high commitment to integrity. Others can add to this list.

In this section of the book, where pictures of mediation in all the different European countries are painted, many differences are expounded. Certain aspects may make you think 'tut-tut' or 'I would never do it that way'. But if all mediators can be coherent in our fundamental framework and core values, then we can afford to let a thousand flowers bloom, and learn from them.

Austria

with Thomas Kustor

Introduction

Mediation in Austria is legally recognised and appreciated as a cost-effective means of avoiding disputes. Surprisingly, mediation could not make the breakthrough in the field of business law although mediation seems to be perfectly suited not only to settle claims, but to constructively structure a 'way forward'. The federal Law on Mediation in Civil Law Matters (Zivilrechts–Mediations- Gesetz (ZivMediatG), hereafter referred to as the Austrian Mediation Act), became law in May 2004, so it has been incorporated into the Austrian legal system for many years.

EU Directive (2008)

The Austrian EU Mediation Act (EU-Mediations-Gesetz) became law in 2011 and covers non-registered mediators in cross-border disputes. Registered mediators are still covered by the Austrian Mediation Act.

The Austrian Mediation Act (2004)

The Act does not stipulate the mediation process or approach – it is up to the parties to decide with the mediator. However, it does stipulate the rights and obligations of Registered mediators, including:

- use of the title 'registered mediator';
- conflicts of interest, particularly acting for or advising, a party in the mediation;
- confidentiality;
- obligations regarding documents and other information;
- prohibition of certain kinds of commission;
- independence and impartiality;
- recording the mediation;
- professional liability Insurance; and
- continuing professional development.

Registered mediators are contained in a list maintained by the Federal Minister of Justice.

Of course, non-registered mediators are not covered by the Act, although non-registered mediators who conduct cross-border mediations are covered separately by the Austrian EU Mediation Act (2011).

Mediation and conciliation

There is often confusion as to the difference between Mediation and conciliation. In Austria:

- Mediation is informal and voluntary. Conciliation is more structured with a formal procedure once the process has commenced.
- Conciliators are members of public authorities, whereas mediators are generally registered under the Act.
- Agreements in mediation are made by the parties, with the help of the mediator. They are the decision-makers. In conciliations the settlement is usually provided by a public official.
- Costs of the mediation are usually shared between the parties whereas in conciliation, if no agreement is reached, they may be claimed as pre-procedural costs.

Definition of mediation

Mediation is defined in the Act as a voluntary process in which a specialised and neutral mediator systematically promotes communication between the parties, with the aim of facilitating an amicable solution of a dispute.

Register of mediators

The Act created the term 'registered mediator' which is a protected term and so can only be used by mediators who have met the necessary criteria and successfully registered. The criteria includes being:

- over 28 years of age:
- professionally qualified;
- trustworthy; and
- insured.

Trustworthiness can be 'proved' by submitting a current extract from the Register of Convictions.

Registration is initially for five years and can then be extended at ten-year intervals. mediators must produce evidence of experience and continued training.

Voluntary/mandatory process

Mediation is a voluntary process. There is no requirement, let alone a mandatory element, for parties to mediate their dispute. Some courts have a mediation presence and may refer cases with the parties' approval, but the voluntariness of mediation is paramount. An Association was formed in 2011 (Verband für Mediation gerichtsanhängiger Verfahren (VMG)) to facilitate court-referred mediation. The mediators registered with the VMG specialise in mediating court-referred cases and the registration conditions are strict – they must have attended several court proceedings, have a basic knowledge of Austrian civil procedure and civil law and must sign up to the code of ethics of the VMG.

Enforceability of mediation clauses

Mediation clauses are enforceable, but overriding this is the acceptance that mediation is a voluntary process and so a clause requiring parties to mediate would fail if one party refuses.

Confidentiality

The Act expressly provides that a mediator has to keep confidential any facts or (other) information which came to their knowledge in the course of the mediation. A mediator who breaches confidentiality, and therefore violates the legitimate interests of another person, is liable to be prosecuted and could face up to six months in prison.

Mediation style and procedure

Given its origin and history in Austria, the normal form of commercial mediation is facilitative, followed by transformative. The type and style of the mediation is decided by the parties, with the mediator, but they tend to be dictated by the level of emotion, transformative style being suited to neighbour and family disputes, facilitative to commercial disputes. Some evaluative mediation is used in commercial disputes although the Act makes clear that the mediator's role is to 'facilitate communication between the parties with the aim of enabling the parties to reach a solution themselves'. The mediator may propose a solution if the parties so request.

Enforceability of Mediated Settlement Agreements

Mediated Agreements qualify as a civil law contract. These are not automatically enforceable but there are several ways to overcome this:

- having the written agreement recorded in the form of a court settlement by any district court;
- having the agreement confirmed in an enforceable notarial instrument;
- having the settlement recorded by an arbitral tribunal; and
- recording the settlement in the form of an arbitral award on agreed terms.

Mediator training, accreditation and post-qualification standards

Anyone can be a mediator but the training requirements for civil/commercial mediators is tough. The requirements are high because of its professional status and depend on the professional background and experience of the person being trained. For example, under the Austrian training regulation for mediators, a lawyer only need to train, with an organisation on the Federal Minister of Justice's list, for 165 hours, whereas a less qualified person may be required to undertake as many as 274 hours. This compares with the requirements in many other EU countries where only 40 hours is common.

The Act stipulates that registered mediators must have a minimum of 50 hours CPD over a five-year period. Evidence must be shown when applying for re-registration.

Mediator exemption

The Act and the Austrian Civil Procedure Code provide that registered mediators are prohibited from disclosing any confidential information to the court, nor can they be summoned to testify regarding the content of the mediation.

Conclusion

In conclusion, Austria has a two-tier system for mediators – registered and non-registered. Registered mediators have a high reputation because of the stringent requirements over qualification and the obligations imposed by the Act. They also have rights and protections that do not apply to non-registered mediators. But in the end it is for the parties to decide – they decide on the mediator, the mediation process, the style of the mediation, the terms on which the mediator is engaged and the terms of the eventual settlement. The power is with the people!

Belgium

Anna Doyle

The Belgian experience – sharing perspective

The purpose of this paper is to outline the current use of mediation, and particularly commercial mediation, in Belgium. It will also comment on its current legal status and the extent to which mediation is used. As mediation is all about promoting shared perspectives, let's take a closer look at what is already published on this subject and easily accessible to the reader, with a view to enlarging our shared perspective in a collaborative spirit.

The following are a number of very interesting and recent publications available, giving an overview of the current state of play in Belgium, as well as the future envisaged for mediation in this country. There is no known analysis available, however, that would establish the common style of mediation that is practiced or the breakdown between mediation styles, eg facilitative, transformative, evaluative, etc. It is too early in the evolution of mediation to say more on this now and, indeed, any such analysis at this stage would be of limited value and would most likely be subjective in nature.

The Future of Mediation in Belgium

FMB (The Future of Mediation in Belgium) is an initiative that aims to provide a joint communication platform to all mediation stakeholders, thereby offering them the opportunity to contribute to identifying best practices (including legal amendments) and setting out a common action plan for the enhancement and promotion of mediation in Belgium. To this end, Belgian mediation stakeholders gather periodically (at least twice a year) in the form of brainstorming sessions and/or working groups. The meetings are held in English, Dutch and French and a copy of the latest FMB Report is available online at: http://www.arbitration-adr.org.

The FMB has proposed a number of positive actions that would reinforce and promote recourse to mediation and these are all outlined in their latest FMB Report. Some of the proposals include promoting greater awareness of the concept of mediation, education and training, possible broadening of existing legislative provisions, improved categorisation of mediators and the services provided in different spheres, as well as learning from the experience of other countries, as portrayed in the in-depth report of the European Parliament which is intended to have the effect of rebooting the Mediation Directive, backed up with a range of both legislative and non-legislative measures.

The latest FMB report also underlines the view that a strong professional body is required to ensure that mediation is functioning at its full potential. This would include taking a range of measures that would entrust more power and resources to the Federal Mediation Commission (FMC), which currently deals with the accreditation of mediators and mediation training.

The FMB Committee has announced its intention to pursue their ideas for further development of mediation in Belgium with the relevant Government Ministries with a view to bringing about an improved Mediation Bill and other wide-ranging measures that would hopefully bring about improvement in the professional practice of mediation in Belgium, as well as promoting greater awareness of the value that it adds, in terms of saving time, costs and enhancing overall relationships in an appropriately flexible framework for the way we live and work today.

The European Parliament perspective

The Policy Department of the European Parliament published in early 2014 (PE 493.042) a very comprehensive study of the state of play of mediation in all the countries of the EU. It is entitled *Rebooting the Mediation Directive: Assessing the limited impact of its implementation and proposing measures to increase the number of Mediations in the EU*.

The study reveals how, more than five years since its adoption, the Mediation Directive (2008/52/EC) has not yet solved the 'EU Mediation Paradox' and that, despite its proven and recognised benefits, mediation in civil and commercial matters 'is still used in less than 1 per cent of the cases in the EU'. This study reflects the views of up to 816 experts from all over Europe, 32 of whom responded from Belgium.

It contains a wealth of very useful information as regards, for example:

- the estimated number of mediations per year;
- a comparison of the average time and money savings of litigation only versus mediation, then litigation; and
- a clear analysis of what currently works, does not work and where there are areas for improvement.

Rather than repeating the findings of the study, the reader is directed to explore the fascinating information contained in this report for themselves, not only in the Belgian context, but also, where feasible, with a detailed comparison across all of the EU Member States.

A detailed analysis of the situation viz-à-viz Belgium, is published in the report as follows:

- mediation legislation (p 72);
- court referral to mediation (p 72);
- confidentiality (p 73);
- enforcement of Mediation Agreements (p 73);
- impact on statutes of limitations (p 73);
- requirements for parties and lawyers to consider mediation as an alternative dispute resolution option (p 74);
- requirements for parties to participate in mediation (p 74);
- accreditation requirements for mediators (p 74);
- mediator duties (p 75);

- duties of legal representative and other professional mediation participants (p 75);
- estimated number of mediations in Belgium and the value (pp 120–127);
- a more detailed analysis of the Belgian respondents to the questionnaire (pp 132–161); and
- the Annex, whch also includes comments made on the national mediation legislation (pp 167–169).

It would appear that the objectives of the European Mediation Directive have yet to reach their full potential in Belgium and that this situation might indeed continue to prevail until such time as there is a concerted drive to incorporate mediation into Belgian law and practice, a situation which is not yet the case.

International organisations' perspective

No comprehensive overview is available yet on the extent to which international organisations have embraced the concept of mediation. The author, however, is the creator of an in-house Mediation Service at EUROCONTROL, the European Organisation for the Safety of Air Navigation, with headquarters in Brussels, Belgium.

The agency's mediation officer at EUROCONTROL heads up the service which was established in 2006. She is responsible to the director general for supporting staff and the agency on issues that would benefit from mediation, so as to overcome any difficulty that may arise in the context of working relations, rights and obligations

The Mediation Service at EUROCONTROL voluntarily commits to the European Code of Conduct, drawn up by the European Commission, which sets out a number of principles to which individual mediators or organisations can voluntarily decide to commit, under their own responsibility. The mediator currently handles about 120 cases a year.

Bulgaria

Eliza Nikolova

Regulation

Legal regulation of mediation in Bulgaria was established in December 2004 when the Mediation Act (MA) was adopted (promulgated in State Gazette No 110/17.12.2004, last amended, SG No 27/1 April 2011). Since then it has been amended several times. The 2006 amendment of the MA authorised the Minister of Justice to issue a regulation on the certification of the organisations providing mediator training and on the training standards for mediators. The Minister of Justice issued this regulation on 15 March 2007 (Regulation No 2). Regulation No 2 covers several areas. First, it specifies the requirements that training organisations should meet to be certified as such. Secondly, it provides for the minimum requirements of mediator training. Thirdly, it establishes an official public uniform register of mediators. Finally, Regulation No 2 sets forth guidelines on the mediation procedure.

On 16 June 2006, the Minister of Justice issued an order approving procedural and ethical standards for mediators.

The new Civil Procedure Code (CPC) (promulgated, State Gazette No 59/20.07.2007, effective 1 March 2008) also had a significant role in increasing the practical implementation of mediation. Several provisions thereof set out the necessary procedural measures for applying mediation in pending court cases and established an initial legal basis for connection between mediation and civil proceedings.

In civil and commercial proceedings, the court has the general authority 'to refer the disputing parties to mediation when scheduling the first hearing of the case in public session'. Additionally, parties may be referred to mediation or decide to use it later on at any time during the proceedings. If the parties agree to use mediation the case may be postponed or stayed depending on the parties' will. In practice, parties are usually able to have mediation sessions in the period between two court hearings.

The CPC states that the judge hearing the case must inform the parties about mediation and other methods for alternative dispute resolution.

Mediation in Bulgaria is voluntary. There is no mandatory pre-action mediation. The court before which a dispute is brought may only propose to the parties that the case be referred to mediation; it does not have the right to order mediation. The same is also true for family law cases, although there is a slight difference, ie an obligation for the judge to refer to mediation, but not for the parties to participate in the mediation procedure.

There are no specific court rules regulating the court-referred mediation. Some private mediation providers have adopted their own rules complying with the MA. Those rules mainly cover the following:

- operation of the mediation provider;
- requirements that mediators need to meet;
- mediation procedure;
- some rules of ethical conduct; and
- fees.

Style

The Bulgarian Mediation Act of 2004 (MA) describes mediation as an alternative method for resolving legal and non-legal disputes (MA, art 1). The notion of mediation is defined in art 2 as a:

> 'voluntary and confidential procedure for out-of-court resolution of disputes whereby a third party – the mediator – assists the disputants in reaching a settlement'.

Three fundamental principles of mediation are stated in some detail in arts 5–7 of the MA:

- voluntary recourse and equal treatment;
- neutrality and impartiality of mediators; and
- confidentiality.

Mediation in Bulgaria is facilitative. Parties have a major influence on decisions made, even more than the parties' attorneys. The mediator is in charge of the process, while the parties are in charge of the outcome. Joint sessions are held in turn with caucuses (if necessary) until it becomes clear whether the parties could reach an agreement.

Who does mediation?

Only natural persons can be mediators. They are allowed to form associations.

In order to be accredited as a mediator, one must be a legally capable person who has successfully passed mediation training, has not been convicted for general crime, has not been deprived of the right to exercise a profession or an activity, and has a permit for long-term (new provision) or permanent residence in the Republic of Bulgaria, in the event the person is a foreign national. Such a permit is not required from nationals of Member States of the European Union or of other states from the European Economic Area and Switzerland. As a direct reflection of the Mediation Directive, the opportunities for foreign nationals to become mediators in Bulgaria were extended by allowing foreign nationals having long-term residence in Bulgaria to acquire the capacity of mediator if they meet the other legal requirements (previously, only persons having permanent residence were allowed to become mediators).

It is important to mention that specific groups of officials are not allowed to serve as mediators. The general prohibition in art 4 of the Mediation Act provides that persons performing functions of administration of justice in the judiciary system may not carry out mediation activities. Thus, judges and prosecutors may not serve as mediators. Other government officials, such as officials in ministries, may not perform mediations, based on the general prohibition that they are not allowed to perform any paid activity in addition to their official service, except for lecturing. However, these government officials could perform pro-bono mediations.

Training

To become a mediator, one must have first successfully completed a mediation training programme. The training takes 60 hours and it includes a theoretical and practical component. The theoretical component consists of three subcomponents. The first is an introduction to mediation that discusses conflict, settlement and mediation as an ADR method. It further covers: the role of the courts; participants in mediation; principles of mediation; and procedural and ethical standards. The second theoretical subcomponent explains the mediation procedure: starting the procedure; the selection of a mediator; the phases of a mediation procedure; the role of the mediator and tools to improve communication; the suspension and termination of mediation; and the settlement agreement. The third subcomponent covers a comparative review of legislation and mediation practice, as well as mediation in different types of disputes. The practical component includes participation in simulations and their subsequent analysis. Each trainee must take part in at least three simulations.

All mediators must be entered in the uniform register of mediators, for which they will receive a certificate from the Minister of Justice.

The organisations that deliver training to mediators need special approval from the Minister of Justice. The terms and conditions for their approval, as well as the requirements for mediation training, are defined in Regulation No 2. Training organisations are also entered in public register.

There is no national statistic about the number and type of mediated cases. The only statistic disseminated is that from the Court Settlement Centre where mediators provide mediations on a voluntary basis. Yet figures are too small to make representative conclusions.

Mediation has its supporters among judges and people devoted to the cause (including some modern thinking attorneys-at-law). The state support however is not enough. The question does not apply only to regulations which comply with EU policies. A scheme of incentives and large-scale pilot projects needs to be implemented, which could only be done by the state.

Croatia[1]

Mladen Vukmir

The Croatian mediation system was largely set up by adoption of the third Mediation Act in 2011 following previous institutional structure development. This endeavour to set up a mediation system started at the beginning of the millennium with the training of the first batch of mediators under the organisational and financial support of the United States (USAid) and EU Member States, and the first phase was rounded off with the adoption of the first Mediation Act in October 2003. The first Act was based on the UNCITRAL Model Law on Mediation and has by far preceded the EU Mediation Directive. This coincided with the founding of the first mediation centre at the Croatian Chamber of Economy Permanent Arbitration Court.

After the adoption of the first Mediation Act, additional mediators were trained thanks to the efforts of those initially trained mediators and with the support of the Ministry of Justice of the Republic of Croatia and EU funds. Numerous mediation centres were gradually founded in the aftermath of ongoing training. During that time, mediation was initiated in practice through pilot programmes, first at

---

1   Some segments of this text were prepared as a write-up accompanying a presentation at the 19th Croatian Arbitration and Mediation Days in December 2011. Its theses were subsequently elaborated at the panel 'Become an even better mediator' on the occasion of the UIA World Forum of Mediation Centres held in Zagreb on 5 and 6 October 2012. Information prepared for various other surveys were incorporated into the present version of the text.

the Commercial Court of Zagreb, followed by the High Commercial Court of the Republic of Croatia and thereafter at many municipal courts.

An umbrella Croatian Mediation Association (Hrvatska udruga za mirenje (HUM)), having as members the majority of Croatian mediators, was also founded early on, around 2003. The Association had an important role in forming the mediation profession in Croatia. Subsequently, HUM has also acquired the authorisation to perform training required for the mediators' certification by the Ministry of Justice of the Republic of Croatia. The mediation system was thus completely set up and all the premises for performing the mediator's profession in Croatia were created. All these systematic endeavours have led to the formation of a network, including today the majority of mediation institutions.[2]

Specifically, in 2006, within the strategy of reform for the legal system, the pilot project 'Mediation before the courts' introduced the mediation centre at the Commercial Court in Zagreb, thus introducing mediation as a dispute resolution method into the legal system for the first time. Based on that project, the implementation of mediation has taken place in a further eight courts throughout the country. In 2007 the implementation of mediation proceedings at the High Commercial Court of Croatia was introduced, making it the first appellate court in the Republic of Croatia with an established mediation centre. Mediation before the Court was conducted mostly by mediators who were judges, but the list also included attorneys, engineers and academics with mediation training.

The role of mediation as a part of the Croatian legal system has become even more prominent after the implementation of the EU project 'Improvement of mediation as alternative dispute resolution' in 2008, through the joint efforts of the Ministry of Justice assisted by some mediation centres. The overall objective of this project was to provide easier access to justice through the development of alternative dispute resolution. Its further purpose was the development of alternative dispute resolution services in Croatia and its adaptation according to best practices in the European Union and the development of alternative dispute resolution before as well as outside of the courts. Amendments to the Civil Procedure Act have introduced mediation as a possibility throughout the entire litigation process.

The second Mediation Act was enacted in 2009 and immediately raised numerous new questions which the newly emerging mediation scene scrambled to answer as quickly as possible. Efforts made to recognise the challenges and develop the appropriate solutions have brought to an accelerated advancement and also new revelations at local level on the nature of mediation. This has brought about a greater experience of local mediators, useful understandings in mediation administration proceedings, and development of materials to raise awareness among potential users.

The third Mediation Act was enacted and came into force from 2011. A few provisions of the Act, related to cross-border mediation came into force with the date of Croatia's accession to the EU on 1 July 2013. Most recently, a new Family Law has been adopted, coming in force from 1 July 2014. This Law introduced strong mandatory mediation in family disputes for the first time. Many mediators

---

2   As listed on the HUM webpage (in Croatian): http://www.mirenje.hr/index.php/o-mirenju/mirenje-u-hrvatskoj/institucije-za-mirenje.html.

received additional, family specific training in the wake of the enactment of the new Family Law.

Although the scope and extent of this section leave no room for further legislative analysis or elaboration of the history of mediation development in Croatia, or a comparison with that of other countries, we are of the view that the foregoing facts should be kept in mind. In fact, the development of mediation in Croatia is a story of success, comparable to successes in other countries. The attainments of the mediation system are such that they almost seem unreal if compared with what seemed likely 20 or even 10 years ago. Many were sceptical at the time towards a successful introduction of mediation, and undervalued the possibility of mediators' education and attraction of clients. The results achieved have completely disproved these fears and today's achievements seem far greater than even the most daring predictions.[3] Let us now briefly look at some of the features characterising the Croatian mediation scene, hoping this can further raise its profile.

One of the formative factors for a mediation scene in any given country would be the mediation training available. Most of the local basic mediation training provides for the facilitative approach and consequently most of the locally conducted mediations are facilitative. This is even more pronounced in the cases of commercial mediation, where the default style is without any doubt facilitative. While most of the mediators will use facilitative approach, some mediators with more traditional styles might use more directive style. Some mediators with a background in the judiciary might use more directive style, and those with a background in psychology might use some transformative elements.

There are no mandatory mediation courses offered by law universities in Croatia so far. The mediation in law universities is usually discussed within family law and labour law courses. Within the civil law process, law mediation issues are discussed in relation to the conclusion of extra judicial settlement between the parties. Only the Faculty of Law in Zagreb offers an elective ADR course. The general amount of hours for basic mediator certification training is 40 hours' minimum basic training; additional advanced training is administered in 20-hour courses.

Sometimes, the directive style might lead a mediator towards evaluative elements. Apparently, this is not necessarily at odds with the expectation of local mediation users. Most frequently, if used at all, the evaluation will be conducted in an informal manner, in the form of general advice from a 'senior/experience' vantage point. Legal opinion rendering has not been used often in mediation, but one can expect more frequent usage in the future as the mediation market develops further.

Regarding the format of mediation sessions, it could be said that the predominant mediation process for commercial disputes involves caucusing. While most of the mediators will use caucusing as a default, some mediators with more sophisticated styles will use joint sessions predominantly.

The standards for the accreditation of mediation institutions as well as mediators are set by the regulations on the register of mediators and standards for the

---

3 See a summary of the ADR situation in Croatia at: http://www.mprh.hr/alternative-dispute-resolution-?dm=2.

accreditation of institutions for mediation and mediators.[4] These also regulate the content, form and manner in which the register of mediators shall be conducted. It is prescribed that the register of mediators is organised under the Ministry of Justice. The register is public and everyone has the right to inspect it without proof of legal interest. In order for a mediator to be inscribed in the register, it is necessary to obtain a certificate issued by an accredited institution on the basis of basic training for mediators.

According to the applicable rules, accredited institutions for mediation are those authorised by the Croatian Mediation Act or those which obtained approval from the Ministry of Justice for conducting basic and advanced training for mediators, conducting training for mediator trainers as well as for conducting mediation in their mediation centres.

While the mediation institutions in Croatia have been set with a vision and following a path that the local mediation community set as a plan, it could be said that market forces played a relatively minor role. Business users of mediation also did not play any important role in setting up the mediation market so it is to be hoped that the liveliness of the market forces will play a bigger role in the future. It can be expected that in the future the markets will work in two directions. It is likely that they will favour certified mediators, and will favour specific experience and styles within that group. Of course, it is possible to imagine that some non-certified mediators will survive market forces, at least as long as certification does not become mandatory.

Generally there are no organisational or competence-related boundaries in using mediation for dispute resolution. Therefore, mediation itself may be entrusted to a mediation centre or organisation or to an ad hoc mediator. It is provided, however, that some mediation procedures can be delegated only to certified organisations or persons who are determined by special mediator lists (ie in family matters, divorce proceedings or collective labour disputes).

Lawyers and others with legal education appear to be mediators in most cases. However, besides lawyers, other professionals are trained and often mediate as well. Sometimes, this option even appears to be preferred by the parties, especially in cases dealing with very sensitive issues (such as family disputes) or in cases where the disputes are of specific and complex nature (like disputes concerning medicine, finance, construction works, etc.) Thus, mediators can be accountants, engineers, architects, social workers, psychologists and experts on labour relations, doctors, consultants, educators, etc. Where parties are accompanied by their lawyers, who supervise the legal aspects of the mediation settlement, it certainly helps mediators who do not have legal education and can thus focus predominantly on conducting the mediation process.

Pursuant to the Mediation Act, a mediation organisation may be a legal person, an entity of a legal person or an organisational unit of a legal person that organises mediation proceedings. So far, they are usually associations, or professional organisations founded by law, such as the Bar Association, Chamber of Craftsmen, etc.

---

4 The Regulations; Official Gazette No 59/11.

Normally, a mediated settlement can qualify as a binding contract, in accordance with the Croatian Civil Code. If the parties have undertaken some obligations by the settlement, they are bound to fulfil them in a timely manner. However, an important feature is the legal mechanism that secures that the settlement agreement in mediation proceedings is a self-executing enforceable title if the prescribed conditions are met. Article 13 of the Croatian Mediation Act prescribes that a settlement agreement concluded in the course of mediation proceedings shall be an enforcement title if it contains a clause setting the obligation to perform an act over which the parties may reach a settlement and if it contains the obligor's statement on immediate authorisation of enforcement (an enforcement clause). In this case the obligor explicitly agrees that on the basis of the settlement agreement, in order to carry out the performance of the due obligation, immediate enforcement may be ordered. Therefore, the enforceable title is not completely automatic, because the enforcement clause has to be incorporated into the agreement. The required formalities are not set by law and are now debated between the mediation system stakeholders, namely the judges and the mediators. The parties need to agree on the inclusion of the enforcement clause, and can even notarise the settlement agreement, although this is not expressly required for its enforceability.

All this has raised quite a few dilemmas in practice and the experts are pointing out some doctrinaire inconsistencies on the side of the law of execution, so it is very likely that this system will be revisited at the next round of legislative changes.

Regarding confidentiality, the regime is set so as to fulfil the traditional internal and external mediation confidentiality requirements. According to art 14 of the Croatian Mediation Act, unless otherwise agreed by the parties, the mediator shall keep all information and data received in the course of the mediation proceedings confidential in relation to third persons, except where the law requires disclosure, or where it is necessary for the implementation or enforcement of the settlement agreement. Furthermore, the mediator shall be liable for the damage caused by his or her violation of this obligation. The above provisions are applied accordingly to the parties and other persons who have participated in mediation proceedings in any capacity. The provisions of art 10(2) of the Croatian Mediation Act regulate the confidentiality in relation to the meetings of the parties and the mediator. This article prescribes that, unless the parties have agreed otherwise, the mediator may communicate information or data received by one party to the other party only with the other party's consent.

The Act also introduces an exemption from obligation to give evidence in court proceedings or arbitration. Article 15 of the Croatian Mediation Act regulates the question of admissibility of evidence in judicial, arbitral or any other proceedings. It prescribes that it is not permitted to make statements, propose evidence or submit any other proof in whatever form regarding any of the following:

- the fact that a party had proposed or accepted mediation;
- the parties' statements of facts or proposals made during mediation proceedings;
- admission of claims or facts made in the course of mediation proceedings if such admissions and observations are not a constituent part of the settlement;
- documents prepared solely for the purpose of mediation proceedings, unless it is stipulated by law that their communication is necessary for the implementation or enforcement of the settlement agreement;

- the parties' willingness to accept the proposals made during mediation proceedings; and
- other proposals made during mediation proceedings.

Such evidence shall be rejected as inadmissible, but according to the principle of autonomy of the parties they can agree otherwise.

Although space constraints do not allow further presentation and analysis of the features of the Croatian mediation system it is hoped that the above will serve as an introduction in Croatia's dynamic and evolving mediation scene. Although the overall number of mediations in any given year remains relatively low, estimated at several hundreds, it is to be hoped that the predicted growth of market-based initiatives will raise mediation's profile and its frequency.

Cyprus

Christos Theodoulou

Mediation in Cyprus, as well as commercial mediation, exists, but, it is not used much, if at all. There is progress, however, concerning the legal framework. Further, there are parties involved in mediation.

The legal framework

According to EU Directive 2008/52/EC of 21 May 2008, for certain subjects of mediation in civil and commercial cases, Member States had to comply with it by 21 May 2011. Cyprus complied to this Directive by Law No 159(I)/2012.

The law follows the provisions of the above-mentioned EU Directive. According to the law, there is a special register kept by the Minister of Justice and Public Order, on which mediators are registered. These mediators are lawyers who exercise the profession and have an annual licence to exercise the profession according to the Advocates' Law and so are duly qualified.

Further, members of the Cyprus Chamber of Commerce and Industry or members of the Scientific Technical Chamber of Cyprus, may become mediators after they follow a special programme for qualification as a mediator for 40 hours, which programme is organised by the Chamber of Commerce or the Technical Chamber or any equivalent programme.

A fee is paid to the Minister for the registration in the mediators' register. A mediator must be independent, objective and fulfil their duties with diligence. There are provisions in the law for compulsory continuous education.

The court may suggest that a case go to mediation. The mediator indicates the venue for the mediation, after examining all the circumstances of the case. The parties may appear by themselves or accompanied by a lawyer.

The procedure of mediation may be terminated in certain cases. Where there is an agreement between the parties, the mediator drafts a written agreement of settlement.

The costs for the mediation are regulated by law.

On application the court may ratify the whole or part of the settlement agreement, executed in the same manner as a judgment of the Court, or reject the application to execute the settlement agreement.

The bodies involved

The bodies involved in mediation are the Cyprus Bar Association, the Cyprus Chamber of Commerce and Industry and the Scientific Technical Chamber of Cyprus. The Bar Council and the Chamber of Commerce also organise seminars and training courses for their members. Further, there is a Cyprus Mediation Association dealing with the subject.

The need for mediation in Cyprus

Litigation in Cyprus is very time consuming and costly. Actually, the time needed for a simple commercial matter is disproportionate to its significance and especially the costs which the parties are asked to pay. For these reasons, alternative dispute resolution (ADR), including mediation, is more than ever needed. Mediation is less costly and quicker than litigation. Unfortunately, up to now, mediation has not been used extensively, even though parties are complaining about the drawbacks of litigation. It is to be hoped that the situation will change with the passing of the time.

Czech Republic

Tatjana Šišková

Soon after the 1989 transformation process started in Czechoslovakia, mediation know-how was brought to the Czech Republic in 1992 by the American NGO Partners for Democratic Change. American mediators also helped to establish the NGO Czech Centre for Negotiation and Conflict Resolution (the Centre). Since then, many mediators were trained overseas (in Europe as well the United States), as well as Czech trainers, thanks to this NGO. Since the state has not been active in promoting mediation in all areas, except in the area of social justice (criminal law), the Association of Mediators of the Czech Republic (AMČR) was established in 2000 by trained mediators and trainers from the Centre. The aim was to maintain the professional level of mediation, teach mediation in 100-hour courses and disseminate adequate information about it. They devised professional standards, a code of ethics, and educational and accreditation standards for mediators and they managed to receive accreditation from various ministries. To date, over 1,000 mediators have accreditation through the AMČR.

Similarly, more organisations working in the area of mediation were established during the first decade of the 21st century. These are NGOs and professional, private and public organisations, including counselling centres providing mediation, as well as various services for people in conflict situations, eg Conflict Management International (CMI), Union for Arbitration and Mediation Procedures of the Czech Republic (URMR), International Resolution Service (ESI), various counselling centres, etc.

Contacts for mediators working in the Czech Republic may be found on various websites by entering the search term 'mediation'. For mediation in civil law matters, you can contact any mediator offering that service. A list of mediators may be found, for example, on the websites of the Association of Mediators of the Czech Republic (http://www.amcr.cz/), the Czech Bar Association (ČAK) (http://www.cak.cz/en), and the Union for Arbitration and Mediation Procedures of the Czech Republic (URMR) (http://www.urmr.cz/), Conflict Management International (CMI) (http://www.conflict-management.org/cs/kontakty/), etc.

Cost

Mediation is a paid-for service; the price level varies a lot. Family mediation cases are much cheaper then commercial cases. The service is offered free of charge in some state counselling centres.

Community mediation

One of the goals of mediators from Partners for Democratic Change was to found conciliation committees in communities, predominantly in interethnic conflicts. The first conciliation committees were established by mediators and trainers from the Centre within municipal authorities in order to be perceived as more prestigious.

The first mediators have now gained some experience. Five conciliation committees were found in the 1990s, but they did not last very long because the new political representatives had other priorities. Unfortunately the new Mediation Act (see below) does not support the existence of conciliation committees.

Act on the Probation and Mediation Service (PMS)

Under Czech law, as in some other Central European jurisdictions, mediation was regulated in the context of criminal victim-offender cases, by the Law on the Probation and Mediation Service, No 257/2000 Coll. (https://www.pmscr.cz). The Probation and Mediation Service of the Czech Republic is the centralised body responsible for mediation as a means of dealing with the consequences of a criminal offence between the offender and the victim in criminal proceedings. The Ministry of Justice has responsibility for this service. A mediator acting within the remit of the Probation and Mediation Service must successfully complete a qualifying examination during the first year of their work. The training of mediators acting within the criminal justice system is ensured by the PMS itself. Mediation provided by the PMS is free of charge, as the costs are paid by the state.

Consumers' mediation

A Pilot project called 'Alternative Dispute Resolution in consumers' cases' was carried out by AMČR together with the Ministry of Industry and Commerce, Chamber of Commerce, consumer associations, the Ministry of Justice and the Court of Arbitration between 2006 and 2008 (http://www.mpo.cz/cz/ochrana-spotrebitele/mimosoudni-reseni/). The foundation of consumer mediation was laid.

Act on Civil and Commercial Matters

The Czech Republic joined the EU Member States that have put the necessary rules in place to transpose Directive 2008/52/EC on mediation in civil and commercial matters. Whereas the Directive's implementation was significantly delayed (Art 12(1) required Member States to complete it before 21 May 2011), the new Mediation Act (Act No 202/2012 Coll, ('the Act')) became effective on 1 September 2012. The Act aims to establish a proper legal framework and thus significantly increase the amount of cases settled through mediation. Mediation is admissible in every area of law (including family and commercial law), except where it is excluded by legislation. According to the Act, the presiding judge may, if practical and appropriate, order the parties to proceedings to hold an initial three-hour meeting with a mediator. In such cases, proceedings may be suspended for up to three months. An agreement between the parties to mediation in a civil case may be submitted to the court for approval in the context of further proceedings.

If a court suspends proceedings in a civil case and orders the parties to hold an initial meeting with a mediator, the first three hours of the mediation meeting are paid at the rate laid down in the implementing legislation (CZK 400 for each hour begun), and this is shared by both parties equally; if the parties are exempt from court fees, they are paid by the state. If the mediation extends beyond three hours, the further costs will be shared by both parties equally, up to the amount agreed between the mediator and the parties to the mediation (ie to the proceedings).

Important features

- Obligatory character of the first mediation session (which may take no longer than three hours), if ordered so by a court (s 100(3) of the Civil Procedure Code, as amended) – the court may then suspend its proceedings for up to three months;
- relatively strict requirements for 'registered mediators': university education with a master's degree, passing the mediator's exam and other requirements (s 16 of the Act);
- explicit administrative sanctions (including fines of up to CZK 100,000 (approx. €4,000) for a breach of a range of mediator's duties, including preserving confidentiality or documentary duties (s 25 (4) of the Act);
- a registered mediator acting in accordance with Act must successfully complete a professional examination before a commission appointed by the Ministry of Justice. The applicants must first complete a written test from basic law, then pass the basic exam on general and then family mediation. According to the

Act all types of mediation cases refer to 'first level of mediation', whereas family cases refer to 'the second level of mediation';
- examination takes two hours. In the first hour mediators present their skills in given model case. Cases are not only from work, corporate or business environment – they also include conflicts in the village, neighbourhood, among relatives and family members or among consumers or inter-ethnics. In family cases, the dispute will relate to parents in divorce and resolve issues such as raising children, contact with parents, alimony, property and finance. In the second hour, candidates receive feedback and evaluation from the committee. That is prepared according to the unified criteria;
- examiners are appointed by the Ministry of Justice. They must be practicing mediators with a master's degree. The Examiner Commission consists of three members: a Ministry of Justice representative, a mediator who is an advocate and a third one who is a mediator with a background other than in law;
- a list of mediators registered in accordance with Act is held by the Ministry of Justice. Among these mediators, approximately 60 per cent are advocates and other lawyers and 40per cent are other professionals;
- various documents, information about examination for registered mediators, list of mediators and other relevant information can be found on the following web pages (http://portal.justice.cz/Justice2/ms/ms.aspx?j=33&o=23&k=5867-).

In the Czech Republic there are different views on this law. Lawyers say the law is one of the most comprehensive and detailed mediation laws in Europe. In contrast to that, the mediators of non-legal professions, especially people who cannot be registered, even if they have mediated long and well, criticise the law for several reasons:
- tests may be passed by candidates with a university degree only:
- practice in working with people and conflict resolution is not taken into consideration, although older workers (perhaps with a high school education or with a B Sc degree) can provide good quality mediation thanks to practical experience;
- mediation is not described as a profession;
- mediation as a multi-disciplinary subject is not universally recognised, with some perceiving it as a sub-discipline of law or as a method of working with people. Professional definition would establish educational and accreditation standards at the state level. Consequently supervision and continuing education are lacking.

The result is that mediation is provided by two different groups. First, one is an officially registered mediator, registered at the Ministry of Justice) and is often recommended by the judge or social worker under the Law about social-legal child protection. The second professional is unregistered mediator who has a license for consulting services. However, in reality, the majority of commercial cases are carried out by the first group, while family cases are usually carried out by mediators with a human background education.

Education nowadays is provided by many institutions offering at least 100 hours' training. Lawyers or other (non-law) professionals undergo mediation training at AMČR, CMI or other institutions, while ČAK provides mediation training to

One Continent, Many Methods

advocates only. Several seminars on mediation are provided by various universities: Charles University in Prague, Masaryk University in Brno, University of Palacký in Olomouc. There is a number of small institutions or individuals who offer mediation training too. However, such seminars are often inadequate, as the courses comprise only a small number of hours, the trainers do not have accreditation themselves, and the seminars are theoretical and lack practical parts and exercises.

Trends in mediation

The most common trend is facilitative mediation. It is promoted mainly by AMČR and CMI. ČAK promotes facilitative and evaluative mediation mostly. A new group of mediators in North Moravia has started to offer transformative mediation.

Time will show whether the new Act will support the spread of mediation as an alternative method of problem resolution. As Czechs are very conservative, the legal framework of mediation is an important step in helping the perception of and a more positive view on mediation.

Thanks to the adoption of the new Law, the Czech Republic has joined other EU States that help people in difficulty and who offer an alternative service.

Denmark

Gerd Sinding

The courts system

Denmark has about six million inhabitants. The Danish court system is a unified system with only two specialised courts in the first instance (The Land Registration Court and the Maritime and Commercial Court), and no specialisation in the second (or third) instance.

Courts of Denmark

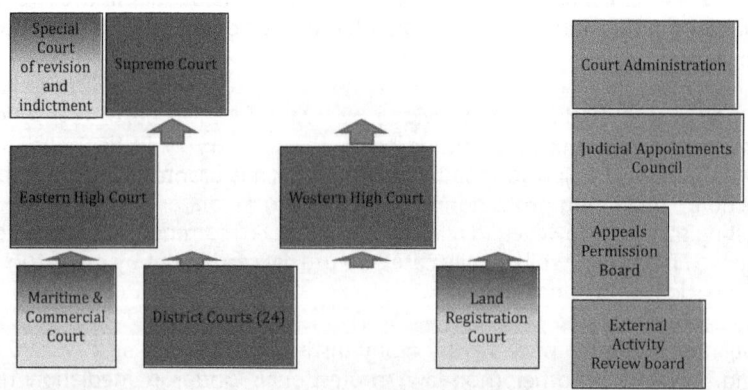

With a few exemptions, all court cases in Denmark – civil and criminal – start in one of the 24 district courts and can be appealed to one of the two high courts. Only in cases where principles are at stake, can a case be referred to one of the high courts at first instance and thus also be brought to the Supreme Court. If a case has started in the district court and then been appealed to the high court, the parties need a permission from the Appeals Permission Board to be able to bring the case before the Supreme Court.

Mediation within the courts

Since 1 April 2008 mediation has been offered to parties within the civil jurisdiction in Denmark. Regulations on mediation within the civil jurisdiction are found in the Administration of Justice Act, s 27.

Mediation is offered in the district courts, the high courts and the Commercial and Maritime Court but not in the Land Registration Court and Supreme Court.

Mediation is only offered in pending civil cases. Thus it is not possible to submit a request for mediation, but the plaintiff can ask for mediation in the writ of summons or the defendant can ask for mediation in his or her defence. In practice the question of mediation will be discussed during the preparatory hearing that is held by teleconference after the courts reception of the writ of summons and the defence. Before the preparatory hearing, the court will send a letter to the parties informing them about the hearing, the possibility of mediation and other issues that are going to be discussed during the preparatory hearing (eg planning of the final hearing, procurement of evidence, survey reports, etc.)

Mediation is only possible in cases where the subject matter of the case is at the parties' disposal. Thus most cases and questions handled in the family jurisdiction cannot be mediated. However, it goes without saying that a lot of informal mediation is performed by judges, lawyers, and other professionals working within the family jurisdiction. Mediation is for the most part not possible in cases concerning administrative law.

It is at the court's discretion to decide that a case should be mediated. Decisions about mediation may be taken on the demand of one or both parties. The court can also suggest mediation, but cannot decide that a case should be mediated against one or both parties' will. In spite of both parties' demand, the court can refuse to mediate a case, eg if the subject matter of the case is not at the parties' disposal or if the principle of equality of arms would be at risk in mediation.

The court is responsible for the appointment of a mediator, but can ask the opinion of the parties before the appointment. Only judges and lawyers who are authorised as court mediators can be appointed. Authorisation is granted for a limited period of four years. The authoriaation is renewable. It is only given to lawyers who have accomplished training and education as a mediator on a certain level. It can be withdrawn if the lawyer neglects his or her duties as a mediator, or if the lawyer stops practicing as a lawyer. A lawyer acting as mediator in a court case will be paid by the court. Ethical guidelines for court mediators have existed since 2008.

There are no regulations in the Administration of Justice Act on how the mediation should be conducted. However, according to the report on the basis of which the legislation was made, the mediator should aim at being facilitative. The training offered to judges is also focused on facilitative mediation. A case study conducted in the courts by a Danish researcher[5] between 2008 and 2010 shows that judges and lawyers can have a tendency to use a more evaluative manner. The case study also shows that mediation within the court system is somewhat affected by the fact that the mediation was initiated by court proceedings, and that the court case will be resumed, if the mediation fails. There is thus a tendency to be focused on facts instead of interests, and to use legal framework and terms in both the conducting of the mediation and when concluding an agreement. However, when asked, the parties feel comfortable about their own involvement, and also that the mediator has listened to them.

This is no wonder considering that judges and lawyers usually work within a legal framework. The fact that it is stated in Danish law that a judge in a civil case in the first instance must explore the possibilities of a settlement before delivering a judgment is probably another influence on the conduct of judges as mediators. The duty of all judges to explore the possibilities of a settlement[6] before delivering a judgment, means that every judge is experienced in discussing different kinds of solutions, including solutions that cannot be obtained by a judgment (if a settlement is obtained, judgment will not be delivered).

Mediation in court must end if any of the parties no longer wish to participate or if the mediator decides to end the mediation. Before the mediator decides to end the mediation, they must invite the parties to state their opinion on the ending of the mediation. The grounds for ending the mediation can be that the parties do not participate adequately, or that the mediator deems it impossible to reach an agreement. The mediator must also end the mediation if it is necessary to prevent the parties in concluding an illegal agreement.

If an agreement is reached, the court case is closed. If an agreement is not reached, the case will continue as an ordinary civil case. A judge who has acted as mediator in a case cannot continue the handling of it as an ordinary civil case, and a lawyer, who has acted as mediator, cannot act as counsel to any of the parties. What has been discussed during the mediation is confident and can, with a few exemptions, not be divulged without consent of the parties.

An agreement reached by mediation can be entered in the court records and can thus serve as basis of execution or enforcement of the agreement.

Mediation outside the courts system

There is a wide and varied range of possibilities of mediation also outside the courts system. The University of Copenhagen offers a masters degree in mediation, but there are several other possibilities to become a mediator. As mentioned above, judges are offered training and education by the Court Administration. The Association of Danish Law Firms, as well as several other organisations and

---

5   L Adrian, *Mellem retssag og rundbordssamtale: Retsmægling i teori og praksis* (Djøf/Jurist- og Økonomforbundet, København, 2012).
6   Possibilities of a settlement will usually be discussed both during the preparatory hearing and the final hearing, but can be discussed at all stages of the case.

companies, offer education and training to a high level that will qualify to act as a mediator.

Many lawyers are trained as mediators and offer mediation to clients, but mediation is also used and practiced in many other contexts and by other professionals, eg by public authorities in disputes about divorce settlements or child custody, by companies in the handling of conflicts with clients or conflicts between departments or employees within the company, and by housing companies in disputes between neighbours. The Danish Institute of Arbitration offers mediation as an alternative to arbitration, and many contracts today includes mediation and/or arbitration clauses.

It is my impression that most courses on mediation in Denmark focus on facilitative mediation, but also on introducing participants to Riskin's grid, Nadja Alexander, and other theories and methods in order to enable participants to adapt their style and concept to the circumstances.

Conclusion

Both within the court system and outside there is still great reluctance in using mediation. For those of us who have been working within the legal framework for many years even though we are enthusiastic about using our new skills as mediators I suppose there is also a tendency to fall back into old habits when handling disputes. Even so I think that being also a mediator makes me a better judge, because of the insights into dialogue, communication, conflict, etc my training as a mediator has given me. I know of many other mediators who have experienced the same in their profession.

Estonia

with Triinu Hiob

Introduction

Mediation is very new in Estonia and rarely used. The only active commercial area is insurance.

Despite this, there is an assumption of negotiation and compromise in all civil proceedings. The general concept is according to the Estonian Code of Civil Procedure that the court must take all possible measures to settle all or part of the case through compromise if this is reasonable in the opinion of the court.

EU Directive (2008)

The EU directive was incorporated into the Estonian Conciliation Act.

The Estonian Conciliation Act

Conciliation and mediation mean the same in Estonia. The Act lays down the procedure for mediation, the legal consequences of mediation and who may mediate. As prescribed by the Act, mediation is a voluntary process in the course of which a mediator facilitates communication between parties to mediation proceedings with the purpose of assisting them in finding a solution to their dispute. Collective labour disputes must be mediated by a public conciliator before employees may strike.

Definition of mediator

A conciliator/mediator may be a natural or legal person, sworn advocate, notary or a specified government or local authority mediation body. In any case, a mediator has to be independent and impartial. Regardless of there being numerous options, it is best to use either a sworn advocate or a notary as a mediator since those Mediated Settlement Agreements are easier to enforce. The mediator may offer a settlement proposal but there is no obligation on the parties to accept.

Voluntary/mandatory process

Under the Act, a mediation clause cannot be enforced if it impairs the parties' right of recourse to the courts. Mediation is generally a voluntary process in Estonia, but the courts may insist that the parties settle their dispute with the help of a mediator. It is only mandatory if the courts insist on the use of mediation as an alternative to trial in court.

Sanctions if parties do not mediate

There are no sanctions. However, if the parties are ordered by the court to mediate, they have no other choice. Despite this, it has to be kept in mind that if a compromise is suggested by the mediator but not accepted by one party and the dispute is eventually settled in court, the court may decide that all or part of the procedural expenses are borne by the party that refused the compromise offer if the court judgment is similar to that suggested by the mediator.

Confidentiality

The mediation proceedings are confidential and the mediator must not disclose facts to which he or she became privy in the course of the proceedings or outside the proceedings.

Mediation style and procedure

The Act regulates the course of the mediation proceedings, but the parties may agree a different process with the mediator if they all agree. Estonian mediators are undoubtedly evaluative in style. In insurance cases the mediator will explain the legally weak points of a party's arguments and propose a (non-binding) settlement. A facilitative style is also recognised but given the lack of commercial mediations generally rarely practised. Most mediations are held in joint session and the mediator is likely to have settlement discussions by phone or email before the joint session is arranged.

Enforceability of Mediated Settlement Agreements

Where the mediator is a sworn advocate or notary, a settlement may be declared enforceable by a county court or other notary. A settlement agreement validated by a mediation body is automatically enforceable.

Where the mediator is an independent neutral, a mediated agreement must be subject of a court hearing in which the mediator and parties speak and confirm that the mediation proceedings were carried out impartially, fairly and lawfully. Should the court determine that these prerequisites are fulfilled, the agreement will be declared enforceable.

Mediator training, accreditation and post-qualification standards

Mediators in Estonia are not required to undertake particular training or have mediation-specific continuing professional development. There is therefore no accreditation or regulation. That said, sworn advocates and notaries have to file an application to their supervisory body if they wish to act as a mediator. This however, is just a formality.

Register of mediators

There is no formal register of mediators or collective membership organisation. The Estonian Bar Association and the Chamber of Notaries publish information regarding who of their members can act as a mediator on their websites.

Mediator exemption

A mediator may be called as a witness but cannot reveal anything disclosed to them during the mediation, unless there is a serious issue of public interest, such as the welfare of children, public safety or criminal matters. Under these conditions, a court may order a mediator to provide information obtained during the mediation

Conclusion

In some ways mediation can be seen as an extension of the work of the legal profession. It is law-based and invariably evaluative. But, compared to most other countries in the EU, Estonian mediation is in its infancy and will develop further with the influence of other countries and the widespread use of mediation as a credible method of resolving business and other disputes.

Finland

Petri Taivaloski

Finland has a strong tradition of using alternative dispute resolution, especially arbitration. The legislative framework and the courts in Finland have generally been very supportive of arbitration, and the Arbitration Institute of the Finland Chamber of Commerce has been administering arbitrations since its establishment in 1911, making it one of the oldest functioning arbitration institutes in the world.

In the commercial context, mediation has long been used in certain specific areas, such as labour disputes, and evaluative mediation has been used in certain sectors such as the construction industry. In civil and commercial matters more generally, it was the Finnish Bar that first introduced facilitative mediation as an alternative for the resolution of disputes in 1998. The use of facilitative mediation is still not very widespread but is growing rapidly through the introduction of mediation by judges in courts of law (court mediation), which was introduced in 2006.

In the following we shall start by describing briefly the legal framework applicable to mediation in Finland, and thereafter first provide an overview of the mediation under the Mediation Rules of the Finnish Bar Association and secondly, address the characteristics of court mediation in Finland.

Legal framework

The Finnish Act on Court Mediation and Confirming Settlements in Courts (394/2011) (as amended, the 'Mediation Act'), which entered into force on 21 May 2011, constitutes the essential legislative framework for mediation in civil and commercial matters in Finland.

Finland implemented the EU Mediation Directive 2008/52/EC (the 'EU Directive') through the Mediation Act. Although the Directive applies only to cross-border disputes, Finland opted to give the Mediation Act a broader scope of application; the Act consequently covers, as a general rule, cross-border and domestic disputes alike. The Mediation Act mainly addresses court mediation (discussed in more detail below) but also includes rules concerning the enforceability of settlement agreements that result from out-of-court mediation. Thus, other aspects of out-of-court mediation remain mainly unregulated.

The implementation of the EU Directive in Finland resulted in two other legislative changes that are worth mentioning. First, to protect the mediator's duty of confidentiality, a new provision was inserted in the Finnish Code of Judicial Procedure, which concerns the admission of evidence in judicial proceedings and provides that the mediator or mediator's assistant may not testify about knowledge gained in the course of the mediation on the subject matter of the mediation, unless particularly compelling reasons require the admission of such testimony. Such particularly compelling reasons could be deemed to exist, eg, if the mediator's testimony is necessary to prevent the conviction of a person of a criminal offence that he or she did not commit.

Secondly, the Finnish Act on Statute of Limitations (728/2003, as amended) provides that the commencement of a mediation procedure falling under the scope of application of the Mediation Act will suspend any period of limitation in the same manner as the filing of a court claim.

Mediation under the Rules of the Finnish Bar Association

The Mediation Rules of the Finnish Bar Association (the 'Finnish Bar Mediation Rules') provide a flexible framework for voluntary and confidential mediation of any kind of civil and commercial disputes. Mediation under the Finnish Bar Mediation Rules is based on a mediation agreement, which can be either a separate agreement to seek to resolve a specific dispute through mediation, or a mediation clause included in an agreement. In the mediation agreement the parties undertake to seek to settle their dispute amicably through mediation and to keep the mediation confidential.

The Finnish Bar Mediation Rules require that the mediator be independent and impartial and that he or she disclose any circumstances that may jeopardise his or her independence or impartiality throughout the mediation. The starting point of the Finnish Bar Mediation Rules is that the parties jointly nominate the mediator. However, upon request the Finnish Bar Mediation Board, a specific body set up by the Finnish Bar, may either appoint the mediator or provide a list of prospective mediators whom the parties may nominate.

The Finnish Bar has been training mediators since the introduction of the Finnish Bar Mediation Rules in 1998. The training, which has been developed in cooperation with CEDR and MATA, is based on the idea of facilitative, interest-based mediation and the use of a structured, voluntary process. To date, over one-third of the approximately 2,000 members of the Finnish Bar have received basic training in mediation, and some 300 have completed the advanced training and have been accredited by the Finnish Bar as mediators.

Court mediation

Under the Finnish Code of Judicial Procedure (4/1734, as amended, the 'Code of Procedure') one of the tasks of the judge is to enhance the possibility of settlement between the parties. There are a number of restrictions as to what the judge may do in this regard. For instance, from a due process prospective it would not be appropriate for the judge who may have to rule on the merits of the case to conduct ex parte (caucus) meetings with the parties if the case does not end up being settled. In addition, the focus of the judge enhancing the possibility of settlement under the Code of Procedure is necessarily on the claims and allegations of the respective parties and their rights and obligations, as opposed to their underlying interests. The major change brought about by the introduction of court mediation in 2006 was that it provides a framework under which the judge may act as a facilitator between the parties in an interest-based, structured process. The solution to the 'Med-Arb' problem, ie the question of the same person mediating and later ruling on the merits, is resolved by prohibiting the mediator-judge from handling the case in the capacity of a judge if it does not settle.

Court mediation may be initiated in two principal ways: through a specific application to the court for the mediation of a given dispute, or by a request of a party in a pending dispute that the handling of the dispute be suspended and the dispute be referred to mediation in the court. In both cases mediation is voluntary and thus requires the consent of all parties.

The Mediation Act does not contain any detailed rules as to how to conduct the mediation process, which may thus be determined flexibly for each case by the mediator-judge in consultation with the parties. The Mediation Act explicitly allows caucus meetings separately with each of the parties, on the condition that all parties agree. In practice the training given by the Finnish Ministry of Justice to mediator-judges is very similar to that of the Finnish Bar Association and is based on the idea of facilitative mediation with a structured process.

The confidentiality of court mediation was a highly debated issue during the legislative process leading to the Mediation Act. Whereas confidentiality can be seen as one of the cornerstones of any effective mediation system, confidentiality of mediation was considered by some commentators to be incompatible with the general principle that court proceedings should be open to the public. The end result in the Mediation Act is a compromise: the Act provides as a starting point for the mediation process to be open to public (except for the caucus sessions) but provides the mediator-judge with wide discretionary powers to 'close the doors' on all or part of the proceedings if necessary.

The Mediation Act stipulates that a court mediation ends:

- when a settlement agreement between the parties is confirmed or the parties inform the mediator-judge that a settlement has been reached;
- if any of the parties informs the mediator-judge that it does not want the mediation to continue; or
- the mediator, after discussing it with the parties, concludes that it is not meaningful to continue the mediation.

In the event that the mediation does not lead to a settlement, the mediator-judge is disqualified from acting as a judge in the dispute in question.

Conclusion

As in many other parts of Continental Europe, mediation has yet to establish itself as a major form of dispute resolution alongside the traditional means, ie litigation, arbitration and negotiation. For example, mediation cases reported to the Finnish Bar Association have remained at a low level at the start of the 21st century and the Arbitration Institute of the Finland Chamber of Commerce, which has the power to appoint mediators (referred to as conciliators in the Institute's Arbitration Rules) in commercial disputes since 2005, has so far appointed a mediator in one case only. However, the future of mediation looks promising. The number of court mediations is increasing rapidly, and the favourable reception of court mediation in Finland is likely to have a positive impact on out-of-court mediation services as well, by raising the awareness of facilitative mediation in general.

France

Thierry Garby

The legal status of mediation in France in 2014

The legal status of mediation in France is directly derived from the EU directive, which was inspired by French law. The main features are:

- Mediation is voluntary; neither the judge nor anyone else can ever compel the parties to go to mediation.

- The judge can suspend proceedings for three months; this period is renewable once.
- When a court orders mediation, the judge determines the remuneration of the mediator.
- There is no condition attached to becoming a mediator other than to have been trained. There is neither a national or other diploma, nor any governmental control on the training, with an exception for 'family mediators' who receive an extensive (over 500 hours) training and can obtain a diploma from the Government. Mediators other than 'family mediators' can mediate in family matters.
- There is no legislation to induce the judge to offer mediation.
- There is no legislation to encourage the parties to use mediation.
- Mediation is confidential unless otherwise agreed by the parties.
- The settlement can be made enforceable by the court, which ordered the mediation, or by the president of the local court or by a notary in case of a mediation agreed directly by the parties.

There is another institution known as 'delegated conciliation', by which the judge delegates his mission to conciliate the parties to a 'delegated conciliator'. These conciliators, unlike mediators, have to be registered on a list held by the court and work pro bono. They are only available for appointment by the small claims courts and the commercial courts.

The development of mediation in France

Although mediation was introduced in France by an act of 1995, its initial development was slow. One of the reasons for that was there are no costs for courts and that lawyers, in the civil law system, are far cheaper than in the common law system. Therefore the financial incentive to go to mediation was certainly not as strong in France as in some other jurisdictions. There was also a cultural resistance to an institution by which the solution would not be imposed from above. There was the usual resistance of lawyers afraid of losing their jobs and of judges afraid of losing their power.

In addition, when mediation was first introduced, everyone thought it would only be useful for family mediation, even though the act considered civil and commercial mediation at large. Therefore, lawyers and judges outside the field of family law despised mediation. The efforts of some Chambers of Commerce to offer mediation services were not followed by major results.

However, since 2013, mediation is booming in France. This seems to be the result of several factors:

- Major companies got tired of the extravagant costs of arbitration. They experienced mediation in the United States and the United Kingdom. They came back convinced and tried it successfully in France. The word spread.
- The introduction of the European Directive in French law convinced many that there was something serious about it.

As a result, mediation proposals by the few lawyers and judges who had been convinced for a long time got accepted by others out of curiosity. As it, of course, worked, the word spread.

Today most courts are developing mediation programmes, as are a number of bar associations and lawyers schools. The results of this phenomenon are varied: for each court where a judge orders many mediations, his colleague next door may never have considered any.

As far as the Bar is concerned, mediation seems to be mainly considered for big, difficult and/or sophisticated cases. This raises the question of why go to mediation in France.

As explained above, the costs of litigation may not always be decisive. The duration can be a factor but French civil and commercial courts work reasonably well and the duration of proceedings is usually not extravagant. The main reason to go to mediation is to try and find a better solution than that offered by litigation.

Such will be the case in shareholders' disputes where the claim never matches what parties really want (a different governance), in inheritance matters which are so much about emotional frustrations, allocation of damages which are always frustrating to both parties when they don't agree to the amount, landlords/tenants disputes, etc.

It will also be the case for extremely complicated cases. Our civil courts are overburdened and our commercial courts are comprised of non-professional judges who work pro bono. As a consequence, it is very difficult for the French court system to properly manage highly sophisticated cases, which require the judges to dedicate a lot of time to them. Mediation is an interesting alternative in the eyes of lawyers for such cases.

Mediation is also developing in the field of revision of contracts. Either because a contract was badly drafted or because some of the circumstances changed, the parties may find themselves in litigious situations, which call for a revision of the contract. Experience shows that, in such cases, when the stakes are high, mediation is needed – litigation will never result in the revision of the ill drafted contract.

Surprisingly, mediation is developing slowly in the construction field as well as for the compensation of physical damages. Apparently insurers are still reluctant to use mediation and keep trying to delay the payment of damages.

The development of mediation in family matters is erratic. Some courts do not use it at all. Some only use family mediators who have obtained the diploma and some also use independent mediators. The choice between both is meaningful. We distinguish 'family mediators' and 'mediators in family matters'. The former have received the diploma and work within associations subsidised by the government. Because their training is so extensive, most of them are originally social workers. Thus the Government pays their training and they are paid by it when training.

Their services are often criticised in two ways:
- In an effort to cover all possible aspects of the dispute, they are some times accused of raising non-existent issues and of making things even more difficult.

With the same intention, some of them would convene the parties to a large number of meetings (for instance seven), each being dedicated to one possible aspect, even if there is no dispute on that aspect. People would then complain that they lost a lot of time and had problems with their employers.

- Most of them being social workers, their normal field of intervention is distressed people. People from middle or upper classes have sometimes complained that 'family mediators' had no sympathy for or understanding of their problems.

In practice, a number of lawyers and even judges tend to refer family cases to mediators who are not 'family mediators' belonging to these associations but general practitioners with experience in family matters. This happens particularly in post-divorce disputes such as the liquidation of common assets.

The structure of the mediation market

It seems to be a general rule that when mediation is still in its infancy, mediation centres are important players to create confidence of the public, the judiciary and the lawyers. They also help make mediation happen through their rules, their rosters and their tariffs. As the market evolves, sophisticated clients and law firms with an extensive experience in mediation get to know the best mediators or, at least, the ones they prefer and appoint them directly. This applies in France just like everywhere else.

Depending on the evolution of the market in the various regions and regional jurisdictions, the role of mediation centres will be more or less decisive. Most of those centres were founded by the local Bars in 1995, when the first mediation act was adopted. As the idea at the time was that mediation would only be for family matters, these centres were trying to keep the family mediation business in the hands of their attorneys. With the adoption of the 'family mediation' regulations, their efforts were in vain and some of these centres almost never did any business.

Recently most of them understood that other civil matters could be suited for mediation and that mediation could be very useful in commercial matters. They therefore decided to have either their initial mediators or new ones trained again and are now developing some interesting business in many regions. Some such centres were also founded by Chambers of Commerce or by an alliance between the local Bar and Chamber of Commerce.

I am confident that if I am asked to write this again in five years, I will be able to describe a mature market.

Germany

Renate Herrmann

Background

In 2008, EU Directive 2008/52/EC on certain aspects of mediation in civil and commercial matters (the 'EU Directive') was passed with the aim of encouraging amicable dispute resolution, particularly through the use of mediation. The EU Directive applies to cross-border disputes in civil and commercial matters, requiring Member States to establish an enforcement procedure for settlement agreements entered into by the parties through mediation, which will allow their mutual recognition and enforcement throughout the EU. The EU Directive further instructs Member States to regulate the suspension of limitation periods for the duration of the mediation proceedings, and the confidentiality of the mediation. It also asks Member States to encourage the training of mediators, as well as the development and application of voluntary codes of conduct for the profession.

The German Mediation Act

In July 2012, the German legislator implemented the EU Directive into national law and adopted the so-called 'Act to Promote Mediation and Other Methods of Out-of-Court Dispute Resolution' (Gesetz zur Förderung der Mediation und anderer Verfahren der außergerichtlichen Konfliktbeilegung, BGBl. 2012 I, 1577; hereinafter the 'Act').

The core elements of the Act are the enactment of the Mediation Act (Mediationsgesetz, MediationsG; hereinafter the 'MediationsG') and amendments to the procedural codes, in particular the German Code of Civil Procedure (Zivilprozessordnung (ZPO)).

The MediationsG is the first codification of mediation and related provisions in German law prescribing, inter alia, basic principles, procedural rules, and minimum duties of the mediator.

The MediationsG does not distinguish between cross-border and domestic mediation, thus differing from the EU Directive. The Act focuses on mediation as a method of alternative dispute resolution. However, the amended provisions in the procedural codes are also open to other methods, such as ombudsmen, adjudication, mini-trial or early neutral evaluation, to name but a few mentioned in the legislative materials.

Next to the standard out-of-court mediation, the Act includes a separate concept of in-trial mediation. Before the Act, different models of in-trial mediation had developed in individual German Federal States, eg models such as court-integrated mediation (gerichtsinterne Mediation) or mediation performed by judges (richterliche Mediation). German Federal States are free to continue with their established models of court-integrated mediation. The Act incorporated such existing practices by referring to three types of mediation or related proceedings: the standard out-of-court mediation, the out-of-court mediation upon proposal by the court, and mediation in judicial conciliatory proceedings, which is a judicial mediation done by judges within or closely connected to court proceedings.

Structure of the German Mediation Act

Article 1 of the Act sets out the MediationsG. The MediationsG establishes general guidelines for the parties and their mediator(s). To ensure the mediator's independence and impartiality, it puts a number of obligations to disclose and restrict activities on the mediator. The MediationsG does not define the mediation procedure: it is left to the parties to agree the procedural process.

A number of different German statutes were changed to judicially recognise the mediator's obligation to strict client confidentiality. Therefore, arts 2 to 8 of the MediationsG define amendments to other acts, including the Code of Civil Procedure (Zivilprozessordnung), the law on the procedure in family matters (Gesetz über das Verfahren in Familiensachen und in den Angelegenheiten der freiwilligen Gerichtsbarkeit) and the Court Fees Act (Gerichtskostengesetz).

The MediationsG: art 1 of the Act

§ 1 DEFINITIONS

The MediationsG defines mediation as a voluntary, confidential and structured process, in which the parties seek an amicable settlement of their dispute with the assistance of a mediator.

Mediators are independent and impartial persons, without decision-making power, who guide the concerned parties through the mediation procedure.

§ 2 CHOICE AND ROLE OF MEDIATOR; THE CONDUCT OF MEDIATION (MEDIATIONSVERFAHREN)

The mediator is chosen by the parties as a neutral person for such proceedings (§2(1)). Unlike an arbitrator in arbitration, the mediator has no authority to impose a decision or other measures upon the parties. The parties are at no time obliged to continue the process (§2(5)).

The MediationsG stipulates basic duties of the mediator to adequately inform the parties and ensure that they are aware of the principles and the course of the mediation (§2(2)).

The mediator is equally committed to all parties. His or her major tasks are to promote communication between the parties and ensure the adequate and fair participation of each party (§2(3)).

If the parties intend to enter into a settlement agreement, the MediationsG requires that the mediator also ensures that such agreement is reached based on the parties' full understanding of the circumstances and content of the agreement (§2(6)).

Mediator's duties

§ 3 DISCLOSURE REQUIREMENTS AND SOME RESTRICTIONS REGARDING OTHER ACTIVITIES (OFFENBARUNGSPFLICHTEN; TÄTIGKEITSBESCHRÄNKUNGEN)

§ 4 DUTY OF CONFIDENTIALITY (VERSCHWIEGENHEITSPFLICHT)

The MediationsG imposes strict confidentiality obligations on the mediator and on those involved in the administration of the case, who also have the right to refuse testifying in civil court proceedings.

Training requirements on mediators

§ 5 EDUCATION AND TRAINING OF THE MEDIATOR, AS WELL AS THEIR CERTIFICATION

§ 6 STATUTORY AUTHORISATION FOR THE FEDERAL MINISTRY OF JUSTICE TO ADOPT BY ORDINANCE MORE DETAILED PROVISIONS RELATED TO MEDIATION TRAINING

The MediationsG sets out training requirements for mediators and the right for training provisions to be made more detailed.

Enforceability of Settlement Agreements

One of the reasons for the long delay between the passing of the EU Directive in May 2008 and its implementation in Germany through the Act in July 2012 was the discussion about a simplified enforcement procedure for settlement agreements.

The Federal Ministry of Justice, on behalf of the Government, prepared to include an additional paragraph into the Civil Procedure Code (§796d ZPO), which would have copied the suggested enforcement procedure of art 6 of the EU Directive. However, the German Parliament, the Bundestag, rejected such approach and stopped the legislative process, conditioning that any further discussions would depend on the deletion of the suggested newly drafted §796d for a simplified enforcement. The main objection raised by Parliament was that parties could, when mutually agreed in writing and recorded by a party-selected court, gain the enforceability of a settlement agreement without any legal representation. Such idea was alien to the parliamentarian, legal advisory commission – a commission formed from a number of highly decorated professors of the law as well as practicing lawyers.

It follows that, unlike the enforcement of arbitration awards, the enforcement of settlement agreements is not separately addressed within the German Civil Procedure Code. However, the existing German civil procedure law recognises two other ways of instant enforceability:

- A lawyers' settlement agreement (Anwaltsvergleichs – §796a ZPO). These are settlement agreements drafted by the parties' legal representatives, which have to comply with a few simple form requirements. For example, such agreements are also used, when issuing arbitration awards made by both parties' consent.
- Recorded settlement agreements, when these are recorded by a German court or a German notary public (Zwangsvollstreckung aus Urkunden – §794(1)(5) ZPO).

Statute of limitation

It is said that, when drafting art 8 of the EU Directive, the draftsmen looked at the German practice of suspending limitation periods for the time parties engage in active settlement negotiations. This practice has a long tradition in Germany and is legislated for in the German Code of Civil Law (Bürgerliches Gesetzbuch, BGB).

A suspension of the statute of limitations during the mediation proceedings can, therefore, be obtained by applying the same statute, ie §203(1) BGB, to mediation proceedings.

However, as there is no explicit rule for mediation procedures, significant uncertainty may arise regarding the exact time frame of the suspension of the statute of limitations, or when one party denies that mediation was still being employed as a serious attempt to settle the dispute. In order to avoid any such uncertainties, the parties are free to make additional arrangements. They are encouraged to explicitly agree on a suspension of the statute of limitations, eg by agreeing institutional rules like ICC ADR Rules or DIS Mediation Rules.

Style of mediations

In general Germans understand mediation to be:

- more facilitative than directive with regard to process; and
- more facilitative than evaluative with regard to content.

The actual role of a mediator may vary depending on the case and the parties: whilst their role may be limited to moderating and enhancing communication between the parties, they are not prohibited from making proposals to the parties as long as the parties request this.

The goal of mediation is generally to seek a future-oriented solution to the dispute, thus allowing the parties to move forward and continue their cooperation. Such forward-oriented perspective is perceived to enable value-added cooperative approaches.

Currently the term 'commercial mediation' covers a wide field of disputes:

- German mediation associations normally concentrate on domestic mediation.
- Due to the dominance of small- and medium-sized companies, who often have very little experience with and budgets for legal representations, their 'commercial' disputes concentrate around shareholder and succession structures as well as internal employee relationships. Such companies are often not aware that mediation could also be used for intercompany contractual disputes.
- There is a long tradition in Germany of buying insurance policies that fund the costs involved in any court proceeding, including the legal representation for such proceedings. This might be one of the reasons why there is a general understanding between arguing parties to meet at court, if they are not able to agree otherwise. In current insurance policies, the insurance companies have the right to refuse the reimbursement of court fees, if their clients did not engage in mediation before going to court. Insurance companies normally keep a list of mediators, to whom they send their clients before agreeing to cover the costs for any further legal proceedings.
- To change this litigious culture is also the aim of the Round Table of the German industry,[7] whose members actively promote the use of mediation to resolve internal disputes, but also their intercompany contractual disputes. However, one of the common complaints raised by the Table members, who include for example Bombardier Transportation GmbH, Siemens AG or SAP AG, is to

---

7   Round Table Mediation und Konfliktmanagement der deutschen Wirtschaft: http://www.rtmkm.de/home/willkommen/mitglieder/.

find the right, commercially minded and competent mediator meeting the circumstances of their dispute. There is currently no forum or search engine that would help parties to match their requirements to the experience of the potential mediator.

Certified mediators

The professional title 'mediator' is not protected by German law. Therefore, everybody more or less trained in mediation skills can provide this service to parties in dispute.

However, the title 'certified mediator' (zertifizierter mediator) may be used only by persons who have completed specific training pursuant to the rules set forth by the German Department of Justice; continuing education is mandatory (§5(2)(6) MediationsG).

As a guideline, but not legally binding, German mediation training takes between 120 up to 200 hours, and includes the following key techniques:
- process skills
- negotiation and communication skills;
- conflict management, ie recognising, handling and solving of conflicts;
- legal aspects of mediation; and
- practical examples, role-play and supervision.

Since the implementation of the Act in 2012 a great number of mediation associations have established themselves, many offering their own training and certification process.

To give flexibility for experimenting, with the aim of initiating a general change within society regarding conflict settlement and developing a code of best practice, the German Parliament allowed a transitional time, during which the different mediation associations are required to agree on a national training and certification procedure for mediators. So far, there has been a lot of completion and rivalry among the associations, but as the deadline for this transitional time approaches more coordinated work has been done.

This coordination was slightly forced by the knowledge of powers transferred to the Federal Ministry of Justice pursuant to §6 MediationsG, which allows the Ministry to issue a legally binding procedure without any further parliamentary consultation, if no other solution has been found in time. At several recent national mediation events, the Ministry confirmed that, although they prefer a best practice code delivered by the association, they will exercise their given power, if such procedure/code has not been presented to them in time.

Types of mediation

The Act refers to three types of mediation or related proceedings:
- the standard out-of-court mediation;

- the out-of-court mediation upon proposal by the court; and
- mediation within judicial conciliatory proceedings.

These three types differ in terms of commencement and acting mediator.

Out-of-Court mediation and settlement negotiations

When a dispute arises, parties may enter into mediation proceedings based on either an ad-hoc mediation agreement or on a mediation clause in a contract underlying the dispute. Mediation may also be agreed upon by the parties as a first step within a multi-tier dispute resolution mechanism, whereby arbitration or court proceedings become permissible only after mediation has failed.

The suspension of the statute of limitations might attract the parties towards mediation. The parties may also be inclined to initiate out-of-court mediation within ongoing court proceedings under §278a ZPO. This might be attractive if a court decision can no longer be expected to be issued within a reasonable timeframe due to the increased complexity of the case.

Mediation in connection with court proceedings

Every statement of claim submitted to a German state court shall now state whether or not the parties are open to mediation or other forms of alternative dispute resolution. Mediation may then be initiated when civil court proceedings have already commenced, upon the court's proposal. Even in the absence of such statement, the newly introduced §278a ZPO empowers the court to propose mediation or any other proceeding for out-of-court settlement, without subjecting the court to any challenge regarding its lack of neutrality on that basis.

If the parties agree to enter into such mediation proceeding, the court is entitled to stay the court proceedings, which will be continued only if a settlement agreement cannot be reached between the parties. If, on the other hand, mediation is successful, the court proceeding will be terminated.

A judge previously involved in a mediation is excluded from serving as judge on the case (§41(8) ZPO).

Mediation within judicial conciliation

This third type of mediation is based on the new §278(5) ZPO. It provides for the possibility of entering or re-entering conciliatory proceedings (ie a form of judicial mediation) before the court upon the referral of the court at any time during the court proceedings.

The conciliatory proceedings are conducted by a judge acting as judicial conciliator (Güterichter), who, in this function, is not authorised to render binding decisions. The conciliation judge need not be different from the judge conducting the court proceeding. Such conciliation is meant to reach a mutual agreement, thus concluding the case other than by verdict.

The new §278(5) ZPO allows the judge in a conciliatory role to make use of the methods of mediation, which is thus a compromise between applying and not applying the concept of in-court mediation.

When it appears that mediation is not advancing a settlement of the dispute, the judge in a conciliatory role can terminate the conciliation proceedings and relegate the matter to court proceedings. Even though the judge in a conciliatory role has no authority to render binding decisions or issue a legal indication, a proposal submitted to the parties could in fact give guidance to the parties and provide valuable support to management seeking to determine whether under the business judgment rule a settlement is appropriate and in the company's best interest.

The judge in a conciliatory role may also access the court files to the case. However, any legal consideration is not binding for the lawsuit itself inasmuch as the judge in a conciliatory role is not functioning as a courtroom judge and can therefore not be heavily relied upon.

The amendments to the Act provide a legal basis for the judge in a conciliatory role when applying mediation, without however establishing particular rules regarding confidentiality or generally applying the duties of a mediator. This might be a concern for the parties, as the procedural rules foster confidentiality only by prohibiting the creation of a transcript in conciliation proceedings unless both parties consent (§159(2) ZPO).

Nevertheless, this mediation-type judicial conciliation may constitute a compromise for circumstances when one party is reluctant to leave the courtroom and is doubtful of the other party's willingness to reach an agreement.

Mediation under the business judgment rule

Referring to the business judgment rule implemented in §93(1)(2) of the German Stock Corporations Act (Aktiengesetz, AktG) more and more emphasis is given to mediation throughout the training of German corporate managers. Modules informing future managers about alternative methods of dispute resolution are included in a number of university and professional courses for managers leading finance, accounting, sales, personnel and other operative units of German companies. Managers are advised to consider factors such as expected outcome, certainty and predictability, time and cost efficiency, and collateral effects such as publicity before litigating or choosing an alternative dispute resolution.

Legal aid/court fees

Article 7 of the Act transfers the decision power with regard to legal aid for mediation to the individual German Federal States, who will not only decide if legal aid is provided to a party wishing to mediate, but also if other financial inducements should be used to tempt parties away from litigation into mediating their disputes (ie reduced or waived court fees in case of settlement, or the reflecting of the parties' behaviour during a court-initiated mediation in a later cost allocation by the court).

Conclusion

With the Act/MediationsG, German legislators have acknowledged that mediation is an established method for dispute resolution.

The MediationsG sets forth minimum legal standards and requirements without limiting the flexibility of mediation. Along with out-of-court mediation, amendments to the Civil Procedure Code (ZPO) have also paved the way for mediation within ongoing court proceedings and allow for a judge in a conciliatory role to apply methods of mediation.

Greece

Introduction

Although civil and commercial mediation is fully incorporated into the Greek legal system and embraced by the courts, it is still very young and experience very small. Although mediation principles have been used by Greeks throughout history, prior to the Mediation in Civil and Commercial Matters Act 2010 mediation was not formally recognised.

EU Directive (2008)

The EU Directive was fully incorporated into Greek law under the 2010 Act. The Act covers all cases (national civil and commercial cases as well as cross-border disputes) and has been extended to cases before the Court of Appeal.

Mediation Act

There have been several additions and amendments to the original Act:

- in 2012, extended in 2013, judicial mediation/court connected mediation was introduced;
- in 2011 conditions were passed for the authorisation and operation of mediator training centres;
- in 2013 an Accredited Mediator's Code of Conduct was adopted;
- in 2012 regulation of fees was introduced; and
- in 2012 the Committee for the Examination of Candidate Mediators was established, which lays down assessment criteria.

As a result, mediation, and mediators, are quite closely regulated in Greece.

Definition of mediator/mediation

The Act describes mediation in general terms and is not prescriptive about the process. Prior to the mediation the parties sign an agreement and the mediator designs the process in co-operation with the parties.

The mediator is bound by the Code of Conduct and is only liable in the case of willful misconduct. If this is found to be the case, the mediator's accreditation may be revoked.

Voluntary/mandatory

Mediation is voluntary in Greece. The courts may invite parties to try to settle their dispute through mediation but they can refuse without penalty. If parties accept the court's invitation, the trial is postponed for a mandatory three months, up to a maximum of six months. If mediation is chosen then court fees are reduced. In any case, the limitation period for cases is suspended during the mediation process.

There is a judicial mediation process, which is also voluntary.

There is a proposal for low-value cases (under €5,000) to be referred to compulsory mediation but this is still in the consultation stage.

In Greece it is compulsory for parties to have legal representation at mediations. The explanation for this is that it should make the process more sophisticated and professional and that it should contribute to the development of mediation generally. It remains to be seen if this is so in practice.

Confidentiality

Mediation is confidential and no record of the procedure is kept. The parties, their lawyers, the mediator and any other person involved in the mediation must all sign a confidentiality agreement.

Mediation style and procedure

The mediator's style is not regulated. Most mediators have been trained in facilitative mediation and so evaluative mediation would be uncommon, at present at least. The mediator may offer a non-binding opinion, but is precluded from offering a binding decision. This applies even to judge-mediators who may well be more evaluative in their style.

Enforceability of Mediated Settlement Agreements

Agreements reached in mediation are binding and enforceable and are signed by the parties, their lawyers and the mediator. The mediator may then, at the request of one party, submit the settlement agreement to the secretariat of the court of first instance in the local jurisdiction where the mediation took place. Once submitted, the agreement is enforceable.

Mediator training, accreditation and post-qualification standards

Mediators are accredited by the Administration Directorate General of the Hellenic Ministry of Justice, Transparency and Human Rights. The Administration licenses mediator training bodies and sets down criteria for accreditation of mediators. It is usual for there to be a final written exam held by the Committee for the examination of candidate mediators. Mediator training courses must be a minimum of 40 hours.

There is an obligation for post-accreditation CPD of a minimum 10 hours over a two-year period.

Register of mediators

Accredited mediators are listed in a public register after approval by the Ministry of Justice, Transparency and Human Rights.

Mediator exemption

The mediator must comply with the Accredited mediator's Code of Conduct. Under the Mediation Act, the mediator cannot be called as a witness or compelled to produce evidence in any subsequent trial or hearing on the same case unless public policy reasons prevail.

Conclusion

It is still too early to detect a common style or to have any reliable statistics in civil and commercial mediation in Greece. It is a process that has been recognised and adopted since ancient times but its formal adoption into the Greek legal framework is new and, so far, experience is limited.

Hungary

Tibor Tajti

Introductory caveats

The following caveats apply to this synopsis of mediation-related post-1990 developments in Hungary. First, the statutory and regulatory environment is comparatively developed but the empirical scholarship is lagging behind, which inevitably leaves its imprint on the text to follow.

Secondly, as it is hard to isolate commercial mediation from its kin at this stage of development,[8] this section on mediation in Hungary is divided into two main parts: while the first part is a general overview of the mediation-related legal environment, only the second focuses on private and commercial mediation specifically.

Finally, within this section on Hungary, the term 'mediation' shall be used in its broader meaning, extending to conciliation and any other structured process

---

8 The Register of Mediators maintained by the Ministry of Justice does not contain data based on which it could be determined how many commercial (or other types of) cases have been Mediated in a given year.

'however named [...] whereby two or more parties to a dispute attempt by themselves, on a voluntary bases, to reach an agreement on the settlement of their dispute with the assistance of a Mediator.'[9] This is in conformity with modern trends as expressed by the 2002 UNCITRAL Model Law on International Commercial Conciliation and the EU Mediation Directive, – with which Hungarian laws and perceptions coincide.

General overview

The post-1990 evolution of mediation in Hungary

The demise of the socialist (communist) regime brought with it increased interest in western law and generally all the successfully working mechanisms of western democratic and market economy-based systems. Although in the realms of dispute resolution, this first meant primarily commercial arbitration and conciliation, it took only a few years for mediation proper to appear and gradually gain an ever stronger foothold. The first discussions, involving the government, public notaries and others, stem from this inaugural phase, culminating in the enactment of Act LV on Mediation in 2002, which still forms the backbone of Hungarian law on mediation.

In the next phase, the Act underwent significant changes especially with the implementation of the EU Directive. Notwithstanding the resulting solid legal background and governmental support, a 2010 Study still reported that 'irrespective of [its] advantages, mediation has not become widespread in Hungary; due primarily to various cultural obstacles.'[10] While it is a fact that the presence of mediation is not as intense as in some of the western European countries, the achievements are significant, especially in some sectors. Mediation is now also normally covered by law school curricula, linked to arbitration, and literature in the Hungarian language is meaningful. Last, but not least, the first foreign publications on Hungarian mediation have also appeared.[11]

Review of the Law on Mediation

Current Hungarian law on mediation comprises three layers of interlinked laws and regulations – general, supplementary and sector-specific laws. The Act on Mediation of 2002 (as amended) provides the general framework and the core principles, although primarily for private and commercial mediation. The Act is then supplemented by provisions in the Code on Civil Procedure and by a host of ministerial orders – to give proper recognition and to incentivise resort to

---

9   Tibor Varady, John J Barcello & Arthur T von Mehren, *International Commercial Arbitration*, 5th Edn (West, Publishing, 2012)
10 "A mediáció és a bírósági eljárások kapcsolata Magyarországon – 2009/2010. évi kísérleti bírósági mediációs program kiértékelése" [the Nexus of Mediation and Court Proceedings in Hungary – the Evaluation of the 2009/2010 Court Mediation Experimental Program] (Budapest, version 3.3. of 17 March 2010), p 5.
11 See Christa Jessel-Holst, 'Mediation in Hungary: Legal Foundations, Recent Reforms, EU Convergence', in Klaus J Hopt and Felix Steffek (eds), *Mediation: Principles and Regulation in Comparative Perspective* (Oxford University Press, 2013), pp 606-627 and Zsolt Okányi and László Gergely, 'Hungary', in Giuseppe di Palo and Mary B Trevor (eds), *EU Mediation – Law and Practice* (Oxford University Press, 2012), pp 162–172.

Mediation. Last but not least, mediation as a dispute resolution method is provided for by sector-specific laws:

- criminal law;
- misdemeanours;
- healthcare;
- labour law; and
- consumer protection.

The role of mediation is meaningful also in the field of child protection and welfare and sports law. Although little empirical evidence is available on the role and importance of industrial codes of ethics, yet these should also be added as secondary sources of law in Hungary.

Private and commercial mediation

What kinds of disputes could be mediated under the 2002 Mediation Act?

Ironically, in Hungary, the mediation of private and commercial disputes (polgári jogviták) is the paradigm, notwithstanding that mediation has so far been more successful in other fields. As Hungary is a monist system and a single Civil Code contains both private and commercial law, the same rules apply to both: all such private and commercial disputes may be mediated that relate to such rights and interests with which the parties can freely dispose of. The 2002 Act on Mediation specifies this by pointing to family law, administrative actions, media-rectification suits, certain types of constitutional complaints, enforcement actions and matrimonial proceedings. The second line of limitation is that the 2002 Act does not apply to mediation – as well as conciliation – regulated by the *lex specialis* listed above and to mediation conducted during arbitral proceedings. Yet the Act extends specifically to court mediation (bírósági közvetítés).

The requirements of the EU Directive

EU Directive 2008/52/EC on mediation was also implemented in Hungary. As the Directive exploited two major components to boost mediation in Europe, it makes sense to analyse Hungarian law from the perspective of these: first, training and quality control of mediators as service-providers, and secondly, adjustment of certain legal principles to fit the Directive's agenda of promulgating mediation.

The licensing and monitoring of mediators in Hungary

Even a cursory review of the 2002 Mediation Act may easily reveal that the backbone of the Hungarian system is the mediator licensing and monitoring system. This is not without reason: in a field where trust in service providers (the industry) is indispensible, ensuring that only properly trained, experienced and – also in Hungary – persons with clean criminal records appear as mediators is essential. However, there are no limitations as far as the fields of expertise or profession of mediators is concerned. Speaking of lawyers, for example, even attorneys and public notaries may serve as mediators, although subject to rules dictated by the very nature of their primary professions.

Register of mediators

The gatekeeper's function is entrusted to the Ministry of Justice,[12] which maintains a register of mediators, decides on requests for entry and issuances of mediators' IDs, and acts as the controller of mediators. Mediators residing in another country within the European Economic Area (EEA) may qualify as well, provided that they file a request with the Ministry, who will then issue a one-year permit. It is important to stress that the entry on the register and issuance of the permit is automatic in the case of both Hungarians and qualifying foreigners provided the statutory requirements are fulfilled: the Minister has no discretion to refuse registration except for the formal reasons listed. Licensed mediators are also subject to quite intense continued professional training requirements. The system otherwise does not impose a centrally-approved tariff system and it is for the parties to agree on the mediator's fees and reimbursement of corollary costs.

The 2002 Act explicitly provides that investigations against mediators may be started either ex officio or following the complaint of parties involved in mediation. However, it fails to list what concrete reasons might trigger investigations (and eventually expulsion). In other words, there are no concrete prudential rules. The Act is also quite succinct on sanctions, as the Ministry may primarily merely warn a mediator and request that they remedy the breach of rules. It may delete somebody from the register of mediators only in case of repeated or grave breaches. Yet the effect of the sanction of deletion is quite severe: re-registration is excluded for five years from the finality of the decision on deletion. The Minister may initiate court or other types of proceedings according to the generally applicable rules. Finally, contrary to attorneys and public notaries, there is no requirement to obtain insurance.

As no media-reported scandals concerning mediators have been heard of as of yet and as the few reported court cases referring to mediation have not denigrated the profession either, it may be tentatively concluded that the licensing-cum-control system works well. However, one may also suspect that this image might partially be ascribed to the confidential nature of mediation, the high success rate (and thus satisfaction of parties) of the otherwise modest number of mediated commercial cases, as well as the media and the general public's unfamiliarity with and thus partial incomprehension of mediation.

Ancillary rules encouraging use of mediation

The other specific requirements of the Directive, serving the ultimate aim of promoting mediation, were also given concrete content by the Hungarian drafters. Thus, the prescription rules were changed to stress that mediation either interrupts or suspends civil procedure and that litigation or arbitral avenues remain available in case of unsuccessful mediations. In the same vein, confidentiality and rules ensuring enforceability of settlements reached via mediation were added as well.

---

12 The website with the list of mediators is at https://kozvetitok.kim.gov.hu/kozvetitok.

Methods of mediation employed in Hungary

Given the lack of empirical studies supported by appropriate quantitative data, it is impossible to determine which model of mediation is prevalent in Hungary at this point in time. Notwithstanding this, some authors suggest that in commercial cases it is the facilitative rather than the evaluative method that is preferred in Hungary. Still, some indirect indicia should also be spoken of.

It may be speculated that the method applied – just as the popularity of mediation – is predetermined by the very nature of the dispute. This might be the reason that while the number of mediated criminal matters is relatively high, the rate is below that expected in private and commercial cases, as suggested mainly by practicing mediators and governmental bodies entrusted with promulgation of mediation.

Mediation may either be transformative (restoration of the relationship), or aimed at resolution of divorce-related disputes (facilitative or evaluative). From the often non-specific formulation of advertisements in brochures or on webpages of practicing mediators, one may furthermore suspect that in the case of commercial mediation, methods may also be combined as facilitative and transformative or evaluative and transformative.

Public notaries form a special class given that they share a common function with mediators: both aim at forestalling litigation. Moreover, in probate the law entrusts notaries explicitly with mediation-related tasks, and they have explicit permission to serve as fee-earning mediators in virtually any type of case, although they cannot appear in both capacities in the same case. Nonetheless, notaries are rarely asked to mediate. Interest in mediation is perhaps more usually expressed by attorneys and consequently the number of attorney-mediators is meaningful, general conclusions with respect to them can hardly be made either.

Conclusions

As may be concluded from the above, mediation has made meaningful progress in Hungary since the fall of the Berlin Wall. Compared to jurisdictions lacking mediation-specific legislation, it has a 'predictable legal framework' as envisaged by the EU Directive aimed at promoting this form of alternative dispute resolution in Europe. Although the (normally only indirect) quantitative data are encouraging, it would be premature to speak of a major breakthrough. It seems that even the number of registered mediators is disproportionately high compared to the number of cases mediated in the last few years, notwithstanding that the strict requirements imposed by the laws implementing the 2008 EU Directive made quite a number of mediators leave the market.

Finally, a brief mention of Hungarian mediation scholarship. Irrespective of the relatively large number of publications, the lack of two important tools is especially noted: databases with concrete researchable case studies, and such tested analytical methods that would be suitable for dealing with the idiosyncratic features of mediation. Although cross-European cooperation in this domain is a fact, foreign experiences that could be exploited to fill these gaps should undoubtedly be welcome in Hungary.

Ireland (including Northern Ireland)

Jim Halley

Introduction

Mediation in Ireland is an active and growing discipline. It is used in several settings, eg commercial/corporate, workplace, community, family, debt, elder and restorative justice. In Northern Ireland, mediation has been used to resolve conflict between members of the nationalist and unionist communities. Most mediators in Ireland use one or more of the following styles of mediation: facilitative, directive, evaluative and transformational. As in many other countries, mediation tends to cost less than the cost of court proceedings. Mediation also tends to be a swift way of resolving disputes, as there are lengthy waiting times for cases to be heard in the Irish Courts.

The Irish Law Reform Commission published its report on 'Alternative Dispute Resolution: Mediation and Conciliation' in 2010. It contains recommendations on how mediation and conciliation may be developed in Ireland.

This overview of mediation in Ireland will consider:

- the main training and accreditation bodies which are active in mediation education in Ireland;
- the development of mediation within Irish law;
- the state of mediation in the domains of commercial, employment/workplace, family and elder mediation in Ireland;
- EU Directive 2008/52/EC which deals with mediation; and
- the most important development in mediation in Ireland to date, which is the publication of the long-awaited Mediation Bill, expected to happen later in 2014. We describe how this will greatly improve the regulation of mediation in Ireland.

Training and accreditation

There are at least four accrediting bodies for mediation in Ireland:

- the Mediators' Institute of Ireland (MII);
- the Chartered Institute of Arbitrators (CIArb)-Irish Branch;
- Edward M Kennedy Institute for Conflict Intervention at the National University of Ireland, Maynooth; and
- CEDR Ireland.

These bodies provide a growing range of innovative accredited training courses in mediation. These courses have very good reputations and have received high praise from participants. These bodies also supply individual mediators or panels of mediators for several kinds of dispute. Many accredited mediators in Ireland are practising solicitors or barristers. Equally though, there are many accredited mediators who do not have a legal background.

The MII Code of Ethics and Practice incorporates the principles that mediation should be both voluntary and confidential. However, it makes allowance for breaches of confidentiality in special circumstances, eg if the mediator suspects that a child has been abused or if the mediator is defending him- or herself against a complaint relating to the mediation. CIArb is a worldwide organisation and also has a Code of Professional and Ethical Conduct (2009). This code is in use in the Irish Branch. It covers dispute resolution in general and does not specifically focus on mediation.

Overview of legal provision for mediation in Ireland

The first reference to mediation in an Act of the Oireachtas (Irish Parliament) occurs in the Industrial Relations Act 1946. This Act provides for the appointment by the Labour Court of 'a conciliation officer to act as a mediator' in trade disputes. In the Judicial Separation and Family Reform Act 1989 there is provision for mediation in relation to separating couples. In several Acts of the Oireachtas since then, provision is made for mediation to resolve a range disputes between parties.

The Commercial Court in the Irish High Court was established in 2004 to deal with large commercial disputes. This court encourages the use of mediation to solve disputes. The Rules of Court have now been amended for the Irish Lower and Superior Courts to allow for mediation in line with the procedure of the Commercial Court. In 2009, the then Minister for Justice and Law Reform, Mr Dermot Ahern TD noted that:

> 'Mediation always has the potential to save on court time and legal costs and that is why rules of court, for example, continue to be developed to facilitate adjournment of proceedings in our courts to permit mediation' (quoted in Law Reform Commission 2010: 51).

The Legal Aid Board was set up in 1979 and is now governed by the Civil Legal Aid Act 1995. The Board provides legal advice at reduced cost to those in financial need. This includes advice on mediation where appropriate.

Commercial disputes

The economic climate in Ireland has been difficult since 2008. In these times, mediation is particularly useful for commercial disputes. This is because mediation generally costs less than court proceedings. Mediation clauses are now often included in commercial contracts; in the past, dispute resolution clauses generally only referred to arbitration. In 2009, the Irish Commercial Mediation Association (ICMA) conducted a survey of approximately 3,500 professionals, entitled 'Commercial Mediation Awareness' (Law Reform Commission 2010: 145). While 97 per cent of those surveyed had an awareness of commercial mediation, only 35 per cent had actually advised their clients to consider mediation. This shows that there is much scope for expanding the practice of commercial mediation in Ireland.

In the construction industry, mediation is now often used in construction disputes. Under the Construction Industry Federation of Ireland (CIF) sub-contract, disputes are referred initially through mediation as a mandatory first step. However, mediation is still not stated in a number of other construction contracts. CIF conducted a survey in 2009 and found that 52 per cent of those surveyed preferred to resolve construction disputes using mediation as opposed to other ADR methods (Law Reform Commission 2010: 150). It can be seen that mediation in the construction industry has major potential.

Employment disputes

The Irish Labour Relations Commission and Labour Court have well-established mediation processes to deal with employment disputes under the Industrial Relations Act 1990. Mediation clauses are now also included in certain employment contracts.

Where there is a complaint of employment discrimination, the Equality Tribunal provides mediation services under the Equal Status Acts 2000-2011 and the Employment Equality Acts 1998-2011. In workplace disputes, one or both of the parties often look for an apology. This is not available through traditional litigation.

Family disputes

The Family Mediation Service exists for disputes within families. The aim is to use mediation instead of court proceedings for *appropriate* family cases, not to divert *all* cases from the courts. There has been a relatively low uptake of mediation offered by this in comparison to the number of family law applications to the court (Law Reform Commission 2010: 111). Nevertheless, there is a long waiting list for the Family Mediation Service. When a case is first heard in the Irish High Court, the court may recommend alternative dispute resolution (ADR), including mediation.

The Family Mediation Service Code of Ethics and Professional Conduct addresses the welfare of children in mediation. This Code also lays out the special considerations for mediation in cases where there have been allegations of domestic violence. If family disputes are resolved by the Family Mediation Service, the Irish State carries most or all of the cost. However, if the parties use private mediation, the parties themselves usually share the cost.

Elder mediation

In 2009, the Alzheimer Society of Ireland launched a pilot elder mediation service for families living with dementia. Caring for a family member with dementia can be stressful and can lead to conflicts within families. This pilot service aimed to deal with this.

Other areas

There are a number of community mediation services in Ireland, eg Mediation Northside, a service of Northside Community Law Centre in Dublin. These services deal with disputes between neighbours or disputes involving community groups.

The Small Claims Court in the Irish District Court provides for a mediation process for certain consumer disputes.

In relation to medical disputes, mediation may be used to resolve certain complaints made under the Medical Practitioners Act 2007. Under the Civil Liability and Courts Act 2004, mediation may also be used in a personal injuries action. However, there have been relatively few such requests for mediation since 2004 (Law Reform Commission 2010).

EU Directive

EU Directive 2008/52/EC deals with mediation (and other ADR processes). The provisions of this directive apply to cross-border disputes but EU Member States may also apply these within their own jurisdictions. This Directive came into effect in Irish law through Statutory Instrument No 209 of 2011, the European Communities (Mediation) Regulations.

Anticipated Mediation Bill

The Irish Government will finally publish the Mediation Bill 2014 later this year. This is eagerly awaited, as it will put structure on mediation practice in Ireland for the future. A Draft General Scheme of Mediation Bill appeared in 2012 and was reported upon by the Oireachtas Joint Committee on Justice, Defence and Equality.

We expect that the 2014 Bill will regulate mediation in the following ways:

- emphasise the facilitative style of mediation, which respects the principle of self-determination by the parties (ie the parties enter mediation freely and come to a resolution themselves; a resolution is not imposed on them by the mediator);
- introduce a code of practice for mediators;
- oblige mediators to inform parties of their training and experience;
- place a requirement for solicitors and barristers to inform clients about the mediation option before court proceedings;
- allow for court proceedings to be adjourned for mediation; this is provided for in the EU Directive;
- stipulate that mediation be confidential;
- allow the parties themselves to determine an agreement in mediation and the enforceability of it. Currently, in Ireland, where mediation agreements are made outside of court proceedings, there is no formal way of enforcing the agreement. In private mediations, Memoranda of Understanding are often used but these too are non-binding. (They are similar to but not exactly the same as mediation agreements.) However, if the mediation agreement is made by order of the court, either party may apply to the court to enforce it, if they believe it has been breached;
- provide that costs of mediation be reasonable and not tied to outcome of process; and
- explain how to involve children in family law disputes.

Northern Ireland

Mediation in Northern Ireland has a number of unique aspects. Mediation Northern Ireland offers its own courses accredited by the College of Mediators UK and Open College Network Northern Ireland. Family Mediation Northern Ireland offers courses accredited by themselves via the College of Mediators UK and the MII. TIDES Training & Consultancy offers accredited training by Open College Network Northern Ireland. University of Ulster Jordanstown (UUJ) and Queen's University Belfast (QUB) offer courses and modules in mediation as part of programmes in Conflict Resolution and Peace Studies. The Institute for the Study of Conflict Transformation and Social Justice is based at QUB and the Transitional Justice Institute is based at UUJ. CIArb-Irish Branch also has a dedicated Northern Ireland Chapter.

Conclusion

Mediation is becoming increasingly popular in Ireland as a swift and cost-effective means of resolving several kinds of disputes. Those at the forefront of mediation education continue to develop the wide range of accredited training courses. Both the Superior and Lower Courts in Ireland now make provision for mediation. Mediation also appears in several Acts of the Oireachtas. Mediation is particularly well established in Ireland for employment/workplace disputes and for family disputes. We have shown the immense scope for the growth of mediation in the commercial sector. When published later this year, the Mediation Bill will be the single most important development for mediation in Ireland since mediation first appeared in an Irish Act of the Oireachtas in 1946. From 2015 onwards, we can look forward to mediation as an exciting and fully regulated discipline in Ireland.

Italy

Carlo Mosca

Introduction

A success story? The 2008 EC Directive half-missed opportunity

Italy has been recently praised[13] as the country where mediation has proved more successful than elsewhere in Europe, following implementation of the EC Directive 52/2008/EC. It is uncontested that the number of mediation cases has rocketed in recent years, mainly thanks to the mandatory scheme Italy has been adopting since Spring 2011.

However, the situation is not as rosy as one might think. The point is that mediation has been conceived by Italian rule makers as a mere tool for cutting the court backlog, more than an authentic way of parties' self-management of the conflict. This original sin is clearly driving mediation towards somewhat unpleasant

---

13 European Parliament DG for Internal Policies (ed), *'Rebooting' the Mediation Directive: Assessing the limited impact of its implementation and proposing measures to increase the number of mediations in the EU*, available at http://www.europarl.europa.eu/RegData/etudes/etudes/join/2014/493042/IPOL-JURI_ET%282014% 29493042_EN.pdf

destinations. In fact, mediation is increasingly characterised as a court-servant process, overruled, and disciplined as if it were something not so different, in the end, from a lawsuit. This clearly seems to diverge from the intentions that animated the EU initiative, in spite of the apparent success of numbers.

How to leash a free market

A cause, and in the meantime, a side effect of this trend is an overregulated market, where mediation services are made available through authorised subjects only, at restricted terms. In the vast majority of the cases, parties are simply not at liberty in selecting their own mediator, or agreeing on relevant costs. Not surprisingly for Italy, quality control on mediators' and mediation centres' activity has been conceived more in terms of formal compliance than adherence to factual standards.

Moreover, the sirens of getting into an controlled market, and chances of getting easy money out of it, initially attracted many unprepared players: legions of would-be mediators needed to be trained, in fact, and earnings from a mass-management of mediation cases determined a typical flowering of thousands of mediation centres. A flash in the pan, more than a true competitive market, and a rather low general quality level as a result.

Although this situation soon deflated, a sense of dissatisfaction and disenchantment still characterises both mediation customers and providers. Mediation in Italy clearly needs a more rigorous approach and a free market confrontation.

The legal framework

The traditional italian approach to mediation

Mediation has been utilised in Italy for decades, in particular as far as interpersonal disputes were concerned, in an almost invariably 'traditional' form, ie either as an exercise of charismatic social control by elders, saviours or other prominent person in a given community, or as a bureaucratic, regulated avenue to control disputes. Intergroup conflicts, such as labour or environmental disputes have experienced more flexible out-of-standard approaches. Finally, some form of court-annexed mediation existed, although more in theory than in practice. In all cases, the actual impact of recourse to mediation has been generally recognised as fairly poor, in terms of positive outcomes and parties' satisfaction. Modern forms of mediation conducted by skilled professionals were virtually absent until the mid-1990s, and randomly practised thereafter until a new regulation was brought in, in 2010.

The 2010 divide

In March 2010 the Italian Government introduced a new regulation on mediation (legislative Decree No 28 of 4 March 2010[14]) with the explicit aim of reducing

---

14   The original text of Decree 28 was published in the Italian Official Gazette (OG) no. 53 of March 5, 2010. The updated version incorporating subsequent amendments can be read, in Italian, at http://www.normattiva.it/uri-res/N2Ls?urn:nir:stato:decreto.legislativo:2010-03-04;28. Unofficial versions in English can be found in the Internet.

the notorious court backlog in both civil and commercial sectors. In fact, at that time it was estimated that 5.5 million cases were laid in front of a judge awaiting a decision. Mediation was clearly seen a way to reduce the input, ranking at an average of 4.8 million cases a year, whereas output was calculated in some 4.6 million per year, definitely interesting, but insufficient to avoid a negative trend generating more and more unresolved cases through the years. Not surprisingly, mediation is defined as 'a process where a neutral assists parties in dispute in reaching an agreement *on the settlement of a dispute'* (emphasis added).

The opportunity for adoption of Decree No 28 was the need to implement the EU Directive No 2008/52, actually intended to create a common ground all over the Community as far as interstate mediation was concerned. However, the Italian rulers took the opportunity to enlarge the scope of the Directive and regulated domestic mediations in a similar vein. Most importantly, mediation was declared as mandatory (indeed, a step to be performed before commencing an action in court) in respect of a fairly diverse number of disputes, ranking from real estate to medical malpractice to car accident cases.

In adopting Decree No 28, explicit reference was made to the problem-solving model; however, a clearly evaluative trait marked the possibility given to mediators to make, in case of impasse, their own settlement proposal, refusal of which would have exposed a party to be sanctioned in costs, where a court would have then found in the proposal's same or similar terms. A distinctive feature of the Italian way of mediation was the choice for a control supply market, whereas only accredited mediation centres (organismi di mediazione) may administrate the process.

Original Decree No 28 and subsequent amendments

Decree No 28 has lasted not very long in its original form. In fact, it has been repeatedly modified in the months following its entry into force in March 2011. In autumn 2012, the whole experiment was frozen following a Constitution Court decision[15] that cancelled any mandatory scheme (which the Government had enacted, the Court said, by exceeding the mandate given to it by the Parliament in this respect). A new bill was adopted in summer 2013 in order to remedy this,[16] although in precautionary terms. As a result, at present mediation is still mandatory, although in a downgraded way: it is no longer necessary to actually mediate a case, being sufficient to participate in a mere free informative meeting; the list of mandated matters has been modified with vehicle accident cases, by far the largest in numbers, no longer requiring prior mediation; and the whole mandatory mediation scheme has been considered as a time-limited test, expiring in four years. Again, lawyers have definitely taken control of the process: where acting as counsel, their presence has been declared as necessary (ie no party can attend unrepresented); where acting as mediator, their professional skills have been considered sufficient (so they don't need to do any further substantial mediator training).

---

15 (Italian) Constitution Court, decision No 272/2012, in OG – Special Series no 49 of 12 December 2012.
16 Law decree No 69 of 21 June 2013, converted into Law No 98 of 9 August 2013 (in OG No 194 of 20 August 2013, Supplement No 63).

The regulating role of the Ministry of Justice

Mediation under Decree No 28 is a fairly highly government-controlled process. In fact, the Italian Ministry of Justice has been given the main tasks of both: (a) controlling mediators' and mediation centres' credentials, which they do more with bureaucratic zeal than actual usefulness; and (b) implementing, and integrating the ground rules of Decree No 28, which in practice has led to the creation of an increasingly overruled system of detailed, and lawsuit-like regulations.

Unregulated mediation

Outside the framework of Decree No 28, it is still possible to have an unregulated mediation put into place. General principles of contract law will apply: the parties are at liberty to choose their own mediator, determine the cost of the process, and keep the process totally in their hands. Some benefits will be lost, of course, namely the possibility of having a settlement agreement put on a fast track, and some fiscal bonuses. There are some doubts whether the confidentiality and no-privilege safe harbour will come into operation: in fact, no such provisions exist for mediation arising out of Decree No 28. However, art 7 of the Directive seems quite clear in requiring all Member States to grant such privilege to all mediation processes as broadly defined in art 3(a).

Recourse to mediation

Some figures

Some significant statistics on mediation in Italy are available only from March 2011. Decree No 28, in fact, enables the Ministry of Justice to collect data with the mediation centres. Unregulated mediations continue to be unmonitored.

Latest available statistics cover the period March 2011 though to the end of December 2013. In 2012, at the peak, some 155,000 requests for mediation were filed throughout the country;[17] the process sensibly slowed down in 2013 as result of the Constitutional Court dictum (see above), and now it seems to have resumed, although not at the 2012 pace. Obviously a request for mediation does not necessarily lead to a mediation: the cases that are actually mediated represent something more of 30 per cent of the total number of filed requests. Success rates, then, are measured in terms of a settlement agreement reached or not in the course of the process (that has to be completed within three months, unless otherwise agreed between the parties). It ranks around some 40 per cent of cases actually mediated.

Mandatory versus voluntary mediations

Stats clearly show that recourse to mediation in Italy has been boosted by its mandatory nature: More than 80 per cent of the 2011-2012 cases were initiated because mediation was mandatory, ie requested as a prior step of a lawsuit.

---

17   In the pre-2011 era, just some 2,000 cases a year were reported.

One Continent, Many Methods

Voluntary mediations still linger in the ratio of some 10-13 per cent and most likely are just a by-product of mandatory ones. Even worse is the situation in respect of court-mandated mediations (just less than 3 per cent).

Regulated versus unregulated mediations

Almost invariably, mediations in Italy seem to fall within the scope of Decree No 28. No data is available in respect of unregulated mediations; however, these seem very seldom utilised, on account of the fact that recourse to mediation still heavily relies on the mandatory side, and the nuances of the process are far from being a common knowledge among lawyers (the main 'providers' of cases) and the public.

The role of mediation centres

As mentioned above, mediations under Decree No 28 may be activated through accredited centres only. There are more than 1,000 presently listed in the register maintained by the Ministry of Justice. Actually a small percentage of them are considered as actually operating, and just a handful may be considered of decent international standard. The Centre's role in the management of the process is crucial. It selects the mediator, and therefore determines the quality of the service. It is rare that the parties ask for a particular mediator: the market is still too young for allowing the parties such choice. The whole Decree No 28 system pushes for discouraging such choice, putting all mediators at the same level provided that they have passed an basic accreditation programme (see below). Unregulated mediations, on the contrary, allow full freedom for the parties' choice.

Mediators' styles and approaches

Styles and approaches

Mediators' style and approach is traditionally the result of their inclination, past experience and, above all, the training they have received (see below). Most of the training available recently has been aligned to a facilitative, problem-solving approach. There are just a couple of centres doing transformative mediation; the rest cannot be considered as training at all, being focused not on skills but on mere analysis of legal aspects of the process (as a result, a fairly large number of mediators are evaluative in style because they simply make recourse to their professional knowledge, lacking any other skills).

Mediators' accreditation

Cases under Decree No 28 may be mediated by accredited mediators only. In order to get accreditation, a minimum school degree is needed, as is 40 hours' of training, released by qualified training centres (enti di formazione); there are some 400 of said centres presently listed with the Ministry of Justice. Again, the number of actually active centres is far less than those on the paper. Moreover, in order to maintain accreditation, a mediator has to take part in 20 cases, and receive 18 hours of refreshment training every two years. An exception to this has been introduced for lawyers: they need to have just 15 hours' initial training, and take part in just two cases.

There is no requirement for mediators selected to run unregulated mediations.

Quality control

Quality control on mediators' activities under Decree No 28 is one of the aims of the Ministry of Justice, and should be a major concern. A feedback system for parties has been put into place, and reports must be quarterly communicated to the Ministry. The quality levels seem unfortunately rather low, with some notable exceptions.

Quality control of unregulated mediations depends on policy adopted by the relevant administering ADR centre, if any. Only the major centres operate, indeed, according to given protocols, and release regularly feedback data.

How to select the right mediator (in a system where one mediator is as good as another)

Apart from other limitations provided for under Decree No 28, from the parties' perspective, it is certainly not easy to accept the fact that their mediator may not be chosen at all, being selected by a mediation centre only. Many centres, however, are reported to respect the possible parties' determination in this respect. In any case, the top-down mechanism may be avoided by carefully selecting the centre itself (a look at its website may be of great help), and by so indirectly choosing, at least, the kind of mediator who is going to be appointed.

Unregulated mediations have no such a kind of drawbacks, of course, as explained above.

Conclusions

Two clearly separate lines of discourse about mediation have been developing in Italy in these recent years.

The first line considers mediation as a useful avenue for supporting the courts' work, and eventually cutting their notorious backlog. In this kind of narrative, mediation is one of the ADR methods it is certainly wise to experiment, along with arbitration, French-style lawyer-assisted negotiation, early neutral evaluation, and so on. As we have seen above, the Italian Government enthusiastically adopted mediation some years ago, in this very mood: results need to be assessed in perspective, but they look quite encouraging. Of course, one must accept this kind of mediation the way it is: do not ask too much to a newly trained army of novice mediators. Settlement is the only appropriate benchmark, irrespective of how to reach it. No surprise, then, that the majority of mediators tend to act more as pushing agents than facilitators. Moreover, lawyers are voicing from a privileged position in the choir. Since mediation has a definite connection with civil lawsuits, it is natural that they will try to control it. In fact, recent developments in regulation clearly show a tendency to attract the process in the court's orbit, with all the consequences one can expect. It is difficult to foresee how mediation, in this perspective, will get through. Should settlement rates turn out not be satisfactory soon, mediation risks being abandoned to its own fate – an unfortunate experiment like many others in the past. There are some encouraging signs, indeed, like the recovery after the abrupt halt in mediations which occurred in 2012 after the above-mentioned Constitutional Court decision. However, the basis on which mediation is grounded seems extremely frail. One blow to the mandatory system (eg the possibility for a lawyer to happily bypass it thanks to a new system of assisted direct negotiation), and everything will crumble down. The fact that most commentaries on mediation insist on dissecting issues relating to mediation centres jurisdiction, instead of maintaining a critical look on mediators' skills and approaches, frankly cannot promise any good.

On a different line of discourse, mediation is a unique approach to conflict, which deserves careful protection from outside influence impairing party self-determination, and ceaseless refinement for neutrals to practice it. In this perspective, settlement rates may have some importance, of course, but only as a way to attract customers. To some, they don't even count too much, because the focus is on customers' overall satisfaction. The focus is on excellency of practice, with little or no attention to the needs of the judiciary. This way of seeing mediation is certainly not a mass phenomenon, yet; however, it seems to attract many, and if only it takes root it can provide mediation with long-term perspectives as a revolutionary practice for managing conflict effectively.

Latvia

Rada Matjušina

Latvia was introduced to mediation approximately 10–15 years ago, when the first mediation association, 'Mediation and ADR' was founded on 7 April 1995.[18] Mediation as a process was quite unpopular till 2006 when the big EU Twinning Mediation Project was implemented by the Ministry of Justice. During this project, mediation training took place. The final mediation conference on 23-24 May 2007 took place and attracted a large number of participants and much interest. After this project and the conference, the leading expert A Trossen (a German) published different articles in Latvia, the film 'Mediation Magic' was shot, etc. After 2007, a new mediation association was founded, whilst other already existing mediation associations changed their activity to mediation.

After the EU Directive of 2008, Latvia started to make every effort to implement the Directive and to implement mediation itself. On 18 February 2009 Decision No 121 The implementation of Mediation in Civil Law Disputes approved the concept and work on the draft Mediation Law was started. EU Recommendation 2001/310/EC provided principles for out-of-court bodies involved in the consensual resolution of consumer disputes. Implementation of the EU Directive happened on 20 December 2010 when Latvia adopted the amendments into the Civil Procedure law, which came into the force on 1 January 2011. The aim of these amendments was to promote mediation in the litigation process in two ways:

18 www.mediacija.lv/adr

- increasing court fees; and
- providing the possibility for parties to recoup 50 per cent of the court fee already paid where conciliation happens.

Practice shows that these measures do not stimulate parties to use mediation, and moreover, theydidn't promote mediation per se, because the dispute parties had no legal information, that conciliation can be brought about not only by themselves, but also with the mediation process.

On 26 January 2012, the draft Mediation Law was announced. On 22 May 2014, the Mediation Law was adopted and came into force on 18 June 2014. Latvia is now at the very beginning of the mediation legislation. Latvia has no mediation history, and as a procedure Latvia only started to use mediation in the past five years.

Under the Mediation Law mediation has to be done by certified mediators. Any person, who is at least 25 years old, has good reputation, received state-recognised higher education, is fluent in the official language at the highest level, passed a mediator training course and obtained the certificate of mediation, can become a certified mediator.

During the dispute, the court or the Mediation Council offers the participants a mediator or the list of certified mediators. The mediator is certified by the Certification Committee. The Certification Committee shall be established by the Mediation Council for three years. Panellists include the representatives of the Ministry of Justice, the district (city) court judge and district courts, the university academic staff representative and two certified Mediation Council representatives.

On 25 July 2011, the Mediation Council (biedrība 'Mediācijas Padome') was set up by all Latvian non-governmental mediation associations. After the foundation, the Mediation Council committees were developed and started to work:

- ethics committee;
- mediators' certification committee; and
- mediation training certification committee.

The aim of the Council is to bring together several Latvian non-profit and non-governmental mediation organisations to promote their cooperation, the development of mediation, to create a Latvian Mediators Ethic Code, to certify mediators, to provide the official list of certified mediators and to ensure mediation popularisation in Latvia.

Under the Mediation Law, the Mediation Council is the organisation that provides the work of the certified professional mediators. Also under the Mediation Law the state, on behalf of the Ministry of Justice, delegates to the Mediation Council several state management tasks:

- mediator examination, certification and attestation;
- issuing certificates to mediators;
- developing a uniform training standard for mediators;
- establishing and maintaining a list of certified mediators;

- mediation service quality monitoring and control, dealing with complaints about mediators; and
- establishing and adopting a code of ethics for mediators.

There is no special style of mediation and mediators choose their own style. It is most important that the mediator has had a training course of at least 30 academic hours per year. At the moment there are no rules on mediators' training qualification.

Under the Mediation Law, the following mediation principles are respected: voluntary confidentiality, parties' equality and cooperation, neutrality and impartiality of the mediator. Under the Mediation Law, the period of claim shall be suspended at the time the mediation proposal is made. The mediator may meet with both parties together or with each side separately. The mediator shall operate under the mediators' professional ethics. The Mediation Council adopted the mediators' professional ethics, influenced by the European Code of Conduct on Mediation.

Lithuania

Natalija Kaminskiene

Introduction

The term 'conciliatory mediation' is used in the Lithuanian legal environment. In common with many other EU countries, the differentiation of mediation and conciliation is unclear, so often in Lithuania they mean the same, but conciliation is mostly understood to be led by judges and the lawyers of the parties within the usual course of the civil case, while mediation is considered to be operated by a professional (mediator) who has no duties or interests in a civil case except to mediate.

The Conciliatory Mediation in Civil Disputes Act of the Republic of Lithuania (2008) amended 2011

The Act lays down the most general principles of mediation, enabling the parties to agree a suitable process with the mediator for their particular dispute. It covers both national and cross-border civil disputes. 'Civil' means any dispute that may be heard in civil proceedings in a court of general jurisdiction.

In addition there is a judicial mediation scheme which operates in all (56) courts of general jurisdiction of the Republic of Lithuania and is regulated by the Act, Code of Civil Procedure (2002) amended 2012 and the Judicial Mediation Rules (2005) amended 2011. Under the scheme the judge who is hearing the case may suggest mediation to the parties but it will only proceed with their written consent. The judge is not allowed to act as mediator in the same case where they render judgement.

EU Directive (2008)

The EU Directive is implemented by the Act, although the Act goes beyond the Directive to include national civil disputes.

Definition of mediation and mediator

Mediation is described in the Act as:

> 'a civil dispute settlement procedure whereby one or several mediators in civil disputes assist the parties to a civil dispute in reaching an amicable agreement'.

A mediator is a third party impartial neutral who is involved in settling a civil dispute between other persons with a view to assisting them to reach an amicable agreement.

Voluntary/mandatory process

Mediation is a voluntary process, so there is no obligation, legal or otherwise, for parties to go to mediation if they so choose. Courts may suggest the parties go to mediation but it is the party's decision. However, if they choose to go to mediation, whether by having a clause in their contract or a separate agreement, they must do so before referring the case to the court or arbitration. If a mediation agreement sets time limits for the termination of mediation, the party to the dispute may refer to court or arbitration only after the expiry of these time limits. Where no time limits for the termination of mediation have been set in the mediation agreement, the party to the dispute may refer to court or arbitration one month after suggesting to the other party to the dispute in writing that the dispute be settled through mediation. However the idea of making mediation a mandatory process in certain types of cases (eg family disputes involving children) is under current discussion by legislative and executive authorities of the state.

Sanctions if parties do not mediate

Currently mediation is voluntary so the courts cannot order parties to go to mediation. There are no sanctions for not mediating.

Confidentiality

All information revealed in, and in connection with, the mediation is confidential except when it is necessary for the execution of the settlement or failure to disclose information would contravene the public interest (particularly where a child's interests need to be safeguarded or where a risk of damage to a natural person's health or life needs to be prevented).

Mediation style and procedure

The most common style for mediators in Lithuania is evaluative/directive, probably because it is seen as a continuation of the mediator's other profession (judge, lawyer, etc). However, mediation is rarely used so it is not possible to identify a generic style.

Mediators can therefore offer an opinion or solution but, because the process is voluntary, such advice is not binding.

Enforceability of Mediated Settlement Agreements

An agreement reached in mediation has a statutory effect on the parties to the dispute. The agreement is treated as a final judgement but it is not enforceable until it is approved by a court.

Register of mediators

A list of judicial mediators (includes judges, assistant judges, psychologists, social workers, lawyers, state child protection specialists and other persons) is maintained by the National Court Administration, and the judge in a case will appoint from that list. The practice shows that most of the judicial mediations are performed by mediator-judges.

Mediators generally are not regulated in Lithuania except under provisions of the above mentioned legal acts and the rules of admittance to the list of judicial mediators (2011) approved by the Council of Judges. One of the main requirements for the person that wishes to become a judicial mediator is a requirement to present a certificate confirming participation in judicial mediation training course. Although the length of such course training is not indicated, according to the practice of the commission that admits persons to the list of judicial mediators the minimum required length of the course training is currently 16 academic hours. Professional background, legal knowledge, education, mediation practice are not relevant.

Mediator exemption

According to the Code of Civil Procedure, mediators cannot be questioned as a witness about the circumstances that they learned during the mediation proceedings.

Conclusion

Mediation in Lithuania is in its infancy and so, along with many other countries in the EU, over time it will grow and become a more accepted method of resolving civil disputes.

Luxembourg

with Alain Grosjean

Introduction

Mediation is enshrined in the Luxembourg Civil Procedure Code (2012). This Act lays down the framework for mediation.

EU Directive (2008)

The EU Directive was absorbed into the Code of Civil Procedure, which covers cross-border as well as national mediation.

The Civil Procedure Code of Luxembourg (2012)

Definition of mediation and mediator

The Code requires that the mediator be independent, impartial and competent. Some judges mediate.

Voluntary/mandatory process

Mediation is voluntary in Luxembourg. Although the court can advise parties to try mediation it cannot be mandated. If parties refuse, the court proceedings will continue. There are no sanctions if the parties refuse mediation.

Confidentiality

Confidentiality within a mediation is enshrined in, and regulated by, the Act.

Mediation style and procedure

Although the Act lays down the mediation procedure, the way the mediation is conducted and the style is not stipulated. Mediation in Luxembourg would generally be considered to be facilitative, the mediator not being empowered to make a decision or recommendation.

Enforceability of Mediated Settlement Agreements

In most cases settlements achieved in mediation qualify as a binding agreement. The agreement must be ratified by the court for it to be enforceable.

Mediator training, accreditation and post-qualification standards

Mediator training is around 60 hours but there is no requirement for structured continuing profession development.

Register of mediators

Mediators are regulated by the Ministry of Justice of Luxembourg

Mediator exemption

There is no exemption for the mediator in giving evidence in court or arbitral proceedings.

Malta

Austin Sammut

The Malta Mediation Act was enacted at the end of 2004 (ie some 10 years ago). It established a Centre for Mediation, which:

> 'shall provide a forum where mediation parties may refer, or be referred to, in order to resolve their dispute through the assistance of a mediator'.

The Act provides for a range of functions for the Centre. Some of those functions are as follows:

- to promote domestic and international mediation as a means of settling disputes;
- to provide the necessary facilities for the conduct of mediation;
- to draw up a list of mediators to assist in domestic and international mediation;
- to provide a code of ethics to be followed by mediators during mediation proceedings; and
- to facilitate better access to mediation procedure through the publication of information, guidelines and related documentation.

These are just 5 out of 16 listed functions assigned to the Centre. To my knowledge, unfortunately, none of the five functions have been fulfilled. The law provides for the appointment of a Board for the Centre, whose members are appointed by the Minister of Justice. Again, to my knowledge, this Board has never functioned effectively or efficiently.

The mediation process is either:

- voluntary; or
- following a decree or order by a court of law or other adjudicating authority; or
- by law.

'Voluntary' is self-explanatory. However, a mediation organisation I had set up with a colleague in a law firm different from my own was unsuccessful in promoting mediation in the media and even in providing voluntary, non-remunerative services to the Malta Chamber of Commerce members. The Maltese Government has always concentrated on (if not been obsessed with) family mediation, while it has ignored the important areas of commercial mediation (above all) and community mediation.

What my organisation did was to organise a number of courses for the training of family mediators with the services of a top British family mediator with great exposure on the European and international mediation platform. These were a success and most of our students provided the nucleus of mediators for the dubious legally imposed mediation process in our Family Court. It seems not to have been a success. I have always been of the opinion that mediation can never be *imposed* but must be *voluntary* all round.

With regard to mediation ordered by a court of law, I believe that such a statement should be clarified. As one of Malta's very few accredited mediators, I have only been assigned around six cases (if that) by the courts (and, in fact, only by one particular judge).

With regard to formal international mediation in Malta I have no comment. It just does not exist or at least I am not aware of it! There are many provisions in the law, of course. To quote the definition in the Mediation Act in full:

> '"international mediation" shall include cross-border disputes of a civil and commercial nature except as regards rights and obligations which are not at the parties' disposal under the relevant applicable law, and other disputes which national legislation may provide from time to time. It shall not extend, in particular, to revenue, customs or administrative matters or to the liability of the State for acts and omissions in the exercise of State authority ("acta iure imperii")'.

An interesting development within the ambit of mediation came in the form of the Restorative Justice Act, enacted in 2012. This has some very interesting provisions, although, to my knowledge, it has not yet taken off. Although restorative justice has been introduced in a number of other countries, this is very innovative for Malta and hence, perhaps, the delay in its implementation.

The Act provides for the introduction of parole, offender assessment and remission for prisoners into the Maltese legal system. For this purpose we have a Parole Unit and Board, an Offender Assessment Board and a Remission Board. These are all totally new and progressive reforms for Malta. But what is of main interest and very positive to us is the Chapter under the Act (also innovative) establishing a Victim Support Unit, in terms of criminal offences, in that it introduces 'victim-offender mediation'.

Some of the functions of the Victim Support Unit are:

- the establishment of a Victims of Crime Charter to regulate the coordination of services to satisfy the needs of victims of crime;
- the drawing up of a code of ethics, in collaboration with the Malta Mediation Centre, to be followed by mediators during victim-offender mediation proceedings;
- the facilitation of better access to victim-offender mediation through the publication of information, guidelines and related documentation; and
- the promotion of victim-offender mediation as a means of reparation for both the victim and the offender at any stage of the criminal justice process.

The provisions of the Act establishing victim-offender mediation are very interesting. A 'Victim-Offender Mediation Committee' shall be established, with the principal duties, among others, being:

- to determine the victim's, the offender's and the offence's suitability for victim-offender mediation;
- to supervise mediators and periodically receive verbal or written reports on the victim-offender mediation processes taking place;
- the responsibility to make recommendations to the responsible Minister and in consultation with the Malta Mediation Centre regarding:

— the drawing up of a list of mediators to assist in victim offender mediation;

— the drawing up of the criteria for the appointment of mediators.

What is interesting is that a Court may, at any stage of criminal proceedings, refer the case to the Committee to determine the suitability and eligibility or otherwise for such case to be referred to victim-offender mediation.

The functions of the victim-offender mediator are the same as those of a mediator in a civil or commercial matter. Further, the same rules regarding the confidentiality of all proceedings, communications and documentation shall apply.

If a victim offender mediation is successful it will result in a 'reparation agreement', which may include a number of very interesting remedies, which I will quote more or less in full:

- the offender providing compensation for damages suffered by the victim;
- the offender providing compensation for non-pecuniary damages suffered by the victim:
- the offender performing personal work for the victim;
- the offender performing community work;
- the offender to undertake any relevant rehabilitation programmes;
- restitution to the victim of any item stolen by the offender; and
- a formal apology by the offender to the victim.

As one can see, there are a whole range of comprehensive remedies.

The mediator is bound to inform their appointing authority whenever an agreement has been reached by the parties, whenever the parties have failed to reach an agreement or where mediation sessions had to be interrupted for any other reason.

Also interesting is the fact that:

- outcomes of victim-offender mediation proceedings during the pre-sentencing stage shall be taken into consideration by the Court when passing judgment;
- provided that, upon the parties having reached a reparation agreement, nothing shall prevent the Court from prescribing any other punishment on the offender which it may deem appropriate; and
- provided further that participation of the offender in mediation shall not be used as evidence of admission of guilt by the offender.

This is a brief overview of the state of mediation in Malta. I started off on a negative note, which, unfortunately, is the reality, but this moved to the positive role of mediation in the field of restorative justice. Hopefully, our domestic mediation, principally, and our international mediation services will finally pick up and move forward. This, however, requires a very big push from the Government, the media, the business sector, local councils and so many other authorities.

Netherlands

with Manon Shonewille and Dr Fred Schonewille

Introduction[19]

Unfortunately this is being written before the new Dutch Mediation Act is passed and so some comments are in anticipation of its final form. However, most of its contents and its intent are known and are described below.

Mediation in the Netherlands jurisdiction has been established for a long time, particularly in family matters. It suits the Dutch approach to justice which maintains an element of 'common sense' and co-operation rather than outright confrontation. In many ways the Act will reflect what has been evolving for nearly 20 years.

EU Directive (2008)

Following the EU Directive a draft mediation law was prepared, aiming to adopt the Directive as a 'light implementation' which would only govern the mandatory aspects of the Directive and, more importantly, introduce a general referral rule which would have offered judges the option of advising parties to try mediation for all cases in every stage of the procedure. This failed to be enacted because it failed to identify any professional standards for mediators. As a result, the Minister of Justice drafted a short new law to implement the EU Directive (Law No 33 320). This only covers cross-border disputes and became effective on 21 November 2012. Interestingly it prescribes, amongst other things, that a judge in a cross-border case is entitled to propose mediation to the parties in every stage of the procedure. Three 'private' draft laws (initiatiefwetsvoorstel, a legislation proposal on initiative of a MP) for the future Dutch Mediation Act (Nos 33 722, 33 723 and 33 727) that have been drafted by MP Van der Steur (Liberal Party) were submitted to the House of Representatives on 3 June 2014 and will be discussed in Parliament after the summer break. These are:

- a law to promote the use of mediation in civil and commercial cases, which proposes changes in the Civil and Civil Procedural Code (No. 33723).

- a law to promote the use of mediation in administrative law (No. 33727).

- a law to regulate and improve the quality of the mediator profession (No. 33722)

This Mediation Act is likely to be introduced in the course of 2014 or in the beginning of 2015; it is currently being discussed in Parliament.

The new Dutch Mediation Act (draft)

Amongst other things, the Dutch Mediation Act will cover:
- definition of mediation;

---

19 This chapter on mediation in the Netherlands incorporates with permission parts of the chapter on the Netherlands in Manon Schonewille and Dr Fred Schonewille (Eds) *The Variegated Landscape of Mediation. A Comparative Study of Mediation Regulation and Practices in Europe and the World* (The Hague: Eleven International Publishing, 2014).

- voluntary/mandatory process;
- enforceability of mediation clauses;
- confidentiality;
- enforceability of mediated settlement Agreements;
- mediator accreditation and register of mediators; and
- mediator exemption.

Definition of mediation

The new Act will describe mediation in terms of procedure, specifically in relation to the Dutch law and court procedure. Mediation is defined as:

> 'Mediation: the structured process guided by an independent neutral third person who on the basis of a mediation agreement is jointly entrusted by the parties, with the objective to enable the parties to find or regain through mutual consultation in a well-considered fashion a mutual norm, or in the absence of such a norm to develop a norm if the parties need this;.'[20]

These definitions are not yet adopted by the Parliament.

Voluntary/mandatory process

The law will introduce a general court referral rule that *urges* a judge, in almost every case, to refer the parties to mediation at every stage of the proceedings if the parties haven't tried mediation before going to court (new s 22a of the Dutch Code of Civil Procedure). Under the Code of Civil Procedure, which goes with the Act, lawyers will have to state whether or not the parties have tried mediation before starting a civil procedure (new ss 111(2)(f) and 278(2) of the Dutch Code of Civil Procedure of the Dutch Mediation Act). So under the draft Law, the judge can advise parties to try mediation but cannot oblige it.

Sanctions if parties do not mediate

If the parties refuse to mediate then the case goes to trial. In some labour conflicts, an 'informal' mandatory element now already exists. There is an expectation that employers will be 'good employers' and that employees will be 'good employees' so if there is a conflict judges will expect the parties to have tried to settle a dispute themselves, for example through mediation, before going to court. Based on this it is probable that a judge, once the Mediation Act is adopted, would generally take into consideration if the parties have not tried mediation for good reason or of it is not considered by the parties 'in good faith'. There are some incentives to

---

20 Unofficial translation prepared by Manon Schonewille for the purpose of this book. The official definition in Dutch is: 'mediation: het in gezamenlijke opdracht van partijen op grond van een mediationovereenkomst door een onafhankelijke neutrale derde begeleide gestructureerd proces, dat als doel heeft partijen in onderling overleg weloverwogen de door hen gedeelde norm te laten vinden of hervinden waar die ontbreekt, terwijl daar bij partijen wel behoefte aan is.'

mediate – not least the access to a judge by electronic means in case the parties need clarification or a decision on the law, getting a quick enforcement order for the mediated settlement and, in divorce cases, the option of getting through the necessary formalities quickly and at considerably lower cost. However, this facility will only be available to registered mediators (see register of mediators below).

Enforceability of mediation clauses

The new Act will introduce the enforceability of a mediation clause (new s 22a of the Dutch Code of Civil Procedure). However, the parties may still jointly choose not to mediate, whether there is a clause, prior agreement to mediate or not.

Confidentiality

At present, confidentiality is only regulated by law for cross-border mediations within the European Union. However the new Dutch Mediation Act will introduce a general confidentiality for mediations conducted by registered mediators (New s 424a(4) of the Dutch Civil Code). Of course, whether the mediator is registered or not, there is nothing to stop the parties from reaching their own confidentiality agreement, both in the Agreement to Mediate and in the eventual Settlement Agreement.

Mediation style and procedure

Traditionally the Dutch mediation style has been facilitative, although the parties may request an opinion, whether it be binding or not (so long as the parties agree it can be either). Although facilitative is still the prevalent, there is a trend towards a mix of styles and therefore towards introducing evaluative aspects in the later stages of a mediation process, especially in commercial cases. Also in business mediation the common view is shifting more towards the necessity of introducing legal or other objective or subjective norms and for mediators to have substantive expertise. Broadly, mediators with a legal background are more directive, mediators from non-legal background tend to be more facilitative.

The common framework is to have an early joint session with a mixture of joint and caucus sessions as the mediation progresses. The new Act leaves the style and procedure up to the parties and mediator.

Enforceability of Mediated Settlement Agreements

A Mediated Settlement Agreement will in most cases qualify as a binding settlement agreement. However, it is not automatically enforceable but parties can ask a civil-law notary or a judge to make their settlement agreement enforceable. The new Act will introduce a quick and easy way to make a mediated settlement enforceable through a special 'e-judge' to whom only registered mediators (see registration of mediators below) will have access.

Mediator training, accreditation and post-qualification standards

Mediator training varies in the Netherlands. On average it is around 50 hours, but the range is probably 40–80 hours. The new Act itself does not regulate training or amount of hours necessary to be trained. This will be regulated at a later stage. At present, only mediators who are accredited and registered by the former Netherlands Mediation Institute (NMI), now part of the Mediators Federation Netherlands (MfN) and who have successfully completed a performance-based assessment, or who have submitted themselves to a peer review (based upon nine mediations in the three years prior to registration) are eligible for court-referred cases. Under the new Act there will be a specific register of experienced and highly qualified mediators (registered mediators) that will be under the auspices of the Justice Department.

In January 2014 all mediator associations merged into the Dutch Mediation Federation (*Mediationfederatie Nederland*), where mediators who are a member of a Dutch Association are now united in a joint register.

Although the standards required by the new Act are not yet known, and each organisation has different levels, the NMI requirement for Continuing Professional Development (CPD) is 48 hours over three years.

Register of mediators

When the Act becomes law there will be three categories of mediator:
- registered mediators who are subject to the Dutch Mediation Act and under the auspices of the Justice Department;
- cross-border mediators, who are subject to the 2012 Minister of Justice Act; and
- mediators who are not (yet) registered.

Mediator exemption

For national cases mediators do not yet have the general right to refuse to give evidence in subsequent proceedings yet. The 2012 Act covering cross-border mediations introduced a general exemption for mediators that are engaged in an EU cross-border mediation to give evidence in judicial proceedings. The new Dutch Mediation Act will introduce a general exemption for registered mediators to give evidence in judicial proceedings. Which leaves the unregistered mediators, who are not covered by the cross-border legislation, unprotected.

Conclusion

Although mediation is established in the Netherlands, probably more so than in most European countries, ignorance is still a challenge. The new Act will raise its profile even more.

Norway

Anna Nyland

Introduction

Civil and commercial mediation is available in Norway both as private (out-of-court, contract-based) and court-connected mediation. Until 2008, private mediation was not regulated: it was considered as private negotiations with at third party facilitator, and any contracts formed were treated as regular contracts. From the late 1990s court-connected mediation was introduced in a few district courts. When the Dispute Act entered in force in 2008, court-connected mediation was introduced in all courts and out-of-court mediation became partly regulated.

The concept of mediation (*megling* or *mekling* in Norwegian) is ambiguous in Norwegian. It has traditionally referred to judicial promotion of settlement, and other activities promoting settlement. Today, mediation refers to both the promotion of settlement and mediation as in facilitative, evaluative or transformative mediation. In this text only Mediation in the latter sense will be discussed.

Legal regulation on out-of-court mediation

Chapter 7 in the Dispute Act has provisions on out-of-court mediation. The provisions are mostly subsidiary. The legislation covers only legal disputes, ie disputes that can be litigated or arbitrated. Although the dispute must be of a legal character, once mediation starts the problem can be defined in an interest-based, need-based or relation-based manner, and the settlement may include remedies not provided by law. The issue can be changed or broadened to cover non-legal aspect and the legal aspect may be dropped if the parties wish so. Therefore, mediation can be conducted according to any mediation model.

The parties can agree to mediate on a general basis, or after a specific dispute has arisen. The agreement to mediate must be in writing. A clause on mediation is not binding for consumers if it is signed before a dispute has arisen. The legal consequences of an agreement to mediate are few.

The foremost advantage is that the parties have direct access to the district courts. The parties can automatically skip the pre-trial lay tribunal, the Conciliation Board, which is normally mandatory. Thus, the parties can save time and money.

If a party is in breach of the agreement to mediate, there are almost no consequences. An agreement to mediate does not affect the possibilities to litigate the case. A case will not be dismissed due to a clause on mediation, as opposed to a clause on arbitration. However, the party who has failed to participate in mediation may be liable to pay some of the litigation costs of the opposing party, regardless of which party wins the case. As an agreement to mediate out-of-court will not affect litigation, the parties may agree to mediate the case while the case is pending at court.

Out-of-court mediation does not have any effect on limitation and prescription periods. Norway is not a member of the European Union, and therefore the

Mediation Directive (Directive 2008/52/EC on certain aspects of mediation in civil and commercial matters) has not been implemented. Consequently, mediation is not a proper method of dispute resolution toward the end of limitation and prescription periods. Alternatively, a party might initiate mediation and file a writ of summons (almost) simultaneously.

According to the Dispute Act, the parties choose the mediator. If the parties do not agree on the mediator, they can request the district court appoint the mediator from its register of mediators. The request must be made in writing and signed by both parties. The parties must give a short description of the dispute.

If the parties agree on a mediator there are no specific requirements for the training of the mediator. To be registered in the court register a mediator must have proficiency and experience in mediation and be suitable for acting as a mediator. Usually, one must have completed mediation training offered by the Bar Association or by the Norwegian Courts Administration, or the equivalent, or document other relevant training or extensive experience. The mediator must be neutral and impartial.

The parties must attend mediation or be represented by a person with authority to settle the case. Mediation is conducted in accordance with any agreement the parties have entered into, ie the parties decide if they want facilitative, evaluative or transformative (or other forms of) mediation, if the focus of mediation be broad or narrow. However, the parties may not turn mediation into de facto arbitration. If the parties have not agreed on the procedure, the mediator decides the process having consulted the parties. The mediator may have private meetings (caucuses) and s/he may suggest solutions or evaluate the case. Taking of evidence is also allowed.

Mediation is confidential. The mediator must keep a record of who is attending mediation, that mediation is closed and the identity of a person giving evidence must be stated. A party making a settlement offer may require that the offer included in the record. The mediator may not testify in court, nor are the parties allowed to testify what happened during mediation, except for what is included in the record. The parties are expressly free to use the information about the existence of evidence (witnesses, documents) gained during mediation. The record stating a settlement offer may be used later to document that the other party has refused a reasonable settlement offer.

The remuneration of the mediator is primarily contract-based. The parties are liable for one-half of the payment each, unless they agree otherwise. The parties can also ask the court to determine the fee. If the mediator wants an advance or a collateral security, the court can order the parties to pay.

The mediated agreement has the same legal status as any contract. It is not directly enforceable and it can be challenged on the same account as other contracts. A party may terminate mediation at any time and the mediator may end the process after a deadlock.

In practice, these rules are almost never used. Most lawyers have either not heard about the rules, or do not know of any cases mediated according to the rules. Consequently, there is no case law on the legislation. The citizens have not embraced the idea of using out-of-court mediation by asking the court to appoint a mediator.

Out-of-court mediation in the private sphere

In addition to out-of-court mediation where the court appoints the mediator, the Oslo Chamber of Commerce and the Norwegian Bar Association offer Mediation services. Both organisations have rules for general civil and commercial mediation and have lists with approved mediators. In practice, parties use the mediation services by the Norwegian Bar Association.

The Norwegian Bar Association requires a 20-hour mediation course or the equivalent of its mediators. The Bar Association offers courses (almost) annually, and there have been some initiatives on continuing education. More than 700 members of the Bar have taken the course on mediation. However, not all are active mediators. The parties agree to mediate either on a general basis or after a dispute has arisen. The parties then agree on a mediator from a list of approved mediators. If the parties cannot agree, the must ask the District Court to appoint a mediator.

The Bar Association has Guidelines for Mediation, which regulate the process of mediation and the conduct of the mediator. The guidelines are to be interpreted in accordance with the Dispute Act. The parties may agree in writing to diverge from the guidelines.

The guidelines on mediation are very open and based loosely on facilitative mediation. The task of the mediator is to facilitate negotiation and dialogue between the parties, and to help the parties find a mutually agreeable interest-based solution. The parties are strongly encouraged to meet in person. However, if the parties chose so, the mediator may offer an opinion on the probable outcome in litigation or suggest a solution, ie use the evaluative model. If the parties have not agreed otherwise, the mediator decides how mediation will be conducted having consulted the parties. In practice, mediation is often evaluative, and only a few mediators have a purely facilitative, broad approach. It seems that mediators often discuss the direct economic aspects of the case, but usually do not discuss the latent economic aspects nor the social or psychological interests and needs of the parties.

Mediation is voluntary and confidential. A party may end the mediation at any time. The parties cannot, unless specifically agreed in writing, refer to any information or suggestions given by the other party or the mediator. The mediator must also adhere to confidentiality, and may not testify in court by a provision in the mediation contract. The mediator must be neutral and impartial, and must disclose any circumstances affecting neutrality. The parties are usually to pay some of the remuneration for the mediator in advance. Each party pays half of the fee, unless otherwise is agreed.

There are no statistics on the use of out-of-court mediation, but a recent poll but the Bar Association suggest its members conduct probably somewhere between 50 and 100 mediations annually. Consequently, mediation seems to be a less attractive alternative in Norway than in many other Western countries.

Court-connected mediation

Court-connected mediation has been available in all courts since 2008. The judge can suggest mediation to the parties in a pending case, or the parties may request the case be sent to mediation. The judge can serve as the mediator, or a mediator may be appointed from the court's register of mediators. According to the law, the parties may request a mediator who is not on the list, but this possibility remains theoretical. In practice, only a few courts appoint mediators from the register, and many courts do not have a register of mediators. Thus, the expertise of outside mediators is not used.

The regulation on the role of the mediator and the conduct of the mediation process is almost identical to the regulation on out-of-court mediation. Section 8-5(3) states that the mediator shall seek to clarify the interests of the parties while trying to find a settlement. The mediator may also identify solutions and discuss the strength and weaknesses of the case. Evidence may be taken with the consent of the parties and of the person giving evidence. The rules on neutrality, impartiality, confidentiality and records of the mediation are practically identical to out-of-court mediation.

The mediation model used is primarily evaluative. Mediation is often based on caucuses: after a brief joint meeting, the parties spend their time in separate rooms, until the case reaches closure. The mediator often gives parties an estimation of how a court would decide the case, or suggest a solution, or discusses strength and weaknesses of the arguments of the parties and the facts of the case. The process is mostly lawyer-driven, but the parties are usually given time to present their views and opinions. Mediation generally has a narrow focus. In some cases, mediation mimics an abbreviated trial. The attorneys give a brief introduction to the case, the legal rules applicable, the evidence and the most relevant arguments. Then the judge-mediator tells the parties what the probable outcome is.

A party can chose to end mediation at any time. The case will continue at the court. If a judge served as a mediator, by rule another judge must be appointed to judge the case. If the case settles, the parties may choose to enter an in-court settlement or an out-of-court settlement. An out-of-court settlement is treated as a regular contract, whereas an in-court settlement can be enforced as a judgment.

Poland

Sylwester Pieckowski

Polish Mediation Law of 2005

Poland was one of the first EU Member States to enact a detailed and complete legislation on mediation in civil and commercial matters by the Law of 28 July 2005 that amended the Civil Procedure Code and introduced mediation as a separate part of the Code (the 'Polish Mediation Law').[21] The Law entered into force on 10 December 2005.

---

21 The Journal of Laws, 2005, No 172, item 1438.

The Law introduces mediation as a new institution into Polish civil procedure, creating an alternative way of resolving disputes in civil matters and in addition to the traditional way of dispute adjudication by state courts. Mediation should result in fast resolution of a number of disputes, in a way which is most convenient and satisfactory to the parties – within a settlement. The drafters intended to make mediation as attractive for the parties involved as well as practicable in order to make mediation a reality. To this end, the provisions of the law were intended to be simple and straight. Mediation should facilitate dispute resolution in civil matters, but at the same time, it requires that the legitimate rights of parties participating in the process are duly protected.

Having in mind such objectives, it was stated that all disputes in civil matters that qualify for amicable agreement can be resolved by means of settlement concluded in front of a mediator. Such settlement, having been confirmed by court, has legal status equal to court settlement. In addition, by embarking on mediation the running of statutes of limitation is interrupted; if mediation proves unsuccessful, it runs anew.

The Law provides for comprehensive regulation of both facets of mediation in civil matters:

- conventional or contractual mediation; and
- mediation in court proceedings (court-annexed mediation).

Financial incentives were also introduced by the Law in order to encourage parties to agreements and disputes to use mediation steadily and frequently. If mediation settlement is reached within court proceedings the plaintiff will recover three-quarters of the court fee already paid.

As a rule mediation is a voluntary instrument of law conducted on the basis of:

- an earlier agreement to mediate future disputes between the parties (contractual mediation); or
- ad hoc agreement to mediate the existing dispute between the parties (contractual mediation); or
- the court has referred the parties to mediation (court-annexed mediation), unless either party can raise an objection against such court decision within seven days, and such objection shall stop mediation. This constitutes evidence that ultimately these are the parties who decide upon whether to embark on mediation or not.

The mediation procedure is regulated in art 183(11)–(15) of the Law as follows:

- The mediator shall immediately establish the date and place of the pre-mediation session. Holding a pre-mediation session is not required if the parties agree to the conduct of mediation without a pre-mediation session.
- A protocol (report) is drawn up after the mediation proceedings, which shall specify the place and time of the mediation, as well as the name, surname and addresses of the parties, name, surname and address of the mediator, and finally the result of the mediation. The protocol is to be signed by the mediator.

- If the parties enter into a settlement before the mediator, such settlement shall be included in or attached to the protocol. The settlement is to be signed by the parties. Any inability to sign the settlement shall be reported by the mediator in the protocol.
- The mediator shall provide the parties with a copy of the protocol.
- In case the court refers a given matter to mediation, the mediator shall deliver the protocol to the court reviewing the matter.
- If the settlement is concluded before the mediator, the court, at a party's request, shall immediately conduct the proceedings aimed at approving the settlement concluded before the mediator. If the settlement is to be performed through a court enforcement, the court shall approve it by stamping an enforcement seal (*klazula wykonalności*) thereon; otherwise the court approves the settlement by a decision during an in camera session.
- The court shall refuse to stamp an enforcement seal or approve the settlement entered into before the mediator, in whole or in part, if the settlement contradicts the law or the principles of social coexistence, or aims at evading the law, or if is incomprehensible or contains contradictions.
- A settlement concluded before the mediator, once it is approved by the court, has the same legal status as a settlement entered into before the court.

General assessment of the Polish Mediation Law vis-à-vis the EU Directive 2008/52/EC

The Law and the Directive voice the same message regarding the need for decisive upgrading of the existing court-based dispute resolution system in civil matters by mediation, which should bring a substantial reduction of tension in national court systems and societies at large, dramatically improve general legal culture throughout the Member States and change civic discourse based more on reasoned conversation and settlement and less on adjudicative power of state court systems.

The scope of regulation of the Law and the Directive is similar but significantly different: the Law covers all civil and commercial matters with one exception contained in the Law, which states that it applies to all civil matters that can regulated by settlement. The Directive, unlike the Draft Directive of 2004, directly applies to mediation in cross-border disputes only.

In accordance with the principle of subsidiarity and proportionality, the Directive is focused on mediation in the court proceedings context, leaving Member States, individuals and business to decide how mediation proper is regulated ie the standards of mediation proceedings, certification and selection of mediators, mediators' training and lists of qualified mediators.

The Polish Mediation Law is broader in its scope: it regulates mediation in the court proceedings context but it also generally approaches the issues of mediation proper ie the mediation agreement, selection of mediator, confidentiality and mediation proceedings.

Definition of civil mediation

The Law does not define civil mediation; rather it describes it. In turn, the Directive defines mediation in art 3. In summary, the Law and the Directive contemplate and regulate a similar 'classic' model of mediation, being viewed as a supportive and supplemental in relation to state court proceedings, with the participation of a neutral and independent person – a mediator – who assists the parties or rather facilitates their discourse aimed at getting a mutually acceptable settlement. The authorities do not regulate or accept other known and accepted forms of ADR such as mini-trial, med-arb, etc. In this sense, this definition of mediation can be connected with the facilitative model rather than the evaluative type.[22]

Referral to mediation

The Directive (art 5) says that the court can invite parties to mediation but it cannot mandate it. At the same time it is stated (art 5(2)) that the Directive does not prejudice national legislation to make mediation compulsory or subject to incentives or sanctions.

The Polish Law goes further than the Directive and stipulates that the state court can mandate the parties to undertake mediation once, even though they have not made a prior agreement to mediate. The voluntary character of mediation is ensured by the parties' right to reject a court referral to mediation made without parties' prior consent or knowledge.

Quality assurance

The Directive (art 4) calls upon Member States to undertake concrete steps aimed at the establishment and improvement of good standards (code of ethics) for mediators and organisations offering mediation services. Secondly, the Directive recognises the necessity of building quality building and supervision mechanisms to protect and promote training of mediators, in order to generally lift the professional level of mediation up, and, specifically, to improve mediation offer for the interested parties.

It should be admitted that the Law is less than satisfactory in this scope. It is expressly stated by the Law that there are no specific qualitative criteria or professional parameters the mediator must meet. In turn, it says that 'Any person with full legal capacity to make legal representations can perform as mediator.'[23] Moreover, in the explanatory memorandum submitted by the Government, it is expressly said that:

> '[a] mediator's abilities do not rest in mediator knowledge but in his personality. Therefore, in order to make it easier for the parties to undertake mediation, no specific requirements as to an mediator's education are foreseen.'

It seems that this patent defect of the Law should be remedied by adequate, active practice of the state courts and their presidents, who will create lists of registered

---

22 The Polish Mediation Law in a descriptive way has adopted a typical form of mediation being rather a facilitative model of mediation in which the mediator acts as a neutral that only helps the parties in conducting their negotiations. It seems that this careful approach is justified by Poland's lack of prior experience in dealing with mediation in civil matters.
23 Article 183(2) § 1.

mediators, also including lists of permanent mediation centres. A good example is provided by US courts and their mediation programmes.[24]

Enforcement of settlement agreements

According to the Law, the settlement agreement constitutes an execution title, equal to an arbitral award; after obtaining a court acceptance the settlement has the legal value of a settlement concluded before the court. The Directive contains similar provisions by saying to this end that the Member States are required to assure in their legislation that mediation settlements are enforceable.

Confidentiality safeguards

Protection of confidentiality for mediators and other participants in the mediation proceedings regarding their exposure as witnesses in civil proceedings is one of the key provisions of the Law and the Directive. These safeguards play a fundamental role in the process making mediation practically safe and available to the parties of civil dispute. Lack of these provisions in the past effectively erased any temptation to try mediation as an effective and legitimate dispute resolution tool.

The provisions of the Law are clear but rather short; they require the mediator to keep confidential all facts learned during mediation and they protect the mediator from testifying as a witness in civil proceedings. The Law does not contain similar provisions for the parties and other participants of mediation process. It is being proposed by the ADR community in Poland that the Law should be corrected by subsequent amendment.

The Directive in art 7 is much more complex and detailed; it prohibits mediators and any person involved in the administering of mediation services to testify or give evidence in civil judicial proceedings except:

- if giving information necessary for the purposes of implementation or enforcement of a mediation settlement, including interpretation of a settlement and its validity; and
- for overriding considerations of public policy of the Member State, eg safety of children, or jeopardy to a person.

The Polish Law envisages a single, different exception to the confidentiality obligation to say that the confidentiality may be lifted if the mediator and the parties so agree.

Interruption of statutes of limitation

According to the Law (art 123 § 1 of the Civil Code): 'The running of the period of limitation shall be interrupted: [...] (3) by commencement of mediation.'

---

24 See US District Court Northern District of Illinois: Mediation Program for the Western Division: 'It is the desire of the court to provide all parties with an opportunity for resolution of their dispute which would occur potentially early in the litigation process in order to keep transactional cost costs at a reasonable level.'

Barriers to successful growth of mediation in civil and commercial matters in Poland

Taking into account the mediation statistics collected by the Ministry of Justice which are focused on mediation in court proceedings, the reported activity of mediation centres and institutions that conduct conventional mediations, and the research studies undertaken by the Civic Council on ADR at the Ministry of Justice, it can be summarised that during 2006–2011 mediation has established its presence in Poland but the actual very low volume of mediation proceedings, compared to the number of all court cases, leads to a painful conclusion that there is a need for deep systemic mediation reform. In order to do it successfully, there are outstanding specific tasks that require vigorous undertaking by the lawmakers, the courts, the mediation institutions, legal professions and the media.

Cognitive barriers

In order to achieve a decisive breakthrough in civil mediation, in its volume and quality, a comprehensive interdisciplinary measure undertaken by *all* interested parties is needed in order to change the picture. On the supply side, new legislation on financing of civil mediation is urgently needed; mediation centres – both existing and new – should be focused on massive training and certification of mediators. Next, acceptance and in-depth understanding of mediation by Polish judges is by far the leading premise for successful take-off and growth of mediation in civil court proceedings. On the demand side, the positive message must reach and convince business leaders, small and big entrepreneurs, and above all, *consumers* that mediation is the first and the best solution for their troubles in getting their disputes resolved in a quick, professional and inexpensive way, before other means like arbitration or litigation are considered. Media acceptance and embracing of mediation as a top issue for societal development and a better legal discourse is a key condition which is absolutely mandatory for the ultimate success of mediation in Poland. On the policy side, mediation cannot significantly grow without a clear and steady support of it by the state and government bodies. In this context, mediation is to be perceived under the notion of ADR that includes all brands of institutions and techniques that serve amicable resolution of civil and commercial disputes, two most important being mediation and arbitration.

Conclusion

Today, it is uniformly accepted within the mediation community in Poland that deep legislative reform is necessary in order to put the institution back on track and to ensure its decisive growth.

Portugal

Ana Maria Maia Gonçalves, François Bogacz and Thomas Gaultier

Overview of mediation in Portugal

Mediation is not a new concept in Portugal. Indeed, Portugal has had legislation governing this aspect of the law since 2001, although limited to very specific branches, primarily with regard to public mediation. Law No 78/2001 of 13 July, the Law of the Julgados de Paz (Justices of the Peace), also set forth the framework for the use of public mediation in small claims cases. In this first mediation legislation dating from over 10 years ago, the scope of which was limited to mediation taking place in small claims court procedures, mediation is defined as:

> 'an extrajudicial means of private, informal, confidential, voluntary, and non-adversarial dispute resolution, in which the parties actively and directly participate, and are assisted by a mediator to find, themselves, a negotiated and amicable solution to the conflict opposing them'.

Moreover, in conjunction with this piece of legislation, a settlement is defined in art 1248 of the Civil Code as a contract in which the parties avoid or settle a dispute through reciprocal concessions.

Portugal was therefore needing more extensive legislation on the issue, which took place in early 2013 with the adoption of Law 29/2013 of 19 April (the 'Mediation Law'), establishing the general principles applicable to mediation carried out in Portugal, as well as the legal frameworks of civil and commercial mediation, of mediators and of public mediation.

Article 2 of the Mediation Law provides a definition of mediation that is quite different from the previous one offered by Law No 78/2001 of 13 July. Indeed, the mediation is now defined as:

> 'a form of alternative dispute resolution, carried out by public or private entities, through which two or more parties who are in conflict seek to voluntarily reach a settlement with the assistance of a mediator'.

The mediator is also defined in the same article as:

> 'an impartial and independent third party, devoid of powers to impose upon the parties, who assists them in trying to construct a final settlement regarding the object of the conflict'.

As mentioned above, although mediation is not a new concept in Portugal, reaching a settlement through the use of a third party neutral is still not common practice in the Portuguese legal environment. Many lawyers and parties are still generally unaware of the potential applications and uses of mediation for dispute, namely of a commercial nature, and mediation suffers from the stigma of being always associated with the public systems of family and labour mediation, which have existed since 2001, and which are not widely popular with the legal community.

As a result, the number of commercial mediation cases is very limited, with certain mediation providers indicating they have handled three mediations in the past five years.

The legal status of mediation in Portugal

Since 2001, the public mediation system in Portugal has been divided into four different systems: the Justices of the Peace, the family mediation system, the workplace mediation system, and the criminal mediation system, each covered by their respective legislation, providing mostly for the procedural rules regarding said systems.

Unfortunately, between 2001 and 2013, although public mediation systems were put in place and granted legislative protection and frameworks, private mediation in itself was never the object of a law, and was thus neither recognised as a private means of dispute resolution nor granted the necessary guarantees for it to be able to function.

As mentioned above, this evolved with the enactment of Portugal's Mediation Law. Regarding mediators, they are now fully considered as a professional category. Since their role is expressly defined by law, alongside their rights and responsibilities as we will also see below, this law will surely trigger a trend towards the professionalisation of mediators, which was not the case until now.

Regarding the scope of the mediations governed by the Mediation Law, art 3 provides that:

> 'the principles set forth in this chapter apply to all mediations carried out in Portugal, regardless of the nature of the conflict which is the subject of the mediation'.

We can therefore assume that they will apply to any mediation in Portugal, whether public or private, in Portuguese or in any other language, by certified mediators and even by non-certified mediators. This Mediation Law now provides all mediation carried out in Portugal with the minimum protection it needed so urgently. The main principles detailed in the Mediation Law are those of voluntariness, equality, impartiality, independence, confidentiality, responsibility and enforceability.

Voluntariness is the first principle appearing in the Mediation Law, in art 4, which provides that the mediation process is voluntary. Article 4 further provides that the parties are free to revoke their consent to mediation at any time during the process, and that such revocation would not constitute a breach of their duty to cooperate under the terms of the Civil Procedure Code. Article 6 of the Mediation Law provides that the parties must be treated equally throughout the entire mediation process, whereby it is the mediator's role to manage the process insofar as to guarantee the balance of powers and the possibility for both parties to participate.

Although the mediator had no power to impose anything upon the parties, being a non-deciding neutral, the mediator must nevertheless manage the process to try and preserve the balance of powers between the parties.

Article 6 of the Mediation Law further provides that the mediator must act impartially, and is not an interested party in the mediation.

Confidentiality

One of the paramount guarantees necessary for mediation to be successfully implemented is to ensure the confidentiality of documents and communications arising out of or in connection with the process. This allows the parties to communicate freely towards reaching a settlement. The Mediation Law, in art 5, contains four sections on confidentiality, the first restating that the mediation process is confidential by nature, and that the mediator must keep confidential all information obtained during the process, not being able to make any use of such information for his or her benefit or for the benefit of others. Section 2 further provides that anything communicated to the mediator in confidence by one of the parties cannot be communicated to the other parties without the first party's consent. Article 5 of the Mediation Law however provides a limit to the confidential nature of mediation, namely for reasons of public policy, for the protection of minors, when the physical or psychological integrity of a person is at stake, or for the purpose of enforcing the agreement in court.

Settlement

In Portugal, mediated Settlement Agreements consist of private agreements signed by the parties to a dispute, and therefore lack the legal effect that would allow them to be directly executed. The Mediation Law clarifies and sets forth a specific article to the end of the enforceability of mediated Settlement Agreements.

Article 9 of the Mediation Law indeed sets forth the provisions on the enforceability of mediated Settlement Agreements. It provides that such Settlement Agreements are automatically enforceable, without the need for acknowledgement by a court, if they fulfil certain requirements.

The first requirement enabling a mediated Settlement Agreement to be automatically enforceable is if the law does not require acknowledgement of that type of dispute. The second requirement is that the parties must have legal capacity to execute the settlement agreement. This requirement is consistent with the fact that settlement agreements are private contracts binding the signing parties. The two following requirements are that the mediation was carried out under the terms provided by law, and that the settlement agreement does not violate public policy. The mediator must also be on the list of mediators managed by the Ministry of Justice. This means that Settlement Agreements will only be automatically enforceable if the acting mediator is recognised and on the lists of the Ministry of Justice.

Mediators

Article 7 of the Mediation Law regards the principle of independence. It provides that the mediator has a duty to safeguard the independence inherent to his or her function, as well as to conduct him or herself with independence, free from any pressure, whether resulting from his or her own interests, personal values or external influences.

The Mediation Law, in art 8, further sets forth certain provision regarding the competence and responsibility of mediators. It provides that mediators can participate in training in specific skills, both in theory and in practice, in order to acquire the adequate skill set for the exercise of their activity. The Mediation Law refers specifically to courses approved by the Ministry of Justice, but is not limiting. It is worth noting that there does not seem to be a general requirement to have attended a mediation course, nor to be a certified mediator to do mediations in Portugal. As such, the door is open to foreign mediators and to individuals with no formal training who can be appointed as mediators.

With regard to the liability of mediators, as mentioned above, art 8 provides that mediators are civilly liable for any damage resulting from the violation of his or her duties in mediation, namely under the terms of the Mediation Law.

Among some of these duties, which are listed in art 26 of the Mediation Law, and that are worth mentioning, mediators must refrain from imposing an agreement on the parties, must inform the parties on the nature, objective, fundamental principles and procedural phases of mediation, and abide by the European Commission's European Code of Conduct for mediators.

Overall, and from a legal perspective, Law 29/2013 of 19 April establishes the general principles applicable to mediation carried out in Portugal, now providing a more complete base of fundamental rights and protections for mediation, mediators and other users.

Use of mediation in Portugal

Although a new legal framework is now applicable as regards mediation in Portugal, with the Mediation Law, mediation as a process has yet to see a significant leap in its development, particularly in commercial matters. Indeed, the lack of awareness, of understanding, and of trust, in the process itself as well as in the mediators, are strong hurdles that will need to be overcome before a more widespread use of mediation is made in Portugal.

For now, the vast majority of mediations taking place are in the family public mediation system, as well as in the small claims courts, the Julgados de Paz. One of the challenges in order to increase the number of commercial mediations in Portugal will be to educate the users as well as the other legal participants in the process, who still feel threatened by mediation and see it as a way to undermine their activity. There has not yet been the much needed mentality shift in recognising mediation as a potential way to satisfy clients in a new manner, thus adapting one's role to what is expected from a modern adviser. In that sense, Portugal is still heavily traditionalist in its approach to novelty, and overall resists this change fervently, as is shown by the recent declarations of the head of the Portuguese Bar Association, who openly criticised mediation on multiple occasions.

Despite the struggling emergence of mediation as a market, and the difficult recognition by the legal community of mediation as a profession, more and more individuals are being trained in mediation and are joining the mediator list published by the Ministry of Justice. Hence, the voice of mediation by mediators is gradually becoming more organised, and mediators are now seeking how to differentiate themselves from their colleagues and competitors in today's practically non-existent, and yet full of potential, commercial mediation market. To that end, mediators are looking towards certifications and accreditations, such as the ones delivered by the International Mediation Institute through local programme providers. Their intent is to provide guarantees and assurances to users, primarily to differentiate themselves, but also to show all stakeholders that a new generation of mediators is growing, one that is trained, prepared and ready to face the demands of the business and legal community. Such mediators do not want to be categorised automatically as a family or small claims mediator just because they have received training in Portugal, but rather as a competent commercial and civil mediator, in addition to any other types of mediation they have been trained in or are comfortable with.

As practitioners in Portugal, our general sense is that the mediation market is still in its definition stage, and the offers in mediation services are slowly becoming more differentiated in terms of area of mediation and style of mediation, although it is still very early to speak about mediation as mainstream or even common in Portugal.

Mediation is still by far the exceptional means of resolving commercial disputes, with only a handful of known cases per year that are not in small claims. As there is no current trend in commercial mediation in Portugal yet, it is also extremely difficult to identify any specific style of mediation as being the most common one in Portugal. Nonetheless, as most of the training provided in Portugal since 2001 has been geared primarily towards family mediation, we would say that most mediators have learned the facilitative approach, although in practice it is hard to say what the training translated into, with so few cases to establish a baseline for a dominant mediation style.

There is still a long road ahead before all stakeholders in the commercial and in the legal fields recognise mediation as a viable path to a satisfactory dispute resolution mechanism, but progress is slowly being made, with a recently enacted legal framework, a new drive by mediators to specialise and obtain accreditations, and more and more mediators being trained.

Romania

Constantin-Adi Gavrilă and Luminita-Jana Trifan

Legal status of mediation in Romania

The current legal status of mediation in Romania is established by Law No 192/2006 on mediation and organisation of the mediation profession. According to the Romanian Mediation Law, mediation represents a way of amicable settlement of conflicts, with the support of a third party specialised as a mediator, in terms of neutrality, impartiality, confidentiality and with the free consent of the parties.

Also, it is stated in the law that mediation relies on the trust which the parties invest in the mediator, as a person capable of facilitating negotiations between them and to provide them with support for the settlement of the conflict, by reaching a mutually convenient, efficient and durable solution.

According to the law in Romania, the mediation is organised within the context of an independent and free standing profession, which is managed by the Romanian mediators. They elect the nine members of the Romanian Mediation Council for terms of four years. The Council was established by law as a quality assurance and steering group for the profession. The Council is not a professional association and its main functions include approving standards, to authorise trainers, training providers and mediators, to monitor the quality of the mediation and mediation training services and to be the official voice of the profession.

The mediators are organised within professional associations in Romania as they can establish local and national professional associations, aimed at representing their professional interests and protecting their status, and they may also join international professional associations. There are almost 10,000 authorised mediators in Romania and they established over 100 professional associations as they are free to choose between joining existing ones or to establish new ones according to their professional interests.

Extent of use of mediation in Romania (particularly commercial mediation)

The extent of mediation services use since 2008 is low and insignificant in terms of number of cases, yet significant in terms of growth rate and potential.

Before 2006, when the Romanian Mediation Law was issued, the mediation services were provided within internationally funded projects managed by different NGOs that in some cases received governmental support. The Mediation Centre from Craiova that was established in 2003 by the Romanian Ministry of Justice as the only pilot centre in Romania and funded with the support of the US Embassy in Romania, local courts and the Dolj Bar Association managed over 1,000 cases until 2007 and achieved an average of 35 per cent settlement rate. The satisfaction rate was excellent, over 95 per cent of the clients were satisfied or very satisfied with the mediation services and stated that they would consider choosing mediation in the future as an appropriate dispute resolution process. The advantage of having statistics in the Pilot Mediation Centre from Craiova was that the mediation cases were administered under an integrated case management programme.

Afterwards, the mediation became an independent profession according to the Romanian Mediation Act, and new challenges arose immediately, including ones regarding the statistics part of the profession. First, most mediators have chosen to work individually in solo firms, as any young system develops, so they had to enhance not only their mediation skills but also their business management experience. Overall, it is known that after the Mediation Act was issued in 2006 very few cases were mediated in Romania because the whole profession was struggling to breach cultures and patterns nationally. Also, the Mediation Council doesn't have much leverage over mediators to structure statistics regarding their practice; it is not completely clear what is the current level of mediation services practice between 2006 and 2011.

The sole recent statistical data on the number of matters settled in the courts of law as a consequence of recourse to mediation were released by the Superior Council of the Magistracy for the year 2010. The Report on the State of Justice in 2010 in Romania points out the fact that:

> 'such alternative procedure for dispute settlement is intended to relieve the burden of the courts, but as per the answers given by such courts to the questionnaire for gathering necessary data for the above report, only a number of 258 case files has been resolved by mediation in year 2010, that is relevant for the reticence of parties to make use of such modality'.

However, it is not specified if such data has been gathered from all Romanian courts. Considering that 258 court cases were settled in 2010 through mediation, taking into account a 50 per cent settlement rate and a 1/1 rapport between court-related mediation and out-of-court mediation, we appreciate that mediation was used in 2010 for an approximate number of 1,000 cases.

The Superior Council of the Magistracy continued to count in the following years and significant growth was registered in 2011 (up to 5,000 mediations), 2012 (up to10,000 mediations) and 2013 (up to 40,000 mediations).

We expect that most of the cases being mediated were family followed by commercial cases. There isn't reliable data available to suggest the level of mediation use only for commercial cases; however, according to the Romanian Mediation Council, a large, national project will be developed starting 2015 in order to gather reliable data from the providers for the purposes of gathering professional mediation use statistics. The project will aim for all types of cases, not only commercial.

Who is doing mediation in Romania?

In Romania, according to art 12(5) of the Romanian Mediation Law no 192/2006, practicing the profession of mediator by persons who have not acquired the capacity of authorised mediator, under the terms of the Law, shall be an offence and shall be sanctioned according to the criminal law.

In order to be authorised as mediators in Romania, mediators have to meet the following conditions:

- they have full capacity of exercise;
- they have university education;
- they have at least three years' length of service;
- they are fit, medically speaking, to pursue this activity;
- they enjoy a good reputation and have not been finally convicted for an offence committed by ill intention, likely to prejudice the prestige of the profession;
- they have graduated from mediator training courses, under the terms of the law, or a post-university masters programme in the field, accredited according to the law and endorsed by the Mediation Council; and
- they have been authorised as mediators, under the terms of the law.

The persons that meet the conditions provided above shall be authorised as mediators by the Mediation Council, after payment of an authorisation fee of a little over €200.

There are almost 10,000 authorised mediators in Romania up to June 2014 and the official list of mediators can be found online at http://www.cmediere.ro/mediatori/.

It is notable that the citizens of EU Member States, the European Economic Area or of the Swiss Confederation, holding a qualification document in the profession of mediator, obtained in one of these states, shall acquire, within the context of the right of establishment, access to the profession in Romania, after recognition of these documents by the Mediation Council, according to Law No 200/2004 on recognition of diplomas and professional qualifications for regulated professions from Romania, as amended and supplemented.

Also, the citizen of a third country, who has graduated from mediator training courses in other countries than Romania or who has acquired the capacity of mediator abroad and wishes to permanently carry on the mediation activity in Romania, shall be allowed access to the mediation profession in Romania under the following terms:

- they present the education title, together with the equivalent certificate issued by the Ministry of Education and Research; and
- they present the contents of the training curriculum covered, including the duration of training and, as applicable, the documents attesting that the capacity of mediator has been acquired.

The Mediation Council shall evaluate the contents of the training curriculum presented, including the duration of training, by comparing the knowledge and skills certified by these documents to the requirements of Romanian law, and it shall decide, if necessary, on access to the profession.

The Mediation Council recognises training programmes in the field of mediation that meet the curricula and the criteria established by the Training Standards in Mediation and the Occupational Standards of the Mediator. In order to develop a capacity to train mediators in Romania, the Mediation Council adopted procedures for accredited specialised trainers in the mediation field and authorised training providers. The accreditation and authorisation procedures are open to all persons proving their capacity as mediators, both from Romania and other countries. In short, an authorised mediator has to prove at least three years of experience and a minimum level of practice (eg a minimum of 25 cases mediated).

Moreover, the Council recognises training programmes in mediation delivered by organisations outside Romania, under the provision to meet the requirements of the procedures, and standards mentioned in the Romanian Mediation Standards.

The common styles of mediation in Romania

The common style of mediation is facilitative in Romania. This is not taken from the Romanian Mediation Law, which does not specifically state anything clear in this matter; it is rather the conclusion of an analysis of the main training formats that were brought to Romania, mostly through facilitative and some through transformative routes.

The law's provisions in this matter are permissive. It is stated that mediation is based on the cooperation between parties and on the use, by the mediator, of certain specific methods and techniques based on communication and negotiation. Also, the methods and techniques used by the mediator must only serve the legitimate interests and objectives pursued by the parties to the conflict. The mediator may not impose a solution on the parties to the conflict under mediation. In addition, the law states that each mediator shall have the right to apply its own model of organisation of the mediation procedure, in compliance with the provisions and principles stated in the Law. No other provisions can be found in the law regarding the priorities between substantive issues and the relation of the parties or regarding the balance between the level of intervention of the mediators regarding the process and the outcome.

As mediation develops in Romania, we expect to see a continuous development of mediation styles. This would be nothing less than normal.

Slovakia

with Renata Dolanska and Slavka Karkoskova

Introduction

Civil and commercial mediation is still in its infancy in Slovakia. There are several Mediation Acts, and several amendments, but the main Act, the Slovak Mediation Act 420, was passed in 2004 and, with amendments, covers civil and commercial mediation. Conciliation (out of the court proceedings) and mediation mean the same thing.

EU Directive (2008)

The 2004 Slovak Mediation Act embodied the EU Directive for cross-border mediations together with the mediation of national cases. There is therefore no distinction and there are no separate requirements for any particular form of mediated cases.

The Slovak Mediation Act (420/2004)

The Act lays down the basic framework law regulating the institution of mediation, its operations, organisation and uses in civil law cases. It deals with disputes arising from civic and legal relations, family relationships and business and working relations. It also deals with cross-border disputes. The Act requires mediators to be registered with the Ministry of Justice.

Definition of mediation and mediator

In Slovakia, there is no professional organisation of mediators which would be established by law. However, there are several voluntary organisations bringing together mediators, eg the Slovak Chamber of Mediators. As their Code states:

- the mediator is there to manage the process, not to make decisions;
- the mediator's role is to create a positive atmosphere and a climate of mutual trust; and
- the mediator must consider carefully any intervention s/he makes.

The mediator is obliged to be independent, impartial and professional and must instruct the parties on any legal rights they may have that could be affected by the mediation. Also to make parties aware of any possible conflict of interest that may exist

The Act states that mediation means extra-judicial action in which the parties settle a dispute, arising from or concerning their contract or other legal relationship, through a mediator.

Voluntary/mandatory

In Slovakia, mediation is a voluntary process but it can only begin when the parties and the mediator have entered into a written agreement. This agreement has to be notarised and then filed with the Central Notary of Deeds before the mediation can start. Under the Act a mediation clause is not binding.

Courts can do no more than challenge parties to try mediation. In fact a law was passed early in 2012 enabling the courts to urge parties to try mediation. But parties can refuse to mediate, in which case the court case will continue. There are no sanctions if the parties refuse.

Confidentiality

Mediation is a confidential process. All parties at the mediation must keep confidential all information that is made available to them in connection with the mediation, unless the parties agree otherwise. Interestingly, if the mediator were to have an action for damages against him or her, the mediator would not be bound by the confidentiality obligation if selective disclosure was necessary for the assessment of the mediator's alleged breach.

Mediation style and procedure

The style adopted by most Slovak mediators is facilitative. The emphasis is on the parties; it is their problem and their solution. They agree with the mediator the style, the framework and the terms of engagement. It is possible for the mediator to offer advice or an opinion, particularly if requested to do so by the parties, but it would not be binding (unless the parties so agreed).

Enforceability of Mediated Settlement Agreements

As with the Agreement to Mediate, the Slovak Mediation Act lays down when the mediation terminates (settlement, written statement by the mediator or written statement by either party). If a settlement is reached and put into writing, the Act qualifies it as a binding written agreement between the parties. However, this is not an enforceable title unless it is:

- drafted as a deed by a notary; or
- approved by a court as a court settlement; or
- made into an arbitral judgement.

The courts have precedence in deciding whether to approve an agreement on mediation as a legal record.

Mediator training, accreditation and post-qualification standards

The Act sets down the requirement of 100 hours' training by a registered provider. There is an exam at the end of the course. There is no performance-based assessment and lawyers are exempt from all but three days' training.

The Act also requires registered mediators to attend a mediation seminar every two years. This is virtually mandatory as the Act requires attendance at two seminars in a five-year period!

Register of mediators

Mediators must be registered with the Ministry of Justice and the Act lays down the criteria for registration, primarily that the candidate must have successfully completed a training course run by a provider that is on the Ministry of Justice register of mediation educational institutions and s/he has to have a master degree education.

Mediator exemption

Mediators are not protected under the Act. There is no special right to refuse to give evidence in court or arbitration.

Conclusion

As in many countries of the EU, the spread of mediation in Slovakia is very slow and many mediators urge for mediation to become mandatory.

Since 1963 conciliation has been an established pre-trial process in certain courts. Conciliation proceedings are regulated as provisional proceedings carried out in court before the start of a legal process. The 1963 Act permits, if the nature of the case allows it, for any court competent to propose such a solution, to attempt an accord through conciliation proceedings, and then to decide whether to approve it if such an accord has been reached. This is rarely used but it could be the way for mediation to be incorporated in the court process.

Slovenia

Simona Mlakar

Place of mediation in Slovenian law

Slovenia implemented Directive 2008/52/EC of the European Parliament and of the Council of 21 May 2008 on certain aspects of mediation in civil and commercial matters in the Mediation in Civil and Commercial Matters Act,[25] in force since 21 June 2008.

The Act (ZMCGZ) applies to mediation in civil, commercial, labour, family and other property relationships with regard to claims that may be freely disposed of and settled by the parties, unless otherwise stipulated for individual disputes by a special law. ZMCGZ does not limit mediation to disputes in the civil sphere, but can also be used for other disputes (for example for relationships with a public element). ZMCGZ applies both to cross-border disputes and domestic disputes and it applies to ad hoc mediations and to institutional providers of mediations (such as court-annexed mediation).

ZMCGZ defines mediation as a proceeding by which the parties voluntarily attempt to reach through a neutral third person (mediator) an amicable resolution of a dispute arising out of or relating to a contractual or other legal relationship, irrespective of whether the term mediation, conciliation, reconciliation, mediation of disputes or other similar term is used for this proceeding (art 3).

Prescription and limitation periods are suspended during mediation. ZMCGZ has provisions on mediator appointment, the conduct of mediation, costs of mediation, etc. It also specifies that the mediator may communicate with parties together or with each party separately, and that they may disclose the substance of the information to any other party to mediation if this benefits the mediation proceedings, unless a party has disclosed the information to the mediator subject to a specific condition that it be kept confidential (art 10). ZMCGZ ensures confidentiality of information and admissibility of evidence (similar to the Civil Procedure Act). ZMCGZ defines the termination of mediation and dispute settlement agreement. The mediator cannot act as an arbitrator in a dispute, unless otherwise agreed by the parties.

Alternative Dispute Resolution in Judicial Matters Act

The Alternative Dispute Resolution in Judicial Matters Act (ZARSS)[26] regulates litigation settlements in the framework of alternative dispute resolution proceedings provided to the parties by the courts on the basis of this Act. This means that it is not possible to apply ZARSS when a lawsuit, an appeal or a proposal is not filed in court.

ZARSS is applied in disputes arising from commercial, labour, family and other civil relationships with regard to claims which may be freely disposed of and settled by the parties, unless otherwise stipulated for individual disputes by a special law. ZARSS does not apply to social disputes. Until a new legal code on family law is adopted in Slovenia, ZARSS also applies to family disputes.

County, district, regional, labour and high courts, as well as the high labour and social affairs court, enable ADR by accepting and implementing the alternative dispute resolution programme. In addition to mediation, courts can also introduce

---

25 (ZMCGZ), Official Gazette of the Republic of Slovenia, No 56/2008.
26 Official Gazette of the Republic of Slovenia, No 97/09 and 40/12 (ZUJF) in force since 15 June 2010 (ZARSS).

other forms of ADR, but until 2014 only mediation was offered to the parties. Courts may adopt and implement the ADR programme as an activity organised directly at a court (court-annexed programme) or they may carry out the alternative settlement of disputes, awarding this task to a suitable provider of ADR with whom they conclude a contract (court-connected programme). In practice all courts have their own court-annexed programme and some courts co-operate with each other. In court-annexed programmes, it is the court that manages the register of mediators. In court-connected programmes, the list of mediators is drawn up and compiled by the programme provider.

The courts refer the parties to mediation in each case, unless the judge deems this inappropriate for a particular case. The court of first instance suspends court proceedings for up to three months if parties agree to start a mediation. During this period the parties have the possibility of solving their dispute with a mediator. This period may be extended with the parties' consent, but only exceptionally.

In all court disputes where ZARSS is applied and where the State is a party, the State Attorney's Office is obliged to give consent for mediation when this is appropriate, given the circumstances of the case. If the State Attorney's Office deems that unsuitable, it must submit a reasoned proposal to the Government of the Republic of Slovenia to make a decision.

The Civil Procedure Act regulates ADR (for out-of-court mediations and for court-annexed mediations) in relation to a settlement hearing, where court proceedings are suspended for up to three months if parties agree to solve their dispute with any form of ADR.

Several other laws implement dispute resolution with the help of a neutral third person in their special field, with subsidiary use of ZMCGZ: the Employment Relationships Act, the Patient Rights Act and Rules on Mediation in Healthcare, the Financial Operations, Insolvency Proceedings and Compulsory Dissolution Act, the Copyright and Related Rights Act, the Financial Instruments Market Act, the Insurance Act, the Investment Funds and Management Companies Act and the Electronic Communications Act.

Who are mediators?

Mediation under the Civil and Commercial Matters Act does not stipulate any necessary mediator qualifications. Article 3 of this Act defines a mediator as a third person that is asked to and accepted to conduct a mediation, regardless of their title or occupation or the way they were appointed or asked to conduct mediation. One or more mediators can conduct mediation. The parties are free to choose the mediator they consider to be qualified for their dispute.

In contrast, there is a list of requirements for mediators who are part of the court programme (court-annexed or court-connected), defined in Alternative Dispute Resolution in the Judicial Matters Act and Rules on Mediators in ADR Programmes of the Courts (Official Gazette of the Republic of Slovenia, Nos 22/2010 and 35/13).

Each court has a list of registered mediators that meet the following criteria:
- have full legal capacity;

- no final judgment was passed to find them guilty of any deliberately committed criminal offence prosecuted ex officio;
- have completed at least the first cycle of a study programme, worth a minimum of 180 credits (ECTS); and
- can verify having obtained mediation training prescribed in the Rules on Mediators in Courts' Programmes.

According to art 2(3) of the Rules, mediators working at court-annexed or court-connected mediation must be lawyers, judges, notaries or other legal professionals who have passed the Slovenian Bar Examination. In complex and difficult family mediations, a mediator has an option to co-mediate with another mediator, who has professional skills and knowledge of psychology or other similar field (such as a sociologist or social worker).

Style of mediators

Mediators are not under legal obligation to declare or describe their mediation style.

The fact that court-annexed mediation is predominantly conducted by judges and lawyers is reflected in their style of mediation. Mostly they use a facilitative and evaluative approach and they adjust it to the needs of a specific case and the clients.

Out-of-court mediations are more colourful in style – therefore mediators also use a transformative style (especially with family mediations, healthcare mediations, etc.) Transformative style is predominantly used to conduct a marriage-counselling interview at Centres for Social Work.

Pursuant to the Marriage and Family Relations Act, Centres for Social Work are entitled to conduct a marriage-counselling interview after receiving the proposal for an agreed divorce or the filing of a suit for divorce from the court.

Although the Marriage and Family Relations Act does not call this marriage-counselling interview mediation, it is conducted in the same way, because lawyers and social workers at the Centres for Social Work follow mediation principles and use mediation techniques and skills. The Centre for Social Work notifies the court on the marriage-counselling interview. In those cases the transformative style of mediation is predominantly used.

The regulations and training that apply

Pursuant to art 22 of the Rules on Mediators in ADR Programmes of the Courts, applicants must attend at least 40 45-minute training sessions, comprising theoretical lectures (conflict theory, psychology, bargaining theory, legal framework, etc) and practical experience, gained by mediating a simulated dispute. Training also includes a final examination and only if an applicant's knowledge is sufficient can he or she successfully conclude mediation training. Mediation training is organised by the Judicial Training Centre as part of the Ministry of Justice.

Other providers also organise basic mediation trainings: the Association of Mediators of Slovenia (64 45-minute training sessions) and private organisations (at least 100 45-minute training sessions and additional 100 or more hours for specific field of mediation).

In addition to the initial basic mediation training, registered mediators who are part of the court programme must also regularly attend further mediation training (organised by the Judicial Training Centre and other providers) in order to enhance and develop their professional skills. Registered mediators are obliged to attend at least one day of advanced mediation training, organised by Judicial Training Centre and one day of advanced mediation training, seminar or conference, organised by other domestic or foreign providers every calendar year.

Pursuant to art 25 of the Rules, a registered mediator is obliged to conduct at least 10 mediations yearly.

Spain

Mari Cruz Taboada

When the judges are frustrated with the judicial system, there is no doubt that change is required. A recent article in *Iberian Lawyer* magazine by judge Pascual Ortuño who represents an association of judges pro Mediation, highlighted that the current justice system in Spain is not adequate for the current social and commercial needs.

Spain enacted a law in July 2012 which enforced the 2008 EU Directive on Mediation and ADR for civil and commercial matters, which was not regulated in detail until December 2013.

This is an important step that brought up lots of different reactions from the different power-groups that are now involved in conflict resolution. The main criticism comes from corporate lawyers who question whether Spain has enough trained and experienced mediators to handle complex disputes.

However, the general feeling is that the new law relates to the current times, and responds to an overloaded judicial system unable to cope with the rising number of claims in times where the Government is decreasing the investment to the justice system and cutting down jobs.

Voluntary/mandatory mediation

When one looks at other countries and wonders what makes mediation successful, there is a common understanding that in the corporate world judges must have a key role in referring cases to mediation in order to incentivise users to take advantage of the alternative dispute resolution mechanisms.

The new Spanish Act, however, does not give a mandate but recommendations. The principle of voluntariness is paramount in mediation, with which I could not agree more, but both lawyers and clients must have the opportunity and responsibility to try reaching pre-agreements before going to court. It is a matter of taking control over the possible outcome and compromising.

With the current system, if an individual or a company currently wants to use mediation it is not clear where to go, how much this process will cost, who the mediators are and what are their credentials. To make the mediation process accessible, these questions must be answered immediately.

Credible institutions

Since the beginning of 2014 the legal community in Spain has started to develop mediation interest groups in key institutions able to provide mediation awareness and services.

The first ones to incorporate a legal framework with capacity to offer mediation services have been the arbitration courts amongst others in Madrid, Barcelona or Valencia.

Newly created Mediation Associations have also been set up around Spain, including a wide range of professionals such as notaries, lawyers, social workers, psychologist and judges that have developed specialist awareness sessions, training and are planning to offer mediation services.

The new regulation does not deal with mediator training properly. Some of the regional governments (Comunidades Autonomas) through their Justice Departments have also set up a guide with registered mediators. In order to join those lists there are a set criteria to follow, but often proven 'real' experience is not included. To be a mediator and enroll in an official list it is enough to have a college degree and have further training in the field for 100 hours.

Universities around the country, have found a great opportunity in the new regulation to offer new executive programmes with a wider offering of postgraduate diplomas to train students on mediation skills and are also developing their own list of accredited mediators.

While the lists of registered mediators are increasing, the confidence in using the service is still not there.

Confidence

Anyone that understands mediation is aware that the skills and ability to mediate is not a question of theory but practical experience, understanding of negotiation and capacity to lead and gain the parties' confidence.

As in Spain there are not yet many professionals with experience in commercial mediation, some have chosen to create 'elite' groups among the most prestigious professionals. The problem is that being the best lawyer or judge, does not make you an excellent mediator.

Article 5 of the Act relates to mediation institutions and the reading is clear; any organised group can develop a mediation service. Some people believe that the law should have been more specific, but in the corporate world confidence is not about strict standards but high level of service and excellence.

In a market where 'word of mouth' is the best reference, the key is to make sure that the diverse offering does not affect negatively on the reputation of mediation. In particular, take into account that companies feel uneasy investing in the 'unknown'.

iIn the latest research with over 200 General Counsel, developed by *Iberian Lawyer*, corporate users highlighted that litigation and disputes are their number one concern and the area of highest legal spend. Considering that the average legal spend is €2m a year, over 75 per cent is spent on litigation or dispute management.

Corporate in-house lawyers confirm that their main experience of mediation has been in disputes outside Spain and often when the conflict is in an emerging country where they do not trust the legal system or when the legal system has mediation as mandatory. So, after all, the corporate in-house lawyers have confidence in the Spanish legal system, which is neutral and independent, and they consider that if they used mediation and it failed to settle, they would have a negative result when reporting to their CEOs.

The role of lawyers in mediation

Mediation is a form of 'assisted negotiation' which requires compromise to reach agreements, but can we say that every conflict is linked to a legal matter? Who has the responsibility to negotiate business deals? Have lawyers the creative and business mind to develop negotiation processes that can add value to their company?

The United States, Canada, Australia and the United Kingdom have already had experience of mediation for long time and have identified the key profile of an effective mediator. The trend is to move away from strict criteria, whether facilitative or directive, and allow flexibility in the process to adapt to the client requirements.

From a user perspective there is one element that is key. The mediation process needs to have the main decision makers involved. Those individuals can understand the business challenges and the opportunities, and the lawyers are advisers that will protect and guide decisions from a legal perspective.

Mediation fees

As in any service provision, mediators in Spain have looked at financial arrangements that would give clients confidence to use the service without much initial investment. The models used have been a fixed fee or retainer, a low fee with a success fee or a success fees agreement. This area has not been regulated by the new law. Therefore, the combination of users' lack of confidence in mediation with the eagerness from mediators to have some experience has had an effect on the fees, with many mediators offering services almost for free.

Endorsement

A handicap for consolidating mediation may also be the reluctance of some lawyers to endorse mediation for fear of possible work loss. Lawyers are suffering from client pressure on legal fees, so an early settlement might not be always in *their* benefit.

Spain's Justice Minister, Señor Gallardon, has not only recently reduced the budget for legal aid but enacted a new law which adds some extra costs when litigating, which it is justified as a way of reducing the trend to claim systematically and try to find agreements outside court.

That means that those with no access to legal aid – the vast majority of the population and businesses – will have to think twice before choosing to go to court. For some, this is an infringement on the right to access to justice, but hopefully alternative dispute resolution methods will be ready to respond to a high percentage of those disputes.

For lawyers, mediation is an opportunity to show clients their ability to add some extra value in managing disputes. However they need to understand clearly how the process works and to make the most without becoming an obstacle to the continuity of business activity.

As the Nobel Peace Price winner Aung San Suu Kyi said: 'If you want to bring an end to long-standing conflict, you have to be prepared to compromise'. The question is whether businesses are ready to compromise to bring disputes to an end.

Sweden

Eric Runesson

For at least the last 100 years, Swedish culture and society has been characterised as quite homogenous in the sense that societal goals and values were shared among almost all actors. The Swedish labour market has for example been known as a peaceful place where the parties have strived to reach consensus and help to build 'the People's Home' (*folkhemmet*). Mediation has not really been on the agenda. Contentious matters have instead to a large extent been resolved in traditional negotiations. This also goes for legal disputes. Legal counsel have lived in a pretty intimate world where they to a large extent have been repeat players. Some reports show that approximately 80 per cent of all cases have settled before the final hearing.

However, for a couple of decades the homogenous culture has given way to heterogeneity. Many different values have to be balanced against each other. As a consequence, conflicts appear as more common or more difficult to resolve.

By an amendment in 1987 to the Code of Procedure, courts were explicitly instructed to encourage settlement and were given the opportunity to arrange for court mediation, subject to consent by the parties. Court-assisted settlement negotiations became usual. In some cases the negotiations in fact became mediations where the parties had caucuses with the judge. Some courts started the practice of arranging formal mediations by having a judge (not sitting in on the case if no settlement was reached) act as a mediator. These court mediations were often of an evaluative nature and few of the judges acting as mediators had any training. The form and nature of court mediations have to a large extent coloured the understanding within the Swedish legal community of what mediation is. It should be added that in some specific areas of law, there have been specific statutory provisions on mediation, eg certain labour law disputes, tenancy disputes and copyright disputes involving collection societies.

In 1999 the Stockholm Chamber of Commerce decided to form the Mediation Institute of the Stockholm Chamber of Commerce as a sister to the much more known Arbitration Institute of the Stockholm Chamber of Commerce. The Mediation Institute was set up as a service to the business community. The Mediation Institute adopted Model Mediation Rules to facilitate mediation agreements and went out to inform about mediation as something more than the traditional court mediation, pointing out the advantages that mediation offered as a first step in any commercial dispute. The Mediation Institute also started to educate a number of interested lawyers as mediators in cooperation with many courts in the Stockholm area. A similar development has been seen in Gothenburg.

It seems that the activities of the Mediation Institute have brought about increased awareness that mediation might be a viable tool for resolving commercial disputes. The message has been that legal counsel do not have to be bad negotiators if they cannot settle in traditional bilateral negotiations. It is just that some negotiations require a neutral to do away with a natural unwillingness to share information, which is a prerequisite to an interest-based outcome.

In 2011, following EU Directive 2008/52/EC, Sweden enacted the Act on Mediation in Certain Civil Law Disputes (Lag 2011:860 om medling i vissa privaträttsliga tvister). The Act and its preparatory works has clarified many of the legal aspects of mediation under Swedish law, inter alia questions on confidentiality and on limitations in the right to invoke what has occurred in a mediation during a subsequent court proceeding. The Act also makes it clear that the initiation of mediation leads to a suspension of statutory limitations and clarifies that a mediation agreement is not an obstacle to litigation or arbitration.

In 2013, the Mediation Institute of the Stockholm Chamber of Commerce merged with its sister, the Arbitration Institute. The merger signifies that different methods for dispute resolution are not incompatible with one another but may be used as complementary options. Revised mediation rules have also been adopted in view of the 2011 Act and the experiences gained since 1999.

If I should try to summarise how mediation today is seen in large parts of the legal community, it can be said that mediation is seen as a form of settlement negotiation with the participation of an independent and impartial third party. Mediation is based on voluntary participation. Each party may at any time terminate the negotiation and chose to initiate or continue a court proceeding or arbitration. The role of the mediator is to facilitate the negotiation process and to provide that the parties make informed decisions, irrespective of whether the decision is to settle or continue the dispute in court or before an arbitral tribunal.

Mediation may be considered at an early or late stage of the dispute. The early mediation effort may be advisable as the dispute resolution costs may still be low at this stage and considering that the parties in the mediation may agree on a structure for the dispute that makes a subsequent litigation more efficient in case a settlement is not reached. Mediation at a late stage of the dispute may be preferred as the parties at that time may be in a better position to evaluate the uncertainties in the legal assessment of the dispute that gradually emerges.

A mediation often commences with each party submitting a brief summary of the dispute to the mediator. The parties, together with counsel, will thereafter meet with the mediator. The parties may at that time further present their case. Typically, the mediation continues with the mediator conferring with each party separately and may, or may not, subsequently reconvene in joint meetings with the parties. The information that has been provided in the separate meetings is confidential unless a party authorises the mediator to share the information with the other party. Through the separate deliberations with each party the mediator will get an understanding of the actual scope of possible agreements between the parties and may in this way assist the parties to increasingly focus the negotiation.

A mediation which is terminated without a settlement may have the effect of concentrating the dispute with costs-saving benefits as a result. A mediator will typically not provide his or her own assessment of the substantial issues in dispute. Further, a mediator will in general not suggest what a settlement may contain. However, a mediator may do so if both parties ask the mediator to suggest a settlement and the mediator agree to do so.

Switzerland

Jeremy Lack

Outline of civil and commercial mediation in Switzerland

Switzerland is a country with a rich tradition of mediation and neutrality, going back to its patron saint, Nicolas de Flue, who mediated a peace agreement at the Diet of Stans in 1481 between warring states, enabling the states of Fribourg and Soleure to join the Swiss Confederation. It has been a preferred venue for hosting international arbitrations for over 100 years, both institutional and ad-hoc. Today, Switzerland consists of 26 cantons, each of which had its own rules of civil procedure until as recently as 1 January 2011, when a new Swiss Code of Civil Procedure (CPC) came into effect and recognised mediation as a form of judicial proceedings at a national level in most civil and commercial cases.[27] Switzerland is also widely recognised as a neutral country in international public affairs. The presence of the United Nations, the International Committee of the Red Cross, and many international governmental and non-governmental organisations in the canton of Geneva have contributed to an international vision of Switzerland as a centre for peaceful and amicable dispute resolution, including arbitration, conciliation and mediation. In the international commercial sector, Switzerland is well known for its adherence to principles of private international law, confidentiality, neutrality and respect for privity of contract. The Swiss Chambers Arbitration Institution, a body set up by the Swiss Chambers of Commerce Association for Arbitration and Mediation (consisting of the cantonal Chambers of Commerce of Basel, Bern, Geneva, Neuchâtel, Ticino (Lugano), Vaud (Lausanne) and Zurich), administers a modern and widely-used international set of dispute resolution rules, the Swiss Rules of International Arbitration (SRIA) and the Swiss Rules of Commercial Mediation (SRCM, jointly referred to as the Swiss ADR Rules), which provide links between mediation and arbitration. Furthermore, the World Intellectual Property Organisation (WIPO), a

---

27 This paper focuses primarily on civil and commercial mediation in Switzerland. For a more detailed analysis of mediation, comparing it to other countries, see M Schonewille and F Schonewille (eds.), *The Variegated Landscape of Mediation: A Comparative Study of Mediation Regulation and Practices in Europe and the World* (Eleven Publishing, 2014). For an official translation of the Swiss Code of Civil Procedure in English, see: http://www.admin.ch/ch/e/rs/272/index.html.

United-Nations agency, offers and administers a broad range of international ADR services, including arbitration, mediation and expert determination. Although its remit relates primarily to cross-border intellectual property disputes, WIPO's ADR rules can be used for any type of commercial dispute and have been approved by its 187 member states. In the field of international sports, the Court of Arbitration for Sports (CAS/TAS) based in Lausanne likewise offers both mediation and arbitration services, and has expressed a growing interest in the use of mediation (as is also the case for the International Olympic Committee, also located in Lausanne). Many other international ADR organizations, such as the World Trade Organisation (WTO), the International Chamber of Commerce (ICC), and the International Centre for Dispute Resolution (ICDR) offer ADR proceedings in Switzerland, with Geneva and Zurich ranking consistently among the most popular venues for international ADR proceedings. Finally, GTSA, the main international commodity trading association in Switzerland, has also recently created a new dispute resolution service with the Geneva Chamber of Commerce and Industry, Alternative Dispute Resolution for Commodity Trading, Shipping and Trade Finance (ACT), which offers mediation and arbitration services.

At a domestic level, Switzerland has four leading associations that provide mediation services and lists of certified mediators for civil and commercial mediations. They are:

- the Swiss Chamber of Commercial Mediation (CSMC/SKWM/SCCM), which is the leading organisation in commercial mediation;
- the Swiss Federation of Mediation Associations (FSM/SDM);
- the Swiss Association for Mediation (SVM/ASM); and
- the Swiss Bar Association, which certifies Swiss lawyers as mediators (SAV/FSA).

Each of these bodies has developed its own set of specialities, accreditation rules and continuing professional development requirements, which set varying best practices, standards and codes of conduct around the country. Some cantons (eg, Fribourg, Geneva and Vaud) also provide a local cantonal registry of certified mediators, who have to swear an oath of office and are accountable to a local supervisory court or commission. The leading association for commercial mediations is CSMC/SKWM/SCCM, which has regional branches in Central Switzerland, Western Switzerland (Suisse Romande), Bern, Ticino and Zurich and cooperates closely with the Swiss chambers of commerce in promoting and implementing the Swiss ADR Rules.

All in all, Switzerland continues to be an active player in the field of civil and commercial mediation, both domestically and internationally.

The current legal status of mediation in Switzerland

At an international level, Switzerland's private and public international laws are highly prized in international commercial dispute resolution circles, leading to the choice of Geneva, Zurich or Lausanne for many international commercial disputes, including for investor-state disputes under the rules of the International Centre for Settlement of Investment Disputes (ICSID). The country's ADR institutions also use updated state of the art rules, which are all compatible with the latest United

Nations Commission on International Trade Law (UNCITRAL) arbitration and conciliation rules.

At a domestic level, the CPC came into effect on 1 January 2011, harmonising the various disparate cantonal approaches to civil and commercial mediation that existed until then. The CPC recognises and distinguishes between three dispute resolution procedures as an alternative to adjudication by a national court. They are:

- arbitration;
- conciliation; and
- mediation.

Arbitration is a binding and evaluative ADR process that is dealt with separately under Part 3 of the CPC, and falls outside the scope of this chapter. Conciliation and mediation, however, are arguably both forms of 'mediation' as defined by art 3 of EU Directive No 2008/52/EC on civil and commercial mediation (the EU Directive). They are dealt with together under Part 2 of the CPC and have been referred to as (non-identical) twin sisters. The distinction between conciliation and mediation is difficult to grasp, as in many languages and countries the two terms are used synonymously. The CPC itself does not clearly distinguish between them either. Both procedures, however, fall within the definition of 'mediation' at art 3 of the EU Directive insofar as they involve a process:

> 'whereby two or more parties to a dispute attempt by themselves, on a voluntary basis, to reach an agreement on the settlement of their dispute with the assistance of a [neutral third party]'.

The primary difference between these two processes, is who the neutral third party will be, and related consequences as described below.

Conciliation is covered by 'Title I: Attempt at Conciliation' under arts 197–212 CPC. The 'conciliation authority' consists of one or more magistrates who are not responsible for the final decision in the matter. The goal of the conciliation authority is defined as follows:

> 'The conciliation authority shall attempt to reconcile the parties in an informal manner. If it helps to resolve the dispute, a settlement may also include contentious matters that are not part of the proceedings.'

In disputes relating to property leases and gender discrimination, the conciliation authority consists of several magistrates who are likely to provide legal advice and their opinions to the parties. Conciliation proceedings are a compulsory prior step in most civil and commercial legal proceedings. In principle, a case will not be heard by a tribunal before an attempt to conciliate has first occurred. There are many exceptions to this principle, however, and a prior obligation to conciliate may also be waived in some instances. Given the fact that the conciliator is a magistrate (who may or may not have had mediation training), a conciliation tends to be a non-binding evaluative process that seldom lasts for more than one hour, although subsequent sessions may be agreed to. The parties must appear in person at the conciliation hearing and need not be accompanied by a lawyer.

The proceedings are not public and the parties' statements may not be recorded or used in subsequent court proceedings. The conciliation authority will normally use the law as a basis to assist the parties in trying to reach an amicable agreement based on an application of legal reasoning, whereby the outcome is based on the findings of fact and law that a tribunal is likely to make. In certain cases the conciliation authority can give a proposed judgment (which can be rejected), or it can even issue a binding decision in certain small claims cases. Although the parties' statements to the conciliation authority are confidential, a proposed judgment or decision (if one is given) may be subsequently used. If an agreement is reached pursuant to a conciliation, the terms of the settlement are recorded by the conciliation authority and the record of settlement has the effect of a binding court decision. It is normal (and even expected) for a conciliator to provide a non-binding opinion and to help the parties to understand what the dispositive issues of the case are likely to be, and who will have the burden of proving what. Although caucusing is not mentioned in the CPC, and is arguably not expressly forbidden, it is unlikely that a conciliation authority would ever consent to meet with one of the parties in private, as it would likely be deemed to be in violation of the *audi alteram partem* rule whereby the other party should always have the right to be present to contest what is presented to a judge, even if the purpose of the caucus would be to do reality testing that would be helpful to the absent party. As a result, a conciliation is not quite equivalent to an evaluative mediation process, although there are clear similarities between these two types or proceedings.

Mediation is covered by 'Title II: Mediation' under arts 213–18 CPC. It is the 'poor' twin sister to conciliation to the extent that there are only six articles in the CPC relating to mediation, and the process is only available if the parties request it as an alternative to a conciliation procedure. That being said, this may also be viewed as a positive thing, giving more strength and flexibility to parties wishing to organise their own private form of mediation, with any mediator of their choice. The court itself may recommend mediation to the parties at any time, or even summon them in family matters involving children, and the parties may also make a joint request for mediation at any time. Unlike conciliation, where the conciliation authority summons the parties and is responsible for organising and conducting a conciliation, the parties are responsible for organising and conducting their own mediation proceedings as they wish. As in conciliation, mediation proceedings are confidential and are kept separate both from the conciliation authority and the court. The statements of the parties may not be used in court proceedings. If a settlement agreement has been reached through such a mediation process, the parties may request that it be approved by the court, in which case the approved agreement will have the same effect as a legally binding decision by the court. Finally, unlike conciliation, where the costs are included in the courts fees, the parties bear themselves the costs of any mediation proceedings they may agree to. The aforementioned provisions relate to court-related mediations. If a mediation is initiated outside of court proceedings altogether (ie without any conciliation proceedings or a court action having already commenced), the provisions of Title II do not apply, and the mediation is not automatically protected by operation of the CPC. It will be subject to any specific contractual or local cantonal provisions that may apply. A settlement agreement that is reached by a mediation outside of court proceedings may still become legally enforceable if it is ratified by the court having personal and subject-matter over the dispute, or if it is converted into an Official Record (in French a *Titre authentique* and in German an Öffentliche Urkunde) under Part 2, Title 10, Chapter 2 of the CPC (arts 347–52), by having it notarised before a public notary. An Official Record is, however, subject to judicial review if there is an objection to its execution. A mediation (whether pursuant to court proceedings or private) can be run in any way that the parties deem fit. (See below).

Although the distinction between mediation and conciliation is thus somewhat unclear, the Federal Council, when publishing the first draft of the CPC, defined mediation in an official communication dated 28 June 2006. Swiss ADR Rules provide some clarification by defining mediation as follows:

> 'Mediation is an *extrajudicial* process. It is essentially characterized by the intervention of a neutral and independent third person. In this way, it resembles classical conciliation. However, whereas an attempt at conciliation is based on an informal negotiation, mediation follows a more formal structure. Unlike the authority of conciliation, the parties find themselves in a *horizontal* relationship with the mediator. Thus, this person does not have any decision-making powers, which also distinguishes mediation from arbitration.'

The Swiss Chambers Arbitration Institution of the Swiss chambers of commerce distinguish mediation from other ADR proceedings as follows:

> 'Mediation is an alternative method of dispute resolution whereby two or more parties ask a neutral third party, the mediator, to assist them in settling a dispute or in avoiding future conflicts. The mediator facilitates the exchange of opinions between the parties and encourages them to explore solutions that are acceptable to all the participants. Unlike an expert the mediator does not offer his or her own views nor make proposals like a conciliator, and unlike an arbitrator he or she does not render an award.'

The major unspoken differences between mediation and conciliation, however, are:

- a typical mediation session will last at least several hours, if not several half days or full days;
- a mediator is unlikely to rely only on norms or a legal reasoning to shape or propose a solution;
- a mediator will often meet with the parties separately and use caucuses or pre-caucuses not to do reality testing (although this is possible) but to coach the parties as to what they could do in joint sessions; and
- a mediator will usually work with the parties to first help them to identify their subjective interests looking to the future (as opposed to their positions), and to generate options based on these interests that could result in long-lasting and viable settlements that will address the parties' interests, rather than seek a compromise between conflicting positions.

The extent and use of mediation in Switzerland

Given that the CPC is still relatively new in Switzerland and that all mediation proceedings are confidential, there are limited statistics on the use of mediation, or on the use of mediation as opposed to conciliation in Switzerland. To the extent that mediation and conciliation are both enshrined in the CPC and that Switzerland is routinely listed as a venue for international ADR proceedings, the use of mediation (in its broadest EU Directive sense) is quite prevalent and continues to grow. As is the case in many other countries, Swiss ADR institutions report a settlement rate of 70–80 per cent for mediation, although a lower settlement rate for conciliation, which varies from canton-to-canton depending on the training that the conciliation authorities will have received. Conciliation is practised in the majority of commercial and civil cases that are pending before the courts. It is believed that extra-judicial mediation (as opposed to conciliation), whether ad-hoc or using private institutional rules is still the exception rather than the norm. Its use has been growing in the last few years, however, and lawyers and arbitrators are beginning to take a growing interest in this form of ADR process, including mediation clauses in an increasing number of agreements.

At a cantonal level, mediation (as opposed to conciliation) is also being increasingly discussed and promoted. Argovie, Fribourg, Geneva, Glaris, Grison, Jura, Neuchatel, St. Gallen, Tessin, Valais, Vaud and Zurich, have all passed supplementary cantonal legislation promoting the use of mediation in civil, criminal and/or administrative disputes. Since 2011, cantonal courts are also increasingly encouraging the use of mediation in family and juvenile courts. As a further sign of the continuing growth of mediation at a local level in Switzerland, the canton of Geneva (which was one of the first to adopt a cantonal law on civil mediation), adopted a new Constitution by popular referendum on 14 October 2012, which contains three mediation provisions:

- the primary means for resolving labour union disputes in the canton in the future will be negotiation and mediation;
- a new independent mediation body will be appointed to handle all administrative disputes; and
- the judiciary and the state must both encourage the use of mediation and other modes of dispute resolution in the future.

Several cantonal universities (eg Geneva, Lausanne, Neuchatel) are also beginning to teach mediation and mediation advocacy. The Neuchatel chapter of the Swiss Academy of Magistrates is teaching mediation to judges, and the Geneva Bar has recently created a vocational advocacy programme for trainees (ECAV), which contains a compulsory 10-hour module on mediation and mediation advocacy for anyone wishing to become a lawyer. From all of these recent initiatives, it appears that the use of mediation in Switzerland is likely to continue to grow at a cantonal and federal level in the coming years.

Common styles of mediation

Given the variety of cantonal approaches that used to exist with respect to conciliation, and the fact that Switzerland is heavily influenced by its neighbouring countries (ie France, Germany, Italy, and Austria) as well as the Swiss tendency to look at other leading jurisdictions in new fields (eg the Netherlands, Australia, Canada, the United States, England and Scotland, when it comes to mediation), it is difficult to speak of one common style of mediation. There is already confusion between conciliation (which is similar to, but not the same as, evaluative mediation), and mediation. All of the Swiss certifying bodies have strict Continuing Professional Development requirements, and over the course of time, most Swiss mediators will have been exposed to many different types of mediation, ranging from facilitative to evaluative, transformative, spiritual, appreciative, solution-focused, constellation-based, systemic-oriented, caucus-based, non-caucus based, etc. Mediations can be ad hoc or institutional (eg using the Swiss Mediation Rules, WIPO, ICC, ICDR, ACT, etc.) Even then, most mediation rules leave the mediator and the parties to their own devices. The parties are free to appoint whomever they wish as their mediator, and it is possible for the parties to appoint a person without any mediation or legal training, unless there are additional local cantonal laws regulating who may act as a mediator. This variation in style is also due to the fact that many Swiss mediators are also used to acting as conciliators and/or as arbitrators, and make a clear distinction between these three forms of ADR. The use of co-mediation and hybrid processes (combining the use of different ADR processes sequentially, in parallel or as part of integrated proceedings, together with mediation) is common in Switzerland, and it is not uncommon for an arbitral tribunal to swap hats and act as a conciliation authority (albeit without caucuses), although not as a mediator. Switzerland has been and continues to be a crossroads where many forms of mediation meet and mix, and where mediators are encouraged to adapt the style of mediation to each case, following a discussion with the parties about their procedural options and preferences, treating the process itself as part of the problem to be jointly solved by the parties, understanding the impact that process can have on the outcomes, and the tendency of conflicts to escalate if the process is not designed to have anti-escalation measures.

United Kingdom with Scotland

England and Wales

David Miles

In the beginning

In 1994, the English Commercial Court introduced a Practice Direction encouraging parties to resolve their disputes by ADR. See Practice Statement (Commercial Cases: Alternative Dispute Resolution) (Cresswell J [1994] 1All ER 34).

In the mid-1990s Lord Woolf was tasked to produce a report on civil procedure in England and Wales. His report was entitled 'Access to Justice'. This led to the introduction of the Civil Procedure Rules in 1998. The rules set out an overriding objective, namely to enable the Court to deal with cases justly. The Court was given a duty actively to manage cases. Active case management included 'encouraging the parties to use an alternative dispute resolution procedure if the Court considers that appropriate, and facilitating the use of such procedure'.

There was much speculation as to the extent of the effect of this objective. The landmark case in 2002 was *Dunnett v Railtrack* which concerned a claimant who had lost at first instance and who had applied for permission to appeal to the Court of Appeal. The Court had suggested ADR. Railtrack rejected the suggestion out of hand. The claimant lost. Railtrack were not awarded their costs. In rejecting Railtrack's application for costs, the Court said:

> 'Skilled mediators are now able to achieve results satisfactory to both parties in many cases which are quite beyond the power of lawyers and Courts

to achieve. This Court has knowledge of cases where intense feelings have arisen, for instance in relation to clinical negligence claims. But when the parties are brought together on neutral soil with a skilled mediator to help them resolve their differences, it may very well be that the mediator is able to achieve a result by which the parties shake hands at the end of the day and feel that they have gone away having settled the dispute on terms with which they are happy to live. The mediator may be able to provide solutions which are beyond the powers of the Court to provide.

It is to be hoped that any publicity given to this part of the Judgment of the Court will draw attention of lawyers to their duties to further the overriding objective in the way that is set out in Part 1 of the Rules and to the possibility that, if they turn down out of hand the chance of ADR, when suggested by the Court, as happened on this occasion, they may have to face uncomfortable cost consequences'.

The courts today

Dunnett v Railtrack was followed two years later by *Halsey v Milton Keynes General NHS Trust*. The claimant's solicitor had written to the Trust before issuing proceedings seeking costs and damages and also proposing mediation. The Trust refused to mediate on the grounds that it was 'an unnecessary waste of both costs and resources'. The Court of Appeal, in a judgment given by the present Master of the Rolls, took the opportunity to review the whole approach to mediation in the English Courts and identified six factors which might be relevant in testing out the appropriateness of mediation. They consisted of:

(1) the nature of the dispute;

(2) the merits of the case;

(3) other methods of settlement that had been attempted;

(4) the cost of mediation would be disproportionately high;

(5) delay; and

(6) whether mediation had reasonable prospect of success.

Some commentators observed that the *Halsey* case was a retreat from the Court's encouragement of mediation. Doubts were also expressed in high judicial circles that the decision may need reviewing. In any event, the Courts said:

'The value and importance of ADR has been established within a remarkably short time. All members of the legal profession who conduct litigation should now routinely consider with their clients whether their disputes are suitable for ADR'.

This is not to say that the courts will penalise every party who refuses to mediate. There are circumstances where the courts feel that it is reasonable for a party to reject mediation. In *Hurst v Leeming*, the case involved a litigant in person who had failed throughout. In rejecting the application for the refusing party to be penalised in costs, the Court said:

'By reason of the character and attitude of Mr Hurst, mediation had no real prospect of getting anywhere. That is not a view which is easily sustainable in any case, but on the facts of this case, it is sustained'.

'Refusal is a high risk to take. But if the Court finds that there was a real prospect (of mediation success) a party refusing to proceed to mediation may, as I have already said, be severely penalised. Further, the hurdle in the way of a party refusing to proceed to mediation on this ground is high, for in making this subjective assessment of the prospects of mediation, the starting point must surely be the fact that the mediation process itself can and does often bring about a more sensible and conciliatory attitude on the part of the parties than might otherwise be expected to prevail before the mediation, and may produce a recognition of the strengths and weaknesses by each party of his own case and that of his opponent, and a willingness to accept the give and the take essential to a successful mediation. What appears to be incapable of mediation before the mediation process begins often proves capable of satisfactory resolution later'.

Who are the mediators?

When ADR was first introduced into the United States, the only mediators were either retired judges (who saw it as some sort of pension arrangement) or lawyers. This was not the case in the United Kingdom. When the ADR Group was formed, they only trained solicitors. The Centre for Effective Dispute Resolution (CEDR), trained both lawyers and non-lawyers.

In the early days, the non-lawyers tended to be from another technical discipline, such as architecture, engineering, quantity surveying and accountancy. This has now broadened to the extent that mediators are trained from all walks of life.

In 2006, the Technology and Construction Court piloted a scheme whereby the judges would assist the parties to try and reach a settlement. If no settlement was reached, then the judge would make a non-binding recommendation which it was open to the parties to accept or reject. If the recommendation was rejected or settlement was not reached, then the case would be assigned to another judge to try.

The procedure gave rise to a lot of criticism from the mediation community. It was pointed out that the judges' function was to try the case. They were not trained mediators. Furthermore, the judges would approach the dispute from a strictly legal point of view. The procedure would only be triggered at a case management conference. Often witness statements and expert reports had been exchanged, which meant that by the time the process was implemented, the parties had incurred a significant amount of costs.

There was also a concern about the preservation of confidentiality. Whilst the process involved the transfer of the case to another judge, if the matter was not settled, doubts were expressed as to whether (inadvertently) there may be breaches of confidentiality as to what had transpired in the mediation between the judges in the judges' Common Room.

Nevertheless the procedure has been implemented and continues. The judges have undergone a very rudimentary form of mediation training. It is also true to say that the more recently appointed judges have had experience of mediation during their practise as barristers before appointment. There will soon be a time when they may even have qualified as a mediator during their time in private practice.

The lawyers

Initially, the lawyer mediators were primarily solicitors. Furthermore, the mediations were conducted by the solicitors without the attendance of counsel. Latterly, barristers began to undergo the training. As the gatekeepers for ADR were lawyers, there was a natural attraction towards appointing a lawyer as it was felt that (despite ADR being a facilitative process), a lawyer would be more evaluative. Arising out of this, more and more QCs undertook the training and became ever increasingly popular as mediators. Some judges trained as mediators when they retired, including Lord Woolf himself, but they had not really had experience of ADR in practice, as it had been introduced after their appointment to the Bench.

The leading lawyer mediators at the moment mostly come from the Senior Bar together with highly experienced solicitor practitioners.

Non-lawyers

Regrettably, there are few successful non-lawyer mediators. One of the exceptions is the author of this book. He had been the first Director of Training at CEDR. Another highly successful, non-lawyer mediator is Mark Jackson Stops, a surveyor by background who formed 'In Place of Strife'. The construction industry saw more non-lawyer mediators than other aspects of the dispute resolution process, but the proportion of non-lawyer mediators is still very small.

The participants

In the early days, it was rare for a mediation to be attended by counsel. However, counsel (and leading counsel) now frequently attend mediations, especially in the larger cases. Their attitude towards mediation is often governed by whether or not they are themselves trained mediators. Whilst some barristers still 'fight the case', this is becoming increasingly rare. Mediators often now value their contribution, finding that their risk analysis helps the parties (and sometimes the solicitors) take a realistic view of their prospects.

Insurers

There are mixed views on the insurer's contribution to the process. It is to be remembered that insurers will be very familiar with mediation whereas it is probably the insured's only experience. Some insurers regard negotiation purely as an arithmetical exercise, some not even bothering to turn up at all. Dealing with insurers remains a vital skill for mediators.

Experts

Experts seem to attend less and less. This is because it is difficult for them to change their opinion during the course of the mediation. Mediators nowadays try to encourage experts to meet prior to the mediation, and if possible to produce a report as to what is and is not agreed, something that most have to do in the litigation in any event.

Confidentiality

Over the past few years confidentiality has been challenged. It arises mainly in circumstances where one party to the mediation, for various reasons, such as clarifying the terms of settlement or whether there has been a settlement at all. Sometimes parties wish to air before the court the conduct of the parties, or indeed what was said in the mediation.

Courts are becoming more and more ready to enquire as to what happened, despite any confidentiality clause in the agreement. Where both parties have agreed to waive confidentiality, which has happened on some occasions, then theoretically there is no problem (although the mediator is also party to the Agreement to Mediate, and therefore bound by the confidentiality provision, whether the parties waive it or not). However, where one party is seeking to discuss confidential matters, the court needs to agree.

Mediator's confidentiality

In *Farm Assist v DEFRA*, in 2008, the judge decided that a mediator's right to confidentiality was capable of being overridden by the court 'in the interests of justice'. In that case, following a 'successful' mediation, the claimant was seeking to overturn the settlement on the grounds that they were put under economic duress.

One of the parties sought to call the mediator as a witness as to what had transpired during the mediation. The mediator objected, relying upon her confidentiality in the agreement. The question arose as to who owned the confidentiality, ie was it the mediators or was it the parties? The court decided that the mediator had a right to confidentiality but was in court to give evidence about the mediation rather than the underlying dispute.

As a result of the case, many mediators' agreements were changed to reflect this danger. Furthermore, agreements were also changed to provide that any costs incurred by the mediator in attending or indeed disputing the requirement to give evidence would be paid by the parties.

Litigation funding

Following the implementation of the Jackson reforms in 2013, there was been a change in litigation funding. Previously some cases were conducted on a Conditional Fee Agreement (CFA) whereby the lawyer acting for a party was entitled to a percentage mark-up (which varied according to the risks of the case) in the event that the litigation was successful. This gave rise, certainly for the mediators, to secondary mediations where the mediator found themselves negotiating between the lawyer and the party as to the extent to which the lawyer could claim fees out of the agreed settlement monies. It was also suggested that a lawyer acting for a party under such arrangement had theoretically a conflict of interest, in that, on the one hand, s/he had a duty to assist in obtaining the best possible settlement for his client, but on the other hand, if the settlement was at a lower figure than anticipated, the percentage proportion of the settlement figure s/he could recover in costs could be lower because of the smaller pot.

Jackson did away with CFAs, though parties are still operating under them. Instead, Damages Based Agreements (DBAs) were introduced. Under a DBA, the lawyer may take a percentage of the damages recovered for their client as their fee, if the case is successful. There is a maximum payment that the lawyer can recover depending on the nature of the case. It is early days at the moment as to whether, and if so to what extent, the difference between CFAs and DBAs will alter the nature of the process. It is suspected not, because there will still be an argument between the lawyer and his or her client as to the lawyer's percentage entitlement.

Mandatory mediation

There have been moves, suggestions and debates as to whether or not mediation should be mandatory, the courts thus far have stopped short of deciding this should be the case. It is anticipated that the position will remain the same for the foreseeable future.

The EU Directive

The Ministry of Justice declared itself satisfied that England and Wales are compliant with the Directive in respect of the majority of its requirements.

However, arts 6 (Enforceability of Settlement Agreements), 7 (Confidentiality of Mediation) and 8 (Suspension of Limitation) were seen to require changes and additions to the English law and procedure to accommodate what the directive requires for cross-border disputes only.

Conclusion

Some busy mediators report that fewer and fewer mediations settle on the day, though often they settle shortly thereafter. Sometimes it is felt that the mediation process is merely regarded as a stage in the litigation/settlement process.

The market amongst mediators remains highly competitive. In a large number of instances the amount of the mediator's fee is a significant factor.

Whilst mediation is undoubtedly now firmly established in the litigation landscape, some solicitors are becoming increasingly casual in the approach, delegating a junior lawyer to find a mediator and delivering position papers either late or not at all.

Scotland

Pamela Lyall

I have been mediating in Scotland for the past 13 years and have been involved in over 200 disputes during that time. Over this period I personally have seen significant change in the landscape. I have undoubtedly learnt much and developed my own practice and remain as passionate about this area of work as when I first started – though I perhaps have learnt that it is not always necessary for parties to be fully reconciled for it to be considered a success! Sometimes, especially in the commercial sector, getting a deal done is enough.

When I first started working as a commercial mediator with Core Solutions, it was necessary to explain what mediation actually was before anyone would ever consider that they needed it, and only after that to suggest that they select me as the mediator in particular! Mediation at that time had established considerable credibility in the family disputes arena but was relatively unheard of in relation to commercial matters. Nowadays, after more than a decade of promotion of commercial mediation, there is a sophisticated group of repeat users, many of whom are lawyers, who understand the process and how it can be of significant benefit to their clients and are consistently promoting its use. Lawyers are involved in the majority of commercial mediations and a number of them have taken steps to train as mediators, so that they better understand the inside track and can work more effectively with the mediator.

This is all most encouraging. But it is clear that commercial mediations cannot continue to grow at the rate that they did in the first few heady years when, starting from a very small base, the numbers doubled year on year. Nowadays, the numbers of mediations have, to some extent, plateaued, although I think mediation is now being seen as a more creative and flexible process than perhaps it was at first. New areas where mediation can be of assistance are opening up, for instance within the planning system and in the conversations around the independence referendum in 2014. It is perhaps being viewed not so much as a narrow process but as a flexible skills set, which can be employed in a number of different ways.

In Scotland, mediation is neither part of the judicial system nor is it mandatory. It is an entirely private and voluntary process though lawyers are now required to consider mediation as an option when advising their clients. The Law Society of Scotland, in November 2013, published new guidance ('Dispute Resolution, Guidance related to Rule B1.9'). It begins:

> 'Solicitors should have a sufficient understanding of commonly available alternative dispute resolution options to allow proper consideration and communication of options to a client in considering the client's interests and objectives.'

Thus, if solicitors do not explore all the possible options that are available, that could be sufficient grounds to establish professional negligence.

Over the years there have been a number of judicial reviews which have looked at the place of mediation within the justice system and the Scottish Government launched its 'Making Justice Work' programme as long ago as 2011, setting out its strategic goals for the civil justice system, including:

'To develop mechanisms which will support and empower citizens to avoid or resolve informally disputes and problems wherever possible, and to ensure they have access to appropriate and proportionate advice, and to a full range of methods of dispute resolution, including courts and tribunals where necessary, and appropriate alternatives.'

However, no specific proposals have been made about the place of mediation within the civil justice system and commercial mediation has grown organically without any trigger from the courts in terms of court processes and rules. As a result, it may be that in Scotland mediation is not viewed so much as simply an alternative to going to court as it might be in other jurisdictions. Matters which would never find themselves in either a court or tribunal are being mediated in Scotland on a fairly regular basis.

The Scottish Government are certainly committed to the development of other forms of dispute resolution. In particular they have heavily promoted Scotland as an international centre of arbitration with a recent bill modernising the process being passed and the opening of new premises in Edinburgh. This focus on arbitration and international disputes should be beneficial to mediation as it provides confirmation that alternative means to litigation for resolving disputes are available to parties. Interestingly, in the Legal Profession and Legal Aid (Scotland) Act 2007, the Scottish Legal Complaints Commission was created and the Scottish Parliament took the bold step of building mediation into the system, this being offered to those who complain about the standard of service provided by a legal practitioner. There has been steady growth from a slow start. In its first nine months in 2008/9, the SLCC scheme completed one mediation, out of 47 eligible complaints. By 2011/12, that figure had reached 55 out of 289 and it continues to increase.

However, there is still a comparatively small number of mediators who make their living from practising mediation in Scotland. Many mediators have mediation as a one of a number of strings to their respective bows. As the demand for mediators is comparatively low, there are a number of trained mediators with little or no experience and they have sought to keep their skills honed by participating in pro bono mediation schemes such as that run through the local sheriff courts and assisting other paid mediators. Apart from Core Solutions, there are one or two other commercial mediation providers operating in Scotland but none with the significant profile or credibility of Core which is based largely on its founder and Chief Executive, John Sturrock. There are no across the board professional standards for mediators in Scotland, although for some time now, the Scottish Mediation Network, an umbrella organisation for all types of mediation, has developed a register for mediators. It is web based and self-certifying and offers a useful resource for those seeking to select a commercial mediator in Scotland.

Most mediators in Scotland would use the facilitative mediation model, which is the default model taught by the main service providers. Overall, the fact that mediation has developed outside of the judicial process and that it is voluntary may well have contributed significantly to the way in which mediation has developed in Scotland. Those that mediate in this jurisdiction do so because they have looked at the alternatives and they have decided that mediation offers them the best possible means of resolving their dispute. They are at the mediation table only because they have chosen to be there. This cannot be a tick box exercise as there are no boxes to tick! This has a positive and significant impact on the number of mediations which achieve a resolution on the day itself or shortly thereafter. That figure is usually at least 85 per cent and often higher across the commercial sector. Although, in my view, it is quite a crude measurement it is of some interest to those who have not used mediation previously or who come reluctantly to the table.

Looking ahead, I can see an increasing use of technology in the mediation field with online and phone based systems being developed for smaller value matters, and mediation skills being used in an expanding number of differing contexts. The future for mediation broadly, and commercial mediation more specifically, in Scotland is, I think, a very positive one as it seeks, under whatever political setup the nation goes forward, a different and more constructive way of social engagement.

Russia

Dr Tsisana Chamlikashvili

Russia has a long tradition of using alternative dispute resolution (ADR). Since ancient times there was a custom of going for arbitration or *treteyskiy sud* (in the context of domestic disputes), which was for centuries regarded as a form of intermediation of a third party in ruling on the dispute. Arbitration has also been traditionally used in international/cross-border commercial disputes. This tradition was not interrupted even in the Soviet era, under the communist regime, when a culture of going to court for protection of an individual's rights on a domestic level was almost lost against the background of lacking private property rights.

With the development of market relations in the second half of the 1980s, legal issues became increasingly important. The court system in the Russian Federation was developing very fast in the early 1990s, when a system of arbitration courts headed by the Supreme Arbitration Court (state courts for commercial cases) was established.

At this time society was undergoing a period of transition, primitive accumulation of capital and rapid redistribution of state property into private hands, and commercial disputes were often resolved outside the legal field, by means of criminal 'showdowns'. By the end of the 1980s 'settlement' of disputes involving criminal authorities had become common practice.

At the same time, by the mid-1990s the development of the commercial court system and legal system in general, huge efforts in the sphere of legal education, legal protection of people's rights and interests, including the right for private property, all contributed to the fact that people started to have recourse to the judiciary much more often, which in its turn led to the steady growth of court congestion. However, a significant number of commercial conflicts were still being resolved not on the basis of law, but with the help of 'shootouts'.

Business communities declared that they wished to settle their disputes without government intervention, in a more flexible, informal and also civilised fashion and even attempted to create mechanisms that would allow this. Commissions on ethics and internal arbitration courts (*treteyskiy sud*) as ADR tools were created in various industries, within business unions, etc. Much attention was paid to the development of this institution by the State and in 2002 a special law on *treteyskiy sud* passed in the hope that the alternative method would help to bring commercial disputes within the legal framework in the country. However, *treteyskiy sud* failed to meet expectations, not having received the support of entrepreneurs and potential users in general. One of the reasons cited is lack of trust by entrepreneurs, sometimes calling arbitral bodies (*treteyskiy sud*) established by various huge corporations 'pocket courts'. All this resulted in the need to revise the current legislation on *treteyskiy sud*. Ongoing discussion about possible changes to the law on arbitration - *treteyskiy sud* - coincided with the reform of the Russian judicial system. A key aspect of the reform was the abolition of the Supreme Arbitration (Commercial) Court and unifying of the State court system under General Jurisdiction.

Over the past 20 years, the burden on the Russian judicial system has been constantly growing (annually Russian courts receive over 20 million claims, including about 1.5 million commercial cases) and Russia became one of the most litigious countries. This fact can be seen as paradox taking in consideration that level of trust towards the existing court system in Russian society is very low.

The last decade was characterised by a decrease in the competitiveness of the Russian legal system (in terms of commercial disputes), which was reflected in the 'escape' of Russian business to other jurisdictions. Also, in the late 1990s another steady tendency emerged of using judicial decisions for unlawful seizure of business and redistribution of property. Against this background, the emergence of opportunities for resolving disputes legally, but without intervention or pressure from outside, in an informal, equitable and confidential process, seems to be a necessary means for supporting businesses, which are eager to maintain and develop their activities in a lawful way. Laying the foundations for civilised and robust business competition, dispute resolution in the legal framework, but with the least intrusive government institutions, would certainly contribute to the development of contemporary Russian society. Mediation is seen as one of the instruments to allow citizens to manage their disputes by resolving them without (or with minimum) involvement of State authorities, minimising corruption and fostering a culture of personal responsibility for decisions and their outcomes.

Since 2004, consistent, comprehensive efforts have been made aimed at the development of mediation in Russia. In 2004, at the All-Russian Congress of Judges, President Putin paid special attention to the need for development of out-of-court and pre-trial dispute settlement procedures in Russia. In early 2005, the First International Conference on Mediation was held in Moscow with participation of government representatives and leading lawyers. The conference was supported by the Presidential Executive Office, and it is often believed to be the formal starting point for integration of mediation in Russia.

The term 'mediation' is found in relation to settlement of disputes between Russian merchants as early as in the nineteenth century. However, it was a procedure similar to arbitration proceedings, where the mediator suggested to the parties a decision based on his own judgement, and the parties then had to follow it. Nowadays, when introducing mediation in Russia, focus is made on the modern voluntary, non-formalised approach to dispute resolution, empowering parties, addressing their interests and needs in dispute, with parties as the sole owners of their dispute and the main actors and decision makers in the process of resolving it. It is parties who have the right to a final vote. They should be able not only to influence the content of the decision, but also to participate actively in the process of developing it, and therefore influence the process as well.

In 2010, the Federal Law on Alternative Procedure of Dispute Resolution with Participation of a Mediator (Mediation Procedure) (No 193-FL) was adopted and on 1 January 2011 it came into force, followed by the Federal Law on Amending Certain Legislative Acts of the Russian Federation in View of Adopting a Federal Law on Alternative Procedure of Dispute Resolution with Participation of a Mediator (Mediation Procedure) (No 194-FL).

Adoption of the Law on Mediation was preceded by an active information campaign aiming to create awareness among citizens and various professional groups, and addressing the main target audiences – the legal community and, of course, the judges. Already, in 2006, several courts had formed a group of judges and their assistants who were ready to support the process of referring parties to mediation, some judges having shown much interest in the development of a new institution, but also regretting the absence of legal grounds for referral to mediation.

Even though, since 2002, the Arbitration Procedure Code (APC) has contained a provision that not only allows, but also obliges, the judge to inform the parties about the possibility that they can apply for conciliation procedures, it was obvious that without the Law on Mediation it would be very difficult to introduce the new institute. Although the practice was still very limited, especially at country-wide level, the adoption of the Law on Mediation was seen on the one hand as a way to legitimise mediation, and on the other as a kind of incentive for the legal community and potential users of mediation, and as a confirmation that the state approved and supported development of a new approach to dispute resolution.

The process of preparing the draft law on mediation was also influenced by the EU Directive on Mediation of 21 May 2008. The Russian law on mediation is a framework law (since great efforts were made to avoid excessive regulation), which defines the basic guidelines for the development of the new institution and supports the facilitative model of mediation:

- the sphere of application is disputes arising from civil relations, including business, commercial, family, and labour (except for collective labour disputes);
- activity status – mediation practice is not entrepreneurial;
- procedure is voluntary and confidential; and
- a mediator cannot be invited to testify as witness at court.

Mediation can be initiated outside the court, before trial (also in accordance with a mediation clause) and after initiating the court procedure, both on the initiative of the parties, and after being referred to mediation by the judge (which is however not compulsory for the parties).

The status of a mediation agreement is that of a contract, and where it is signed after going to court the parties may submit the mediation agreement for approval as a settlement agreement, which gives it the power of an execution writ.

The mediator's role is assisting the parties to develop their own mutually satisfactory, viable solution. They will not offer solutions for resolving the dispute to the parties, and if they turn to him or her with such a request, they reserve the right to decide. In addition, the mediator, even if they are a lawyer, should not (and has no right to) advise the parties on legal issues.

Mediation activity is subject to self-regulation. Mediators and mediation service providers can be organised in non-profit organisations. In 2011, the non-commercial Partnership 'National Organisation of Mediators' was created. Among its founders were the Russian public organisation 'Association of Lawyers of Russia', the non-governmental organisation 'Chamber of Commerce and Industry of the Russian Federation', the Russian public organisation 'Russian Union of Industrialists and Entrepreneurs' and the autonomous non-profit organisation 'Scientific and Methodological Centre for Mediation and Law'. By 2013, the organisation has acquired the status of self-regulatory organisation.

Only a person at least 25 years old, with any higher education and trained according to the Program of Mediation Training can act as a professional mediator.

With the adoption of the Law some hoped for rapid growth of demand for mediation, especially in the sphere of commercial and business disputes. These expectations had no solid ground, which has become obvious in the past three and a half years.

Integration of mediation is a progressive process which take time and that requires the joint efforts of judges, lawyers, professional mediators and representatives of potential clients. The wide spread of mediation practice requires changes in habitual patterns of behaviour and ways of responding to conflict. Despite the fact that mediation in its modern sense really places emphasis on the interests and needs of the parties themselves, by empowering them, these changes take time, specially so for the society with quite a high level of mistrust, which is aggravated by the low level of willingness to take responsibility.

With the law coming into force, the courts became more involved in the work on integration of mediation. Quite surprisingly, for the most part these are courts of general jurisdiction while commercial courts are less active with some exeptions. For instance some Commercial courts have referal programmes, several courts increased the level of settlements from 3 per cent (average across the country) to 30 per cent due to the mediative approach (developed by the Centre for Mediation and Law). In March 2014, with the assistance of the Centre for Mediation and Law, a mediation room was opened at the newly established Federal Court for Intellectual Property Rights (The Court for IP was established in 2012 and opened for business in June 2013).

Today in more than 25 per cent of the constituents of the Russian Federation, in the courts of general jurisdiction, efforts are made to refer parties to mediation. In some courts mediation/reconciliation rooms have opened. It should be noted that confusion with the terms, to which mostly representatives of the legal community contribute, is another obstacle to bringing the essence of the new approach to the public. Serious damage to the ongoing efforts is made by using familiar words denoting procedures which are not popular with people and evoking associations with an attempt to influence decision-making and directive approach, while mediation is aimed at facilitating the free will of the parties themselves.

In 2011–2012, the possibility of introducing mandatory mediation was actively discussed. Perhaps such a measure could be helpful for increasing awareness in citizens, potential users of mediation, although it should not be disregarded that mediation is by nature a voluntary process and that by introducing mandatory mediation we reject the first level of voluntariness – voluntary recourse to the procedure, but in any case never to the detriment of the most significant level of voluntariness –the voluntary decision to agree and to enter the agreement.

However, recourse to judicial protection is a constitutional right of citizens. Mandatory mediation should be complemented by the possibility of obtaining mediation assistance (at least 3–4 hours' mediation session) at no charge (obviously with an option for the parties to choose a mediator for a fee). Today in Russia there is no infrastructure capable of providing quality and free of charge mediation services across the country. Finally, a decision was made against counterproductive and untimely introduction of mandatory mediation. At the same time, efforts are made to introduce, at least in the mode of pilot projects, mandatory information sessions on mediation; in some courts mediators offer their services on a free of charge (pro bono) basis or for a very low (symbolic) fees.

Awareness of citizens and demand for mediation are growing, but it is a long and progressive process.

As far as commercial disputes are concerned, acceptance of mediation procedure by the business community is much lower than it could have been, even at the early stages of integration of the new institute. Despite the fact that public organisations and business associations declaratively support the development of a new institution, the strategy of behaviour remains in the paradigm of 'the strongest wins' – the winner being the one who has more power and influence. Under such conditions parties are quite rarely guided by considerations of expediency and pragmatism, which can more often and better be realised in cooperation with opponents – an opportunity given by mediation. Corporate lawyers are very reluctant to apply for mediation, although using it can improve their own efficiency.

This situation is somewhat contradictory. After all, if for a lawyer and external counsel mediation creates some conflict of interests (which on a deeper level is untrue, if we consider professi onal ethics), for the corporate lawyer mediation, that is able to reduce the risks arising from disputes and escalation of conflicts, is an integral part of the work and professional competence. But in Russia very few corporate lawyers embraced mediation yet in their every day work. It is the same with Russian branches of large international companies and corporations, whose offices in other countries do a nice job for prevention of disputes and ADR (and even among those who signed the CPR pledge).

Yes, Russia has very 'affordable' judicial proceedings (inexpensive, fast enough), but the level of enforcement of court decisions is very low. Almost every audience asks a question about compulsory execution of a mediation agreement. This question shows lack of understanding of the mediation process and the nature of a mediation agreement as that which is produced on the basis of consent, reflecting parties' own interests and needs. Therefore, along with the work with the legal community in whole, great efforts are made to inform and involve the business community, corporate lawyers, etc.

Mediation may contribute to increasing the independence of the business community from the judiciary and the state in general, growing business efficiency, and reducing corruption factors. It is corporate lawyers who are 'gatekeepers' of this approach for companies, no less so than the legal community, for potential users in general. The same situation can be observed not only in Russia but also all over the world, including those countries where mediation has been developing for decades, but still is underused.

The real need for mediation is very high, including in terms of social and economic development. However, the potential user is often unable to benefit from the 'product' that is useful, because either they are not aware of its existence or the product that they are offered, advertised as 'proper' and 'useful', is a substitute.

Since the adoption of the Mediation Law a number of organisations promoting themselves as mediation and mediation training providers has grown to more than 50 all over the country. Most of the regions have one or sometimes more organisations providing mediation. Several Chambers of Commerce are suggesting mediation along with arbitration. Lawyers are supporting mediation if they are well educated.

Choice of strategy for responding to conflict should not be the prerogative of lawyers. The choice is to be made by those whose business, reputation and dividends are directly affected, and the choice should be informed. This is the responsibility of lawyers and even a question of their professional ethics to assist clients in the execution of informed choices.

Mediation must become accessible to potential users, that is, each of us. Since 2006, due to the efforts of the Centre for Mediation, law students of the main universities and law schools have an access to mediation courses (Moscow State University, Moscow State Academy of Law, School of Private Law, etc), all over the country special courses for judges are organised, and chambers for lawyers and notaries are invited for collaboration.

Great attention is paid to developing a culture of amicable dispute resolution in society in general. 'School mediation' method is integrated into the educational system, and introductory courses in mediation are taught not only at law schools, but also to managers and representatives of most diverse professions, primarily socially oriented.

In 2013, the Federal Institute for Mediation was established as a state governmental body. The Institute is aiming to shape policy for the implementation and development of mediation and ADR in the Russian Federation.

Currently, application of mediation in general and in commercial disputes in particular is negligible compared to the number of cases in the courts. But this does not mean that mediation is not needed in Russia. On the contrary, a process which, unlike most countries with a well-established legal system, in Russia started as 'top-bottom', is gradually acquiring more and more allies in society and has a tendency to become a 'bottom-up' movement. We are still at the stage of 'scattering seeds', which with patient and continuing care, are sure to yield prominent results.

Turkey

Deniz Artan Ilter and Samil Demir

Background overview

Turkey's legal system belongs to the civil law family based on statutory and legal enactments. Turkish Law is a written law and is not based on precedents. However, verdicts of the Supreme Court constitute precedents for the lower courts to follow in legal interpretations of the codes. The Turkish Constitution prescribes the separation of powers, and the judiciary is an independent branch of the state.

Following the establishment of the Turkish Republic in 1923, Turkish Law was constituted by adopting the civil law of continental Europe, such as the Swiss Civil Code and Code of Civil Procedure, the Italian Penal Code, the German Code of Criminal Procedure and Code of Commerce and French administrative law with due adaptations. Substantial amendments and modifications have been effected since, particularly in the last decade within the framework of the EU accession process. Some of these are the new Civil Code and Code of Civil Procedure in 2001 and the Obligations Code and Code of Commerce in 2012.

Commercial cases are heard in the commercial courts, which have jurisdiction over the disputes listed in art 4 of the Turkish Commercial Code, including commercial transactions, acts and affairs related to any trading firm, factory, or commercially operated establishment. These specialised courts are structured only in cities where the number of commercial cases reach a certain level. Therefore in the cities where no commercial courts are founded, the civil courts are authorised to try commercial cases. Moreover, some chambers of the Court of Appeals are specialised for appeals in commercial disputes.

Legal status of mediation

The EU Directive on Mediation

In 2008, the European Parliament and the Council adopted the Directive on Certain Aspects of Mediation in Civil and Commercial Matters The objective of this Directive is to facilitate access to alternative dispute resolution and to promote the amicable settlement of disputes by encouraging the use of mediation and by ensuring a balanced relationship between mediation and judicial proceedings. The Directive applies to civil and commercial matters except as regards rights and obligations which are not at the parties' disposal under the relevant applicable law. The Directive comprises the base rules to be adopted by the Member States for the implementation of mediation concerning the referral to mediation, ensuring the quality of mediation, the enforcement of the settlement agreements and suspension of limitation periods. As a part of the adoption of the EU Acquis process, a draft Mediation Law has been prepared by the Turkish Ministry of Justice predicated on the Directive and this constituted the first comprehensive legislation on mediation in Turkey.

The draft Mediation Law

Work on drafting a Mediation Law first commenced on 27 January 2004 by the constitution of a commission mandated by the Ministry of Justice, for drafting a Code of Civil Procedure (CCP). Initially contemplating addressing mediation in civil disputes as a chapter within the CCP, the commission later decided to regulate mediation under a separate act and authorise a dedicated sub-commission for its drafting.

Besides the UNCITRAL Model Law and the pertinent Proposal for a Directive of the European Union, the Green Paper on alternative dispute resolution in civil and commercial Law, the Austrian Federal Law on Mediation in Civil Disputes, the Baden-Württemberg Conciliation Act of 1999, the Bavarian Mandatory Alternative Dispute Resolution Act in Private Law, the Hungarian Law of Mediation and the recently adopted mediation Acts of Slovakia and Bulgaria were taken into consideration while drafting the Law. Besides these sources, meetings were held at various occasions with specialists from countries such as the United States, the United Kingdom, Italy, Spain, Canada, Germany, the Netherlands and Austria, and the developments in comparative law were monitored.

Finally, at the end of 2007, the Draft Law on Mediation in Civil Disputes (Draft Mediation Law) was issued for discussion and consultation of relevant parties. The Law on Mediation in Civil Disputes No 6235 (Mediation Law) was enacted in the Turkish Grand National Assembly on 7 June 2012 and published in the Official Gazette dated 22 June 2012; sections concerning the organisation of the Ministry of Justice came into effect on the same date, while the rest commenced on 22 June 2013. The Minimum Wage Tariffs for Mediation came into effect on 22 June 2013 and was subsequently updated on 20 December 2013. The Model Ethics and Professional Rules for the Mediation System and the Mediators was issued on the same date in the official website of the Mediation Department of the Ministry.

Criticism and revisions

The Mediation Law has been subject to unprecedented criticism and discussion. Criticism, apparently resulting from lack of sufficient information on the institution of mediation, was mostly based on concerns for opening the door to onset of parallel legal systems, for mediation being potentially instrumental in creating an alternate justice system that will unfairly serve the mighty, for being unconstitutional in that it means a transfer of the exclusive authority of the courts to judge, etc. Mediation also came under criticism with the consideration that the lawyers already struggling under dire economic circumstances due to harsh competiton would be harder pressed by further increased competition and ensuing loss of business.

Mediation also receives ideologically based criticism in that it is viewed and presented as an instrument of a neo-liberal agenda. The capitalists, it is argued, in their quest to vitiate any hindrance posed by the fundamental branches and agencies of the state to their endeavours, as embodied in their global pursuit for deregulation, have found an invaluable implement in mediation for undermining an effective and functional judiciary. Their stance against litigation in court amounts to impairment of a functional judiciary, which they are bent on derogating on the grounds that it is slow and costly and problematic in many ways and hence ineffectual and inefficient. This, accompanied by the promotion of extra-judicial solutions, will surely facilitate the pursuance of capitalists' interests, making it easier for the mighty to sustain their domination over the weak. Another point made against mediation is that in unitary states with diverse ethnicities, each group will be urged to recourse to a mediator of their own ethnicity rather than to the courts, thus conducing polarisation of the society and disintegration of the nation on an ethnic basis.

Severe reprobation of the law, especially by the lawyers, during the drafting stage led to changes in the final draft. Whereas the first draft allowed anyone with a four-year graduate degree to be eligible for being a mediator, the final draft laid down a law faculty diploma and five years of professional experience as conditions for legibility.

To preclude possible queries regarding validity and binding nature of the formal agreement reached through the mediation process, it is stipulated that such agreement may be brought to a court to obtain a commentary of enforceability, rendering it equivalent in force to a court judgment. The final draft also brought down the minimum duration of mediator training from 150 to 48 hours.

The Mediation Law

PRINCIPLES

The Mediation Law has been formulated with the purpose of fulfilling the requirements of modern mediation activity, with voluntariness/willingness and equality of the parties and the confidentiality of statements and documents introduced during the process being among its prominent features. The Mediation Law has laid down the principle of voluntariness in resorting to mediation. Contrary to what has been adopted in various countries it does not stipulate compulsory mediation for disputes subsumed under specified categories or for those less than a threshold value in pecuniary terms. The parties are totally free to resort to mediation as well as to continue it or withdraw therefrom.

In the management of the mediation process, the Law has adopted the principle of equality for the parties in bearing the due expenses and wages, in the rights and privileges they will enjoy and in their reception and treatment by the mediator. Any party who deems itself being treated with less than complete equality and impartiality has at its discretion the absolute freedom to terminate the process at any time.

The Law specifies in detail the confidentiality of the opinions and proposals put forth and imparted by the parties or the mediator during the mediation process. The parties, by default, are forbidden to utilise the statements and documents introduced during mediation in possible subsequent litigation or arbitration, however they are also entitled to jointly decide against such prohibition.

The mediator is held liable to discharge their duty diligently and impartially. In case of any doubt arising as to her/his impartiality, it is the obligation of the mediator to explicitly inform the parties so as to dissipate any such suspicion. The mediator is required to always keep the parties well informed during all stages of the mediation process, and especially explain the principles and possible outcomes at the beginning of the activity.

The Law only allows mediators registered in the Ministry of Justice registry to use the mediator title. The mediator is entitled to ask for part of the wage and expenses in advance as down payment. The mediators are forbidden to advertise in any manner, akin to the similar prohibition in the profession of advocacy.

SCOPE

The Law on Mediation in Civil Disputes specifies that mediation is applicable only in private law cases where the parties may freely have a disposal, ie where they can end the dispute by an agreement, including those possessing the element of alienage, and where a court verdict is not needed for the agreement to come into effect. The parties, for instance, cannot take a divorce case to a mediator, where a court decision would be needed for the divorce and the custodianship of children to legally come into effect. Likewise, mediation is not applicable when the dispute arises from domestic violence and not subsumed in the Law for Criminal Procedure under the matters appropriate for conciliation. Cases, for instance, involving compensation claims due to violence between spouses and intimates, weapon inflicted injuries or manslaughter cannot be taken to a mediator.

Recourse to mediation is possible, however, in the resolution of disputes involving all credit contracts, bargain and sale contracts, consumer disputes, intellectual property agreements, rent and lease disputes, maritime commerce and insurance disputes, trademark and patent disputes, disputes in sharing property following divorce, and in the resolution of disputes on compensation for criminal cases subject to complaint for prosecution like those involving reckless injury, unarmed assault occasioning injury, insult, threatening, breaking in a residence or disclosure of trade secrets.

MEDIATION MODEL

According to the Mediation Law, mediation is a negotiation process directed by the mediator, an impartial third party, who employs in a systematic manner the communication techniques they have acquired through specialist training. The mediator, using the said techniques, aims to bring the sides together, facilitate their communication so that each gains a better understanding of the other's point and eventually lead the parties towards finding a common solution. These principles set forth in the Law suggest that it is the *facilitative mediation* model that is adopted in the Law.

Considering the general principles of mediation, and particularly those explicitly adopted and endorsed by the Law, the mediator does not make any decision concerning the solution of the dispute, or force the parties to a formulated agreement. The mediator assists the courts in cases of disputes under adjudication in a court. The purpose of mediation activity is not to tell right from the wrong but try and reach the best resolution that satisfy the parties' interests. It is at the absolute discretion of the parties to reach an agreement at the end of the negotiations or to altogether abort the mediation activity.

These principles have been emphasised in s 19.5 of the By-Law under the Mediation Law as follows:

> 'The mediator, may not, in the process of mediation, give legal advice to the parties; may not develop a proposal for resolution or a catalogue of proposals and impose them on the parties, nor may he force the parties to agree on a resolution alternative that has taken shape during the negotiations'.

This corresponds to a preclusion of the mediation model that is designated as 'evaluative mediation' in the doctrine. It is to be inferred that the legislature has adopted facilitative mediation as the Turkish mediation model, and that the By-Law, likewise, has rejected the evaluative mediation model by explicitly disallowing its principles of practice.

PROCESS

The disputing parties are totally free in selecting a mediator. They may agree on a mediator themselves or authorise a third party to decide on the mediator. Recourse to mediation is possible during litigation in court as well as prior to it. Mediation stops the elapse of time with respect to time bars or other specified time periods during which a claim or right may be exercised in court cases. The judges, in every court case suitable for mediation, are obliged to inform and encourage the parties on resorting to mediation. When the parties decide to take their case to a mediator, the judge postpones the case for a maximum of two to three months, after which the litigation in court resumes should the parties fail to reach a resolution in the meantime. In case of a succesful mediation, the mediator prepares an agreement document and instructs the parties on the validity thereof. Should they so desire, the parties are entitled to have the resolution ratified by the court to secure its execution with the force of a court judgment.

MEDIATORS

A new professional occupation is introduced by the regulations of the Mediation Law. In order for this profession to accomplish the intended social function, it is stipulated in the Law that its practitioners have appropriate training and qualifications, and that the registers of the trade are held by the State.

Registering as mediator requires Turkish citizenship, a law faculty diploma with five years of seniority in the profession, possession of full legal capacity, not being convicted of an intentional crime, having completed the mediation training and passed the written and practical examinations held by the Ministry. The mediators bearing these qualifications are permitted to practice mediation at the date of their registry, as per s 20/11 of the Mediation Law. The Mediation Department established under the Legal Affairs General Directorate of the Justice Ministry holds the register of the persons authorised to practice mediation. The information on people in this register is published online by the Department, as per s 19/1 of the Law.

Mediator candidates are given a training covering the basic information on the conduct of the mediation activity, communication techniques, methods of negotiation and dispute resolution, lessons in psychology and other theoretical and practical items indicated in the relevant sections of the By-Law. Upon completion of this 48 hours or more training, the candidate mediators are given a document by the training institutions certifying successful consummation of the training, as per s 25 of the Mediation Law. This certificate qualifies the candidate to enter the mediation examinations held by the Ministry.

The Law delimitates the institutions authorised to provide mediation training to the law faculties, the Turkish Academy of Justice and the Union of Turkish Bar Associations. An official permission from the Ministry is needed to start a mediator training programme. The Ministry accords each permission for a maximum validity period of three years and publishes a listing of the authorised institutions on its website. The total number of currently licensed training institutions is 49.

Current practice of mediation

Considering that the Mediation Law came into effect on 22 June 2013, the onset of mediation practice in Turkey is quite recent. As at publication there are 1,035 registered mediators, and the total number of reported resolutions stand at a mere 24, the bulk of which pertain to labour and alimony disputes, with no resolutions on commercial disputes yet recorded. Of these mediation cases, 21 ended with an agreement. Mediation cases took place in 11 different cities, including Istanbul with seven cases. Such information comes from a Mediation Department database where the mediators are required to file a copy of each agreement for statistical purposes.

Observations on the ground verify the statistics in that, especially with respect to commercial disputes, people tend to approach this untrodden method with caution and a wait-and-see attitude. In the rare cases, for instance, that a construction company suggests mediation as a possibility to another construction company with whom they have run into dispute, they are typically told squarely by the latter's attorney that they would like to wait for the court decision. Insurance executives, when approached for mediation on a car insurance dispute, for instance, predictably turn the offer down on the grounds that it will push the costs up, meanwhile very likely delivering an upbraiding tirade assuring there was nothing to negotiate, otherwise they would have done it best themselves. Consumer disputes constitute a category which suitably could have been fertile ground for mediation if it were not for the possibility of applying to a court free of fees for these cases, and had not the Consumer Arbitration Board been authorised to issue binding decisions on disputes less than TRY 3,000, again free of any fees. The prevalence of the described business ethos vis-à-vis mediation suggests time is needed for the establishment of mediation as a viable alternative, particularly in commercial disputes, and also some further maturing of the legal infrastructure, following the gigantic step forward taken by the enactment of the Mediation Law.

Chapter 8

Using Interpreters in Mediation

Dr Xiaohui Yuan

Once I learned to pronounce her name, I grew to know Xiaohui well and to respect her knowledge and commitment to intercultural mediation. Much of what she writes connects with other papers in Part 3. She is well tuned to the cultural subtleties and challenges of mediating with parties of differing cultures. She is a very interesting and cheery person. (DR)

> 'I told him to just translate what is said. No more! No less! But he seldom did!'[1]

Introduction

Mediators who have used interpreters for international mediation may not always find the experience smooth and helpful, and can probably relate to the above comments very well. Interpreters are often perceived as language conduits, ie the purpose of their presence is merely to bridge language differences. Such a perception can lead to certain prescriptive expectations of how an interpreter should conduct the tasks during the mediation:

> 'The crucial point is that the interpreter must maintain neutrality. They must not add their own spin to what is being translated but at the same time must be skillful in conveying the nuances of what is being said'.[2]

Nevertheless, the truth is, in reality, interpreters seldom do this. Ultimately, interpreters are human agents. They carry their cultures, values, beliefs and other social and anthropological factors when endeavouring to facilitate successful interactions. They make efforts to coordinate interactions by distributing turns of talking, clarifying misunderstanding, and even leaving miscommunication unresolved when it is believed not to cause any issues for the interaction. These roles of an interpreter, which are clearly beyond the expectation of a language conduit,

---

1   A mediator's comments on her experience of working with an interpreter at a mediation where Chinese and British parties were involved.
2   Another mediator's comments on his expectation of how an interpreter should undertake the translation.

have been studied and evidence found in medical,[3] court[4] and police[5] settings. Probably unbeknown to other professions, interpreters are considered mediators in the realm of translation and interpreting practice in view of their functions of mediating linguistic, cultural and interactional differences/gaps. This could create confusion and/or uncertainty in relation to what an interpreter is supposed to do vis-à-vis what a mediator is responsible for when the two mediators work together.

Bearing the above in mind, as an interpreter trainer and mediator, I intend in this chapter, through explaining an interpreter's roles and how interpretation is done with examples, to help international mediators to develop effective skills and strategies working with interpreters. I do not wish, however, to focus on the poor interpretation quality as this can be rectified by using trained, qualified and registered interpreters with courts and professional interpreter associations.

Interpretation versus translation

The similarities and the differences of the use of these two terms are often bewildering for a lay person. So I believe it is necessary to explain, at the outset, the contexts and activities where these two terms are employed.

Although they are used by many in an exchangeable way, translation, at a higher level, constitutes the umbrella term referring to the switching between two or more languages in both writing and oral modes. In a more strict sense, interpretation or interpreting is used only to denote language-switching activities in the oral manner, *not* the writing manner, such as a court interpretation or a medical interpretation. On the other hand, the word 'translation' may be used to specifically mean language-switching activities in the writing mode, such as literary translation, legal translation, and so on. Moreover, translation can also be adopted for the oral mode where the use of translation and interpretation is interchangeable.

In this chapter, we focus on the oral translation, ie the interpretation for the mediation. When the word translation is used, in this context, it is equivalent to interpretation.

Two types of interpretation may be deployed in mediation and mediation training. They are simultaneous interpreting (SI) and consecutive interpreting (CI). In the simultaneous mode, the interpreter speaks and finishes at almost the same time with the speaker with a short lag behind dependent on the syntactic characteristics of the language combination. The most significant advantage of SI is time-saving. But professional booths and interpreting equipment are prerequisites for fulfilling SI tasks. Moreover, due to multi-tasking of active listening, message processing and retention, and delivery, an interpreter's cognitive capacity will constantly reach saturation, which could lead to information loss and mistranslation. According to the International Conference Interpreters Association (AIIC), the accuracy of a professional SI performance is around 60 per cent to 70 per cent. SI is often adopted

---

3   C Angelelli, *Medical Interpreting and Cross–Cultural Communication* (Cambridge: Cambridge University Press, 2004).
4   S Berk-Seligson, *The Bilingual Courtroom: Court Interpreters in the Judicial Process* (Chicago: The University of Chicago Press, 1990/2002).
5   C Wadensjö, *Interpreting as Interaction* (London: Longman, 1998).

in mediation training provided outside the United Kingdom. In contrast, in the consecutive mode, an interpreter alternates their turn of talking with the speaker. Therefore, in CI, the length of an interaction may be doubled. But information tends to be retained at a higher rate, and the interpreter has the opportunity to liaise with the speaker for clarifying messages and intentions. Hence, CI is often used in mediation sessions.

Interpretation in arbitration versus in mediation

Most of us are probably more familiar with interpretation in the arbitration context where an interpreter is sworn to stick to verbatim. As arbitration involves a more rigid and pre-set procedure with a heavy focus on legal and technical aspects, verbatim interpretation is, most of the time, suitable and sufficient. Moreover, an interpreter may have more accessible resources for preparation such as any submissions, court orders, or legal papers, and they are less likely to be involved in coordinating interactions as the arbitrator holds the power and authority. In contrast, interpretation for mediation is a much more complex activity since mediation involves a more flexible process with a strong focus on interpersonal dynamics and rapport management. Under such circumstances, an interpreter has less resources for preparation since the human dynamics of the mediation are unpredictable and fluid. *A mediator and an interpreter must work together as a team to facilitate communication.* Verbatim interpretation is seldom appropriate or sufficient. This aspect will be further delineated in the next section with examples to demonstrate the reasons for and the features of non-verbatim interpretation.

Confidentiality constitutes another important aspect for mediators to pay attention to. When another human agent is involved in the confidential process, in this case the interpreter, *it is essential for the mediator to sign a separate confidentiality agreement with the interpreter and to show the agreement to all the parties as an assurance.* The mediator also bears the responsibility to educate the interpreter on the content of the rules of confidentiality. So far, no interpreting training programmes provided at the British universities or professional associations offer interpreting training tailored for mediation services. This is an important gap to fill in view of the unique features of the mediation process and rules involved. This also reveals the fact that most interpreters are not informed of how mediation is conducted, its relevant procedure and rules. Therefore, *a mediator should meet the interpreter prior to the mediation to educate the interpreter in this respect.*

Non-verbatim interpretation for rapport management

There are usually three main reasons why interpreters deviate from verbatim translation in mediation, which can appear to add spins to what is said:

- to bridge cultural differences;
- to protect a party's face and emotional needs; and
- to defuse potential conflicts or to enhance rapport.

Now I shall give examples to illustrate how interpretation is done to achieve the above three purposes.

Using Interpreters in Mediation

Example 1: bridging cultural differences in building rapport

This example shows the exchange between the mediator John and the Chinese party Chen at the end of a private meeting prior to the mediation. The communication is facilitated through an interpreter. The exchange is transcribed as follows to enable my readers to experience the vicarious dynamics of the interaction as it happened.[6]

Chen: 多谢你到我办公室来，这次会面很有用。

Interpreter: Thank you for coming here to meet me. This meeting is very useful.

John: You are very welcome. It has been a great pleasure to meet you and to talk with you through the matter.

(John rises from his chair to shake hands with Chen and the interpreter before his departure. He notices a painting on the wall and makes comments on it.)

John: That's an interesting picture.

Chen: 您喜欢吗？

Interpreter: Do you like it?

John: I like the style. Is it contemporary?

Chen: 有三四十年了，这位画家刚去世不久。 生前是中国美术界挺知名的人物。

Interpreter: It's 30 or 40 years old. The artist died recently. He was quite well known in Chinese art circles.

John: Ah, we don't have anything to compare with this in the West. My wife likes that type of painting. Anyway, I must go back now.

Chen: 请收下吧。不成敬意。我派人送到您酒店去。

Interpreter: It is my gift to you. I will have it sent to your hotel.

John (slightly taken aback and smiles): I couldn't possibly accept such a gift.

Chen: 不行。一定要收下。

Interpreter: No, please. I insist.

John (whispers to the interpreter): Oh, I feel very awkward about taking the painting.

Interpreter (whispers to Chen in Chinese): Mr Chen, it's probably not a good idea to insist on him taking the painting.

---

6   For ease of reading, I have omitted the Chinese translation of John's utterances.

Chen (to the interpreter in Chinese): Why? He just said his wife would like it and he seemed interested as well. I just wanted to be generous and make sure he's happy with me.

Interpreter (to Chen in Chinese): I think he was just being polite.

Chen (to interpreter in Chinese): So you mean he didn't really want to have my painting?

At the end of this first private meeting building up to mediation, John's efforts to build rapport with Chen seemed to have paid off till the last moment when this unexpected 'painting incident' cropped up. This is a clear example of misconnection of one party's intention to pay compliments (being polite) and its cross-cultural reception and interpretation by the other party. In Chinese culture, showing generosity underpins one of the most important constituents of politeness[7] A Chinese person would feel obliged to demonstrate such generosity by offering his or her possession as a gift (or to pay for some shared service such as a meal or a taxi ride) when the other has expressed admiration towards the possession, provided both parties assess the value involved to be appropriate as a gift. Such a manifestation of politeness not only impacts interactions between adults but also children. I still vividly remember that as a five or six-year-old child, I scribbled on my favourite doll with mixed feelings in fear that my mother would offer it as a gift to her friend's daughter who showed great interest in my doll! I felt absolutely awful and guilty doing it but believed that it would be the only choice I had to keep my doll. Unbeknown to myself, I was already protesting in my way to a Chinese politeness principle. If I am brave here, I dare say that many Chinese disapprove of such a practice quietly but must follow for the sake of face. This explains Chen's interpretation of John's compliments to the painting and Chen's reaction by offering it as a gift to John and his wife, which is shown to be completely out of John's expectation and puts him in a difficult position to respond appropriately as an English person.

In this case, were the interpreter to follow the verbatim interpretation rule, ie faithfully interpreted John's utterance expressing his awkward feelings in front of Chen, it would very probably arouse a sense of offence in Chen. Instead, the interpreter allowed himself to get involved in the interaction, becoming a cultural mediator for John and Chen by bridging the gap of misunderstanding and by clarifying two parties' respective intentions implied in their words.

Example 2: protecting a party's face needs and defusing potential conflicts

This example is extracted from the press conference given by the Chinese Premier in 2010. The journalist from AFP asked a highly face-threatening question to the Premier at this conference attended by thousands and watched via television by millions. It serves as a good example, illustrating how an interpreter may handle

---

7   According to Gu Yueguo ('Politeness Phenomena in Modern Chinese', (1990) 14(2) *Journal of Pragmatics*, 14(2) 237), there are four constituents made up of Chinese politeness: respectfulness, modesty, attitudinal warmth (showing generosity) and refinement.

such challenging utterances by mediating the use of certain linguistic markers in the interpretation. The following is the original question in verbatim.

Journalist: Thank you very much, Prime Minister, for accepting this question by AFP. Over the last year, there has been a spate of self-immolation in the Tibetan areas of China. Is this a matter of great concern to you personally? What do you think your government can do? What's the best way for your government to address this situation? Thank you very much.

Interpretation: 我是法新社记者。自去年以来，我们看到在中国藏区出现了一系列藏人自焚的现象。我想问您本人是否对这一现象深感关切。 您领导的政府将采取什么措施，您认为政府觉得是什么样的方式才能最好地应对这一局面？

Idiomatic translation of the interpretation: I am from AFP. Since last year, we have seen a series of phenomena where some Tibetans carried out self-immolation in China's Tibetan area. I'd like to ask whether you (deferent form) personally are very concerned about this matter. What measures will be taken by the government led by you, (hesitance and rephrase) according to you, what does the government believe to be the best method for dealing with this issue?

In the journalist's utterance, negative descriptor 'a spate of' was used to stress the grave situation in Tibet. This posed a great threat to the Premier's face needs and his government since there had been severe criticisms of Chinese government's policy on Tibet within the international community. This question entailed a highly controversial political issue. Moreover, the questions were initiated in a rather direct manner with personal pronoun 'your' (government) explicitly pinpointed. In the interpretation, 'a spate of' which has a negative connotation was replaced by a neutral expression 'a series of' to mitigate face threats. The deferent form of the second person pronoun 您 was also adopted. Furthermore, when interpreting the last two questions, the interpreter started off with translating verbatim but then showed hesitance, followed by rephrasing the wording she just used in the interpretation, i.e., changing 您领导的政府 (the government led by you), in which the Premier's leading role in the government that had adopted the controversial policy was highlighted, to 您认为政府觉得 (according to you how does the government feel) where the Premier's knowledge of the government's thinking was sought, and the Premier and the government were treated separately in this manner. Such hesitance and rephrasing in the interpretation serve as good evidence of the interpreter's conscious efforts to protect a party's face needs and to defuse potential conflicts.

The above two examples show clearly that when a context is highly oriented towards interpersonal interactions, verbatim interpretation is seldom possible or desirable. Interpreters, in fact, constantly make decisions to coordinate interactions by participating in the interaction or mediating party's use of language to achieve three purposes highlighted at the beginning of this session. Therefore, the expectation of interpreters to behave merely as language conduits and not to add any spins to what is said constitutes a misreading of the nature of interpreting activities.

Mediators are recommended to discuss with and inform interpreters prior to the mediation how they should handle the interpretation of certain salient use of language by parties such as sarcasm, jokes and humour, banter and irony, and emotionally charged comments. Mediators may wish to use the corridor time to learn/gain knowledge from the interpreter of a party's uncoloured utterances for access to the party's intentions, emotions or attitude.

Working with interpreters on deciphering body language

Studies, such as that carried out by Yuan,[8] have shown that people of different cultural backgrounds may use different body language to achieve the same pragmatic intentions, and they do have cross-cultural difficulty in interpreting the meanings of paralinguistics. For example, I investigated this by showing a group of British viewers and a group of Chinese viewers two film clips respectively.[9] One clip is from the film *Kramer vs Kramer* with and without Chinese subtitles. And the other clip is from a Chinese language film with and without English subtitles. Both British and Chinese viewers watched the same clips twice. Nevertheless, they produced very different interpretations of the speaker's body language shown on screen. Specifically, the British viewers were able to notice many subtle movements and changes in the speaker's body language in the English language film clip, such as his half-hearted attempt to laugh, hearing the words but not really listening, his scant engagement and little eye contact, types of smile displayed on his face at certain points, his nervous cough, his tone, his playing with the stem of his wine glass, his constant looking down to avoid eye contact when saying certain things, his stiff and upright gestures. The pragmatic meanings communicated through such body language, as reported by the British viewers, informed them of his attitude, emotions and intentions. They helped the British viewers to make their minds up about the speaker as a 'shifty, sneaky, calculating, emotionless, and unsympathetic individual'. Via the same images on screen about the same speaker, the Chinese viewers commented on his body language as his manners being sincere, his facial expression showing he is sorry, full of pain and reluctance, his having no mood for lunch, and his listening to the other person with patience. Such interpretations have contributed to the Chinese viewers' impressions of the same speaker as 'a sympathetic and humane individual with good people skills'. This demonstrates that the Chinese viewers, who are from a very different cultural background from that of the speaker on screen, were not able to decipher accurately many subtle activities in the speaker's use and change of his body language. This conclusion witnesses/gains its validity in the experiment on the British viewers' with the Chinese language film clip.

Such challenges also baffle people's efforts when they try to read facial expressions in cross-cultural contexts.[10] I once presented the picture below showing contrasting facial expressions of two groups (rows) of women, one being Eastern Asian and the other Western Caucasian'.[11]

---

8   X Yuan, *Politeness and Audience Response in Chinese-English Subtitling* (Oxford: Peter Lang, 2012).
9   For details of the experiment and the findings on cross-cultural understanding of body language, please refer to Chapter 5 in X Yuan, *Politeness and Audience Response in Chinese-English Subtitling*. n 8 above.
10 R Jack, R Caldara and P Schyns, 'Internal Representations Reveal Cultural Diversity in Expectations of Face Expressions of Emotion' (2012) 141(1) Journal of Experimental Psychology 19.
11 The picture is drawn from Jack et al (n 10 above), 21.

Using Interpreters in Mediation

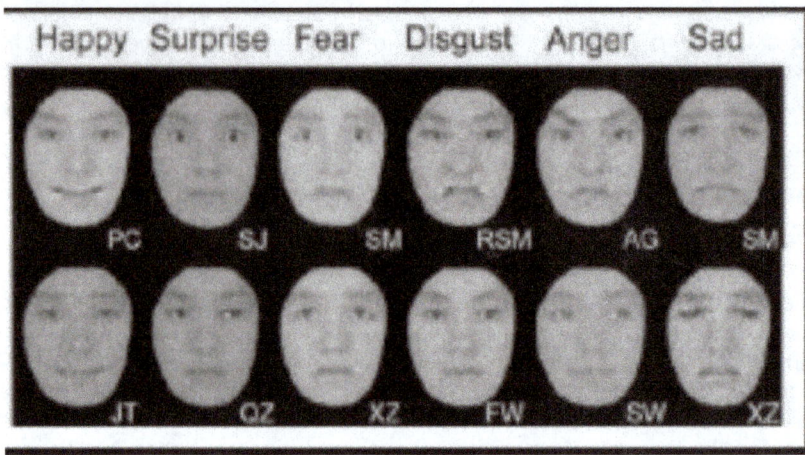

I asked 10 British mediators to identify which facial expressions belong to Western Caucasians. The same question was repeated with 10 Chinese mediators. Both British and Chinese mediators were able to accurately discern that the top group belongs to the Western Caucasians and the bottom to the Eastern Asians. However, when I asked how they could identify them or what helped them to reach the answer, they all reported that the group which comes from the same cultural background as theirs, the facial expressions make sense to them, but they cannot understand or are not familiar with the facial expressions displayed in the other group.

The above two experiments illustrate the great difficulty and challenges we face when trying to understand other's body language and facial expressions in cross/inter-cultural contexts. The correct interpretations of body language and facial expressions are indispensible if we want to understand the other's intentions, attitude, emotional status, personalities, or simply what the person is like and what they are thinking. Guesses and conjectures without informed knowledge can be dangerous and misleading. In international mediation, they certainly should be avoided. Therefore, *when working with an interpreter, the mediator should take full advantage of the interpreter's cultural knowledge and skills in this respect.* The interpreter can be a huge help providing useful comments on a party's body language as in most occasions, the interpreter would come from the same cultural background with that of the party for which they are interpreting.

Pitfalls of using party's relatives or lawyers as interpreters

In practice, there can be pragmatic reasons for discouraging the use of interpreters. For example, parties may be reluctant to involve another human agent during the discussion of private and sensitive matters. Use of interpreters will simply incur extra costs, which parties may not be aware of beforehand. Parties may not be convinced or trust that the interpreter will faithfully and accurately represent what they are trying to communicate. Instead, a party's relative or lawyer may be called on to do the interpretation. There are many pitfalls doing this. First, and obviously, a party's relative or lawyer may not be a trained interpreter, and so they would not be skilled in faithfully representing the party's voices and intentions. For example, in professional interpreting, the first pronoun 'I' is always used to communicate the party's voice through the interpreter. Nevertheless, an untrained person may draw upon various pronouns which could confuse the person referred to in the discussion and cause confusion as to who is spoken to. At one instance, during a family mediation, a party used her nephew as the interpreter since he is bilingual and familiar with the major issues at dispute. However, it turned out that the nephew mainly did summarisations of what the party said, incorporated his own understanding and comments on the issues, asked questions and made requests that he believed as necessary and appropriate. This caused confusion for the mediator who had difficulty in discerning what was actually originally said by the party which accurately manifested her thinking and interests. Throughout the mediation, the mediator was visibly frustrated by having to ask the nephew repeatedly to clarify what was added/omitted to the party's descriptions of events and/or comments.

A professional interpreter is trained not to add or delete the messages communicated. An untrained person may well do so for various reasons, particularly in view of the fact that lawyers are trained to represent their clients from their own perspectives or even with their own agendas. For example, during a commercial mediation where the lawyer interpreted for the party, the lawyer was so confident about his knowledge of the party's interests and bottom line, he spoke most of the time on behalf of his client rather than interpreting for him. Fortunately, the co-mediator present was bilingual and able to encourage the party's direct involvement in the communication. Should there be no bilingual co-mediator at a mediation, the interactional dynamics can be very unhelpful. *Therefore, it is highly recommended to use, ideally a qualified mediator and trained interpreter, as the co-mediator in intercultural mediation.*

In essence, to ensure the effective representation of the party's positions and interests, the mediator should inform the parties of the necessity of using a professional interpreter when the party cannot sufficiently understand the language used for mediation. The mediator should also build relationships with professional interpreting associations to draw on competent interpreters for their international mediation services.

Dos and don'ts for using interpreting in mediation

In summary, at the end of this chapter on use of interpreting in mediation, the following bullet points will hopefully provide a useful checklist for mediators when considering to use or preparing to work with an interpreter:

Dos

Before the mediation:

- choose a professional interpreter;
- build rapport and trust as you do with parties;
- decide the mode of interpretation;
- decide the seating arrangement;

Using Interpreters in Mediation

- clearly brief impartiality and confidentiality;
- explain the mediation process;
- sign a separate confidentiality agreement;
- instruct how certain expressions to be interpreted;
- share background documents if possible; and
- define the responsibilities of managing interactions.

During the mediation:

- explain the interpreter's job at the beginning;
- assure the parties of confidentiality;
- remind the parties to use simple language, avoiding Shakespeare or biblical language, etc;
- take advantage of the interpreter's bi-cultural capability;
- make sure of the interpreter's reasonable working conditions; and
- use corridor time to exchange with the interpreter on a party's use of verbal and nonverbal language.

Don'ts

- Don't omit your work with the interpreter at preparation stage;
- don't go with the party's suggestion of using a relative or a lawyer;
- don't assume your interpreter will act merely as a language switcher; and
- don't assume your interpreter is familiar with the mediation process

Rules of thumb

- Make sure you use interpreters when one party cannot sufficiently speak the working language used for mediation.
- Make sure you use qualified trained and professional interpreters from recognised organisations, such as:
    — ITI (The Institute of Translation and Interpreting); and
    — AIIC (International Association of Conference Interpreters).

Chapter 9

Enhancing the Political Process

John Sturrock QC

I have known John since he trained in the mid-1990s and he quickly became one of the best commercial mediators and trainers in the United Kingdom. His intelligence and thoughtfulness have enabled him to use his skills in many ways beyond business disputes, not least in and around government and parliaments. He has also worked extensively in sport and with the churches. He has been a staunch advocate of co-operation rather than confrontation in all these fields. No wonder he is known as 'Mr Mediation' in Scotland. (DR)

In an excellent examination of Nelson Mandela's leadership style (*Mandela's Way: Lessons in Life*), his biographer Richard Stengel writes:

> 'Shades of grey are not easy to articulate. Black-and-white is seductive because it is simple and absolute. It appears clear and decisive. Because of that, we will often gravitate toward yes or no answers when a 'both' or a 'maybe' is closer to the truth. Some people will choose a categorical yes or no simply because they think it appears strong. But if we cultivate the habit of considering both – or even several – sides of a question, as Mandela did, of holding both good and bad in our minds, we may see solutions that would not otherwise have occurred to us. This way of thinking is demanding. Even if we remain wedded to our point of view, it requires us to put ourselves in the shoes of those with whom we disagree. That takes an effort of will, and it requires empathy and imagination. But the reward, as we can see in the case of Mandela, is something that can fairly be described as wisdom.'

These words reflect the philosophy and insights of one of the greatest political leaders of any generation. They have great resonance for those of us who are mediators. We recognise the wisdom in the narrative. Black-and-white, categorical assertions, the paradigm of right/wrong, fault and blame, are familiar to us. They underpin many, if not most, of the disputes we are called upon to help resolve. The culture of adversarialism is familiar and often destructive, to business and professional relationships, commercial initiatives, joint ventures, partnerships, workplaces, boardrooms, neighbourhoods and families.

Mandela could see that it was also destructive to a nation:

> 'I never sought to undermine [the president] Mr de Klerk, for the practical reason that the weaker he was, the weaker the negotiations process. To make peace with an enemy one must work with that enemy, and the enemy must become one's partner.'

Enhancing the Political Process

The idea that many of the world's problems are much more complex than dualist thinking (yes/no) permits is not new. In reality, many of the conflicts within and between nations, whether political, economic or social, are multi-dimensional, finely nuanced, layer upon layer. There are no easy, right or wrong solutions. There are, literally, several sides to most stories, many vantage points and differing perspectives. The dirty filters of assumption, history, culture, (mis-) perception, bias and all the other cognitive illusions, abound. What is 'good' to some is 'bad' to others – and vice versa. That is the reality, and we know that no one side is ever as clearly 'right' or 'wrong' as others may think.

'You never really understand things from another person's point of view…until you climb into his skin and walk around in it,' said Atticus Finch in *To Kill a Mockingbird*. How often do we mediators encourage parties in mediation to do just that, using a variety of techniques designed to induce different thinking, help a party to acknowledge a different point of view, break a deadlock or unlock impasse? 'It's not our differences that separate us but our judgments about each other,' writes Margaret Wheatley. We know how hard it can be to shift judgment, to challenge assumption, the 'effort of will', 'empathy' and imagination' it requires…and yet we also know how valuable and transformative viewing matters from your protagonist's perspective can be. It can result in solutions that would 'not otherwise have occurred'. Helping people to do these things is what mediators do.

It seems obvious, therefore, that the skills and techniques we use as mediators ought to be ideally suited to helping to address political issues. Doug Noll, in *Elusive Peace*, argues as much. But, generally, mediation skills are not sought in political controversy. To be fair, we do hear of mediators in international conflicts. And, sometimes, they have heroic achievements. However, as Noll has argued, these individuals seem often to lack the deep training and process awareness that many professional mediators would regard as essential. If we turn more to domestic issues, such as allocation of scarce resources, inter-departmental or local/national government disputes, trades union/management uncertainties, large-scale development projects, scrutiny of public expenditure, etc, how often is highly professional, top quality mediation a resource on which decision makers as a matter of course rely? Rarely? And yet helping other people to untangle complex problems and find extra value is what mediators do.

It's not easy of course. Politics, or a certain style which we might describe as 'Westminster politics', thrives and indeed is sustained by confrontation, partisanship, the finding of fault, personal attack, party discipline and a largely binary system. Careers are made and broken by this system. Whole structures exist to maintain it, and are dependent on it. And it is said that this system is necessary to hold those in power to account. However, all the anecdotal evidence and some good recent writing[1] suggest that this is not so. Indeed a common expression on the back cover of these two books is 'cock-up'. As we often see paralleled in the commercial, family and community worlds, the adversarial model produces simplistic analyses, defensiveness, a culture of right/wrong and unattractive politics. Worse than that, it leads to some pretty disastrous policies and decisions, and a culture of cover up and hubris.

---

1   Anthony King and Ivor Crewe, *The Blunders of our Governments* (Oneworld Publications, 2013) and Richard Bacon MP and Christopher Hope, *Conundrum: Why Every Government Gets Things Wrong* (Biteback Publishing, 2013).

Enhancing the Political Process

The great lateral thinker, Edward de Bono, captures well the alternative of maximising gains, in a way that addresses mutual interests, in his principle of co-opetition. Transcending both competition with its zero sum connotations and the kind of cooperation which results in compromise, de Bono challenges us to think differently as we seek to find added value in a way which literally expands the notional pie and builds on the real underlying needs, hopes and aspirations of people, most of whom will welcome encouragement and recognition. This approach requires those involved to move away from simply building up their own arguments while knocking down those of others with whom they (apparently and perhaps only superficially) disagree – as classical politics necessitates. That should no longer be the name of the game. We need to move on from 'right' or 'wrong', 'either/or' solutions. These are not, says de Bono, efficient. Helping people to understand these ideas is what mediators do.

The same theme is picked up by leading Harvard mathematician and biologist, Martin Nowak, in his powerful book about altruism, *Super Cooperators*.[2] Survival is not of the fittest with their selfish genes, but of those who find ways to collaborate successfully. However, through its apparent inability to evolve in this way, politics runs the risk of extinction, or at least of wholesale indifference, in the minds of those to whom it should matter most, the electorate.

Richard Rohr, the Franciscan priest, tells us that the contemporary mind has almost no training in how to think paradoxically, being stuck with dualist thought and locked into making seemingly clever distinctions, while devoid of wisdom. Hence, he says, our angry politics – and our angry religion. So, reflecting the reality of complexity, how do we help politicians and others to build on their opponents' suggestions and look for multiple options where both – or many – ideas may be valid? How do we find common criteria to help them assess their choices and make decisions together and imaginatively? Well, that is what mediators do.

As we have already noted, a shift in culture to an interest-based, collaborative approach in politics would not be easy. Indeed, many of you reading this now will be saying to yourselves: 'We have heard all of this before', 'This is the usual fantasy stuff', 'Even if some did this, he/she/they would not', 'It will never work'.

And, of course, these are all true if we allow them to be. Nelson Mandela faced similar choices. He decided – and had the character and willpower – to do and be something, someone, different. These paradigm shifts need exceptional people doing and being just that, different. That is what mediators are – or should be.

Consider the utility of the following questions in modern politics, questions like:

What are the real needs and objectives underlying this policy?

How can these be achieved realistically?

What are the alternatives to such and such a course of action?

How much will each cost?

---

2   Martin Nowak, *Super Cooperators: Altruism, Evolution, and Why We Need Each Other to Succeed* (Free Press, 2012).

What other risks are there?

How can we add value?

What in the 'opposition's' criticisms might be valid?

How could we involve 'them' in improving this policy?

How do we achieve the desired outcome in a complex world?

How can we build on our counterparts' suggestions and look for multiple options, where 'both' – or many – ideas may be valid?

By what criteria can multiple options be analysed?

What common criteria can we find to assess our choices and make decisions rationally and imaginatively?

How can we set boundaries and hold people properly accountable and, at the same time, acknowledge their humanity and imperfection?

We all make mistakes, don't we?

How do we minimise the risks and maximise the potential?

These questions are not easy to ask and answer if you live and die by the point-scoring ritual of the dispatch box. Arguably, the only people who can ask these sorts of questions are those without a stake, genuinely disinterested in the outcome but committed to a world-class process or, perhaps, those who learn the skills to do so because their positions in the political system require it. This hints at the kind of process where 'debate' in the classic meaning ('to resolve by beating down') carries less weight, and is understood to be less effective, than genuine dialogue, which enables multiple ideas to flow, seeking meaning in relationships which are built and maintained in the common interest. Helping people to engage in this sort of dialogue – or learn to do so – is what mediators do.

My own work has taken me into the legislatures of many of the assemblies and parliaments in the countries of the United Kingdom, to train and coach members in 'scrutiny skills'. I believe that many politicians do understand the real value of this training at an individual level. I believe that they wish to move away from the time-consuming, energy-depleting, morale-sapping and often futile game of positional politics. They sense that this change is what their constituents want too. The whole mood was summed up by an elderly lady, as she passed me on her way out of a public meeting which was part of a mediation process in which I was engaged. The issues were heavily political, and also social and economic. 'We should have had this meeting two years ago, before ...'.

I have also been privileged to work with many of Scotland's business, political and public sector leaders in the activities of Scotland's 2020 Climate Group, which I facilitated for four years. While not strictly mediation, the role was, in a light touch way, to help the disparate players to work together and find common interest in addressing this most pressing of human problems. The work of the group has become a beacon in a world where self-interest and posturing still dominates and threatens our very survival as a species.

From these and other experiences, I know that many politicians and civil servants have an inclination to be, and an aptitude as, interest-based negotiators. The so-called 'Edinburgh Agreement' between the UK Government at Westminster and the Scottish Government at Holyrood, governing the conduct of the independence referendum in Scotland, is a fine example of Getting to Yes (or, for balance, The Power of a Positive No!) in practice. Much of which is done behind the scenes in politics does reflect good practice in collaborative problem-solving. But it is not the norm, nor are most people sufficiently skilled in the genre. Indeed, as with any other difficult problems or crucial conversations, people in politics suffer the same stresses and strains as those others with whom mediators regularly mediate.

We now understand that, in straitened circumstances or when feeling threatened, many of us will tend to resort to 'fight or flight' evasive behaviour, just as our predecessors would when they faced unpredictable predators. For example, the success of Nobel-laureate Daniel Kahneman's *Thinking, Fast and Slow*[3] has brought to our living rooms many examples of what have become known as cognitive illusions or 'traps'. Reactive devaluation, attribution error, confirmation bias, over-reliance on intuition, risk aversion, missing the obvious – all of these ways in which our brains can trick us wait for politicians, perhaps especially politicians, given the febrile atmosphere in which they operate, as they do for the rest of us. This understanding helps us to appreciate why, in a tense, binary, political debate, proponents of different views (yes/no, right/wrong) might behave in ways which seem unattractive and evasive. This can all be understood, acknowledged and managed. Helping people to understand, acknowledge and manage these sorts of things is what mediators do.

In the charmingly-titled *The Dance of Opposites*[4], one of the great heroes in our field of conflict resolution, Kenneth Cloke, sums all this up eloquently:

> 'Successful political decision-making and conflict resolution require not silence or rage but dialogue, not aggression but collaboration. ... Indeed, it is arguable, ... that in the absence of improved conflict resolution skills it will prove difficult, if not impossible, for us to survive as a species. ... [it is not] utopian or presumptuous to imagine that we can expand and evolve dialogue techniques in ways that will allow us to discuss and resolve contentious political issues without resorting to violence or coercion.'

So, what can mediators do?

- Challenge our own assumptions about what we do and how we do it.
- Be prepared to move into other spheres.
- In particular, transfer our thinking about mediation to the political sphere.
- Consider our language and attitudes and how we can engage with politicians and those who serve them – and us.
- Offer to help – not presumptuously but with humility and with the same understanding we would extend to others to whom we offer our skills and services.

---

3   Daniel Kahneman *Thinking, Fast and Slow* (Penguin, 2012).
4   Kenneth Cloke, *The Dance of Opposites: Explorations in Mediation, Dialogue and Conflict Resolution Systems* (Goodmedia Press, 2013).

Enhancing the Political Process

- Be realistic, shaping what we do to the real world of political decision making in tough situations.
- Explore the underlying needs of, and tensions within, the political systems.
- Help politicians and others understand the benefits of moving from the win/lose paradigm of political power to interest-based, collaborative decision-making.
- Challenge the idea of right/wrong, single truth outcomes.
- Encourage dialogue rather than debate wherever possible.
- Identify the gains which could be made with such changes.
- Talk about choices, opportunities and responsibility.
- Write, talk, train, coach, whenever and wherever opportunity arises.
- Build relationships, get to know people and remain independent.
- Continue to be bold, exceptional and different.

After all, these are all things that mediators can do, and the reward, to paraphrase Richard Stengel, as we saw in the case of Mandela, might just be something that can fairly be described as 'wisdom.' That, at least, is an aspiration worth aiming for.

Note

The work of Collaborative Scotland (www.collaborative-scotland.org) in promoting respectful dialogue in the campaign on the question of Scottish independence has revealed a deep-seated desire among many in my country for a new way of doing politics. This initiative seeks to engage ordinary folk in discussing politics in a different way, valuing uncertainty, paradox, and non-dualist approaches to decisions, encouraging consideration of *how* we do things as much as the outcome and moving towards a more 'interest-based' context.

Chapter 10

Beyond Mediation

Tony Willis

Tony was the first big name in commercial mediation. His stature, intellect and presence make him a formidable mediator and it has led to international recognition and involvement in some huge mediations. I originally asked him to write about deal mediation but he rightly grew the brief to include many other possibilities for commercial mediators. (DR)

Introduction

Mediation in the commercial field usually involves an actual or potential dispute, a disagreement that could be decided by a judge if required. It may not be in litigation or arbitration or it could be close to or even in trial. Two or more parties, each legally represented. Such matters probably make up most cases undertaken by experienced commercial mediators in the United Kingdom, the United States, Australia, Canada and New Zealand and probably elsewhere. The Woolf Reforms to the Civil Procedure Rules in effect in England and Wales[1] from 1999 encouraged it, the case law since has emphasised it and experienced law firms and counsel are practiced in the arts of representing their clients in those processes.

Such cases tend to follow a well-trodden path, with initial discussion, documents, briefing papers (mostly exchanged but sometimes confidential to the mediator from one or more parties), meetings with senior representatives present and face-to-face and private meetings. An experienced mediator will move to meaningful negotiation when he or she senses the parties are or should be ready. If there are insurers involved, they usually want early engagement on numbers.

It is arguable that the mediation process has become too formulaic. Some mediation institutions and others are guilty of rule building and definition confusion but that is a different subject. Some of the most experienced mediators have moved increasingly in major cases to more engagement with the parties and their lawyers to plan a suitable process before any formal meetings take place. In other cases, it may be sensible to abandon complex briefing notes with all the cost involved in their preparation. The reality is that the mediation process conducted by experienced and respected mediators is powerful. It leads to results in many to most cases and considerable benefits even where no agreement is reached.

---

1   Not in Scotland where moves to encourage mediation in the civil justice system have been more recent and comparatively limited.

Possible new fields to conquer

Deal mediation[2] is a term spoken about occasionally among commercial mediators[3] to describe use in a wider business context of the well-used tool kit we deploy every day in achieving settlement of commercial disputes. The same question is usually asked. Why not use our skills and experience in non-contentious negotiations, in negotiating long term commercial contracts for example – or perhaps in the labour relations field now occupied to a significant extent by ACAS in the United Kingdom?

What about negotiations involving sovereign states or governmental organisations? Sovereign states regularly show all the signs of needing expert advice and help in some of their international dealings. How many suggested negotiations never start when they need to because one or other suggested participant insists on some pre-condition being satisfied before even one word is spoken? That and other existential negotiating mistakes abound. As I write this the Middle East is on fire again with horrifying consequences for many innocents, including children, yet participants regularly refuse frank discussions.

Then there is acting as settlement counsel, when an experienced mediator is hired to assist, to counsel one party to a dispute on negotiation tactics and strategy.

These four fields – sovereign state negotiations, collective bargaining, contract negotiations and acting as Settlement Counsel – seem likely to be sensible outlets for the immense practical experience which experienced mediators can bring to bear. All involve a search by negotiation for a deal.

Sovereign state negotiations

We know too little about the use of experienced private mediators in the governmental and sovereign state context. My experience is limited. That it does happen there is no doubt. Private mediators have been working at least in Scotland in the climate change field for some time. There are doubtless other examples but they are exceptions.

There are particular reasons for this. It might be thought for example that an experienced mediator could make a better job than the US Government in mediating between Israel and the Palestinians. The record speaks for itself – endless attempts, lots of commitment, lots of failures, no agreement which sticks. Every two steps forward seems to lead inexorably to three steps back, with The United States heavily conflicted.

---

2   Sometimes called 'facilitating difficult discussions'.
3   Examples include a column written by Associate Professor Scott Peppet at the University of Colorado School of Law published in 'The Colorado Lawyer' for October 2003, Vol 32, No 10, p 81 under the heading 'Transactional Mediation', research published by Howard Raiffa in 1982 as 'The Art and Science of Negotiation' containing a detailed conceptual framework for the negotiation process, and not least a piece by my old and respected friend Professor Moti Mironi from Israel entitled 'Deal Making Mediation'.

Private Norwegian mediators (albeit supported by their government and doubtless with other state encouragement and support) were successful, where nearly everyone else had failed, in establishing a communication channel between Israel and the Palestinian Liberation Organisation (PLO), establishing sufficient common ground to justify private discussions and then conducting secret negotiations at private locations in Norway which led to the Oslo Accords in August 1993. They then handed over the process to the sovereign states who are the prime actors.[4]

Although the Norwegian mediators deserve much praise (and if one is optimistic the accords are not entirely dead) there are particular reasons why the role of private mediators in such matters will be limited. The international geopolitical order is a forum occupied by states who will always seek to operate in a rule-free environment consistent with their sovereign status. Yet only such entities can provide guarantees, resources, pressure and all the indicia of statecraft to such negotiations. Obtaining sufficient legitimacy for a few private individuals to act in secret will always be extraordinarily difficult. The Norwegian example is a shining exception to the rule that international political dispute resolution is unlikely to provide a sustainable career to private mediators. My hope remains nonetheless for future exceptions.[5]

Collective labour negotiations

My instructive experience of involvement as a private mediator in mediation between a major employer and its many employees on particular issues suggests that there is a somewhat greater role for private mediators than might be thought.

Such matters are ordinarily dealt with between employer (acting through its senior management's HR function) and employees (acting through the unions involved). Whether or not a forum already exists in which such matters can be raised, any serious issue is likely to lead to hard negotiations. All the behaviours to be expected from protagonists in a dispute will be present and so all the stages expected by an experienced mediator are likely to occur. In the United Kingdom, ACAS may become involved and a conciliation may follow. As a private mediator, direct and indirect discussion, private meetings to obtain insights into each side's position, the use of proposals and suggestions, negotiation coaching, setting the scene and guiding the tone, encouraging the climate for constructive dialogue in a problem solving fashion, refining possible outcomes, encouraging the parties to put possible agreements on paper and chasing down possible difficulties implementing the deal all arise. These and many other things are the experienced mediator's stock in trade.

It is possible that a private mediator carries with him or her a greater sense of neutrality when compared with an ACAS conciliator or equivalent with a history

---

4 See 'Against conventional wisdom: mediating the Arab-Israeli conflict' by Ezzedine Choukri-Fishere published as part of the Oslo Forum 2008 hosted by the Royal Norwegian Ministry of Foreign Affairs and the Centre for Humanitarian Dialogue.
5 See the text from the ever optimistic Doug Noll, 'Elusive Peace; How Modern Diplomatic Strategies Could Better Resolve World Conflicts' published by Prometheus (2011). Also the posting on the website of the Middle East Round Table, www.bitterlemons-international.org, Edition 20 Vol 9 – July 7th 2011 entitled 'the role of the mediator'.

Beyond Mediation

of that type of assignment. Against that, a private mediator may not be as familiar with the dynamics of negotiation with a group of unions. A great deal will depend on the mediator as always, but my experience suggests that collective bargaining matters are entirely appropriate for private mediators.

Commercial deal making

Much more has been written about the use of private mediators to assist parties engaged in commercial contract negotiations, what is usually described as deal mediation. My experience of a considerable number of such matters strongly suggests mediation can be of real assistance in this context.

In any mediation, the parties will always know far more than the mediator will know about themselves, the background, their business and the history of the reasons why a mediator is involved. In deal mediations, this factor is magnified and the mediator must be aware at all times of his or her limitations. While it does enable the mediator to ask what I sometimes call the 'damn fool questions from the back row', there are limits to that ploy.

In one such case, I was engaged after some months of what was proving to be very difficult negotiations concerning a long-term and major contract for services between two large multinational groups. The contractual history went back a very long way. The parties knew each other very well. The regulatory background had introduced some further uncertainties. The negotiating teams had made some progress but not sufficient to identify clearly all the blockages and some of the outcomes. Deadlines had passed and serious financial and other practical consequences were starting to intrude on the arrangements about to expire. Relationships between some (but by no means all) of the principals had started to fray. Fundamental attribution mistakes were multiplying along with many other roadblocks which mediators deal with every day.

Most mediators would have recognised the process that emerged. That process used all the usual tools of plenary and private meetings and private discussions with smaller groups. The end after a period was agreement on nearly all matters that had caused the blockages. The remaining matters were administrative in nature, so expected to be solved quickly.

Looking back at that matter, I think the most important (and arguably simple) contribution I made was to change the tone of the discussions from adversarial to problem solving. One member of one team said to me early on: 'That meeting was so different from the ones we have been having for many months'. It was clearly a relief. By contrast my contribution to the detailed issues in negotiation was less of a task than usually arises. Such is the power of mediation: the simple but sometimes difficult task of sitting protagonists round a table with a neutral chair guiding a process of solving problems which they both had a strong interest in solving.

In another matter concerning strategic direction within a group of companies and disagreements at Board level in several places, nearly all meetings took place in plenary session with the assistance of one chairman who had become alarmed by the level of dysfunction and its impact on business performance. Outcomes were unexpected including significant changes to Board composition. Lawyers were involved but much more as observers than is usual. On this occasion over several days many difficult conversations were had, allegiances started to change and my hope was that the changes about to take place would allow the businesses to continue as most hoped.

Neither of these matters involved claims for money or legal proceedings. In both cases, the real issues were how to solve problems, in one case leading to the best way to give effect to an agreed strategy (namely, to continue the long term agreement) and in the other leading to changes which would enable a somewhat changed strategy to be put into effect.

Settlement counsel

A party to litigation or arbitration will occasionally reach out for consultants in various fields, including negotiation. Experienced mediators can bring real hands on experience of the negotiation process and so are prime candidates to advise. Sometimes the role is behind the scenes; sometimes (as in the cases I have undertaken) settlement counsel has been in the negotiation team for the party concerned. Not only does this add to the negotiation firepower of the party concerned but it is invaluable experience for a mediator to see negotiation from a different perspective.

Conclusions

Mediators who seek to expand the roles we might play into different fields are right to try. They are correct in advancing the utility, the power and the merits of mediation techniques. Anyone who doubts that this is the case might go back to the inspirational text from that master of mediation in a broader context Andrew Acland, *A Sudden Outbreak of Common Sense*,[6] in which he described use of the techniques of mediation to a universe of circumstances.

One final and cautionary word to the mediation community. We should be beware of the increasing tendency to commoditise mediation, to apply complex rules and definitions. The wholly sterile debate concerning the supposed difference between conciliation and mediation is one example, as is the useless debate concerning the difference between evaluative and facilitative mediation. The mediation community itself is diverse and needs to give serious thought to its organisation and structure. There is not a simple answer to this but any structure must divide some sensible regulation (if it comes) from promotion (of which there has been far too much of the unthinking kind in years past). Whatever the structure, it must embrace all kinds of circumstances, including flexibility and new innovations.

The mediation process is extraordinarily powerful and in a time of much dangerous, confusing and tragic conflict in many parts of the world it is a valuable process holding great promise in many fields.

---

6   Andrew Acland, *A Sudden Outbreak of Common Sense: Managing Conflict Through Mediation* (Hutchinson Business Books, 1990).

Chapter 11

Standards and Regulation

I wanted Phillip Naughton to write this, or at least some of it, but at the time of concluding this draft he was too poorly to do so. He might not want me to dedicate a chapter on standards and regulation to him but he has been there from the beginning, helping to establish mediation in the UK legal system and then to help it grow into a credible profession. So this is for him. (DR)

As I write this in 2014, nearly 25 years after the introduction of commercial mediation to the United Kingdom, talk of regulation is gaining strength. The 'logic' is that, if we are to become a profession, regulation is part of the package. It adds credibility to being professional, so it is said, and with Government expecting the use of mediation to increase, if only to reduce the cost of 'official justice' (ie the courts), the fear is that politicians (or rather, civil servants) will impose regulation from a position of ignorance, rather than it be devised by the profession itself. Fear is the worst possible driver for anything, most of all the regulation of a profession.

My belief is it is much more important to ensure that people entering the profession have achieved a high standard and been rigorously assessed, than to be regulated once they are practicing.

High standards

Other chapters in this book try to identify what it is that makes a good mediator. Indeed the purpose of Part 3 is to change 'good' into mastery. Even a 'natural' needs some training, so where do we start?

There have been efforts in recent years to set minimum standards in the training and practice of commercial mediators. The Civil Mediation Council (CMC) recently decided that 40 hours' training, 50 per cent being role play, with two separate assessments, is the minimum standard of training and that six hours' continuing professional development and a minimum of two mediations a year would be sufficient to ensure a professional service.

It is my view that 'minimum' anything will not set high standards, indeed may well drag down standards to the lowest agreed criteria, whilst we trainers and practitioners, and the CMC in particular, should be seeking to identify the highest standard. A 'natural' mediator will be good after perhaps only 20 hours' training whereas a bad mediator will still be bad after 100 hours' training. My view is that minimum hours training with a set percentage of role play case studies, will never ensure high quality or a uniformity of standard.

Standards and Regulation

But we have to start somewhere, and setting high standards, both in training and assessment, is not a bad start. The trouble is, there are significant commercial pressures in play – a successful accreditation rate of 50 per cent or less is not attractive to most people who are investing a lot of money in a training course. High standards should mean fewer accredited, which should mean fewer less-than-competent mediators at work. Unfortunately, with only minimum standards being considered, mediocre mediators abound. it is not sufficient to assume that the market will sift out the good from the bad – the market is still largely ignorant of mediation, let alone good mediation.

But what makes a good mediator? Ironically, most good mediators don't know because they do it without thinking. It comes naturally, admittedly after a lot of practise, but it is still difficult to properly identify what it is that makes it work. Part 1 of this book covers the basic skills and process, and what follows builds on that:

- The effective mediator will be able to build such *rapport* with the parties and their advisers that everyone in the mediation feels they are not only a safe pair of hands that will guide them through difficulty but also that they are open, accepting, have only the interests of the parties in mind and no agenda of their own. A person who can be trusted with the most sensitive of information knowing that it will never be used to the party's detriment.

- The effective mediator will be a person who can *use information strategically* (when to give, when to hold, when to reframe) and be 'flexible' with confidentiality.

- The effective mediator will be a firm and confident *manager* of a flexible process, maintaining confidence that the process works whilst also giving confidence by managing the time efficiently and ensuring everyone is engaged in the process and focussed on achieving an outcome to which everyone can sign up – a person who can manage difficult people in a way that still values their contribution and who can have or encourage difficult conversations with and between the parties.

- The effective mediator makes time and space for parties to tell their story, to encourage *relationships* being valued and restored, and ensures that the process does not focus entirely on settlement but also on the humanity of the dispute.

- The effective mediator will be an experienced *negotiator* who can coax, coach, reframe and manipulate offers and counter offers so that they have a positive and beneficial effect on the negotiations, who can help parties see the shape of an emerging deal before the detail is discussed, so that when the detail is discussed it encourages co-operation, who resists giving opinions and who ensures that the parties take responsibility for the problem and the outcome.

Of course, there are other indicators of a good mediator, including how the mediator prepares for the mediation and follows up afterwards (including obtaining feedback and undergoing regular peer reviews), the minimum (or maximum) number of mediations that ensure the mediator is best every time, continuing study and development and so on. But being effective in those areas, and being assessed to be competent under rigorous criteria, should enable the mediator community to stand tall and know that they are the best. And the end user can be confident that they are going to get a mediator who gives them the best chance of achieving a resolution. Unfortunately that is not (currently) the case, although some may say that the settlement data of around 70–80 per cent is sufficient, good mediator or not. What is needed is the agreement of assessment criteria against which all mediators are assessed, and professional assessors who will apply that criteria rigorously. So agreeing the criteria, and training the assessors to apply it uniformly, is the answer to achieving confidence in the mediator profession, and we are a long way from that in 2014.

But if a mediator aspires to be the best, rather than just good, what else is required?

Aspirational standards

This is even more difficult, but I would like to see the CMC website have a statement on its website about the aspirational standards for mastering mediation. What is it that causes the 'magic' that is so often mentioned when a mediator helps parties in dispute break through deadlock and misery to finding a deal that puts an end to their dispute? What is it that gets the mediator in such harmony with the parties that it is almost spiritual? What is it that allows the mediator to know when a risky move or statement is right, and when it is not? And how can it be into words that are meaningful to anyone else?

This is all about feelings and instinct, about confidence and selflessness, about humanity and spirituality about self-awareness and trust. Most of those have different meanings to different people and they are 'soft' human skills, which are so hard to describe. But although some have been described in detail elsewhere in this book, so this is a reminder:

- **Feelings and instinct**

  We all have feelings, sometimes good, sometimes bad. An early lesson that I learnt was that good people can have bad feelings, and that doesn't matter. We mediators cannot expect to empathise greatly with every person involved in a mediation. Sometimes they are downright horrible, but rarely evil. The art is for the mediator to ensure that whatever feelings they have are filtered and generally not shown. I sometimes have to say to my assistant 'kick me if my irritation shows,' because it is difficult, but mediators have to demonstrate neutrality (or should that be independence?) at all times whilst also demonstrating empathy with the parties – a challenge and another paradox. Instinct is different. It comes from the soul – when to do something, say something, or not. There are times in a mediation when the mediator does or says something that is unpremeditated, but absolutely right. That is instinct, and the best mediators have it.

- **Confidence and selflessness**

  Parties need to feel that they are in safe hands, that when they feel vulnerable, they will not be hurt and when they express strong feelings, they will be understood. So much of the mediator's work is in modelling other's behaviour and a confident mediator will breed confidence in others. The paradox is that at times the mediator needs to fade into the background and allow parties the space and opportunity to be at the centre of the process. It is quite difficult for the mediator to become anonymous in a process that they are managing, even orchestrating, but this is a party-centred process (or should be) and the mediator is often required to be in the background. The irony is that the opposite may apply to another party, where encouragement and coaching may be needed. But the mediator needs to accept that the party is most important, and that at times they are unimportant. As has been mentioned in many places in this book, humility is a sign of a master mediator.

- **Humanity and spirituality**

    Mediation brings common sense back into the dispute resolution process. The mediator is able to put the parties into the centre of the process and they are able to take control. Not all do but fundamentally it removes the mystery and fear of the legal process and returns the dispute to a more human and understandable arena. And when it really works, the mediator is able to connect with the parties at a level of harmony that is almost spiritual. A connection – not a sympathy – that creates a trust and understanding that is well beyond the functional.

- **Self-awareness and trust.** Self-awareness is covered in more detail in other chapters, as is Bias in Chapter 5, but the message is that the mediator knowing her/himself, recognising that we all have principles and assumptions that are ingrained and generally unchangeable, is an important step in becoming an open, accepting, non-judgemental facilitator of the mediation process. Being open, accepting and non-judgemental builds trust with the parties and their advisers, which in turn results in them being more open and candid in what they share with the mediator. More of that later.

Trust brings me on to regulation.

Regulation

Most professions are regulated but the big question is: Why? It must be to protect the public, or rather, the users of the professions services. Logic then says that the users are being protected from abuse and incompetence so that the services provided are both good and appropriate. The opposite, it seems to me, is trust. If a party trusts the professional, in this case the mediator, then regulation is unnecessary. Add to that the existence of codes of conduct and easily accessible complaints procedures, and the suggestion of regulation seems irrelevant, if not irreverent! The trouble is we live in a blame culture (problem = someone is to blame = they must pay) and this culture of suspicion tends to result in the cry for more regulation. The fact that it doesn't work (eg the financial/banking industry in 2008 and the Maxwell pension scandal years before) seems to be ignored. Other professions (eg solicitors) have become burdened with increasing and ever more detailed rules that have to be administered by an increasingly expensive bureaucracy, and still the rogues prevail. The trouble is that when rules exist, people find ways to avoid them, and so more rules are created. If a person is trusted simply because there are legal sanctions against them acting in an untrustworthy way, we just do not trust them at all. We create trust that we will do the right thing simply because it is the right thing to do, not because it is a rule. So regulation can undermine real trust, or rather, real trust makes regulation unnecessary. So the challenge is to build a trustworthy profession. To me, regulation is a sign of failure rather than success and so I am against it.

But there are, and will be, rogues who profess to be effective mediators, and they will get the publicity. The counter to this is a robust filtering at training stage (ie assessment), regular peer review that is honest and courageous, and a preparedness for practitioners to challenge unacceptable practice and behaviour. The best-developed form of accountability is a willingness on the part of colleagues to voluntarily hold each other to account. I fear that we may all be too nice, or too fearful, to properly do that. And that is the danger – if we don't have the willingness and courage to hold each other to account, someone else will do it for us.

Chapter 12

What We Do Changes the World

David Richbell and Stephen Ruttle QC

Stephen is a big man, charismatic and (at times) loud. He usually arrives at meeting in shorts and cycling helmet (and other clothes according to the weather), but he has infectious enthusiasm and devotion to the cause of non-violent solutions to the world's problems. His vision of local peace centres staffed by mediators of mixed disciplines and funded by income from mediations carried out pro-bono by its mediators has yet to be established. But it will come. He makes things happen. (DR)

This final part of the book has been about mastery, about getting there and staying there and about pushing boundaries and visioning a distant horizon. Several chapters touch on the possibilities, the challenge and the exciting potential of using mediation skills beyond dispute resolution. John Sturrock (Chapter 9) writes of the potential for mediation skills in the political and international arenas. 'It is what we do,' he writes. Tony Willis writes about how these skills are already being used in deal making and other areas.

Together with Stephen, Bill Marsh, Andrew Acland and several others (and John Sturrock in Scotland), I have recently been involved in a series of facilitated conversations in the Church of England. They will continue for at least a further two years but the change in the quality of discussion was remarkable. Synod is used to a Westminster-style debate, with debaters for and against a particular motion. Suddenly, in quite small groups, people were talking to each other and being prepared to listen and accept differences. Paul Gibson (Chapter 5) calls it 'constructive disagreement' – being able to have positive conversations to enlarge understanding and create co-operation in finding solutions. And even if there are no solutions, the greater understanding and acceptance of difference creates an atmosphere of friendly coexistence. How the world needs to learn from this! How desperately we need to use these tools of understanding and co-operation instead of the violent and tragic ways that seem to be 'normal' both in human relations and in the use, or rather abuse, of this delicate planet called earth.

I have also recently been used as a 'dispute manager'. This is a new but, dare I suggest, wise use of a mediator. It was a multi-party case involving several areas of dispute and numerous legal arguments. Quite apart from the 20 or more lawyers, well over 30 experts were involved. I, and my co-mediator, were employed to co-ordinate the various lawyers' and experts' meetings to ensure that each had a common purpose so that when the mediation actually took place their advice was helpful and, within reason, consistent for every party. As a result, the experts were not involved in the two mediation days (although 76 other people did attend!) Alongside mediators using their skills in dispute avoidance, dispute management is yet another area where our experience can be invaluable to parties who disagree.

Stephen Ruttle has long been an evangelist for mediator peace centres and for the removal of the distinctions between commercial, community and other strands of mediation. Here he writes on his vision for mediation.

The potential of mediation

I was first introduced to community mediation in 1998 by the extraordinary Tony Curtis, the charismatic CEDR commercial mediator and trainer. Tony's observation, when seeking to put commercial mediation into the broader mediation scene, was that it was *community* mediation, not commercial mediation, that was 'the coal face; where the real work of transforming relationships took place'. This was not to undervalue commercial mediation, he said. Although most commercial disputes primarily have to do with money and the avoidance or settlement of Court cases, in a significant proportion of such disputes there will have been a breakdown in personal relationships and this breakdown may well need to be addressed in order to reach a settlement. Community disputes on the other hand usually had little to do with court cases and everything to do with how people, particularly neighbours, lived with and related to each other.

Early in my mediation career I was given a definition of mediation, I think both by Tony Curtis on my CEDR course, and by Bill Wakely, a community mediator, that I have gone back to again and again. 'Mediation' they told me 'is helping people have difficult conversations'. This is the most helpful summary that I have ever been given of what it is that we are there to do; whether we call ourselves mediators, facilitators, conciliators, conflict resolution specialists, negotiation coaches, or whatever. It is a definition, I think, that gives us a profound insight both into what is happening in our societies and cultures, and into how this mediation phenomenon, and we as the mediators involved to implement it, can best be used to make a real difference. We are 'conversation enablers'. We help people have proper conversations; talking to each other and listening to each. (I have elsewhere suggested that the mediation phenomenon is a sort of 'social antibody'; what we are seeing is the emergence in our societies of groups of people (mediators in their various guises) whose role is to help combat, and then heal, a profound social disease or malaise).[1]

This point can perhaps be illustrated by reference to four different disputes, each of which would typically be viewed as falling within a distinct type of mediation.

(1) A commercial dispute[2] between a large independent trader and the operator of a pool of large vessels. The trader chartered a vessel for the carriage of goods from Europe to Japan. The pool operator had itself chartered in the vessel in question from her registered owner. This owner then defaulted on its mortgage with its funding bank. The bank foreclosed on the mortgage and seized the vessel as the trader was preparing to load cargo upon her. The trader, thus deprived of the vessel, was obliged to charter in replacement tonnage to cover its open position. This led to considerable problems because of the complex nature of the trader's business at the loading port. However by working hard and by juggling other cargoes and vessels the trader was able to keep its losses down to a relatively modest level (about $1.5m). The trader claimed

1   See Roebuck Lecture, Chartered Institute of Arbitrators 2013; published in *Arbitration*, August 2013.
2   The facts are modelled broadly on a recent commercial mediation.

these losses from the pool operator, contending that the pool operator was in breach of contract in failing to procure that the vessel lifted the intended cargo. The commercial relationship between the two parties was of long standing and of very significant benefit to both groups, greatly exceeding the value of the sums involved in this dispute. Both sides had, however, appointed lawyers who took a profoundly differing view of the proper construction of the charterparty and the true extent of the traders' losses. There were suggestions in correspondence that the trader had inflated its claim and that it had acted unreasonably in seeking to mitigate its loss, and that, in any event, the claim had absolutely no prospect of success. The parties, now viewing each other though the lenses of their respective lawyers' correspondence, decided that they were better apart. They did however decide to mediate the dispute before issuing proceedings.

(2) Vicky and Chloe live next door to each other on the same street. Vicky and her partner have lived on the street for a long time and their two children often played with other children in the street. Chloe has lived on the street for two years and in that time their children had played together and both mums had become friends. More recently Chloe's partner Mike had moved in. Vicky had complained to Chloe about the noise coming from Mike's hi-fi and they got into an argument. The argument became more serious when another neighbour got involved saying she needed to defend Vicky. All three parties started to call the Housing Association most days to report on each other. The children became involved and started calling each other names. Vicky and Chloe tried to avoid meeting because when they did meet insults began to fly.

(3) Jim was withdrawing money at about 10.00pm from a cash point outside Euston Station. Ben, who had had a history of drug addiction and minor criminal behaviour, was desperate for money with which to buy drugs. He waited until Jim had removed the cash from the cash point, knocked him to the ground with a baseball bat, stole the money and ran off. He was arrested by the police and pleaded guilty to GBH. Jim in the meantime had suffered nightmares and was particularly ashamed (in his own view of himself) that he had not been able to stand up for himself and prevent himself from being knocked down 'into the gutter'. He thought that he could quickly get over his memories and move on with his life. Nine months later it was not happening.

(4) Playground bullying was rife in an inner city primary school in Battersea. Particular children were being targeted by others and the situation had got to the stage where both teachers and parents were involved. The bullying was serious, with the victims frightened to return to school with one in particular playing truant.

Each of these disputes, typically, would be given a different label: commercial, community, restorative justice/victim offender, and peer/schools. Those involved in helping the protagonists seek some resolution would probably describe their mediation practices by reference to the same terms. But each situation has the same fundamental issue in common: in none of these situations is there any or any effective conversation between the protagonists.

(1) In the 'commercial' dispute the lawyers have taken over. Typically they will advise their clients not to talk directly to each other because of the risk that there might be said something that would impair their respective legal cases. Conversation between the two parties is now 'mediated' by the lawyers; in the sense that the trader talks to their lawyer who talks to the pool operators' lawyer

who talks to the pool operator. So what the two parties are saying about each other, what they think about each other and the like is now communicated not face-to-face, but through the conduit of two separate lawyers.

(2) In the 'community' dispute the anger and resentment between Vicky and Chloe has developed to such an extent that conversation, if any, is restricted to slagging each other off when they meet in front of their houses or in the communal gardens.

(3) In the third instance (the 'restorative justice' situation), there has never been any previous conversation between Jim and Ben, brought together as they are by Ben's assault on Jim. However, Ben's violent act has caused Jim to demonise his shadowy assailant and to turn him instead into a shadowy figure of power, violence and looming threat. Ben, on the other hand, has no sense of Jim as a person, seeing him only as a hand holding desperately-needed banknotes.

(4) The children in the playground in all likelihood have never previously been taught how to learn to use words constructively rather than aggressively; as building blocks rather than as offence and abuse.

In each of these situations what is missing is conversation. In each case this missing conversation is difficult *even to consider* having, and still harder to be a part of. There are of course degrees of difficulty; conversation is usually easier where the dispute is about money or legal rights and where the parties have had a previous business relationship. However, where a relationship that had previously existed has broken down because of abuse, anger, or, even worse, violence, then the conversation will be much harder.

In each of these situations the role of the mediator is exactly the same: to help the protagonists begin to talk to each other, to help them listen to what the other is saying, to help them express emotions that are likely to make them more or less vulnerable, and so on. Such conversations by their very nature are threatening. Although the ultimate object of each of these conversations may be different (settlement of the litigation and mending of the business relationship; peaceable co-existence, and possibly reconciliation between the neighbours; closure, and, possibly, healing and forgiveness between victim and offender; and playground harmony and the emotional development that comes with learning a language that is constructive rather than negative) the task of the mediator in each case is the same: to enable the parties by virtue of their conversations to begin to work out their own solutions to the problems in which they find themselves.

The social and cultural context in which this discussion takes place is of importance. In the United Kingdom, as indeed in most of Europe and North America, there is an increasingly rights-focussed culture. At the same time the world is shrinking; multiculturalism and increasing ethnic and religious diversity is a significant feature of most of our communities. Difference invariably leads to disagreement and often to dispute. Add in the increased focus on rights (religious, moral, social and legal) and conflict is an inevitability. 'How do we live at peace?' is becoming one of the more profound cries of an age in which we are aware of increasing conflict at all levels.

Another trend can be seen. Cultural, family and community ties have degraded and often disintegrated. The communication technology boom seems to be co-existing with (and some would say causing) a noticeable decrease in relational and emotional capability. As conflict increases, so too does the demand for the emotional intelligence with which to commit to, and then to hold, what will frequently be a difficult conversation. A modern irony is that the need for such conversations seems to be increasing at exactly the same time as the ability to hold them is decreasing. The consequence is what I call a 'turning of backs'. Individuals, family groups, indeed cultural groups and nations are turning their backs on each other. As soon as that happens, conversation stops. It cannot begin until both are prepared to turn around and face each other. This is extremely difficult and usually does not happen. The consequence of this 'backing away' (often associated with 'triangulation' where each of the individuals in the dispute engages with a third party about the wrong doing of the other) is polarisation. Middle ground becomes empty and turns into a vacuum. In the words of the Irish poet WB Yeats: 'Things fall apart, the centre cannot hold, mere anarchy is loosed upon the world'. At such a time, communities, and indeed the societies made up of such communities, urgently require help for the holding of difficult conversations. Seen in this way mediation, in the wide meaning of the term, is indeed a social antibody.

The potential therefore for mediation has never been greater. Commercial mediators, typically those mediating cases which are high profile and which may involve very large sums of money, are tempted to think too highly of themselves and to regard the work they do as being of undue significance. This is a bad mistake! Commercial mediation, though more visible, is little more than the tip of the iceberg. The real work, Tony's 'coal face', takes place at local and community level where individuals, partners, families and faith groups, polarised and separated by reason of increasing divergences of view and behaviour, start again to talk to each other and thereby begin to create solutions. Mediators, invited by the protagonists to stand between them in the empty middle ground, walk towards (rather than away from) the forcefields of pain and anger, and act both as bridges and buffers. The resulting conversation often draws the parties together, re-colonising the middle ground, and starting to re-establish stable social structures.

The potential of mediation coincides with an enormous increase of interest in it. Today, across all levels of society and across all ethnic, religious, cultural and social divides, there are numerous individuals prepared to provide time as volunteer mediators to help make their own communities more peaceful. This resource, if mobilised, would have a huge effect showing that society could indeed be 'big'.

I have argued for many years for the creation of local 'peace centres' that form a loosely associated network of what might be described as a community peace service. Each of these peace centres would be backed by panels of mediators competent to mediate different types of dispute. Ideally the centre would be a sort of 'one-stop-shop' for the referral of *all* disputes that affect that community, whatever label (for instance family, community, work place, legal, etc) might currently be applied to them. The lowest common denominator on each of these disputes is the absence of conversation. The role of the relevant mediator – and of course particular types of training would be required for the type of dispute referred – is to enable these individuals to begin and then to develop these conversations.

I offer two observations by way of conclusion. The first is the need to confront division. There are of course different practices (and the need for different mediation training) between different sorts of mediation. What is unhelpful is the mindset that sees these practices as quite separate disciplines and not as aspects of a larger whole. Why is this important? First, because it emphasises the need (for all of us facilitators/conciliators/mediators) to work together. We cannot afford either to ignore each other or to squabble. What we have is too important to be wasted. There is mutual inter-dependence; and with that comes mutual inter-responsibility. Secondly, by experiencing different applications of what is essentially the same process, our own skills as mediators are deepened and our own practices enriched and broadened.

The second is the need for a bigger vision, namely to take more seriously, rather than less seriously, the significance of what we are doing as mediators. Why? Quite simply, what we do changes the world! Not usually in headline grabbing ways, but in the way in which the having of a difficult conversation, the mending of an impaired relationship, even the ability of neighbours or erstwhile litigants now to be able to sleep well at night, always changes the worlds of those individuals.

What we do changes the world. Just get on with it!

Index

Achieving excellence 341–345
  balance 341
  choices 344–345
  guide through time 344
  momentum 343
  process issues 342
  tone of mediation 343
Active listening 14
  balance of air time 14
Aftercare 83–84
Agreement to mediate 35–37
Alternative dispute resolution
  meaning 5–6
Amygdala 123–124
Appointment
  confirming 28–29
Appointment of mediator 25
Arithmetical error 62, 109
Armed Forces disputes 167–170
  operational effectiveness, and 168
  reforms, and 168
  Royal Navy 169
  value of mediation 170
Assertive lawyer 62
Assistants 27–28, 34, 309–312
  appointment 310
  debriefing 312
  procedure 310–311
  reasons for 310
  role of assistant 311–312
ATE insurance 33
Austria 395–398
  confidentiality 397
  definition of mediation 396
  enforceability of mediated settlement agreements 398
  enforceability of mediation clauses 397
  EU Directive 2008 395
  Mediation Act 2004 396
  mediation and conciliation 396
  mediation style and procedure 397–398
  mediator exemption 398

Austria – *contd*
  mediator training, accreditation and post-qualification standards 398
  register of mediators 397
  voluntary/mandatory process 397
Authority 44

Banking and financial disputes 170–172
  emotional factors 170
  inter-bank transactional disputes 172
  mis-selling claims 171–172
  types of 171
  understanding transaction 172
  wider interests 171
Belgium 399–401
  European Parliament perspective 400–401
  future of mediation 399–400
  international organisations' perspective 401
Bias 369–381
  acceptance 380
  awareness 380
  common personal biases 373–374
  conscious 372–373
  dealing with 379
  identification 375
  meaning 371
  mindfulness 380–381
  necessary purpose of 371–372
  neutrality 371–379
  rules and standards 375
  unconscious 372–373
Body language
  matching 18–19
Breaking up 48
Brown envelope 27, 51, 107
Bug 77, 111
Bulgaria 401–404
  mediators 403
  regulation 401–402
  style 402–403
  training 403–404

Index

Case study 23–24
Caucus sessions 53–54
CAVNNN 44–46
Changing the world 543–548
Charity sector disputes 173–175
Civil Mediation Council 143–144
   accreditation with 25
Civil Procedure Rules 94–96
   disobedience 96
   fast track 95
   multi task 95
   small claims track 95
   tracks 94–96
Clinical negligence disputes 175–178
   expert opinion 175–176
   fundraising v fiduciary duties 174
   gauging mood 176
   high rate of settlement 178
   lawyers' views of 177
   management v trustees 174
   preparation 176
   profit v principles 174
   service v trade 174–175
   technicality of claims 177
   volunteers and management 173
Coaching 67
Collective labour negotiations 535–536
Commercial deal making 536–537
Commercial dispute 545–546
Commercial mediation
   dispute resolution landscape 5–6
Communication skills 157–164
   acknowledging emotion 162
   body language 161
   challenging own assumptions and judgements 158–159
   conductive atmosphere 161–164
   depersonalise to defuse 163
   establishing and developing rapport 160–161
   eye contact 160
   matching language 160–161, 163–164
   meaning 157
   openness 160
   phrasing patterns 162–163
   prepare and plan 158
   presence 158–160
   self-awareness 158–160
   self-confidence 158–160
   telling people you have heard and understood 161–162
Community dispute 546

Community mediation 7, 255–261, 304–309
   benefits 305–306
   challenges 306
   concluding 308–309
   exploring 308
   nature of 255–256
   negotiating 308–309
   opening-joint session 308
   overview of process 256–257
   particular features 260–261
   parties 259–20
   process outline 258
   tools for mediation 258–259
Competence 336–337
Competition disputes 178–180
   cost estimates 180
   experts 179
   follow-on cases 178–180
   future relationship of parties 179–180
   group mediating 180
   types 178
Concluding stage 79–87
   deals with dignity 79–80
   getting the deal 79
   mediator recommendation 80–81
   pain-pain 80
   settling, or not 83
   summary 84
Confidentiality 44, 103–104, 337–339
Confirming appointment 28–29
   standard email 28–29
Conflict 122
Conflict of interest 41, 105, 335–336
Consent order 82
Consideration 102
Construction/engineering disputes 180–183
   bespoke process 181–182
   co-mediation 182
   experts 182
   larger costs 181
   numbers 182–183
   papers 182–183
   peculiarities 181
   smaller costs 181
Contingency fee agreement (CFA) 33, 86, 113
   costs, and 100
Contract 102
Core skills 11–22

Costs 98–99
    assessment 98–99
    CFA, and 100
    damages based agreement, and 100
    employment tribunals, and 101–102
    settlement offers, and 99
    standard basis 98
Counsel 51, 87, 106–107, 113–114
    role of 34
Court Rules 94–96
Court system 93–94
    funding 99
        alternatives 99
    jurisdiction 93–94
    redress through 96–97
Croatia 404–409
    accredited institutions 406–407
    confidentiality 408
    effect of mediated settlement 408
    Mediation Acts 404–405
    training 406
Cross-cultural
    meaning 145–147
Crowd control 52
Cultural aspects 70–71
CV 25–26
Cyprus 409–410
    bodies involved 410
    legal framework 409–410
    need for mediation 410
Czech Republic 410–414
    Act on Civil and Commercial Matters 412
    Act on the Probation and Mediation Service 411
    community mediation 411
    consumers' mediation 412
    cost 411
    important features 412

Damages 96
Damages based agreement
    costs, and 100
Dates 27
Deadlock, overcoming 69–70
    breaking problem down 69
    change the group 69
    food 69
    identify emotional blockage 69
    identify tactical deadlock 69–70
    take a break 69
    techniques 69–70
Deal mediation 534

Deals with dignity 87
Decision maker 51
Demonised party 52
Difficult conversations 131–135
    conflict can be positive 133
    different stories 133
    end positively 135
    face the demon 133
    key points 132
    look out for and avoid 135
    look to the future not back at the past 134
    prepare and rehearse 134
    save face 134
    separate people from problem 133
    step into other's shoes 133
    turn assumptions into facts 134
    types 132
Dispute manager 543
Dispute resolution landscape 5–6
Documents
    Electronic calendar 27
    Emotions 122–124
    influence of 123
    mediator's eyes only, for 30

Empathy 12–13
    meaning 12
    sympathy, and 12–13
Employment disputes 183–187
    aim of mediation 184
    employee perspective 185–186
    employer perspective 186
    employment tribunal claims 184
    handling emotional and relational aspects 185–187
    managing own responses 187
    meaning 183
    mediation not appropriate, when 187
    on the day 185
    power of good ending 187
    tips 184–185
Employment tribunals 101–102
    awards 101
    costs 101–102
    powers 101
    time limits 101
Energy disputes 187–190
    advantages of mediation 188–189
    emotional needs 189
    long-term projects 188
    main objectives of mediation 189–190

Index

England and Wales 497–502
  confidentiality 501
  courts today 498–499
  EU Directive 502
  experts 501
  insurers 500
  lawyers 500
  litigation funding 501–502
  mandatory mediation 502
  mediator's confidentiality 501
  mediators 499–500
  non-lawyers 500
  participants 500
  Practice Direction 497–498
English legal system 93–104
Entertainment and media sector disputes 190–194
  content 193
  creative 191
  divergent practices or laws 193
  entertainment industry 191–192
  industry's attitude towards litigation 192
  industry's attitude towards mediation 192
  money 193
  suitability of mediation 193–194
  terminology 191–192
  typical industry disputes 192–193
Environmental and public policy mediation 292–297
  ADR, and 296
  contexts 293
  engagement 296
  facilitation 293
  multiple uncertainties 293–294
  process design 294–295
  third-party involvement 292–293
Environmental mediation 7
Equipment 31
Equitable remedies 96–97
Ethical code 325–326
Ethics 325–340
  impartiality 334–335
  mediator's obligation 331–333
  monitoring settlement agreement 330–331
  regulation 327
  types of mediation 326–327
  United States experience 328–330
European Code of Conduct for Mediators 327–328

European countries 393–395
  background of mediators 394
  extent and nature of regulation 394
  focus of mediation discussions 394
  framework 395
  joint versus private meetings, use of 394
  training 394
  values 395
Evaluative mediation 6, 247–255
  commissioning 252
  consequences 254–255
  dealing privately with lawyers or technical experts 250
  form 253–254
  mediation and decision making 248–250
  merits 250
  preparation 252–253
  reality testing 250
  using within facilitative mediation 250
Experts
  role of 34
Exploring stage 53–63
  moving on 56
  purpose 53
  summary 56–57
  variety of meetings 54

Facilitative mediator 129
Facilities 30, 43–44
Faith community mediation 288–292
  bespoke process 291
  choice of mediator 290–291
  commercial mediation, and 291–292
  expectations 290
  extended preparation 291
  facilitating conversations 292
  issues behind disputes 290
  issues commonly in dispute 289
  mediation process 291
  nature of 288–289
  needs 290
  patience 292
  relationships 292
Faith disputes 7
Family mediation 7, 262–272
  accreditation 265–266
  Children and Families Act 2014 264–265
  civil mediation, and 271–272
  compulsory referral 264

Family mediation – *contd*
  couple 268–269
  court, at 270
  direct consultation with children 266–267
  facilitative versus evaluative 271
  funding 272
  history of 262–264
  legal aid agency recognition 265–266
  managing process 269
  MIAM, and 263
  models 265
  nature of 262
  process 266
  property and financial 267–268
  right time to mediate 270
  shuttle mediation 269
  training 265–266
  types 266–267
Farming disputes 165–167
  challenging factors 166
  mediator's perspective 166–167
  variety 165–166
  volatility 165–166
  volume 165–166
Fault 123
Fees 26–27
  brown envelope 27
  payment in advance 26
  significance of 26
  success fees 27
Finland 419–422
  court mediation 421–422
  legal framework 420
  Rules of Finnish Bar Association 420–421
First contact 38–39
First open session 48–50
  purpose 43
First private meetings 35
Flipchart 21–22, 46–47
  use of 46–47
Food 30
  energy-raising 30
Forgiveness 366–367
France 422–425
  development of mediation 423–425
  legal status of mediation 422–423
  structure of mediation market 425
Franchise disputes 194–196
  BFA Panel 196
  intellectual property 195–196

Franchise disputes – *contd*
  law 195
  licences 194–195
Full and final settlement 87, 114
Future
  controlling 19

Germany 425–433
  certified mediators 430
  court fees 432
  enforceability of settlement agreements 428
  legal aid 432
  Mediation Act 426
    structure 426–428
  mediation in connection with court proceedings 431
  mediation under business judgment rule 432
  mediation within judicial conciliation 431–432
  mediator's duties 427
  out-of-court mediation 431
  statute of limitation 428–429
  style of mediations 429–430
  training requirements on mediators 428
  types of mediation 430–432
Greece 433–435
  confidentiality 434
  definition of mediator/mediation 433–434
  enforceability of mediated settlement agreements 434
  EU Directive 2008 433
  Mediation Act 433
  mediation style and procedure 434
  mediator exemption 435
  mediator training, accreditation and post-qualification standards 434–435
  register of mediators 435
  voluntary/mandatory mediation 434

Heads of Agreement 81–82
Hearing
  listening, and 13
High conflict disputes 136–141
  attachment disorganisation 137–138
  boundarised empathy 139
  cautions 139
  dealing with party's world view 140
  directiveness 140

Index

High-conflict disputes – *contd*
  distinguishing high conflict from other factors 137
  endings 141
  help personal and analytical responses 141
  high conflict personalities 137
  high conflict, special meaning 136–137
  maladaptive traits 138–139
  personality disorders 138–139
  proactivity 140
  records 140
  relevant strategies 141
  reservations 139
  small incremental steps 140
  strategies 139–141
  structure 140
History 19
Hitting the zone 17
Horror stories 360
Hungary 435–439
  introductory caveats 435–436
  post-1990 evolution of mediation 436
  private and commercial mediation 437–439
  review of Law on Mediation 436–437

ICC Mediation Rules 376–377
Idle time 45
Impartiality 334–335
Incompetence 359–363
  dangers 361–362
  learning ladder 354
Inflammatory summary 42, 106
Insolvency disputes 196–200
  costs 199
  statement of affairs 198
  timing of mediation 198–199
  types 196–197
  typical issues 197–199
  valuation issues 198
Insurance/reinsurance disputes 200–205
  brokers 202
  direct insurance as opposed to reinsurance 201
  historic view 200–201
  insurance 201–202
  reinsurance 203
  retrocession 203

Intellectual property and IT disputes 205–208
  experts 207
  IT mediation 207
  know the law 206
  love the product 206–207
  process design 208
  time management 208
Intercultural mediation 145–156, 383–391
  Aboriginal communities 155–156
  acknowledgement 389
  assumptions 154–155
  broad cultural approach 148–149
  case study 147–148
  challenge 145
  communication styles 154
  conditions underpinning 385
  conflict with local communities 391
  correct approach 148
  demystification, and 149
  digest of theory and practice 383–391
  ethno-specific approach 148
  expectations 154–155
  five dimensions of national culture 152–153
    collectivism
    femininity 152
    individualism 152
    long-term orientation 153
    masculinity 152
    power distance 152
    short-term orientation 153
    uncertainty avoidance 152–153
  flexibility 149
  gap between expectations and behaviour 149
  group dynamics 386–387
  high and low context communication 150–151
  high context cultures 150–151
  Hofstede's model, insights based on 153–154
  impact of group identity on perception and cognition 386–391
  intentions 154–155
  intercultural, meaning 145–147
  invitation nets 390
  Japanese and American parties 151–152
  low context cultures 150–151

Intercultural mediation – *contd*
  prolonged contact 388
  role of culture in conflict situations 387–388
  self-awareness 149, 384
  shift in climate 389
  turban, removal 147–148
Interests 55–56
Interpreters 517–526
  arbitration, in 519
  bridging cultural differences 520–521
  deciphering body language 523–524
  defusing potential conflicts 521–523
  non-verbatim for rapport management 519–523
  party's relatives or lawyers 524
  protecting party's face needs 521–523
  translation, and 518
Ireland 440–444
  anticipated Mediation Bill 443
  commercial disputes 441–442
  elder mediation 442
  employment disputes 442
  EU Directive 443
  family disputes 442
  legal provision for mediation 441
  training and accreditation 440–441
Italy 444–450
  EC Directive 2008 444
  free market 445
  legal framework 445–447
  mediators' style and approaches 448–449
  recourse to mediation 447–448

Joint session 51

Key document 51

Latvia 450–452
  Mediation Council 451
  Mediation Law 451
Lawyer
  centre of mediation 142–143
  role of 4–5, 34
Legal expenses insurance 99
Limitation periods 97–98
  breach of contract 97
  negligence 97
  personal injury claims 97
Limits of authority 33

Listening
  active 14
  hearing, and 13
Lithuania 452–454
  Conciliatory Mediation in Civil Disputes Act 452
  confidentiality 453
  enforceability of mediated settlement agreements 454
  EU Directive 2008 453
  mediation, definition 453
  mediation style and procedure 4543–454
  mediator, definition 453
  mediator exemption 454
  register of mediators 454
  sanctions if parties do not mediate 453
  voluntary/mandatory process 453
Litigation
  disadvantages 121
Love 366
Low offer 66
Luxembourg 454–455
  Civil Procedure Code 2012 455
  confidentiality 455
  enforceability of mediated settlement agreements 455
  EU Directive 2008 455
  mediation, definition 455
  mediation style and procedure 455
  mediator, definition 455
  mediator exemption 455
  mediator training, accreditation and post-qualification standards 455
  register of mediators 455
  voluntary/mandatory process 455

Malta 456–458
  Centre for Mediation 456
  international mediation 457
  Mediation Act 456
  restorative justice 457–458
  Victim Support Unit 457–458
Managing emotion 15–16, 47
  emotional investment 15–16
Mandatory mediation 7–8
Marketing 91
Mastery
  achieving 356
  being rather than doing 355
  building on foundations 354–355
  debrief 357

Index

Mastery – *contd*
  doing rather than being 355–356
  external mediator 355–356
  internal mediator 355
  meaning 353–354
  peak-performance 362
  peer review 356–357
  receiving feedback 358
  review, giving 357–358
  reviewer, role of 357
Mediation
  advantages 5
  definition 544
  human activity, as 22
  male of the species, and 4
  meaning 8
  nature of 8
  non-evaluative 4
  reason for 3–4
  social and cultural context 546
  solitary profession, as 9
Mediation models 6–8
Mediation practice 89–91
  create experience 89–90
  profile 89–90
  setting up 89–91
Mediator
  appointment 25
  centre of mediation 143
  CV 25–26
  fees, see Fees
  profile 25–26
Mediator as communicator 17–20
Mediator as 'friend' to all 11–16
Mediator as manager 20–22
  patience 20–21
  routine issues 20
  tenacity 20–21
Mediator as negotiator 16–17
Mediator challenges 41–42, 51–52, 62–63, 77, 86–87
  arithmetical error 62
  assertive lawyer 62
  authority 86
  better deal 87
  brown envelope 51
  bug 77
  CFA 86
  conflict of interest 41
  counsel 51, 87
  crowd control 52
  deals with dignity 87
  decision maker 51

Mediator challenges – *contd*
  demonised party 52
  first and final offer 77
  full and final settlement 87
  giving a steer 77
  inflammatory summary 42
  joint session 51
  key document 51
  key information 77
  mediator not wanted 77
  needs 62
  no honest intent 51
  papers 41–42
  no money 62
  participants 51
  ratification 86
  relaying offer 77
  responses to 105–114
    arithmetical error 109
    assertive lawyer 109
    authority 112
    better deal 113
    brown envelope 107
    bug 111
    CFA 113
    conflict of interest 105
    key information 110
    papers 105
    participants 106
    ratification 112
    relaying offer 111
    room allocation 107
    second thoughts 112–113
    serial user 114
    support documents 105
    tears 113
    too late for deal 114
    unrepresented party 110
    VAT 114
    walk-out 111–112
  room allocation 51
  second thoughts 86
  serial user 87
  supporting documents 42
  tears 86
  too late to deal 87
  unrepresented party 63
  urgent text 52
  VAT 87
  walk-out 77
Mediator groups 90
Mediator panels 90
Mediator, role of 8–9, 360–361

Index

Mediator's eyes only
   paper for 30
Mentoring 358
Mismatching 19
Modelling other's behaviour 19–20

Needs 62
Need to be heard 125–126
Negligence 102–103
Negotiating stage 65–77
   coaching 67
   cultural aspects 70–71
   first and final offer 66
   low offer 66
   mediator's advice 66–67
   power imbalance 70
   reality testing 67–69
   salami slicing 66
   shaping the deal 65
   strategies 65–67
   styles 65–67
   summary 71
   techniques 65–67
Negotiation
   failure of 4
Neighbourhood mediation 7
Netherlands 459–462
   confidentiality 461
   Dutch Mediation Act 459–460
   enforceability of mediation clauses 461
   enforceability of mediation settlement agreements 461
   EU Directive 2008 459
   mediation, definition 460
   mediation style and procedure 461
   mediator exemption 462
   mediator training, accreditation and post-qualification standards 462
   register of mediators 462
   sanctions if parties do not mediate 460–461
   voluntary/mandatory process 460
Neutrality 45
NMAS Practice Standards 376
No imposed settlement 45
No interruptions 45
No money 62
Non-binding 45
Non-evaluative commercial mediation 6
Non-evaluative mediator 130–131

Non-lawyer mediators
   avantages of 17
Non-verbal communication 18–19
Northern Ireland 444
Norway 463–466
   court-connected mediation 466
   legal regulation on out-of-court mediation 463–465
   out-of-court mediation in private sphere 465

On the day 35, 41
Open meeting 84–86
Opening stage 43–52
   summary 48
Opening statements 46
Outline of the day 45–46

Pain-pain 80
Parties
   centre of mediation 142
Partnership and family business disputes 208–211
   attachment 210
   high emotion 209–210
   historic relationships 210
   justice 210
   law 211
   separating people and problem 209
Peer mediation 7
Peer mediation in schools 282–285
   peace work programme 284–28
   process 285
   secondary schools 284
   teams of mediators 283
Perceptions 127
Personal injury claims 102–103, 211–214
   costs mediation 213–214
   early process management 212
   Lord Justice Jackson on 214
   negotiations 213
   people 211–212
   who should be there 212–213
Personal network 90
Planning related disputes 214–218
   continuing management of expectations 215–216
   examples 216
   information 216
   Lands Chamber 217–218
   litigation, and 217
   rapport building 215

Planning related disputes – *contd*
  reality testing 215
  third parties 215
  who pays 217
Poland 466–471
  barriers to successful growth of mediation 471
  civil mediation, definition 468–469
  confidentiality safeguards 470
  enforcement of settlement agreements 470
  interruption of statutes of limitation 470
  Mediation Law 2005 466–468
  quality assurance 469–470
  referral to mediation 469
Political process 527–532
  collaborative approach 529
  Collaborative Scotland 532
  'fight or flight' 531
  mediation skills, and 528
  mediators, role of 531–532
  questions in modern politics 529–530
  scrutiny skills 530
  style of 528
Portugal 471–476
  confidentiality 473–474
  legal status of mediation 472–473
  mediators 474–475
  settlement 474
  use of mediation 475–476
Positions 55–56
Post-transaction warranty claims 235–237
  accounting evidence 235–236
  adviser's ambiguous position 236
  date of valuation 235
  essential law 235
  joint and several liability 236–237
  remorse 237
  reputational risk 236
  tax advice 236
Potential of mediation 544–548
PowerPoint 31
Powers imbalance 70
Pre-mediation contact 31–33
  content 32
  reason for 32
Preparation
  summary 37–38
Preparing stage 25–42
Principled negotiation 55

Private meetings 57–62, 71–76
  timing 53–54
Private sessions 53–54
Probate and trust disputes 218–220
  break-state 220
  common ground 219
  disengagement 220
  emotional closure 218–219
  families 219–220
  lawyers, role of 219
Problem solving 16
  bringing logic and clarity to issues 16–17
Professional indemnity disputes 220–224
  advisers 222
  causation 221
  commercial considerations 223
  component parts of claim 221
  coverage disputes 223
  errors and omissions cover 221
  experience of defendants 221–222
  grievance, sense of 222–223
  novice claimants 222
  quantum 221
Profiles 25–26
Property disputes 224–229
  choice of mediator 227–229
  domestic 224–225
  landlord/tenant 226
  neighbour disputes in multi-occupied buildings 225–226
  non-domestic property 226–227
Providers
  centre of mediation 143
Psychology 121–127
Public funding
  abuse of 100
Public sector disputes 229–231
  attendees 231
  authority 230
  decision-making 230
  post-mediation approval 231
  public accountability 230
  statutory framework 229–230

Questioning
  appropriate 17–18
  challenging questions 18
  closed questions 18
  hypothetical questions 18
  open questions 18
  types of questions 18

Rapport building 12
  physical dimension 12
  purpose 12
Ratification 86
Reading list 115–116
Reality testing 67–69
  potential danger 68
  questions posed 68
  techniques 68
Recommendation 80–81
Reflecting 15
Reframing 14
Refreshments 45
Regulation 542
Relationships 129–144
Relationships v problem solving 56
Restorative justice 297–304, 546
  commercial mediation compared 299–300
  enhancing commercial mediation 303–304
  from retribution to restoration 297–298
  limits of adjudication 297
  personal engagement 302
  shared values 298–299
  standards for practitioners 303
  timing 301
  to caucus or not to caucus 302–303
Risk analysis 313–323
  anchoring 315, 322–323
  approaches to 317–321
  asymmetric attitudes to gains and losses 315
  be prepared 323
  communication tool 322
  confirmation bias 316
  determine best decision 319
  example decision tree 318
  flexibility 322
  fundamental attribution error 316
  garbage in, garbage out 322–323
  groupthink 316
  increased clarity 322
  negotiation advantage 322
  numeracy requirement 322
  outcome values 319
  overconfidence 315–316
  probabilities 318–319
  pros and cons 322–323
  quantifying qualitative results 323
  rational, barriers to 314
  reasons for 313–314

Risk analysis – *contd*
  risk neutral answers 323
  structure 318
  sunk cost fallacy 316
Romania 476–480
  common styles of mediation 479–480
  extent of use of mediation 477–478
  legal status of mediation 476–477
  mediators 478–479
Room allocation 51, 107
Russia 505–510
  Arbitration Procedure Code 507
  courts, role of 508
  Law on Mediation 507
  mandatory mediation 509
  nature of mediation 506
  role of mediator 507
  school mediation 510

Salami slicing 66
Saving face 17, 54
Scotland 503–505
  facilitative mediation model 504
  international centre of arbitration, as 504
  judicial reviews 503–504
  nature of mediation 503
Seating 43–44
Self-esteem 124–126
  corporate 124–125
  nature of 124
  need to be heard 125–126
  protection 125
Serial user 87
Setting the scene 44–46
Settlement Agreements 81–83
  pro forma 33
  precedent 83
  writing 81
Settlement counsel 537
Shareholder disputes 231–235
  bartering, and 340
  Companies Act 2206, ss 260–264 232
  Companies Act 2006, s 994 232
  date of valuation 235
  dominance of accountancy evidence 233–234
  essential law 232
  golden goose paradox 232
  Insolvency Act 1986, s 122(1)(g) 232
  managing experts 234

Shareholder disputes – *contd*
  O'Neill letters 234
  remedies 232
  thinking outside the box 234
  winning can be worse than losing 233
Shipping disputes 237–240
  advance strategy 239
  overpopulation of mediation 238
  parties from different countries 239–240
  potential for success 238
  preservation of relationships 237–238
  rapport 238–239
  ultimate problem 239
Side meetings 54
Silence 15
Site visit 35
Slovakia 480–482
  confidentiality 481
  enforceability of mediated settlement agreements 481–482
  EU Directive 2008 480
  Mediation Act 480
  mediation, definition 480
  mediation style and procedure 481
  mediator, definition 480
  mediator exemption 482
  mediator training, accreditation and post-qualification standards 482
  register of mediators 482
  voluntary/mandatory 481
Slovenia 482–486
  Alternative Dispute Resolution in Judicial Matters Act 483–484
  mediators 484–485
  place of mediation in Slovenian law 482–483
  regulations and training 485–486
  style of mediators 485
Sovereign state negotiations 534–535
Spain 486–489
  confidence 487
  credible institutions 487
  endorsements 488–489
  fees 488
  role of lawyers 488
  voluntary/mandatory mediation 486–487
Sports disputes 240–242
  commercial and social imperative 241

Sports disputes – *contd*
  concentration on parties' interest 241
  public domain 241–242
Standards 539–542
  aspirational 541–542
    confidence 541
    feelings and instinct 541
    humanity 542
    self-awareness 542
    selflessness 541
    spirituality 542
    trust 542
  high 539–541
Stimulating dialogue 46
Storytelling 285–288
  DNA 287
  layers 286–287
  mediation process 286
Strategic use of information 16
Strategy for idle time 33
Success fee 27
Summaries 29–30
Summarising 13–14
  function of 13–14
Supporting documents 29–30, 42
Sweden 489–491
  Act on Mediation 490
  court mediations 489
Switzerland 491–497
  civil and commercial mediation 491–492
  common styles of mediation 496–497
  current legal status of mediation 492
  extent and use of mediation 495–496
  mediation, definition 495
Sympathy
  empathy, and 12–13

Tailing 55
Telling stories 46
Time constraints 45
Time management 21
Tomlin Order 82
Topping 55
Transformative mediation 6–7, 131, 243–247
  client centred 246
  constructive dialogue 245
  destructive dialogue 245
  lessons for commercial mediators 247

Transformative mediation – *contd*
  nature of 244–245
  scenarios 243–244
  self determination 245–246
  skills 246
  tools 246
Trust 365
Truth 365–366
Turkey 510–516
  current practice of mediation 515–516
  legal status of mediation 511–515
  Mediation Law 513–515
  mediation model 514
  mediators 515
  process 515

Unrepresented party 13
Urgent text 52

Values 126–127
  sedimented 126
  shared 126

VAT 87, 114
Venue 30
Victim-offender mediation 7
Visual aids 21–22
Voluntary 44

War 122
Who attends 34
Who is at centre of mediation 141–144
Without prejudice 103–104
Workplace mediation 272–282
  business case for 277–278
  emotional needs, and 276
  employment mediation, and 276
  future of 281–282
  historical context 272–273
  operational level 279
  organisational background 274
  return on investment 278–279
  strategic level 279
  terminology 276